ROYAL MANUSCRIPTS
THE GENIUS OF ILLUMINATION

ROYAL MANUSCRIPTS
THE GENIUS OF ILLUMINATION

Scot McKendrick, John Lowden and Kathleen Doyle
with Joanna Frońska and Deirdre Jackson

BRITISH LIBRARY

First published in 2011 by
The British Library
96 Euston Road
London
NW1 2DB

On the occasion of the exhibition at The British Library:

'Royal Manuscripts: The Genius of Illumination'
11 November 2011 – 13 March 2012

978 0 7123 5816 3 (HB)
978 0 7123 5815 6 (PB)

Frontispiece
The Earl of Shrewsbury presenting a book to Queen Margaret, seated in a palace beside King Henry VI, from the Shrewsbury Book, British Library Royal 15 E. vi, f. 2v (detail). See cat. no. 143.

Page 3
Alexander unhorsing King Porus, from *Historia de prelis* in a French translation *(Le Livre et le vraye hystoire du bon roy Alixandre)*, British Library Royal 20 B. xx, f. 53 (detail). See cat. no. 75.

Page 6
The coat of arms of the Arundel family (see cat. no. 148) is incorporated in the bookplate.

Designed and typeset by Andrew Shoolbred
Colour reproduction by Dot Gradations Ltd, Essex
Printed in Italy by Printer Trento S.r.l.

Contents

Dedicated to

The Pigott Family

'Royal' supporters of the British Library

Foreword

The present publication and the accompanying exhibition, *Royal Manuscripts: The Genius of Illumination*, are the result of productive cross-sectoral collaboration and generous philanthropic support. The research project that informs both publication and exhibition was based on a partnership between the British Library and the Courtauld Institute of Art and funded for three years, 2008–11, by the United Kingdom Arts and Humanities Research Council (AHRC). A fundamental aim of the project was to translate the knowledge gained from new academic research on the Library's world renowned collection of illuminated manuscripts into a major public exhibition. We are grateful to the project leaders, Dr Scot McKendrick, Head of History and Classics at the British Library, and Professor John Lowden of the Courtauld Institute of Art, for ensuring that our collaboration achieved its aim of advancing both knowledge and cultural enrichment. We are pleased to present an innovative interpretation of medieval and Renaissance painting in Royal manuscripts in the first dedicated exhibition of illuminated manuscripts at the British Library's St Pancras site.

Our Royal manuscripts project has greatly benefited from the generosity of others: Melvin R. Seiden, whose support underwrote this catalogue, the American Trust for the British Library, the Helen Hamlyn Trust, and an anonymous donor. Several important loans from institutions across the United Kingdom have also enhanced our exhibition. For each of these critical contributions we are extremely grateful. We appreciate the belief and trust you have shown in our project.

We are thankful for the Pigott Family's generous support of the exhibition: *Royal Manuscripts: The Genius of Illumination*. We share in their knowledge, passion and enthusiasm for the British Library.

Dame Lynne Brindley
Chief Executive
The British Library

Professor Deborah Swallow
Märit Rausing Director
The Courtauld Institute of Art

BRITISH LIBRARY

THE COURTAULD Institute of Art

Arts & Humanities Research Council

Lenders to the Exhibition

The British Library would like to acknowledge the generous loans to the exhibition made by

Her Majesty the Queen

Syndics of the Fitzwilliam Museum, Cambridge

Culture and Sport Glasgow on behalf of Glasgow City Council

Museum of London

The National Archives, London

The Trustees of the Natural History Museum, London

Trustees of Sir John Soane's Museum, London

Luton Culture, Wardown Park Museum

The Governing Body of Christ Church, Oxford

Principal and Fellows of Jesus College, Oxford

Mark Pigott, OBE

The National Trust, Stourhead, Wiltshire (item on indefinite loan to the Victoria & Albert Museum, London)

The Dean and Chapter of Westminster

Warden and Scholars of Winchester College

Picture Credits

All images are © The British Library unless otherwise stated. pp.12–13 Mercer Design, London © The British Library; p.20 Mercer Design, London © The British Library; p.26 Bibliothèque nationale de France; p.28 © Patrimonio Nacional; p.29 Leiden University Library; p.30 Musée Condé, Chantilly, France / Giraudon / Bridgeman Art Library; p.31 Bibliothèque nationale de France; p.34 akg- images / Pierpont Morgan Library, New York; p.36 © Katholieke Universiteit Leuven / Bruno Vandermeulen; p.43 Bibliothèque nationale de France; p.45 © Bibliothèque Sainte-Geneviève, Paris; p.46 Bibliothèque nationale de France; p.48 Bibliothèque nationale de France; p.49 John Rylands University Library, Manchester; p.50 Bibliothèque Mazarine, Paris; p.51 Stadtbibliothek Nürnberg; p.52 Bibliothèque municipale de Lyon; p.55 Bodleian Library, University of Oxford; p.161 © The Principal and Fellows of Jesus College, Oxford; pp.170–1 © Luton Culture; p.176 The Governing Body of Christ Church, Oxford; p.191 (diagram) Mercer Design, London © The British Library; p.204 and p.205 Courtesy of the Trustees of Sir John Soane's Museum; p.355 © Dean and Chapter of Westminster Abbey; p.360 © Fitzwilliam Museum, Cambridge.

Notes to the Reader

Biblical quotations are taken from *The Holy Bible: Douay Rheims Version*. References are to Vulgate books and chapters, with the modern numbering and book titles appearing in brackets.

Abbreviations used

BnF	Bibliothèque nationale de France (Paris)
KB	Koninklijke Bibliotheek (The Hague)
KBR	Koninklijke Bibliotheek van België / Bibliothèque Royale (Brussels)
ÖNB	Österreichische Nationalbibliothek (Vienna)
TNA	The National Archives (London)

All other references to manuscripts include the institution's full name and location, except for British Library manuscripts, which include the collection and shelfmark only.

f. or ff.	folio or folios
v.	verso
r.	recto (only used when the reference is to both recto and verso of one folio

The abbreviation 'Fig.' refers to illustrations within the essays; illustrations within the catalogue entries are unnumbered.

Contributors to the Catalogue

N. B.	Nicolas Bell, The British Library
S.J.B.	Sarah J. Biggs, The British Library
A.B.	Alixe Bovey, University of Kent
A.C.	Andrea Clarke, The British Library
J.C.	Justin Clegg, The British Library
S.D.	Sonja Drimmer, Columbia University
K.D.	Kathleen Doyle, The British Library
J.F.	Joanna Frońska, The British Library
R.G.	Richard Gameson, Durham University
J.H.	Julian Harrison, The British Library
D.J.	Deirdre Jackson, The British Library
J.L.	John Lowden, The Courtauld Institute of Art
S.McK.	Scot McKendrick, The British Library
J.O'D.	Joshua O'Driscoll, Harvard University
S.P.	Stella Panayotova, Fitzwilliam Museum, University of Cambridge
L.S.	Lucy Freeman Sandler, New York University

Regnal Dates

England

Anglo-Saxon

Alfred (871–99)
Edward the Elder (899–924)
Athelstan (924/5–39)
Edmund I (939–46)
Eadred (946–55)
Eadwig (955–59)
Edgar (957/9–75)
Edward the Martyr (975–78)
Æthelred II (978–1013 and 1014–16)
Swein Forkbeard (1013–14)
Edmund Ironside (1016)
Cnut (1016–35)
Harold Harefoot (1035–40)
Harthacnut (1035–7 and 1040–2)
Edward the Confessor (1042–66)
Harold II (Godwineson) (Jan–Oct 1066)

Norman and later

William I (1066–87)
William II (1087–1100)
Henry I (1100–35)
Stephen (1135–54)

Henry II (1154–89)
Richard I (1189–99)
John (1199–1216)
Henry III (1216–72)
Edward I (1272–1307)
Edward II (1307–27)
Edward III (1327–77)
Richard II (1377–99)

Henry IV (1399–1413)
Henry V (1413–22)
Henry VI (1422–61 and 1470–71)

Edward IV (1461–70 and 1471–83)
Edward V (Apr–Jun 1483)
Richard III (1483–85)

Henry VII (1485–1509)
Henry VIII (1509–47)
Edward VI (1547–53)
Mary I (1553–58)
Elizabeth I (1558–1603)

James I (1603–25)
Charles I (1625–49)
Interregnum (1649–60)
Charles II (1660–85)
James II (1685–88)
William III (1689–1702) and Mary II (1689–94)
Anne (1702–14)

George I (1714–27)
George II (1727–60)

France

Hugh Capet (987–96)
Robert II (996–1031)
Henry I (1031–60)
Philip I (1060–1108)
Louis VI (1108–37)
Louis VII (1137–80)
Philip II Augustus (1180–1223)
Louis VIII (1223–26)
Louis IX (Saint Louis) (1226–70)
Philip III (1270–85)
Philip IV (1285–1314)
Louis X (1314–16)
John I (15–19 Nov 1316)
Philip V (1316–22)
Charles IV (1322–28)

Philip VI (1328–50)
John II (1350–64)
Charles V (1364–80)
Charles VI (1380–1422)
Charles VII (1422–61)
Louis XI (1461–83)
Charles VIII (1483–98)
Louis XII (1498–1515)
Francis I (1515–47)

Valois Dukes of Burgundy

Philip the Bold (1363–1404)
John the Fearless (1404–19)
Philip the Good (1419–67)
Charles the Bold (1467–77)

The French Royal Family

- **Philip II Augustus** (1180–1223) m. Isabel of Hainault
  - **Louis VIII** (1223-26) m. Blanche of Castile
    - **Louis IX (Saint Louis)** (1226–70) m. Margaret of Provence
      - **Philip III** (1270–85) m. (1) Isabel of Aragon m. (2) Mary of Brabant
        - **Philip IV** (1285–1314) m. Joan of Navarre
          - **Louis X** (1314–16) m. (1) Margaret of Burgundy m. (2) Clemence of Hungary
            - **John I** (1316)
            - Joan of Navarre
          - **Philip V** (1316–22) m. Jeanne of Burgundy
          - **Charles IV** (1322–28) m. (3) Jeanne d'Évreux
            - Blanche of France m. Philip Duke of Orleans
          - Isabel m. Edward II King of England
        - **The Valois**
        - Charles of Valois m. Margaret of Anjou-Sicily
          - **Philip VI** (1328–50) m. Jeanne of Burgundy
            - **John II** (1350–64) m. Bonne of Luxemburg
              - **Charles V** (1364–80) m. Jeanne of Bourbon
                - **Charles VI** (1380–1422) m. Isabel of Bavaria
                  - **Charles VII** (1422–61) m. Mary of Anjou
                    - **Louis XI** (1461–83) m. (1) Margaret of Scotland m. (2) Charlotte of Savoy
                      - **Charles VIII** (1483–98)
                - Louis Duke of Orleans m. Valentine Visconti
                  - Charles Duke of Orleans m. Mary of Cleves
                    - **Louis XII** (1498–1515) m. (3) Mary Tudor
                  - John Count of Angoulême m. Margaret of Rohan
                    - Charles Count of Angoulême m. Louise of Savoy
                      - **Francis I** (1515–47)
              - Louis Duke of Anjou m. Mary of Blois
              - John Duke of Berry
              - **Dukes of Burgundy**
              - Philip 'The Bold' (1363–1404) m. Margaret of Flanders
                - John 'The Fearless' (1404–19)
                  - Anne m. John Duke of Bedford
                  - Philip 'The Good' (1419–67) m. (3) Isabel of Portugal
                    - Charles 'The Bold' (1467–77) m. (2) Isabel of Bourbon m. (3) Margaret of York
                      - Mary of Burgundy
          - Jeanne m. William of Hainault
            - Philippa of Hainault m. Edward III King of England
        - Margaret of France m. Edward I King of England (1272–1307)
          - Edward II m. Isabel of France
    - Charles of Anjou King of Naples m. Beatrice of Provence
      - Charles II of Anjou King of Naples
        - Robert of Anjou King of Naples

The Ruling Houses of England

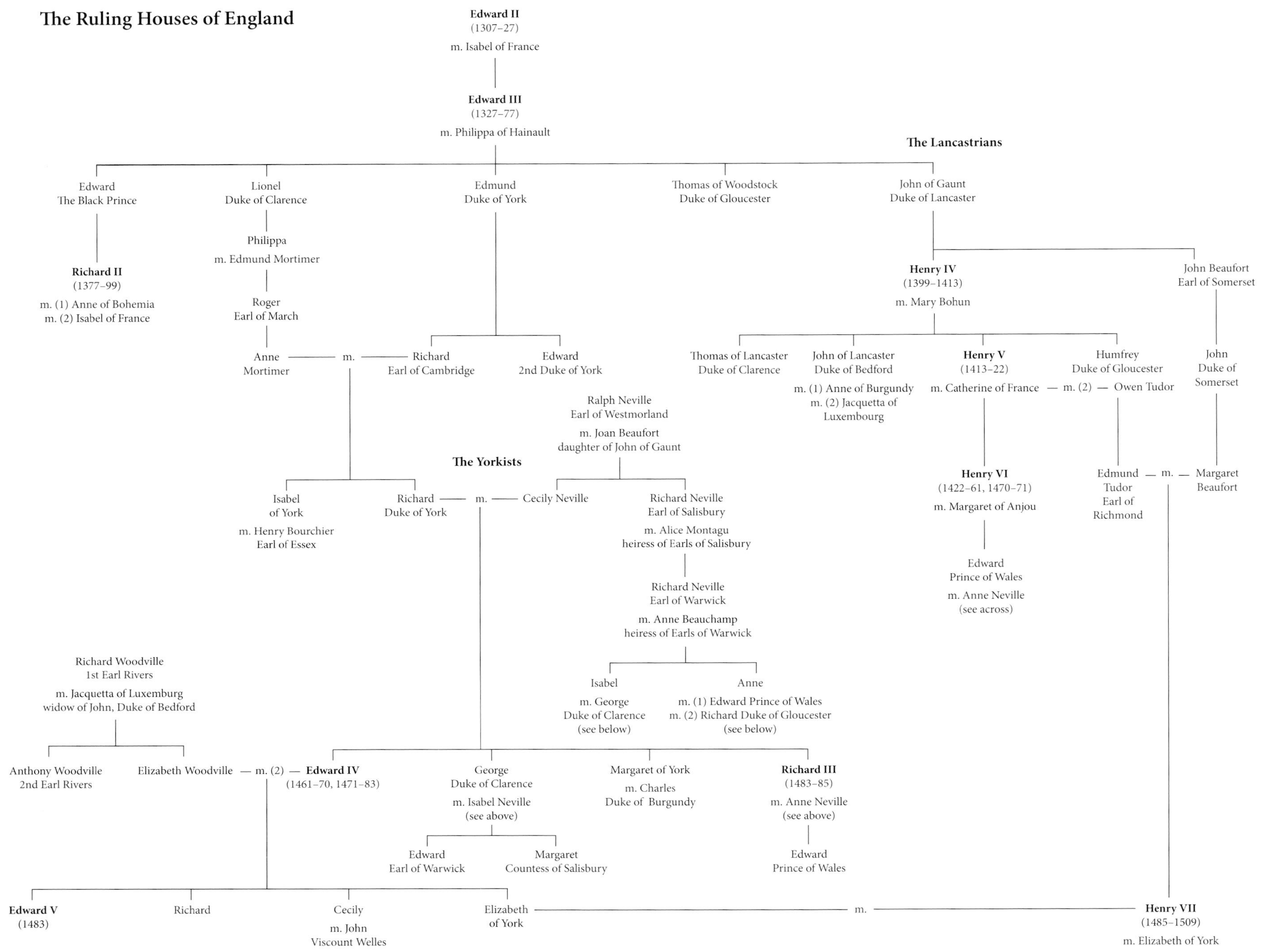

Royal Manuscripts: The Genius of Illumination

SCOT McKENDRICK

Surviving manuscripts associated with successive kings and queens of England form a remarkable inheritance. Together they offer by far the largest body of evidence for the interplay between two critical parts of British cultural heritage: its monarchy and its medieval art. Parts of the built legacy of the British monarchy from the Middle Ages – for example, the White Tower of London, Westminster Abbey and Windsor Castle – have a high profile in national and international public consciousness. Royal manuscripts in contrast have much lower public recognition, concealed from all but scholarly view for centuries in libraries, the very means of their preservation. Yet their survival is a miracle worthy of much greater recognition. Despite centuries of warfare, social, religious and cultural disruption, royal manuscripts still exist in large numbers. Tens of thousands of pages in them bear some of the most outstanding examples of decorative and figurative painting that survive in Britain from the eight hundred years between the eighth and sixteenth centuries. The state of preservation of these remarkable illuminations is moreover notably high, their colours often as vivid as when they were first painted and their gold still making their pages glow and flicker in the light for us, as they did for those who first viewed them so many centuries ago. The achievement of the creators of these great works is manifest to this day. As one contemporary inscription puts it, 'The beauty of this book displays my genius.'

Yet royal manuscripts do much more than declare the artistry of their makers. They offer unique insights into the life and aspirations of those for whom they were made. In them we have the most vivid surviving sources for understanding royal identity, moral and religious beliefs, learning and politics. Through careful interpretation of their texts and images, we can deepen our understanding of what it was to be a king in the Middle Ages and find answers to some key questions about medieval monarchs. How, for example, did they relate to the ultimate ruler of all, God, and to his representation on Earth, the Church? What was expected of young princes of the blood, born to power? To whom did they look to inform their conduct as rulers? What knowledge did rulers need, and seek, to enhance their power and authority? How did they shape their multiple identities as dynast, crowned king, law-giver, supreme military commander and pinnacle of the most exclusive and fashionable part of society? How did they give visible expression to their political rivalry with their Continental cousins? Complemented by documentary evidence, royal manuscripts greatly enrich our knowledge of the history of Britain and its monarchy.

Thanks to a generous gift to the nation by George II in 1757, most surviving royal manuscripts are still preserved together as a group. Now held by the British Library and kept as a discrete collection, the Royal manuscripts number nearly two thousand volumes. Each of the volumes is denoted as 'Royal' and identified by a shelfmark assigned to it as part of that collection. Together with some nine thousand printed books also donated by George II, they form what has become known as the Old Royal library. Within it are the books inherited by the Hanoverian monarch from his royal predecessors. Subsequently his grandson George III built up his own vast personal library. It too is now held by the British Library and retained as another discrete collection, this time called the King's collection. The collections of books formed by subsequent British monarchs are retained elsewhere, in the Royal Collection held in trust by HM Queen Elizabeth II for her successors and the British nation, most notably in the Royal Library, Windsor Castle. Of these three English royal libraries the Old Royal library is by far the most significant for its medieval illuminated manuscripts and associations with the monarchs of the Middle Ages.

The present volume and accompanying exhibition showcase illuminated manuscripts associated with the English royal family principally through those still forming part of the Old Royal library. From this collection 111 volumes have been selected from around 1200 that are in some way decorated. To complement them and enhance the thematic and chronological presentations we have chosen thirty-seven volumes that now form parts of other collections in the British Library, but were also once associated with English monarchs. Several of these formerly belonged to the Old Royal library. Also forming part of this catalogue are six royal manuscripts now held by other institutions in England that are so closely related to Royal manuscripts in the British Library that it was important that they be presented together with them. Some of these volumes will be reunited with their fellows for the first time since the early modern period. With these exceptions, such is the wealth of material available within the Royal and other collections of the British Library that we were able to formulate and explore the role of illuminated manuscripts owned by English monarchs solely from the Library's resources. The British Library's manuscript collections have, yet again, proved that they have much to offer those prepared to engage in first-hand research on them.

The indispensable foundation of this publication has been nearly three years of thorough reappraisal of the manuscripts and secondary literature on them. Only through examination of some 600 volumes were we able to select 154 manuscripts that would elucidate the questions posed above. Only through detailed and painstaking re-examination of each of these chosen few have we come to understand the distinctive voice of each of these witnesses to our royal and artistic narrative. Both the wide overview and particular focus have enabled us to shape and refine the present work. In this respect our approach was empirical; for our story available primary evidence was always the touchstone.

That said, our reappraisal did not start from a blank sheet. Indeed, as the bibliography at the end of this volume makes clear, our work rests on broad shoulders – the contributions of many generations of scholars support our efforts. Most notably our research, and indeed that of most other modern scholars, could not have been undertaken without the monumental four-volume *Catalogue of the Royal and King's Manuscripts* that was compiled by successive Keepers of the Department of Manuscripts in the British Museum, Sir George Frederic Warner and Julius Parnell Gilson. Although published ninety years ago, in 1921, this catalogue is still one of the most outstanding scholarly catalogues of early manuscript books ever produced. Almost every entry in the present work has benefited from the insights that Warner and Gilson brought to their subject. The essays too are deeply indebted to their work. Several other major contributions made more recently to the study of royal manuscripts need to be highlighted. The publication probably most often cited by us is James P. Carley's *The Libraries of King Henry VIII*. Since its publication in 2000, Carley's work has provided students of the Old Royal library with a map with which to navigate their way through its historical complexities. Like many others, we owe him a particular debt of gratitude. Other researchers who have made significant contributions to our understanding of the English royal library before the time of Henry VIII are Jenny Stratford and the late Janet Backhouse. Just as Stratford enriched our knowledge of its documentary history in the fourteenth and first half of the fifteenth centuries, so Backhouse stimulated the reappraisal of the extant manuscripts of both the recognized founder of the Old Royal library, Edward IV, and his Tudor successor, Henry VII. To single out these authors is perhaps incautious. In doing so we have, however, no wish to deny the significant work that others have made and continue to make in the field. Indeed one of the aims of this catalogue is to create new juxtapositions and comparisons, thereby stimulating the development of further insights into and understanding of the production and reception of these manuscripts, and their place in the national collection. We trust that it will suggest new avenues of research and inspire others to embark on further investigations and research into this material.

The present publication presents its subject in two distinct, but complementary ways. It opens with essays that take a broad view of the subject and continues with separate analyses of individual works. As much as we have been able, we have sought to integrate the two parts of the volume, in particular employing repeated cross-references within the essays to the catalogue entries and within each catalogue entry to other entries. This strategy is intended to underscore the complex interdependency of the available evidence. Previous exhibition catalogues on the subject, such as those published in 1957 to mark the two hundredth anniversary of the donation of the Old Royal library and in 1977 to celebrate the twenty-fifth anniversary of the accession to the throne of HM Queen Elizabeth II, have been summary publications. The first comprised merely eleven pages of text and eleven black and white illustrations; the second offered just three pages of discursive text, supplemented by fifty-one black and white plates. In the second case the exhibition encompassed a wider royal heritage than manuscripts, or even books. Our publication is the first monographic treatment of the subject. All 154 manuscripts featured in the catalogue and many comparative manuscripts not included in the exhibition are illustrated in colour. Essays and entries are supplemented with extensive bibliographies.

Three essays exploring key research questions form the first section of the book. In the first essay John Lowden reviews a long chronology of royal engagement with books, from the formative commission of Constantine the Great from Eusebius of Caesarea for fifty copies of Holy Scripture to gifts of various books made to Henry VIII. Spanning over one thousand years, his analysis seeks both to categorize contexts within which royalty engaged with books and to illustrate the almost infinite number of variations on these categories that pertained. To do so it considers the wider European context of royal patronage and association with finely illuminated manuscripts, drawing on examples of works related to monarchs of France, Italy and Spain, as well as those of England. The second essay also reflects on the Continental context. More narrowly focused in chronology than that of his co-editor, Scot McKendrick's essay considers the reasons why so many manuscripts in English royal possession during the late Middle Ages issued from Continental sources. In his contribution McKendrick presents the wider evidential context, both documentary and artefactual, within which illuminated manuscripts from the Old Royal library need to be seen. Building on this, he seeks to explain the evident dependency of English royalty on Continental books. In the third and final essay Kathleen Doyle explores the history of illuminated manuscripts in the Old Royal library from the time of its foundation under Edward IV to its donation to the British nation by George II. In particular she considers which monarchs engaged with the collection of illuminated manuscripts and thereby contributed to its remarkable status as a major repository of medieval art. She also traces the vicissitudes of the collection during the problematic period when the library temporarily lost its royal status during the Commonwealth. In an appendix to her essay Doyle presents an annotated list of the principal booklists of the Old Royal library from after the time of Henry VIII.

Within the second part of the present publication the manuscripts we have selected are presented in six thematic sections. The first considers illuminated manuscripts as evidence of the evolving interaction of English monarchs and the Christian Church. Taking a long chronological view, from Anglo-Saxon to Tudor times, and comprising forty-six works, this section presents different aspects of royal religious patronage and personal devotion. The second focuses more tightly on a key moment in the history of the engagement of English monarchs with books. In it we present sixteen of the south Netherlandish manuscripts that were acquired for Edward IV in the final prosperous years of his reign and that came to form the foundations of the Old Royal library. In the third we return to a thematic approach, exploring through twenty-five case studies the ways in which books contributed to the shaping of young royal princes and offered mature royalty models on which to base their lives and actions. The fourth section explores books from the Old Royal library that transmitted medieval knowledge on a wide range of topics. Encompassing twenty-six manuscripts that range in date from the eleventh to the sixteenth centuries, this part of the exhibition looks at English royal engagement with an evolving corpus of texts, the authors of which built on the learning of classical Greece and Rome and developed their own distinctive contribution to western European thought. Fifth is a section of twenty volumes that illustrate the different ways in which books contributed to the complex nexus of identities developed by English monarchs. In this we focus on illuminated manuscripts that aided men to present and understand their identity as monarchs, distinct from other men through genealogical descent and formal coronation, and through their roles as supreme law-giver, military leader and arbiter of chivalric conduct and courtly taste. The final section explores twenty-one particularly beautiful manuscripts of Continental origin acquired by English monarchs. Through them we observe both their close affinity with fashionable Continental styles and particular efforts at appropriation of the art and culture of their longstanding political rival, France.

The present volume is one of the outputs of a major three-year research project funded by the United Kingdom's Arts and Humanities Research Council. Led by Scot McKendrick, Head of History and Classics at the British Library, as the Principal Investigator, and John Lowden, Professor of Art History at the Courtauld Institute of Art, University of London, as the Co-Investigator, this project had as its principal aim the presentation of new scholarly research in a major exhibition for the general public. As a fundamental part of our preparations, two post-doctoral research assistants, Joanna Frońska and Deirdre Jackson, undertook summary descriptions of the illuminated manuscripts from the Old Royal library now in the British Library. Chantry Westwell contributed additional summary descriptions of manuscripts in the Royal collection. As a result of this work nearly six hundred manuscript descriptions accompanied by over 10,000 images now feature in the British Library's online Catalogue of Illuminated Manuscripts. Frońska and Jackson then proceeded to research and prepare catalogue entries for many of the manuscripts selected for the present publication. In all these endeavours they were directed by Kathleen Doyle, Curator of Illuminated Manuscripts at the British Library, and assisted by Sarah J. Biggs, who was instrumental in coordinating new digital images of all the exhibited manuscripts, and two interns funded by the American Trust for the British Library, Sonja Drimmer and Joshua O'Driscoll. Together these individuals formed the core curatorial team responsible for the intellectual shaping of the present volume and accompanying exhibition. Also offering critical scholarly and curatorial support to the project was an international advisory board, comprising Thierry Delcourt (Paris), Richard Gameson (Durham), Thomas Kren (Los Angeles), Stella Panayotova (Cambridge), Jane Roberts (Windsor), Lucy Freeman Sandler (New York), Jan Van der Stock (Leuven) and Lieve Watteeuw (Brussels). We are much in their debt for both their commitment to the project from the outset and their continuing advice and support over the past three years. Three of them, Richard Gameson, Stella Panayotova and Lucy Freeman Sandler, have also generously contributed entries to the present catalogue. Other contributors to this publication who require full recognition are Alixe Bovey, of the University of Kent at Canterbury, and Nicolas Bell, Andrea Clarke, Justin Clegg and Julian Harrison, all of the British Library.

For their significant support and advice many others deserve our grateful thanks. At the British Library we thank

Jenny Lawson for all that she has done to help shape the present volume. In addition we acknowledge the invaluable contributions of members of the Library's exhibition project board: Claire Breay, Greg Buzwell, Kathleen Doyle, Jon Fawcett, Clive Izard, Geraldine Kenny, Yasmin Khan, Miki Lentin, Catherine McMahon, Heather Norman-Soderlind, Jane Richardson, Pamela Stephenson, Alan Sterenberg, Roger Walshe, Mark Walton, David Way, Colin Wight and Julie Yau. We also thank our other colleagues Wieke Avis, Peter Barber, Kate Bower, Mark Browne, Susan Dymond, Laura Fielder, Moira Goff, John Goldfinch, Kristian Jensen, Chris Lee, Karen Limper-Hertz, Philippa Marks, Barbara O'Connor, Charlotte Orrell-Jones, Jennie Patrice, Cordelia Rogerson, Lara Speicher, David Wilkerson and Chris Wootton. At the Courtauld Institute of Art we would like to thank Deborah Swallow, and colleagues and students in medieval art history. Elsewhere our thanks are extended to Elizabeth Adey, François Avril, Nancy Bell, Paul Binski, James Carley, Thomas Charles-Edwards, Gregory Clark, Linda Clark, Abbie Coppard, Tony Edwards, Natalia Elagina, Sarah Ereira, Hazel Forsyth, Suzanne Foster, Anne D. Hedeman, Martin Kauffmann, Michael Kauffmann, Peter Kidd, Jenny Knight, Patricia Lovett, Ellen McAdam, Owen McKnight, Janet McMullin, Michael A. Michael, Marigold Norbye, Susan Palmer, Ann Payne, Catherine Reynolds, Mary Robinson, Jane Rowlands, Kathryn Rudy, Richard Sabin, Desmond Shawe-Taylor, Tony Trowles, Anne-Marie Turcan-Verkerk, Linda Voigts and Paul Williamson.

Others have played a key part in making this project come to fruition. In addition to the crucial British support from the Arts and Humanities Research Council, American belief in its key aims has been critical in three ways. First, we thank the Pigott Family for their commitment to the British Library and for their remarkable generosity in funding this exhibition. We are honoured to have your support. Second, we thank the American Trust for the British Library for funding a sequence of internships that enabled three American doctoral students to contribute to and develop through their participation in the project. Since 2005 the Trust's support has been invaluable in opening up the Library's vast and rich collection of illuminated manuscripts not only to these interns but through their work to researchers across the world. Third, we thank the late Melvin R. Seiden whose enthusiasm for our work on medieval manuscripts at the British Library culminated in two generous grants to support the present catalogue and exhibition. It is our great sorrow that he did not live to share with us the result of his generosity. By way of tribute to him and to all that he has done to foster the love of fine books and manuscripts we offer this catalogue to his memory. Last, but by far not least, all the members of the Royal Manuscripts project thank those who have journeyed through life alongside them as they worked on this publication and exhibition. They know who they are and how they have contributed. For their tolerance and love we offer them our deepest gratitude.

In memory of Melvin R. Seiden

Cy cõmence la bible en francois translatee selon les hystoires escolastres. Et premierement

The Royal Manuscript as Idea and Object

JOHN LOWDEN

The Old Royal library, including almost two thousand manuscripts previously owned by English sovereigns, was given to the nation in 1757 by George II. It is now part of the British Library. All these manuscripts are easily identifiable, for they have shelfmarks beginning with 'Royal'. In addition, some retain their mid-eighteenth-century binding, and bear on the spine indications of their provenance, from Edward IV, Henry VII, and other early collectors (see fig. 1.1).

It is characteristic of the hand-made book, and in particular the manuscript, that each is unique in format and appearance and has its own individual history. If we were to write the biographies of these volumes we would need to begin with the craftsmen who designed and made them, then speak of their original owners and users, and finally take account of those who possessed them over the course of the centuries. How and when these widely divergent manuscripts were obtained by members of the English royal family is known in many cases, but in other instances these two fundamental questions remain unanswered.

The focus of the present publication is on manuscripts from the Old Royal library, but it also encompasses several manuscripts owned by English royalty and now held in other British Library collections, such as the Cottonian and Harleian, as well as a handful on loan from other institutions. In the following discussion, any manuscript for which there is any evidence of a royal connection at any point in its history, will be considered 'royal'; the adjective is not restricted to those books commissioned directly by kings or queens. A book can therefore be termed royal because, for example, it is mentioned in a royal inventory or comparable source, even if the first such mention was many centuries after the book was manufactured – the Cotton Genesis (cat. no. 46), briefly in the English royal collection in the sixteenth century, is a case in point. Alternatively, a book may be identified as royal because

Opposite: Detail from cat. no. 24

Fig. 1.1
Bindings of some Royal manuscripts

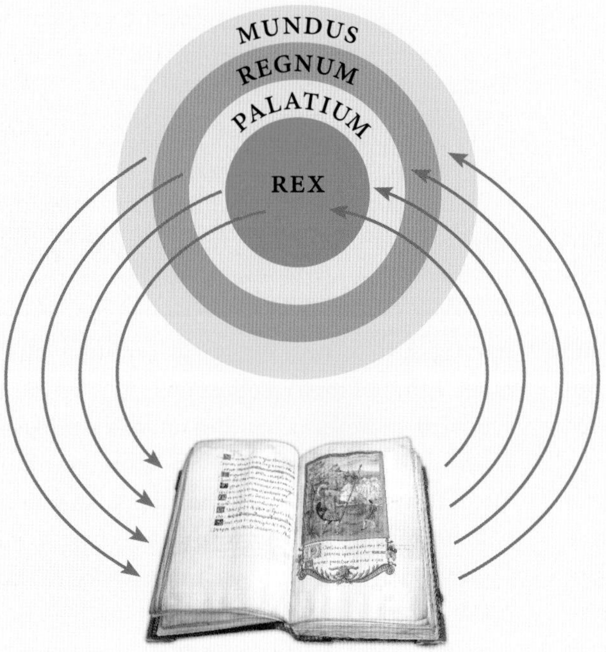

Fig. 1.2
Patterns of production and consumption of royal manuscripts

it contains a dedicatory inscription, a note of royal ownership, royal heraldic devices or mottos, an image of a contemporary king or queen, or any one of numerous pointers to a specific royal aspect to its history.

It is important to consider the precise nature of the link between (royal) persons and (royal) books, for there are many possible scenarios. For purposes of clarification, some of these possibilities can be represented diagrammatically in a modern version of the sort of image sometimes used in medieval books for pedagogic and mnemonic ends. As befits a product of the twenty-first century, however, the logic of the Venn diagram is also not wholly absent. In brief, the *Rex, Palatium, Regnum, Mundus* diagram (fig. 1.2, which I constructed some years ago for a different project) is intended to suggest some of the varied patterns of circumstance under which royal books might have been produced and used.[1] We see a representative royal book at the bottom of the diagram, and above four circles or spheres, representing the King at the centre, and the progressively wider categories of the Palace, the Kingdom and the wider World. (As we shall see below, this is far from exhausting the range of possible categories.) The arrows curving down to the image of the book indicate a variety of possibilities with regard to that book's origin and manufacture. The arrows curving upwards indicate some possibilities for its destination and use. We can see that a royal book might have been commissioned by a king, and have been intended for use by that same figure (the order to make the book went out from *Rex*, and the book, when made, returned to *Rex*). This would be the pattern defined by the innermost arrows of the diagram. But it is quite possible that this royal book was commissioned instead by a figure in one of the outer spheres, a royal adviser in the palace, some important magnate in the kingdom or perhaps a patron somewhere further afield. In addition, but independent of the circumstances of its production, our hypothetical royal book might not have been intended for consumption and use by a royal personage, but instead by someone in one of the outer spheres of the diagram.

So what can be learned from the diagram? First, it is important to distinguish the making of a book from its use. Second, any visual argument made by the images and decoration of a royal book will differ, depending on what path within the diagram the book was expected to follow. A royal book with images intended originally to instruct, let us say, the king's son and heir apparent, will have been viewed in a significantly different way should the king's son have died unexpectedly and the book then have been given to the king's daughter (e.g. cat. no. 17). Third, every book has its own history and many royal books have changed hands on several occasions, making, in effect, several journeys round the diagram or at least on the second leg of the diagram, and quite likely following different routes on different occasions. Fourth, a book may originally have had no royal connections, and become royal (such as the Cotton Genesis, cat. no. 46) or Royal (such as Codex Alexandrinus, fig. 1.3, overleaf) only centuries later. The corollary (a fifth possibility) is also true: a book may appear to modern scholars to have been royal in all likelihood, and yet now bear no explicit record of this fact, thus threatening to slip through the net, unobserved. The fifth possibility is not considered here. What we can state unequivocally, in the light of the diagram, is that it is important when considering any royal book to consider in what sense it is 'royal', and to allow for a wide range of differing possible circumstances in the commissioning and consumption of the book, especially if these factors are not explicit. This essay will therefore consider in a broad historical context some of the differing circumstances that pertain to royal books.

There is, however, one crucial element of enquiry which the diagram does not call to our attention: namely the 'Why?' of the production and consumption of royal books. This will nonetheless be the second focus of the essay. We shall want to know why a certain royal book was made, why it was decorated with certain images, why it changed hands when it did; and to ask further 'Why?' questions as may be appropriate.

Royal books as gifts by or from kings – the beginnings to c. 1050

Gift exchange is as old as human society.[2] The giving specifically of books as gifts by or from kings, however, is a more recent phenomenon. Remarkably, we can pin down the origins of the practice to precise historical circumstances in the fourth century AD. The royal book as gift may be associated with the conjunction of three triumphs: the triumph of the Emperor Constantine over his rivals for dominion in the late Roman Empire, the triumph of the book-as-codex over the book-as-scroll, and the triumph of Christianity over other religions in the Roman world. These three triumphs involve the mingling of complementary historical factors: the political/personal, the technical/practical and the religious/metaphysical.

We can begin with the technical/practical factor. The book-as-codex, the still familiar volume composed of folded rectangular sheets sewn in gatherings and bound between protective covers, the use of which we take so much for granted, was an invention of the first century AD.[3] Using specially prepared animal skins (parchment) in preference to the much less durable papyrus, initially the codex seemed advantageous because it offered a much more compact means of storing information than the traditional papyrus scroll. The first codices seem to have been relatively inexpensive volumes of small format, like the readily portable, wooden, wax-filled writing tablets in diptych form from which they took their name (*caudex/codex* – note that the terms are Latin, not Greek, suggesting where the terminology was, and was not, developed). The Roman poet Martial remarked in an epigram composed *c.* 80–100 (and doubtless employing some poetic licence) that the vast works of Livy, which his entire library of scrolls could not contain, were contained in a single parchment codex.[4]

The codex form was particularly popular among Christians in the first centuries AD.[5] Whereas Jews retained the scroll form, most notably for the Torah – the first five books of what became the Christian Bible, from Genesis to Deuteronomy – Christians found the codex to be eminently practical in their mission to proselytize, for not only were the Christian Scriptures in codices easy to carry, but they were easy to consult. In preaching, study and the liturgy, as well as disputation with proponents of competing book-based religions (such as Judaism or Manicheism), it would have been much easier to locate scattered texts in a codex than in one or more scrolls. The Messianic nature of Christianity – with many citations of the Old Testament in the New – made such cross-referencing particularly important. So when Constantine directed imperial patronage to benefit Christianity after his victory over Maxentius in 312, he gave a decisive boost to the authority of the codex. This support also took a practical form. According to the panegyric *Life of Constantine* by Eusebius, Bishop of Caesarea in Palestine (d. 339–40), the Emperor ordered the Bishop to supervise the production of fifty copies of the 'sacred Scriptures' for distribution around the churches of the new imperial city of Constantinople.[6] Constantine specified that they be on parchment in a 'convenient portable form'. Eusebius describes them as 'magnificent and elaborately bound'. They were indisputably gifts from the ruler, and directed to institutions rather than to individuals. They were going from *Rex* to *Regnum*.

Constantine's patronage of Christianity established various norms for his successors: divine approval was held

Fig. 1.3
Layout of Codex Alexandrinus.
Royal 1 D. viii, ff. 5v–6

to be essential to successful rule; correct belief and practice were essential for divine approval.[7] Hence the distribution of imperially sanctioned religious books was, by extension, advantageous to emperor and empire. These actions and ideas provided a model for Christian kingship that held sway until the Protestant reformation.

If the codex-book was for Martial a handy small volume, by the time Eusebius made the fifty copies of sacred Scriptures for Constantine the codex was very different. One copy that gives an idea of what the Eusebian volumes may have been like has survived: the Greek Codex Sinaiticus (mostly now in the British Library as Additional 43725).[8] This Bible is a massive volume (even with half of the Old Testament missing it comprises some four hundred folios of large format, 380 x 345 mm), and the craftsmanship is superb. Although now very plain in appearance, it seems likely that it would originally have been decorated with various diagrams: notably canon tables, devised by Eusebius, in which parallels between the Gospels were listed in columns, and possibly plans of Jerusalem and of the Temple.[9] In the seventeenth century, when Codex Sinaiticus was as yet undiscovered by western scholars, the greatest treasure of the royal collection was the somewhat similar four-volume Greek Bible (Royal 1 D. v–viii, known as Codex Alexandrinus; fig. 1.3), which was presented to Charles I in 1627 by the Patriarch of Constantinople.[10] It is now dated to the fifth century, and thus was more than eleven hundred years old when it first became a Royal book (there is no record that it was royal before this date, although this of course is possible). The book's antiquity and completeness ensured that it was held in high esteem.

By the end of the fourth century the taste for what might be termed 'luxury' books of Christian content, ignited by Constantine's patronage, had developed to an extraordinary degree. Jerome specifically condemned the practice of writing the holy books with letters an inch tall and gold and silver as the ink, and on parchment dyed purple (leaving the naked Christ to die outside the door, as he expressed it in a different context).[11] Burdens, rather than handy codices, he termed these books. A surprising number of such luxury books, or fragments of them, have survived. They date mainly from the sixth century rather than the fourth, but this is likely to

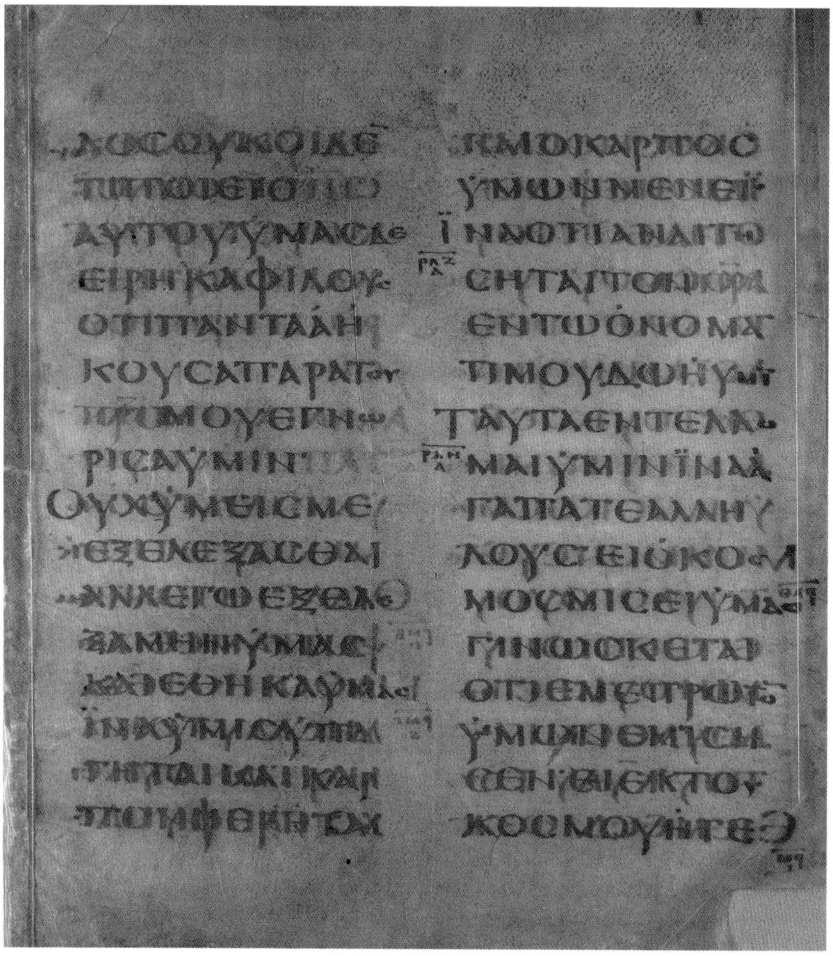

Fig. 1.4
Gospels written in silver on purple parchment.
Cotton Titus C. xv, f. 5

be the result of greater production in the later period, rather than evidence of the effectiveness of the strictures of Jerome in the earlier. Most such survivors are written with silver ink rather than gold, but the effect is still sumptuous and the cost must have been very high (fig. 1.4).[12] Unfortunately these books are silent as to their origins. But there is good reason to suppose that a silver, gold and purple copy of the Gospels in Gothic translation, now in Uppsala, was made on the instructions of and for the use of the Gothic King Theoderic, who ruled Italy from his palace at Ravenna (493–526).[13] Most of these luxury books probably had diagrams and possibly images within them, as well as on their covers. The covers were probably fashioned of gold or silver-gilt revetments, with or without precious stones, or alternatively revetted with thin sheets of often figurative ivory.[14] Such books proclaimed themselves royal (or imperial) primarily by their materials, rather than their images. They seem to have been considered appropriate as gifts not so much to earthly rulers, but to the heavenly ruler, God, visualized in the form of Christ. In terms of the diagram, therefore, such gold or silver and purple books could be seen as going from an earthly king to a divine one, or from a mundane to a divine sphere (a possibility not anticipated by the four circles of the diagram, and difficult to represent). Yet although the intended recipient was invisible, the gift itself probably remained very visible, carried in processions and displayed on the altar for all to see, when not in use. These luxury books have survived when so many other books have not, it must be said, precisely because they were considered so remarkable. Workaday volumes were made and used until they were worn out; they stood virtually no chance of surviving.

The interpenetration of ideas about earthly and heavenly attitudes to luxury books was not restricted to the Roman (later the Byzantine) Empire. In the period when the Germanic settlers of northern Europe were being converted to Christianity by missionaries from Ireland and England, St Wilfred (d. 709) is said to have commissioned for the house of God which he founded at Ripon, and 'for his soul's good', a Gospel-book written in gold on purple parchment, with a gold and jewelled binding.[15] Clearly St Wilfred was offering the divine ruler a gift so splendid that he was confident it would meet with approval. His younger contemporary,

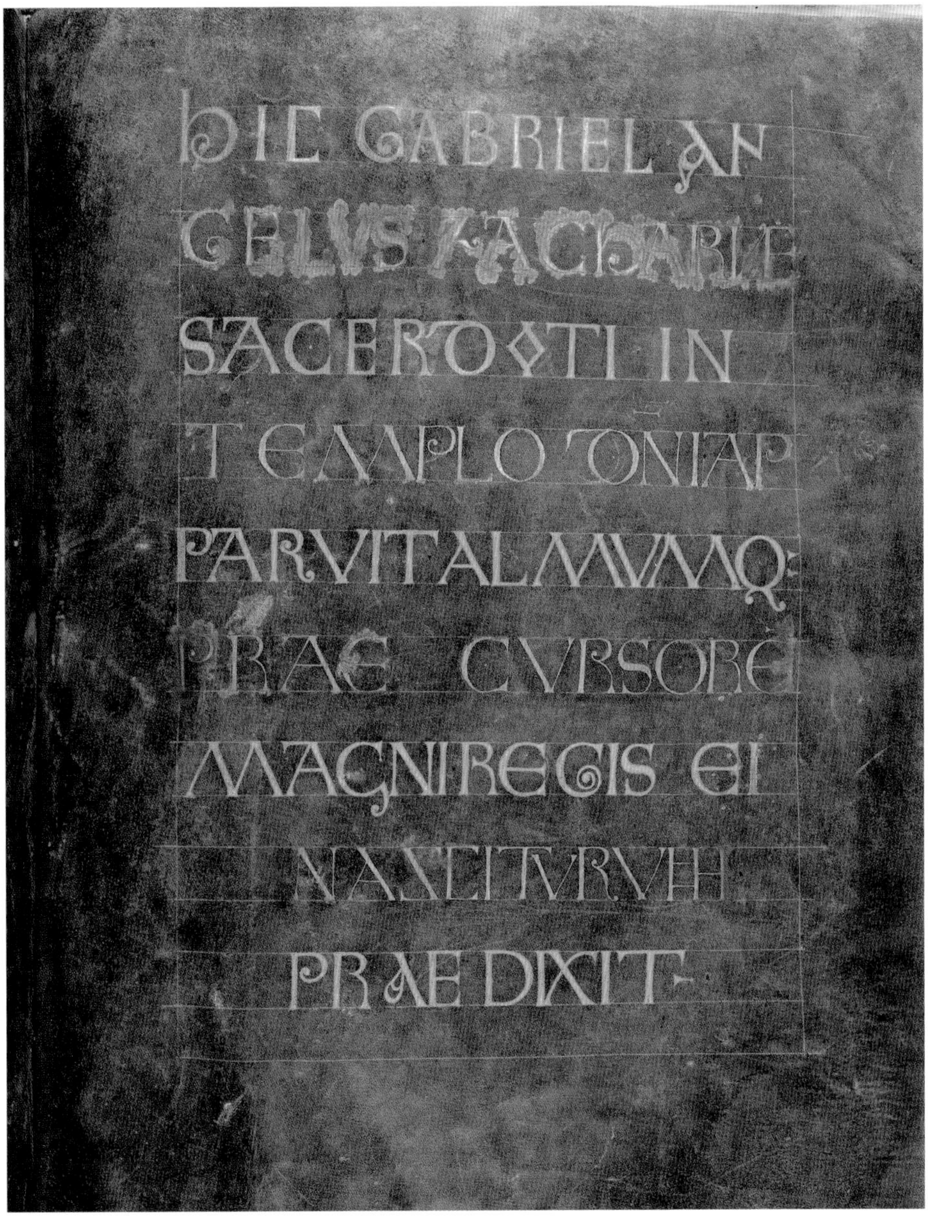

Fig. 1.5
Page of gold text on purple parchment, in the Canterbury Royal Bible.
Royal 1 E. vi, f. 44

St Boniface, later known as the 'apostle of Germany', in 735/6 commissioned the Abbess of Minster-in-Thanet to have made for him a copy of the Epistles of Peter, written in gold 'to secure honour and reverence for the Holy Scriptures when they are preached from before the eyes of the heathen'.[16] What for St Wilfred would impress the heavenly King, for St Boniface would help to convert the illiterate pagan ruler. The ninth-century so-called 'Royal Bible' (fig. 1.5 and cat. no. 2) gives some idea of what the gold and purple pages of such a book might have looked like.

In 800 the Frankish Charles the Great (Charlemagne) was recognized as 'Emperor of the Romans' – the first such ruler since late Antiquity – and crowned in Rome by Pope Leo III. He pursued a policy of *Renovatio imperii romani* (renewal of the Roman Empire), not merely by conquest but in part through the making and distribution of various types of luxury book, providing a model that later rulers would follow. Large-format Bibles of a standardized type were copied at and distributed from the monastery of St Martin at Tours.[17] Illustrated Gospel-books of superb craftsmanship and the costliest materials – gold and silver inks, purple-dyed parchment, ivory covers – were produced in series, it would seem, at Charlemagne's palace at Aachen (fig. 1.6).[18] Both Bibles and Gospels sometimes included images of the royal sponsors of such books. For example, the Bible seemingly presented as a gift by Charlemagne's grandson, Charles the Bald, to Pope John VIII on Charles's coronation in 875 has a full-page image of the Emperor with personified Christian

Fig. 1.6
Opening of Mark's Gospel, in the Harley Golden Gospels.
Harley 2788, ff. 71v–72

virtues above.[19] The miniature is accompanied by verses in gold on a purple ground. This book has been at the church of St Paul's outside the walls of Rome for more than a thousand years.

Of special significance as royal gifts in an English context are three related late Anglo-Saxon manuscripts. Written in gold, the Winchester New Minster Charter, dated 966, has a prefatory image on a faded purple-painted page which represents King Edgar offering the charter in book form to a figure of Christ in Majesty, supported by angels (cat. no. 5).[20] The King is flanked by the church's dedicatees, the Virgin and St Peter. The composition has striking parallels with the dedication image in the Carolingian Bible (datable *c.* 845–46) of Count Vivian, which was presented to Charles the Bald (Paris, BnF, MS lat. 1, f. 423; fig. 1.7).[21] Christ is supported in a nimbus-like mandorla by angels in the New Minster manuscript, much as Charles on his throne is supported by two courtiers; Edgar, seen from behind with arms raised, resembles the choir master in the centre foreground of the miniature in the Bible; St Peter in the charter echoes Count Vivian (at the right) in the Bible. In terms of our diagram, we can be certain that the charter/book was going to the New Minster at Winchester, hence to a destination in the Kingdom (*Regnum*). But was it a gift coming directly from Edgar? Edgar's support in reforming the New Minster was crucial, and doubtless Bishop Æthelwold wanted it to be recorded visually. Most likely, therefore, the book was made both in and for the New Minster. Thus the charter/book, although

it might appear to be a product of the King, was rather a product of the Kingdom or, given the role of the bishop, by a member of the equivalent of the Palace (*Palatium*).

The book of benefactors and others whose names were to be recalled in masses at Winchester (the cathedral's *Liber Vitae*, probably dateable 1031; cat. no. 8) has a frontispiece image of King Cnut and his Norman Queen, Ælfgyfu (Emma), presenting a gold and silver altar cross beneath a Christ in Majesty, flanked as before by the Virgin and St Peter.[22] Two angels place a veil and crown on the heads of the royal couple, while indicating Christ above. Doubtless this image too was made in and for Winchester, and in addition with direct knowledge of the charter of King Edgar, discussed above. In this case there is no doubt that the image records the gift of the altar cross. Was the book with an image of the cross also a gift? Or was it commissioned by the recipients as a record of the gift? It is striking that the book, the *Liber Vitae*, has survived to ensure the perpetual remembrance of the King and Queen and others, whereas the gold cross, surely far more costly to produce than the book, perished in 1141. In terms of our diagram, the book was commissioned in the Kingdom, quite probably at the cost of the King, and destined for the same recipient in the Kingdom. Unlike gold and silver and precious stones, which could easily be stripped off a book's binding, the cost of labour and materials that went into a book's production could not effectively be recovered.

Fig. 1.7 (opposite)
Presentation of the Bible to Charles the Bald.
Paris, BnF, MS lat.1, f. 423

Fig. 1.8
Opening of John's Gospel, in the Cnut Gospels.
Royal 1 D. ix, f. 111

Also connected with King Cnut is a lavishly decorated Gospel-book made at and for Christ Church, Canterbury (datable 1013–19; cat. no. 7).[23] It probably originally contained images of the four Evangelists, which would have faced the surviving incipit pages (figs 1.8, 3.6). The manuscript still contains two Old English texts on parchment left blank between the Gospels of Matthew and Mark. One is a lengthy recognition of Christ Church properties, witnessed by King Cnut, and the other is a brief note that Cnut and four companions have become members of a fraternity. In terms of the diagram, the link between the Gospels and the King is debatable. Did Cnut commission the book, and then have the texts relevant to him added? Or did the monks of Christ Church take advantage of a visit from the King to record in the book a deed, relevant to themselves, and a fraternity note, relevant primarily to the King? The latter seems more likely. In terms of our diagram, the book was commissioned in the Kingdom, for use in the Kingdom.

On the continent of Europe, it was particularly the Ottonian and Salian successors to the Carolingian rulers who most conspicuously used images to enhance the books they gave as gifts.[24] They represented rulers accompanied by personifications of their virtues and their territories, or recorded in acts of piety at the feet of images of Christ in Majesty. These, like the Anglo-Saxon examples, were executed in major centres of illuminated manuscript production, associated with monasteries or cathedrals. For example, Henry III and Queen Agnes presented a book of the Gospels, written in gold, to the cathedral at Speyer founded by Henry's parents, the Emperor Conrad and Empress Gisela (El Escorial, MS Vitr. 17, datable 1045–46).[25] Henry is shown presenting the volume to the enthroned Virgin against a stylized background of the cathedral (fig. 1.9). The Virgin accepts the gift and crowns Agnes. The image is framed by an inscription invoking the Virgin's aid for the one bearing gifts, and there are medallions with personifications of Justice, Prudence, Fortitude and Temperance. Facing this page in diptych form is an image of Henry's parents, Conrad and Gisela, who kneel in prayer (their words are recorded in the framing text) and kiss the feet of Christ in a mandorla. Christ's mandorla is inscribed with a quotation from Psalm 71:19 ('And blessed shall be the name of his majesty for ever: and the whole earth shall be filled with his majesty') in Latin,

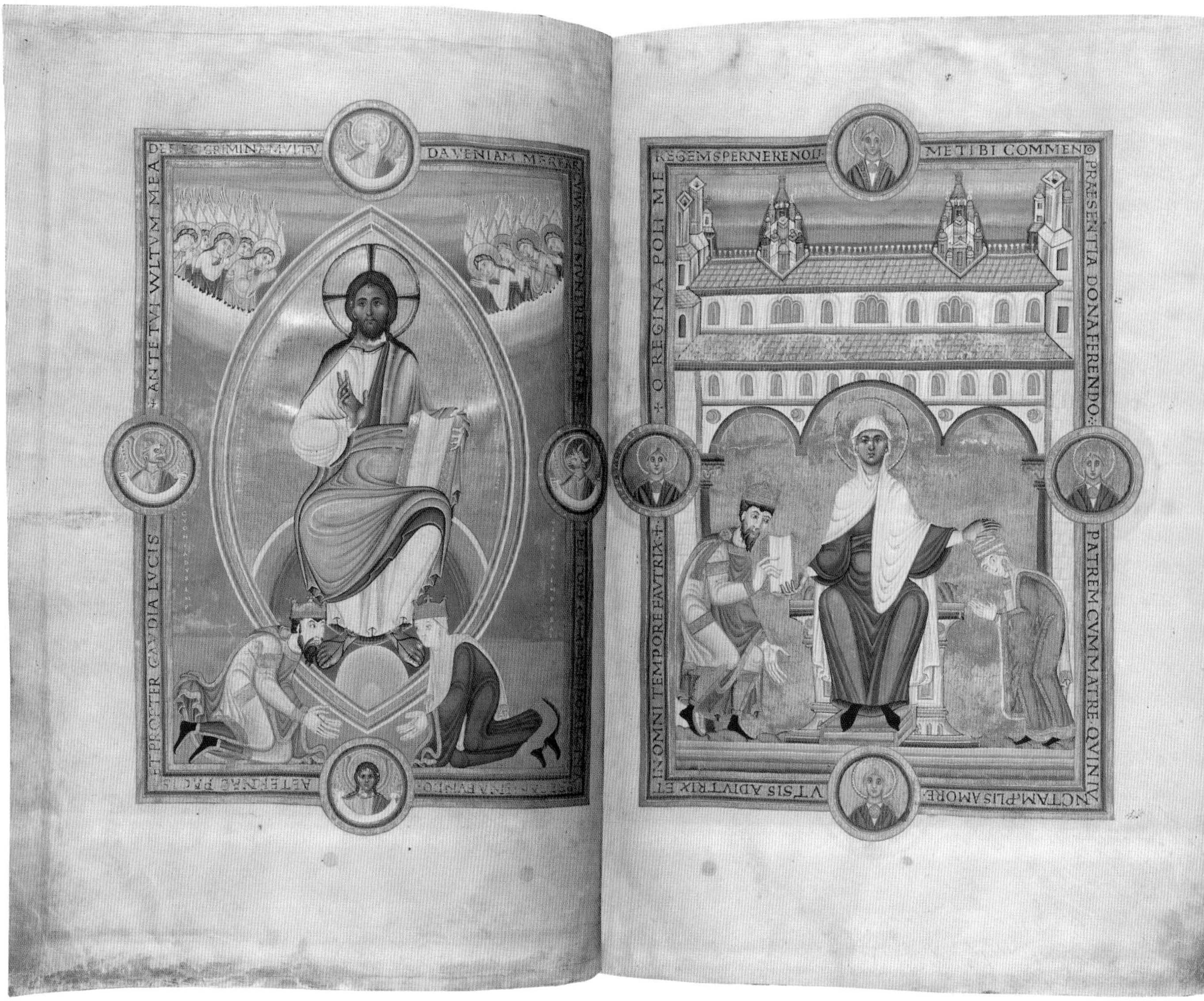

Fig. 1.9
Christ in Majesty with Conrad and Gisela, and Mary with Henry and Agnes.
El Escorial, MS Vitr. 17, ff. 2v–3

but written phonetically in a western version of Greek script. It is possible that the book held by Christ is the one presented to the Virgin by Henry. The book was made at the abbey church of Echternach, near Trier, a considerable distance from Speyer. It is explicit as to why it was made. Inscriptions were used to ensure that there could be no doubt as to the identity of the royal figures and their motives. The book was commissioned by the King for use in the Kingdom.

Royal books as gifts to or for kings (c. 1200–1300)

Books as gifts *from* kings continued to be made throughout the long millennium of the illuminated manuscript, roughly from the fifth to the sixteenth century. But books as gifts *to* or *for* kings followed a different historical pattern. This was because a book, unless it was composed entirely of pictures (which was rarely the case), implied or presumed a high level of literacy on the part of its recipient. In late Antiquity the Bible circulated in the mother tongues of many of its users (not just Greek, but Armenian, Coptic, Ethiopic, Gothic, Latin, Syriac and so forth). But in the West, after the collapse of Roman rule, the Bible circulated not in the various vernaculars of the West, but almost exclusively in Latin. Increasingly over time Latin was a language that had to be learned. Functional literacy in Latin amongst western rulers could not be assumed before, very approximately, the second half of the twelfth century, even if there were some exceptions (King Alfred is an outstanding example).[26] The Psalter, which usually contained various prayers and litanies along with a liturgical calendar and the 150 Psalms, was not only the primary text of private devotion; it was also the primary text from which Latin was learned in the Middle Ages, at least

Fig. 1.10
Scenes from the Nativity cycle, in a Psalter of St Louis.
Leiden, Universiteitsbibliotheek, MS BPL 76A, ff. 16v–17

until the rise in popularity of the Book of Hours, notably from the early fourteenth century.[27] The luxury Psalter, at least from the mid-eleventh century, also often contained prefatory images. These were generally not illustrations to the Psalms, nor images of the owners/donors, but pictorial cycles assembled from the Old and/or New Testaments. Such cycles were intended to reward and instruct the viewer/reader of the book. It is no coincidence, therefore, that beginning around 1200 a series of magnificent 'royal Psalters' are associated with the names of, in particular, French kings and queens, and their offspring.[28]

Several such Psalters became known as Psalters of St Louis (Louis IX of France, who was canonized in 1297). The earliest of these is now in Leiden (Universiteitsbibliotheek, MS BPL 76A).[29] It seems to have been made in northern England for Geoffrey Plantagenet, Archbishop of York (d. 1212), illegitimate son of Henry II (fig. 1.10). From Geoffrey it came by some means into the possession of Blanche of Castile, Queen of France, mother of Louis IX (the obit of her father, Alfonso VIII, d. 1214, was added to the book's calendar). Blanche was brought up in France from the time of her marriage in 1200 as a twelve-year-old to Louis VIII, son of Philip II Augustus. It may have been from this richly decorated book that Blanche herself learned to read Latin. This would not be inconsistent with the statement by a later hand that this was the Psalter of St Louis (b. 1214) from which *he* learned to read. (A further member of this group of manuscripts – Paris, Bibliothèque de l'Arsenal, MS 1186 – is called the Psalter of Blanche of Castile, and is a lavish book which she may have commissioned for her own use, around 1215–20).[30] After the calendar in the Leiden manuscript there are twenty-three pages of images, from the Creation to Samson in the Old Testament (occupying eight pages), followed by a New Testament cycle. The images are painted

Si come abraham uit trois angeles 7 un en aora.
Abrah
Si come il leur dona a maingier.

on one side of the parchment only, a sign of conspicuous consumption. This book passed through the hands of a series of royal or noble women: Agnes, Duchess of Burgundy (d. 1327), daughter of Louis IX; Jeanne de Bourgogne (d. 1349); and Blanche of Navarre (d. 1398), the latter two both queens of France; until reaching Philip the Bold, Duke of Burgundy.[31] Archbishop Geoffrey would surely have been astonished to learn that this book was used by so many women, and possibly by their children too. Such manuscripts have a more detailed provenance because they came to be considered quasi-relics of Louis IX, and later owners wanted to claim literary as well as religious kinship to their saintly forebear.[32] The Leiden Psalter repeated the second part of the journey in our diagram to successive royal women, and its archiepiscopal origins were forgotten as it became increasingly royal.

Related in terms of some of its pictorial content to the Leiden manuscript is the Psalter of Queen Ingeborg (Chantilly, Musée Condé, MS 1695), made in northern France (fig. 1.11).[33] Ingeborg was the wife of King Philip II Augustus of France; the Psalter was very probably commissioned either as a wedding gift to the Danish Princess (in 1193) or, more likely, to mark her reconciliation with her husband (in 1213). Its origin and royal destination are recognizable thanks to the obits in the calendar of Ingeborg's parents, Waldemar, King of the Danes (d. 1182), and Sofia, Queen of Dacia, as well as of Ingeborg's supporter Eleanor, Countess of Vermandois (after whose death in 1213 Vermandois lapsed to Philip II). A remarkable non-liturgical or devotional record of the Battle of Bouvines (the text is in French) was inserted in the calendar for 27 July: 'In the year 1214, Philip, King of France, conquered in battle King Otto and the Count of Flanders and the Count of Boulogne and numerous other barons.' The Ingeborg Psalter contains twenty-four full pages of miniatures executed (like those in the Leiden Psalter) on only one side of the parchment, with inscriptions mainly in French and frequently starting: 'Sy come ...' (Here is how ...). Most of the images are of the Life of Christ, but they are preceded by five pages of Old Testament scenes, and rounded off by two pages with the Theophilus legend (a priest sells his soul to the devil, but is saved by the intervention of the Virgin). It was twice noted by a later hand that 'This was the Psalter of St Louis'. It probably came to him on Ingeborg's death in 1236. It was in the French royal library when the first inventory was drawn up in 1373 (see below), when it was listed as the Psalter of St Louis.[34] In terms of our diagram the book was royal by origin and subsequent history, but the uses to which it was put by Ingeborg doubtless differed markedly from the pattern of possible use by Louis IX and subsequent royal owners.

Also identified as a Psalter of St Louis is a volume in Paris (BnF, MS lat. 10525), the most splendid of the books that are claimed to have been his (fig. 1.12).[35] The connection with the royal saint is noted in an early fifteenth-century inscription that records the history of the book from its ownership by Jeanne d'Evreux, Queen of France (d. 1371), who gave it to Charles V, who gave it to his son Charles VI, who gave it to Mary of France, a religious at the royal foundation of Poissy. Obits of Louis IX's father, grandfather, mother and brother (Robert of Artois) are original entries in the calendar. The latest elements in the calendar are the obits of his mother Blanche (d. 1253) and the feast of St Peter Martyr (also 1253). Although only half the size of the Ingeborg Psalter, this later St Louis Psalter has more than three times as many illustrations, as before on only one side of the parchment, and with vernacular captions: 'En ceste ymage est comment ...'. The Psalter has a prefatory cycle of seventy-eight full pages of Old Testament scenes, from the Sacrifices of Cain and Abel (Genesis 4:3–5) to 1 Kings (1 Samuel) 11:15 (Saul becomes

Fig. 1.11 (opposite)
Abraham and the angels, in a Psalter of St Louis (Ingeborg Psalter).
Chantilly, Musée Condé, MS 1695, f. 10v

Fig. 1.12
Abraham and the angels, in a Psalter of St Louis.
Paris, BnF, MS lat. 10525, f. 7v

King of Israel), but it is possible that some quires may be missing. It has never been doubted that this manuscript is a royal commission, and probably intended for a royal consumer. But given that the other Psalters of St Louis were definitely not made by or for Louis IX, we should be wary of concluding that this manuscript was an exception. Louis was a noted ascetic.[36] There were several royal women, for example, who may have been the book's intended recipient. The Psalter may have been a royal gift from rather than to Louis IX.

Although the first 'Psalter of St Louis' was an English manuscript, there was no English equivalent of Blanche of Castile to promote the making of royal Psalters in England, at least until the late thirteenth century. From this later period comes the lavish Psalter of Alphonso (cat. no. 17).[37] Alphonso was the son and heir apparent of Edward I of England and Eleanor of Castile. The Psalter was commissioned by either the King or the Queen (who died in 1290), or possibly both, to celebrate the forthcoming marriage of Alphonso to Margaret, daughter of Floris V, Count of Holland. The arms of Alphonso and Margaret appear together on the opening page of Psalm 1. But the marriage was prevented by Alphonso's premature death in 1284, and the manuscript, which may have been intended for either Alphonso or Margaret, appears to have been left unfinished. A second dynastic marriage between England and Holland was arranged in 1285, in this case between the young royal Princess Elizabeth (b. 1282) and John, the infant son of the Count of Holland (b. 1284). The coats of arms of England and Holland could therefore be reused, if one overlooked the significance of the label in the English arms (symbol of a son). John of Holland was brought up in England, almost as much hostage as guest. When his father Floris V was murdered in 1296, he was succeeded as Count of Holland by John, who was duly married to Elizabeth in 1297. John of Holland, however, died in 1299, aged fifteen, without children. Elizabeth then married Humphrey de Bohun, Earl of Hereford and Essex, in 1302, bearing him at least ten children before her death in 1316.

The complex and unpredictable history of the Alphonso Psalter can be read in its images. The book must have been written in 1284, but decorated at that point only in the first two quires (the standard of the craftsmanship here is superb) (fig. 1.13). To these quires of text with a few marginal images were later added prefatory pages comprising full-page images of predominantly female saints (including Margaret but not Elizabeth), and thirty small images of Christ's Passion, six to a page (fig. 1.14). Most remarkable, the Passion scenes must have been cut from the pages of a diminutive book and then pasted into the Psalter. Each scene is on a separate leaf measuring just 45 x 35 mm overall, and their frames are just 32 x 24 mm. The presence of the Bohun arms in one of the Passion scenes shows this phase must date from or after Elizabeth's second marriage. The strongly female character of the book is confirmed by the inclusion in the calendar of obits of Elizabeth's grandmother, mother and sister and, in due course, of herself. In terms of our diagram, the book was commissioned by a king or queen as a gift for her or his son, a king-to-be, or for his wife, but it never set off on that journey, instead being diverted to her or his daughter, first as Countess of Holland (in the World), then as Countess of Hereford and Essex (in the Kingdom), at which point new images were added, and some recycled from another book. The recycled images, which include the Bohun arms, may have been from a picture book that was another royal gift to Elizabeth.

Fig. 1.13
Text and marginal decoration, in the Alphonso Psalter.
Additional 24686, f. 13

Fig. 1.14 (opposite)
Six scenes from the Passion with the Bohun arms, in the Alphonso Psalter.
Additional 24686, f. 4

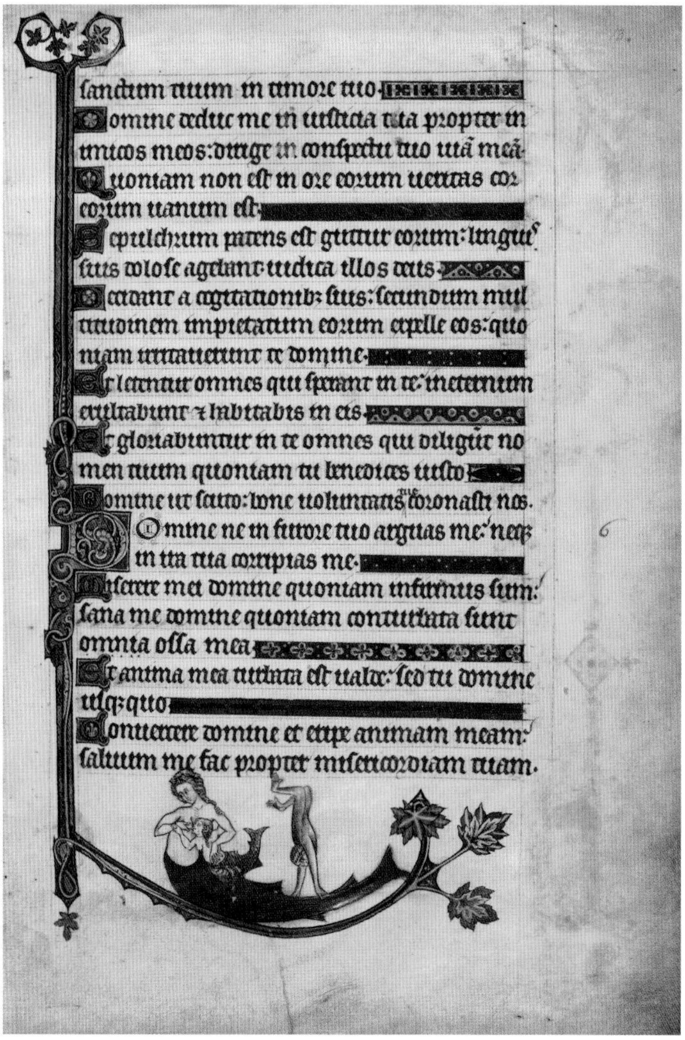

Fig. 1.15
Visual colophon, from the *Bible moralisée*.
New York, Pierpont Morgan Library, MS M. 240, f. 8

A remarkable example from the same period of a radically different type of French royal biblical picture book is provided by the moralized Bibles.[38] These were books of large format, the exact opposite of the biblical images pasted into the Alphonso Psalter, but they also had an English royal phase. There were no detailed precedents for these works before production on them was begun in the 1220s. The first such book (Vienna, ÖNB, cod. 2554) had texts purely in the vernacular, and may have been commissioned by Blanche of Castile, around 1220.[39] It used an unprecedented layout, with eight medallions of images, flanked by brief texts, on every page. Beginning with the Creation, the biblical account was followed as far as 4 Kings 4:20 (2 Kings), every biblical image and caption being accompanied by a visual and verbal parallel with a moralizing flavour. Although many leaves are missing, this book still contains 1032 medallions. The next surviving *Bible moralisée* was made for Blanche's husband, Louis VIII, with texts exclusively in Latin (Vienna, ÖNB, cod. 1179).[40] It was a more ambitious volume, including additional Old Testament books, plus the Apocalypse, and, despite losses there are 1950 medallions. Subsequently a pair of expanded versions of the *Bible moralisée* in three volumes, and originally with over five thousand images each, were made for Louis IX and his Queen, Margaret of Provence, probably at the instigation of Blanche of Castile once more (Toledo, Tesoro del Catedral + New York, Pierpont Morgan Library, MS M. 240; Oxford, Bodleian Library, MS Bodley 270b + Paris, BnF, MS lat. 11560 + Harley 1526–1527).[41] Initially the plan for the Toledo *Bible moralisée* was that every Latin text should have a vernacular equivalent, but this plan was abandoned as too ambitious. One of these three-volume moralized Bibles retains its visual colophon, in which a king and queen preside over the work of a religious, who is instructing a lay craftsman at work on making the book (fig. 1.15). Of the two surviving copies of the three-volume version, one was given by Louis IX to his cousin Alfonso X of Castile and León (grandson of Alfonso IX, the brother of Blanche of Castile), and the other may have been given by Margaret of Provence (wife of Louis IX) to Henry III of England and/or his wife, Margaret's sister Eleanor of Provence.[42] Most remarkable, the English fascination with illustrated manuscripts of the Apocalypse seems to have taken its cue from the *Bible moralisée* sent by Margaret, Queen of France, to Eleanor, Queen of England, around 1255.[43]

Production of these *Bibles moralisées* continued into the late fifteenth century.[44] All seem to have started out as royal books and to a great degree they remained royal books as they changed hands. To judge by their difference in layout and content from Psalters, moralized Bibles were presumably used in very different ways. In particular it seems probable that the latter would not have been employed for solitary contemplation and private devotion. More likely, a favoured household priest would have helped the royal consumer in her or his reading, understanding and interpreting of texts and images. In terms of our diagram, queens may have been more important than kings.

Royal books for royal use (c.1300–1470) – amassing a royal library

Luxury books such as royal Psalters and moralized Bibles were commissioned with the specific requirements of their users clearly in mind, and continued to be produced in the later centuries of the manuscript era. The role of women, especially royal women, in the commission and transmission of such books was particularly important, and merits still greater attention than it has received.[45] It may even be helpful to consider the principal intended audience for such illuminated manuscripts to have been women, not men. These books came to be considered of dynastic significance, and were passed on from one royal generation to the next. The process led to an accumulation of books, possibly multiple copies of the same texts (as with Psalters, for example). It was very different, however, from the type of systematic collecting and commissioning of books necessary to form a useful library, royal or otherwise. Indeed, it cannot have seemed obvious before the fourteenth century that a royal library, as distinct from a royal collection of treasure books, was necessary. What then were the factors that led to the founding of such an institution or institutions?

Taking the long view, we can say that monastic libraries were almost as old as the practice of monasticism itself. [46] St Benedict in his Rule (*c.* 540) had laid down that monks must spend considerable time every day in *lectio divina*.[47] A large community thus needed many books supplementary to those needed for the celebration of the monastic offices and the liturgy. In addition to volumes of biblical commentary and exegesis, it was necessary to study and understand God's creation and man's role through encyclopaedias, as well as works of history, chronology, science and so forth. But if by the later Middle Ages numerous such libraries already existed (in monasteries and in cathedral and other schools), what prompted the formation of specifically royal libraries? The answer lies, it would seem, partly in the growing use of the vernacular in books, and partly in the actions of a few monarchs who cultivated a name for wisdom.

The principal biblical model for medieval rulers was King David. Not only was David a model of penitence, he was especially familiar in visual terms owing to his repeated appearances in images in Psalters. Royal children were brought up on David as they learned to read from the Psalms. But it was Solomon, David's son, who was the model of a specifically wise king. Solomon was the author of three of the five Old Testament wisdom books: Wisdom (of Solomon), Proverbs 'To know wisdom' (Proverbs 1:2) and Ecclesiastes. The exceptions were Job and Ecclesiasticus. The role of wisdom was clearly of great importance, yet few medieval monarchs were termed 'the Wise' by their contemporaries (with hindsight the number was greater). One exception, whom we have encountered before, was Alfonso X, known as *el sabio* (the learned, wise), who ruled Castile and León from 1252 to 1284. Alfonso organized the compilation of encyclopaedic works of law, history, hunting, chess, astronomy and astrology, and of music and religious verse, which were produced in the vernacular, some of them in luxury illuminated copies. In the *Libro de las Piedras* he is described as *Alfonso amador de sciencias y de saber* (lover of knowledge and wisdom).[48]

The Angevin King Robert of Naples, who ruled 1309–43, perhaps took his inspiration from Alfonso X.[49] Known as Robert the Wise, he was represented in a frontispiece image in the Anjou Bible now in Leuven, surrounded by virtues who drive off vices (fig. 1.16).[50] In an inscription he is described as *Rex expertus in omni scientia* (King expert in all knowledge). He promoted the vernacular writings of Boccaccio and Petrarch, as well as artists such as Simone Martini and Giotto. He was particularly renowned for his preaching and authored works of philosophical, theological and devotional content. Most notably in the present context, he built up a library, now known largely through payments in account books.[51] He supplemented the books acquired by his father and grandfather with works of moral instruction, devotion, liturgy, hagiography, theology, history, geography, medicine, canon and civil law and classical texts, including some costly works in the vernacular for his son, Charles of Calabria. Paolo da Perugia, a proto-humanist scholar, who had been a royal secretary from 1324, was from 1332 his librarian. In 1347 the Angevin collection in Naples was looted and dispersed by Robert's cousin, King Louis of Hungary. Some of the most remarkable books found their way to France, and a few to England; an example is the mid-fourteenth-century copy of the *Histoire ancienne* (cat. no. 135).

When in 1373 Giles Mallet drew up an inventory for Charles V (1364–80) of the books in the French royal collection, located primarily on three floors in a tower of the Louvre, the librarian's list ran to 965 items.[52] About 10 per cent of these have been identified among surviving volumes. Other royal books were housed elsewhere – notably some treasure books, such as the Ingeborg Psalter, at Vincennes. Clearly these books must have been accumulating for some time to have reached such numbers. Charles V's father, John II (r. 1350–64, but held hostage in England from 1356), was a systematic bibliophile, who before 1356 commissioned translations into French of the Bible with commentary (by Jean de Sy, unfinished), the *Bible moralisée*, Aristotle, Augustine's *City of God*, classical texts (Valerius Maximus, Pierre Bersuire's translation of Livy) and works of instruction (*Jeu des échecs* / Game of chess). Some overlap with the types of book translated by Alfonso X is notable. John II certainly inherited a taste for collecting and commissioning vernacular translations of books from his parents, Philip VI and his Queen, Jeanne de Bourgogne (d. 1349). Jeanne did not merely act as a consort in these activities, she was a very important patron in her own right. For example, she commissioned Jean de Vignay to translate Vincent of Beauvais's *Miroir historial*, a vast undertaking, intended specifically for the education of her son John (see cat. no. 57). Between them Philip VI and Jeanne commissioned from Jean de Vignay translations of the *Golden Legend* (saints' lives) (see cat. no. 79), the *Miroir de l'église* of Hugh of St Cher, the Epistle and Gospel lections for Sundays and feast days, and an anthology of crusade-

related texts, with over 160 miniatures, which was compiled in 1333–34 (cat. no. 91).[53]

At the same time as Charles V was enriching the French royal library, his younger brothers – notably Philip the Bold, Duke of Burgundy, and John, Duke of Berry (d. 1416) – were doing something very similar with ducal libraries. The extent of their libraries can be gauged through inventories.[54] Although John of Berry's library was dispersed after his death, the Burgundian library remained a focus of ducal attention throughout the fifteenth century. As Ghent and Bruges (in Burgundian territory) gradually overtook Paris as the most important centre of luxury book production, the tastes of the dukes of Burgundy were aped by the nobility – Louis of Gruuthuse, Anthony of Burgundy ('the Great Bastard'), Philip of Cleves, the counts of Chimay (De Croÿ) – who spent fortunes building up their collections of books.[55]

Royal books as gifts to or for kings (c. 1470–1550)

To recognize that a particular book was given *by* a king, and to understand why, may prove to be no more difficult perhaps than identifying and translating an inscription. But to understand why a particular book was given *to* a king – in the absence of an inscription – can be much more difficult to fathom, because there are many possibilities. For example, a donor might wish to present a king with a copy of a text which he knew was already of interest. Alternatively, the gift might represent something hitherto entirely unknown, a composition by the donor, perhaps. If the giver wished to flatter the royal recipient, it is conceivable that the gift might imply skills and/or interests that the ruler did not in fact possess. Over time the types of books that were given to kings became progressively wider, and hence the possibilities became ever greater. It is not feasible in the present instance to do more than highlight a few variants on the theme of royalty as recipients of books.

The *Carmina regia*, an address in verse (cat. no. 134; fig. 1.17) is a magnificent gift to King Robert of Naples from the city-state of Prato, in Tuscany, which was at the time (*c.* 1335–40) seeking the King's protection. The question of why such a book was made is thus easily answered in this case. Unlike commissioning, for example, an illustrated Psalter, this was an overtly political act. The book was clearly calculated to impress, by its very large format and its numerous large-scale miniatures and extensive use of gold. Doubtless the Pratese, as they planned the book, felt that Robert would pay special attention to a full-page image of himself. The image that the book presents of Robert, seen in profile, thin lipped, wrinkled and somewhat desiccated, is clearly based on an

Fig. 1.16 (opposite)
King Robert the Wise, in the Anjou Bible.
Leuven, M. Sabbe Library, Anjou Bible, f. 3v

Fig. 1.17
Mounted knight of Prato, in the *Carmina regia.*
Royal 6 E. ix, f. 24

'official' Angevin/Neapolitan portrait-like representation, as may be seen in comparison with the frontispiece of the Anjou Bible (fig. 1.16). In terms of the diagram, therefore, the gift is more complex than at first appears. It comes from the World beyond the Kingdom, but from a corporation that seeks to be part of that Kingdom. It is destined for the King, and seeks to represent him in a manner with which he would already be familiar. The donors must therefore have consulted the Palace to discover what the King would find most appropriate and pleasing. This manipulation of the categories for the production and consumption of a royal book suggests the book's makers were indeed thinking in terms similar to those of our diagram.

Another book of political significance, intended for a royal viewer and coming from outside the Kingdom, is the *Epistre au roi Richart* (datable 1395; cat. no. 140). The lengthy and detailed 'Letter' to Richard II of England by the

French royal counsellor Philip de Mézières, runs to eighty-two folios. It proposes that Richard found a new crusading order with Charles VI and promotes the case of a marriage between Richard and Isabel of France. An image of the author presenting the book to Richard – anticipating the event – faces a rich frontispiece in which the name of Jesus is set against a heraldic ground bearing the arms of France and England. Above, the royal crowns of France and England flank the bloody crown of thorns. The kings of France and England flank the 'King of Peace'. This gift/letter, addressed unequivocally to the King (Richard II), and originating from outside the Kingdom, was coming from de Mézières, doing the bidding of Charles VI. Doubtless, as in all diplomatic correspondence, the most important aspects of the message were not committed to parchment, but presented verbally by the messenger. In terms of our diagram, this manuscript was accompanied by a cryptic message which negotiated the route to the King in secrecy. In terms of politics, Richard and Isabel were married in 1396, but neither King participated in the disastrous crusade of the same year.

On occasion, gifts coming to a king from outside the Kingdom failed to reach their intended audience. An example is a humanist manuscript of a Latin verse translation of a Hellenistic ekphrasis of images by Filippo degli Alberici of Mantua, the *Tabula cebetis* (cat. no. 110). This was dedicated to Henry VII, but it appears that Alberici, who came from Paris – where the book had been illuminated – to England in 1507, failed to gain an audience with the King. In 1508 he wrote to Richard Foxe, Bishop of Winchester, asking him to support him in his desire to enter the service of Henry VII, a request that he followed up in 1509 with a presentation copy of a poem, *De homine condito*, dedicated to the Bishop,[56] but his petitioning was never successful. The *Tabula cebetis*, meanwhile, seems to have been given to Joachim Bretoner, a Cambridge-based humanist. The manuscript was royal by intended destination, but never, it would seem, Royal.

A product of the Palace sphere of our diagram, which differs greatly from what one might expect, is a volume of moral instruction entitled *Enseignement de la vraie noblesse* (cat. no. 69). It was written at the palace of Sheen by the librarian of Henry VII, Quentin Poulet (who had been trained in Lille), as a presentation copy for the King. The script and high-quality decoration are typical of south Netherlandish work. Despite the proximity of craftsman/donor to royal recipient – Palace and King in terms of our diagram – it is notable how few elements of the book's appearance are specific to Henry VII or even to England. Were it not for the introductory dedication, and the presence of royal arms, one would be hard pressed to identify the book as a product of London, not Bruges.

To be the recipient of gifts from beyond the confines of his Kingdom, a king had to be known internationally. Henry VIII was probably better and more widely known in his own time than any other English monarch.[57] It is not surprising, therefore, that a range of luxury manuscript books was sent to him for a variety of reasons.

In 1542 Jean Rotz of Dieppe presented to Henry VIII an atlas with twelve double-page maps of the world (cat. no. 95).[58] The book had originally been intended for presentation to Francis I of France, but Rotz adapted it for a new destination, adding full-page images of the English royal coats of arms, supported by a white hound and red dragon, and the Tudor rose. Rotz's subsequent appointment as hydrographer to the English King suggests that his gift of the costly book could be seen as a successful investment. In this case the book travelled from the World to the Kingdom to the Palace to the King himself. At the same time, the donor made a comparable journey, sought an audience with the King, and presented himself to the monarch, much as he also presented his book. The King accepted both.

The success of Jean Rotz's gift was by no means without precedent or parallel. Another is the loosely speaking scientific volume, the *Cosmographie* of Jean Mallard in French verse (cat. no. 96).[59] It was presented to Henry VIII in 1539, after Mallard (like Rotz) switched allegiance from the court of Francis I, where he had been a court poet, to that of Henry VIII, where he petitioned for a similar role through the presentation of this book. His move can be seen to have been a success. Once established in England, Mallard wrote the illuminated Psalter of Henry VIII (cat. no. 45), utilising an elegant French Humanist script. The fact that Henry was represented in the image to Psalm 52 ('The fool said …') with William Somer, the King's fool (fig. 2.14), indicates that whereas Mallard's *Cosmographie* had come (in terms of the diagram) from the World, the Psalter he made for the King came from the Palace.[60]

A gift to Henry VIII that came from a much greater distance was a presentation copy of moral/philosophical dialogues of Lucian of Samosata (d. *c.* 180), and of the humanist Pandolfo Collenuccio (d. 1504) (cat. no. 113).[61] This book was produced in Italy by some of the most skilled craftsmen of the early sixteenth century: the scribe Ludovico degli Arrighi, and the artist Attavante degli Attavanti (d. *c.* 1520–25). The scribe was based in the papal chancery at Rome, the artist in Florence. The book was commissioned, however, not by an Italian (the term is anachronistic, but convenient), but by a chamberlain of Henry VIII, Geoffrey surnamed Chamber, while the latter was in Italy. It was presented to Henry VIII on his return to England by Chamber. The circumstances are recorded in a prefatory text written by Arrighi. That the book was commissioned for presentation to Henry (it was not an off-the-peg volume

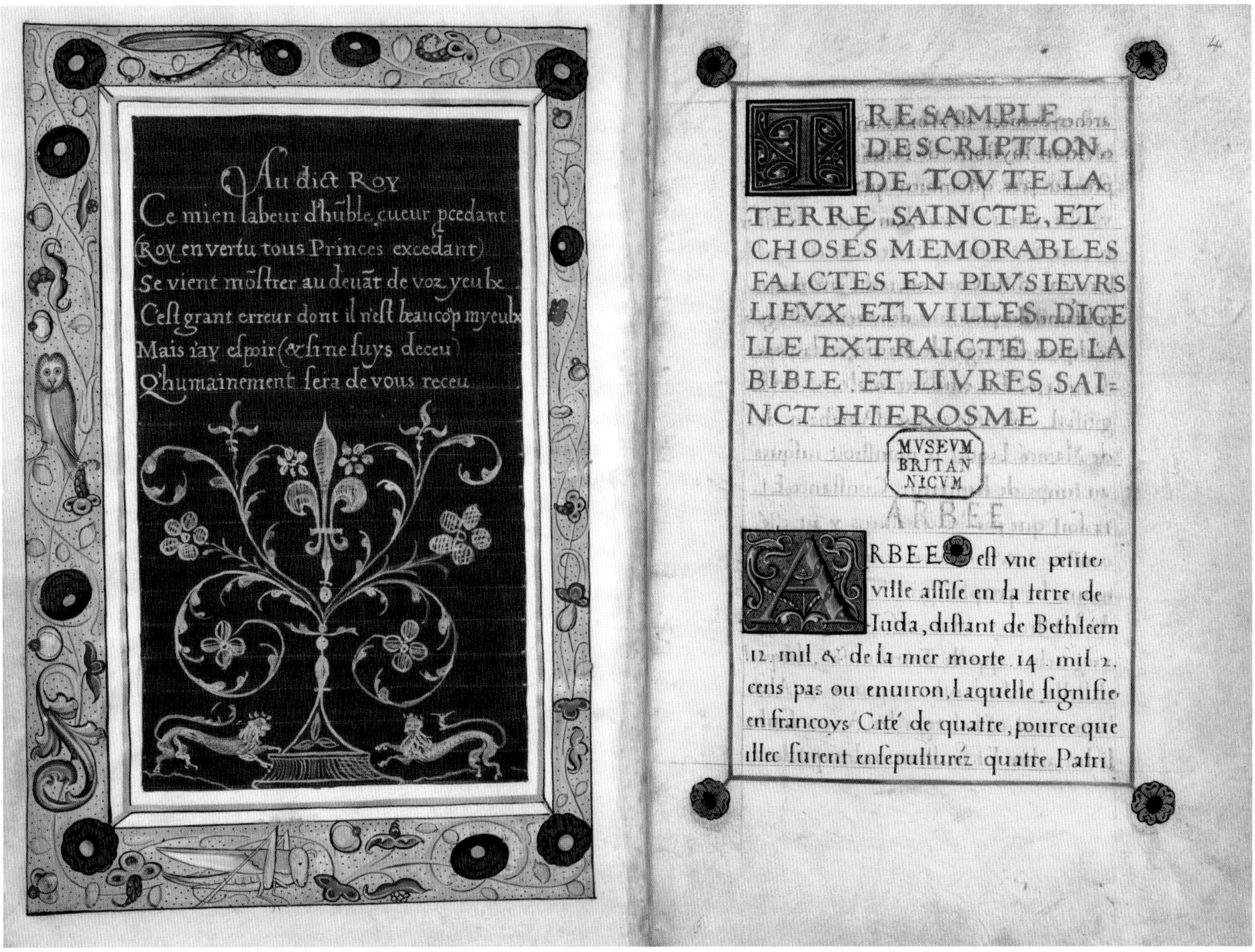

Fig. 1.18
Martin de Brion, *Tresample description de toute la Terre Saincte.*
Royal 20 A. iv, ff. 3v–4

with an added preface) is shown by the Tudor roses on later folios, as well as the royal arms supported by the white hound and the red dragon. Thus although in geographical terms the book came from far beyond the borders of the Kingdom, in fact it was devised by a member of the Palace.

Among the books from overseas presented or dedicated to Henry VIII is a copy of the *Description of the Holy Land*, in French, by Martin de Brion of Paris (dated *c.* 1540; cat. no. 146; fig. 1.18).[62] Not knowing Henry VIII personally, de Brion relied on extravagantly flattering language, and luxury of materials, to ensure his gift was noticed. The prefatory text was written on four pages in gold on a red-painted ground, and records the author's admiration for Henry VIII. A short excerpt gives an idea of the author's tone: 'Certes bien est digne d'estre Roy du monde le Roy qui cherche scavoir tout ce qui est contenu en iceluy' (Certainly the king who seeks to know everything that is in the world is worthy to be king of the world). The opening of the prefatory dedication was placed opposite a full-page image of the arms of England, crowned, and set within the Order of the Garter, flanked to left and right by a gold 'H', with a Tudor rose in each corner. To ensure the intended recipient noticed the book, it was bound in crimson velvet and embroidered partially with gold thread with the same English royal design as within, including embroidered Tudor roses in each corner. Remarkably, the embroidered design was repeated on both covers (it would not matter which way up the volume was laid), and then, for protection, the book was placed within a black leather case, itself decorated with the royal arms once again, to attract attention. (Sadly, the case does not survive.) Of all the books in the royal collection, it is this volume, sent from Paris for reasons that are now obscure, that declares itself most unambiguously to be an English royal book.

Royal books in non-royal contexts?

The final category to be considered here comprises royal books, in particular those with royal images, which appear to be circulating in our diagram solely in the non-royal outer spheres – in other words, royal books that do not appear to have a direct connection with royal persons. What was the function of royal images in such books?

The register of the fraternity of the Holy Trinity, Luton (cat. no. 36), founded in 1474, has a superlative frontispiece image.[63] The body of the crucified Christ is supported by the enthroned God the Father, with the dove of the Holy Spirit between their heads. Two angels lift and draw back the hangings around the Trinity. The divine Trinity is echoed by a mundane trinity in the foreground: a bishop in the centre is flanked by a king and queen, the three kneeling in prayer, each at a prie-dieu. The Bishop, Thomas Rotherham of Lincoln, holds the end of a long narrow scroll on which is written:

: Blessod : Lord : in : Trenete [trinity]
: Save : all : thes : fretarnete [fraternity]

The fraternity included a chantry to pray for the souls of Edward IV and Queen Elizabeth as well as for Thomas Rotherham and all other members of the fraternity. The image represents the King and Queen in prayer, as members *of* the fraternity. They would become objects of prayer *by* the fraternity after their death. In terms of our diagram, the book can be said to have been commissioned in the Kingdom sphere, in a part of that sphere very close to the Palace, given the eminence of Thomas Rotherham – who became Lord Chancellor in 1474 (a coincidence?). As for its function, the fraternity book went to Luton, for use in the Kingdom. But it is hard to believe that before going to Luton, Bishop Thomas would not have shown the image – doubtless made in the Low Countries – to Edward and Elizabeth as evidence of his support for the Crown. Indeed, when viewed from Bishop Thomas's point of view, that short moment of display may have been a primary purpose of the book.

Conclusion: object and idea

The Old Royal library includes many individual manuscripts of superb quality. These objects were made at different times, in different places, for different purposes, by and for different people, over the entire millennium of the handwritten codex-book. It is a truism, but nonetheless worth bearing in mind, that it is only possible to understand the past by simplifying it. When it comes to understanding Royal (or royal) books this is especially the case. Handwritten books are extraordinarily complex artefacts, the products of innumerable decisions, and infinitely variable. In almost every case we now see only the results of decisions, not the processes by which those decisions were reached. We must keep a sharp look-out if we wish to observe evidence that can provide insights into how and why such books were made and how they were subsequently used. In particular we need to avoid the temptation to assimilate variety, and gloss over inconsistency, so as to make the objects fit a single, simple overall plan. The diagram (fig 1.2), which may initially have seemed quite complex, proved to be not nearly complex enough to represent the many patterns that we observed. We need to allow the books to tell their own stories.

The individual history of every Royal book is undeniably important. Yet a broader context of ideas must not be overlooked. The British Library's Royal manuscripts can best be understood as a subset of the category of 'royal manuscript book', of which the British Library has many important examples. The formalization of the English royal library in the fourth quarter of the fifteenth century transformed individual books into an assemblage: the royal book was reformulated as an idea, the royal library.

NOTES

1 Lowden, 'Image' (1993), p. 215.
2 For recent contributions on (later) medieval gift-giving see, for example, Chattaway, *Order* (2006); Wild, 'Gift Inventory' (2010).
3 A story many times re-told. See, first, Roberts and Skeat, *Birth* (1983). For general orientation see also Brown, *In the Beginning* (2006); Klingshirn and Safran, *Early Christian Book* (2007); Gamble, *Books and Readers* (1995).
4 Martial, *Epigrams*, Book xiv, no. CXC.
5 A fine recent survey is Parker, *New Testament* (2009), esp. pp. 13–25.
6 Conveniently accessible in Schaff and Wace, *Eusebius* (1979), pp. 548–49, chaps 36, 37.
7 On Constantine's beliefs see Barnes, *Constantine* (1981).
8 See first the online site: http://www.codexsinaiticus.org. Also Parker, *Codex Sinaiticus* (2010).
9 Schaff and Wace, *Eusebius* (1979), p. 42. For the plan of the Temple, see Bede, 'In Templo', ii, pp. 28–30, and reference to Cassiodorus's *pictura* of the Temple in his single-volume Bible (pandect). Cassiodorus also mentions his painted image of the tabernacle in his

Expositio Psalmorum, lxxxvi.1. See also Sed-Rajna, 'Tabernacle/Temple' (1997–98), pp. 23–24.
10 McKendrick, 'Codex Alexandrinus' (2003), pp. 1–16.
11 Thompson, *Introduction* (1912), p. 32.
12 See the online publication: http://www.ub.uu.se/codexargenteus.
13 Lowden, 'Beginnings' (1999), p. 48.
14 Lowden, 'Word made Visible (2007), pp. 13–47, pls 1–15.
15 *English Historical Documents* (n.d.), according to Eddius Stephanus's *Life of St Wilfrid*, no. 154 (p. 694), chap. 18.
16 *English Historical Documents* (n.d.), no. 172 (p. 747).
17 Kessler, *Illustrated Bibles* (1977).
18 Koehler and Mütherich, *Karolingischen Miniaturen*, 2, pp. 56–69, pls 42–66. Further bibliography in http://www.bl.uk/catalogues/illuminatedmanuscripts.
19 Kessler, *Illustrated Bibles* (1977), pp. 135–38; Jemolo and Morelli, *La Bibbia* (1981); Diebold, 'Ruler Portrait' (1994).
20 Miller, *Charters* (2001).
21 Kessler, *Illustrated Bibles* (1977), pp. 125–35.
22 See Gerchow, 'King Cnut' (1992); Keynes, *Liber Vitae* (1996); Parker, 'Gift' (2002); Karkov, *Ruler Portraits* (2004); and http://www.bl.uk/catalogues/illuminatedmanuscripts.
23 See Brooks, *Early History* (1984); Heslop, '*De luxe* Manuscripts' (1990); Gerchow, 'King Cnut' (1992); Dumville, *Caroline Script* (1993); and http://www.bl.uk/catalogues/illuminatedmanuscripts.
24 See in general Mayr-Harting, *Ottonian Book* (1991).
25 For the Speyer Golden Gospels, see Serrano, *El Códice Aureo* (1987); Boeckler, *Das goldene Evangelienbuch* (1933); Dodwell, *Pictorial Arts* (1993), pp. 144–46.
26 Invaluable starting points on the question of literacy are McKitterick, *Carolingians* (1989); Clanchy, *Written Record* (1993).
27 See the useful collection ed. by Büttner, *Illuminated Psalter* (2004).
28 Stirnemann, 'Les Bibliothèques' (1989). On royal Psalters see Lowden, *Making* (2000), pp. 51–52; and, more recently, Vidas, *Christina Psalter* (2006).
29 Morgan, *Early Gothic Manuscripts* (1982), 1, no. 14.
30 Martin, *Les Joyaux* (1909).
31 De Winter, *Bibliothèque* (1985). Wijsman, 'Psalter' (2006), pp. 32–42, on the continuing use of the Psalter by princes and princesses into the early sixteenth century.
32 In general, see Kauffmann, 'Image' (1993), and specifically pls 9–17.
33 Deuchler, *Ingeborgpsalter* (1967); Conklin, 'Ingeborg' (1997). See also the Getty Psalter: Kren, *French Illuminated Manuscripts* (2007), pp. xi, 12–14.
34 Deuchler, *Ingeborgpsalter* (1967), pp. 6–7; see also pp. 183–84.
35 Stahl, *Picturing Kingship* (2008). See also review by Patricia Stirnemann, who kindly made the text available before publication.
36 Le Goff, *Saint Louis* (1996).
37 Bond, 'Description' (1863); Hutchinson, 'Attitudes toward Nature' (1974); Sandler, *Gothic Manuscripts* (1986), I, pp. 24, 27; 2, no. 1; Alexander and Binski, *Age of Chivalry* (1987), no. 357; Goodall, 'Heraldry in Decoration' (1997); Parsons, *Eleanor of Castile* (1997).
38 In general, see Lowden, *Making* (2000). See also the Electronic Bibliography: http://www.courtauld.ac.uk/people/lowden_john/bibliography.shtml; and Haussherr, *Bible moralisée* (2009).
39 See Haussherr, *Bible moralisée* (1973).
40 See Lowden, *Making* (2000), pp. 55–94.
41 *Biblia de San Luis* (1999); De Laborde, *Bible moralisée* (1911–27).
42 On the *Bibles moralisées* as dynastic books, see Lowden, *Making* (2000), ii, pp. x–xi, 201–3, 208–9.
43 Lowden, 'Apocalypse' (2004).
44 Lowden, '*Bible moralisée*' (2005).
45 A point considered in more detail and with references in Scot McKendrick's essay, below. Most manuscript scholars have explored the significance of female patronage, but the general use in manuscripts of masculine forms, especially in Latin prayers, seems to have been assumed unquestioningly to reflect or even indicate a generally male readership. In practice female users of such books would have known enough to have been able to substitute *peccatricem* for *peccatorem* and so forth. Plentiful evidence to support this view is provided by books known to have been passed down in the female line, which nonetheless retain masculine endings.
46 Still useful is the wide-ranging study by Thompson, *Medieval Library* (1939).
47 See the Holy Rule of St Benedict, especially chaps 48 and 42, conveniently available online: http://www.ccel.org/ccel/benedict/rule2.html.
48 Burns, *Emperor of Culture* (1990).
49 Kelly, *New Solomon* (2003).
50 Watteeuw and Van der Stock, *Anjou Bible* (2010).
51 Coulter, 'Library' (1944). Kelly, *New Solomon* (2003), pp. 26–31.
52 Delisle, *Recherches* (1907); Avril and Lafaurie, *Librairie* (1968). In comparison, the papal library at Avignon grew from nothing to 2053 manuscripts between 1309 and the inventory of Urban V in 1369. The papal library was also housed in a tower. See Faucon, *Librairie des papes* (1886–87), i, pp. 93–262. In general see *Histoire des bibliothèques* (1989).
53 Rouse and Rouse, *Manuscripts* (2000), i, pp. 244–47.
54 Guiffrey, *Inventaires* (1894–96); de Winter, *Bibliothèque* (1985).
55 Kren and McKendrick, *Illuminating the Renaissance* (2003), pp. 68–69. See also Wijsman *Luxury Bound* (2010).
56 Rundle, 'Filippo Alberici' (2005), pp. 147–49.
57 Essential context provided by Carley, *King Henry VIII* (2004); *Henry VIII* (2009).
58 Wallis, *Maps and Text* (1981); Wallis, 'Rotz Atlas' (1982); Carley, *Libraries* (2000), H2. 994; Toulouse, *Marine Cartography* (2007).
59 See Taylor, *Tudor Geography* (1930), pp. 71–72, pl. opp. p. 72; Cooper, 'Jean Mallard' (2003); Doran, *Henry VIII* (2009), no. 241 (entry by James P. Carley); Carley, *Prayer Book* (2009), pp. 44–59.
60 See Backhouse, 'Two Books' (1966–67); Tudor-Craig, 'Henry VIII' (1989), pp. 194–205; Carley, *Libraries* (2000), p. 192, H2 1098; pp. 171–72; Doran, *Henry VIII* (2009), no. 194 (entry by James P. Carley); Carley, *Prayer Book* (2009); Sharpe, *Selling* (2009), p. 73.
61 See Wolpe, 'Royal Manuscript (1958); Kren, *Renaissance Painting* (1983), no. 17; Rummel, *Erasmus* (1985), p. 50; Starkey, *Henry VIII* (1991), no. ii.15; Alexander, 'Foreign Illuminators' (1999), p. 55.
62 See Davenport, 'Embroidered Bindings' (1904), pp. 268–69; Karrow, *Mapmakers* (1993), pp. 94–95; Backhouse, 'Robert Cotton's Record' (1997), p. 232; Carley, *Libraries* (2000), H5. 140.
63 See Gough, *Register* (1906); Sotheby's, *Catalogue of Bute Collection* (1983), lot 19; Lunn, 'Luton Fraternity' (1984); Campbell, *Early Flemish Pictures* (1985), p. 45; Marks, 'Guild Registers' (1998); Alexander, 'Foreign Illuminators' (1999), p. 57; Scott, 'Illustration and Decoration' (2000); Marks and Williamson, *Gothic* (2003), no. 347.

A European Heritage: Books of Continental Origin collected by the English Royal Family from Edward III to Henry VIII

SCOT McKENDRICK

The Old Royal library, which was given in 1757 to the British nation and is now held by the British Library, is an eloquent witness to the development of English culture and identity. Yet for many who first encounter the manuscripts from that collection it may come as a shock that most of their late medieval splendour is of Continental rather than English origin. Why, they may ask, is so much of their artistic merit the result of foreign rather than native English hands? Also, why are the texts of so many volumes in this English royal library the works of Continental, not English authors, and their language French, not English? Specialists, on the other hand, have long recognized the Royal manuscripts as a critical resource for the study of the art, literature and language of late medieval France and the southern Netherlands. For them the collection has provided a rich seam of research materials on which to base their studies of particular Continental authors, texts or artists. However, the question as to why such volumes ever came to be in English possession – this is essentially what lies behind any shock felt in a first-time encounter with the Royal manuscripts – has been only recently perceived as worthy of study and further understanding.[1] The present essay seeks to progress that line of research, and thereby enrich our national story.

To date, much emphasis has been given to two episodes in that story. First among these is the acquisition by the younger brother of Henry V of 'the grete librarie that came oute of France' and the patronage by him of such treasures of French manuscript illumination as the Bedford Hours (cat. no. 142; fig. 2.1) and Salisbury Breviary (fig. 2.2).[2] Renowned among art and book historians, John, Duke of Bedford, has become the starting point for much discussion of English engagement with French art and culture during the late Middle Ages. As Regent of France, he took the opportunity to appropriate for himself and for England the best that France had to offer – not only to acquire the entire library of the French King, but to continue French royal patronage of the leading French illuminators of their time. The second focal point in the story of English engagement with Continental book culture in the late Middle Ages has been the acquisition by Edward IV of up to fifty deluxe manuscripts produced in the southern Netherlands (see the section below 'Edward IV').[3] Constituting some of the most lavish works to survive within the Royal manuscripts, the Flemish illuminated manuscripts of Edward IV have demanded historical explanation. In response, scholars have cited the close dynastic and political ties between Edward and the Valois dukes of Burgundy, as well as the strong commercial links between Yorkist England and the Netherlandish territories of the dukes. Yet, as the present essay seeks to demonstrate, these well-known episodes

Fig. 2.1 (opposite)
Clovis, in the Bedford Hours. Additional 18850, f. 288v

Fig. 2.2
The Adoration of the Kings, in the Salisbury Breviary. Paris, BnF, MS lat. 17294, f. 106

are merely the mountain peaks that we see rising above the mists of time. Around and below these imposing eminences are less easily visible, but fertile slopes. To explore them adds colour and resonance to the mighty peaks.

The historical background

Before undertaking our climb up the lower slopes it is necessary to review the wider landscape. First and foremost we must take in the long historical view. For, though long separated from Continental Europe by the intervening waters of the Channel, England has been the subject of constant interaction with the Continent. Indeed it is an anachronism to see the Channel as a barrier rather than as a natural conduit that facilitated easier passage between England and the Continent than between many parts of the island itself.[4] Invasion and domination by men from over the seas is a critical part of England's story – whether as a part of the Roman Empire for nearly four centuries, as the subject of a vast migration of Germanic peoples in the fifth century or under threat from Viking raiders from the eighth to the eleventh centuries.

As regards the subject of this essay, the most significant period of foreign domination was that following the Norman Conquest. From the time of William's famous victory at Hastings in 1066 until the thirteenth century England was ruled as merely one part of a wider domain that extended across both sides of the Channel. Indeed, from the reign of Henry II it became subject to the most powerful dynasty in Europe, the vast majority of whose territories lay in France, encompassing the duchies of Normandy and Aquitaine and the counties of Anjou, Maine and Touraine. While the other territories within the so-called 'Angevin Empire' owed feudal homage to the king of France, Plantagenet England remained a kingdom. Yet its king spent most of his life in France, and even in death ensured that he would be best remembered there. The bodies of Henry II and Richard I were buried not in England, but in the Angevin abbey of Fontevrault, where their French wife and mother, Eleanor of Aquitaine, had herself been laid to rest; the famous lion-heart of Richard became one of the relics of the Norman cathedral of Rouen. Despite his disastrous losses of Normandy and Anjou to Philip II Augustus of France, John continued to show special favour to his remaining French domains. Henry III formally renounced his claims to Normandy, Anjou and Poitou, but only after his son Edmund had become titular King of Norman Sicily and his brother Richard, King of the Romans. His perspective remained that of a Continental potentate.

Gradually the perspective of English monarchs changed. While retaining some territories in Aquitaine, most notably Gascony, each became the head of an English nation fighting to retain its Continental lands against sustained aggression by successive French kings. Edward III's opportunistic claim to the title 'King of France', which was based on his mother's more direct descent from the Capetian kings of France than that of the Valois King Philip VI, led to the so-called Hundred Years War between the kingdoms of England and France. Major military victories for the English at Sluys (1340), Crécy (1346) and Poitiers (1356) culminated in the humiliating capture of the French King John II and gave England an ascendancy, which they reinforced with favourable truces. Yet more advantage was to come to the English. Exploiting the political factionalism that emerged in France under the mentally unstable Charles VI, Henry V achieved through his famous victory at the Battle of Agincourt the re-conquest of Normandy and through his marriage to Charles VI's daughter the right of inheritance to the French throne, which passed to his son Henry VI. As dual monarch of both England and France, the young Henry VI established a title for English monarchs that continued until 1802. Yet the reality of that claim was short-lived. French fortunes revived under Charles VII and Joan of Arc. The conclusive defeats at Formigny (1450) and Castillon (1453) lost Henry first Normandy, then Gascony. After that the only English toehold on the Continent was Calais and its Pale. Their subsequent loss in 1558 marked a critical stage in the evolving status of the king of England and the relationship between his kingdom and the Continent.

French manuscripts in English royal collections

Documentary evidence, including surviving inventories, proves that the many French illuminated manuscripts that are still preserved within the Old Royal library form part of a long and consistent engagement on the part of English royalty with such books. Together, documents and surviving manuscripts provide important insights into the cultural life of the English monarch and his family. In them we catch glimpses of books as diplomatic and courtly gifts, symbols of military and political ascendancy, unique remnants of the personal worlds of successive French brides of English kings, objects of the commercial trade in luxury goods, and evidence of evolving English royal ambition and taste. That they are of French origin should come as no surprise. As outlined earlier, successive English monarchs were deeply conscious of their French dynastic affinities. Many had regular first-hand experience of French court culture. For much of the late medieval period French was also their principal vernacular language; for the rest it was an important vernacular alongside English.

Moreover, Paris was renowned across the courts of western Europe for the refined quality and sophistication of its luxury goods. Among these were the illuminated manuscripts that the city's most talented artists provided for the most socially elevated and wealthy patrons.[5]

Many French manuscripts passed into English royal ownership as part of the complex practice of gift-giving at court during the late Middle Ages.[6] Some were exchanged by social equals, either within the English royal family or between them and the French royal family. As might have been predicted, given his privileged position within France, John, Duke of Bedford, was particularly important in the dissemination of French books within English royal circles. Most spectacular was the Bedford Hours (cat. no. 142; fig. 2.1), the gift from him and his wife, Anne of Burgundy, to the young Henry VI on Christmas Eve 1430. Also presented by him is what now forms one of the greatest treasures of the Bibliothèque Ste-Geneviève in Paris (fig. 2.3).[7] Still bearing the signature of Charles V of France, this lavishly illuminated copy of Pierre Bersuire's French translation of Livy's *History of Rome* was given by Bedford in 1427 to his brother Humfrey, Duke of Gloucester. Humfrey's praise of Bersuire's translation in a letter sent in 1445 to Alfonso V of Aragon[8] shows that this gift was not only used by its recipient, but also made a significant impression on him. Bedford may also have been the source from which Humfrey obtained Charles V's personal copy of the *Songe du vergier* (cat. no. 139).[9] The text's academic exploration of the relationship between secular and ecclesiastical power must have been of interest to one of the most powerful men in England.

Other manuscripts formed one side of gift-giving between English and French royalty. One of the most beautiful fourteenth-century manuscripts to pass from France to England was the Breviary partly illuminated by Jean Pucelle for Jeanne de Belleville (fig. 2.4).[10] Almost certainly confiscated by Philip VI after the execution of Jeanne's husband in 1343, the two-volume Breviary was recorded first in Charles V's study at Vincennes and later as a gift from Charles VI to Richard II. An untraced Missal that also came from the Belleville family and left French royal possession sometime after 1380 may well have passed to Richard II at the same moment.[11] Unlike those of the famous Breviary, the splendours of the Belleville Missal can now only be imagined. The context of the presentation of both Breviary and Missal was most likely the truce with France and in particular the marriage, in 1396, of Richard II to Charles VI's daughter, Princess Isabel. Just as he had lavished tapestries and other luxury goods of Continental origin on Richard and his uncles during cross-Channel negotiations leading up to the truce and marriage,[12] so Philip, Duke of Burgundy, Charles's powerful uncle, may also have presented them with deluxe

Fig. 2.3
The Macedonian Wars, in Livy's *Ab urbe condita*, translated by Pierre Bersuire.
Paris, Bibliothèque Ste-Geneviève, MS 777, f. 316

manuscripts. The widow of Thomas, Duke of Gloucester, Eleanor Bohun, left in her will a *Chroniques de France* with clasps bearing the arms of the duke of Burgundy.[13] Hence, it is possible that at least part of the splendour recorded in the 1397 inventory of Gloucester's books at Pleshey reflects further gifts from the Continent.[14] Some of those that still survive are certainly of French origin (see cat. nos. 129, 131).

Periods of intense diplomatic exchange between England and France also provided a context for gifts to the king of England from French visitors of lower social station.[15] Like other such presents, gifts of books were made with a view to obtaining personal favour and even full remuneration. Arising from Richard II's peaceful relations with France were gifts of lavish copies of the writings of both Philip de Mezières and Jean Froissart. Though they had different purposes – Mezières wished to turn brothers in peace into brothers

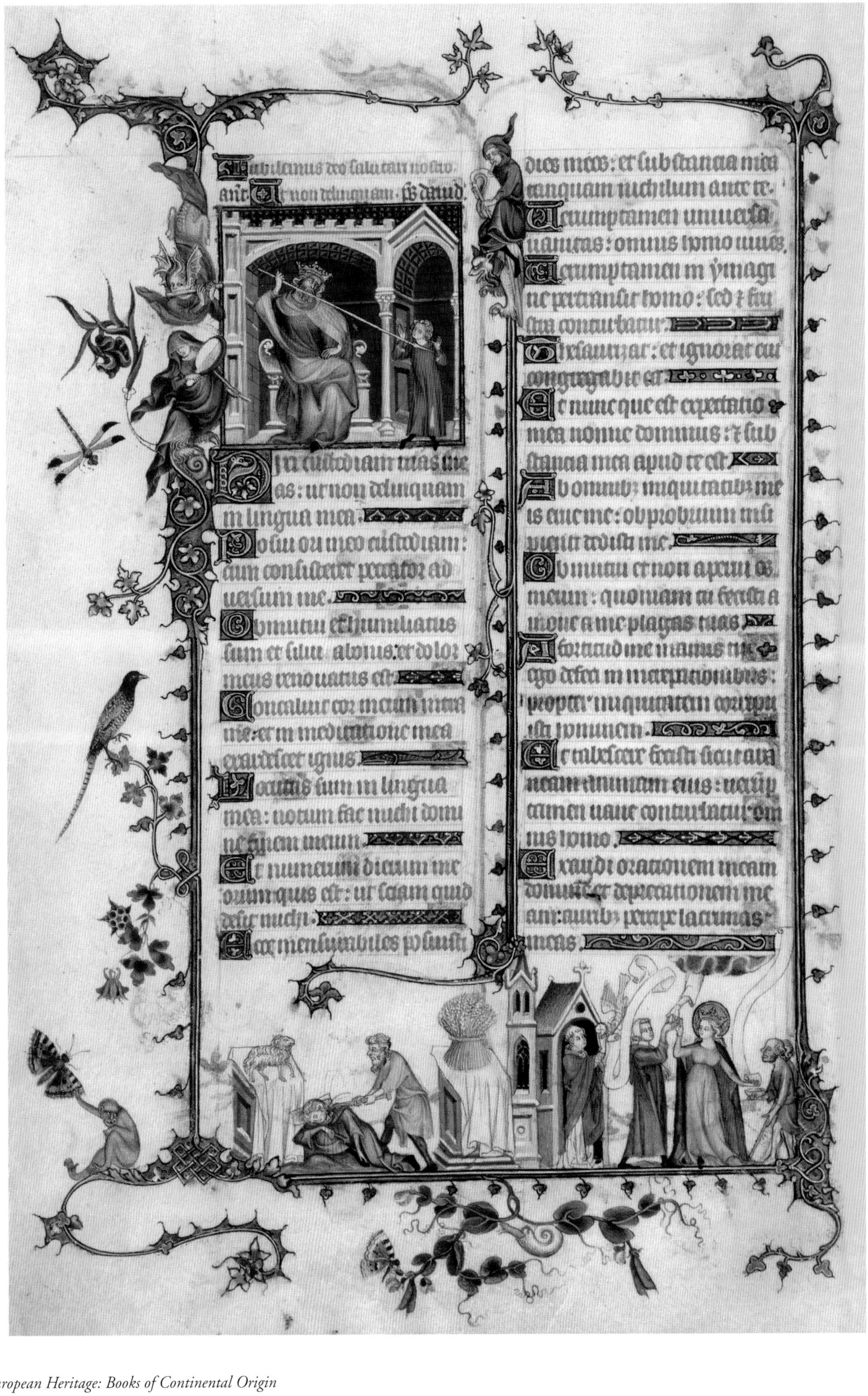

in arms (see cat. no. 140) and Froissart to gain Richard's patronage – both men recognized the persuasive, even seductive power of such books over the King. If we are to believe Froissart's own account, his presentation made the intended impact on Richard. According to him, what impressed the King first of all was that Froissart's volume (untraced) 'was illuminated, well-written and illustrated, and covered with red velvet embellished with ten bosses of richly gilt silver bearing roses of gold at their centre and two great gilt clasps richly worked at their centre with roses of gold'.[16] Enticed by its French luxury, Richard was encouraged to dip into the volume's courtly text and be further charmed by its French language. Much later such French authors as Claude de Seyssel, Jean Mallard, Jean Rotz, Martin de Brion and Louis Le Roy similarly employed French style to win English royal favour for their texts and themselves (see cat. nos. 145, 96, 95, 146, 147). In each case they employed the same means of persuasion with the king of England as they did with the French monarch.

Other gifts of French books to English royalty came from their own English subjects. In the same year that he received Charles V's copy of Livy from John, Duke of Bedford, Humfrey of Gloucester also had presented to him a finely illuminated *Bible historiale* (Paris, BnF, MS fr. 2). According to an inscription still in the volume, it was given to him during a visit to Chester Abbey by Sir John Stanley (d. 1437), K.G., Justice of Chester 1426/7. However, since the book appears previously to have been owned by Humfrey's stepmother Joan of Navarre, its presentation to the Duke may not have been a personal gift from Stanley, but rather another manifestation of Humfrey's profiteering from the dowager Queen during the minority of Henry VI.[17] Humfrey also received from the executors of Sir John Cornwall (d. 1443), Baron Fanhope, a richly illuminated *Grandes chroniques* that had been produced for John II of France before he acceded to the French throne in 1350 (cat. no. 136). In doing so he became the possessor of a book that had once been owned by not only his great adversary, the King of France, but also the husband of his aunt, Elizabeth of Lancaster. By Richard Beauchamp (d. 1439), Earl of Warwick, Humfrey was given an unfinished, illustrated *Decameron* in French translation that is apparently the first copy of Boccaccio's famous text known to have reached England (Paris, BnF, MS fr. 12421).[18] As for Henry VII, between 1505 and 1509 he had presented to him by one of his chaplains, George Strangeways, Archdeacon of Coventry, an extravagant Parisian Book of Hours that had previously been adapted for René, Duke of Anjou (cat. no. 144; fig. 2.5). Although we do not know how Strangeways came to have it in his possession, it may have passed to England together with René's daughter, Margaret, who married Henry VI in 1445.[19] Given Henry VII's vigorous promotion of his Lancastrian namesake, such an association with Henry VI may have been at least equal to the splendid illumination of the Book of Hours in making it attractive to Henry VII.

Fig. 2.5
The Visitation, in the Hours of René of Anjou.
Egerton 1070, f. 29v

Fig. 2.4 (opposite)
David threatened by Saul; Cain Killing Abel; the Eucharist, and Charity, in the Belleville Breviary.
Paris, BnF, MS lat. 10483, f. 24v

Another route by which French books came to England and into very close proximity to the king was marriage. Successive medieval monarchs of England wed women of Continental, especially French, birth. In doing so, they opened up an important channel of French cultural influence over not only their own taste and preferences, but also those of their children and heirs. After her marriage to Edward II in 1308, Isabel of France was particularly powerful in this respect.[20] As the daughter of Philip IV, sister of three successive kings of France, cousin of another and sister-in-law of numerous queens of France, Isabel had connections with the inner French royal circle that were sustained over several decades, well beyond the brutal death of her husband into the

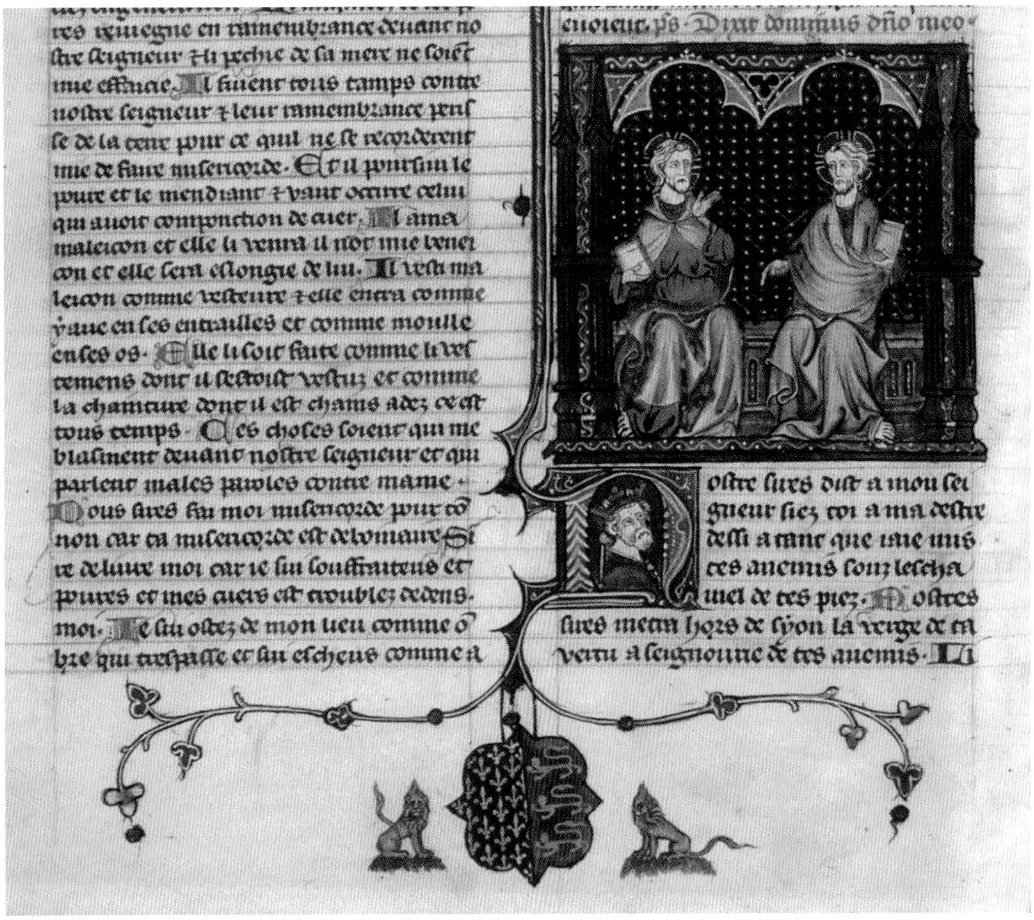

Fig. 2.6
God and Christ, with the arms of France and England, in the *Bible historiale*.
Paris, BnF, MS fr. 156, f. 275 (detail)

Fig. 2.7 (opposite)
Scenes from the Life of Christ, in the Crawford Psalter.
Manchester, John Rylands University Library, MS lat. 22, f. 9

long reign of her son, Edward III. Like several of her female contemporaries amongst the French aristocracy, she appears to have gathered together a small, but important, collection of books, including several French romances. Very soon after his arrival in England in the summer of 1357, her cousin's captive son, John II, turned to Isabel to lend him two of these romances, a *Lancelot* and *Sang real* (or *Holy Grail*).[21] Upon her death she bequeathed some of her books to Edward III and others to her daughter Joan, by then Queen of Scotland, and subsequently several of these bequests, both to Edward and Joan, passed to Richard II. Although it has not yet proved possible to trace most of these books and thereby confirm their origin, the stated liturgical use of some strongly suggests that they were produced in France; an Apocalypse in French has also been identified as a finely illuminated volume from Paris (Paris, BnF, MS fr. 13096).[22] In addition, one previously unremarked *Bible historiale* (Paris, BnF, MS fr. 156; fig. 2.6) appears to preserve part of a lavishly illustrated two-volume set that was made for her in Paris. After her death it remained in England, passed first to Joan, then to Richard and finally became an heirloom of the male line of Sir John Cheyne of Beckford, Speaker of the Commons and member of the King's Council.[23] If Isabel was the original patron of either one or both of two spectacularly illuminated Psalters of English origin (Munich, Bayerische Staatsbibliothek, cod. gall. 16; cat. no. 85), they too are a telling witness of her impact on book culture in English royal circles.

Other royal brides of French origin also brought to England important books from their homelands. In 1396 Isabel of France's trousseau included a lavishly furnished Book of Hours.[24] A little later Joan of Navarre, the second wife of Henry IV, brought to England a finely illuminated Psalter of earlier Parisian manufacture (Manchester, John Rylands University Library, MS lat. 22; fig. 2.7) and a *Bible historiale* of similar origins (Paris, BnF, MS fr. 2).[25] Also probably amongst the possessions with which she left France was a Breviary that she had been bequeathed in 1396 by her aunt, Blanche of Navarre, dowager Queen of France (untraced),[26] and a manuscript of Jean de Meun's *Testament* (Cambridge, Mass., Houghton Library, MS Typ 749).[27] As for Henry V's French bride, Catherine of France, she may have been responsible for bringing into English royal possession at least two manuscripts that had been lavishly illuminated in Paris for her brother, the Dauphin Louis of Guyenne (cat. nos. 67, 141; fig. 2.8). She may well have done so to impress on her young son his position as the true heir of St

Fig. 2.8
Prince with St Catherine before the Virgin and Child, in the Psalter of Henry VI.
Cotton Domitian A. xvii, f. 75

Fig. 2.9
David in the wilderness, in the Mazarine Hours.
Paris, Bibliothèque Mazarine, MS 469, f. 83 (detail)

Louis. Also perhaps brought to England by Catherine were a lavishly illustrated French Book of Hours now back in Paris (Bibliothèque Mazarine, MS 469; fig. 2.9) and another now in Nuremberg (Stadtbibliothek, MS Solger 4.4°; fig. 2.10).[28] Just as the Mazarine Hours is a fine representative of the art of Parisian illuminators of the early fifteenth century – indeed the volume has now become the name manuscript of an artist whose works were long conflated with those of the celebrated Boucicault Master – so the Nuremburg Hours is now renowned for the attribution of its illustrations to the much earlier leading exponent of Parisian illumination, Master Honoré. Later, in 1445, Henry VI's French wife, Margaret of Anjou, brought with her to England a truly monumental book of French texts that had been illuminated in Rouen by one of its leading painters and presented to her upon her marriage (cat. no. 143). As noted earlier, Margaret may also have been responsible for bringing to England a Book of Hours that had been beautifully illustrated in Paris around 1410 by an exceptionally talented artist – who now takes his name, the Egerton Master, from this book – and later, in the 1440s, was embellished for Margaret's father, René, Duke of Anjou, by another accomplished artist whom many scholars now identify as Barthélemy d'Eyck (cat. no. 144; fig. 2.5).[29] Even the briefest of marriages of an English princess to the king of France could result in French books coming to England. In 1530 Mary Tudor, the sister of Henry VIII, presented to her brother a fine Book of Hours that may have been given to her by Louis XII after their marriage in October 1514 and before his death in January 1515 (Lyons, Bibliothèque Municipale, MS 1558; fig. 2.11).[30] For Henry this book, with miniatures attributed to the Parisian illuminator Jean Poyer and the Master of Claude de France, would have served as a reminder of not only what had once been the height of French fashion, but also the days when England and France had been at peace.

Whereas women brought French books to England as the result of peace between the two nations, men did so also as the wages of war. Because of the male focus of much early scholarship, relevant narratives have often been dominated by the more spectacular achievements of warrior kings and their commanders. Only more recently has the impact of women as potent agents of cultural transmission been acknowledged and studied. Taking their lead from pioneering synthetical studies of the subject,[31] a succession of mainly female scholars has greatly progressed our understanding of the collection, patronage and dissemination of deluxe books by leading French noblewomen.[32] Yet the idea that it was men who, for better, or more often for worse, drove events remains largely accurate. Men had greater access to military might, political power and monetary wealth, and men caused the most far-reaching social, political and economic changes. With these resources their impact on the history of books and libraries was bound to be significant. As the spoils of war, books offered them both substantive trophies and memorials of victory and also potential vehicles of cultural appropriation.

During the Hundred Years War and within the context of the conflict over who was the rightful king of France, hundreds of French books were seized by the victorious English. The culmination of these depredations was, as has already been stated, the acquisition by John, Duke of Bedford, of the French royal library established at the Louvre by Charles V. Purchased by Bedford as Regent of France after the death of Charles VI in 1422, together with such other effects of the French King as his extensive collection of tapestries and opulent chapel goods, the library was first kept in Paris and then, in 1429, moved to the English headquarters at Rouen. When Paris was retaken by the French in 1436, the royal cupboard was found to be bare. Sometime before Bedford's death in 1435 the library and other French royal goods were moved further out of reach of the French and brought across the Channel to England. Bedford's acquisition had several precedents. In 1361–62 Edward III presented to King's Hall, Cambridge, three books that were said to be from Calais.[33] These volumes were almost certainly the result of the English capture of Calais in 1347 and unlikely to have been the only ones taken from there by the English. Later, in 1417, when the English seized Caen, Henry V reserved for himself from the plunder a 'goodly French Booke'[34] and, again, in 1422, when they took Meaux, the King appropriated 110 books that he subsequently presented mainly to King's Hall, Cambridge, and All Souls', Oxford.[35] Victory at the Battle of Poitiers in 1356 presented the opportunity for the English not only to capture the French King, but also books in his baggage. John II's magnificent *Bible historiale* (cat. no. 137) was certainly obtained by the English after that battle. His mother's beautiful copy of Gautier de Coincy's *Miracles de Notre Dame* (Paris, BnF, MS n.a.fr. 24541), which was said in 1380 to have been bought back from the English, had probably been taken as plunder at Poitiers.[36] The *Grandes chroniques* that John II had had made before acceding to the throne (cat. no. 136) may also have passed into English hands at this point. If, as some scholars have argued, it was produced for Philip VI, the French crusading compendium now amongst the Royal manuscripts (cat. no. 91) – which we know had reached England long before Bedford obtained the French royal library – may have been another of the early spoils of war with the French. Other spoils of the French wars, as yet unidentified, very probably lurk within the Old Royal library.

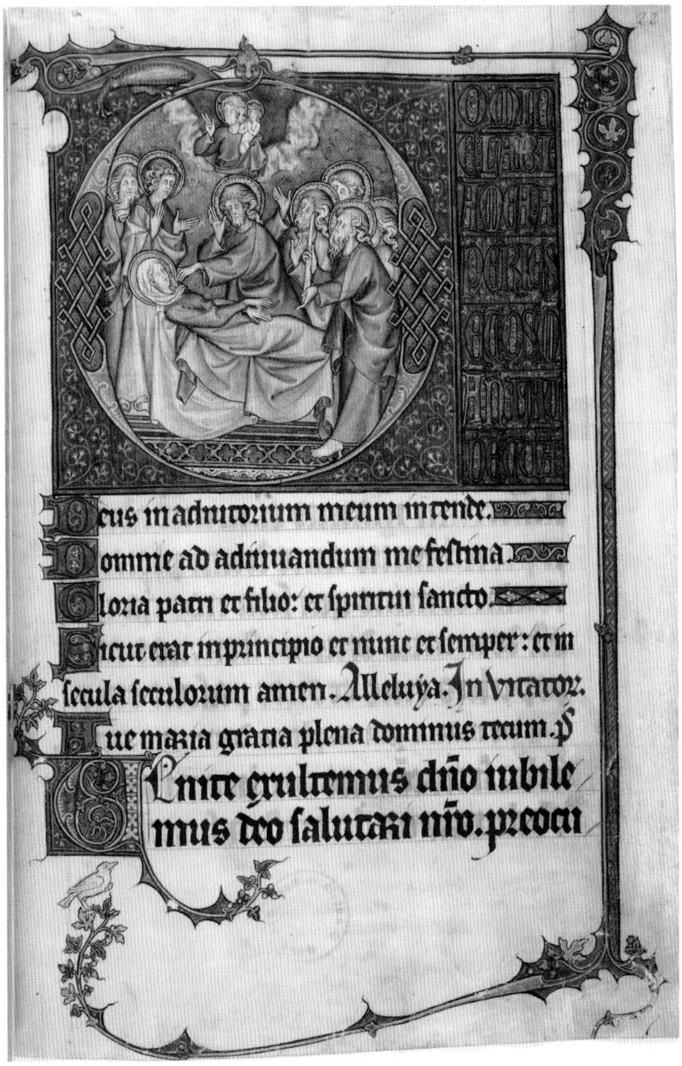

Fig. 2.10
The Dormition of the Virgin, in the Nuremberg Hours.
Nuremberg, Stadtbibliothek, MS Solger 4.4°, f. 22

French booksellers and book producers also came to understand the commercial opportunities that greater English patronage of deluxe French books offered them. Even before the English occupation of Paris and re-conquest of Normandy, two leading Paris *libraires* separately ventured to England to conclude the sale of two expensive books.[37]

Fig. 2.11
St Jerome, in the Hours of Mary Tudor.
Lyons, Bibliothèque Municipale, MS 1558, ff. 7v–8

In 1398 or early 1399 Regnault du Montet left the French capital for Calais, where he crossed the Channel to obtain payment of 60 *écus* from the King's cousin Edward, Earl of Rutland (d. 1415), for a *Chroniques de France.* A little later, in August 1399, Pietro da Verona travelled to England with the specific purpose of selling to the King himself a Bible that the *libraire* had already sent to London for safe-keeping. Although Pietro was unsuccessful in doing so because of the unfavourable turn of events in England and Richard's subsequent overthrow, his continued efforts to find a buyer for the Bible suggest that what he wished to sell to the King was a work of the highest quality and Continental fashion. On its safe return from England, the Paris *libraire* certainly thought his volume worth showing to Philip the Bold, Duke of Burgundy. In the end he managed to sell it to the most discriminating of French bibliophiles, John, Duke of Berry. Later, during English embassies to Paris in 1414 and 1415, both Regnault and Pietro signalled the response of the trade to the changing political landscape. In his enthusiasm to sell books to members of the delegation, Regnault sought out the head of the English delegation, Richard Courtenay, Bishop of Norwich, at his Paris residence. Subsequently, both Regnault and Pietro managed to sell to the English visitors to Paris several volumes, including expensive copies of *Tristan* and texts by Froissart and Ovid. Pietro too managed to entice the Bishop and his fellow ambassadors – who included Thomas Langley, Bishop of Durham, Thomas Montagu, 4th Earl of Salisbury, and Thomas Beaufort, Earl of Dorset – to view his stock at his premises at the heart of the Paris book trade in the Rue St Jacques.[38]

During the English occupation of France, French craftsmen produced numerous deluxe books for their new masters. Most notably, the Bedford Master not only completed the Bedford Hours for the English Regent of France (cat. no. 142; fig. 2.1), but also undertook for him anew the Salisbury Breviary (Paris, BnF, MS lat. 17294; fig. 2.2), the so-called

Fig. 2.12
David at prayer, in the Hours and Psalter of John, Duke of Bedford.
Additional 74754, f. 201 (detail)

Fig. 2.13
Presentation scene, in Boethius, *De consolatione philosophiae* in French translation.
C.22.f.8, A2

Pontifical of Poitiers (now lost) and an Hours and Psalter (Additional 74754; fig. 2.12).[39] While the English retained control of Paris, other artists also produced manuscripts for English royalty. The Master of the Harvard Hannibal (or Master of the Royal Alexander), for example, was responsible in the early 1420s for the illumination of at least one of the copies of the *Livre doré* by Jean Galopes that were made for Henry V (cat. no. 29) and also for a copy of another work by Galopes dedicated to John, Duke of Bedford (London, Lambeth Palace Library, MS 326).[40] Later, after the English headquarters had moved to Rouen, artists based there supplied the English with numerous lavish works.[41] The Talbot Master in particular was responsible for the illumination of several significant volumes, some of which remain in the royal library (see cat. nos. 37, 72, 143; and Royal 16 G. ii).[42] Other less accomplished Rouen artists decorated two volumes for Bedford himself.[43] Distinctively the Fastolf Master appears to have followed his English clients in not only their withdrawal from Paris to Rouen, but also that from France to England itself, where he resumed work alongside English book producers.[44]

Finally, the long-standing affinity of English monarchs and their families with French culture cannot be overemphasized. Gifts, marriage and conquest undoubtedly made a significant contribution to the numbers of deluxe French books in English royal possession. However, they can be seen as merely providing further opportunities for the exercise of royal preference for the best that the French market in luxury goods could supply, whether of the French texts they so coveted for their pastimes and instruction, or of the devotional or liturgical texts that were critical to their religious life. As early as 1281 the wife of Edward I, Eleanor of Castile, resident in England for twenty-seven years, ordered from Paris not only fruit and cheese, but also a manuscript of the French romance *Isembart*.[45] After the introduction of printing in the fifteenth century Henry VII turned to France

Sed ſperauit in multitudine diuitiaꝝ
ſuarum: & preualuit in vanitate ſua.
Ego autem ſicut oliua fructifera in
domo Dei ſperaui in miſericordia Dei
in eternum, & in ſeculum ſeculi.
Confitebor tibi in ſeculum quia feciſti
& expectabo nomen tuum quoniam bonū eſt
in conſpectu ſanctorum tuorum. Gloria
patri. Sicut erat.
Dixit
inſipieſ
in corde
ſuo nō
eſt Deꝰ
Cor-
rupti ſūt

Fig. 2.14
Henry VIII with his fool, in the Psalter of Henry VIII.
Royal 2 A. xvi, f. 63v

Fig. 2.15 (opposite)
Scenes from the Life of Alexander the Great, in Alexander Miscellany.
Oxford, Bodleian Library, MS Bodley 264, f. 43v

for the supply of this new type of book, over forty of which still survive (fig. 2.13).[46] Whereas various other details – including date of publication, name of the printer and even name of the publisher – were erased by the producers of Henry's books, the place of publication was always retained. As one recent critic has remarked, it was 'as if their Parisian origin was valued'.[47] As late as 1540 Henry VIII turned to an *émigré* from the court of Francis I to write and illuminate his personal copy of the Psalms (cat. no. 45; fig. 2.14). Even later, in 1565, a French artist working in a style favoured by the French royal court was engaged to illuminate a copy of the same text for the godson of Henry VIII: Henry Fitzalan, Earl of Arundel (cat. no. 148).

Given the copious evidence for English royal interest in deluxe French books, what are we to make of the early departure of many of these books from royal ownership? Although remarkable for the very large number of volumes involved, the dispersal of the French royal library after the death of John, Duke of Bedford, was far from a unique event. Other earlier and contemporary royal collections of books were similarly dispersed by executors and heirs. They were after all regarded as personal possessions. In such dispersals many Continental books passed out of royal ownership, often transferring to new owners of significantly lower social status.[48] Thus, for example, a *Bible historiale* successively owned by Joan of Navarre and Humfrey of Gloucester (Paris, BnF, MS fr. 2) was purchased in London by an equerry of Philip the Good in 1461.[49] Similarly, a *Bible historiale* made for Isabel of France and subsequently owned by her son and great-grandson (Paris, BnF, MS fr. 156) came to be owned by members of the Cheyne family of Gloucestershire.[50] Within that context the acquisition by Continental aristocratic collectors of books once belonging to Charles V is interesting not because it demonstrates English lack of interest in such works, but because it suggests that the volumes, especially ones previously owned by prestigious individuals, had some particular additional value for such collectors. As French exiles hungry for vestiges of their own culture, Charles, Duke of Orleans, and his brother John, Count of Angoulême, had a clear interest in acquiring French manuscripts that were available in England.[51] A sense of pride is evident in John's inscription recording his purchase in London in 1441 of one of Charles V's books (Paris, BnF, MS fr. 437).[52] If Louis of Gruuthuse's visit to England in 1472 was the context for his acquisition of so many of Charles V's books,[53] his success says more about his very individual bibliophilic tastes in seeking out such by-then unfashionable works than about the willingness of the English to let them go. At that same time he may well have acquired several older manuscripts of English origin.[54] That Louis had the opportunity to acquire so many of these works may be a further indication of the special privileges that he was granted during his visit.

Netherlandish manuscripts in English royal collections

For many centuries close commercial, political and dynastic relations bound England to the Low Countries. The English wool and Flemish cloth trades were highly interdependent. Edward III's claim to the French crown played very well with the independently minded towns of Flanders who aspired to free trade with England and opposed their francophile Count. One of Edward I's daughters married the Duke of Brabant and another the Count of Holland. Edward III himself wed the daughter of the Count of Hainault and Holland. Cultural

links also were strong. From the fourteenth century deluxe Netherlandish books found English royal owners. Around the time of Edward III's betrothal to Philippa of Hainault in 1326 a compilation of instructive texts was put together by a team of English and Netherlandish artists working in Hainault (Paris, BnF, MS fr. 571).[55] A spectacularly illustrated miscellany of texts relating to Alexander the Great (Oxford, Bodleian Library, MS Bodley 264; fig. 2.15) that was produced probably in Bruges between 1338 and 1344 also has strong links to the English royal family.[56] Not only did it come into the possession of Thomas, Duke of Gloucester, but later additions to it, partly by Master Johannes, may have been made for Henry IV.[57] One recent scholar has even argued that its original patron was Edward III.[58] In parallel with the commercial export of illuminated devotional books from the Low Countries to England,[59] more lavish, customized volumes were also made there for English aristocrats (see cat. no. 25). Two immigrant artists who had the most formative impact on English manuscript illumination in the early years of the fifteenth century, Master Johannes and Herman Scheerre, were either of Netherlandish origin or trained in a Netherlandish context. Both are associated with important royal books (see cat. nos. 21, 23, 26–28).

Yet it was not until the reign of Edward IV that English royalty and their closest associates chose south Netherlandish manuscripts consistently and in large numbers.[60] That they did so was the result of several factors. In the 1460s Edward and the new Yorkist regime sought political alliance with the Duke of Burgundy and commercial alliance with his northern territories. By now the most powerful ruler in western Europe, Philip the Good offered the Yorkists a means of reviving the economic and political fortunes of England after the nadir of Lancastrian misrule, and of reasserting the magnificence of England's monarch and royal court. In 1468 the election of Edward to the select Burgundian Order of the Golden Fleece and the marriage of his sister, Margaret of York, to Philip's son and heir, Charles the Bold, marked a key turning point in that revival. Such a dynastic alliance with Burgundy was not unprecedented. John, Duke of Bedford, had married Philip's daughter, Anne, in 1423. Yet much had changed since then. Most notably France was now almost entirely lost to the English King and had gained in Louis XI a wily and effective adversary to oppose England. Moreover, when Edward temporarily lost power to a Lancastrian coup in 1470, it was in the Duke of Burgundy's northern territories, if not directly from the Duke himself, that Edward found greatest support. Bruges in particular was later to be thanked personally by Edward for the 'great kindness and courtesy' that he and his retinue had enjoyed during their exile in the Low Countries in the winter of 1470–71. The Flemish nobleman Louis of Gruuthuse was rewarded by Edward for acting as his host at Bruges by the exceptional honour of an English peerage.

Although the foundations had been laid for a realignment of royal artistic and cultural patronage by 1471, Edward appears not to have begun collecting manuscripts from Bruges until around several years after his stay there. Reflecting his much greater ease of circumstances and financial resources than in the earlier part of his reign (an annual pension of 50,000 crowns extracted by Edward from Louis XI in 1475 made a significant contribution), Edward also undertook his most significant expenditure on building, furnishings and jewels during this period.[61] Of the twenty-one illuminated volumes produced there that bear Edward's arms and devices, five are dated 1479 and one 1480 (e.g. fig. 2.16). Virtually all the rest are very closely related to the six dated manuscripts in either the style of their illumination or the format and style of execution of their heraldic painting. Also dating from 1479 is a payment of £80 to 'Philip Maisertuell merchant stranger in partee paiement of £240 for certaine boks by the said Philip to be provided to the kings use in the partees beyond the see'. Recent scholarship has offered further evidence to support my tentative identification of this foreign supplier of books with the Bruges illuminator Philippe de Mazerolles.[62] Heraldic evidence in at least two of the books acquired by Edward during this period (cat. nos. 50, 52) clearly points to Louis of Gruuthuse's having played some part in the English monarch's collecting of books from Bruges. Given the political crisis and economic uncertainties that faced Bruges after the death in battle of the last Valois duke of Burgundy in 1477, Louis may have been prompted to do so as much by concern for the financial position of the scribes and illuminators – whose works he himself collected so extensively and clearly valued – as by a wish to promote cross-Channel cultural exchange.

Despite their Netherlandish origins, Edward's manuscripts can be seen to continue the traditions of book collecting of previous English monarchs. Their texts were still in French and formed part of the established reading matter of Francophone aristocrats, including those of the English court. Their format was in essence that of the distinctive type of deluxe library book that had been produced at Paris since the fourteenth century and, as outlined earlier, had proved attractive to English royalty. Large in size, long in length of text and lavish in illustration, Edward's volumes complied with this French tradition as it was continued in the southern Netherlands during the fifteenth century in response to the

Fig. 2.16
The translator in his study, in Valerius Maximus, *Facta et dicta memorabilia*, in French translation. Royal 18 E. iii, f. 24

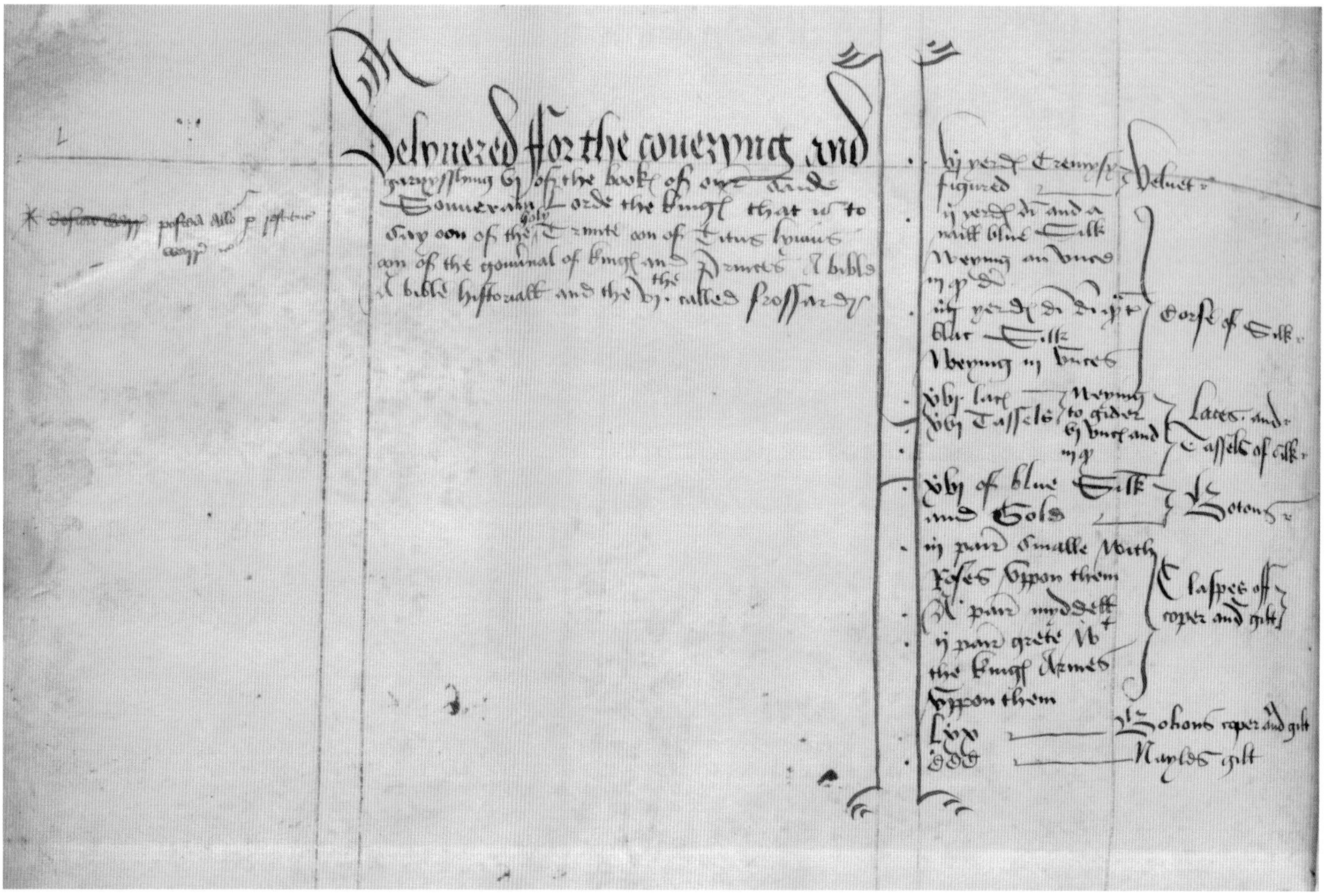

Fig. 2.17
Record of delivery of stuff for the covering and garnishing of Edward IV's books, in the Great Wardrobe Accounts.
Harley 4780, f. 40v (detail)

patronage of Philip the Good and his family, the presumptive heirs of their French royal ancestors.

Nevertheless, the works that Edward brought to England from the Low Countries were in several important respects different from what had previously been on offer from French sources.[63] The painters responsible for the illustration of his volumes spoke a different artistic language from their French predecessors. They drew on the achievements of the by then well-established tradition of early Netherlandish art, as epitomized in the work of such painters as Jan van Eyck and Rogier van der Weyden. Mirroring the painters' highly developed interest in the depiction of the natural world – the human form, landscape and the effects of light – Netherlandish miniaturists brought new life to the pages of manuscripts in both their illustrations and their naturalistic borders. In addition, the texts that Edward's Netherlandish manuscripts contained brought new horizons into view. These texts reflected a change of emphasis in the interests of the French-speaking nobility towards the subjects and lessons of ancient and modern history. The movement had led to the revival of earlier texts, such as the translation of Valerius Maximus's compilation of anecdotes from history begun for Charles V, the chronicle of the Hundred Years War written by Jean Froissart between 1370 and 1400, and the anonymous biography of Julius Caesar, the *Faits des Romains*, compiled as long ago as 1213–14 (see cat. nos. 49, 50, 60). This shift of interest also made popular among the nobility such new historical texts as Vasco da Lucena's translation of Quintus Curtius Rufus's biography of Alexander the Great, Jan Du Quesne's translation of Julius Caesar's autobiographical account of his military and political successes, and Jean de Wavrin's history of England from legendary times (see cat. nos. 149, 76, 47, 48).

In his collecting of south Netherlandish manuscripts Edward both conformed to wider cultural trends within western Europe and made an individual contribution. Several of his closest associates turned to Netherlandish book producers to satisfy their desire for books of the highest quality

Fig. 2.18
The Castle of Love, in a verse miscellany completed for Henry VII.
Royal 16 F. ii, f. 188

and fashion. William, Lord Hastings, and Sir John Donne certainly did so, as did Edward's own sister as Duchess of Burgundy.[64] Gruuthuse was also to become a renowned patron of Netherlandish illuminators.[65] Each preferred handwritten books and, although Margaret of York apparently encouraged William Caxton's printing of his *Recuyell of the Historyes of Troye*, each showed little interest in collecting works produced by the more modern method of printing with movable type.[66] Yet, to judge from what survives, Edward's collection was significantly different from any of these other collections. In part this is explained by his greater wealth than Hastings and Donne enjoyed, his different gender and contemporary expectations from his sister, and his shorter period as a collector than Gruuthuse. That said, Edward's collection has a distinctive cohesion both in visual appearance and textual content that is lacking in all these other collections apart from that of his sister. For just as Margaret's manuscripts are famous for their devotional texts and rich, religious imagery, so Edward's are notable for their texts containing the narrative and lessons of history and the artistic contributions of the Master of Edward IV and Master of the White Inscriptions.[67] Most notably, the vast majority of his manuscripts focus on the history of Rome and its empire from its beginnings under Romulus up the time of Constantine the Great.[68] In this respect Edward appears to have taken over from his ill-fated brother-in-law, Charles the Bold, an overwhelming fascination with empire and imperial ambition.

In the records of Edward's reign we also find one of the deepest insights into the contemporary appearance of English royal books.[69] Judged by even the most extravagant standards of the Burgundian court, Edward's books were magnificent in their opulence. According to a Great Wardrobe Account of 1480 (fig. 2.17), which records the work undertaken on them in England, six large volumes were specially bound and the edges of their pages finely gilded. Each book then required an average of 2 yards (1.8 m) of expensive fabric for its covering. Three volumes covered in red velvet had added to them small pairs of gilt copper clasps bearing the King's device of the white rose. One covered in blue silk had two medium-sized clasps. Two others covered in black silk were embellished with pairs of large clasps bearing the King's arms. In addition, each volume was equipped with silk laces and tassels, silk buttons (*botons*) and gilt copper bosses affixed to their covers with gilt nails. Only then could the books be dispatched in specially prepared fir chests in the King's carriage to his palace at Eltham. Such outer splendour would have paled in comparison only with that of books intended for the extravagant Richard II. Fourteen of these were covered in blue and white satin lined with red satin and garnished with blue silk, gold buttons and silk tassels, and four covered in gold cloth, lined with gold buttons and tassels.[70] Each volume was kept in a specially made bag of Reims cloth and Brabant linen. The years have not been kind to such outer manifestations of royal luxury and, with very few exceptions (see cat. nos. 45, 146, 147), opulent bindings like these have been lost without trace. While the preservation of the volumes themselves is a major achievement, the loss of their original coverings prevents us from experiencing the full visual impact that they must have made on the King and his contemporaries.[71]

Returning to our account of English royal collecting of Netherlandish manuscripts, we find a notable shift of emphasis during the reign of Henry VII away from the importation of works produced in the Low Countries to the patronage of works made in England in Netherlandish styles.[72] Although there was no sustained production within the royal library of deluxe manuscripts by Netherlandish or Netherlandish-trained artists resident in England, Henry did employ during his reign a librarian from Lille who produced or completed some such books for him (cat. nos. 69, 133; fig. 2.18). The

Fig. 2.19
Hours of the Sorrow of the Virgin.
Royal 2 A. vii, ff. 20v–21; flap of blind-stamped binding

Tudor king commissioned and came to own works characteristic of the immigrant illuminators working in the style of the Dutch artist now known as the Master of the Dark Eyes (cat. nos. 38, 41). Among Henry's surviving books are also several works undertaken by illuminators trained in Netherlandish styles (cat. nos. 99, 120).[73] All these observations confirm that, despite Henry's acquisition of many books of French origin and fashionable French style in both manuscript (cat. nos. 144, 145) and printed form (fig. 2.13),[74] the first Tudor monarch retained a taste for Netherlandish styles. Under his successor, Henry VIII, Netherlandish artistic styles, partly transmitted by such immigrant artists as the Horenbouts,[75] continued to shape the King's most precious books (cat. nos. 43, 153, 154).[76] The ultimate artistic legacy of Netherlandish artists to England was to be the translation of the courtly art of book illumination into the intimate art of limning and the English portrait miniature.

Other Continental manuscripts in English royal collections

Manuscripts illuminated elsewhere in Continental Europe during the late Middle Ages appear to have formed a remarkably small part of English royal collections. Indeed, almost no books illuminated in Byzantium, Germany or Spain – all major centres of manuscript production – seem ever to have entered royal possession.[77] The late antique Cotton Genesis was a real exception within the royal collection (cat. no. 46). To my knowledge the Royal manuscripts now include only one modestly decorated volume of Spanish origin: a previously overlooked Hours of the Sorrow of the Virgin with a fine blind-stamped binding that was probably brought to England by Catherine of Aragon (fig. 2.19).[78] As a result of this general situation the distinctive styles of the illuminators of these regions made little, if any, impact on English royal artistic taste. In itself a lack of manuscripts from other centres should not surprise us; throughout the Middle Ages most manuscripts were produced for local consumption.[79] Texts in vernacular languages were certainly only read by those conversant in them; Greek was an impenetrable language for most of the late Middle Ages in northern Europe. Yet, in the context of the presence in English royal collections of so many French and Netherlandish books and of the establishment of a cross-European book trade during the second half of the fifteenth century, the dearth of illuminated books from elsewhere is striking. Perhaps more than anything it underscores the significance of the ownership by English royalty of so many manuscripts from France and the Netherlands. It

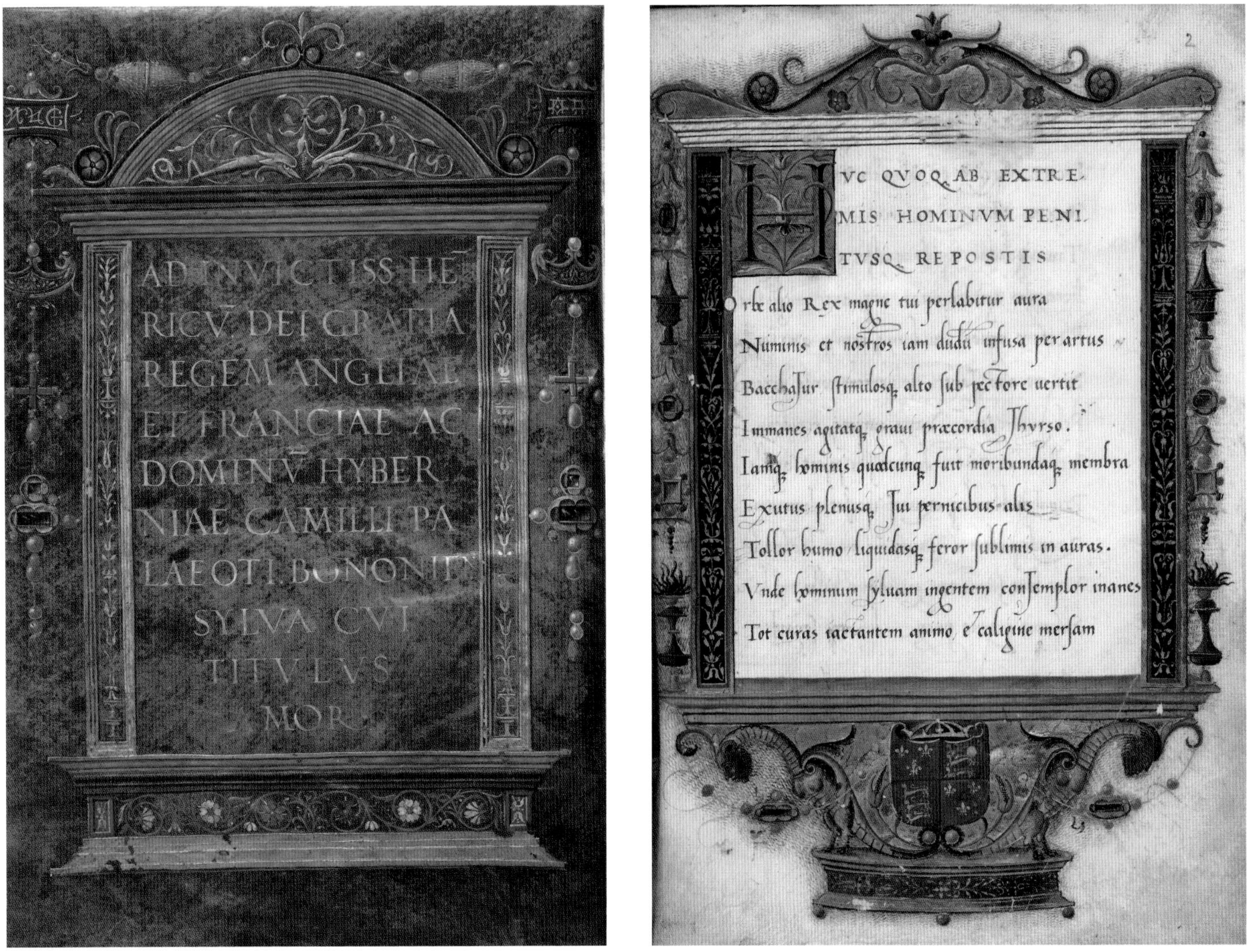

Fig. 2.20
Dedication to Henry VIII, and opening of text. Camillo Paleotti, *Sylva cui titulus amor.* Additional 30067, ff. 1v–2

also puts into context those few manuscripts that did enter the royal library from other parts of the Continent.

Most notably, several finely illuminated manuscripts from Italy did make it into English royal possession. The earliest of these are three fourteenth-century books. Two are exceptionally lavish works associated with the Angevin rulers of Naples (cat. nos. 134, 135); the third is a more modest but important early copy of Brunetto Latini's *Trésor* (Oxford, Bodleian Library, MS Douce 319).[80] At least one of the Angevin manuscripts came to England via France, having successively formed part of the collections of Charles V and John, Duke of Berry. The *Trésor* was given to Thomas, Duke of Gloucester, by William Montagu, 2nd Earl of Salisbury, before the end of the fourteenth century.[81] In Gloucester's post-mortem inventory of 1397 it was valued at only 3 shillings,[82] in sharp contrast to the *Bible historiale* of John II of France (cat. no. 137), which Montagu had earlier bought for 100 marks. Later, Humfrey, Duke of Gloucester, attracted to England several manuscripts of Italian origin and had others made in England by Italian scribes and artists (see cat. no. 109).[83] Although the artistic styles of these books had some impact on contemporary English production and taste (see cat. nos. 32, 33), that impact was very limited and short-lived.[84] Even by the early sixteenth century very few illuminated books from Italy had come into English royal hands. A striking exception is the handsome copy of the statutes of the Hospital of Santa Maria Nuova in Florence, which the foundation's patron Francesco Portinari had illuminated in Florence for Henry VII in connection with the King's plans to found a similar hospital in London (Oxford, Bodleian Library, MS Bodley 488).[85] Also noteworthy are two volumes containing Johannes Michael Nagonius's verses celebrating the triumphs of Henry VII (York Minster Library, MS XVI.N.2) and Baldassare Castiglione's *Life of Guidobaldo,*

Duke of Urbino (Philadelphia, Rosenbach Museum and Library, MS 239/25).[86] The first was almost certainly written and illuminated at Rome and the second at Urbino. Thereafter, several fine volumes did find their way to Henry VIII. Most notable among these are the copy of the works of Collenuccio and Lucian illuminated at Rome that Geoffrey Chamber brought back from Italy for Henry (cat. no. 113), Francesco Roseti's volume of verses on St Ursula that his son conveyed to England from Verona (Royal 13 A. ix), and two volumes now attributed to the Renaissance scribe Pier Antonio Sallando, both of which were presented to Henry by the Italian authors of the texts that they contain (Additional 19553 and 30067; fig. 2.20).[87] Both Henry VII and Henry VIII received their Italian manuscripts as unsolicited gifts. Although they appear to have been pleased with what they received (Henry VII confirmed this about Nagonius's volume in a letter to the future Paul III[88]), neither showed any interest in commissioning or actively acquiring further manuscripts from Italy.

Concluding remarks

Having reviewed the evidence for the collecting of books of Continental origin by the English royal family, what general observations can we make? First, English royalty were consistently best placed to undertake such acquisitions. According to one modern study, personal contacts of individuals with the Continent were the principal reason why individual books were brought to England before the middle of the fifteenth century.[89] Successive English monarchs and their families had such contacts in abundance. More than any other English individuals, they were deeply connected to the Continent. Moreover their connections were visceral – those of blood, marriage, language and land. While English merchants might have spent more time going back and forth to the Continent than the monarch, their contacts were ultimately superficial in comparison with those of the king of England. As long as these connections continued, English royalty would view the Continent as a natural source of luxury books. With the notable exception of Henry VI, they also recognized the importance of such books in reinforcing the status of the English monarchy in comparison with their European counterparts. To compete in terms of magnificence with their greatest rival, France, English kings needed to be seen to value and to seek out works of the same content and appearance as those collected by the king of France.[90]

Yet to continue to do so through the fifteenth century led to an increasing dislocation of royal taste in the content, format and artistic elaboration of their reading matter from those of their subjects – the majority who collected and read books in England. As Harris so perceptively stated, 'The continuing allegiance of the bilingual English nobility to earlier French literary forms, and their taste for the fashionable exclusivity of contemporary (largely imported) French culture, only highlight the radical nature of the divorce of that culture, for all its aesthetic (and social) attractions, from the main concerns of the growing reading public.'[91]

As the fifteenth century progressed, non-royal readers increasingly engaged with English texts in books produced in England, in manuscript or printed form, and Latin texts printed on the Continent and imported as part of a wholesale trade. More and more of what they acquired was shaped with a view to mass circulation and had limited scope for personalization. English monarchs, on the other hand, while also patrons of some English writers such as Thomas Hoccleve and John Lydgate (see cat. nos. 30, 64, 65, 73), continued to seek out manuscripts produced by scribes and illuminators working in France or the southern Netherlands or in England in the artistic styles developed in France or the Low Countries. For most of the fifteenth century the non-devotional texts that they acquired by this means were ones written in French by authors favoured by the French-speaking courts of the Continent. At the beginning of the fourteenth century the texts that English royalty selected were courtly romances; by the end of that century they had been supplemented by vernacular histories and instructional manuals, and translations of earlier Latin works. In the fifteenth century the monarch and his family continued to prefer such texts and the traditional deluxe manuscript format. Even such a supporter of academic and humanistic learning as Humfrey of Gloucester was known for his strong personal interest in and knowledge of French texts.[92] As noted earlier, such interest was pursued by him through the collecting of manuscripts of a very traditional appearance, lavishly decorated and illustrated in French style.

By the second half of the fifteenth century English monarchs were not alone in being out of step with most of their subjects with respect to their reading matter. Their Continental counterparts were equally so. Harris's 'fashionable exclusivity' of the English aristocracy captures, therefore, two aspects of their book collecting: their exclusivity of taste within England and their fashionability with respect to their counterparts on the Continent. Elsewhere I have argued that on the Continent this fashionable separateness with respect to their book collecting was deliberately sought by the nobility.[93] In England it seems similarly to have been part of an effort of the monarch and the upper echelons of society to mark out and define their distinctiveness. Neither English merchants nor English gentry collected deluxe copies of French library texts.

Furthermore, many of the devotional books that English monarchs obtained from the Continent were of a quality well beyond that of the devotional books acquired by the majority of their subjects. While many English merchants and gentry obtained numerous such books from the Continent, they did so mainly thanks to the expanding export trade in books from the Low Countries. Any customization for such owners was based on standard offerings. The purges of 'superstitious books' under Edward VI significantly reduced the number of devotional books owned by English royalty that are extant. Those that survive, however, are indicative. Although not originally produced for English royalty, such outstanding manuscripts as the Belleville Breviary, Egerton Hours and Bedford Hours (Paris, BnF, MSS lat. 10483–10484; cat. nos. 144, 142) were works in which English royalty could rightly take pride. Such lavish books were certainly capable of putting the English on a par with their Continental rivals.

Yet all such royal collecting of Continental books had its price. While members of the blue-blooded Bohun family appear to have offered significant and consistent patronage to native scribes and illuminators (see cat. no. 20), their practice seems distinctive in England by the end of the fourteenth century. Others of similar aristocratic status, including the royal family, seem not to have fostered native artistic talent for the production of their luxury books.[94] There is certainly no evidence of such support in England as was given by the French royal family during the reigns of Charles V and Charles VI. Instead, English monarchs frequently turned to either France or the Low Countries for this kind of book. Did they do so because what was on offer from the Continent was so much more attractive to them than English work? Had English illumination lost its allure? It is certainly the case that no surviving manuscript illuminated in England in the fifteenth century attains the outstanding artistic achievements of earlier examples – say, the Queen Mary, Luttrell, Gorleston, De Lisle or Macclesfield Psalters.[95] Whereas French illumination went from strength to strength through the fourteenth century and into the fifteenth, English illumination did not, despite the innovations of such immigrant artists as Herman Scheere. Moreover, for some considerable time through the fourteenth century English royalty had become aware that if they wished to own certain fashionable texts, they needed to do so by acquiring foreign works. Subsequently the royal family's increasing acquaintance with foreign books and their developing artistic styles through gifts, marriage and plunder may have encouraged a more general taste for foreign books that encompassed a wider selection of texts, some of which could have been, and were in the past, supplied by native production. Confronted by foreign success in both the luxury and wholesale book markets from the middle of the fifteenth century, English illuminators seem to have suffered a loss of confidence in their own abilities and those of their artistic tradition, deriving more and more of their visual vocabulary from foreign artistic styles and losing the power of independent invention based on an existing native tradition.[96] Such was the national price paid for the ambition of English royalty to be at least the equals of their Continental cousins.

The present essay has sought to answer a simple question. The answer has proved complex. Many factors contributed to so many manuscripts owned by members of the English royal family being of Continental origin. How we respond to this situation is for each of us to decide. To Sir Thomas Elyot in 1531 it would have been regarded as part of a broader national failure – the result of constrained individual choices – in which no pride could be taken. For him the key point was that 'in the ... artes englisshmen be inferiours to all other people'; because of that it was necessary 'to resorte us unto strangers'.[97] I would want to draw something more positive from the legacy of the past. Like successive English royalty, I would take pride in the European heritage that lies at the heart of the Old Royal library and at the heart of this part of our national story.

NOTES

1 On fifteenth-century English collecting of Continental manuscripts see Harris, 'Patrons, Buyers and Owners' (1989), pp. 180–82; Meale, 'Patrons, Buyers and Owners' (1989), pp. 201–08; Alexander, 'Foreign Illuminators' (1999), pp. 47–64. For English royal collecting see Alexander, 'Manuscript Illumination' (1983), pp. 141–62; Stratford, 'Early Royal Collections' (1999), pp. 255–66; Backhouse, 'Royal Library' (1999), pp. 267–73; Stratford, 'Royal Books' (2003), pp. 180–81; Stratford and Webber, 'Bishops and Kings' (2006), pp. 209–17.

2 See Stratford, 'Manuscripts' (1987), pp. 329–50, and Stratford, *Bedford Inventories* (1993), pp. 91–96.

3 See Backhouse, 'Founders' (1987), pp. 23–41; McKendrick, '*Grande Histoire*' (1990), pp. 109–38; McKendrick, 'Lodewijk van Gruuthuse' (1992), pp. 153–54; McKendrick, 'Romuléon' (1994), pp. 149–69; Backhouse, 'Royal Library (1999), pp. 267–70.

4 On this ease of passage see Barron, 'Introduction' (1995), p. 1.

5 See Rouse and Rouse, *Manuscripts* (2000).

6 On this practice see Buettner, 'Past Presents' (2001).

7 Morrison and Hedeman, *Imagining the Past* (2010), pp. 174–76 no. 24.

8 Samaran, *Pierre Bersuire* (1962), p. 153.

9 Bedford may also have supplied Humfrey with a copy of Jean de

Vignay's *Légende dorée* that was finely illustrated in Paris in the late fourteenth century (Paris, Bibliothèque Mazarine, MS 1729). According to Delisle, *Recherches* (1907), 1, pp. 56, 284–85), this volume may have been made for Charles V.

10 See Leroquais, *Breviaires* (1934), 3, pp. 198–210; *Fastes du Gothique* (1981), pp. 293–96 no. 240.

11 Stratford, 'Royal Library' (1994), p. 190.

12 See McKendrick, 'Tapestries' (1995), p. 45; and Stratford, 'Gold and Diplomacy' (2000).

13 Cavanaugh, 'Study of Books' (1980), p. 110; also McFarlane, *Nobility* (1973), p. 236.

14 For the inventory see Dillon and St John Hope, 'Inventory' (1897).

15 On one type of such exchanges see Prud'Homme, '*Donnez*' (2009).

16 My translation from de Lettenhove, *Oeuvres de Froissart* (1867–77), 15, p. 167: 'et voult veoir le roy le livre que je luy avoie aporté. ... Il l'ouvry et regarda ens, et luy pleut très-grandement et bien plaire luy devoit, car il estoit enluminé, escript et historié et couvert de vermeil velours à dix clous attachiés d'argent dorés et richement dorés et roses d'or ou milieu, à deux grans frumaus dorés et richement ouvrés ou milieu de roses d'or.'

17 On Humfrey and Jeanne see Jones, 'Entre la France' (1999), pp. 68–69.

18 See Branca, *Boccaccio visualizzato* (1999), pp. 230–35; also Farnham, 'England's Discovery' (1924), pp. 123–39; and Petrina, *Cultural Politics* (2004), p. 188.

19 Backhouse, 'Illuminated Manuscripts' (1995), p. 182.

20 See Cavanaugh, 'Royal Books' (1988), pp. 309–11). For her documented books see Cavanaugh, 'Study of Books' (1980), pp. 457–60; and Vale, *Edward III* (1982), p. 170. For more speculative treatment of Isabella's connection with extant manuscripts see Stanton, 'Isabelle of France' (2003). In general see Bennett, 'Isabelle of France' (2001), pp. 215–25.

21 Bond, 'Notices' (1854), p. 468; also Bennett. 'Isabelle of France' (2001), p. 219.

22 Lewis, 'Apocalypse' (1990).

23 For the documents relating to a two-volume French Bible belonging successively to Isabel, Joan and Richard see Cavanaugh, 'Study of Books' (1980), pp. 280, 459, 725, and Cavanaugh, 'Royal Books' (1988), p. 313. In Richard's time the manuscripts were highly valued, at over £26. The extant volume includes an inscription relating to Sir John Cheyne (Paris, BnF, MS fr. 156, f. 3v), which links to two references in the wills of Sir John Cheyne and his son Edward. For these references see Roskell, 'Sir John Cheyne' (1956), p. 71; and Cavanaugh, 'Study of Books' (1980), p. 124. There is significant variation in the marshalling of the arms of England and France through the Paris volume: some have France ancient in the sinister part, whereas others show it in the dexter. Those in the first section of the manuscript, which correspond to Isabel's arms as consort of Edward II, have been taken as evidence of her ownership.

24 Delisle, *Recherches* (1907), 1, p. 207.

25 Delisle, 'Notice' (1897), pp. 381–93. See also James, *Descriptive Catalogue* (1921), pp. 64–71, pls 48–50. Whereas the Bible returned to Continental possession in 1461, the Psalter remained in Britain, being rebound there late in the fifteenth century and having its Litany mutilated in the time of Henry VIII.

26 Delisle, 'Notice' (1897), pp. 392–93.

27 Sotheby's, London, 3 April 1957, lot 9. I am grateful to Bill Stoneman and Joshua O'Driscoll for tracing the present whereabouts of this volume. A lavishly illustrated copy of Pierre's Bersuire's translation of Livy (Paris, BnF, MSS fr. 269-272) includes an inscription that has been misattributed to Joan (*pace* Delisle, *Cabinet* [1868–71], p. 14; also Booton, *Manuscripts* [2010], pp. 137, 160 n. 13, 201, 312). *Pace* ibid., p. 312, BnF, MS fr. 610 was owned by Joan of Navarre (d. 1305), wife of Philip IV.

28 On these two volumes see Meiss, *French Painting* (1968), pp. 113–14; and Simmons, *Heures de Nuremberg* (1994).

29 Margaret may also have been the means by which French texts came to England and to royal attention. See Legaré, 'Les Deux Épouses' (2009), pp. 68–69.

30 See Wieck *et al.*, *Hours* (2000), pp. 26–27; and Hofmann, *Jean Poyer* (2004), pp. 35–36, 117–21, pls 70–81.

31 See in particular Bell, 'Medieval Women' (1988); also Buettner, 'Women' (2001), pp. 9–31.

32 See, for example, Holladay, 'French Queens' (2006); Keane, 'Most Beautiful' (2008); Field, 'Marie of Saint-Pol' (2010).

33 Cavanaugh, 'Royal Books' (1988), p. 315.

34 Cavanaugh, 'Study of Books' (1980), p. 415.

35 For the full list of books seized see Harriss, 'Henry V's Books' (1972); also Cavanaugh, 'Study of Books' (1980), pp. 417–20.

36 Delisle, *Recherches* (1907), 1, pp. 290–92; see also Focillon, *Le Peintre* (1950); and *Fastes du Gothique* (1981), p. 296 no. 241.

37 For what follows see Rouse and Rouse, *Manuscripts* (2000), 1, pp. 287–90, 297–300; also Meiss, *French Painting* (1967), pp. 64–65.

38 For one volume that Langley may have acquired by this means see Gameson, *Manuscript Treasures* (2010), pp. 146–49.

39 See Reynolds, 'Salisbury Breviary' (1986); Reynolds, 'Workshop' (2006), pp. 443–49; Reynolds and Stratford, 'Le Pontifical de Poitiers' (1988); Stratford and Reynolds, 'Foyle Breviary' (2007), pp. 351–62, figs 1, 6–8.

40 Stratford, 'Manuscripts' (1987), p. 348, states that it is improbable that the Lambeth volume is Bedford's presentation copy of 1427. More recently she has described it as 'very probably the presentation copy'; Palmer and Brown, *Lambeth Palace* (2010), pp. 60–63.

41 In general see Reynolds, 'English Patrons' (1994).

42 On the Talbot Master see Avril and Reynaud, *Les Manuscrits* (1993), pp. 169–71; Reynolds, 'Shrewsbury Book' (1993), pp. 109–16; Reynolds, 'English Patrons' (1994), pp. 305–07.

43 Stratford, 'Manuscripts' (1987), pp. 348–49.

44 On the Fastolf Master see Reynolds, 'English Patrons' (1994), pp. 307–08; also Alexander, 'Lost Leaf' (1971), and Alexander, 'Foreign Illuminators' (1999), p. 49.

45 Cavanaugh, 'Royal Books' (1988), p. 306.

46 See Winn, *Anthoine Vérard* (1997), pp. 138–53.

47 Winn, *Anthoine Vérard* (1997), p. 148.

48 On this general movement of books down in the social scale see Harris, 'Patrons, Buyers and Owners' (1989), p. 170. Later (p. 174) she qualifies her argument by acknowledging that the fate of 'volumes prized as "joyaux"' did not necessarily conform to this pattern.

49 On the embassies to England of this equerry (variously described as Philippe de Loan, Louhan or Lowyn) see Scofield, *Edward IV* (1923), 1, pp. 190, 277–78, 298 n. 4.

50 See above at note 23.

51 On their acquisitions see Delisle, *Recherches* (1907), 1, p. 140; in general see Ouy, *Librairie* (2007).

52 On John's volume see Jackson, 'Traité du Sacre' (1969), p. 307.

53 See Delisle, *Recherches* (1907), 1, p. 140; Lemaire, 'Lodewijk van Gruuthuse' (1981), pp. 211–13); McKendrick, 'Lodewijk van Gruuthuse' (1992), p. 159 n. 102.

54 For example, Paris, BnF, MSS fr. 1, 123, 403; lat. 4976, 6049. In England he may also have acquired Paris, BnF, MS fr. 156.

55 See Avril and Stirnemann, *Manuscrits enluminés* (1987), no. 187.

56 See James, *Romance of Alexander* (1933).

57 On these additions see Dutschke, 'Truth' (1998), pp. 278–300.

58 Melis, 'Alexander Manuscript' (2002), pp. 973–77.

59 On this trade see Harris, 'Patrons, Buyers and Owners' (1989), pp. 181–82; and Alexander, 'Foreign Illuminators' (1999), pp. 52–53.

60 For what follows see the literature cited in note 3 above.

61 See Ross, *Edward IV* (1974), pp. 270–77; also McKendrick, 'Edward

IV' (1987); and Campbell, *Henry VIII* (2007), pp. 45–64.

62 Hans-Collas and Schandel, *Manuscrits enluminés* (2009), p. 175.

63 For such works see McKendrick, 'Reviving the Past' (2003).

64 On Hastings and Donne see Backhouse, 'Memorials' (2001); see also Backhouse, 'Sir John Donne' (1994), and Morgan and Panayotova, *Catalogue* (2009), p. 158 no. 207 (noting the ownership by Hastings of Corpus Christi College MS 91). On Margaret see Kren, *Margaret of York* (1992), also Legaré, 'La librairye' (2005), pp. 207–10.

65 See Hans-Collas and Schandel, *Manuscrits enluminés* (2009); and Martens, *Lodewijk van Gruuthuse* (1992).

66 On Margaret see Lowry, 'Sister' (1992), pp. 103–10; also Hellinga, *William Caxton* (2010), pp. 19–26, 35–38, 42–45. On Louis and contemporary printing see Le Loup, 'De Relatie' (1992), pp. 149–52.

67 On both artists see Kren and McKendrick, *Illuminating the Renaissance* (2003), pp. 289–91, 295–305; on the Master of Edward IV see Hans-Collas and Schandel, *Manuscrits enluminés* (2009), pp. 204–21.

68 See McKendrick, 'Grande Histoire' (1990), and McKendrick 'Romuléon' (1994); also Hughes, *Arthurian Myths* (2002), pp. 238–63.

69 What follows is based on a fresh analysis of Harley 4780, which I shall publish at greater length elsewhere. For the parts relating to books see Nicolas, *Privy Purse* (1830), pp. 117, 125–26, 152. For earlier discussion of the Harley manuscript see Backhouse, 'Founders' (1987), pp. 28–29. The stationer responsible for binding, gilding and dressing Edward's books is elsewhere documented as renting a property in Paternoster Row in the City of London, see Christianson, *Directory* (1990), p. 68.

70 Cavanaugh, 'Study of Books' (1980), p. 727.

71 For descriptions of the earlier velvet bindings of books from the Old Royal library see Carley, *Libraries* (2000), pp. xxv–xxvii, 5–6. A manuscript in Paris bearing the arms of Henry IV (BnF, MS fr. 25447) retains its red velvet binding (Avril and Stirnemann, *Manuscrits enluminés* [1987], no. 217). Another once owned by Henry VII (cat. no. 38) was still bound in red velvet in 1715. For red velvet bindings on Henry VII's printed books see Carley, *Libraries* (2000), p. 3.

72 For what follows on Henry VII see Backhouse, 'Founders' (1987), pp. 32–39, and Backhouse, 'Illuminated Manuscripts' (1995). For the popularity in England of Netherlandish illumination and English imitations of it see Alexander, 'Foreign Illuminators' (1999), pp. 62–63; and Trapp, *Erasmus* (1991), p. 83.

73 For other examples see Scott K., 'Manuscripts' (2007), pp. 280–83.

74 See Backhouse, 'Illuminated Manuscripts' (1995), p. 179; also Winn, *Anthoine Vérard* (1997), pp. 138–53.

75 On the Horenbouts see Kren and McKendrick, *Illuminating the Renaissance* (2003), pp. 427–39.

76 In addition, two of Henry's sisters successively owned a lavish Netherlandish Book of Hours now in Vienna, see Kren and McKendrick, *Illuminating the Renaissance* (2003), no. 110.

77 For the general lack of manuscripts imported to England from Germany see Alexander, 'Foreign Illuminators' (1999), p. 54. The only decorated manuscript of German origin still in the royal collection (Royal 15 B. vii) is a late addition. An important escapee is the tenth-century purple Gospels from Trier once owned by Henry VIII (New York, Pierpont Morgan Library, MS M. 23).

78 *Pace* Warner and Gilson, *Western Manuscripts* (1921), 1, p. 27; and Carley, *Libraries* (2000), p. 65. This volume is not of Italian origin. Its script, decoration and binding all indicate a Spanish origin. I am grateful to Andrea Clarke, Laura Nuvoloni and James Carley for their advice on this volume.

79 Alexander, 'Foreign Illuminators' (1999), p. 58.

80 On the *Trésor* see Pächt and Alexander, *Illuminated Manuscripts* (1966–73), 2, no. 154.

81 The means by which Montagu acquired this volume is unknown. Sometime before 1388 he had acquired a *Roman de la Rose* that had formerly belonged to the French royal library – Delisle, 'Notice' (1907), 1, p. 121; 2, p. 192 no. 1183.

82 Dillon and St John Hope, 'Inventory' (1897), p. 300.

83 Trapp, 'Humanist Book' (1999).

84 Alexander, 'Foreign Illuminators' (1999), p. 54; and Reynolds, 'England' (2003), pp. 83–84.

85 Alexander, 'Foreign Illuminators' (1999), p. 55, fig. 2.6.

86 See Gwynne, 'Frontispiece' (1992); and Clough, 'Baldassare Castiglione' (1981), pp. 1–5.

87 On the two Sallando manuscripts see Nuvoloni, 'Pier Antonio Sallando' (2008).

88 Gwynne, 'Frontispiece' (1992), p. 270.

89 Harris, 'Patrons, Buyers and Owners' (1989), pp. 180–81. Harris argues that the numerous Books of Hours produced in the Low Countries that came to England and Scotland during the first half of the fifteenth century were part of a mass import trade fed by speculative production that addressed individual needs by means of minimal customization.

90 Meale, 'Patrons, Buyers and Owners' (1989), p. 204.

91 Meale, 'Patrons, Buyers and Owners' (1989), p. 166.

92 Petrina, *Cultural Politics* (2004), pp. 181–84.

93 Kren and McKendrick, *Illuminating the Renaissance* (2003), pp. 72–73; see also Wijsman *Luxury Bound* (2010).

94 Meale, 'Patrons, Buyers and Owners' (1989), pp. 202–06; Alexander, 'Foreign Illuminators' (1999), p. 61.

95 Alexander, 'Foreign Illuminators' (1999), pp. 60–61.

96 For a different perspective see Scott, *Later Gothic Manuscripts* (1996), 1, pp. 23–25, 62–64.

97 Reynolds, 'England' (2003), p. 84.

The Old Royal Library: 'A greate many noble manuscripts yet remaining'[1]

KATHLEEN DOYLE

Of the nearly 2000 manuscripts in the Old Royal library, around 1200 are illuminated or from the early medieval period, and about a third of these contain significant decoration or illustration. The rather complicated but fascinating history of how these illuminated manuscripts came to be assembled as a single collection is the focus of this essay. One of the surprising aspects of this group is that in the main, only three kings and one prince were responsible for it, and of these only one reigned in the medieval period. The first and only medieval contributor was Edward IV, now typically remembered, if at all, as the father of the 'little Princes', whose large, lavish vernacular manuscripts are examined in the previous essay, 'A European Heritage'. The second collector is as famous as Edward is obscure: Henry VIII, whose search for biblical and legal support for his divorce and subsequent sequestration of the goods of those failing to support the Act of Supremacy resulted in the incorporation of a significant number of monastic manuscripts into the royal collection. The two other acquisitions of large numbers of illuminated manuscripts were made by Stuarts: Prince Henry Frederick, the son of James I, who died when he was only eighteen; and a more well-known figure, although not for his interest in books, Charles II, the 'Merry Monarch'. Both Prince Henry and Charles II collected medieval illuminated manuscripts somewhat indirectly, through the purchase or gifts of extesive collections of books and manuscripts assembled by others.

This is not to say that the medieval kings of England did not own, commission and collect illuminated manuscripts – there is abundant evidence that they did. However, their manuscripts do not survive in any significant numbers in the Old Royal library. In the introduction to the magisterial catalogue of the collection in 1921 Gilson commented that there are 'probably not more than half a dozen' manuscripts 'for which is it possible to establish even a probability of their having been continuously in the Royal possession since an earlier date than Edward IV's reign'.[2] With perhaps a few additions to Gilson's list, his assessment remains true today. Nor is the surviving evidence for these earlier collections systematic, in the form of surviving library catalogues or book lists. Some of the possible reasons for these lacunae will be explored in this essay.

Other interesting facets of the history of this manuscript collection are how late it came together in one central royal library space, how it survived the vicissitudes of the Commonwealth period and how it was organized in the various libraries (or other spaces) in which it was kept. What follows is an attempt to trace these various strands to determine when the various royal collections and libraries became the Old Royal library. This will involve an analysis of the various motivations for the assembly of manuscripts, together with an assessment of how their function and use changed over time, particularly at the point when manuscripts were no longer being produced and had become, instead, 'used' books. These issues are not straightforward, because in many cases crucial evidence is missing or partial. Nevertheless, the miraculous survival of the manuscripts themselves demonstrates the ultimate success of the inclination to collect and preserve illuminated manuscripts as a body in a royal library.

Early history

Some of the earliest detailed evidence for the storage, if not the collections, of manuscripts comes from accounts of the Keeper of the Privy Wardrobe for the Tower of London, John de Flete, for the period 1324 to 1341, during the reigns of Edward II and Edward III.[3] De Flete's records reveal that a large number of manuscripts and unbound quires (340) were kept in the Tower. The account provides some description of the books, though the majority (211) were simply summarized as 'De libris [or quaternis] diversis', and 'De libris et peciis de romancie' (59).[4] The account does not specify the room in the Tower in which these books were kept, but it is clear that they were stored in chests, and some also within sealed sacks.

Stratford's careful analysis of the entries demonstrates that by 1341 only eighteen books remained in the collection; all the others had been distributed, some apparently as gifts and others as the return of sequestered property (three

Opposite
Detail from fig. 3.2

went to Queen Philippa, and several to Edward III's mother, Queen Isabel).[5] The only manuscripts that may have been delivered to the King for his use (marked 'opus') were four rolls of *mappa mundi* with 'portraitures' issued to Edward in 1338. Perhaps these rolls included genealogical trees, like the two that were made before or during his reign (cat. nos. 117, 118). De Flete's records reveal a picture of Edward as a distributor, rather than a collector of manuscripts. Whatever may be said of his motivation, he did not, like Henry VIII, take the opportunity to turn sequestered goods into a royal library. Moreover, the regular dispersals of these manuscripts and their partial storage in sealed bags suggest that they were being kept in the Tower more for safe-keeping in custody than as a working library or study to be used by the King.

The first mention of a study for books in a royal residence, if not a library proper, comes at the beginning of the fifteenth century.[6] In 1401–02 the first Lancastrian king, Henry IV, furnished a new study (*novum studium*) next to his chamber at Eltham Palace with one small and one large desk, the latter with two 'stagez' in which to store books.[7] The desk had sections (perhaps shelves) *pro libris*, which suggests that it was designed for bound volumes rather than for unbound documents in a kind of muniment room, although these may have been books of accounts rather than of literature, history or theology. However, the records for the stained-glass windows in the study show that the windows were decorated with depictions of saints, biblical scenes and animals, and make it clear that it was a handsome room, perhaps more appropriate for the King's reading or study of handsomely illustrated illuminated manuscripts than of governmental papers or account books. One of the volumes kept there, if not in the chapel, may have been the huge 'Great Bible' mentioned in Henry V's will as having been owned by his father, possibly cat. no. 23; if so, its size would have necessitated a large shelf and desk for its storage and consultation.[8] Something is known of a few other of the books that Henry IV may have owned, but the Great Bible is the only illuminated manuscript associated with the King that survives in the Old Royal library.

Henry had a keeper of books (*custos librorum*), Ralph Bradfield.[9] It is possible that this post was more of a book-keeper, in the sense of keeping books of accounts, as Gilson argues was the case for Henry VIII's 'Keeper of the King's Books', John Porth (as opposed to the Keeper of the King's Library).[10] However, Stratford's identification of Bradfield's involvement in a 1419 lawsuit to recover missing royal books supports her identification of Bradfield as the first known royal 'librarian', though the term was not used until the end of the century (see below).[11]

Henry IV's son, Henry V, also had a book collection, which was, according to McFarlane, 'for his time, rank, and other tasks, remarkably well stored and, it was believed, much read'.[12] Much of it was bequeathed to religious foundations that he founded and to Oxford University (for example, sermons useful for preaching and books for meditation went to his foundations of Brigittines at Syon and the Charterhouse at Sheen, and his legal and scholastic books were given to the University of Oxford).[13] All of Henry's manuscripts not specifically bequeathed were left to his unborn child, in order to form a library for him ('omnes libri nostri … filio nostro remaneant pro libraria sua'), though this did not include the service books from the chapel, which were listed separately.[14] Both Henry IV and Henry V have been characterized as 'bibliophiles and founders of the royal library', but the dispersal of both collections and the generous distributions made by Henry V suggest that these book collections may have been viewed more as personal libraries, rather than as a royal library to be preserved intact and held by successive monarchs.[15]

The *libraria* inherited by Henry VI and other manuscripts he may have received were subject to even more thorough diffusion through donations than his father's had been. This collection included at least 140 manuscripts in Latin (as well as around 110 manuscripts from Meaux confiscated by Henry V after the city's capture in 1422) that were kept in the Treasury during Henry VI's minority.[16] However, perhaps as a result of what Stratford characterized as the King's 'dangerous tendency towards excessive open-handedness', apparently most of this library was given away during the King's lifetime.[17] Indeed, of the six illuminated manuscripts given to Henry VI included in this catalogue, only two remain in the royal collection (the others are Cotton, Harley or Additional manuscripts).[18] In 1440 the King gave seventy-seven of the Meaux books to King's Hall, Cambridge, and twenty-seven to All Souls' at Oxford.[19] Other royal books appear to have served as a sort of 'lending library' for clerks and secretaries and other men associated with the royal household and kept in the Receipt of the Exchequer at Westminster, rather than in one of the King's private rooms or closets.[20] Perhaps Henry was more interested in devotional books than those in the collection he had inherited, although three of the four illuminated manuscripts illustrated that are no longer in the Old Royal library are devotional texts or lives of saints. Alternatively, it may be that his own incapacity, the civil war and the shifting control of power between Henry and Richard, Duke of York, and his son Edward, Earl of March (the future Edward IV), later in Henry's reign were factors in Henry's disinterest in creating or preserving a royal library. Whatever the cause, his unwillingness or inability to maintain the manuscripts that he received as a royal collection may have been part of a more general failure to create a magnificent royal court.[21]

Edward IV

In sharp contrast, Henry's successor Edward IV consciously created a court that would be the equal of any in Europe, as McKendrick demonstrates in his essay 'A European Heritage'. The best surviving material record of this endeavour is the remarkable collection of large-scale historical and literary manuscripts in French ordered by or associated with the King (see 'A European Heritage', pp. 42–65). These illuminated manuscripts, totalling nearly fifty, are perhaps the best known of the Royal manuscripts as a group, and are remarkable for their survival as a collection. This first 'coherent collection' of royal books provides the basis for the generally accepted view of Edward IV as the 'founder' of the Old Royal library.[22]

The related questions of where this library was kept, whether it was in one place only, and how it was organized are more problematic, and can only be the subject of speculation. Thurley asserts that 'although Edward IV had been a keen collector of books he carried books from place to place and there was no permanent establishment', perhaps on the basis of entries in the Wardrobe Accounts for 1480 of payments for 'the Kinges carreman for a reward awaiteing uppon certen of the Kinges books put in the Kinges carr', and for fasten ings for 'divers cofyns of fyrre wherein the Kinges books were conveyed and caried from the Kinges grete Warderobe in London unto Eltham'.[23] However, because of the weight, size and general unwieldiness of the manuscripts commissioned by Edward and the building work being carried on at Eltham, one of the King's favourite residences, Backhouse argued that the payments reflected a more permanent transfer of the manuscripts to Eltham.[24] Based on Continental precedents of centralized library collections, this seems more likely. Moreover, the high rate of survival of Edward's books may suggest that they were kept together in one library. Whichever is the case, Edward, like Henry IV, had a designated yeoman to 'kepe the kinges bookes'.[25] His Household Ordinances of 1478 specify that there were to be twenty-four yeomen, chosen as 'most semely persones'; some of the duties of the other yeomen included keeping the robes, the beds, the armory, the 'bowes' and the dogs.[26] The specific duties of the keeper of books are unknown, and could have involved the supervision of the transportation of books from place to place instead of (or in addition to) their care at a particular library. That this unknown keeper indeed kept the King's books carefully is evidenced by their survival in the Old Royal library as a group.

In contrast to Edward's surviving manuscript collection, only a small number of his brother and successor Richard III's books can be traced. Further, as Backhouse put it, Edward V's and Richard's brief reigns 'offer no recorded contribution to the development of the royal library'.[27] Only one illuminated manuscript commissioned by Richard survives in the royal collection, a copy of Vegetius's *De re militari* in an English translation decorated with the arms of England supported by boars, Richard's badges cat. no. 127).[28] Backhouse also commented that Richard's books 'may in fact be regarded as the contents of a private bookshelf', unlike Edward's assemblage of 'very grand manuscripts appropriate to the furnishings of the public rooms in which they would have been used and displayed'.[29] If so, perhaps Edward IV can be credited not only as the founder of the Old Royal library but also as the first English monarch to conceive of a royal library as a more permanent aspect of monarchy belonging to the rank or position of king rather than to an individual.[30]

The Tudors

With the Tudors there is increasing evidence of dedicated library spaces in multiple royal residences. According to Thurley's study of royal palaces, Henry VII had libraries at his new palace of Richmond, built on the site of the destroyed palace at Sheen; at the Tower of London, in a new block overlooking the river; and probably also at Windsor and Greenwich.[31] There survives a contemporary description of the 'Kinges goodly Manoir of Rychemond' in a *c.* 1502 account of the celebrations of the marriage of Prince Arthur and Catherine of Aragon, *The Receyt of the Ladie Kateryne.*[32] While the court was staying at Richmond, in order to console the Princess after the departure of the Spanish entourage the King took Catherine, her ladies and 'dyvers ladies of Englond and brought them to a lybrary of is, wherin he shewed unto her many goodly pleasaunt bokes of werkes full delitfull, sage, mery, and also right cunnyng, bothe in Laten and in Englisse'.[33]

The location of this library in the residence is unspecified; it may have been in one of the King's 'secret closettes most richely enhaungid, dekkyd, and beseen'.[34] A second, short description of one of Henry VII's libraries – perhaps also that of Richmond – is included in the dedicatory preface to a French translation of Xenophon's *Anabasis* (cat. no. 145), given to the King a few years later by the French Ambassador Claude de Seyssel, in which the Ambassador remarked that 'ayant veu votre libraire que je trouvay tres belle et tres bien acoustree' (having seen your library I found it very fine and very well appointed).[35] Even discounting the flattery embedded in a dedication of this type, it appears from these two accounts that, like Edward IV, Henry VII was also deliberately building up an impressive library collection and library rooms; what Starkey has called 'a display library'.[36]

Like his predecessors, Henry had a keeper, the scribe and illuminator Quentin Poulet of Lille, appointed in 1492.[37]

Manuscripts written for Henry VII by Poulet survive, such as the presentation copy of the *Enseignement de la vraie noblesse* made by Poulet in 1496 or 1497 (cat. no. 69). Like those of the earlier keepers, Poulet's duties are unspecified, although in his case the keeping of books became 'services in keeping the king's library'.[38] The wording of the patent of office for Poulet's successor in 1509 specifies further that the library in question is that of Richmond: 'For Giles Duwes. To be keeper of the King's library at his manor at Richemounte, during pleasure, with 10l. a year from the customs of the port of Bristowe, as held by Quintin Paulet.'[39] As Duwes's appointment was made at the very beginning of Henry VIII's reign (13 September 1509), the specific mention of Richmond may well reflect that his father's principal library was also located there.

Around nineteen illuminated manuscripts (a few in several volumes) in the Old Royal library can be associated with Henry VII or his wife, Elizabeth of York, Edward IV's daughter – a smaller number than those commissioned by Edward IV. (A number of Old Royal manuscripts with the monogram 'HR' [for *Henricus Rex*] formerly associated with Henry VII have now been identified more securely with his son, Henry VIII, as will be discussed below.)[40] Many others survive in other libraries or collections (see cat. no. 99), and reflect Henry's patronage of works made in England in Netherlandish styles, as McKendrick demonstrates (see 'A European Heritage', pp. 59–60).[41] A greater number of Henry VII's printed books survive (around seventy), leading Backhouse to conclude that Henry 'seems to have been more interested in the acquisition of printed books than in contemporary manuscripts'.[42] Yet several of these printed books include illumination, such as the Vérard copies produced in Paris (see fig. 2.13), indicating Henry's interest in acquiring illuminated books, albeit on not quite such a grand scale as Edward IV's.[43]

Henry VIII

Henry VIII's impact on the structure of his kingdom was prodigious, and his transformation of the composition of the Old Royal library is equally significant. Indeed, Carley observed that it is only with Henry VIII that 'the Royal Library really began to take form', and the large number of surviving manuscripts assembled in his reign, together with the evidence of their more systematic arrangement, supports this conclusion.[44] The manuscripts Henry collected now in the Old Royal library (over 400, or around 20%) outnumber those that can be associated with any other monarch.[45] This acquisitive King also appears to have had more libraries in which to put them, with over sixty residences at his death.[46]Many of these – at least the greater houses, as opposed to hunting lodges and the like – presumably contained libraries or book collections.[47] Henry also created new libraries at Whitehall, Hampton Court and Greenwich, in addition to the existing subsidiary ones.[48] Moreover, it is also from the period of Henry's reign that the first book lists or inventories survive, allowing more detailed analysis of the contents of the royal library and of where these books and manuscripts were kept.

Like earlier monarchs, Henry received and commissioned illuminated manuscripts. Several spectacular examples are illustrated, such as his personal Psalter with his portrait in the guise of David, and two music books, one with a hymn in Henry's honour, and the other with the royal arms of England and Henry's devices (cat. nos. 45, 154, 153). But what set his library apart from those of his predecessors and increased the scale of it dramatically was his systematic acquisition of monastic books on a particular topic. Henry's collection was what Roberts called an 'issue-driven library – or libraries' assembled to enable the King and his advisers to research grounds for his divorce, and thereafter the question of royal supremacy.[49] To achieve his aims, Henry sent out the antiquary John Leland to 'peruse and dylygentlye to searche all the lybraryes of monasteryes and collegies' throughout the kingdom, as Leland recalled.[50] While these manuscripts were not sought for their illumination, many are handsomely decorated with historiated or pen-flourished initials (for example fig. 3.1), even if not, in Ker's phrase, 'finely illuminated'.[51]

As a result of these various acquisitions, a large proportion of the manuscripts in the Old Royal library collected by Henry VIII are monastic in origin (around 250).[52] Ironically, then, one of the greatest collections of English medieval monastic manuscripts was assembled by the monarch responsible for the destruction of their original libraries. This transfer resulted in the first large acquisition of 'used' books for the royal library, in contrast to the new commissions, gifts and presentation copies that survive from the collections of Henry's predecessors. Interestingly, at least for the first tranche of monastic manuscripts sought out and collected specifically for their content, the primary function of these books did not change – they remained part of a working library to be studied and read. Of course, the readers and the purpose for which these manuscripts were consulted changed dramatically. Nevertheless, this usage distinguishes Henry's acquisition of medieval manuscripts from those of his successors.

Henry VIII had a huge number of residences in which to deposit his books. Yet Leland identified only three as major repositories for the monastic manuscripts Henry collected: Westminster (or Whitehall), Greenwich and Hampton Court.[53] After its acquisition from Cardinal Wolsey in 1529,

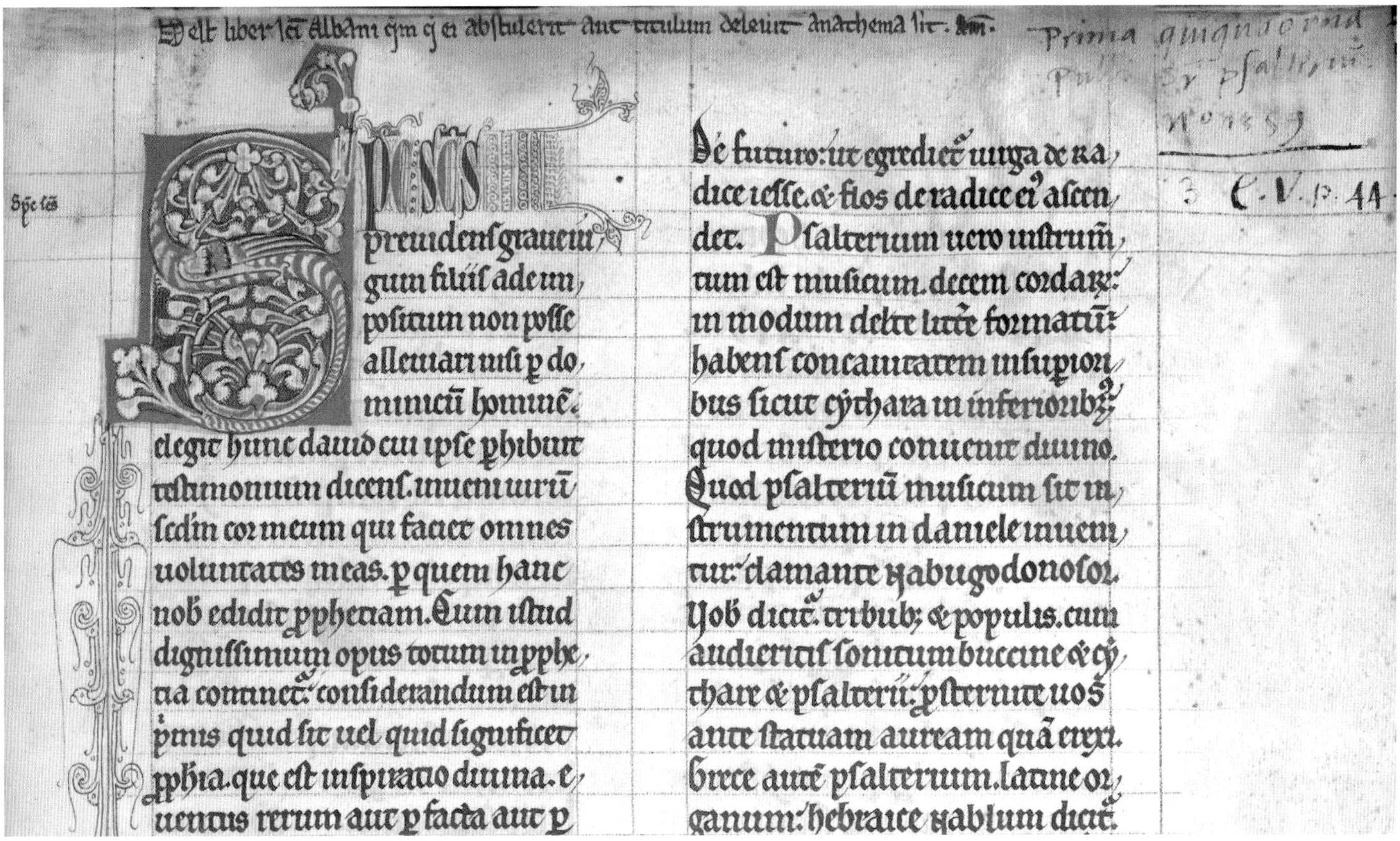

Fig. 3.1
Decorated initial, ownership inscription of St Albans, Henrician title and Westminster inventory number. Royal 3 C. v, f. 1

Whitehall – close to the site of the former Westminster Palace, which had been destroyed by fire in 1512 – quickly became Henry's main residence.[54] In 1536 by Act of Parliament it was designated the King's principal seat.[55] According to the post-mortem inventory of Henry's possessions, there were in fact two libraries there: 'the highest Library' and 'the little Study called the newe librarye'.[56] This new library may have been a more personal one, or a muniment room for papers and documents rather than books, as Jervis and Selwyn and Selwyn have argued.[57] In any event, for the 'highest' or 'upper' library there is a precious record of the earliest surviving systematic inventory or catalogue of both printed books and manuscripts in the royal collection.

The importance of this inventory as a source and Carley's invaluable edition of it for the history of the royal library can hardly be overstated. The inventory permits both a reconstruction of one of Henry's libraries at a particular palace at a particular time, and the identification of manuscripts that were present there that remain part of the Old Royal library. The list is part of a more general inventory of the goods at Whitehall Palace made in 1542, and was included as part of 'Stuff of sondry natures as well founde within the kinges upper library'.[58] Crucially, while most of the listings are very short (typically only a few words of description), many manuscripts and printed books still in the Old Royal library can be identified because the order of the entries, corresponds generally to numbers entered into surviving volumes[59] (for an image of this type of number see fig. 3.1 and cat. no. 103).

The inventory is divided into two groups, both organized alphabetically, with 573 titles in the first group, and 335 in the second, making a total of 908 books and manuscripts.[60] Printed books and manuscripts are intermixed in each group, but Carley has shown that printed books are predominant in the first, while the second consists primarily of monastic manuscripts.[61] Carley has suggested that this segmentation 'almost certainly reflects the layout of the room itself'; however, it is possible that it indicates the placement of the smaller group in another room that was also considered part of the Upper Library.[62] Or, some type of segregation of manuscripts and printed books may have been the aim of the groupings: the title of the second grouping includes the phrase 'quidam inculti, quidam ex antique impressione'.[63]

Sadly, similarly detailed inventories and numbering systems do not survive for Henry's other palaces. For example, while Greenwich Palace was one of the King's favourite palaces, the only record of the books kept there is a reference

Fig. 3.2
HR monogram. Royal 20 C. iv, f. 1

in the post-mortem inventory to 329 books 'in the highest library' stored in seven desks and two tables, and identified, if at all, by the colour or material of their bindings rather than by their contents.[64] Thus, although there was apparently more than one library at Greenwich, as at Whitehall, it is not possible to determine the contents of what was kept in them. Even less information is preserved about the library at Henry's third principal palace, Hampton Court, for which the post-mortem inventory records succinctly: 'Item a greate nombre of bookes.'[65]

The Whitehall numbers are the only ones that can be identified confidently with a surviving list. Henry's librarians may have employed other systems of markings or numberings at other of the royal libraries. For example, fourteen manuscripts, eleven of them illuminated, and twenty-two printed books in the Old Royal library have a large added monogram 'HR', usually on the first page (fig. 3.2).[66] Carley has shown that this monogram must refer to Henry VIII rather than Henry VII, because it appears in nineteen books printed after Henry VII's death.[67] The monograms are not in Henry VII's hand, so they may have been added by a librarian(s), perhaps to identify books kept in a particular place or even a chest or, as Carley suggests, those that may have been of particular interest to the King.[68] If the marks are related to some kind of library arrangement, it was a much more rudimentary system than that employed in the Upper Library at Whitehall.

Some further information about the contents of the library at Richmond comes from another surviving booklist of a slightly different type – a list of books made by a French visitor, perhaps to be identified as the Treasurer of Brittany, in 1535.[69] This list, which may be incomplete and in turn be a copy of a lost, more inclusive inventory, includes around 143 volumes (there are 125 items, but some may describe books in multiple volumes).[70] The list is described as an inventory ('Inventaire des livres estans ou chasteau de Richemont en *Angleterre*'). Most of the items are in French, so the list could consist of a selection of books from the library reflecting the particular interests of the French compiler or copier, or the section of the library containing French manuscripts only. Moreover, unlike the Whitehall books, it is more difficult to identify surviving manuscripts with this list because there do not appear to be any corresponding numbers in surviving books to tie them securely to the concise descriptive titles (such as 'La Bible', 'Listoire scolasticque' or 'The Bible in Englisshe').[71] Nevertheless, Carley's painstaking research demonstrates that in many cases the descriptions are likely to correspond with manuscripts ordered by Edward IV and other manuscripts still extant in the Old Royal library.[72]

As noted above, Henry VIII's first librarian was appointed to an office specifically at Richmond. However, shortly before Duwes's death in 1534 the reversion of his office was granted to William Tyldesley on slightly different terms: as 'the office of keeper of the King's library in the manor of Richmond or elsewhere' (although when the grant was renewed two years later the reference was to Richmond only).[73] This change in the wording of the patent for the keeper may reflect the build-up of libraries in other residences, such as Whitehall, Greenwich and Hampton Court. Early in Henry VIII's reign Richmond was one of the residences that the young King visited more frequently, and it was one of the six 'greater houses' specified in the Eltham Ordinances of 1526 where hall should be kept.[74] However, Thurley argues that after the fall of Wolsey, Richmond was viewed as old fashioned, perhaps due to its medieval plan, and had 'almost fallen out of use'.[75] Henry spent only 5% of the important New Year's celebrations during his reign at Richmond (in contrast, around 60% of them were celebrated at Greenwich).[76] Moreover, in around 1525 Wolsey was allowed to occupy the Palace, possibly in exchange for Hampton Court, and Anne of Cleves was granted a life interest in it as part of her annulment settlement in 1540, but this was revoked by Edward VI's Council after Henry's death.[77]

If the identifications of Edward IV's manuscripts in the 1535 list are correct, as seems likely, they raise the intriguing question of why such grand and at one time important manuscripts – interesting enough to have been listed by a foreign visitor – were present at a palace not often frequented by the King towards the end of his reign, and in fact given over by him for others' use. The simplest explanation would be that they had been assembled there by Henry VII or Poulet and left in a dedicated library space. Later evidence from late sixteenth- and seventeenth-century visitors indicates that this may be what occurred. The Richmond library was one of two (the other was Whitehall) most often mentioned by travelling foreign dignitaries and visitors touring various royal palaces. For example, one visitor in *c.* 1610 listed the sights at Richmond as follows: 'The most curious thing to be seen is Henry VII's Library; here is also his glass, in which they tell us he could see everything passing in the world; it was broken at his death. The Genealogy of the Kings of England from Adam. Henry VII's inkstand, and his bed-chamber sprinkled with his blood.'[78] Another visitor in *c.* 1606 recorded that Richmond possessed 'many old written and printed books'; a third in *c.* 1614 instructed others visiting Richmond to 'remark the Library of King Henry VII, for the most part consisting of manuscripts, of which Library nothing was known until the time of Queen Elizabeth' (the mirror and blood-spattered bedchamber also featured in these reports).[79] On the basis of these and other accounts, Carley concluded that 'the library [at Richmond] stayed virtually intact into the 17th cent'.[80]

Thus, if the 'foundation' royal collection of Edward IV's illuminated manuscripts, together with others apparently added by Henry VII, remained in a palace not often used by Henry VIII's court at the end of his reign, this may indicate that practices had changed from the communal reading of large historical and literary French illustrated texts to more private individualized reading in smaller, more personal books. In his *c.* 1506 gift of the Xenophon manuscript to Henry VII, de Seyssel explained that he had heard that the King 'entendant aussi que prenez grand recreation et passe temps a lire et ouyr histoire et aultres chouses apartenant a ung noble et saige prinpce' (was well entertained in reading and hearing history and other topics appropriate for a noble and wise prince).[81] Judging from the pristine condition of the manuscript, and the possible loan to Wolsey and Anne of the Edward IV and other manuscripts in the Richmond library during their occupancy of the Palace, it may be that this practice of hearing history read aloud was not continued at Henry VIII's court, at least in the later period.[82] In turn, this would indicate a change in the function of these manuscripts from Backhouse's 'appropriate cultural dimension of the luxury furnishings of the rooms where they were designed to be read out' to objects to be kept (perhaps unread) as valuables or even 'curiosities' collected by previous monarchs.[83]

Edward VI, Mary and Elizabeth

The accession of Edward VI in 1547 marked a significant change in policy towards illuminated manuscripts and other types of book in the royal libraries, effected by an authorization for the centralization of certain types of books to Whitehall, and a systematic deaccessioning of others from the royal collection. The terms of the appointment of Edward's librarian, Bartholomew Traheron, in December 1549 included an unusual provision encouraging the centralization of the collection at Whitehall. It stated that because 'in his singular love for good letters the King has determined to stock his library of Westminster with notable books to be kept conveniently to his use', Traheron was authorized to 'take books from the king's other libraries to furnish the library or promote the king's studies provided it may be done without damage'.[84] There are no contemporary records indicating whether transfers were accomplished pursuant to this authorization and, if so, what sort of books was considered useful for the King's studies; yet as Carley has suggested, the higher range of Whitehall inventory numbers indicates that transfers did occur.[85]

Contrariwise, in 1550 as part of the establishment of the use of the Book of Common Prayer, an 'Acte for the abolishinge and puttinge awaye of diverse Bookes and Images' required that:

> all Bookes called Antiphoners, Myssales, Scayles [grails], Processionalles, Manuelles, Legends Pyes Portuyses Prymars in Lattyn or Inglise Cowchers Journales Ordinales, or other bookes or writings whatsoever heretofore used for Service of the Churche, written or prynted in the Inglishe or Lattyn tongue, other than suche as are or shalbe settforthe by the Kings Majestie, shalbe by authoritie of this present Acte clerelye and utterlye abollished extinguished and forbidden for ever to be used or kept in this Realme.[86]

The King's own library was not exempt. In 1551 the Privy Council ordered 'the purging of his Highnes Librarie at Westminster of all superstitiouse bookes, as masse bookes, legendes, and suche like and to deliver the garnyture of the same bookes, being either of golde or silver, to Sir Anthony

Aucher, in the presence of Sir Thomas Darcie'.[86] Technically, as is clear from the 1542 inventory of the Upper Library and Henry VIII's post-mortem inventory, these types of service book generally were not kept in the library, but in other of the King's private chambers or closets, or in the chapel, or if particularly valuable, in jewel houses for safe-keeping. As noted above, the service books from the chapel bequeathed by Henry V were not part of his *libraria*. Similarly, eighty-nine service books itemized in the post-mortem inventory of Henry VIII were located in the vestry at Whitehall, with two 'masse bookes' characterized as 'ornamentes for chaples and closettes'.[87] Manuscripts and books in the library at Richmond and other royal libraries may also have been unaffected, as it seems unlikely that liturgical or Latin devotional manuscripts would have been considered 'notable books' to be moved to the Whitehall library. Nevertheless, whether these manuscripts were deemed to be included within the ban or left the royal collection in other ways, almost no decorated liturgical or devotional book survives in the Old Royal library – those that do are almost all Jacobean acquisitions.

For example, there are no illuminated Missals at all, except for two leaves that survive through their use as flyleaves in another manuscript, which itself entered the royal library with Charles II's acquisition of the Theyer collection.[88] There are only eight other illuminated liturgical manuscripts (four Breviaries, one Lectionary, two folios from a Lectionary now used as flyleaves, two Martyrologies, and one Gradual and Troper), again with two or three of these entering the collection in the seventeenth century.[89] Illuminated Books of Hours are even less well represented, with only eight copies.[90] These are significant lacunae. By comparison the great Harley library, assembled in two generations in the eighteenth century by two earls of Oxford, includes 103 illuminated Books of Hours. Similarly, even though Psalters were amongst the most common of all medieval manuscripts, there are only eighteen illuminated copies in Old Royal library, compared to sixty-one in Harley.[91] Again, nearly half of these entered the royal collection in the Jacobean period. While some of the losses may be the result of gifts of particularly personal books, or of the abandonment of liturgical books that had become obsolete through changes in liturgical practice, it also seems likely that Traheron, 'a protestant of the most advanced views', contributed to the dearth of these types of manuscripts in the royal collection through fairly diligent compliance with the Council's order, whether or not these manuscripts were kept in the Whitehall library or in other libraries or chambers.[92]

A few magnificent pre-Edwardian escapees survive, perhaps due to their very close royal associations. For example, Henry VIII's personal Psalter mentioned above,

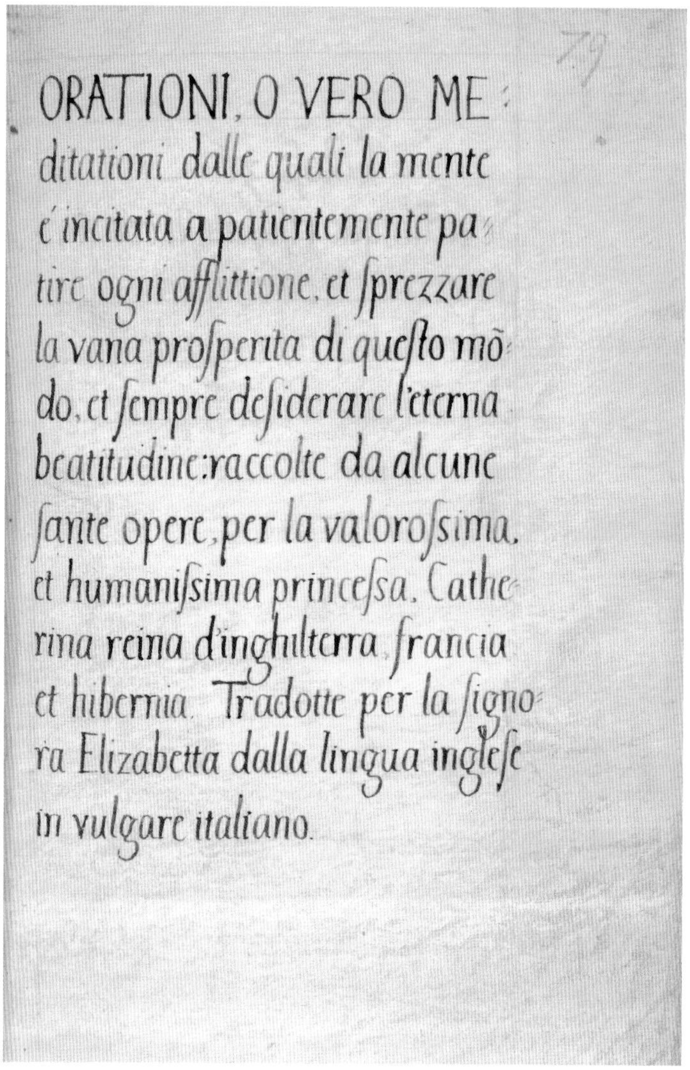

Fig. 3.3
Elizabeth I translation. Royal 7 D. x. f. 79

ORATIONI, O VERO ME:
ditationi dalle quali la mente
è incitata a patientemente pa:
tire ogni afflittione, et sprezzare
la vana prosperita di questo mõ:
do, et sempre desiderare l'eterna
beatitudine: raccolte da alcune
sante opere, per la valorosissima,
et humanissima principessa. Cathe:
rina reina d'inghilterra, francia
et hibernia. Tradotte per la signo:
ra Elizabetta dalla lingua inglese
in vulgare italiano.

with its portraits of the King and his extensive handwritten marginal notations (cat. no. 45) remains, as does the lavish copy of a selection of Psalms made by Humfrey, Duke of Gloucester, Henry V's younger brother (cat. no. 32). Another Psalter, owned by Isabel, the sister of Richard, Duke of York (cat. no. 34), is also part of the Old Royal library. The first may have been exempted from the purge by a proviso to the Act that 'any Prymars in the Englishe or Lattyne tongue set forthe by the late Kinge of famous memorie Kinge Henrie theight' may be retained as long as the prayers to the saints were 'blotted or clerelye put out'.[93] Although this clause was certainly not designed for Henry's personal Psalter, it may have been applied to it.

Further, in another of the ironies of the Old Royal library, the Act and the Privy Council's order may have provided the impetus for the reintroduction of these types of illuminated manuscripts into the royal collection following Mary's accession in 1553. For example, the new Queen was presented with at least two illuminated Psalters, one of which is arguably the most lavishly decorated illuminated manuscript in the Old Royal library, with over a thousand illustrations. As Gilson put it, 'if a single book could compensate for the losses suffered in the Edwardian purgation, it would be the magnificent Psalter 2 B. VII, the most beautiful MS. in the whole collection'.[94] This Psalter, now known as the Queen Mary Psalter (cat. no. 85), was saved from the national purge and rescued from export by a quick-thinking customs official, Baldwin Smith, who presented it to the Queen in 1553 after the arrest of its owner.[95] It may have been well known that Mary would value these survivals, for another, earlier but less lavishly illuminated Psalter (cat. no. 82), was presented to her by a London grocer, who inscribed the manuscript 'God save the Quene / Be me your humbull and poore orytur Rafe, Pryne, grocer, of Loundon, wushynge your gras prosperus helthe' (f. 1v).[96]

It seems probable that the main body of the Henrician library remained at Whitehall during the reigns of Henry's children, even if Richmond Palace was more favoured by them and retained a library. Only one partial catalogue of printed books survives from Elizabeth's reign: a small quarto-size list in faint ink of books in 'the newe librarye placed by T. Kny. [probably Thomas Knyvett (b. 1545/6, d. 1622), a household officer who was appointed Keeper of Whitehall Palace by 1597] the 20th of December, 1581' (see Appendix, no. 1, for a summary description).[97] This 'newe librarye' is presumably Henry VIII's 'newe librarye' (as distinguished from the 'upper library' catalogued in 1542) and, if so, the short alphabetical listing by title or subject of seventy-four printed books, with numbering system, gives at least a slight indication that it continued to be used as a library after his death.

In 1598 a German visitor, Paul Hentzner, commented that the royal library at Whitehall was 'well stored with Greek, Latin, Italian, and French books'.[98] He noted that 'all these books are bound in velvet of different colors, though chiefly red, with clasps of gold and silver; some have pearls and precious stones, set in their bindings'.[99] Hentzner also remarked particularly on a 'little one in French, upon parchment, in the hand writing of the present reigning Queen Elizabeth', dedicated to her father.[100] Like the manuscripts, mirror, genealogy and ink stain in 'Henry VII's library' at Richmond, this book featured in the accounts of other Continental visitors. Commenting on a trip to the Palace made in around 1610, another visitor mentioned that 'in the library is kept a little book written by Queen Elizabeth, in French, and dedicated to her father, Henry VIII'.[101] Similarly, the Duke of Saxe-Weinberg, who visited Whitehall in 1613, was shown the manuscript written by Elizabeth although, interestingly, he described the room in which it was kept as 'a small chamber where the books belonging to the Queen stood' instead of the library proper, and the book as a copy of 'the Dialogus fidei of Erasmus of Rotterdam'.[103] Another young Duke visited the 'Queen's cabinet' at Whitehall in 1602 and was shown 'a number of beautiful books bound in velvet and mounted with gold', including a 'Latin prayer book, that the Queen had written very nicely with her own hand and, in a beautiful preface, had dedicated to her father'.[104] The copy of Erasmus apparently does not survive, but the Latin prayerbook may be the translation of Katherine Parr's *Prayers and Meditations* (published in 1545) that Elizabeth translated into Latin, French and Italian and dedicated to her father (see fig. 3.3).

These visitors went to other palaces such as Greenwich, Hampton Court and Windsor, but only one comments on a library other than Whitehall and Richmond. (The Duke of Stettin-Pomerania mentioned briefly 'Henricus octavus' library' at Hampton Court, which had a 'very large Bible'.[105]) These various accounts, while apparently both somewhat formulaic, may suggest that Whitehall and Richmond were the two principal, or at least more 'public', royal libraries from the middle of the sixteenth century.

Prince Henry Frederick

Following the 'doldrums' of the royal library under Elizabeth, the accession of James I brought the third important influx of illuminated and other medieval manuscripts into the royal library.[106] In 1604 James gave his eldest son, Prince Henry Frederick (b. 1594, d. 1612), the palace of St James, which had been used by Henry VIII's children, for his residence (James and Prince Henry are pictured in fig. 3.4).[107] Despite his relative youth, Prince Henry set about creating a fitting court there. The Prince collected works of art, including paintings and bronzes, as well as 'curiosities' such as antiquities, coins and medals, with what has been called an 'insatiable appetite'.[108] Whitaker and Clayton comment that Henry 'gained a reputation as a discriminating collector who wanted to build up a princely collection in emulation of that of Rudolf II in Prague or the Florentine court under the Medici grand dukes'.[109] According to a contemporary, Prince Henry was interested in 'building and gardening, and in all sorts of rare musique, chiefly the trumpet and drumme; in limming, painting and carving, in all sorts of excellent and rare pictures, which he had brought unto him from all countries'.[110]

The building up of this court included the creation both

Fig. 3.4
James I and Prince Henry Frederick.
Additional 36932 (detail)

of a splendid library collection and a library space. Prince Henry had a large annual allowance of at least £10,000, and in 1610 he spent over £1000 of it on creating or refurbishing a 'new Lybrary Gallery and altering of officers lodgings', probably under the supervision of the Prince's Surveyor, Inigo Jones.[111] The space was ornamented with a fireplace and 'four greate arches over the passages in the library with architrave round aboute them and the Princes armes in the spandrils', together with Ionian and Corinthian capitals, sculpted pendants and satyrs completed by Maximilian Colt, the 'King's Sculptor or Master Carver'.[112]

Though the room itself does not survive, Sir Christopher Wren annexed a plan of the library at St James's to his 1706 report to the Treasurer concerning a proposed move of the library (fig. 3.5).[113] If this is the same room, which seems likely, the Prince's library was above the kitchen, facing the river, and measured 25 x 30 feet (7.6 x 9.1 metres). Wren's plan also shows what appears to be a long bookcase running down the centre of the room. The Prince's new or remodelled library was important enough to have featured in a tour of his painting collection given to the visiting representative from the duchy of Tuscany, Ottaviano Lotti, in March 1610, even though it was still under construction at that time.[114]

The books and manuscripts to be placed in this new grand space included the collection of John, Lord Lumley, which the Prince had acquired – perhaps as a gift from the childless Lumley – in 1609 (the wording of the relevant reference to the transfer leaves it unclear whether it was a gift or a purchase: 'the librarie whiche his highness hade of my lord Lumley').[115] This collection of nearly 400 manuscripts and 2400 printed books was one of the largest Elizabethan libraries.[116] Not all of it came to the Prince, as duplicate printed books were eliminated, but probably around two thousand volumes, including slightly more than three hundred manuscripts,

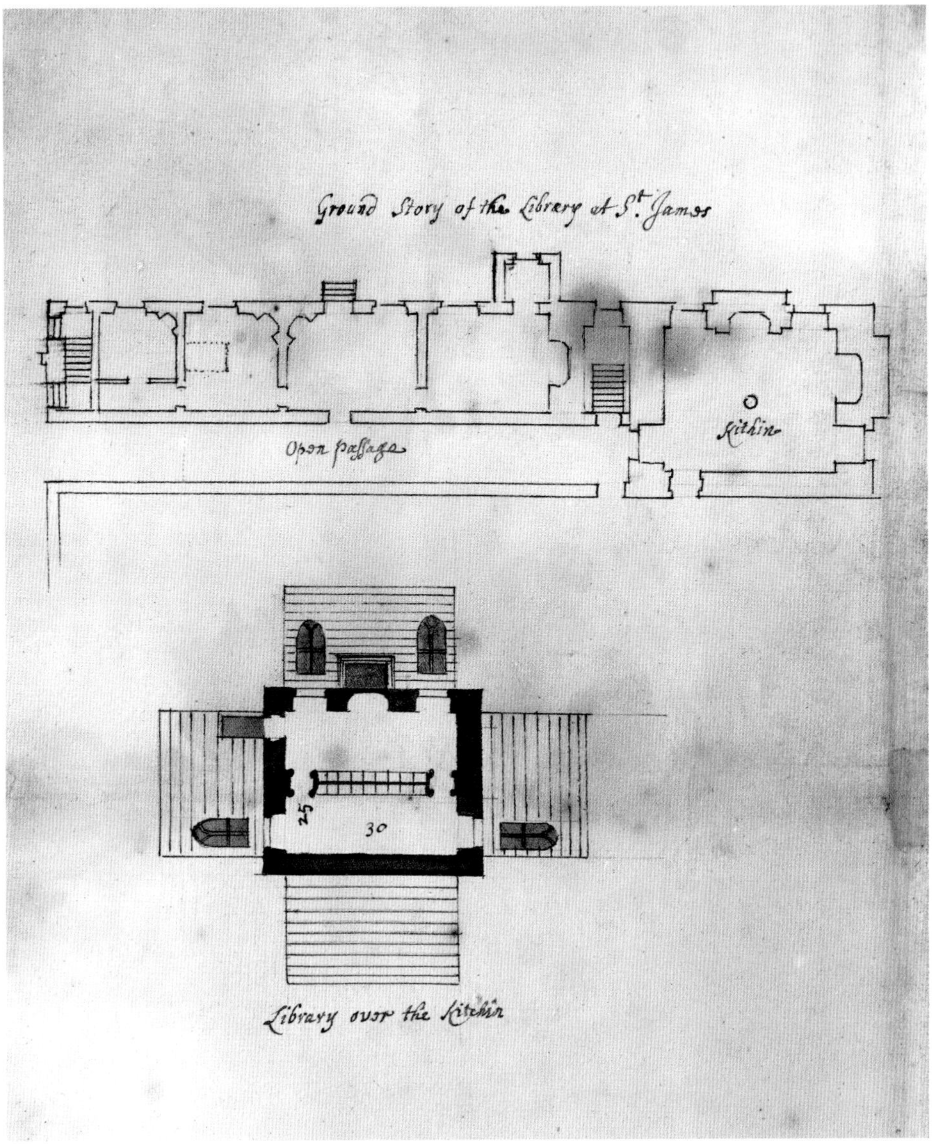

Fig. 3.5
Wren drawing of St James's Library.
Facsimile Supplement II (d) (2)

were included in the library at St James's.[117] As a result, this acquisition indirectly provided an Elizabethan collection of manuscripts as part of the Old Royal library.

Lumley's library was particularly rich in medieval material, because it included two other significant collections, most notably that of Lumley's Catholic father-in-law, Henry Fitzalan, 19th Earl of Arundel (d. 1580). Arundel served as Chamberlain under both Henry VIII and Edward VI until 1550, and as Lord High Steward under Mary.[118] The Earl's collection included approximately fifty manuscripts acquired at the dissolution of the monasteries and, in addition, the books and around one hundred manuscripts of Archbishop Thomas Cranmer that had been confiscated by the Crown after Mary's accession, including twenty-one illuminated ones.[119] A group of monastic manuscripts from Bury St Edmunds is also in the collection.[120] As noted above, a large percentage of the liturgical and devotion illuminated manuscripts in the Old Royal library are Lumley or Arundel manuscripts, such as the latest manuscript illustrated in this publication, the vividly illuminated Psalter of the Earl of Arundel, made in 1565 (cat no. 148); two much earlier works, a glossed Genesis and Exodus (cat. no. 14) and the impressive copy of Smaragdus's commentary on the Rule of St Benedict, with its full-page portrait of St Dunstan (cat. no. 101). Many manuscripts from Lumley's collection are recognizable by an added inscription of his name (fig. 3.6) or that of his father-in law (fig. 3.7). These names may have been added when Lumley's collection was merged with that of Arundel *c.* 1557 in connection with Lumley's move to Arundel's residence at Nonsuch Palace.[121] Around a thousand of Prince Henry's printed books, exclusive of those in the acquired collection, also survive in the Old Royal Library.[122]

The Prince's acquisition of the Lumley library was certainly consistent with his 'well-known penchant for learning'.[123]

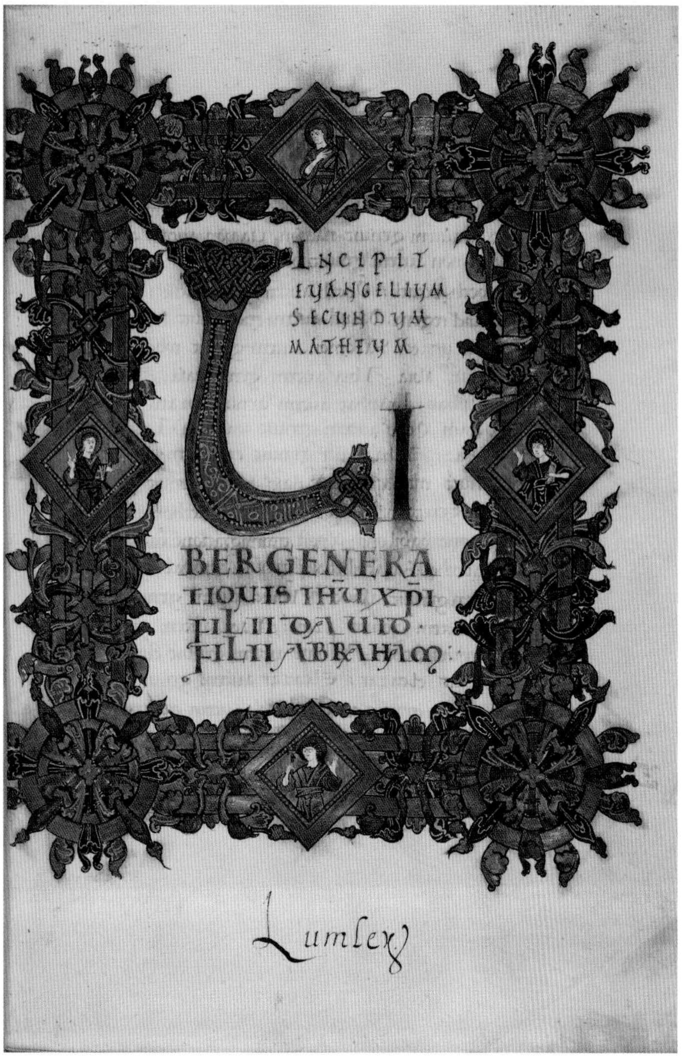

Fig. 3.6
Lumley inscription. Royal 1 D. ix, f. 6

Fig. 3.7 (opposite)
Arundel and Lumley inscriptions. Royal 3 C. i, f. 1

In addition, the possession of a great library housed in a grand and suitably princely venue appears to have been an important motivation for the Prince and his advisers in creating his library, in both senses of the term. The essential element, or 'the defining characteristic', of antiquarian libraries in the period 1580 to 1640, according to Ovenden, was the inclusion of medieval manuscripts; this element was provided by the Prince's acquisition of Lumley's collection.[124] Whether the illumination in some of these manuscripts was as important to Henry as their composition as a group, and indeed as a component of a larger collection of books and manuscripts, is less clear. It is certainly conceivable that the Prince was as interested in the 'limming' in the Lumley collection as he was in paintings on canvas and in other art objects. Alternatively, the illuminated manuscripts within Prince Henry's library may have been as much 'curiosities' as his medals, coins and other items appropriate to his position as a Renaissance prince.

At the Prince's death his collections went to his younger brother Charles, later Charles I, and presumably like Henry's painting collection, remained at the palace of St James.[125] At the same time, a new library was being built at Whitehall Palace for James I, but no catalogue of the contents of that library remains.[126] In 1622 the King sent out his librarian, Patrick Young, to search cathedrals for 'old manuscripts and ancient records' and to make an inventory of them.[127] If this occurred it does not appear to have resulted in the appropriation of manuscripts into the royal library. In 1617 James I did acquire part of the library of Isaac Casaubon, which included twenty-eight of the forty-three Greek manuscripts in the Old Royal Library, but these are mainly later manuscripts on paper without significant illumination.[128]

The only written indication of what was added to the royal library by Charles I is a short list of 237 predominantly English manuscripts and 93 printed books in English labelled 'Whitehall' amongst Young's papers, now at the Bodleian Library (see Appendix, no. 2).[129] The latest book on the list was published in 1641, so this list probably represents only a portion of what was at Whitehall during Charles's reign. These manuscripts are principally plays, verses and theological tracts, including funeral verses for King James and epigrams (in Latin) for Queen Elizabeth.[130] From their short titles, none is noticeably the sort of manuscript that would be illuminated. One of the oldest – and most famous – of manuscripts in the Old Royal library did enter the collection during this time, in 1627: the fifth-century Codex Alexandrinus, the earliest complete copy of the Bible (fig. 1.3).[131] While some of Alexandrinus's endpieces are decorated with heavily stylized, simple pictorial content, such as a palm tree, it is not an illuminated manuscript in the traditional sense of the term.[132] Other manuscripts did 'continue to migrate' out of the collection, but not in any systematic way.[133]

Commonwealth

The temporary end of the monarchy and the institution of a Commonwealth government effected a major change in the location, but happily not the loss of the royal collection of illuminated manuscripts. One of the first acts of the new government was to determine which royal goods could be sold, and this included a valuation of royal manuscripts and books. In September 1649 the King's former librarian was directed to prepare an inventory of the library.[134] Part of a 1650 catalogue of books and a few manuscripts, perhaps

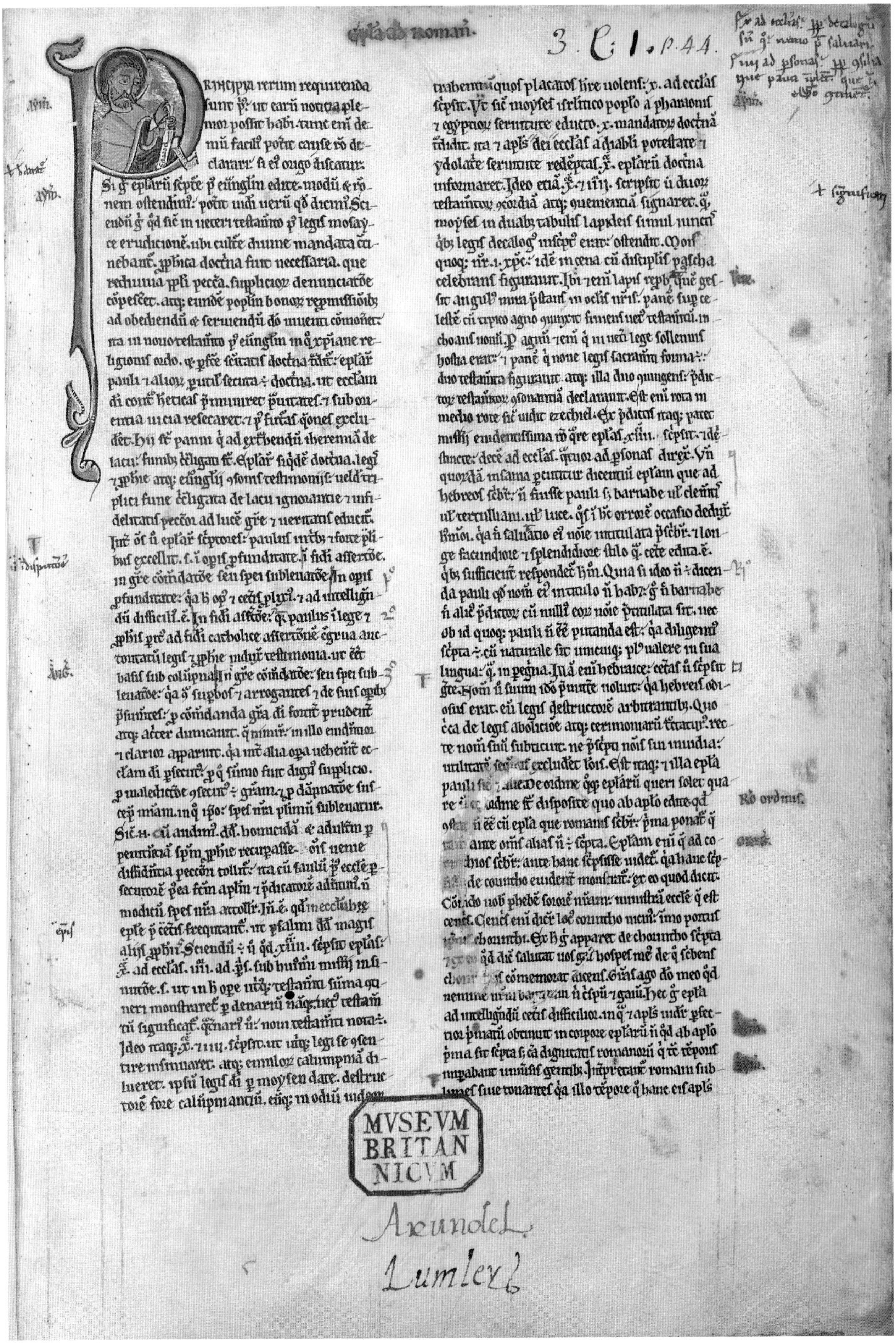
3. C. I. p. 44.
MVSEVM
BRITAN
NICVM
Arundel
Lumley

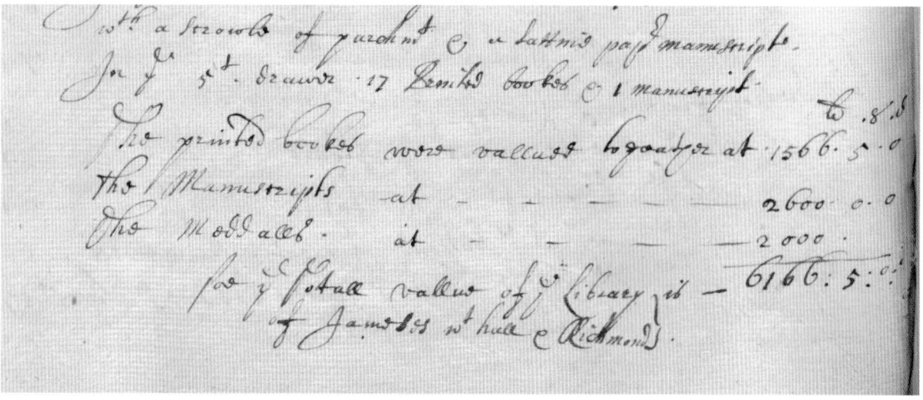
With a scroule of parchment & a Lattin paper manuscripte.
In ye 5th drawer 17 Printed bookes & 1 manuscript
The printed bookes were valued togeather at 1566.5.0
The Manuscripts at 2600.0.0
The Meddales at 2000.
for ye totall value of ye library is 6166.5.0
of Jameses Whall & Richmonde.

Fig. 3.8
Valuation of St James's Library.
British Library C.120.h.6(1), p. 206 (detail)

Young's list or a copy of it, survives as C.120.h.6(1). This 1650 list of the printed books of the St James's library appears to be a shelflist, and therefore includes some clues about the placement of books in the library rooms there, such as 'Bookes of St Jameses Librarie under 3 Sydes of Arches in Folio' and 'Bookes in the Closet' (see Appendix, no. 3). Unfortunately, Wren's plan is not sufficiently detailed to allow these areas to be identified.

Similarly, there is a tantalizing glimpse of the number and arrangement of manuscripts at the Palace on an added page at the end of these lists of printed books. The page contains an undated list, headed simply 'Manuscripts', and is literally a shelf (and drawer) count, with totals at the end of each line (see Appendix, no. 3). For example, the eleven shelves 'between the chiminey and the doore' contained a total of 585 manuscripts, while the nine shelves and one drawer in the 'Middle row fronting the Chimney' held 677 manuscripts. Some manuscripts, rolls or 'scroules' or books are grouped together, making it impossible to give a total number. Nevertheless, the list includes at least 1274 manuscripts. There is no indication of the room from which this survey was made, but the various indications of placement in each list suggest that the manuscripts were housed in a different area from that of the printed books, and were apparently the subject of a separate inventory. This makes a change from the arrangement of printed books and manuscripts alphabetized together in the Upper Library at Whitehall in 1542.

Other printed books were listed in a separate catalogue of 'Bookes that were brought from Whitehall'. Apparently the Richmond books and manuscripts were also moved to St James's as part of the assessment process; there is no library mentioned in the otherwise fairly detailed 1649 inventory of Richmond Palace (although books may have been kept in the Privy Chamber or the Prince's Closet).[135] These volumes may all have been stored in another room, perhaps in the new chapel at St. James's, which was to be fitted out as a library.[136] Alternatively, they may simply have been deposited or stored in piles on the floor in the existing library space. In his petition to obtain the keys to the library in 1651, the Library Keeper John Durie wrote that:

> The books and manuscripts will be utterly spoiled if not immediately looked after, as they lie upon the floor in confused heaps, so that not only the rain and dust but the rats, mice, and other vermin can easily get at them, and none of these inconveniences can be prevented unless you order the trustees for the sale of the late King's goods to deliver me the keys.[137]

At the bottom of the verso of the page listing manuscripts is a summary valuation of medals, printed books and manuscripts in the library, giving the total values of each: the medals were worth £2000, the printed books £1566 5s., and the manuscripts £2600 (fig. 3.8). If made *c.* 1650, as seems likely, this indicates that the library was worth considerably less than the royal collection of around 1570 paintings, which was valued at £37,000.[138] Indeed, the most valuable painting, Raphael's *Madonna della Perla,* was valued at £2000, less than the value of the manuscripts but more than the entire collection of printed books.[139] The line giving the total also states that it is a total value of '£6166.5.00', 'of Jameses Wthall & Richmonde', indicating that the manuscripts must have been brought together in one place, presumably St James's, to complete the valuation.

In his reminiscences or *Memorials*, Bulstrode Whitelocke explained that he accepted the position of Library Keeper from the Council in order to prevent a 'design in some to have them [the medals and books] sold and transported beyond Sea'.[140] The fact that printed books, manuscripts and medals were inventoried and assessed for their value may indicate just how real the danger of dispersal of the then former royal library may have been. Thus, ironically enough, it appears that the first centralization of at least the principal royal libraries took place with a view to their dismantling and sale. However, unlike Charles I's collection of paintings, sold in the 'Commonwealth Sale' conducted at Somerset House from late 1649 to 1651, the King's books and manuscripts escaped this fate.[141] Like some of the paintings reserved for the Protector, the books and manuscripts instead were preserved 'for publick Use'.[142]

Charles II

At the Restoration this now centralized library once again became a royal library. Presumably the first task in re-establishing it was to determine what remained, and a rough 'transfer inventory' signed or verified on each page by both the outgoing Commonwealth Keeper, John Durie, and his successor, Thomas Ross, suggests that this occurred fairly quickly.[143] The inventory is a 'Sundry Catalogue of Books' of lists of printed books and manuscripts in which the location of the library is not given, although it seems unlikely that the volumes had been moved from St James's. As a verification rather than an initial compilation, this inventory may well have been based on a list made by Patrick Young, or another list compiled during the Interregnum. Only one page of manuscript listings survives. Nevertheless, there is some indication of where the manuscripts were placed in the library. The short group of 'Engl: Man: in octavo' were 'in the 5. press on the west wall' and the 'Lat: in octavo' were 'those in the 3d press against the chimney'. The different listings may reflect a physical separation of manuscripts and printed books in the library, either in separate rooms or in different parts of the same room, or at least placement on different shelves. Another list, Royal Appendix 71, dated 1666, lists titles in similar groups that appear to correspond to twenty-six bookcases or shelves, and in fifteen 'scrin[ia]', presumably another kind of case (see Appendix, no. 9).

In addition to being catalogued, the royal library was also being supplemented with new acquisitions. In 1660 or 1661 the collection of John Morris (d. 1658), an antiquarian and book collector who described his library as 'the cheife pleasure and imployment of my life', was purchased for the royal library.[144] Morris's collection consisted of over 1400 principally French, Italian and Spanish printed books, but included a few manuscripts.[145] Charles II also acquired at least two book collections from the bookseller Robert Scott (d. 1709/10). In a letter to Archbishop William Sancroft (b. 1617, d. 1693), Scott enclosed a list, no longer extant, of the library of the great bibliophile Jacques-Auguste de Thou (b. 1553, d. 1617), Keeper of the French royal library, which Scott had been asked to view 'by my Ld Chancillor Hydes direction'.[146] Scott writes that 'he shall be very happy (if I cannott purchase it my selfe) to be assisting in buying itt for his ma[jes]tie ... though I believe itt noe convenient tyme to mention the Purchase of this Library for his Ma[jes]tie'.[147] In order to support his case, Scott reminded Sancroft that 'About 7 years since I bought out of Monsr. Montmores [Pierre de Montmaur (b. 1576, d. 1648), professor of Greek at the Collège Royal] Library in Paris, most of the french Historians, etc. all of the Royale pap[er] and richly bound, w[hi]ch his Ma[jes]tie bought of mee w[i]th great pleasure'.[148] The letter itself is undated, but de Thou's library was sold in 1680, so presumably this earlier sale occurred in the early 1670s.[149]

The second collection purchased from Scott was the library of John Theyer (b. 1597, d. 1673), of Cooper's Hill in Gloucestershire, probably in 1678.[150] With this acquisition the last significant group of illuminated and other medieval manuscripts was added to the Old Royal library. Theyer was an antiquarian who had collected 'all the relics of monastic libraries that he could secure', which included, as Gilson put it, 'a great number of useful mediaeval manuscripts'.[151] Like the manuscripts of John, Lord Lumley, many of Theyer's manuscripts are also identified by an inscription of his name or a monogram (fig. 3.9). The collection comprised around 334 manuscripts, most of which had belonged to around twenty monastic houses, particularly from the west of England; the bookseller's list with Scott's individual valuations and those of the appraisers survives as Royal Appendix 70.[152] The whole collection was valued by Scott at £841, and at £560 by William Beveridge, the rector of St Peter's, Cornhill, and William Jane, a canon of Christ Church, Oxford, who were presumably acting for the King as assessors.[153] Despite these relatively low values (for comparison, in the period from 1670 to 1677, the King spent £36,073 on gifts to his mistress Louise-Renée de Kérouallle and in 1674 made a gift to Nell Gwyn of silver ornaments for her bed worth £2265),[154] these 'useful' manuscripts include many important illuminated, monastic and early medieval manuscripts, such as the *Bible historiale* of Charles V (cat. no. 22); an early thirteenth-century bestiary with eighty miniatures (cat. no. 80); a glossed Epistles with the commentary of Peter Lombard with elegant historiated initials (cat. no. 104); and – perhaps most famously – the Westminster Psalter, with added notes in Theyer's hand (cat. no. 12).

Shortly after this acquisition, in 1681, the King wrote to Henri Justel, a former secretary to Charles's cousin Louis XIV, appointing Justel a 'chief inspector of the ancient MSS.' and 'curator of all other his MSS.'[155] Charles explained that because 'he had many ancient and rare manuscripts in the learned languages' in the royal library at St James's, he wished Justel 'to range and digest the said MSS. there into such method and indexes as shall be most convenient to render them useful towards the advancement of learning'.[156] But Justel's duties extended beyond cataloguing and indexing. He was also to inspect 'other MSS. in the custody of the Bishop of London and other subjects' in order to 'report how they may be disposed in the said library at St. James'.[157] As part of this inspection Justel was empowered to supplement the royal library with manuscripts 'from the libraries of the Universities at home or from foreign libraries', and to this end to require 'all keepers of libraries and others to assist him'.[158] A number of catalogues or lists of various parts of the royal library – some for printed books, some for manuscripts organized by different principles, such as subject or title, and in various states of drafts and completeness – survive from the second half of the seventeenth century. None is dated, but dates of printed books in some of the lists provide *termini post quem* of 1648, 1652, 1669 and 1679 (see Appendix, nos. 6–12 for descriptions). Whether or not any was prepared by Justel, these various inventories and catalogues testify to the interest in classifying and organizing the royal library during Charles's reign.

The terms of Charles's letter to Justel make it clear that the principal repository of the newly re-established royal library remained at St James's Palace after the Restoration, despite the fact that the King's principal residence in London was Whitehall.[159] This is supported by a comment made in 1684 by Thomas Tenison, later Archbishop of Canterbury, who mentioned only three 'noted' libraries in Westminster: those of Sir Robert Cotton, Westminster Abbey and 'St James (which belongs to his Majestie and to which there is noe easy access)'.[160] Interestingly, however, Charles also developed a personal library at Whitehall. In September 1680, when the King was away at Windsor, the diarist John Evelyn spent several days examining Charles's 'private library at Whitehall'.[161] Evelyn noted that there were 'about a thousand Volumes' there and commented that these books 'consisted chiefely of such books as had from time to time ben dedicated, or presented him'.[162] Although presumably most of this library would have consisted of printed books and the sort of verses and tracts included in the earlier Whitehall list now in Young's papers, the collection did include medieval illuminated manuscripts, for Evelyn mentioned in particular '3 or 4 Romish Breviaries with a great deal of *Miniature* & Monkish Painting & Gilding; one of which is most exquisitely don, both as to the figures, Grotescs & Compartiments, to the uttmost of that curious art'.[163] Gilson suggested that this highly illuminated manuscript might be the Queen Mary Psalter (cat. no. 85).[164]

Charles's acquisition of various collections of books, including the Theyer collection of manuscripts, his appointment of a curator to classify and supplement the manuscripts at St James's, and his development of what must have been a newly formed personal library at Whitehall are at odds with his reputed 'distaste for reading', which according to one modern biographer 'he could never overcome'.[165] A contemporary, Gilbert Burnet (b. 1643, d. 1715), Bishop of Salisbury, wrote that the King 'is very little conversant in books, and young and old he could never apply himself to literature'.[166] Similarly, George Savile, 1st Marquess of Halifax (b. 1633, d. 1695), in his *Character of King Charles the Second*, commented that the King's 'Wit was not acquired by *Reading*'.[167] Charles may not have been entirely comfortable reading Latin; in a letter to Evelyn, John Mordaunt, 1st Viscount Mordaunt of Avalon (b. 1626, d. 1675), reported that upon Evelyn's presentation of a panegyric for Charles's coronation the King had enquired whether it was in Latin, and commented that he 'hoped it would not be very long'.[168]

Fig. 3.9
Theyer inscription. Royal 3 A iv, f. ii (detail)

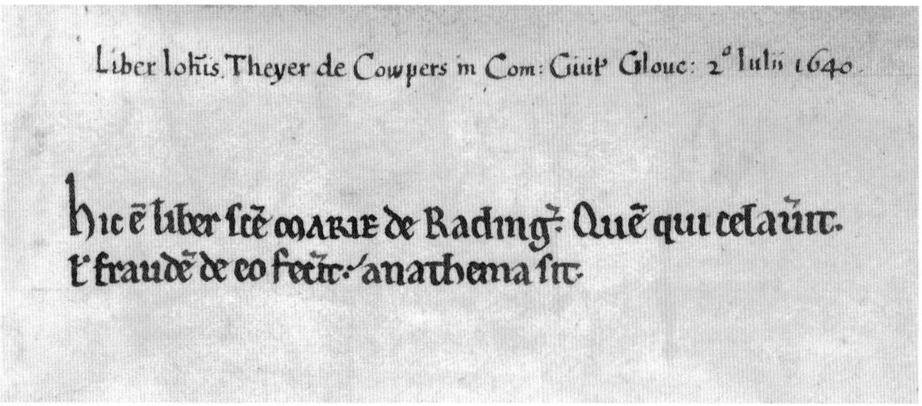

The rationale given for Justel's appointment may help to explicate this apparent conundrum. Charles was concerned that manuscripts in the royal library 'dissipated and embezzled in the late civil wars … have not since been sought after and recovered'.[169] Secondly, manuscripts in the collection that were 'imperfect or mutilated' were to be replaced by copies from the universities or foreign libraries.[170] This effort was akin to that undertaken to recover the royal collection of paintings, which Charles 'set about reassembling', or acquiring comparable works, immediately upon his restoration in 1660.[171] An additional enterprise was the binding, or rebinding, of around a thousand books with the King's arms, a project that Birrell argues was supervised by the King, on the basis of the design of the binding.[172] A bookbinder to the King, Samuel Mearne (b. 1624, d. 1683), was appointed quickly after the Restoration in June 1660; from May 1675 Mearne and his son Charles were granted the new office of Bookbinder, Bookseller and Stationer to the King.[173] These various initiatives of cataloguing, supplementing and rebinding suggest a deliberate policy of restoring the royal library and indeed of enhancing and improving it to an appropriately grand and royal collection.

What is less clear is the role and importance of the illuminated manuscripts within this strategy. Charles shared with his father 'a love of art', filling a small room off his bedchamber at Whitehall with painting and statuettes, and the rooms next to the library with 'divers of the best pictures of the greate *Masters*'.[174] He collected drawings as well; his is the foundation collection of drawings in the Royal Collection at Windsor.[175] Perhaps this appreciation extended from drawing and painting to illustration in books. According to the biography of Nicholas Ferrar, when Charles was a young boy the Prince so admired one of the illustrated Ferrar books of biblical harmonies that another was commissioned specially for him. However, the author stresses the content rather than the illustration as the rationale for the selection (and some of these books are unillustrated).[176] Moreover, because only around sixty of the three hundred-plus Theyer manuscripts have painted decoration and just half of those contain miniatures, historiation, diagrams or drawings, it seems unlikely that this was the sole motivation for the King's acquisition of medieval manuscripts.

Because the new bindings did not include the King's arms, Birrell concluded that the King himself must have been involved in the design decision, and that he 'wanted to show that his library was to be that of a private gentleman – a gentleman virtuoso, a patron of the Royal Society – in other words a gentleman who happened to be a king'.[177] However, the rebinding programme and the other initiatives undertaken by Charles or at his direction may represent the opposite impulse – to continue the tradition going back to Yorkist precedents of maintaining a magnificent court, including a royal library appropriate for a king. The fact that Charles may not have been particularly interested in reading or studying individual manuscripts in the collection (particularly the Latin ones, which predominate) may have been less important than the enhancement of the re-established royal library.

Later history

The Theyer acquisition represented the last major addition to the collection of illuminated manuscripts in the Old Royal library.[178] This library apparently remained primarily at St James's Palace for the balance of the seventeenth century. In August 1689, in a very long letter to Samuel Pepys, John Evelyn lamented the lack of 'good libraries' in England, describing in some detail notable exceptions. In London, he singled out Cotton's library as 'without dispute the most valuable in MSS.', but adds that 'there is hope his Ma[jes]ties at St James's may emerge & be in some measure restor'd againe, now that it comes under the inspection of the learned Mons. Justell [appointed Keeper the previous month]'.[179] Evelyn concluded that there were in the royal library 'a greate many noble manuscripts yet remaining' at St James's.[180] He did not include the library at Whitehall or any other royal palace in his survey. Similarly, the antiquary John Bagford, in an essay on libraries in London published in 1708, commented that although kings had their books at several palaces, including Whitehall, the library at 'St James' was the chiefest'.[181] Likewise, the 1698 publication of the union catalogue *Catalogi librorum manuscriptorum Angliae et Hiberniae* includes only an entry for the King's library at St James's.

From early in the eighteenth century the Old Royal library began a series of seven moves to various non-royal buildings. Initially these plans were necessitated by the insufficient space and apparent incommodious state of the library at St James's. In 1696 the Keeper, Richard Bentley, complained that the library was 'not fit to be seen' and moved Codex Alexandrinus into his own rooms so 'that persons might see it without seeing the library'.[182] In 1706 Sir Christopher Wren was engaged to advise on a move to Cotton House, and surveyed 'her Majesty's library at St James'. He reported that 'the library at St James was a lofty room, and shelved as full as it could well be, and yet a great number of bookes remained in heapes for want of room'.[183] As a result, in February 1707 Wren was paid £288 'to put in hand the repairs necessary at Cotton House [in Westminster] for the reception & preservation of her Majesty's Library at St James's into the said House'.[184] The Old Royal library was stored there with the collection of Sir Robert Cotton, which had been accepted by Parliament as a public library in 1700.[185] Cotton House, in turn, was considered unsuitable as a venue and in 1722 the two collections were moved to Essex House in the Strand, and in 1729 to Ashburnham House in Little Dean's Yard, Westminster, after the expiry of the lease of Essex House.[186] Two years later a fire broke out at Ashburnham House, but most of the Old Royal library escaped damage, apparently as a result of being thrown out of the upstairs window into the courtyard below, with the retired Bentley in his nightshirt reportedly rescuing Codex Alexandrinus.[187] An example of a manuscript that was damaged is Royal 9 C. x (fig. 3.10). The surviving books and manuscripts of both collections were moved immediately across the street, and then to the New Dormitory at Westminster school.[188] Shortly thereafter they were transferred to the school's Old Dormitory, where they remained until the move to the British Museum at Montagu House in 1757.

Fig. 3.10
Manuscript damaged in the Ashburnham House fire. Royal 9 C. x

Conclusion

In a review of the first modern catalogue of the Royal collection, Poole commented that 'a great library has a history of its own, in some ways independent of the value of its contents'.[189] In this essay I have attempted to draw out aspects of both the history of the Old Royal library and the role and significance of illuminated manuscripts within it. There are a few surprises in how the books were used and assembled. Edward IV's sumptuous illuminated manuscripts may have been intended as some of the 'noble Stories, as behoveth a Prince to understand, and knowe' that the King commanded be 'read before' the Prince of Wales after meals.[190] However, this particular use of illuminated manuscripts appears to have ceased near the end of Henry VIII's reign. The copious surviving notes in Henry's own hand in manuscripts – including illuminated ones – demonstrate that manuscripts were still being read, but perhaps not aloud, in the later periods.

It is also noteworthy that only a relatively small number of individuals made a significant contribution to the collection of illuminated manuscripts in the Old Royal library, and that the last two of these enhanced the collection at a point when illuminated manuscripts were no longer being produced. Prince Henry's acquisition of the Lumley collection is particularly important after the losses suffered under Edward VI and the 'seventy years' of inactivity under Elizabeth, even if it is not quite the 'virtual refoundation of a Royal Library' articulated by Miller and later by Strong.[191] Similarly, the popular view of Charles II as a monarch who does not 'rank highly' either as a patron or a collector must be revised, at least in relation to the manuscript portion of the library, whatever his motivation and whether or not this collecting was due to a personal interest in illumination.[192] Interestingly, the acquisition by both of existing or 'residual' collections that included manuscripts indicates the shifting importance and function of illuminated manuscripts within the royal library.

A more continuous strand in the history of the Old Royal library is the function of the library and the manuscripts within it as indicia of kings' (or princes') position and a manifestation of the appropriate magnificence of their courts. The best surviving material evidence of what has been called the late medieval 'cult of magnificence' and was understood so well by Edward IV and Henry VIII is the manuscripts they ordered and collected and are still in the Old Royal library.[193] That this remained one of the functions of illuminated manuscripts is illustrated by Charles II's pride in his 'ancient and rare MSS', demonstrated by his interest in supplementing, organizing and arranging them. In turn, this aspect of the library is related to the ongoing importance of the example of other royal, Continental libraries, as McKendrick demonstrates in his essay 'A European Heritage'. Awareness of the collections of their fellow rulers, if not competition with them, surely informed the centralization of an English royal library. It is reasonable to conclude that at least some kings believed that assembling a royal library 'was the sort of behaviour expected of people in their position, that it would be shaming not to play the same game as the French kings or the Burgundian dukes'.[194] In this regard it is perhaps significant that medieval illuminated manuscripts and the contents of royal libraries were amongst the items to be 'shown off' to foreign dignitaries and other visitors.

A final shared objective of the collection of medieval manuscripts in the Old Royal library has been that it be 'useful towards the advancement of learning', as Charles II phrased it.[195] George II's donation to the nation of this tremendous assemblage of manuscripts and books ensured that the Old Royal library continues to be used for this purpose.

NOTES

1 Letter of Evelyn to Pepys, 12 August 1689, in Wheatley, *John Evelyn* (1906), III, p. 449. I should like to thank James Carley, Scot McKendrick and John Lowden for reading a draft of this essay and for their very helpful comments and suggestions.
2 Gilson, 'Introduction' (1921), p. xi.
3 Additional 60584, f. 24, printed in summary in Vale, *Edward III* (1982), Appendix 9.
4 See discussion Vale, *Edward III* (1982), pp. 49–50; Stratford, 'Royal Library' (1994), p. 189 n. 12. Stratford, 'Early Royal Collections' (1999), pp. 257–58.
5 Stratford, 'Early Royal Collections' (1999), pp. 258–59; see also Stratford, 'Royal Library' (1994), pp. 189–90; Stratford and Webber, 'Bishops and Kings' (2006), p. 202.
6 Stratford, 'Royal Library' (1994), p. 191; Stratford, 'Early Royal Collections' (1999), pp. 260–61; Stratford and Webber, 'Bishops and Kings' (2006), p. 209.
7 London, TNA: PRO E101/502/23, mm.3–4, 'in uno magno deske facto de ij stagez pro libris regis intus custodiendis', cited in Stratford, 'Royal Library' (1994), p. 191; Stratford, 'Early Royal Collections' (1999), pp. 260-61; see also Stratford and Webber, 'Bishops and Kings' (2006), p. 209.
8 For the identification of this manuscript see Stratford, 'Early Royal Collection' (1999), p. 263.
9 Stratford, 'Royal Library' (1994), p. 192; Stratford and Webber, 'Bishops and Kings' (2006), pp. 209, 215.
10 Gilson, 'Introduction' (1921), p. xiii n. 5.

11 Stratford, 'Royal Library' (1994), p. 191; Stratford, 'Early Royal Collection' (1999), p. 261; Stratford and Webber, 'Bishops and Kings' (2006), pp. 209–10.
12 McFarlane, *Lancastrian Kings* (1972), pp. 116–17.
13 Eton, Eton College Records 59, f. 4, will clause xxx, edited in Strong and Strong, 'Last Will' (1981) p. 94; cited in Alexander, 'Manuscript Illumination' (1983), p. 159; Stratford, 'Royal Library' (1994), p. 193; Stratford, 'Early Royal Collections' (1999), p. 262.
14 Eton, Eton College Records 59, f. 7, 1422 codicil, clause [3] edited in Strong and Strong, 'Last Will' (1981), p.100, and cited in Stratford, 'Royal Library' (1994), p. 193; Stratford, 'Early Royal Collections' (1999), pp. 262–63; see also Stratford and Webber, 'Bishops and Kings' (2006), pp. 210, 216, where they conclude that liturgical books were regarded as distinct and kept separately.
15 Stratford, 'Early Royal Collections' (1999), p. 266.
16 London, TNA: PRO Exchequer K. R., Various Accounts, E101/335/17, printed in McFarlane, *Lancastrian Kings* (1972), pp. 234–38; see also Alexander, 'Manuscript Illumination' (1983), p. 159; Stratford, 'Royal Library' (1994), pp. 193–95; Stratford, 'Early Royal Collections' (1999), pp. 263–64.
17 Stratford, 'Early Royal Collections' (1999), p. 265.
18 Cotton Tiberius A. viii (Capgrave); Cotton Domitian A. xvii (Psalter of Henry VI); Additional 18850 (Bedford Hours); Harley 2278 (Metrical lives of Sts Edmund and Fremund); Royal 15 E. vi; (Shrewsbury Book) Royal 13 B. iii (Life of St Louis) (cat. nos. 119, 141, 142, 30, 143, and 67).
19 Stratford, 'Royal Library' (1994), p. 195; Stratford, 'Early Royal Collections (1999), p. 264.
20 Stratford, 'Royal Library' (1994), pp. 195–96; Stratford, 'Early Royal Collections (1999), p. 265.
21 Cf. Sir John Fortescue, *Articles sent from the Prince to the Earl of Warwick*, in Plummer, *Governance of England* (1885), Appendix B, p. 352, cited in Thurley, *Royal Palaces* (1993), p. 12.
22 Stratford, 'Royal Library' (1994), p. 187; Gilson, 'Introduction' (1921), p. xi; Backhouse, 'Founders' (1987), p. 23; see also Stratford, 'Early Royal Collections' (1999), p. 255; Stratford and Webber, 'Bishops and Kings' (2006), p. 213, and Barker, *Treasures* (2005), p. 25; but see Strong, *Henry* (1986), p. 211, for Henry VII as the founder of the 'first Royal Library'.
23 Thurley, *Royal Palaces* (1993), p. 141; for the accounts see Nicolas, *Privy Purse* (1830), p. 125; see also Kipling, *Triumph of Honour* (1977), p. 32, where he states that Edward 'made no attempt to provide special quarters for his books, much less to establish a library as an institution with a staff of its own'.
24 Backhouse, 'Founders' (1987), p. 29; Backhouse, 'Royal Library' (1999), p. 269; but see Carley, *Libraries* (2000), p. xxv, where he states that 'it is not clear where Edward himself housed his books'.
25 Section 37, 'Yomen of Crowne' in Myers, *Household* (1959), p. 116; I thank Scot McKendrick for this reference; see also Stratford and Webber, 'Bishops and Princes' (2006), p. 215. But see Gilson, 'Introduction' (1921), p. xiii, where he states that 'of the arrangements made by Edward IV or Richard III for the custody of the books we have no information'.
26 Myers, *Household* (1959), p. 116.
27 Backhouse, 'Founders' (1987), p. 32; for Richard's books see generally Sutton and Visser-Fuchs, *Richard III's Books: Ideals* (1997).
28 Another illuminated manuscript, Royal 20 C. vii, was probably originally made for Richard's uncle, Edward (Edward of Langley, Edward of York), Earl of Rutland and 2nd Duke of York, and was acquired by Richard while he was Duke of Gloucester; it is inscribed 'Richard Gloucestre' (f. 134).
29 Backhouse, 'Royal Library' (1999), p. 271.
30 Cf. Brown and Scheele, *Old Royal Library* (1957), p. 4, where they observe that 'the statement that the University of Oxford asked Duke Humphrey to procure the library of Henry V after his death suggests that the idea of a Royal Library as a continuing institution had not yet emerged'.
31 Thurley, *Royal Palaces* (1993), pp. 25–37; see also Carley, *Libraries* (2000), pp. xxv–xxvi; lxiii n. 129; Starkey, 'Preface' (2004), p. 8.
32 Kipling, *Receyt* (1990), p. 71; for the date and background see pp. xlii–l.
33 Kipling, *Receyt* (1990), p. 77; see discussion in Carley, *Libraries* (2000), p. 141.
34 Kipling, *Receyt* (1990), p. 73, cited in Thurley, *Royal Palaces* (1993), p. 29.
35 Royal 19 C. vi, f. 19. The entire preface transcribed in Dionisotti, 'Claude de Seyssel' (1995), pp. 90–95. Although this is often cited as a specific reference to the library at Richmond (see, e.g., Kipling, *Triumph of Honour* (1977), p. 33, and Carley, *Libraries* (2000), pp. xxvi, 3, 141), no place is mentioned in the dedication, although this may be clear from other evidence of the places de Seyssel visited.
36 Starkey, 'Preface' (2004), p. 8.
37 7 April 1492; 20 January 1493, in Lyte, *Calendar of Patent Rolls, Henry VII* (1914), II, pp. 378, 455–56.
38 7 April 1492; 20 January 1493, in Lyte, *Calendar of Patent Rolls, Henry VII* (1914), II, pp. 378, 455–56. It may be on this basis that Poulet is often referred to as the first royal librarian or keeper of the royal library; see, e.g., Brown and Scheele, *Old Royal Library* (1957), p. 4; Carley, *Libraries* (2000), p. 4.
39 20 September 1509, Brewer, Brodie and Gairdner *Letters and Papers*, Foreign and Domestic, Henry VIII, (1862), I, p. 74, no. 513.
40 Carley, 'Marks' (1997).
41 See also Backhouse, 'Illuminated Manuscripts' (1995); Scott, *Gothic Manuscripts* (1996), 2, pp. 365–66; Scott, 'Manuscripts' (1997).
42 Backhouse, 'Founders' (1987), p. 33; for his printed books see Birrell, *English Monarchs* (1987), pp. 5–12.
43 On Henry VII's Vérard books see Backhouse, 'Founders' (1987), p. 33; Backhouse, 'Illuminated Manuscripts' (1995), p. 179; Birrell, *English Monarchs* (1987), pp. 5–6; Carley, *Libraries* (2000), p. xxvii; Winn, *Anthoine Vérard* (1997), pp. 138–53.
44 Carley, *Libraries* (2000), p. lxiii.
45 Ker, *Medieval Libraries* (1964), p. xi, for the number of manuscripts.
46 Thurley, *Royal Palaces* (1993), p. 1.
47 See Carley, 'Royal Library' (1999), p. 274, for the number of residences as fifty 'each presumably with its own collection of books'.
48 Thurley, *Royal Palaces* (1993), p. 141.
49 Roberts, 'Extending' (2006), p. 296; see also Carley, *Leland* (2010), pp. li-liii; Ferdinand, 'Library Administration' (2006), p. 568.
50 Leland, *The Laboryouse Journey* (1549), sig. B viii, cited in Carley, *Libraries* (2000), p. xliv, and Carley, *Leland* (2010), pp. liii; on Leland generally see pp. xxi-clx.
51 Ker, *Medieval Libraries* (1964), p. xii.
52 Ker, *Medieval Libraries* (1964), p. xi.
53 Leland *Antiphilarchia*, Cambridge, University Library, MS Ee.5.15, pp. 335–36, cited in Carley, 'Royal Library' (1999), p. 275; Carley, *Libraries* (2000), p. lxiii.
54 Thurley, *Royal Palaces* (1993), p. 54; Carley, *Libraries* (2000), p. 30.
55 Statutes of the Realm, 28 Henry VIII, c. 12, cited in Thurley, *Royal Palaces* (1993), p. 56.
56 Harley 1419A, f. 62v (for the 'highest Library'); Harley 1419A, ff. 186–188 (for the 'newe librarye'), cited in Jayne and Johnson, *Lumley Library* (1956), p. 292 n. 2.
57 Jervis, 'English Country House' (1999), p. 13; Selwyn and Selwyn, 'Profession' (2006), pp. 503–04; see also Carley, *Libraries* (2000) p. 283.
58 London, TNA: PRO, Augmentation Office, Misc. Books 160 (E.315/160), f. 105v, ed. in Carley, *Libraries* (2000), p. 31.
59 See Carley, *Libraries* (2000), pp. lxvi–lxxiv, p. 34.

60 Carley, *Libraries* (2000), p. lxvi.
61 Carley, *Libraries* (2000), pp. 31–32.
62 Carley, *Libraries* (2000), pp. 32, lxxii.
63 Carley, *Libraries* (2000), p. lxxii.
64 London, TNA: PRO, Augmentation Office, Misc. Books 160 (E.315/160), f. 62v, ed. in Carley, *Libraries* (2000), pp. 282–83. On Greenwich see Carley, *Libraries* (2000), p. 27.
65 London, TNA: PRO, Augmentation, Misc. Books 160 (E.315/160), f. 245, edited in Carley, *Libraries* (2000), p. 288.
66 The illuminated manuscripts with this monogram are Royal 15 D. ii, 16 E. vi, 16 E. xii, 19 B. xii, 19 C. i, 20 A. xv, 20 B. iii, 20 B. xx, 20 C. iv, 20 D. ix, and 4 C. xi.
67 Carley, 'Marks' (1997), pp. 599–605; see also Carley, *Libraries* (2000), p. 33.
68 I am grateful to Andrea Clarke for confirming that the marks are not in Henry's hand.
69 For the tentative identification of the author see Carley, *Libraries* (2000), pp. 4–5; Carley, *Libraries* (2000), p. 26.
70 Paris, BnF, MS Moreau 849, ff. 166–167; ed. in Carley, *Libraries* (2000), pp. 5–29. Carley, 'Royal Library' (1999), p. 274, states that the list 'seems to cover the whole contents of the library', but in Carley, *Libraries* (2000), p. 141, xxvi n. 14, he states that the inventory 'is only a partial one' and uses the *Receyt* of *the Ladie Kateryne* (see note 32) as evidence that the library contained more than French manuscripts.
71 Items 67, 31, 19, in Carley, *Libraries* (2000), pp. 6–29.
72 Carley, *Libraries* (2000), pp. 6–29; see also Omont, 'Manuscrits' (1891).
73 March 1534, 25 Henry VIII, Brewer, Brodie and Gairdner, *Letters and Papers,* VII (1883), p. 175 no. 11; Undated grants, 27 Henry VIII, Brewer, Brodie and Gairdner, *Letters and Papers,* X (1887), p. 327, no. 776.5.
74 Thurley, *Royal Palaces* (1993), p. 73.
75 Thurley, *Royal Palaces* (1993), pp. 73, 31–32; for the King's progresses generally see Samman, 'Progresses' (1995).
76 Carley, *Libraries* (2000), pp. xlvi n. 86; 25.
77 For the dates of the Wolsey exchange see Carley, *Libraries* (2000), p. lxiv; for Anne's settlement see Warnicke, 'Anne' (2004); Thurley, *Royal Palaces* (1993), p. 78; see also Carley, *Libraries* (2000), pp. 4, 289.
78 Zinzerling, *Itinerarium Galliae* (1649), trans. in Rye, *England as Seen by Foreigners* (1865), p. 134.
79 Grasser, *Frantzösische und Englische Schartzkammer* (1610); Eisenberg, *Itinerarium Galliae et Angliae* (1614), both trans. in Rye, *England as Seen by Foreigners* (1865), pp. 128, 172.
80 Carley, *Libraries* (2000), p. 5.
81 Royal 19 C vi, f. 19. See also translation and discussion in Winn, 'Paint, Pen' (2006), pp. 205 n. 28; 206.
82 See Starkey, 'Preface' (2004), p. 8 on the change from public to private reading.
83 Backhouse, 'Founders' (1987), p. 31.
84 14 December 1549, Public Records Office, *Calendar of Patent Rolls, Edward VI,* III (1925), pp. 74–75.
85 I thank James Carley for this observation.
86 An Acte for the abolishinge and puttinge awaye of diverse Bookes and Images, 3 & 4 Edward VI chap. 10.
87 25 February 1550/1, *Acts of the Privy Council,* II (1891), p. 224.
88 Nos. 95–107, 127–28, in Carley, *Libraries* (2000), pp. 280, 284.
89 Royal 5 A. xii, ff. iii–vi.
90 Breviaries: Royal 2 A. x–xiv (probably Theyer); Lectionary: Royal 2 B. xii and xiii (in two volumes), Royal 15 B. xiv (flyleaves, from the Theyer collection); Martyrologies: Royal 2 A. xiii, Royal 7 E. vi; Gradual: Royal 2 B. iv.
91 Royal 2 A. i, Royal 2 A. iv (Theyer), Royal 2 A. vii, Royal 2 A. viii, Royal 2 A. xvii, Royal 2 A. xviii, Royal 2 B. xv, Royal 2 D. xl.
92 Royal 1 B. x, Royal 1 D. x, Royal 13 D. i*, Royal 2 A. iii, Royal 2 A. v, Royal 2 A. vi, Royal 2 A. xvi (Psalter of Henry VIII), Royal 2 A. xxii (Westminster Psalter), Royal 2 B. i (Selection of Psalms of Humfrey of Gloucester), Royal 2 B. ii (Theyer), Royal 2 B. iii (possibly a gift to Mary I), Royal 2 B. ix (Earl of Arundel's Psalter, Lumley), Royal 2 B. v (Cranmer/Lumley); Royal 2 B. vi (Theyer); Royal 2 B. vii (Queen Mary Psalter), Royal 2 B. viii (Princess Joan Psalter), Royal 2 B. xiv (Isabel, sister of Richard, Duke of York), Royal 2 B. x. (This is excluding glossed versions.)
93 See Carley, *Libraries* (2000), p. lxxvii; cf. Barker, *Treasures* (2005), p. 30; Gilson, 'Introduction' (1921), p. xvi, who concludes that the loss of 'fine work of medieval artists' as a result of the purging process 'was probably considerable'; Brown and Scheele, *Old Royal Library* (1957), p. 5.
94 An Acte for the abolishinge and puttinge awaye of diverse Bookes and Images, 3 & 4 Edward VI chap. 10.
95 Gilson, 'Introduction' (1921), p. xvii.
96 A detailed inscription gives his name and the date of the gift (f. 319v).
97 I thank Scot McKendrick for this suggestion.
98 Royal 17 B. xxviii, ff. 128v–145; see Gilson, 'Introduction' (1921), p. xviii; for Knyvett see Nicholls, 'Knyvett' (2008).
99 Walpole, *Paul Hentzner's Travels in England* (1797), p. 21.
100 Walpole, *Paul Hentzner's Travels in England* (1797), p. 21.
101 Walpole, *Paul Hentzner's Travels in England* (1797), p. 21; see discussion Backhouse, 'Royal Bookshelf' (1992), pp. 232–33.
102 Zinzerling, *Itinerarium Galliae* (1616), trans. in Rye, *England as Seen by Foreigners* (1865), p. 133.
103 Neumayr von Ramssla, *Des durchlauchtigen hochgeborenen Fursten* (1620), trans. in Rye, *England as Seen by Foreigners* (1865), p. 165.
104 Von Bülow, 'Diary' (1892), p. 25.
105 Von Bülow, 'Diary' (1892), pp. 55–57, cited in Carley, 'Royal Library' (1999), p. 278.
106 On Elizabeth see Ovenden, 'Libraries' (2006), p. 549.
107 Thurley, *Royal Palaces* (1993), p. 81.
108 Wilks, 'Art Collecting' (1997), p. 31; see also Strong, *Henry* (1986), pp. 184–219, for the Prince's collections.
109 Whitaker and Clayton, *Art of Italy* (2007), p. 17; on the contents of his library see Birrell, *English Monarchs* (1987), pp. 30–40.
110 Cornwallis, *Life and Death of Prince Henry* (1809 reprint), p. 250. Cornwallis was Henry's treasurer. Note that Strong, *Henry* (1986), p. 173 ascribed the account to John Hawkins, and the original as Additional 30075; however, that manuscript omits the first and last paragraphs of the published text, and may instead be a fair copy of another manuscript, as is Additional 11532, dated 1613, which includes the last paragraph and the valediction but omits a signature.
111 For the Prince's income see 21 August 1610, in Green, *Calendar of State Papers, James I* (1857), p. 629: 'The King intends to settle on the Prince of Wales, lands to the amount of 10,000*l* per ann.' For the payment of £1025. 13s. 1d 'for the new Lybrary Gallery and altering of officers lodgings from the first of June 1610 unto the Last of Aprill 1611' see Jayne and Johnson, *Lumley Library* (1956), p. 17 n. 3.
112 Cited in Strong, *Henry* (1986), p. 210; Selwyn and Selwyn, 'Profession' (2006), p. 507.
113 Report and plan referred to in 15 December 1706, Redington, *Calendar of Treasury Papers,* III (1874), p. 476; copy of the report and plan of the same date in MS Facsimile Supp. II(d) (1) and (2).
114 Strong, *Henry* (1986), p. 190; cf. Wilks, 'Art Collecting' (1997), p. 33.
115 On the vexed question of whether this was a gift or a purchase, and by whom, see Jayne and Johnson, *Lumley Library* (1956), pp. 14–17; Gooch, *A Complete Pattern* (2009), p. 63. For the acquisition as a purchase, see Gilson, 'Introduction' (1921), p. xix; De Ricci, *English Collectors* (1930), p. 19 (both for a purchase by James I for his son); Brown and Scheele, *Old Royal Library* (1957), p. 7 (an acquisition by

James I); and Strong, *Henry* (1986), p. 200 (a purchase by Henry). Recent scholarship has followed Jayne and Johnson, *Lumley Library* (1956): see, e.g., Evans, *Lumley Inventory* (2010), p. 15 (although as a bequest). On Lumley see Gooch, *A Complete Pattern* (2009); Strong, *Henry* (1986), p. 200, who states that Lumley was one of the Prince's tutors, a point disputed by Jayne and Johnson, *Lumley Library* (1956), p. 15 and Gooch, *A Complete Pattern* (2009), p. 62.

116 See Jayne and Johnson, *Lumley Library* (1956), pp. 10–11 for the number of volumes; see also Gooch, *A Complete Pattern* (2009), p. 61; for it as the second-largest Elizabethian library see Selwyn and Selwyn, 'Profession' (2006), p. 518; Strong, *Henry* (1986), p. 200.

117 See Jayne and Johnson, *Lumley Library* (1956), pp. 12–19; for the number of manuscripts in the royal collection as 308 see Gilson, 'Introduction' (1921), p. xix n. 2.

118 Jayne and Johnson, *Lumley Library* (1956), p. 3; see also Roberts, 'Extending' (2006), p. 308.

119 See Jayne and Johnson, *Lumley Library* (1956), pp. 2–4; Roberts, 'Extending' (2006), p. 308; on Cranmer's library see Selwyn, *Cranmer Library* (1996).

120 Ker, *Medieval Libraries* (1964), p. xiii; Gilson, 'Introduction' (1921), p. xix (putting the number at 17).

121 Jayne and Johnson, *Lumley Library* (1956), p. 5; but see De Ricci, *English Collectors* (1930), p. 19, where he states that all of Lumley's manuscripts 'bore his signature on the title'.

122 Birrell, *English Monarchs* (1987), p. 30.

123 Jayne and Johnson, *Lumley Library* (1956), p. 15.

124 Ovenden, 'Libraries' (2006), pp. 530–31.

125 For the paintings see Wilks, 'Art Collecting' (1997).

126 For the reference to the 'makeing a new Library for the Kinge', see London, TNA: PRO E. 351/3247, cited in Cox and Norman, *Survey of London* (1930), pp. 41–115 n. 196.

127 For quotation see Boren, 'Young' (2004); see discussion Gilson, 'Introduction' (1921), p. xx.

128 On the Greek manuscripts see Brown and Scheele, *Old Royal Library* (1957), p. 8; on the Causabon acquisition see generally Grafton and Weinberg, 'Isaac Casaubon' (2009), p. 27; Birrell, *English Monarchs* (1987), p. 58; Boren, 'Young' (2004).

129 Oxford, Bodleian Library, MS Smith 34, pp. 105–12.

130 Cf. Murdoch, 'Royal Bibliophiles' (1907), p. 59, where he comments that 'by far the greater number of Charles the Second's books were plays'.

131 See Gilson, 'Introduction' (1921), p. xx.

132 See *Sacred* (2007), p. 68.

133 See Carley, 'Source for Cotton' (1992), p. 208.

134 29 September 1649, Green, *Calendar of State Papers, Domestic*, II (1875), p. 323.

135 The survey of 1649 is printed in the *Vetusta Monumenta* (1747), II, following pl. XXIV.

136 See 21 November, 1650 no. 12, in Green, *Calendar of State Papers, Domestic*, XI (1876), p. 436, cited in Gilson, 'Introduction' (1921), p. xxii n. 5: 'Mr Durie the library keeper is to … receive instructions for the safe preservation of the library and medals and to prepare directions to be given to the surveyor of works for fitting the new chapel for the use of a library.'

137 6 (?) October, 1651, in Green, *Calendar of State Papers, Domestic*, XVI (1877), p. 468, cited in Gilson, 'Introduction' (1921), p. xxiv n. 1.

138 Brown and Scheele, *Old Royal Library* (1957), p. 8, date the valuation to 'about 1650–1652'; for the paintings see Whitaker and Clayton, *Art of Italy* (2007), p. 28.

139 On the value of the painting see Whitaker and Clayton, *Art of Italy* (2007), p. 28.

140 Whitelock, *Memorials* (1732), p. 415, cited in Gilson, 'Introduction' (1921), p. xxi n. 2.

141 See Whitaker and Clayton, *Art of Italy* (2007), p. 28, for the Commonwealth sale.

142 Whitelock, *Memorials* (1732), p. 415, cited in Gilson, 'Introduction' (1921), p. xxi n. 2.

143 Royal Appendix 86 (see Appendix, no. 5 for description).

144 Bremmer, *Morris* (2004); Birrell, *John Morris* (1976), p. xv.

145 Birrell, *English Monarchs* (1987), pp. 56–58.

146 Letter to William Sancroft, Oxford, Bodleian Library, MS Tanner 314, f. 94 (Summary Catalogue 10141), cited in part in Rostenberg, *Literary, Political* (1965), p. 290.

147 Letter to William Sancroft, Oxford, Bodleian Library, MS Tanner 314, f. 94.

148 Letter to William Sancroft, Oxford, Bodleian Library, MS Tanner 314 f. 94.

149 Goyau, 'de Thou', (1912). The de Thou library was acquired by Jean-Jacques Charron (b. 1643, d. 1718), vicomte, then marquis de Ménars, and subsequently dispersed; 152 de Thou bindings for printed books and at least three illuminated manuscripts from Charron's collections are held at the British Library.

150 See Jayne and Johnson, *Lumley Library* (1956), p. 22; Gilson, 'Introduction' (1921), p. xxvi; Poole, 'Review' (1922), p. 452.

151 Poole, 'Review' (1922), p. 452; Gilson, 'Introduction' (1921), p. xxvi.

152 For the collection generally see Gilson, 'Introduction' (1921), p. xxvi.

153 'Wee whose names are heer underwritten do certify, that wee, having been appointed to view a parcell of manuscripts belonging to Mr Robert Scott containing about three hundred thirty six volumes (A Catalogue whereof is hereunto annexed) have accordingly perused them, and judg that they may bee very well valued at five hundred and sixty pounds. In witness whereof we have hereunto sett our hands this 29th day of July 1678', signed 'Will. Beveridge Reck of St Peter's Cornhill Lond'. [William Beveridge (bap. 1637, d. 1708), rector of St Peter's, Cornhill, from 1672 to 1681, later bishop of St Asaph] 'Will: Jane Canon of Christ Church in Oxford. (f. 2). There follows an individual valuation of each volume by Scott (£841; 'Mr Scotts valuation'; ff. 29–30v); and 'Mr Jane and Mr Beveridge valution' (£572; ff. 31–32v). An earlier inventory was commissioned from Edward Bernard by Theyer's grandson Charles; it lists 312 manuscripts, and notes that there were some others of lesser value. It is this list (without the note) that is apparently the basis for a figure of 312 for the number of manuscripts. See Gilson, 'Introduction' (1921), p. xxvi; Poole, 'Review' (1922), p. 452.

154 Hutton, *Charles the Second* (1989), p. 335.

155 Letter to Justel, 3 December 1681, in Daniell, *Calendar of State Papers Domestic* (1921), p. 601.

156 Letter to Justel, 3 December 1681, in Daniell, *Calendar of State Papers Domestic* (1921), p. 601.

157 Letter to Justel, 3 December 1681, in Daniell, *Calendar of State Papers Domestic* (1921), p. 601.

158 Letter to Justel, 3 December 1681, in Daniell, *Calendar of State Papers Domestic* (1921), p. 601.

159 See also Poole, 'Review' (1922), p. 452, for St James's as the 'place of deposit of by far the greater part of the manuscripts'.

160 Cited in Ramsay, 'Libraries for Antiquaries' (2006), p. 147.

161 Evelyn, Diary, 2 September 1680, in De Beer, *Diaries* (2000), IV, pp. 214–17 (p. 214).

162 Evelyn, Diary, 2 September 1680, in De Beer, *Diaries* (2000), IV, p. 215.

163 Evelyn, Diary, 2 September 1680, in De Beer, *Diaries* (2000), IV, p. 215.

164 Gilson, 'Introduction' (1921), p. xxv n. 11.

165 Hutton, *Charles the Second* (1989), p. 453; see also Ollard, *Image* (1979), p. 54, who states that 'like his father, he read little'; but see Miller, *Charles II* (1991), p. 3, who commented that the King 'in later life read widely (if not deeply)'; Murdoch, 'Royal Bibliophiles' (1907), p. 56, who characterized the King as a 'lover of books'.

166 Cited in Ollard, *Image* (1979), p. 173.
167 Savile, *Character* (1750), p. 25, cited in Ollard, *Image* (1979), p. 166.
168 Mordaunt to Evelyn, 23 April 1661, cited in De Beer, *Diaries* (2000), III, p. 284 n. 4.
169 Letter to Justel, 3 December 1681, in Daniell, *Calendar of State Papers Domestic* (1921), p. 601.
170 Letter to Justel, 3 December 1681, in Daniell, *Calendar of State Papers Domestic* (1921), p. 601.
171 Whitaker and Clayton, *Art of Italy* (2007), p. 7.
172 Birrell, *English Monarchs* (1987), pp. 54–58.
173 Foot, 'Mearne' (2004); Nixon, *Restoration Bookbindings* (1974).
174 Evelyn, in De Beer, *Diaries* (2000), IV, p. 216; Miller, *Charles II* (1991), p. 2; Hutton, *Charles the Second* (1989), pp. 450, 133.
175 Whitaker and Clayton, *Art of Italy* (2007), pp. 33–34.
176 Mayor, *Nicholas Ferrar* (1855), p. 123. An example of an unillustrated one from the Old Royal library is Royal Appendix 65.
177 Birrell, *English Monarchs* (1987), p. 56.
178 Around twenty-four Oriental manuscripts entered the collection from the library of Thomas Hyde (b. 1636, d. 1703), according to Brown and Scheele, *Old Royal Library* (1957), pp. 8–9.
179 Evelyn, Diary, in Wheatley, *John Evelyn* (1906), III, pp. 448–49.
180 Evelyn, Diary, in Wheatley, *John Evelyn* (1906), III, p. 449.
181 Harley 5900, f. 45, the manuscript cited in Ramsay, 'Libraries for Antiquaries' (2006), p. 148; see also Gatch, 'Bagford' (1986), p. 165.
182 Bentley, *Dissertation on Phalaris,* p. lxv, cited in Gilson, 'Introduction' (1921), p. xxvii.
183 15 December 1706, in Redington, *Calendar of Treasury Papers*, III (1874), p. 476.
184 9 February 1707/1708, in Shaw, *Calendar of Treasury Books*, XXII (1952), p. 131.
185 An Act for the better settling and preserving the Library kept in the House at Westminster called Cotton House, 12 and 13 William III ch. 7 'for the benefit of the publick', cited in Gilson, 'Introduction' (1921), p. xxviii.
186 Jayne and Johnson, *Lumley Library* (1956), p. 22; Gilson, 'Introduction' (1921), p. xxx.
187 Dr Robert Friend, headmaster of Westminster School, in a letter to Lady Sundon, in Nichols, *Literary Anecdotes,* IX (1815), p. 592, cited in Gilson, 'Introduction' (1921), pp. xxx–xxxi (where he also states that the damage was confined to shelves 9A–9C).
188 Gilson, 'Introduction' (1921), p. xxxi.
189 Poole, 'Review' (1922), p. 450.
190 Ordinances, in Sloane 3479, f. 53v, cited in Kekewich, 'Edward IV' (1971), p. 486.
191 Miller, *Noble Cabinet* (1973), p. 55; Strong, *Henry* (1986), pp. 184, 211 (for the quotation).
192 Hutton, *Charles the Second* (1989), p. 450.
193 On the concept of magnificence see Thurley, *Royal Palaces* (1993), pp. 11–23; Carley, *Libraries* (2000), p.xxiii.
194 Davies, 'Review' (2009), p. 1445.
195 Letter to Justel, 3 December 1681, in Daniell, *Calendar of State Papers Domestic* (1921), p. 601.

Appendix

Notes on selected catalogues, inventories or lists of parts of the Old Royal library

This is a brief summary of selected catalogues, inventories or lists of the Old Royal library or manuscripts in the royal collections, presented in chronological order. It is based in part on the *History of the Royal Collection 1471–1761* table, Appendix B, in Jayne and Johnson, *Lumley Library* (1956), pp. 292–96, and Goldfinch, 'Contemporary Sources' (2009).*

PRINTED SOURCES INCLUDE:

1324–41 Records of John Fleet
British Library, Additional 60584

References to books mentioned in the final account of John Fleet, Keeper of the Privy Wardrobe, to the Auditors of the Chamber for receipts and issues of the Privy Wardrobe; 16 July 1324–1 July 1341, are printed in part in a summary table in Vale, *Edward III* (1982), Appendix 9, p. 169.

1535 list of books at Richmond Palace
Paris, BnF, MS Moreau 849, ff. 166–167

A list of 125 items described as an inventory 'Inventaire des livres estans ou chasteau de Richemont en *Angleterre*', primarily of books in French edited in Carley, *Libraries* (2000) pp. 3–29, as 'H1'.

1542 inventory of the Upper Library, Whitehall Palace
London, TNA: PRO, Augmentation Office, Misc. Books 160 (E.315/160)

This inventory is part of the general inventory of the goods at Whitehall Palace as 'Stuff of sondry natures as well founde within the kinges upper library', and edited in Carley, *Libraries* (2000), pp. 30–226, as 'H2'.

1547 Post-mortem inventory of Henry VIII's Palaces
British Library, Additional 48348; London, Society of Antiquaries, MS 129 and British Library, Harley 1419A and 1419B

Extracts from the post-mortem inventories of Henry VIII's palaces 1547–50, British Library Additional 48348, are printed in Carley, *Libraries* (2000), pp. 265–96, as 'H5'.

The full inventory from London, Society of Antiquaries, MS 129 and British Library, Harley 1419, is edited in Starkey, *Inventory of King Henry VIIII* (1998).

***Catalogi librorum manuscriptorum Angliae et Hiberniae*, 2 vols, *Bibliotheca Jacobaea* (Oxford: Sheldonian, '1697' [1698?]), II, pp. 239–48 [pp. 443–47 if bound together]**

A printed edition of the titles (not the volumes) of the manuscripts in St James's library. Warner and Gilson speculate that this was based on Royal Appendix 71 and specify the order in which the titles correspond to the shelves. The first published catalogue of the manuscripts in the Old Royal library.

BIBLIOGRAPHY: Warner and Gilson, *Catalogue* (1921), I, p. xxxiv; Jayne and Johnson, *Lumley Library* (1956), p. 295.

Casley, *A Catalogue of the Manuscripts of the King's Library* (1734)

UNPUBLISHED SOURCES INCLUDE:

1
Short alphabetical list of printed books in the New Library, Whitehall, 1581
British Library, Royal 17 B. xxviii, ff. 128v–145

200 x 150 mm

Paper codex.

A partial listing of printed books with a short preface, including the statement that these are books in 'the Newe librarye placed by T. Kny. the 20th of December, 1581' (f. 128v). Seventy-four books are listed alphabetically by title or subject. The date and place of publication of the volumes range from 1517 (f. 133) to 1564 (f. 141).

BIBLIOGRAPHY: Warner and Gilson, *Catalogue* (1921), II, p. 231; Jayne and Johnson, *Lumley Library* (1956), p. 292 (but not a title page only, as stated there).

2
List of Manuscripts and English printed books, Whitehall, after 1641
Oxford, Bodleian Library, MS Smith 34, pp. 105–112

315 x 195 mm

Paper codex.

Entitled 'Shefe Following [av e] Manuscript in the floure:' (p. 105), with a list of 237 manuscripts. There is also a list of ninety-three English printed books, entitled 'Whytehall/English bookes printed:' (p. 111), with the latest book dated 1641. Given to [Thomas] Smith [b. 1638, d. 1710] by William Atwood, Patrick Young's grandson, 23 February 1704–05 (see also inscription, p. 286).

BIBLIOGRAPHY: Madan, *Summary Catalogue*, III (1895), no. 15641 item 6; Jayne and Johnson, *Lumley Library* (1956), p. 293; Goldfinch, 'Contemporary Sources' (2009), p. 425.

* I thank Scot McKendrick for the suggestion that the Huntington manuscript is a Phillipps manuscript; Philippa Marks for her identification of the Stuart bindings; Moira Goff, John Goldfinch, Martin Kauffmann and Karen Limper-Herz for their review and advice on various parts of the manuscripts in this summary; and Mary Robinson for the transcription and dating of the Huntington flyleaf inscription, flyleaf information and measurements of that manuscript.

3
Inventory of printed books from Whitehall and St James's, 1650
British Library, C.120.h.6(1)

300 x 195 mm

Paper codex. pp. [208] [paginated in part, and in groups].

Despite its classmark, this is a paper manuscript in a limp vellum binding listing printed books, with a title on the upper outside cover of 'A Catalogue of the Bookes in St James Liberarie'. (It is not a vellum manuscript, as stated in Jayne and Johnson, *Lumley Library* [1956], p. 288).

The first leaf is a title page inscribed 'The first Catalogue containeing the Bookes that were brought from Whitehall' viz: Theologici/ Libri Hebraici/ Histories/ Philosophies/ Philologies/ et Politici' (p. [i]). The heading on the first page is 'Catalogus Liborum Bibliothaecae Albanta 1650**'** (pp. 1–68). Following this are four separate catalogues of St James's, paginated individually: 'the first Catalogue of Bookes belonging to ye Liberarie att St Jameses' (p. [71]); 'The 2nd Catalogue of Bookes in St. Jameses (p. [127]) paginated as 1–29; 'The Third Catalogue of Bookes belonging to the Liberarie att St Jameses' (p. [162]), paginated as 1–20; 'The 4th Catalogue of Bookes belonging to the Liberarie att St Jameses' (p. [168], which lists 'Books of St Jameses Liberarie under 3 Sydes of Arches in Folio' (p. 1), paginated as 1–18). This fourth catalogue includes a small group of thirty-two manuscripts (pp. 16–17), and 'Bookes in the Closet (pp. 23–35). On p. 36 of this fourth catalogue is a note of the medals of 'Gold silver and Copper' 'found in the Library at St James's. Following are two stubs, then two pages of lighter paper, slightly smaller (295 x 195mm), perhaps a gathering of four, with the first two leaves removed. The first leaf has a list of manuscripts, and the second is blank (pp. [205–208]).

BIBLIOGRAPHY: Jayne and Johnson, *Lumley Library* (1956), pp. 288, 293; Brown and Scheele, *Old Royal Library* (1957), p. 8 [citing this as a manuscript catalogue and total values]; Goldfinch, 'Contemporary Sources' (2009), p. 425.
See fig. 3.8.

4
Catalogue of printed books at St James's
British Library, C.120.h.6(2)

310 x 210mm

Paper codex. Unpaginated.

A copy of the catalogue in C.120.h.6(1) of the printed books at St James's, dated 1650, but in two columns, ending with 'Bookes in the Closet'.

BIBLIOGRAPHY: Jayne and Johnson, *Lumley Library* (1956), p. 288; Goldfinch, 'Contemporary Sources' (2009), p. 425.

5
Verification of books and manuscripts, no place given, no date [*c.* 1660]
British Library, Royal Appendix 86, ff. 2–44

310/325 x 190/205 mm

Paper codex. Mounted on guards.

Signed on most rectos as 'reviewed and found compleat J. Durie; Thom. Ross'. There is some variation in the wording, e.g., 'these were reviewed and found compleat' (p. 51); 'reviewed and found to agree with the Catalogue (f. 41v); some pages contain just the signatures. Imperfect, and possibly in the wrong order (there is earlier ink pagination in a different order). The lists are of printed books, except for a few English and Latin manuscripts (f. 35r–v). Warner and Gilson 1921 date the list to *c.* 1661–66. The titles are sometimes listed in groups of roughly ten or twenty, perhaps corresponding to shelves.

BIBLIOGRAPHY: Warner and Gilson, *Catalogue* (1921), II, pp. 399–400; Jayne and Johnson, *Lumley Library* (1956), p. 293; Goldfinch, 'Contemporary Sources' (2009), p. 425.

6
Catalogue of printed books, no place given, no date [*c.* 1660]
British Library, C.120.h.6(3)

325/30 x 205/10 mm

Paper codex.

An undated paper catalogue of printed books, with added non-sequential 'A-D' shelfmarks in four-digit numbers in the left margin. Heavily annotated.

The titles in Latin are organized by subject, and within that alphabetically: theology, history, lives of the saints, history, mathematics, philosophy, medicine, law, politics, rhetoric, grammar, poetry, letters dictionary, library and library catalogues, and miscellaneous.

Jayne and Johnson, *Lumley Library* (1956), p. 293, state that this is a rough draft of the manuscript now San Marino, Huntington, MS HM 180, with only the portion dealing with Latin printed books surviving, and speculate that the hand is that of Patrick Young. They state that it may have been kept as an acquisition list as late as 1704, and that it may have served as the basis for Tab.1281.b.1 (no. 13 below). They note that the latest date is 1648 and comment that the added pressmarks are in Bentley's hand (appointed 1693).

BIBLIOGRAPHY: Jayne and Johnson, *Lumley Library* (1956), p. 293; Goldfinch, 'Contemporary Sources' (2009), p. 425.

7
Subject catalogue of printed books and manuscripts at St James's, *c.* 1660
San Marino, Huntington Library, MS HM 180

365 x 240 mm

Paper codex. pp. 395 (+ 12 unfoliated leaves at the beginning and 19 at the end).

Entitled *Bibliothecae Regiae in Palatio d Iacobi/Codd./Tam Mss Quam Impress/Catalogus.*

A large book in a fair hand, in which the manuscripts are grouped by language (Latin, French, Greek, and English) but then listed by broad subject headings: for Latin, theology (533), history (73), law (78), and arts (106), and for French, theology (80), history (38), romance (13), and miscellaneous (44). Fourteen Greek and twenty-one English manuscripts follow these listings.

The latest printed book in the list is dated 1652. Jayne and Johnson state that it was compiled by Thomas Ross *c.* 1660 (Jayne and Johnson, *Lumley Library* (1956), p. 21; see also Goldfinch, 'Contemporary Sources' (2009)).

Eleven Bibles, eight 'Evangelia', and fourteen Psalters are listed, but there are no books of hours. Only a handful of the descriptions contain any indication of illumination. A Psalter is listed 'cum picturis variys', and another 'eleganter scriptum anno 1565 ', probably Royal 2 B. ix, the Psalter of the Earl of Arundel (cat. no. 148), although if so it is interesting that the script, rather than the illumination is what is noted (pp. 360, 359).

The only subjective comment about the illumination or perhaps the script is of a copy of 'Vegetius de re militari et de mulomedicina', which is described as 'codex pulchre sed hori scriptus' (p. 387), probably Royal 12 C. xxii.

Provenance:
Charles II: the catalogue is in a brown turkey leather binding with the simple Charles II cypher of two 'C's back to back between palm leaves surmounted by a crown, characteristic of Mearne bindings (for a similar binding see Nixon, *English Restoration Bookbindings* [1974], pl. 2); discussion p. 12.

? Colonel Lovelace: inscribed 'Formerly belonged to Colonel Lovelace 17th cent.' And 'From the Libraries of Charles I/ Charles II/ Colonel Lovelac' in a nineteenth-century hand (f. [i]).

? Included in *A Catalogue of the Valuable and Highly Interesting Library of Printed Books and MSS., removed from Leeds Castle, in Kent; a great part of which was collected at different times by the Lords Fairfax, and added to by the Rev. Dr. Wilkins, of Suffolk*, Christie's, 10 January 1831, lot 113, in the section 'Curious MSS. On Vellum and Paper' as 'Bibliothecae Regiae Calalog [sic]' with 'a parcel of MS. Catalogues, etc.'; purchased by Phillipps, according to a note of provenance in the 1837 edition of *Phillipps's Catalogus Librorum Manuscriptorum,* cited in Munby, *Formation of the Phillipps Library* (1954), Appendix A, p. 165 as 'Mss. Fairfax & Wilkins, from Leeds Castle, Kent'. The sale included a number of other royal papers, such as 'A Commission, signed by Charle II, 1680' and drafts of 'Letters in the Duke's [of Buckingham] own hand to Charles II' (lots 145, 146).

Sir Thomas Phillipps, Baronet (b. 1792, d. 1872), collector of books and manuscripts: his MS 10307; his sale Sotheby's, London, 19 May 1913, lot 612 as 'CHARLES I. BIBLIOTHECAE REGIAE IN PALATIO D. JACOBI CODD. TAM MSS. QUAM IMPRESS. CATALOGUS, *old red morocco gilt, g.e., a fine volume*, 395 *pp. folio.* XVII Cent. This is apparently the original Catalogue of KING CHARLES THE FIRST'S printed books and manuscripts in the library at St. James's Palace. At each corner of the central panel and on the back are crowns with the letters C.C. intertwined.' According to notes in the annotated copy of the sale catalogue in the Department of History and Classics, it was sold to Sabin for £47.

Dr. A.S.W. Rosenbach (b. 1876, d. 1952) and his brother, Philip (b. 1863, d. 1953), dealers in books and manuscripts: sold to Huntington on 16 March, 1918: Huntington Library records.

Henry E. Huntington (b. 1850, d. 1927), businessman with interests in railroad companies, utilities, and real estate; purchased by him in 1918; transferred in trust to the Huntington Library by indenture in 1919.

BIBLIOGRAPHY: Jayne and Johnson, *Lumley Library* (1956), pp. 293, 294; Goldfinch, 'Contemporary Sources' (2009), p. 425. (The Phillipps manuscript reference has been listed previously as a *c.* 1690 St James's catalogue, probably by Justel and location unknown.)

8

Possibly a catalogue of manuscripts at St. James's, 1661, now untraced

Formerly Lansdowne 1219, ff. 94–110

In the Catalogue of the Lansdowne manuscripts MS 1219, item 20 is described as 'Catalogus MSS. Graecorum, Latinorum, et Gallicorum, A. D. 1661. fo. 94 i. e. An old Catalogue of the Manuscripts in the King's Library.' This item was removed by Sir Frederic Madden and from 1952 has been untraced (typed note in the copy of the catalogue kept in the Manuscripts Reading Room). Jayne and Johnson state that this was a copy of the list now in Harley 694, Pepys MS 2427, Trinity College, Cambridge MS O.5.38, and in part in Royal Appendix 86, item 14, presumably on the basis of the Lansdowne catalogue entry.

BIBLIOGRAPHY: [Henry Ellis and Francis Douce], *A Catalogue of the Lansdowne Manuscripts in the British Museum* (London: British Museum, 1819), p. 293; Jayne and Johnson, *Lumley Library* (1956), p. 293; Goldfinch, 'Contemporary Sources' (2009), p. 425.

9

Catalogue of printed books and manuscripts, no indication of place, 1666

British Library, Royal Appendix 71

(Formerly Additional 6415; moved by Sir Frederic Madden in 1852 (inscription, f. [iv verso]))

320 x 190 mm

Paper codex. ff. 21.

Entitled 'Catalogus Liborum MSS. Bibliothecae Regiae 1666'. The list of shelves (or presses) are numbered sequentially, and books are listed in groups, usually of 10 or 20. There are twenty-six bookcases or shelves, located mostly on the west side of the room, and fifteen '*scrin[ia]*'. Each numerical listing has two parts, 1, and 2 (e.g., 1.1 and 2.2) They number 1.1 to 38.1, with 10–13, 19–24, and 33.2–35.2 omitted (shelves 28.1 and 28.2 contain English printed books); 1 to 33.2 were located for the most part on the west side of the room 'Lat[us] Occid[entale] (f. 2), while the last three (36–38.1) were on the east side (Lat[us] Orient[ale] (f. 14). The manuscripts are grouped by language (Latin, French, and Greek, with English manuscripts in the French section).

There is no indication of place, but it can be identified as the library of St James's through its close correlation with the entry for St James's in the *Catalogi librorum manuscriptorum Angliae et Hiberniae*, according to Warner and Gilson.

BIBLIOGRAPHY: Warner and Gilson, *Catalogue* (1921), II, p. 396; Jayne and Johnson, *Lumley Library* (1956), p. 293.

10

Alphabetical list of books [probably not of the royal library], no place or date [after 1669]

British Library, Harley 4180

365 x 225 mm

Paper codex. ff. 53 (+ 2 unfoliated modern and three earlier paper leaves at the beginning and one ruled leaf at the end).

An alphabetical list in ink of books A-Y, with only one entry with a date (of 1669). At the far right-hand side of each page three columns have been ruled in red, labelled 'D', 'sh' and 'book', respectively. Letters in the D column range from A to F; shelves from 1–9, and books from 1–51.

Watermark of a crowned fleurs-de-lis.

Murdoch identified this as a royal catalogue, but it does not correspond with the pressmarks or printed books in Royal (See Jayne and Johnson, *Lumley Library* (1956), p. 293; Birrell, *English Monarchs* (1987), p. 66 n. 23.

Provenance:

Charles II: binding of brown leather with a gold-tooled central lozenge, and in the centre of the upper and lower covers the Stuart royal arms tooled in gold used by Charles I and Charles II supported by a lion and a unicorn, with 'CR' above, possibly by Samuel Mearne (compare the arms on C.120.h.6(5), no. 13 in this Appendix; C.68.112, on <http://www.bl.uk/catalogues/bookbindings/Results.aspx> [accessed 12 April 2011]; Nixon, *English Restoration Bookbindings* (1974), pls 3, 4, 9, 11, 12, and 30).

? Samuel Mearne, publisher and bookbinder (b. 1624, d. 1683): some of the books and manuscripts delivered to the Mearne bindery are listed alphabetically in a paper manuscript 'Catalogue of Bookes in Mr Mernes Custody', British Library C.120.h.6(4). Under 'C' is a 'Catalogue of Books' (f. [1v]). Apparently Mearne was not paid for all of the books delivered to him; and the books delivered were sold. See Nixon, *English Restoration Bookbindings* (1974), p. 12.

The Harley Collection, formed by Robert Harley (b. 1661, d. 1724), 1st Earl of Oxford and Mortimer, politician, and Edward Harley (b. 1689, d. 1741), 2nd Earl of Oxford and Mortimer, book collector and patron of the arts, inscribed as usual by their librarian, Humfrey Wanley, '13 Aug. 1724' (f. [i]).

Edward Harley bequeathed the library to his widow, Henrietta, née Cavendish Holles (b. 1694, d. 1755) during her lifetime and thereafter to their daughter, Margaret Cavendish Bentinck (b. 1715, d. 1785), Duchess of Portland; the manuscripts were sold by the Countess and the Duchess in 1753 to the nation for £10,000 (a fraction of their contemporary value) under the Act of Parliament that also established the British Museum; the Harley manuscripts form one of the foundation collections of the British Library.

BIBLIOGRAPHY: Murdoch, 'Royal Bibliophiles' (1907), p. 56 n. 3; Jayne and Johnson, *Lumley Library* (1956), p. 293; Birrell, *English Monarchs* (1987), p. 66 n. 23.

11
Draft alphabetical catalogue of manuscripts, no place given, 2nd half of the seventeenth century
British Library, Appendix 73
(Formerly K. R. 3.g (transferred by Sir Frederic Madden (f. 1). Formerly Add. 5011, but returned to Royal by Madden.)

305 x 90 mm

Paper codex. ff. ii + 151 (f. ii is at the end).

Perhaps a draft for an alphabetical catalogue of the Royal manuscripts, with a few of the printed books. There are entries in four main alphabets (ff. 1, 45, 78, 121) with many blank pages, but the rationale for the groupings is unclear. All of the entries are crossed out, presumably as entered in a far copy, as Warner and Gilson suggested. Gilson, 'Introduction' (1921) p. xxvii suggests it may be a rough draft of part of a catalogue made by John Postlethwayt, High Master of St Paul's School, and Richard Wright, a schoolmaster at St James's after the death of Justel and before the appointment of Bentley.

BIBLIOGRAPHY: Warner and Gilson, *Catalogue* (1921), II, p. 397; Gilson, 'Introduction' (1921), p. xxvii; Jayne and Johnson, *Lumley Library* (1956), p. 294 dates it to *c.* 1692.

12
List of printed books and of manuscripts, no indication of place, after 1679
British Library, C.120.h.6(5)

360 x 230 mm

Paper codex. pp. 296.

Seventeenth-century brown leather binding with gold tooling by Samuel Mearne, Royal Bookbinder to Charles II (on Mearne see Brown and Scheele, *The Old Royal Library* (1957), p. 83 and this Appendix, no. 10), the central coat of arms excised on the upper cover. The arms block-tooled in gold on the lower cover is of the Stuart royal arms used by Charles I and Charles II, supported by a lion and a unicorn, with a crowned 'CR' and crowned bird, perhaps a dove, holding a branch in its beak above. The crowned CR and bird are tooled in gold alternately on the spine.

A list of printed books and manuscripts. The books and manuscripts have an indication of placement in a column on the right, from 'A–D' for the Latin printed books, of 'E' for the manuscripts, of 'F' for French books, 'I' for Italian books, and 'S' for Spanish books, each followed by an Arabic number. The books in Latin are arranged by subject (pp. 1–78; and 131–219). Books in French (pp. 220–252), Italian (pp. 253–286), and Spanish are grouped together (pp. 287–296).

The 1802 manuscripts are grouped by language, and to a certain extent by subject: *MSS Latini* E 1-922 (pp. 79–105); *MSS Latini Comentarii in Biblia,* E 955–1196 (pp. 106–111); *MSS Graeci,* E 1197–1236 (p. 112); *MSS Gallici,* E 1251–1484 (pp. 114–120); *MSS Italici,* E 1485–1508 (p. 121); *English MSS,* E 1509–1802 (pp. 122–130). A few manuscripts are also included with printed books; after A 1–169 is a short list entitled *Biblia MSS* , A 920–954 (p. 6). These include a *Psalteriam cum Picturis* (A 933), and a *Biblia Lat. Scripta a Will de Hales 1254* (A 939), presumably Royal 1 B. xii.

The latest date for printed books in the original hand appears to be 1679 (no. 317, p. 39). However, additions, sometimes at the bottom of pages, or in darker ink, often lined out, are included of books printed up to 1707 (no. 360, lined out, p. 41).

Jayne and Johnson speculated that this is a *c.* 1694 St James's shelflist 'now mixed up by the binder, but includes entire library in all classes: A, B, C, D, E, F, S, and I.'

BIBLIOGRAPHY: Jayne and Johnson, *Lumley Library* (1956), p. 294; Goldfinch, 'Contemporary Sources' (2009), p. 425.

13
Catalogue of printed books, no place, no date (the Italian binding and paper before 1547; the catalogue *c.* 1709)
British Library, Tab.1281.b.1

440 x 355 mm

Paper codex. ff. 260 (+ an unfoliated limp parchment binding with the royal arms, and numerous unfoliated lined paper folios at the end).

Red Florentine morocco binding with gold tooling and stamping, with a curved fore-edge flap and leather bands and lacings of the account book style, with a Tudor rose in colours and 'HR' on the inside upper cover. (See description Nixon, *Early English Bookbindings* (1964)).

A catalogue of printed books, organised by language, and within the Latin books, by subject, with columns for size, place of publication, date, and placement (A–D). The contents are Latin books (ff. 2–157); English books (ff. 158–183); and in a different hand, French books (ff. 184–214); Italian books (ff. 215–247), and Spanish and Portuguese books (ff. 248–260). There is no indication of the location of the library, or of the date of the compilation of the list. In the English books' section are references to books published in 1699 (f. 158); 1700 (f. 183, on the first line) and 1709 (f. 170, on the last line), the latter two both apparently in the same hand as the rest of the list but lined out. According to Jayne and Johnson, with the same numbers as in C.120.h.6(5).

BIBLIOGRAPHY: Jayne and Johnson, *Lumley Library* (1956), p. 295; Nixon, *Early English Bookbindings* (1964), pp. 305–06, pl. VIII; Carley, *Books of King Henry VIII* (2004), pl. 71; Goldfinch, 'Contemporary Sources' (2009), p. 425.

The Christian Monarch

The arrival of St Augustine of Canterbury (the Roman missionary sent by Pope Gregory I) at the court of Æthelberht, King of Kent, in 597 marked a formal start to the process of converting the Anglo-Saxons to Christianity. The intimate relations between royalty and churchmen that ensued drew the former into contact with the world of finely crafted books. Though continually redefined and sometimes stormy (most famously in the case of Henry II and Thomas Becket), the relationship between monarchy and church remained fundamental to both institutions: the fact that the most radical change of all involved a king (Henry VIII) becoming head of the English church underlines the point.

Members of the royal family, whose deeds were chronicled by monastic historians, sought counsel from esteemed churchmen, attended Church councils and backed clerical and monastic reforms (cat. nos. 5, 6, 101). They also established monasteries and convents and supported the friars (cat. nos. 16, 17, 68, 151) and fraternities (cat. nos. 36, 39). In addition, like their continental counterparts, English royalty financed other ecclesiastical building works (cat. no. 41), collected relics (cat. nos. 1, 3) and commissioned liturgical furnishings (cat. no. 8), artworks and manuscripts. Many of the latter are luxurious volumes that reflect the wealth and high status of the individuals who paid for them. At the same time, these books attest to the desire of their makers and users to glorify God, the divine ruler, whose eternal kingdom was mirrored by the earthly court.

Presented mainly in chronological order, the manuscripts described in this section, which date from the eighth to the sixteenth century, vary in appearance and use, but all are decorated, some extravagantly so. Several were employed in Christian worship, while others were perused by individuals in the course of their devotions. The inclusion of twelve Psalters reflects the great importance assigned to this text (cat. nos. 3, 11–13, 17, 19–21, 26, 33, 34, 45) throughout the Middle Ages and well into the sixteenth century. Bibles and Gospel Books also span the entire period (cat. nos. 1, 2, 4, 7, 9, 10, 14, 15, 18, 22–24, 43). Books of Hours are represented by five examples (cat. nos. 20, 25–28), three of which are associated with royal women.

Some of these volumes were gifts from monarchs (cat. nos. 5, 8). Others were gifts to them (cat. nos. 17, 30, 46). Yet others were books commissioned by royalty for their own use (cat. nos. 22, 23, 26, 27, 31, 32, 34, 45). All bear witness to the centrality of Christian religion and the Church in the lives of English monarchs and the importance of English royalty in the creation of richly ornamented and illustrated copies of Christian and Church texts.

King David as royal paradigm (cat. no. 12)

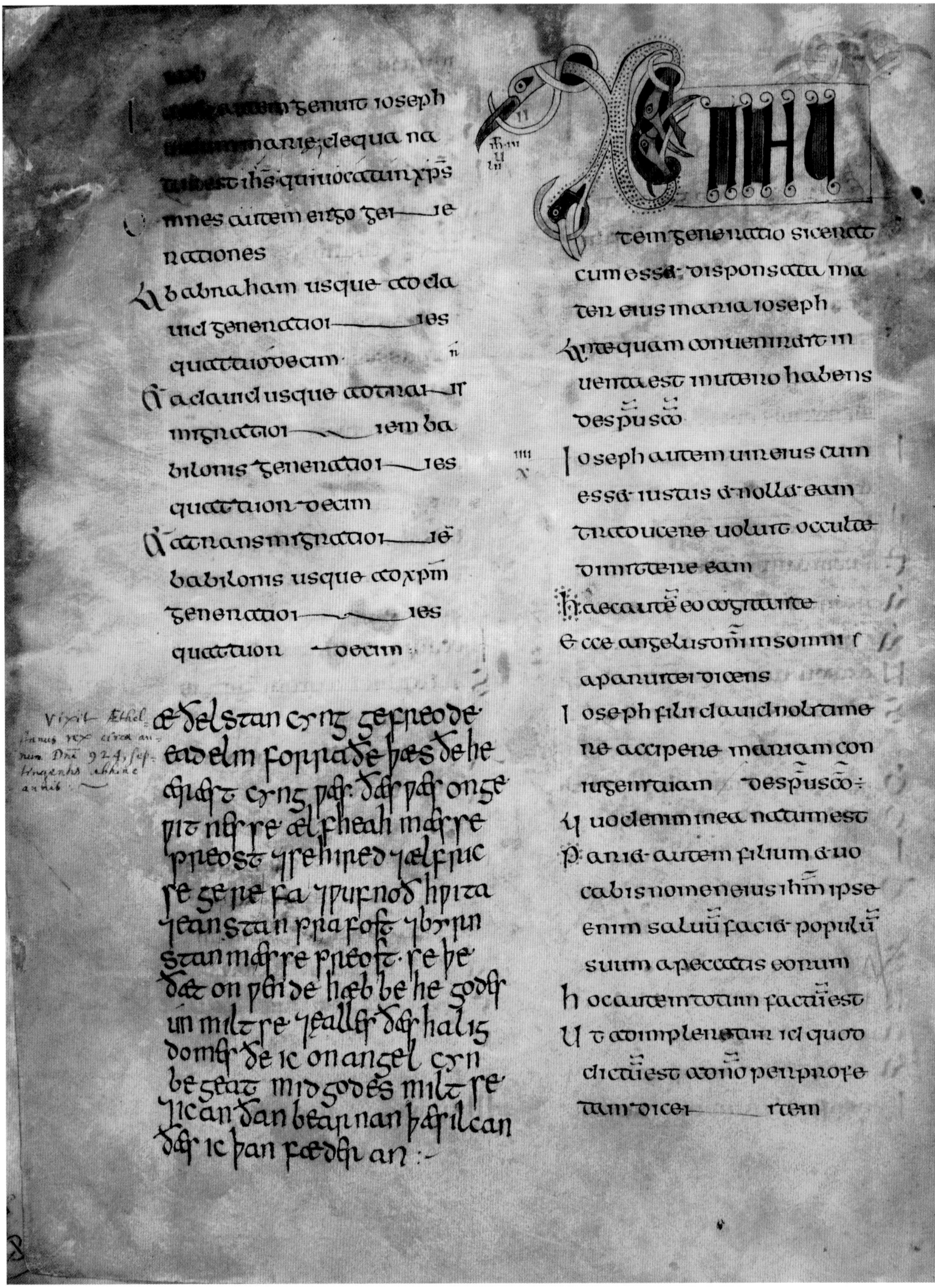

1 An Insular Gospel-Book

Northumbria (?Lindisfarne), 1st half of the 8th century
280 x 220 mm

BRITISH LIBRARY, ROYAL 1 B. vii

Linked to the Lindisfarne Gospels (Cotton Nero D. iv) by text type, chapter summaries and lection list (a distinctive set that specifies liturgical occasions, but not the readings to go with them) – though with a different type of canon tables – the present volume was evidently produced in the same milieu, possibly at Lindisfarne itself. Whereas the Lindisfarne Gospels is a work of supreme artistry, the Royal manuscript is more utilitarian. Ornamentation is limited to a set of line-drawn canon tables, and to simple decorated initials plus display script marking the start of each Gospel, most prefatory texts and *Christi autem* (Matthew 1:18 – the first mention of Christ's name and the beginning of the narrative proper). Yet, less treasured over the centuries than their deluxe counterparts, 'workaday' Insular Gospel-books are now, paradoxically, rarer than higher-grade ones; indeed, Royal 1 B. vii is a unique survival of the sort of volume that saw daily use in the churches of early Christian Northumbria. Clearly written, its text set out *per cola et commata* (each new sense unit starting on a new line), each subdivision marked by a line of orange script, with liturgical rubrics in the relevant margins and interlinear *sigla* to guide performative reading of the Passion according to Mark, the book is eminently practical. Its weathered state betokens extensive service.

The early provenance of the manuscript is undocumented; by 925, however, it was somewhere in the dominions of the King of Wessex, as an addition reveals. In order to position *Christi autem* at the top of column two on fol. 15v, the original scribe had left a gap at the foot of column one after the genealogy of Christ (Matthew 1:1–17). Into this space was inserted the record (in Old English) that 'King Athelstan freed Eadhelm straight away, as soon as he became king', naming witnesses to the act and invoking God and 'all the holy relics' that the King had acquired in England to fortify it. This is the earliest extant English manumission.

Athelstan's accession to the throne of an imperfectly unified England, still partly dominated by Vikings, may not have been entirely smooth. When his father, Edward the Elder (son of Alfred the Great), died in July 924, Athelstan was acclaimed king in Mercia; but in the dynasty's heartland of Wessex his younger half-brother Ælfweard was preferred. Although the latter died within a month, the fact that Athelstan was not crowned until September 925 (and the Bishop of Winchester apparently absented himself) hints at continuing tensions between the two recently united kingdoms. The act of freeing a slave with reference to a personal relic collection had additional value if Athelstan were facing, or had recently overcome, resistance to his succession; the circumstance that the record was inscribed in a Gospel-book surely reflects a desire to apotheosize the King's clemency as much as to reinforce the beneficiary's freedom. The phrase 'straight away, as soon as he became king' clearly conveys the idea that Athelstan was magnanimous from the very beginning of his reign; however, it is debatable whether this means following initial recognition in Mercia, after acknowledgement in Wessex as well, or in the aftermath of his coronation at Kingston-upon-Thames. The nature of the act and the composition of the witness list suggest that the manumission occurred within Athelstan's household – which in turn raises the possibility that this Gospel-book may have pertained to the King's 'chapel'.

That this copy of the Gospels continued in active service after Athelstan's day is indicated by subsequent interventions. Neums (staffless musical notation) were added over Mark 15:46 (f. 77), a few damp-damaged words were recopied (ff. 75–75v, 76v, 77) and one reading and a couple of spellings corrected (ff. 75, 76v), all seemingly in the eleventh century. This activity focuses on one section of the book. It is surely no coincidence that around the same time *positurae* (punctuation marks) were inserted into the same place, Mark's account of the Passion (chs 14–15, ff. 73–77) – and also into that of John (chs 13–15, ff. 146v–149v). Such revision suggests reconditioning for public reading, though the fact that only two passages were thus updated hints at limited use: a utilitarian volume had become a venerable one with royal connections, deployed only on selected occasions. *R.G.*

PROVENANCE:
Charles II.

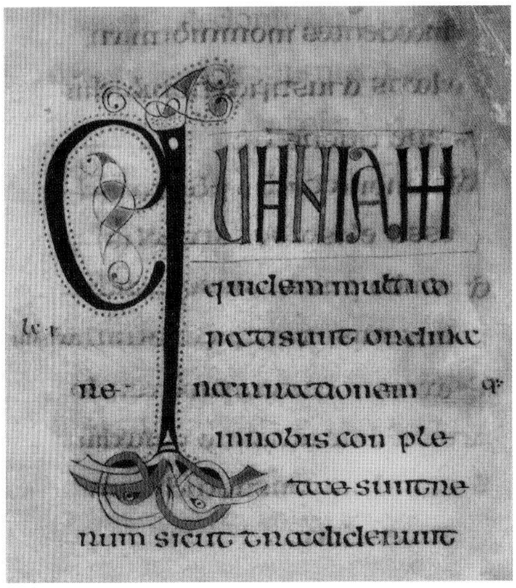

Above:
Decorated incipit to the Gospel of Luke, f. 84 (detail)

Opposite:
Matthew 1:16–22, including the decorated *Christi autem* (1:18) and added manumission, f. 15v

2 The Canterbury Royal Bible

Canterbury (St Augustine's Abbey), early 9th century
470 x 355 mm

BRITISH LIBRARY, ROYAL 1 E. vi

Though long reduced to an imperfect copy of the Gospels, this manuscript was once a Bible. In the early Middle Ages, when the books of the Bible generally circulated individually or in subgroups (the Pentateuch, the Gospels, etc.), whole Bibles were rarities, and only one example (Codex Amiatinus – Florence, Biblioteca Medicea Laurenziana, MS Amiatino 1) survives intact from pre-Viking-Age England. Requiring a huge investment of time and resources – including the possession of exemplars for the whole text – such a volume was necessarily the product of a well-endowed centre, in this case Canterbury, cradle of English Christianity.

Still impressive for its sheer scale (and originally it had over 900, as opposed to the present seventy-eight, leaves), the Royal Bible fragment also boasts suites of ornamental pages executed in gold and silver inks on purple parchment, the acme of opulence (see fig. 1.5). Though the loss and reordering of relevant leaves renders the details debatable, each Gospel was seemingly preceded by at least two such leaves (one bearing a descriptive *titulus*, the other the incipit of the text) and possibly four – depending on whether a missing illustration page and the Evangelist portrait were done on purple or ordinary parchment. Another purple *titulus* page, facing a lost miniature, prefaced the Gospels as a whole. Whether every biblical book started thus is unknowable; however, it is likely that some of them did, and inconceivable that Genesis did not. Notwithstanding the royal, indeed imperial, associations of these materials, they were equally rich in Christian symbolism, and purple-adorned volumes were more often produced for churches than for princes.

This and other aspects of the book's design reflect late antique sources on the one hand, and Carolingian ones (themselves echoing antique models) on the other. St Augustine's Abbey apparently possessed a two-volume Bible associated (rightly or wrongly) with Gregory the Great (d. 604), which contained a number of purple leaves, while purple pages are a feature of a pair of 'Theodulf Bibles' made in Orléans or Fleury *c.* 800. If the poor survival of all such material, plus the truncated state of the Royal Bible itself, prevents a definitive evaluation of its sources and affiliations, the volume unquestionably attests to the availability of exotica in Canterbury at the beginning of the ninth century.

The *titulus* on the first surviving purple page (f. 1), which celebrates 'four masters [who] with concordant voice chant the mighty works of God', evokes the harmony of the Gospels, as doubtless did the miniature it once accompanied. The canon tables (ff. 4–6) convey the same message (pictured). Displaying which passages were common to multiple Gospels and which unique to one, they demonstrate the essential unity of the four accounts. Their presentation here highlights their symbolic, as opposed to utilitarian, value. Whereas most versions (e.g. those in cat. no. 1) included crossbars to subdivide the runs of numerals, here there is no such assistance (customary subgroupings are merely signalled by discreet 'ticks'). The numbers themselves are not scrupulously accurate: the first canon contains twenty-three errors, the last (theoretically the easiest to get right) twenty-seven. Moreover, the final twenty-three pairs of numbers in Canon V are not presented in parallel but rather with all those from Matthew preceding those from Luke, thus sacrificing their role as a reference tool in order to fill the final unit of a three-column design. Nor, with a couple of exceptions, was the corresponding apparatus of section numbers and cross-references supplied in the margins of the Gospels themselves – rendering it impossible to move from the tables to the relevant sections of text. Visually, however, the tables are magnificent: enriched but not overwhelmed by panels of insular ornament, the imposing architectural framework exhibits the Gospels symbolically as a harmonious and mighty edifice.

When and why the Bible was dismembered is unclear. However, the supply of an Evangelist portrait (plus doodles) in the eleventh century hints at early damage, while by *c.* 1300 a leaf from Acts (now Oxford, Bodleian Library, MS lat. bib. b. (P)) had been recycled as flyleaves. The coeval addition of a St Augustine's Abbey pressmark and ownership inscription to the front of the present volume, plus the note 'Quatuor evangelia vetera', indicates that this part was already close to its current form – and was perceived as 'old'. The failure to insert the standard chapter numbering promulgated in the thirteenth century suggests that it saw limited service in the later Middle Ages (the numbers were eventually added in the early modern period).

Still majestic despite truncation and mutilation, and representing the swansong of a great Kentish scriptorium in the face of incipient Viking raids, the Canterbury Royal Bible is the Ozymandias of early Anglo-Saxon book production. *R.G.*

PROVENANCE:

St Augustine's Abbey, Canterbury; John, 1st Baron Lumley (d. 1609); Henry Frederick, Prince of Wales (d. 1612).

Opposite:
Canon table, containing Canons III–V, f. 5

Incipit
canon · III · in quo · III ·
Incipit
canon · V · in quo · II ·
matth
luc
iohan
matth
luc
matth
Finit
Incipit
In quo
matth
Finit
In quo
luc
matth
luc

3 The Athelstan Psalter

North-east Francia (?Reims), middle of the 1st half of the 9th century;
(additions) southern England (?Winchester), early 10th century
130 x 95 mm

BRITISH LIBRARY, COTTON GALBA A. xviii

The core of this manuscript (a Psalter preceded by prayers and followed by Canticles, creeds and further prayers) was made in north-east Francia, probably at Reims, within a decade either side of 825. Its diminutive scale indicates that it was designed for individual rather than communal use, and a possible clue to its early ownership is offered by the inclusion of two Kings of Italy – Pippin (d. 810) and Bernhard (d. 818) – in a short list of added obits (f. 28). Interest in Italian affairs need not necessarily indicate, however, that the book was in Italy: Frankish expansion into the province under Charlemagne meant that many northern Europeans had Italian concerns. The man created Margrave of Friuli towards the middle of the ninth century, for instance, a certain Eberhard, had his ancestral lands in northern France and it was there that he was buried; his will reveals that he had a substantial book collection, including several Psalters.

By the beginning of the tenth century the volume had reached southern England, as substantial supplements reveal. Prefixed to it then was a metrical calendar, the date and saint for each day of the year being given in 365 hexameters. As Alfred the Great (d. 899) and his consort, Ealhswith (d. 902) are commemorated in the work, it was presumably composed in Wessex, and not before 902. The style of the script indicates that this copy of the calendar – in which each month is adorned with a zodiac sign and a standing saint – was made shortly thereafter. Full-page miniatures, mainly by the hand responsible for decorating the calendar, were inserted before Psalm 1 (the *Nativity*, now Bodleian Library, MS Rawlinson B.484, f. 85), Psalm 51 (lost, possibly the *Crucifixion*) and Psalm 101 (the *Ascension*; pictured), with two more preceding the original prefatory prayers and the volume as a whole. This latter pair (pictured) shows the choirs of heaven (angels, patriarchs, prophets, then apostles, confessors, virgins) adoring a figure of Christ accompanied by instruments of his Passion. A visual litany, they complement the content of the prayers sandwiched between them which – after addressing Christ, Mary and John the Baptist – invoke apostles, martyrs, confessors and virgins. A decade or so later a further supplement of prayers – together with transliterated Greek litany, Pater Noster, creed and Sanctus – was appended to the volume (ff. 178–200).

In 1542 the manuscript belonged to Thomas Dackcomb, a canon of Winchester Cathedral, who, presumably reflecting information since lost, described it as the Psalter of King Athelstan (f. 1). Could there be any truth in this claim? The Anglo-Saxon additions demonstrate that the volume had reached England before Athelstan's reign (924/5–39) and its presence at Winchester is shown by the circumstance that its imagery of the choirs of heaven was reprised in the Benedictional of Æthelwold (Additional 49598), a manuscript made there between *c.* 971 and 984. An earlier connection with Winchester is suggested by similarities in style between the artwork of the added miniatures and a wall-painting fragment that was reused in the foundations of New Minster and is datable to before 903. While the implements of the Passion in the first added miniature offer a seductive parallel to the relics of the true cross, the crown of thorns, a sacred nail and the holy lance that Athelstan received from Duke Hugh of the Franks in 926, this gift arrived too late to have informed the image in question. Potentially more telling is the fact that the added Greek texts reappear in a dossier of material associated with a certain Israel the Grammarian (e.g. Paris, Bibliothèque Ste-Geneviève, MS 2410, ff. 118–121), an itinerant scholar who enjoyed Athelstan's patronage; it is possible, therefore, that he copied them from this very manuscript while at the West Saxon court.

Thus, although certainty is impossible, there is some evidence to link the book with Winchester and Athelstan's court. Whether or not it belonged to the King himself, it certainly forms part of the evidence for an influx of Frankish manuscripts into southern England that started in the later years of Alfred's reign (871–99), and it stands at the beginning of a revival, possibly with royal sponsorship, of an indigenous tradition of figural illumination. *R.G.*

PROVENANCE:

Old Minster, Winchester; Thomas Dackcomb (d. *c.* 1572) in 1542; Sir Robert Cotton (d. 1631) in 1612; bequeathed to the nation by Sir John Cotton, 1702.

Opposite top:
Christ with choirs of heaven; metrical calendar, ff. 2v–3

Opposite below:
The Ascension; Psalm 101, ff. 120v–121

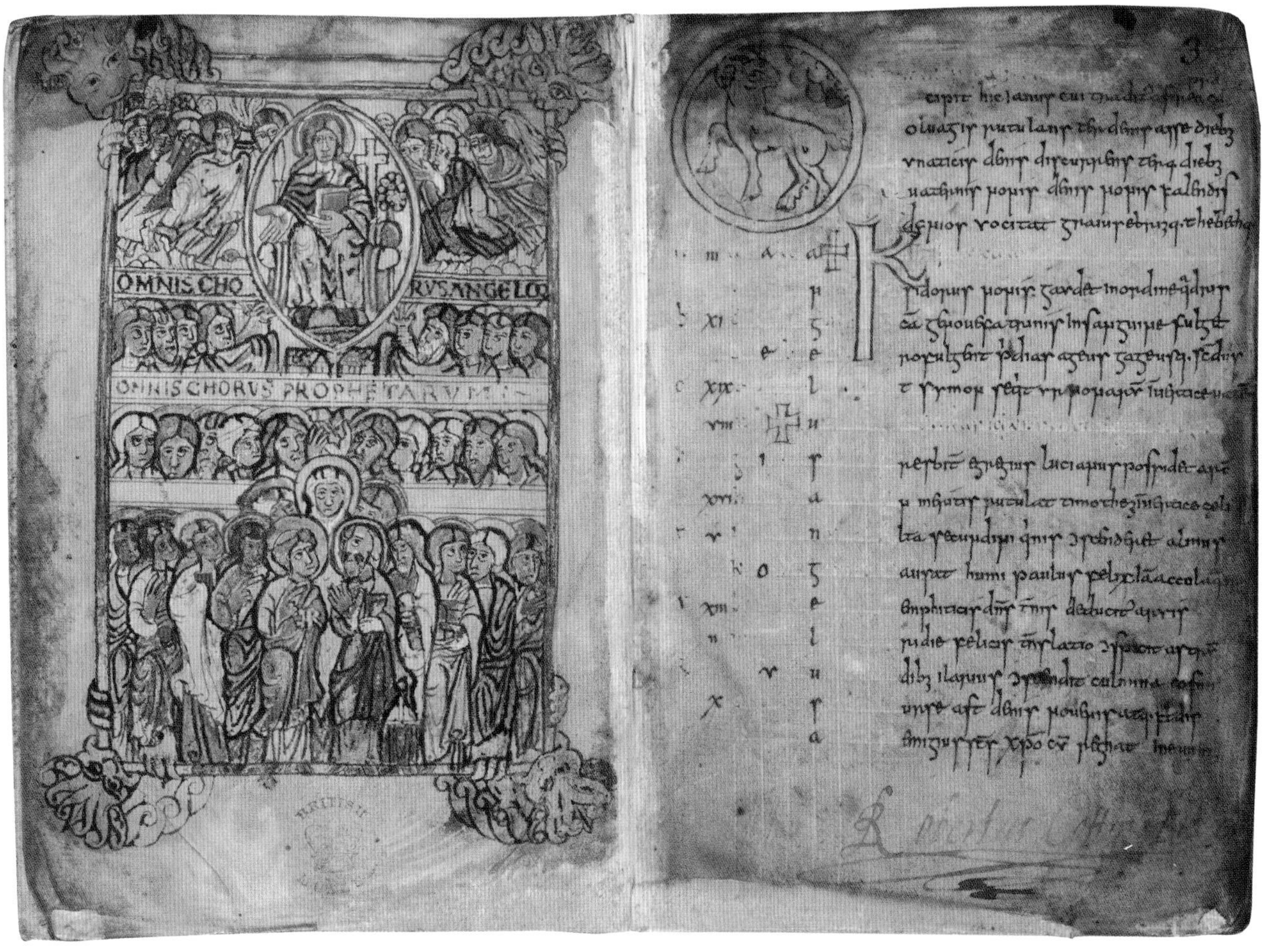
OMNIS CHO
RUS ANGELO
OMNIS CHORUS PROPHETARUM

120
121
NE
EX
AV
DI
ORA
TIONEMMEA

4 The Athelstan or Coronation Gospels

Lobbes (?), last quarter of the 9th century or 1st quarter of the 10th century
230 × 175 mm (maximum size of original parchment as preserved)

COTTON TIBERIUS A. II, FF. 3–218; COTTON CLAUDIUS A. III, FF. 2–7, 9*;
AND COTTON FAUSTINA B. VI, VOL. 1, FF. 95, 98–100

The manuscript known variously as the Athelstan Gospels or Coronation Gospels has a convoluted history, from its manufacture in late Carolingian Francia to its present resting-place at the British Library. Perhaps made at Lobbes (in modern-day Belgium), the Gospel-book arrived in England at an early stage, since it was presented by King Athelstan to the monks of Christ Church, Canterbury, in the 930s (see inscriptions, Cotton Tiberius A. ii, ff. 15–15v). At Christ Church several documents were entered into the book in the eleventh and early twelfth centuries, written on hitherto blank pages and newly inserted leaves. During the seventeenth century the manuscript was acquired, and disassembled into three separate volumes, by Sir Robert Cotton (d. 1631). At the same time there originated the mistaken belief that this Gospel-book had been used in the coronation ritual of the Anglo-Saxon kings. Finally, the major portion of the Athelstan Gospels was damaged by fire in 1731 – albeit not grievously – and remounted in paper frames in 1848.

The Gospel-book was made in late ninth- or early tenth-century Francia, to judge by its Caroline minuscule script and its decoration. In the Gospel-book proper the handwriting of two contemporaneous scribes can be identified, the first of whom wrote most of the manuscript and the second six leaves that form part of the Gospel of John (Tiberius A. ii, ff. 167–172v). The work of two separate artists can also be distinguished, one being responsible for the miniature prefacing the Gospel of Matthew (f. 24v) and the other for the remaining three Evangelist portraits (ff. 74v, 112v, 164v) and the major initials. It has been plausibly argued elsewhere (Wormald 1952; Puhle 2001) that the figure-types employed by both artists resemble the portrait of John in the Vienna Coronation Gospels (Vienna, Kunsthistorisches Museum, Schatzkammer Inv. XIII 18) and the Evangelists depicted in the early ninth-century Aachen Gospels (Aachen, Domschatzkammer, Inv. 4). The most likely intermediaries between those two books and the present volume are Gospel-books produced at Reims in the middle of the ninth century. Such a direct source may explain why the Evangelist figures in the Athelstan Gospels are less crisply executed than their counterparts in Vienna and Aachen.

There is no question that this Gospel-book passed through King Athelstan's hands. A compelling argument for the manuscript's arrival in England has been devised by Keynes (1985), based on two inscriptions reading *ODDA REX* and *MIHTHILD MATER REGIS* respectively (Tiberius A. ii, f. 24). Odda is most probably Otto I, who became King of Germany in 936 and Emperor in 962, and who died in 973; in turn, Mihthild may be identified as Otto's mother Matilda, who died in 968. The orthography and script of both names is English, the appellation *rex* suggesting that they were inscribed in the manuscript no earlier than 936 (Lapidge 1981). Otto was closely connected to the English royal court, having married Athelstan's half-sister Eadgyth in 929 or 930. We may surmise that the Gospel-book was presented to Athelstan by Otto or his father, Henry the Fowler (d. 936), at the time of the marriage celebrations or in the years immediately following.

The tradition that the kings of Anglo-Saxon England swore their coronation oaths on this manuscript has been described as a 'romantic invention' of Sir Robert Cotton (Wormald 1951). There is neither internal nor external evidence to support Cotton's claims for such usage, as stated in the earliest catalogue of his collection and on the title-page made at his instruction. Cotton nonetheless attempted to present the Athelstan Gospels to Charles I at his coronation in 1626.

Study of the Gospel-book is complicated by another Cottonian intervention, namely the removal of those leaves containing papal bulls and Anglo-Saxon charters. Cotton rebound these documents with unrelated material in two separate volumes (Claudius A. iii and Faustina B. vi), both of which escaped the ravages of the 1731 fire that damaged the remainder of the Athelstan Gospels. Adding insult to injury, Cotton supplied his own frontispiece to the Gospel-book, comprising a miniature removed from the Psalter of Henry VI (now Cotton Domitian A. xvii, f. 98; see cat. no. 141) and a cutting of the Breviary of Margaret of York, Duchess of Burgundy (d. 1503) (Brown 1998). This association with the Psalter of Henry VI provides further testament to Robert Cotton's desire to bolster the royal credentials of the Athelstan Gospels. The miniature taken from the Psalter was restored to its rightful home in the middle of the nineteenth century. *J.H.*

PROVENANCE:

Otto I (d. 973) (?); King Athelstan; Christ Church, Canterbury; Sir Robert Cotton (d. 1631); bequeathed to the nation by Sir John Cotton, 1702.

Opposite:
Evangelist portrait of Mark, f. 74v

5 The New Minster Charter

Winchester, 966
225 x 165 mm

BRITISH LIBRARY, COTTON VESPASIAN A. viii

Nominally a royal charter, this exquisite little volume is a potent expression of the late Anglo-Saxon monarchy's relationship to the contemporary Church. It commemorates the revolutionary replacement of secular clerics by Benedictine monks at New Minster, Winchester, a transformation instigated by the dynamic monastic reformer Bishop Æthelwold of Winchester (d. 984), and enforced by King Edgar (see cat. no. 6). According to the *Anglo-Saxon Chronicle*, this occurred in 964; whether because the transformation was a lengthy process or because it subsequently needed bolstering, the present document was drawn up two years later.

Whereas charters normally occupy a single sheet of parchment, this one is presented as a luxurious book. It is the only late Anglo-Saxon manuscript to be written entirely in gold, an unequivocal projection of its importance. Likewise the scripts – Caroline minuscule for the main text, Uncials for chapter headings and the rubric (f. 3v), and Square Capitals for the prologue (f. 4) – all types recently introduced or reintroduced to England and redolent of Continental culture – were potent symbols of a new order. The lengthy text (doubtless composed by Æthelwold, and set out as verse) first casts the events into the cosmic time-frame of the Creation, Fall and Redemption of mankind, and then notes Edgar's replacement of clerics by monks in general before turning to New Minster in particular and going on to define the respective responsibilities of the monks and the King.

The text is prefaced by a pictorial frontispiece that shows King Edgar holding a book (presumably this charter) and flanked by the Virgin Mary and St Peter (New Minster's patron saints) in the presence of Christ who, enthroned on an arc and globe within a mandorla upheld by angels, and with the wounds of his Passion visible on his hands and feet, is a cosmic figure of power and judgement. The relationship between the two central figures is spelled out by golden verses on the facing page: 'Thus he who established the stars sits on a lofty throne. King Edgar, prostrate and venerating, adores him.' The opulence of the frontispiece is enhanced by its elaborate frame and (now weathered) ground of purple, a colour rich in regal symbolism with overtones of Christ's suffering.

At one level this is a potent image of an Anglo-Saxon monarch who enjoys a direct relationship with the deity. Yet, while Edgar (and by extension his kingship) is being blessed, this is because he performs good works and acknowledges his subordination to Christ. Underlined within the text of the document by formulae such as 'king by the favour of divine grace', the latter point is broadcast by the verses quoted above, and by numerous details in the picture – ranging from the relative positions of deity and monarch to the fact that Christ wears a golden mantle while the King has only a gold edging to his cloak. Edgar receives divine blessing here precisely because he is supporting the monastic reform instigated by his Bishop; and the text spells out a reciprocal relationship between the King and the new monks: he defends them in the world (§§ 14 and 16) and they protect him from the Devil (§ 15) – a spiritual support evoked in the miniature by the patron saints who flank the King.

For the reformed community of New Minster – the owners of the book, to whom the text was regularly to be read (§ 22) – the image shows that the supreme powers of heaven and earth were united in supporting their new regime. This is reinforced on the next opening (ff. 3v–4, the rubric and preface) where Edgar's name in capitals on the verso is balanced on the recto by the *Chrismon* (the traditional symbol for Christ on charters) and by a circumlocution for God ('Almighty founder of all creation').

One of several houses reformed around this time, New Minster may indeed have been of particular interest to Edgar, not only because of its proximity to his palace, but also on account of its role as a mausoleum for the West Saxon dynasty. Be that as it may, this volume advertises the extent to which the image of a monarch could be modelled by the Church and used for ecclesiastical as well as political purposes. *R.G.*

PROVENANCE:

New Minster, Winchester; Sir Robert Cotton (d. 1631); presented to the nation by Sir John Cotton, 1702.

Opposite top:
Pictorial frontispiece with King Edgar; descriptive verses, ff. 2v–3

Opposite below:
Introductory rubric and prologue, ff. 3v–4

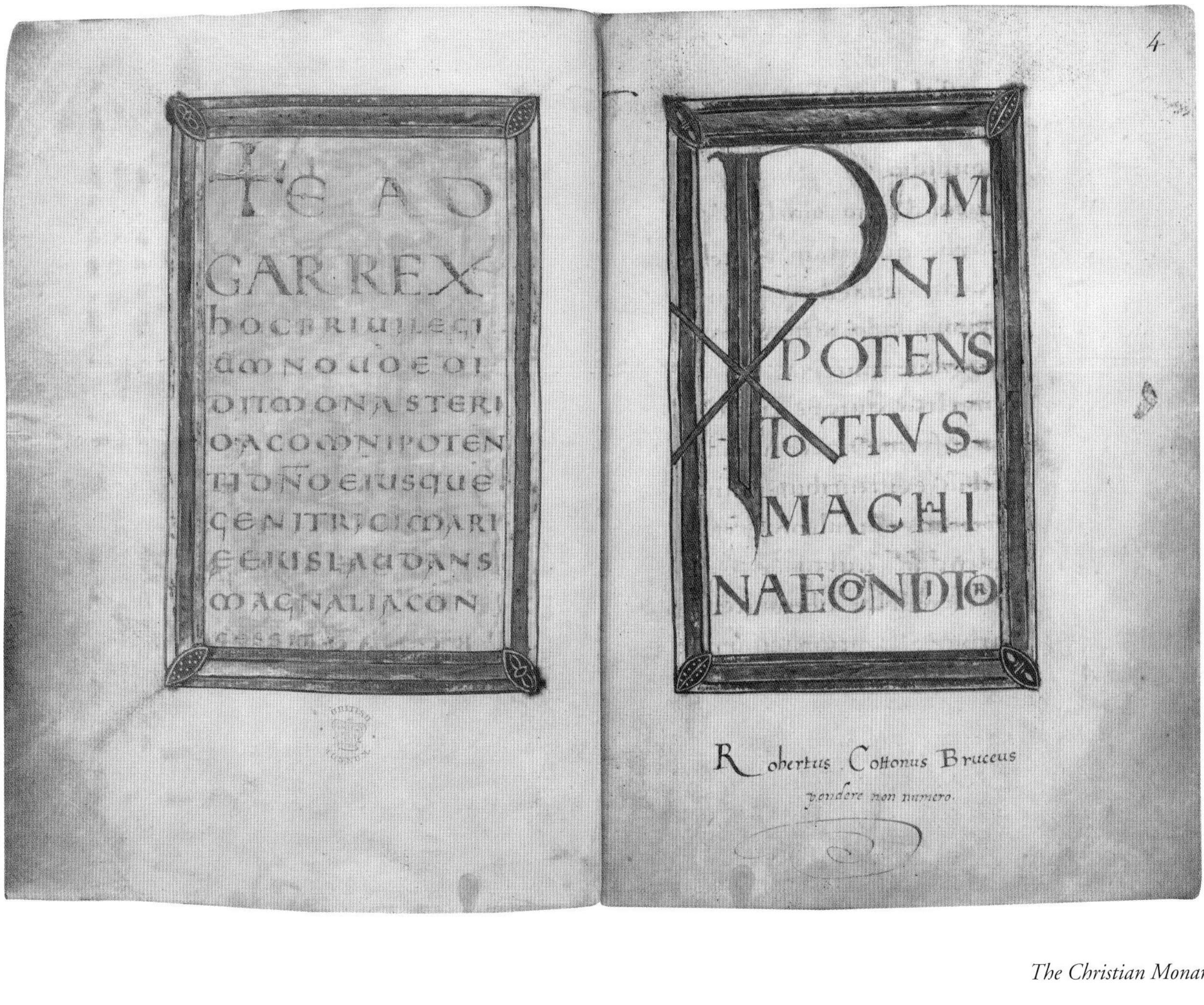
TE AD
GAR REX
DOMINI OMNIPOTENS TOTIUS MACHINAE CONDITOR
Robertus Cottonus Bruceus
pondere non numero.

6 *Regula S. Benedicti*, *Regularis concordia* and other Devotional, Practical and Educational Texts for Monastic Use

Canterbury (?Christ Church), 2nd quarter of the 11th century
c. 245 x *c.* 185 mm (maximum size of original parchment as preserved)

BRITISH LIBRARY, COTTON TIBERIUS A. iii, ff. 2–173

This compendium sheds searching light on the late Anglo-Saxon Church and its relationship to the monarchy. Though dominated by a suite of texts on the organization of monastic life along with other devotional material, it also includes prognostics that reflect folkloric beliefs. There are texts in the vernacular as well as in Latin; many of the latter have a continuous Old English gloss (plus, occasionally, construe marks to assist with word order), and one of them is a colloquy designed to teach Latin to beginners. The book thus evokes a monastic Church in which spiritual aspirations were balanced by superstition, and where the learning of a few was tempered by the struggle to inculcate basic Latin to the many. It also reveals one where 'independence from secular domination' meant relying on the favour of the king.

The first two texts of the volume as originally constituted, the *Rule of St Benedict*, then the *Regularis concordia*, were introduced by full-page miniatures, the first (now f. 118v) fully painted within an elaborate frame, and the second (now f. 2v, pictured) a delicately tinted line-drawing in a plain one. The latter features a king seated between a bishop and an archbishop, doubtless Edgar (d. 975), Æthelwold (d. 984) and Dunstan (d. 988) respectively.

With the accession of Edgar to the throne of all England in 959 (from 957 he had been King north of the Thames only), a clique of monastic reformers, whose influence had hitherto been limited, swept to prominence. Dunstan, the former Abbot of Glastonbury who had briefly been Bishop of Worcester, then London, when Edgar ruled north of the Thames, was collated to Canterbury (960); his disciple Æthelwold, former Abbot of Abingdon, was made Bishop of Winchester (963). With Edgar's support, Æthelwold energetically converted communities of secular clergy into Benedictine monasteries (see cat. no. 5) and revived lapsed foundations such as Peterborough and Ely. In addition to perceived spiritual benefits, the process gave Edgar unimpeachable grounds for weakening some of his nobles by removing lands from their possession to 'restore' them to these monasteries.

At a synod held in Winchester, probably in the early 970s, a supplement – the *Regularis concordia* – to the *Rule of St Benedict* was promulgated. It was designed to ensure uniformity of observance among the reformed communities. It also codified the devotions that they would perform to fortify the King. Beginning 'Glorious Edgar, by the succouring grace of Christ king of the English', the lengthy preface (in Æthelwold's rumbustious style) is lavish in its praise of the monarch and his spirituality. Crediting Edgar with the initiative behind, and wise advice to, the council, it formalizes his role in the election of abbots and abbesses, designating him the protector of monasteries (his queen was to fulfil this role for nunneries – a sensible precaution given the King's reputation as a womanizer).

The pictorial frontispiece encapsulates the idealized alliance of Edgar, Æthelwold and Dunstan articulated in the text. All three hold, and so endorse, the one scroll, doubtless representing the *Regularis concordia*. Its acceptance is indicated by the kneeling monk below, who embraces (literally and hence figuratively) a corresponding scroll. The King's key role is shown by his central position, and by the fact that all three ecclesiastics look towards him. While Dunstan and Æthelwold are haloed and hold stylized croziers, Edgar is ostentatiously crowned and brandishes a palm, suggesting that he has attained the courts of heaven. Unlike imagery that stressed the special status of rulers by juxtaposing them with some aspect of the Divine (cf. cat. nos. 5 and 8), here the King is apotheosized as a Solomonic figure, his spirituality articulated through his wise direction of a particular ecclesiastical policy.

The pictorial frontispiece to the *Rule of St Benedict*, which shows a commanding figure of that saint instructing monks from his *Rule*, is plainly related to a version of the subject that was made at Christ Church a generation earlier (Arundel 155, f. 133). The *Regularis concordia* image may likewise echo an earlier model. If so, the model was probably created at Winchester in connection with the initial publication of the text, reflecting ideals current in the 970s. When the present version was made it had new resonances: in the context of Edward the Confessor's reign (1042–66), as the royal dignity was threatened and eventually outmanoeuvred by over-mighty earls (the Godwins) and as Benedictines were losing ground to secular canons, the alliance of Edgar and his monk-bishops here depicted evoked the regal and monastic virtues of a former golden age.

R.G.

PROVENANCE:

Christ Church, Canterbury; Sir Robert Cotton (d. 1631); bequeathed to the nation by Sir John Cotton, 1702.

Opposite:
Frontispiece to the *Regularis concordia* featuring Bishop Æthelwold, King Edgar and Archbishop Dunstan, f. 2v

7 The Cnut Gospels

Southern England, early 11th century (before 1017–20)
350 x 270 mm

BRITISH LIBRARY, ROYAL 1 D. ix

This large and handsome volume, lavishly conceived with gold initials throughout and decorated openings for each Gospel (pictured and figs 1.8, 3.6), is one of a small group of predominantly high-grade manuscripts linked by the recurrence of a pair of scribal hands. Active at the beginning of the eleventh century, these scribes have proved difficult to localize; the textual affiliations of one of their volumes point to a connection with Ely or Peterborough (the latter was also the early provenance of another of their manuscripts), while the provenance of a couple of the others is certainly or possibly Canterbury. The only internal evidence for the origin of the present volume – the emphasis given to Sts Martin and Andrew within the list of readings – is ambiguous. However, the fact that it belonged at a very early date to Christ Church, Canterbury, is demonstrated by two short Old English texts that were added to originally blank pages between the preface to, and the beginning of, Mark's Gospel; both relate to Cnut, King of England.

The first (f. 43v, pictured) states in Latin and Old English: 'In the name of our Lord Jesus Christ, here is written CNUT the king's name / who is our dear lord before the world and our spiritual brother before God', going on to name Cnut's brother, Harold, and then three other Scandinavians, each described as 'our brother'. It thus immortalizes a bond of confraternity between the monastic community and the King, along with his brother and followers (see cat. no. 8).

Such acts were generally reciprocal in some respect, and Cnut was a generous benefactor to Christ Church, apparently giving it rights at the port of Sandwich, and notably his own golden crown. Moreover, on the very next page of the present manuscript (f. 44v) was inscribed his general confirmation of the community's liberties. After the greeting clause, this declares (in Cnut's voice): 'The Archbishop spoke to me about the freedom of Christ Church … I gave him permission to draw up a new charter of freedom in my name. Then he told me that he had charters of freedom aplenty … I myself took the charters … and laid them on Christ's own altar'. Reflecting its importance, this document was penned by Christ Church's master scribe of the time, a certain Eadwig Basan (see cat. no. 10).

Having seized the English throne by force, Cnut used all available means – ranging from political and military reorganizations, through guarantees of traditional English law and government, to marrying his predecessor's widow (see cat. no. 8) – not just to keep it, but to underline the legitimacy of his position. Conspicuous generosity to the Church was a powerful tool to this end, advertising his Christian credentials and winning the favour not only of influential churchmen, but also (in principle) of heaven itself. In this connection it has been suggested that Cnut, like Athelstan (see cat. no. 4), may have been a great donor of books to religious houses. However, though he was generous to the Church in other ways – certainly sending two splendid volumes to Cologne, and possibly giving another to the Duke of Aquitaine – there is little hard evidence to support the theory. Had Cnut donated the present manuscript to Christ Church, we might expect this to have been mentioned alongside the added records relating to him; but neither there nor anywhere else is this suggested.

Whatever its origin, this manuscript was surely selected to receive these documents as the newest and most luxurious copy of the Gospels that Christ Church then possessed (gold had been used only sparingly in the products of its own scriptorium during the tenth century), providing the most opulent and hence resonant repository for all-important records of mutual support between the King and the community. The practice of immortalizing key transactions by copying them into Gospel-books (cf. cat. no. 1) was here used to the advantage of all parties involved, providing a vivid illustration of the interplay of sacred and royal authority. *R.G.*

PROVENANCE:

Christ Church, Canterbury; John, 1st Baron Lumley (d. 1609); Henry Frederick, Prince of Wales (d. 1612).

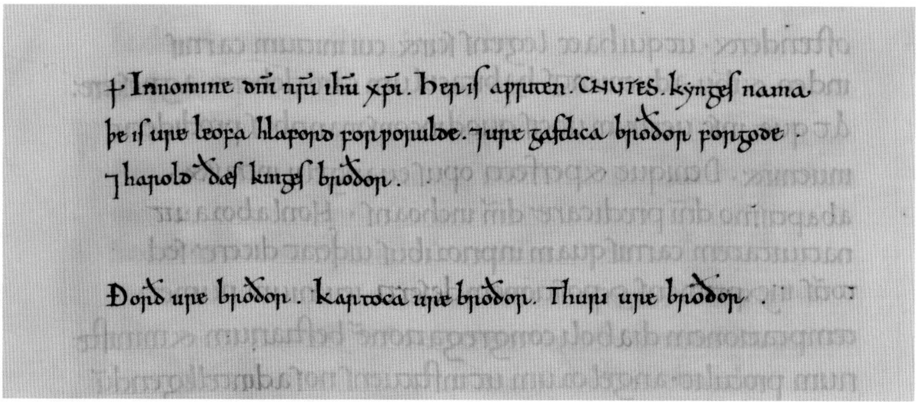

Above:
Added confraternity record, f. 43v (detail)

Opposite:
Incipit to the Gospel of Mark, f. 45

8 The New Minster *Liber Vitae*

Winchester (New Minster), 1031
255 x 150 mm

BRITISH LIBRARY, STOWE 944

At the core of this volume are the lists of names of those who enjoyed a bond of confraternity with the New Minster, Winchester. A preface (ff. 13–13v) explains that 'by making a record on earth in written form, [those named] may be inscribed into the pages of the heavenly [book of life]', going on to specify that the individuals in question would be commended to God at the high altar every day during mass. In accordance with its liturgical function, the original stratum of the book included a Gospel Lectionary with readings for the principal feasts of the Church year; while, reflecting its role as a vehicle of communal memory, it contained several historical texts. Amidst much else, the collection proclaims the close ties between the community and the West Saxon monarchy: a history of New Minster celebrates the role of the kings in its development; the first class of people to be named in the *Liber vitae* proper are West Saxon rulers; and there is a copy of Alfred the Great's will, a West Saxon regnal list and a vernacular record of the establishment of New Minster by Edward the Elder. Above all, the volume opens (f. 6, pictured) with a depiction of King Cnut (d. 1035) and Queen Emma–Ælfgifu (d. 1052).

The royal couple present a cross to the altar of New Minster – a real donation that survived until the siege of Winchester in 1141. The offered cross, highlighted by its size, centrality and colour, is shown bridging the gap between heaven and earth. Above, the Virgin Mary and Peter, the community's patron saints, intercede with Christ on behalf of the Queen and King, while angels place a veil on Emma's head and a crown on Cnut's. Below, the community of New Minster acclaim the act, the central monk holding an open book – doubtless the *Liber vitae* itself – paralleling the heavenly book on Christ's knee above. The words 'Ælfgifu regina' and 'Cnut rex', prominently inscribed around the royal couple, are the first names to appear in this earthly *Liber vitae* – doubtless to be transferred to its celestial counterpart. The advantages of this are underlined on the very next opening (ff. 6v–7), where vivid drawings delineate the possible fates of the soul – joyfully saved or miserably damned.

Destined for use at the altar of New Minster, the image is a pendant to the frontispiece of the New Minster Charter (cat. no. 5), advertising the continuing royal favour that the community enjoyed, while drawing parallels between Cnut and 'good' King Edgar. Significantly perhaps for a conqueror, Cnut (unlike Edgar) is shown with a sword; grasping this with his left hand while holding the cross with his right, he is a ruler of military force as well as spirituality. The fact that he is crowned by an angel shows that heaven endorses his kingship. The arch atop his crown parallels the design of that of the Ottonian–Salian dynasty of contemporary Germany (and Cnut had attended the coronation of Conrad II in Rome in 1027), though whether it bore imperial connotations here (styling Cnut's North Sea dominion an empire) is an open question.

The inclusion of the Queen also distinguishes this depiction from the New Minster Charter, while assimilating it to some Ottonian–Salian imagery, such as an ivory of 982/3 with Otto II and Theophanu or the Pericopes Book of between 1007 and 1012 with Henry II and Cunigunde. Cnut's marriage in 1017 to Emma of Normandy, formerly the wife of Æthelred II, was one way for the Danish conqueror to forge links with the regime he had supplanted. Interestingly, Emma is here shown in the favoured position at Christ's right hand, below the Virgin Mary. While this may reflect an enhanced share of royal power brought by her unusual position as twice Queen and an embodiment of continuity (and she does appear to have played a more important public role than any previous consort), the point should not be overstated for only Cnut is crowned by heaven (Emma receives a veil), Cnut alone touches the giant cross, and his name is the more prominent (centrally placed and written in Square Capitals, the top of the late Anglo-Saxon script hierarchy). Whatever the precise balance of honour, both enjoy uniquely prominent inclusion in a *Liber vitae* that, additions and supplements attest, continued in active service until the eve of the Reformation. *R.G.*

PROVENANCE:

New Minster, Winchester; (?) Walter Clavell of Smedmore (d. 1740); George North of Codicote (d. 1772); Michael Lort (d. 1790); Thomas Astle (d. 1803); George Grenville (d. 1813); Bertram, 4th Earl of Ashburnham (d. 1878); bought for the nation in 1883 from Bertram, 5th Earl of Ashburnham.

Opposite:
King Cnut and Queen Emma–Ælfgifu presenting a cross to the altar of New Minster, Winchester, f. 6

CNVT
REX

platearum & in sinagogis stantes orare ut uide
antur ab hominib; amen dico uob pceperunt
mercedem suã. Tu autẽ cũ orabis intra in cu
biculum tuum & clauso ostio tuo ora patrẽ
tuũ & pater tuus qui uidet in absconso reddet
tibi Orantes autẽ noli multũ loq sic ethni
ci putant enim q in mul loquio suo exaudi
antur noli te ergo adsimilari eis scit enĩ
pater noster quid uob opus sit antequam
petatis ab eo sic autem orabitis;
PATER NOSTER
qui es in celis scificetur nom tuum.
Adueniat regnum tuum. Fiat uoluntas
tua sicut in celo & in terra panem nrm co
tidianum da nob hodie & dimitte debita
nra sicut & nos dimittimus debitorib; nris
& ne patiaris nos in duci in temptationem
sed libera nos a malo amen;
Si enim dimiseritis hominib; peccata eorum
dimittet uob pater uester caelestis delecta
ura si autem non dimiseritis hominibus nec
pater ur caelestis dimittet uob peccata ura
Cum autẽ ieiunatis nolite fieri sic hipocritae
tristes. Demoliuntur enim facies suas ut pareant

9 The Goda Gospels

South-east England, 1st half of the 11th century
320 x 210 mm

BRITISH LIBRARY, ROYAL 1 D. iii

Written in the first half of the eleventh century, this Gospel-book is a fascinating volume with a complex history, about which little can be stated with certainty. Some scholars have placed its origin in Canterbury, as internal evidence indicates that it is a close copy of a ninth-century Gospels from St Augustine's Abbey (now Royal 1 A. xviii), with which it shares nearly all of its rare textual variants. Such an attribution, however, does not take into account the common practice of regional monastic houses borrowing and copying one another's manuscripts, with many documented loans from the particularly well-equipped libraries of Canterbury. In addition, the decorative programme in the Goda Gospels, mostly coloured or decorated initials in yellow, red and brown, detailed with geometric patterns and rough knotwork (pictured), is significantly different in style from that of contemporary Canterbury.

Certain further features of the Goda Gospels suggest that the manuscript may have been created by a less accomplished scriptorium, or in some haste. The opening canon tables contain several considerable errors and omissions, and chapter numbering that was clearly entered after the surrounding arcades were finished (McGurk 1993). Originally, these tables were followed by three ruled but otherwise blank pages; this space was utilized by a twelfth-century scribe to include a version of the 'Exultet' with musical neums (ff. 7v–8). The programme of decoration is also incomplete. Most notable is the unfinished 'Beata' page (f. 9), with other major decorative initials only extant until f. 66. Following this, the text is characterized by large blocks of space left by the scribes for the artists to illuminate. Some of these spaces (in no clear pattern) contain preliminary sketches for future decoration, but most are utterly empty.

The Gospels take their name from their purported original owner, the Countess Goda (otherwise known as Godgifu; d. *c.* 1055), a sister to Edward the Confessor and the daughter of Æthelred II. Goda's ownership of the Gospels is attested to by a thirteenth-century note (f. 9): 'Text[us] de ecc[lesi]a Roffen[si] p[er] Godam comitissam. III.' It was not unusual in this period for *textus* to be used to describe Gospel-books, but it seems to have held a particular meaning in thirteenth-century Rochester, used sparingly to denote books of special esteem (Richards 1988). The further designation *de ecclesia*, rather than the more common *de claustro*, appears to indicate that the Gospels were part of a select group of manuscripts stored in the cathedral church rather than the monastic library, a suggestion strengthened by the absence of these Gospels from later library inventories.

The Countess Goda was evidently an important patron for Rochester, and for St Andrew's Priory in particular (see also cat. nos. 81, 102). Her name is mentioned in the *Textus Roffensis* (Rochester, Cathedral Library, MS A.3.5), a twelfth-century legal compilation and cartulary, which notes her gift of a manor in Lambeth. That Rochester Abbey took great pride in their close ties to this daughter and sister of kings is further evidenced, as Richards notes, by the fact that Goda is the only female donor whose largesse is described as being her own, rather than her husband's or family's.

The Gospels, however, are unlikely to have been a gift made by Goda during her lifetime. The manuscript did not arrive in Rochester until some decades after her death, following a reconfirmation of her donation of the Lambeth manor by William Rufus, the current king (r. 1087–1100). The entry relating to the Gospels in the early thirteenth-century *Registrum Roffensis*, a list of donations to St Andrew's Priory (Cotton Vespasian A. xxii, ff. 60–129), hints at further complications. According to the *Registrum*, the Gospels were taken from this Lambeth estate and removed to Rochester by the monk Ralph, who served as the estate's first *custos* on behalf of the Abbey. After their arrival in Rochester, the Gospels were encased in an ornate binding of jewels and silver ('text[us] evangelior[um] argento et lapidib[us]p[re]ciosis ornatos'), which has since been lost. At some point in the following decades, the *Registrum* tells us, the Gospels were pawned, apparently the victim of a theft. They were eventually redeemed by Prior Helyas in the first decade of the thirteenth century and returned to the Abbey. The Rochester ownership inscription attributing the manuscript to the Countess Goda (f. 9) was probably added shortly after the volume's return. This complicated provenance, as well as the manuscript's decorative imperfections, has raised several questions in the minds of subsequent scholars. However, it is clear that the monks of Rochester entertained no such doubts about the royal Countess's legacy, and highly honoured the Gospels as a relic of their distinguished patroness. *S.J.B*

PROVENANCE:

Countess Goda (Godgifu; d. *c.* 1055); Cathedral priory of St Andrew, Rochester; Henry VIII.

Opposite:
Decorated initial 'P' at the beginning of the 'Pater Noster' (Matthew 6:9–13), f. 23v

10 The Grimbald Gospels

Southern England (?Christ Church, Canterbury), 2nd or 3rd decade of the 11th century;
(added letter) Winchester (New Minster), *c.* 1100
320 x 245 mm

BRITISH LIBRARY, ADDITIONAL 34890

Alfred the Great (d. 899) is the first English king whose literary activities are well documented and with whom extant books can be associated. While the tale recounted by the King's biographer, Asser (d. 908/9), about the infant Alfred winning a volume of poetry by memorizing it cannot be accepted at face value, it nevertheless raises the possibility that a fifth son with little chance of coming to the throne could have had greater exposure to literature in childhood than his elder brothers. Certainly, concern for learning was to be a key theme of his kingship.

Acceding to the throne of a realm overrun by Vikings, Alfred was eventually driven into hiding (in 878), only to re-emerge triumphant at the Battle of Edington later in the same year. Subsequent military and defensive reforms were accompanied by a suite of educational initiatives – all practical means to the same end. The root cause of the heathen onslaught, in Alfred's view (eloquently expressed in the prose preface to his Old English translation of Gregory the Great's *Pastoral Care*), was that the English had incurred divine punishment by failing to love wisdom. He recalled that before everything was ravaged and burned, the churches of England had been full of books, yet few people had been using them since command of Latin had atrophied.

In order to regain God's favour while Latin learning was at a low ebb, Alfred spearheaded a drive to translate key texts, being personally involved in producing vernacular versions of Gregory's *Pastoral Care*, Boethius's *Consolation of Philosophy*, Augustine's *Soliloquies* and the first fifty Psalms. Such works had symbolic resonance as well as practical value, articulating spiritual and philosophical dimensions to Alfred's regime and apotheosizing the fortunes of the English under his direction. The inclusion of the *Pastoral Care* implied that, just as Pope Gregory had sponsored the conversion of the Anglo-Saxons three centuries earlier, now Alfred was reconverting them. The King's prefaces to this work, along with the extant manuscripts, reveal a plan to send copies to all the bishoprics in his realm, where it might be further multiplied. Believing not just that those destined for the Church should be literate in Latin, but also (more radically) that all free-born boys should learn to read English, he attempted to make literacy a precondition of state office, establishing a royal school towards this end.

In order to realize his plans, Alfred gathered scholars from Mercia (a previously independent kingdom now increasingly under his sway), Wales and overseas. Whereas Asser simply states that Alfred's envoys identified and recruited Grimbald of St-Bertin, a letter to the King from Fulco, Archbishop of Reims (883–900), offers an alternative perspective. Alluding to the desperate terms in which Alfred had begged for help, the Archbishop clearly felt he was doing the King a great favour by responding to his appeal – to the extent of requiring guarantees that his protégé Grimbald would be suitably honoured.

The Grimbald Gospels is so called because it contains the earliest copy of Fulco's letter (pictured). The original manuscript is one of the most lavish and sophisticated late Anglo-Saxon Gospel-books, with a carefully maintained hierarchy of scripts and initials flagging the many subdivisions throughout the text. Since it was entirely written by the master scribe Eadwig Basan, whose localizable work was accomplished at Christ Church, Canterbury (see cat. no. 7), that was probably where the volume was made. Fulco's letter, however, was a later insertion, added on a specially prepared supplementary quire. Since this was written by a scribe associated with New Minster, Winchester (he was responsible for adding two charters to its *Liber vitae* (cat. no. 8, after *c.* 1080), and this was moreover where the cult of Grimbald was celebrated, the volume was evidently then in Winchester. Joining this flattering letter to a magnificent Anglo-Saxon Gospel-book was a potent act of memorialization: if the upheaval of the Norman conquest did not motivate New Minster to reaffirm the status of its learned holy man in this way, the disjunction when the community relocated outside the city walls in 1110 may have done so.

While the Grimbald Gospels itself was the product of an ecclesiastical scriptorium, the added letter attests to the key role that had been played by the royal court in the initial revitalization of English book production at the end of the ninth century. Immortalized by Asser as regularly either reading himself or listening to others doing so, and concerned not only to gather texts but to translate and disseminate them, Alfred was central to this phenomenon. As transmitted by later chroniclers, the monarch's bookishness became the stuff of myth, culminating in the claim that he had founded Oxford University – with Grimbald as its first professor of divinity or chancellor. More pertinently, the image of Alfred with which Matthew Paris (see cat. 114) headed a genealogy of English monarchs in his *Chronica majora* shows the King instructing a group of men, while brandishing a book at them. *R.G.*

PROVENANCE:

New Minster, Winchester; Thomas Ford (d. 1747) of Wells; the Carew family of Crowcombe Court, Somerset; purchased for the nation in 1896.

Opposite:
The start of Fulco's letter, 'To the most glorious and most Christian King of the English, Alfred', f. 158

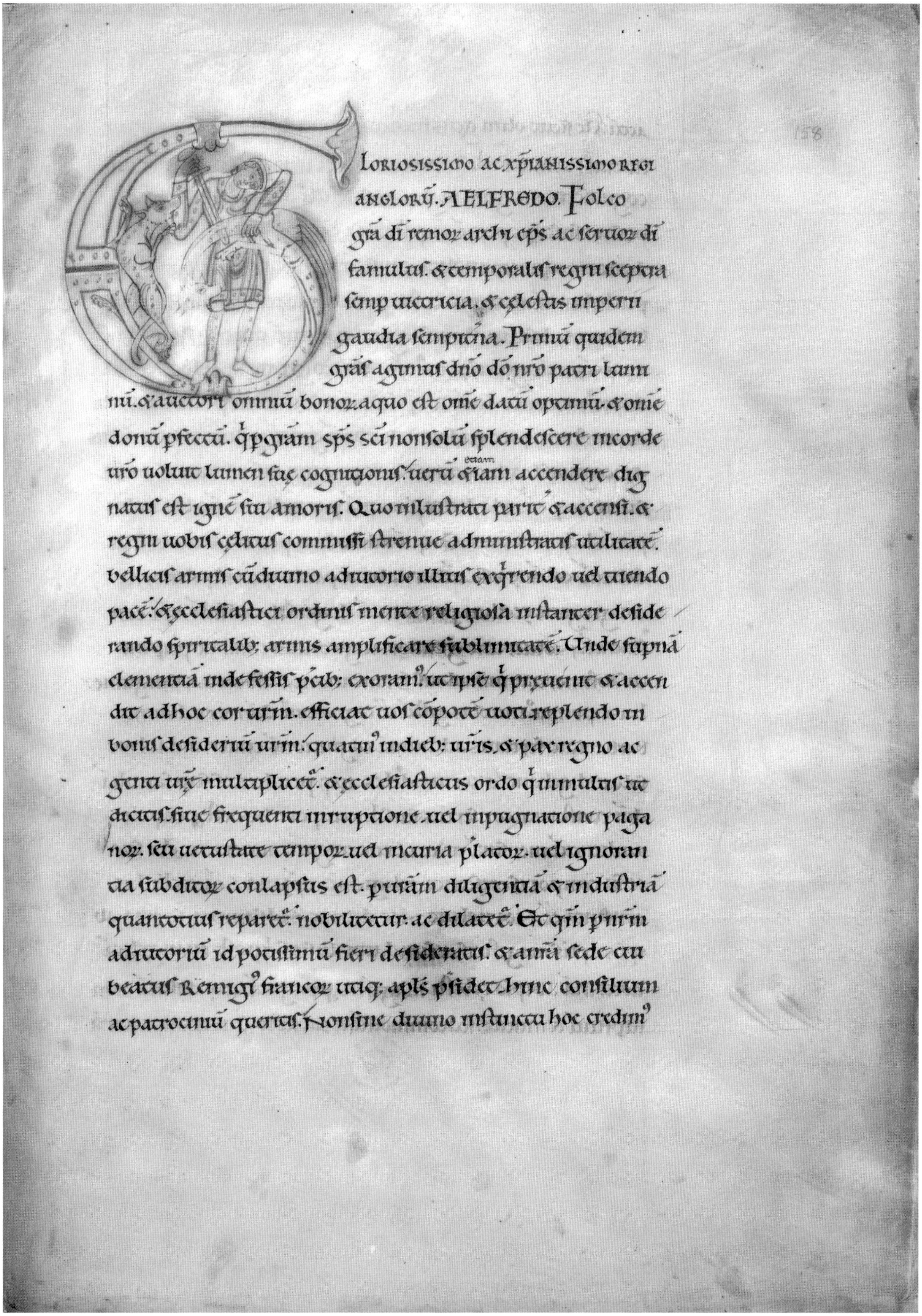

BRITISH
MUSEUM

11 The Shaftesbury Psalter

Southern England (?West Country), *c.* 1130–40
225 x 140 mm

BRITISH LIBRARY, LANSDOWNE 383

Around nine hundred years ago, the woman depicted in this Psalter uttered the Psalms and prayers inscribed on its pages. She is shown kneeling before Christ (f. 14v), and supplicating the Virgin Mary in the miniature pictured (f. 165v). Whether she was a member of a religious community or a laywoman is uncertain, although her elegant attire in the first 'portrait' supports the latter identification. Regardless, such a lavish devotional book could only have been made for a wealthy patron, probably a woman of aristocratic or royal birth. Warner (1903) was the first to suggest that it was made for use at the nunnery of Shaftesbury, Dorset, which was dedicated to the Virgin Mary and St Edward, king and martyr (d. 978). Edward, the first English king to be canonized, was enshrined there and features prominently in the calendar and litany of the present Psalter.

The manuscript opens with a calendar listing saints' feasts, followed by a table for calculating the date of Easter, the Psalter, Canticles, a Litany, Collects (short petitions), and various longer prayers. Gaps in the text point to at least three missing leaves (Kauffmann 2001), but these textual deficiencies are minor compared to the loss of miniatures. An extensive series of full-page miniatures depicting events in Christ's life most probably preceded the Psalter, but only six survive and these do not always follow a logical sequence. A miniature of the three holy women visiting Christ's tomb, for example, follows abruptly after the first one in the series, which shows God sending Gabriel to the Virgin Mary to announce Christ's impending birth. Holes along the top edges of the extant miniatures show that silk curtains, now lost, once protected the painted surfaces. Evidently, the surviving prefatory pictures are vestiges of a much more ambitious cycle. Judging from comparable manuscripts, the losses are significant. The St Albans Psalter (Hildesheim, St Godehard), for example, made *c.* 1120–30, and featuring three similar compositions, contains forty prefatory miniatures.

Although the original prefatory cycle cannot be reconstructed, it is possible to pinpoint where other miniatures are missing, something that seems to have been overlooked by scholars thus far. These pictures would have illustrated prayers in the final section of the Shaftesbury Psalter and conformed in style, size and arrangement to the two that survive: a full-page miniature of a female suppliant with the Virgin and Child facing a prayer addressed to her (ff. 165v–166), and another of the archangel Michael illustrating a prayer invoking him (ff. 168–169). The first missing miniature, probably depicting the Crucifixion, would have occurred after f. 153 and faced the prayer on the Holy Cross, now bound in the wrong place after f. 15, but belonging before f. 154. Furrows in the parchment at the top of f. 153v provide vital clues. Thread used to secure a silk curtain to the face of the missing miniature left these indentations. On the front side of the miniature where the silk curtain hung, the thread was cushioned by the cloth, but on the back of the missing miniature where the thread protruded, it pressed into f. 153v and left a tell-tale mark.

It is probable, too, that a miniature of St Peter preceded the prayer addressed to him on f. 170. A third missing miniature would have occurred after f. 171 and accompanied a prayer to St Lambert, of which only the final lines remain on f. 172. Indentations left by thread on f. 171v are proof that a miniature, probably depicting Lambert, has been lost, and the gap in the text indicates that an additional page with the first part of the prayer to the saint is also missing.

The textual emphasis on St Lambert, the martyred Bishop of Maastricht (d. 705), led Kauffmann (2003) to argue that the book, though following a Shaftesbury model, was made for someone devoted to this saint, possibly the widow of Henry I, Adeliza of Louvain (d. 1151), who was from the southern Netherlands where Lambert was enshrined. If the Psalter had retained all of its miniatures, including one of Lambert, the devotional affiliations of its original owner would have been even more explicit.

The fact that almost all of the missing leaves had illustrations strongly suggests that they were deliberately removed. We cannot determine when these losses occurred, but it is possible that the person responsible was motivated by piety rather than avarice. Isolated from the Psalter, the full-page miniatures may have served as independent devotional aids. Prayers added in the fourteenth century reflect the preoccupations of later medieval owners, and inscriptions on the front flyleaf show that the Psalter continued to be used into the seventeenth century. *D.J.*

PROVENANCE:

The Benedictine nunnery of St Edward, Shaftesbury, Dorset, or made from a Shaftesbury model for Adeliza of Louvain (d. 1151), widow of Henry I; William Adlard, 1612; Dorothy Berington, 1627; William Petty (formerly Fitzmaurice), 2nd Earl of Shelburne and 1st Marquess of Lansdowne, Prime Minister (b. 1737, d. 1805); purchased for the nation in 1807.

Opposite:
The enthroned Virgin and Child with a female suppliant, f. 165v

12 The Westminster Psalter

London, *c.* 1200 (Psalter) and 1250 (tinted drawings)
230 x 155 mm

BRITISH LIBRARY, ROYAL 2 A. xxii

This manuscript is the oldest surviving Psalter associated with the Benedictine Abbey of St Peter, Westminster, where St Edward the Confessor is enshrined and English monarchs from William the Conqueror onwards have been crowned. Over a thousand years ago Benedictine monks established a community on the site. In the eleventh century Edward the Confessor rebuilt the abbey, built his palace alongside it, and chose to be buried there. Royal patronage continued to influence the political affairs and physical fabric of the abbey – notably under Henry III, who replaced the Confessor's church with a Gothic building and erected a magnificent shrine in Edward's honour.

Written around 1200, the Westminster Psalter was almost certainly commissioned by a monk of high standing or an abbot. Possible candidates are William Postard (r. 1191–1200) and his successor, Ralph de Arundel (r. 1200–14). Shown kneeling before Christ and holding a scroll inscribed 'Lord, hear my prayer', the unidentified patron is depicted (f. 116) beneath the text of Psalm 101.

The images that decorate the Psalter are the result of three separate campaigns. The first, begun as soon as the text had been copied by the scribe, was executed by one or more artists who painted the roundels in the calendar and the initials that mark the ten-fold division of this Psalter (on English Psalter divisions see cat. no. 83). The second campaign, concurrent with or begun shortly after the first, consists of five full-page devotional images located at the beginning of the volume. The hand of the artist who painted these superb images appears in no other part of the manuscript. Since the pages on which they are painted form a separate gathering, they were almost certainly created independently before being bound into the book. The artist of the second campaign was probably an itinerant lay professional – gilded initials by him also occur in a Bible made *c.* 1200 at the Benedictine Abbey of St Albans (Cambridge, Trinity College, MS B. 5.3; Binski and Panayotova 2005). Some scholars think his work was influenced by some of the greatest painters of the period – masters who worked on projects as diverse as initials in the Winchester Bible (Winchester Cathedral Priory, MS 17) and a cycle of wall-paintings at the convent of Sigena in Aragon.

The style of the artist of the second campaign is particularly close to that of the so-called Master of the Gothic Majesty and the Morgan Master, two of the painters who decorated the Winchester Bible. As noted by Eric Millar (1926), for example, the ermine lining of the robe worn by Saul on a leaf that is now detached from the Bible (New York, Pierpont Morgan Library, MS M. 619) is identical to that of David's garment in the Westminster Psalter image (f. 14v, pictured). Equally striking, though unremarked by Millar, are similarities between the rendering of the face of David and that of Saul on the reverse of the Morgan leaf, and the identical treatment of the pink foliate borders in both manuscripts. Evidently the individuals who painted the Winchester Bible, *c.* 1160–75, exerted an influence on other artists working in southern England in subsequent decades.

Approximately fifty years after the Westminster Psalter was completed, five drawings – among the most celebrated in medieval English art – were added to previously blank pages at the end of the volume (ff. 219v–221v, pictured overleaf). These images of Christ, various saints and a king were executed in pen with washes of colour – a popular technique of the middle of the thirteenth century, and one also employed in a Life of St Edward the Confessor made at Westminster *c.* 1255 (Cambridge, University Library, MS Ee.iii.59) and in copies of the Apocalypse made for aristocratic or royal patrons (e.g. London, Lambeth Palace Library, MS 209). We do not know who commissioned this third and final artistic campaign, but any number of artists could have made the drawings because, *c.* 1250, Westminster was a hub of artistic activity: Henry III was rebuilding the abbey and also embellishing his adjacent palace.

Prayers and antiphons added in the fourteenth and fifteenth centuries attest to the Psalter's continued use in a monastic context, and the volume appears alongside other liturgical books in an inventory of the vestry of 1388 (Legg 1890). A second Psalter, with an Apocalypse, is also mentioned in the same inventory. This manuscript, now lost, is said to have been a gift of Henry III. Perhaps the artist or artists who decorated that thirteenth-century Psalter also updated the present one by adding the drawings to the pages at the end. Almost certainly, from its creation in 1200 until 1540 when Henry VIII dissolved the monastery, the Westminster Psalter was used in services there. *D.J.*

PROVENANCE

The Benedictine abbey of Westminster; John Theyer d. 1673), antiquary; Charles II.

King David playing the harp; Beatus page, ff. 14v–15

A knight paying homage to a king (added drawings, *c.* 1250), ff. 219v–220

220.

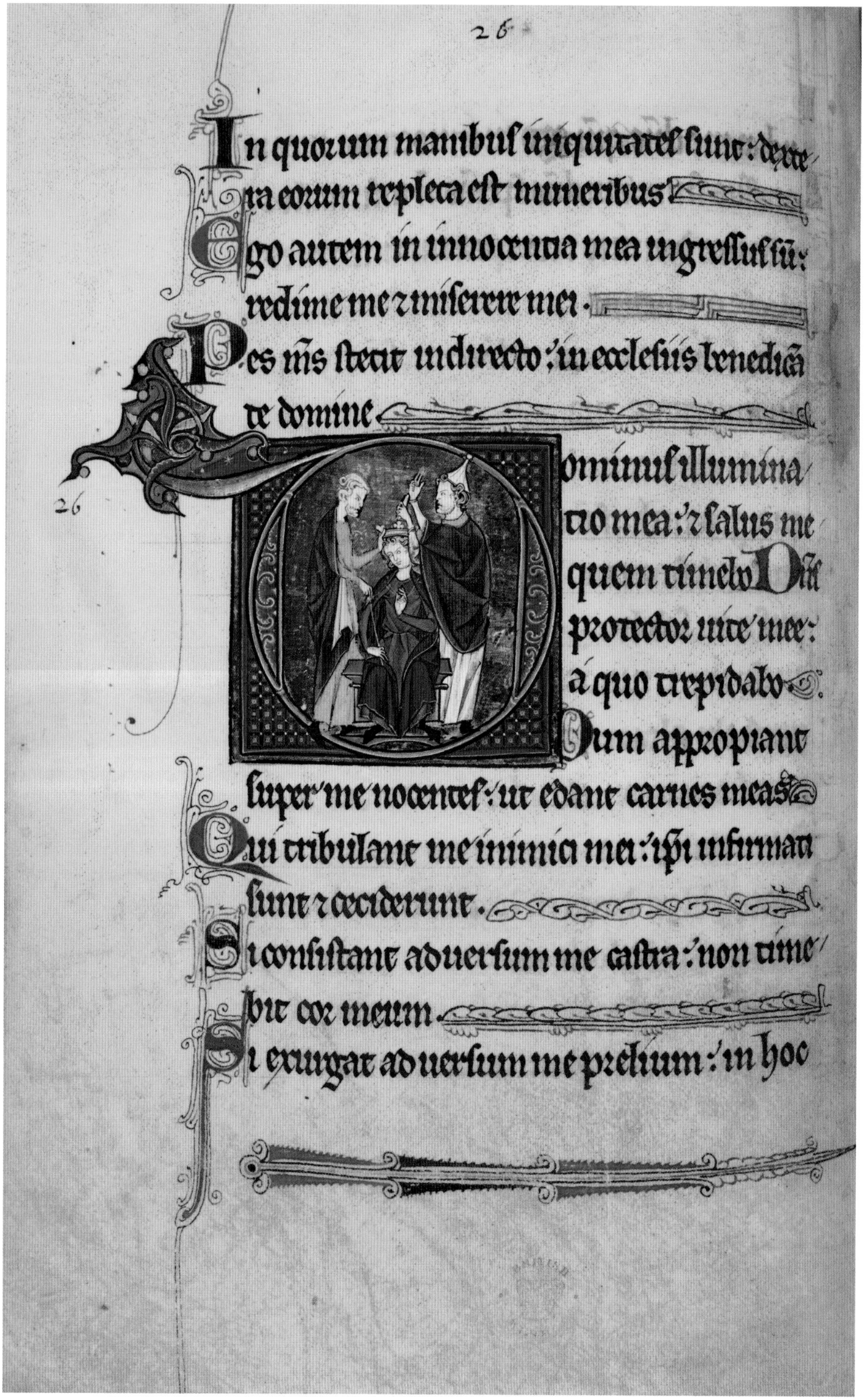
26

In quorum manibus iniquitates sunt: dextera eorum repleta est muneribus.
Ego autem in innocentia mea ingressus sum: redime me et miserere mei.
Pes meus stetit in directo: in ecclesiis benedicam te domine.
26 Dominus illuminatio mea: et salus mea quem timebo. Dominus protector vite mee: a quo trepidabo.
Dum appropiant super me nocentes: ut edant carnes meas.
Qui tribulant me inimici mei: ipsi infirmati sunt et ceciderunt.
Si consistant adversum me castra: non timebit cor meum.
Si exurgat adversum me prelium: in hoc

13 Psalter

Paris, middle of the 13th century
250 x 130 mm

BRITISH LIBRARY, ROYAL 2 B. ii

Above:
Psalm 97, Priests chanting, f. 105 (detail)

Opposite:
Psalm 26, Anointing and crowning of David, f. 29v

No biblical book played a more important part in the liturgy of the medieval Church than the Psalms. Attributed to King David and first chanted by Jews in the Temple and synagogue, these poems of praise and penitence were recited by Christ and his disciples and came to form an integral part of Christian services. The Psalms also occupied a particularly important place in the lives of medieval monks and nuns who devoted themselves to the *Opus Dei* (Work of God). As stipulated by St Benedict (d. *c.* 547), the father of western monasticism, this entailed chanting all 150 Psalms every week, beginning with Psalm 1 at Sunday Matins. In order to complete the task, the Psalms were divided into groups and recited during the Divine Office – a series of services conducted over the course of each day.

Different ways of dividing the Psalter were conceived over the centuries and are reflected in surviving manuscripts. An important development was the decision to mark specific Psalms with illustrated initials whose subjects reflect the opening verses. This became standard practice in France from the early thirteenth century onwards and then spread to England, Italy, Flanders and Germany. Large gilded initials at the eight principal divisions (Psalms 1, 26, 38, 52, 68, 80, 97 and 109) adorn this French Psalter from the middle of the thirteenth century. Each initial was once protected by a silk curtain; some curtains remain in whole or in part.

The subjects of the initials are drawn from a traditional repertoire. Among the most beautiful is that of Psalm 26, which shows a youthful King David being crowned and anointed (f. 29v, pictured). Three slim priests, whose garments cascade to the floor, chant together at the initial for Psalm 97: 'Cantate domino canticum novum' (Sing to the Lord a new song). It was customary to illustrate this Psalm with an initial depicting monks or clerics singing, but the artist has gone beyond the traditional formula by adding a crucifix on an altar (f. 105, pictured). Stationed in front of this object, the priests literally sing to the Lord. The image, which reflects contemporary devotional practices, gives us a glimpse of how Psalters could be employed in public worship.

A calendar at the front of the Psalter lists the main liturgical feasts and saints' days. Pictures showing appropriate tasks to be performed each month, and medallions with the signs of the zodiac are rendered on burnished gold grounds. The subjects of the calendar conform to a set formula. Certain details, however, are imaginative additions – including the inquisitive dog watching a pig being slaughtered on the December calendar page (f. 6v).

Given the style of the paintings, scholars have deduced that the Psalter was made in Paris, the leading European centre of manuscript production at the period. Workshops clustered around the cathedral of Notre Dame were staffed by professional scribes and artists. These catered to a wide range of customers, from local university students needing textbooks to high-ranking ecclesiastics and members of the aristocracy wanting sumptuous volumes. One scribe appears to have written the entire Psalter and a single artist painted the major initials. According to Branner (1977), the latter may have been an associate of the chief illustrator of a volume of civil law (Copenhagen, Kongelige Bibliotek, Gl. kgl. S. 393 2°).

The Psalter was almost certainly made for a nun since it includes two prayers for the welfare of 'abbatissam nostram' (our abbess). The inclusion in the calendar of Sts Donatian and Rogation, who were venerated primarily at Nantes – but also in Meaux, about twenty-five miles from the centre of Paris, in the department of Seine-et-Marne in the Île-de-France – suggests that the nun who owned the Psalter may have resided at a convent there. Reference to St Fara, who was venerated in Faremoutiers (also in the department of Seine-et-Marne), points to the same general location. On 10 May 1422, during the Hundred Years War, Henry V captured Meaux and seized among other goods 110 manuscripts, many of which were later given to King's Hall, Cambridge, and All Souls, Oxford, and others loaned to court functionaries (Stratford 1994). It is possible that the Psalter was brought to England with other Meaux manuscripts at this time. Certainly it passed to an English owner in the fifteenth century, as attested by the deletion of references to the papacy and by obits added to the calendar, including that of the London draper Clement Lyffyn (8 October 1450). It was later acquired by the antiquary John Theyer and entered the Old Royal library in the seventeenth century.

D.J.

PROVENANCE:

Probably made for a nun from Meaux; Lyffyn family of London by 1450; John Theyer (d. 1673), antiquary; Charles II.

14 Genesis and Exodus, with the *Glossa ordinaria*

Oxford, *c.* 1250–75
455 x 290 mm

BRITISH LIBRARY, ROYAL 3 E. i

Above:
Eleazor Avaran killing an elephant, Royal 3 E. iii, f. 160v (detail)

Opposite:
Days of Creation and the Crucifixion, f. 3

Although the production of ponderous, multi-volume Bibles encompassing the entire sacred text reached its zenith in the twelfth century, such Bibles continued to be produced in the thirteenth century. Many were commissioned by wealthy ecclesiastics or lay people who donated them to religious communities. Made in Oxford in the mid-thirteenth century, the manuscript illustrated is one of a set of six volumes containing books of the Bible with glosses (Royal 3 E. i–v, 3 E. viii). The present binding dates from the eighteenth century, but the phrase stamped in gold letters on the spine, *OLIM. CONVENT./ PRAED. LONDON* (Formerly [belonging to] the Convent of Preachers, London) presumably reflects the evidence of an earlier binding and lends support to the idea that in the Middle Ages the set was acquired by a Dominican house in the metropolis. The additional word *COMITISSAE* (Countess) is perhaps an allusion to a noblewoman who commissioned these volumes and/or gave them to the friars.

The page reproduced shows the first chapter of Genesis, which begins: 'In principio creavit Deus' (In the beginning God created). The primary importance of the biblical text – believed by Christians to be the Word of God – is reflected by its central placement on the page and the large size of the script. Because the gloss appears alongside the sacred text it may be scanned with ease. An anthology of the works of various Church Fathers compiled in France in the middle of the twelfth century, it is known as the *Glossa ordinaria* (standard gloss) because it was then the most widely read. The large initial 'I' features six medallions that depict the Creator at work. The final one, at the base of the initial, portrays God enthroned, and the miniature below shows the crucified Christ flanked by Mary and John the Evangelist. Four decorative extensions, sprouting from the initial, offer perches for birds and other creatures.

The beginning of each biblical book in the multi-volume set is marked by a large initial with an apposite scene. For example, the initial at the first book of Maccabees (pictured) shows the Jewish warrior Eleazar Avaran disembowelling an elephant with a tower strapped to its back – an animate war-machine employed by his Greek enemies. Set in Judaea in the second century BC, the books of Maccabees tell the story of Jewish warriors who led a revolt against their Greek overlords when forced to relinquish their customs and religion. A perennial favourite, the narrative was embraced by medieval audiences who saw Judas Maccabaeus and his brothers as forerunners of Christian knights and warmed to tales of harrowing battles and heroic deeds. In the thirteenth century, for example, Edward I had episodes from I–II Maccabees depicted on the walls of the Painted Chamber of the royal palace at Westminster.

In the left margin, near the illuminated initial, appear the faint outlines of the elephant's trunk, soldiers, and the audacious Eleazar Avaran. This sketch served as a guide for the artist, ensuring that the correct subject was painted on the appropriate page. The initial 'E' for 'E'(t), inserted alongside the sketch, likewise served as a visual cue. Similar sketches and guide letters occur in five of the six manuscripts in the set.

Further insight into the methods employed by medieval illuminators is supplied by an inscription on the final folio (f. 239v), which records the number of decorated initials in the manuscript: 3206 small letters and paragraph marks and 534 big letters (i.e., pen-flourished initials). All but the fourth volume (Royal 3 E. iv) feature a note of this type. Undoubtedly these annotations were written by someone involved in the book's manufacture because only a craftsman paid by the piece or a master overseeing the work would require such a detailed tally. Close observation of the manuscripts reveals a series of numbers written in brown ink. These provided a running total and enabled the craftsman to calculate the final number of small initials and paragraph marks for each volume, namely: 3890, 4028, 3206, 4100, 1782 and 7345.

It is difficult to say where the workshop that produced the Bible was located, but a note in the fifth volume (Royal 3 E. v, f. 102v), referring to a certain 'Reginald of Oxford', offers a clue. Reginald could have worked outside his native city, but the style of the initials evokes Oxford. De Hamel (1986) identified the artist with Reginald, an illuminator who lived at 94 High Street, Oxford, *c.* 1246–70. *D.J.*

PROVENANCE:

Dominican priory, London, perhaps given by an unidentified countess; Henry Fitzalan, 19th Earl of Arundel (b. 1512, d. 1580); John, 1st Baron Lumley (d. 1609); Henry Frederick, Prince of Wales (d. 1612).

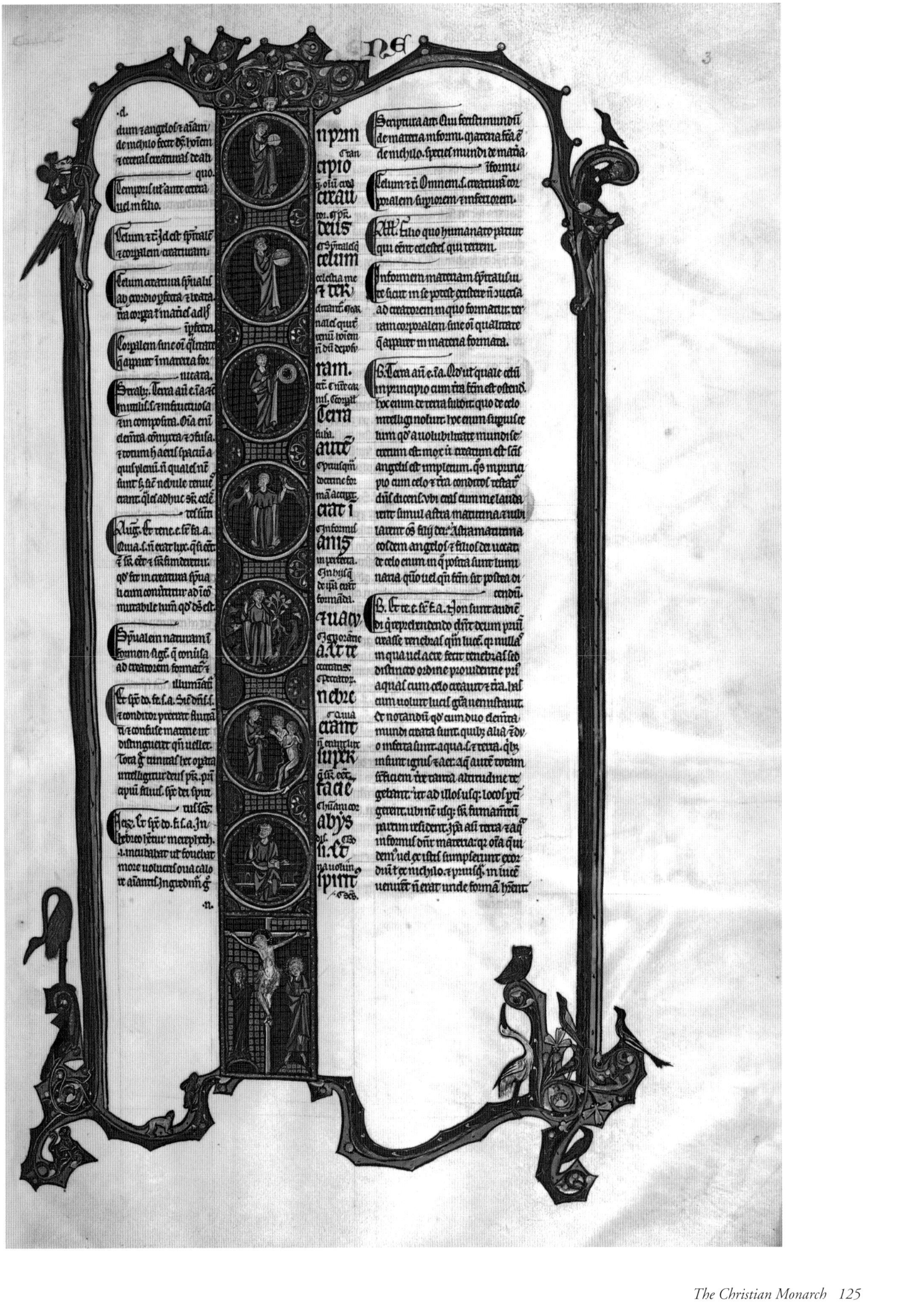

PROLOGUS

15 The Bible of William of Devon

Oxford (?), *c.* 1260–70
315 x 205 mm

BRITISH LIBRARY, ROYAL 1 D. i

Made in England around the middle of the thirteenth century, this Bible is unusually grand, exquisitely decorated and almost perfectly preserved. Its large size and elegant miniatures suggest that it was commissioned by a wealthy patron. Bar-borders throughout provide convenient perches for animals, birds and fanciful creatures, and the penwork decoration is executed in gold, in addition to red and blue. An inscription at the end of the Bible (f. 540v) supplies the name of the scribe: William of Devon. Regrettably, neither the name of the artist who illuminated the volume nor those of his assistants were likewise recorded. Some of them, though based in England, may have been born and trained in France. They certainly, drew inspiration from French models: the historiated initials in the manuscript conform in style and subject matter to initials in Bibles illuminated in Paris (Branner 1972).

Despite the artists' general dependence on French models, the manuscript's first page is idiosyncratic. Inscribed with St Jerome's Epistle to Paulinus, the standard prefatory text for Bibles by this date, the page features a large initial depicting Jerome writing. Although this is the customary illustration for this text, the four pairs of friars included in the margins are unusual. Balanced on four gold columns are pairs of Franciscans, Dominicans, Pied Friars or Trinitarians, and Carmelites (Bennett 1972). To date scholars have offered no satisfactory explanation for their presence here. If, however, we read Jerome's letter the reason becomes clear. Jerome begins by describing various pagan sages who travelled in search of wisdom. Next, he alludes to the preaching ministry of St Paul, and insists that wisdom comes from studying the Scriptures. Finally, he urges Paulinus to forsake his possessions and devote himself to God. Both the pagan sages and St Paul may be viewed as precursors of mendicant friars who also travelled 'with minds willing to learn', forsaking material goods and preaching wherever they went. Only one other surviving Bible (Oxford, Bodleian Library, MS Auct. D 1. 17) has a comparable illustration and it was produced by the same group of artists, who seem to have invented the composition. It is not necessary to argue, as some scholars have done, that the friars reflect the patron's interests, or to prove that the Bible was made in a town where all four orders were based; the text itself justifies their inclusion.

Two large miniatures, without exact parallels, offer further evidence of the artists' creativity; the first serves as a visual preface to the Bible proper (f. 4v), and the other to the Psalms (f. 230v). The frontispiece to the Bible, reproduced here, occurs on a page ruled by the scribe for two columns of text, but largely left blank: the text he wrote on it occupied only the first thirteen lines of the first column. Working within the boundaries of the ruled lines, the chief illuminator transformed this large expanse of parchment. At the top right, to balance the block of text on the left, he painted an image of the Coronation of the Virgin Mary. Below, he placed the Crucified Christ, flanked by the Virgin and St John. Beneath he situated the enthroned Virgin and Child, with Sts Peter and Paul on either side, and, in the bottom register, St Martin clothing a beggar. In the lower margin, on the same vertical axis as the beggar, is a kneeling cleric who likewise supplicates St Martin. Almost certainly he is the unidentified man who commissioned the manuscript. Could he have been named Martin or associated with St Martin in the Fields, London? From 1222 the parish church of St Martin's was under the jurisdiction of the abbot of Westminster, and the monks' extensive gardens (now Covent Garden) lay adjacent to the churchyard. The prominence assigned in the miniature not only to Martin but also to Peter (to whom Westminster Abbey was dedicated) and Paul (whose cathedral lay to the east), may reflect the devotional allegiances of a London-based cleric. The arrangement of saints in tiers almost certainly echoes contemporary rood screens 'such as the lost example at Westminster Abbey' (Morgan 1982–88).

Many questions surround the Bible of William of Devon, including where it was made. Scholars have identified six manuscripts illuminated by the same workshop, among them liturgical books with texts linking them to patrons in the Midlands. Although the workshop may be assigned to Oxford, this is not absolutely certain (Morgan 1982–88). Apart from the image of the patron, no marks of ownership appear in the Bible. Its handsome binding of purple velvet is thought to have been applied in the sixteenth century after the volume had been acquired for the Old Royal library. *D.J.*

PROVENANCE:
Henry VIII.

Opposite:
Virgin Mary, Christ and Saints with a kneeling suppliant, f. 4v

16 Peter Comestor, *Historia scholastica* ('The Ashridge Peter Comestor')

Southern England (?London), 1284–1300
400 x 265 mm

BRITISH LIBRARY, ROYAL 3 D. vi

Peter Comestor, priest and theologian of Troyes, rose rapidly to prominence and became chancellor of the cathedral school of Notre Dame, Paris, *c.* 1164. His most famous work, the *Historia scholastica*, is an abridged version of the Bible augmented by information drawn from various sources, and describing events from the Creation of the world to the Ascension of Christ. Because the *Historia scholastica* made intelligible even the most complex sections of the Bible, it appealed to scholars and laypeople alike. Endorsed by the papacy at the Fourth Lateran Council (1215), it was required reading for students of theology throughout Europe. An estimated eight hundred copies of the work survive in manuscripts dating from the twelfth to the sixteenth centuries (Sylwan 2005).

The present manuscript, one of the finest copies made in the thirteenth century, was commissioned by Edmund, 2nd Earl of Cornwall (b. 1249, d. 1300), who had inherited his father's wealth, vast estates, and lucrative tin mines and was the wealthiest nobleman in England. Decorated initials occur throughout the volume, which features borders with foliate motifs, birds, animals and fanciful creatures. The subjects – including a splendid peacock, blue jay, and goldfinch (f. 234, pictured) – reveal an interest in naturalism apparent in other English manuscripts of a comparable date (e.g. cat. no. 17). Large initials illustrating episodes described in the text are placed at the beginning of almost every book, and an additional one depicting the author, Peter Comestor, appears at the beginning of the manuscript (f. 3, pictured). It is not a conventional author portrait of a writer at his desk. Instead, as if to stress the authoritative nature of the work, it shows Comestor in his role as chancellor, holding a stave surmounted by a fleur-de-lis.

Instructions to the artists, written in Latin, are inscribed in the margins of the present volume near most of the large initials with figurative scenes. This suggests that the artists who painted them could read the language of the literate elite or were given verbal instructions by someone who could.

Most impressive visually is the first page of the Gospels (f. 234, pictured). In the historiated initial the angel Gabriel announces to the priest Zachariah that he and his barren wife, Elizabeth, will be blessed with a son – the future John the Baptist. The story, recorded by Luke, who explains that Elizabeth was related to the Virgin Mary, is the first in a series of miraculous events that culminate in the birth of Christ. Four shields in the border bear, in turn, the arms of Edmund of Cornwall, his father Richard, his cousin Edward I, and the heir apparent: either Prince Alphonso, who died on 19 August 1284 when he was only ten years old (see cat. no. 17), or his brother Edward of Caernarvon, born on 25 April 1284.

The pairs of shields emphasize the ties between fathers and sons, a theme also underlying the subject of the initial: Gabriel's annunciation to Zachariah of the birth of his son, John. Medieval Christians considered Christ and John to be first cousins, a relationship reflected by that of Edward I and Edmund, whose fathers, Henry III and Richard, 1st Earl of Cornwall, were brothers, and whose mothers, Eleanor and Sanchia of Provence, were sisters.

An inscription on the flyleaf shows that the manuscript was once owned by Ashridge College, a religious house founded by Edmund in 1283 and built about a mile from his castle in Berkhamsted, now Hertfordshire. Scholars have assumed that Edmund created the volume for presentation to the rector and canons of Ashridge, but it is possible that the Earl – who kept apartments there – commissioned the manuscript for himself and that it passed to the canons when he died at Ashridge in the late autumn of 1300. The manuscript could have been commissioned to mark the occasion when in 1290 Edward I celebrated the feast of Christmas at the college and held parliament there. Since Edmund died without an heir, his property passed to his cousin, Edward I, and in the following decades Ashridge continued to be patronized by the royal family. Given the links between the Crown and Ashridge, it is possible that the manuscript came into the royal collection before the dissolution of the house in 1539. *D.J.*

Above:
Peter Comestor at the beginning of the preface, f. 3 (detail)

Opposite:
Annunciation to Zachariah, f. 234

PROVENANCE:

Edmund, Earl of Cornwall; Ashridge College, Hertfordshire; Henry VIII.

17 The Alphonso Psalter

London, *c.* 1284 (ff. 11–25v); East Anglia (?), *c.* 1297–1316
245 x 165 mm

BRITISH LIBRARY, ADDITIONAL 24686

In October 1254 Edward, son of Henry III, travelled from London to the city of Burgos in northern Spain. His purpose was twofold: to be knighted by Alfonso X, King of Castile and León at the royal abbey of Las Huelgas; and to take in marriage Eleanor of Castile, Alfonso's half-sister, who was only thirteen years old. Although the marriage had political objectives, it proved to be an affectionate one.

Edward, who became king in 1272, embarked on one crusade or military campaign after another, and Eleanor generally travelled with him. She gave birth to sixteen children. Most were girls and many died in infancy, so the arrival of a son, their second, on 24 November 1273 was cause for celebration. Born in Gascony, the Prince was christened Alphonso after his illustrious uncle and godfather, the King of Castile, who attended his baptism. When his elder brother, Henry, died in 1274, Prince Alphonso became the heir apparent to the English throne, and as the years passed his parents sought a suitable bride for him, deciding after protracted negotiations on Margaret, daughter of Florent V, Count of Holland and Zeeland.

In 1284, in honour of the young Prince who was soon to be wed, the present Psalter was commissioned, and his arms and those of his bride-to-be were emblazoned on the opening page (f. 11, pictured). The gull at the centre is possibly an additional allusion to Holland or Zeeland (literally 'land of the sea'). English royal patrons commissioned countless sumptuous manuscripts, but relatively few of a comparable date are extant (see cat. no. 16). Decorated by an artist who used the finest of lines and subtle washes to endow his figures with grace, the first section of the manuscript is exquisite. Portraits of David harping and waging battle with Goliath are juxtaposed with naturalistic depictions of animals and birds. Even imaginary creatures, such as a dragon and a griffin, are rendered with such precision that they are entirely credible. Combat scenes abound, surely designed to excite the imagination of the young Prince, but another dominant theme, that of fecundity – appropriate for a betrothal – is expressed in the nesting woodpigeon (f. 11), the mermaid nursing her child (f. 13, fig. 1.13), and the doe suckling a fawn (f. 13v).

The Psalter is best seen in the context of the court whose opulence is reflected in surviving household accounts. Alphonso's mother, Eleanor of Castile, delighted in fine objects: mirrors in ivory cases, a chess set of crystal and jasper, vases, carpets and textiles, and enamel caskets from Limoges. The life-like lions in the borders of her son's Psalter may have been inspired by those in the royal menagerie, and the birds by specimens in her aviary at Westminster.

In addition, the contents of Alphonso's Psalter reflect his mother's devotional allegiances, with both Dominic (Domingo de Guzmán), the Spanish founder of the Dominican Order, and Peter Martyr featured in the litany (the calendar, a later addition, also points to the Blackfriars). Eleanor founded priories in Chichester and London, and Dominicans served as confessors to Eleanor and Edward I and as tutors to their children.

Sadly, on 19 August 1284, only months before the planned wedding, Prince Alphonso, then a boy of ten, died. His body was buried in Westminster Abbey and his heart was enshrined at the Dominican priory in London, where his mother later elected for her own heart to be buried. Although more than seven hundred years have passed since it was made, the Prince's Psalter still bears witness to his untimely death. Scribes had completed the Psalms, Canticles and Litany, but the artist responsible for its vibrant marginal scenes stopped short after f. 18. A second, closely related artist supplied decorated initials for the next seven leaves, but then he too abandoned the task. There was no impulse to continue and the commission languished for over a decade.

Eventually, in 1297, another dynastic marriage was arranged between England and Holland: Alphonso's sister Elizabeth married John I, son of Florent V and the brother of Alphonso's intended bride. The arms emblazoned on the manuscript were no longer obsolete, and the Psalter was adapted for the new bride by artists working in a different style (Sandler 1986). Portraits of saints were inserted in the front of the volume, along with pictures of Christ's Passion cut from a late thirteenth-century French manuscript and pasted onto the pages (fig. 1.14). The calendar, added to the book around the same time, includes in a fourteenth-century hand obits of Elizabeth's grandmother, mother and sister, as well as her own: 5 May 1316. *D.J.*

PROVENANCE:

Alphonso (b. 1275, d. 1284), son of Edward I and Eleanor of Castile; Elizabeth (b. 1282, d. 1316), sister of Alphonso, wife successively of John I, son of Florent V, Count of Holland and Zeeland (1296/7) and Humphrey de Bohun, 4th Earl of Hereford and 3rd Earl of Essex (1302); the Bohun family, 14th century; – Mannynge, d. 1584; Edward Graveley, 16th century; Thomas Tenison, Archbishop of Canterbury (d. 1715) (his sale, 1 July 1861); purchased for the nation in1862.

Opposite:
Psalm 1, David harping, f. 11

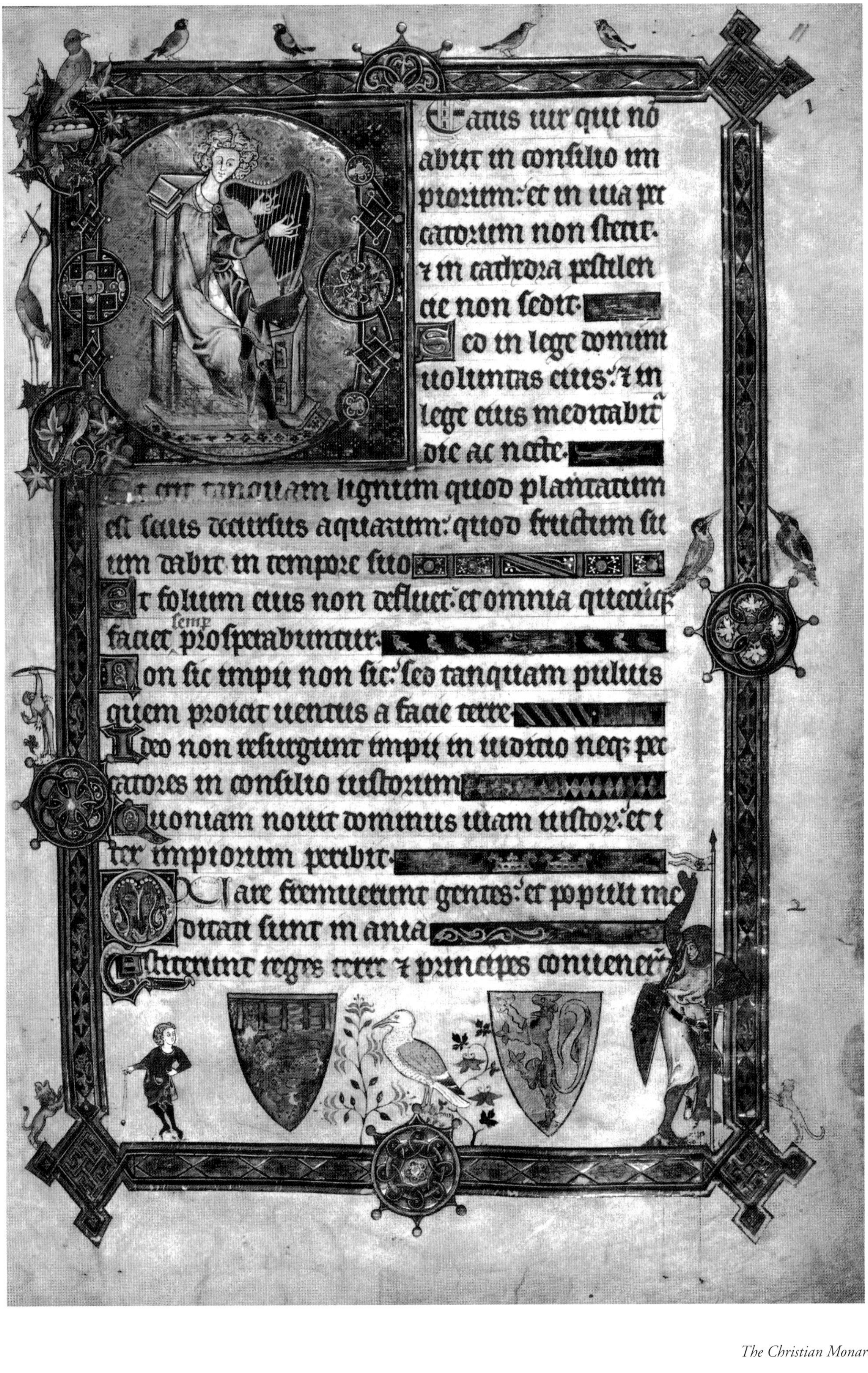

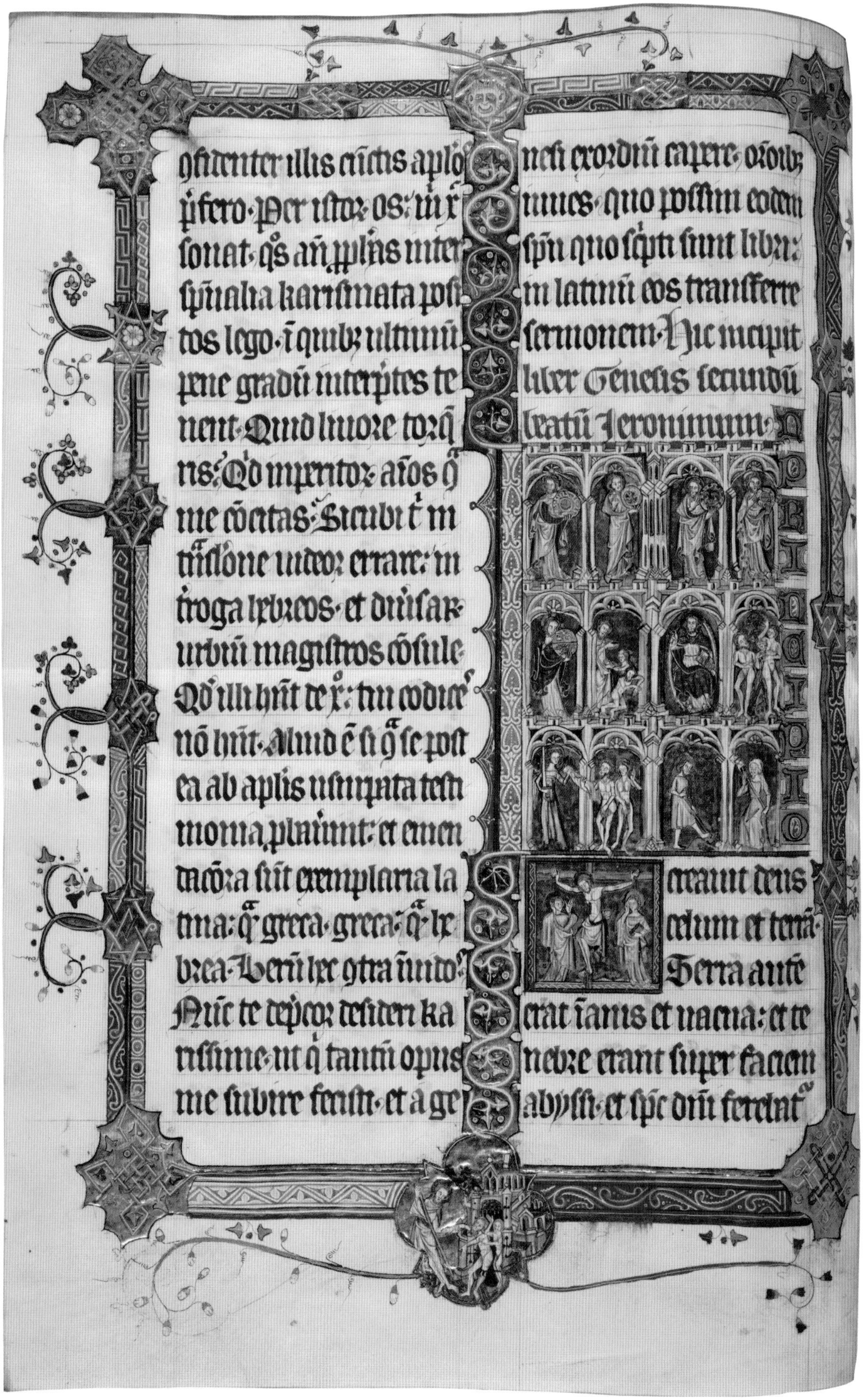

18 Genesis to Ruth

East Anglia, *c.* 1345–50
445 x 290 mm

BRITISH LIBRARY, ROYAL 1 E. iv

Judging from its impressive weight and size, this manuscript, containing the first eight books of the Bible, was intended to be placed on a lectern and read aloud. As recognized by Michael (Sotheby's 1980), it was conceived as part of a set of four volumes comprising the entire text of the Bible. The present manuscript is the only one to have survived intact, but detached leaves from the third volume (Proverbs to Job) are dispersed in various collections worldwide, including the Bodleian Library, Oxford, and the Pierpont Morgan Library, New York. The appearance of the detached leaves proves that different scribes and artists were responsible for the third volume, but similarities in layout and ruling patterns between the leaves and the Royal manuscript substantiate the idea that they once formed part of the same four-volume Bible. The unconscionable mutilation of the third volume seems to have occurred *c.* 1927, when it was deemed lucrative to sell piecemeal the 413 pages (Manion *et al.* 1989).

Large initials featuring appropriate subjects occur at the beginning of each of the eight biblical books in the Royal volume. The initial for Judges, for example, shows the Lord commissioning the warrior, Judah, to lead his people into battle against the Canaanites (f. 321v). Judah wears plate armour and a bascinet with a visor, a type of helmet worn widely by the middle of the fourteenth century. The one depicted is a relatively early type with a piece of chain-mail (aventail) protecting the neck. In addition, a portrait of Jerome – not, as described by Warner and Gilson (1921), 'a nun in the act of writing' – appears at the beginning of the preface (f. 1). The style of the figures points to a date *c.* 1345–50, and to East Anglian artists who also illuminated manuscripts for the Bohun family (Sandler 1986; Dennison 1988). Most of the historiated initials conform to standard compositions invented by artists in the thirteenth century. Even the large initial 'I' at the beginning of Genesis (f. 12v, pictured), which seems unusual at first sight, features the same scenes that appear in thirteenth-century Bibles. The main differences are that in the Royal manuscript the scenes are arranged in a rectangular, rather than a vertical, format and a miniature of the Harrowing of Hell appears in the lower margin.

By the middle of the fourteenth century, most religious institutions in England would have been well supplied with biblical manuscripts (Pächt and Alexander 1973). Consequently, there must have been a specific reason, now unknown, for someone to commission this volume and its companions, possibly for the use of a religious house. Scholars have been unable to determine for whom the book was made, but the portrayal of what appears to be a white friar on one of the detached leaves (New York, Pierpont Morgan Library, MS M. 741, f. 2) may offer a clue.

The initials 'TC' (for Thomas Cardinalis), inscribed on the first folio, show that in the sixteenth century the volume was owned by Thomas Wolsey (b. *c.* 1471, d. 1530), adviser to Henry VIII, Archbishop of York and Cardinal. From 1521 Wolsey also served as the Abbot of St Albans and helped himself to at least eleven manuscripts held by that monastery (Carley 2000). It is likely that he also acquired this manuscript at the expense of a monastic establishment.

In 1527, after eighteen years of marriage, Henry VIII convinced himself that his union with Catherine of Aragon (the widow of his older brother, Arthur) contravened divine law, and that his lack of a male heir was a direct result of this sin. The King's interest in Anne Boleyn offered further impetus for divorce. Wolsey was charged with the task of compiling texts and arguments to bolster Henry's case and resolve the so-called Great Matter. Discussion centred on certain passages from the Old Testament (Rex 1991), including Leviticus 18:16, which, in some Vulgate copies, but not in the original Hebrew or Greek, included the statement: 'Et uxorem fratris sui nullus accipiat' (Nobody may marry his brother's wife). Andrea Clarke recently noticed that a *maniculum* (little hand) drawn in brown ink had been inserted in the margin of f. 159v of this manuscript to draw attention to this very statement, which suggests that the volume was consulted by Wolsey or other supporters of Henry's case. According to Clarke, the *maniculum* could have been added by Henry VIII himself. Impatient with delays in securing his divorce, Henry charged Wolsey with treason and had him arrested. The latter's death on 29 November 1530 probably spared him execution. Afterwards, thirty-one manuscripts owned by Wolsey, including this one, were appropriated by the King (see also cat. nos. 89, 92). *D.J.*

PROVENANCE:

Cardinal Thomas Wolsey (b. 1470/71, d. 1530); Henry VIII.

Opposite:
Days of Creation, Temptation, Expulsion from Paradise, Labours of Adam and Eve, and the Crucifixion, f. 12v

19 The Psalter of Philippa of Hainault

England, *c.* 1330–40
250 x 165 mm

BRITISH LIBRARY, HARLEY 2899

This Psalter was made for Philippa of Hainault (b. 1314, d. 1369), Consort of Edward III, whom she married in 1328. The daughter of William the Good, Count of Hainault, and Jeanne of Valois, Philippa was born in the Low Countries, probably at Valenciennes, where she received an education befitting a noblewoman. Evidence of Philippa's esteem for learning survives in various forms. To commemorate her betrothal to Edward III in 1326, for example, she presented him with a miscellany of texts (Paris, BnF, MS fr. 571). Fifteen years later, her chaplain Robert Eglesfield founded in her honour the 'Hall of the Queen's Scholars at Oxford' (now Queen's College), to which she granted endowments.

In addition, documents relating to her household expenses include a payment in 1343 to Master Robert, whom the Queen calls '*nostre elumynour*' (our illuminator) and another in 1350 to his widow for various works completed by him (Vale 1982). Some scholars have speculated that Master Robert illuminated the present manuscript, one of two surviving Psalters owned by the Queen (the other is London, Dr William's Library, MS Ancient 6), but nothing else is known of this artist and the Psalter bears no resemblance to other manuscripts made for Philippa or Edward (Michael 1985).

Nine shields in the border (f. 8, pictured) attest to the Queen's ownership of the Psalter. One is damaged and indecipherable, but the others show the arms of England (twice), France (once), Hainault (twice) and England impaled with Hainault (three times). Since the arms of England are not quartered with those of France, the manuscript was probably made before January 1340, when Edward III, pressing his claims to the French throne, adopted the new charge (Alexander 1983). The arms of Hainault impaled with or quartered by the arms of England also occur in various initials, as do portrait busts of a queen. Although similar busts are found in other English manuscripts of a comparable date, those in the present Psalter probably represent a specific queen, Philippa, rather than a generic one.

Historiated initials of standard subjects mark the eight liturgical divisions at Psalms 1, 26, 38, 52, 68, 80, 97 and 109. The initials reflect the artist's awareness of French models, but were probably painted by an English craftsman. Continental models would have been readily available to an artist working for the English court. At the start of the Hundred Years War both Philippa and Edward stayed in her native region for extended periods; their son Lionel was born in Antwerp in 1338 and their son John (of Gaunt) in Ghent in 1340.

The illustration for Psalm 1 includes a depiction of David slaying Goliath (in the lower margin) and David playing the harp (in the smaller of the two *Beatus* initials). Elements of the design that are less conventional include the men crowded together in the lower half of the larger letter 'B'. The fact that there are twelve seems significant, but they are probably not intended to represent Christ's disciples since they lack halos, or prophets since they lack scrolls. A clue to their identity is possibly provided by the text of the antiphon that appears in an abbreviated form at the top of the page and is written in full on f. 10. It repeats words that the dying patriarch Jacob spoke to his twelve sons. According to Genesis 49:10, he addressed each one in turn, prophesying that the Messiah would be born of the descendents of his son, Judah. 'Non auferetur sceptrum de iuda ... donec veniat qui mittendus est' (The sceptre shall not be taken away from Judah ... till he come that is to be sent). David, the first King of Judah, and the other monarchs portrayed in the margin, may allude to this prophecy fulfilled by Christ: 'the Lord God shall give unto him the throne of David his father; and he shall reign in the house of Jacob for ever. And of his kingdom there shall be no end' (Luke 1:32–33).

Antiphons with musical notation are included throughout the Psalter. These short chants were sung before and after individual Psalms or groups of Psalms during the Divine Office. Their inclusion suggests that Philippa, known for her charity and compassion, may have used the book during services in the royal chapels.

D.J.

PROVENANCE:

Philippa of Hainault (b. 1314, d. 1369); Robert Harley, 1st Earl of Oxford (b. 1661, d. 1724), in 1723; Edward Harley, 2nd Earl of Oxford (b. 1689, d. 1741); purchased for the nation in 1753.

Opposite:
Psalm 1, David enthroned, Fourteen seated kings, David slaying Goliath, and the Arms of England, Hainault and France, f. 8

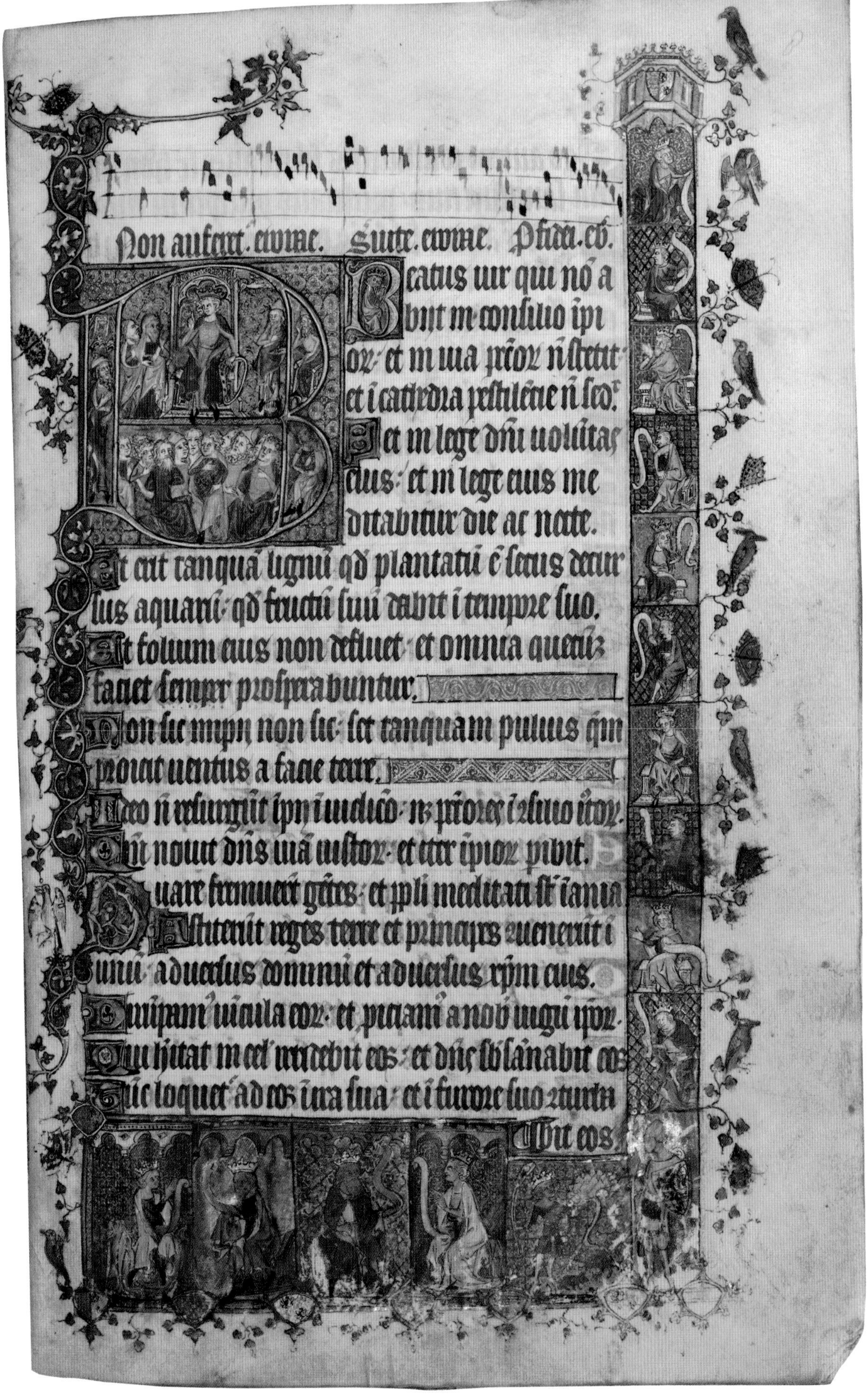

spectu meo semper. Quoniam iniquitatem
meam annunciabo: et cogitabo pro peccato me
o. Inimici mei uiuunt et confirmati sunt
super me: multiplicati sunt qui oderunt me in
ique. Qui retribuunt mala pro bonis detra
hebant michi: quoniam sequebar bonitatem.
Ne derelinquas me domine deus meus: ne
discesseris a me. Intende in adiutorium me
um: domine deus salutis mee.
ixi cus
todiā
uias
meas
ut nō
delin
quam
in lin
gua
mea. Po
sui o
ri meo custodiam: cum consisteret peccator ad
uersum me. Obmutui et humiliatus sum:
et silui a bonis et dolor meus renouatus est.

20 Bohun Psalter and Hours

Pleshey Castle, Essex, *c.* 1361–73 and 1380s
340 x 230 mm

BRITISH LIBRARY, EGERTON 3277

Above:
Psalm 118k, Ark of the Covenant entering the Temple, f. 84 (detail).

Opposite:
Psalm 38, Saul and David, arms of England, Bohun and France, f. 29v

Virtually a royal manuscript, the Egerton Psalter and Hours was made for Humphrey de Bohun (b. 1342, d. 1373), 7th Earl of Hereford, Essex and Northampton, great-grandson of Edward I and father of both Eleanor Bohun, wife of Thomas of Woodstock, youngest son of Edward III, and Mary Bohun, wife of Henry of Bolingbroke, later Henry IV. The manuscript is one of ten surviving devotional books illustrated for successive generations of Bohun earls in the second half of the fourteenth century by a group of artists who worked in the chief Bohun residence at Pleshey Castle, Essex. It is an extraordinary witness to the practice of illumination by artist-retainers of a noble family, perhaps reflecting similar though undocumented productions in other noble families, and even the royal household.

Along with two other large-format Psalters illustrated by the same group of artists (Vienna, ÖNB, cod. 1826* and Oxford, Exeter College, MS 47), the Egerton manuscript contains memorial prayers on behalf of 'Himfridus' (Humphrey), as well as heraldic shields with the arms of the Bohun family and the noble families to which they were related by marriage, including the English royal family. Of the three books, the present manuscript is the one most likely to have been begun for Humphrey 'the seventh' after he acceded to the earldom in 1361 upon the death of his uncle, another Humphrey, the sixth Earl. However, it probably remained unfinished on his death in 1373. The main illustrated pages were painted only in the 1380s, possibly at the command of Humphrey's widow, Joan Fitzalan (d. 1419).

The extensive pictorial programme, in the form of large and small historiated initials with marginal extensions for every Psalm and subdivision of the Hours of the Virgin, consists of two cycles, originally totalling nearly four hundred subjects (some illuminated pages have been excised). The Psalter illustrations are pictorial equivalents of the narratives of the first three Old Testament Books of Kings (in the Vulgate), and those of the Hours of the Virgin are drawn from the New Testament Gospels of Luke and John, and the Acts of the Apostles. In some cases the figural motifs in the adjacent areas respond in subject to the themes in the initial fields, enriching the meaning of the whole. For example, on the page for Psalm 38 (pictured), marking one of the main divisions of the Psalter text, human and hybrid musicians at the outer edges of the initial accompany the chanted text with viol, horn, cymbals and harp (instruments mentioned in the Psalter). The initial field contains four scenes illustrating I Kings 24: Saul entering the cave at Engedi in pursuit of David; David cutting off the end of Saul's garment as he relieves himself; David showing Saul the cut fragment; and David swearing fealty to Saul. The point of the story is that while David might have killed Saul, he chose not to, remaining faithful to his sovereign, the anointed king. The artist introduced a layer of topical meaning by inserting shields with the arms of England, Bohun and France into the initial frame, positioned so as to equate the honourable David with the English King and his loyal Bohun subjects, and the evil yet legitimate overlord Saul with the French ruler, in this way reflecting pictorially the ideological struggles of the Hundred Years War.

For Psalm 118 *Coph* (a subdivision of this long Psalm), the various figural components within and outside the initial frame again respond to each other (pictured). In the initial field, King Solomon accompanies the Ark of the Covenant, represented as a treasure chest, into the Temple of Jerusalem (III Kings 8:6). The treasure theme is parodied in the marginal image of an ape holding a purse as he moves in the same direction as the biblical procession. The ape also holds an owl; the combination of purse and owl would have been recognized in the Middle Ages as a reference to an ironic saying, 'Pay me no less than an ape, an owl and an ass.' Serving as an 'anti-model', the vignette in fact focuses attention on the biblical subject it mimics. The ape-worker, and the bear-scribe below him, may also allude to the artist (artists were called 'apes of nature') and the scribe of this self-same book, as on other pages – for example the bear-scribe 'catchword' at the end of the first gathering (f. 13v), and the entwined ape, bear and lion (the Bohun emblem) adjacent to the initial for Psalm 42 (f. 32v). Humphrey de Bohun may have recognized the ape and the bear as members of his household, and found amusement in their disguised self-representation as playmates of their noble employer. *L.F.S.*

PROVENANCE:

Humphrey de Bohun (b. 1342, d. 1373); (?) Joan Fitzalan (d. 1419); Sir Philip Stephens, Bart (b. 1723, d. 1809); the Rev. Thomas Zouch (b. 1737, d. 1815); William Lowther, 1st Earl of Lonsdale (b. 1757, d. 1844); John Manners, 9th Duke of Rutland (b. 1886, d. 1940); purchased for the nation in 1943.

21 The Princess Joan Psalter

London, *c.* 1400–25; *c.* 1462
275 x 185 mm

BRITISH LIBRARY, ROYAL 2 B. viii

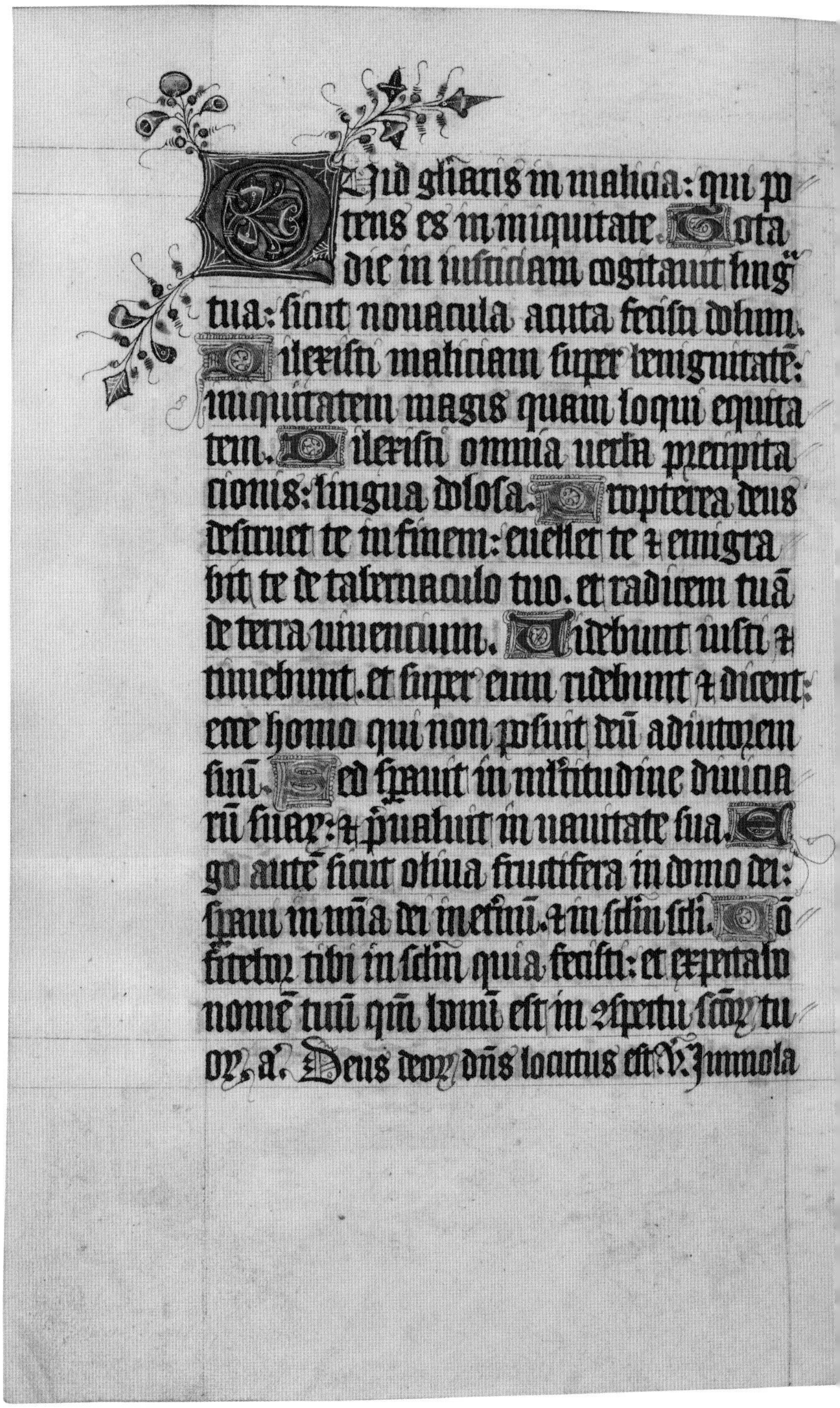

Psalms 51–52, King David and the fool, ff. 53v–54

The Princess Joan Psalter has the honour of being named after a Princess who never owned this exquisite prayerbook. However, the misnomer did not originate without reason. At the front of this volume, preceding the Psalter proper, is John Somer's *Kalendarium*, a series of tables that assist the calculation of eclipses, movable feasts, leap years and the angle of the moon, from 1387 to 1463. Somer (d. after 1409), who was a monk at the Grey Friars' convent in Oxford and may have attended Merton College, dedicated this treatise in 1380 to Princess Joan (d. 1385), mother of Richard II. Of the thirty-four complete or near-complete copies of his text that survive, eight including the Royal manuscript have the prologue that contains this original dedication. The present manuscript, perhaps because it is one of the most lavish books to contain Somer's *Kalendarium*, was long believed to have been the copy presented to Princess Joan.

Close inspection of the manuscript in more recent years has revealed it to comprise two separate parts, each produced long after Princess Joan's death. The earlier part of the volume is a Psalter that contains eight historiated initials at the head of the usual English divisions in the Psalms and a ninth marking the beginning of the Office of the Dead. The artistic style of these accomplished illuminations allies the manuscript with several Psalters that were produced in London in the first quarter of the fifteenth century for a clientele that included members of the royal family. According to Scott (1996), all these volumes appear to have been made in part by or under the supervision of the artist Johannes, who signed his name in additions to a manuscript of tales from Marco Polo's travels and the life of Alexander (Oxford, Bodleian Library, MS Bodley 264; fig. 2.15). One manuscript within this group (Oxford, Bodleian Library, MS Don. D. 85) clearly shared the same pictorial models as the present volume. For example, in their respective initials for Psalm 52 ('The fool said in his heart: There is no God') the fool is depicted as a jester and straddles his stick as if riding a toy horse (pictured). However, while scholarship on the Princess Joan Psalter has assigned this part of the manuscript to a particular artistic grouping, little else has been discovered about the circumstances of its commission.

An inscription at the back of the Psalter may provide a clue to its original owners. In a note added at the end of the volume (f. 150), Mary Courtenay (d. 1572), wife of Sir William Courtenay of Powderham (d. 1535), beseeches an 'especyall good lady'

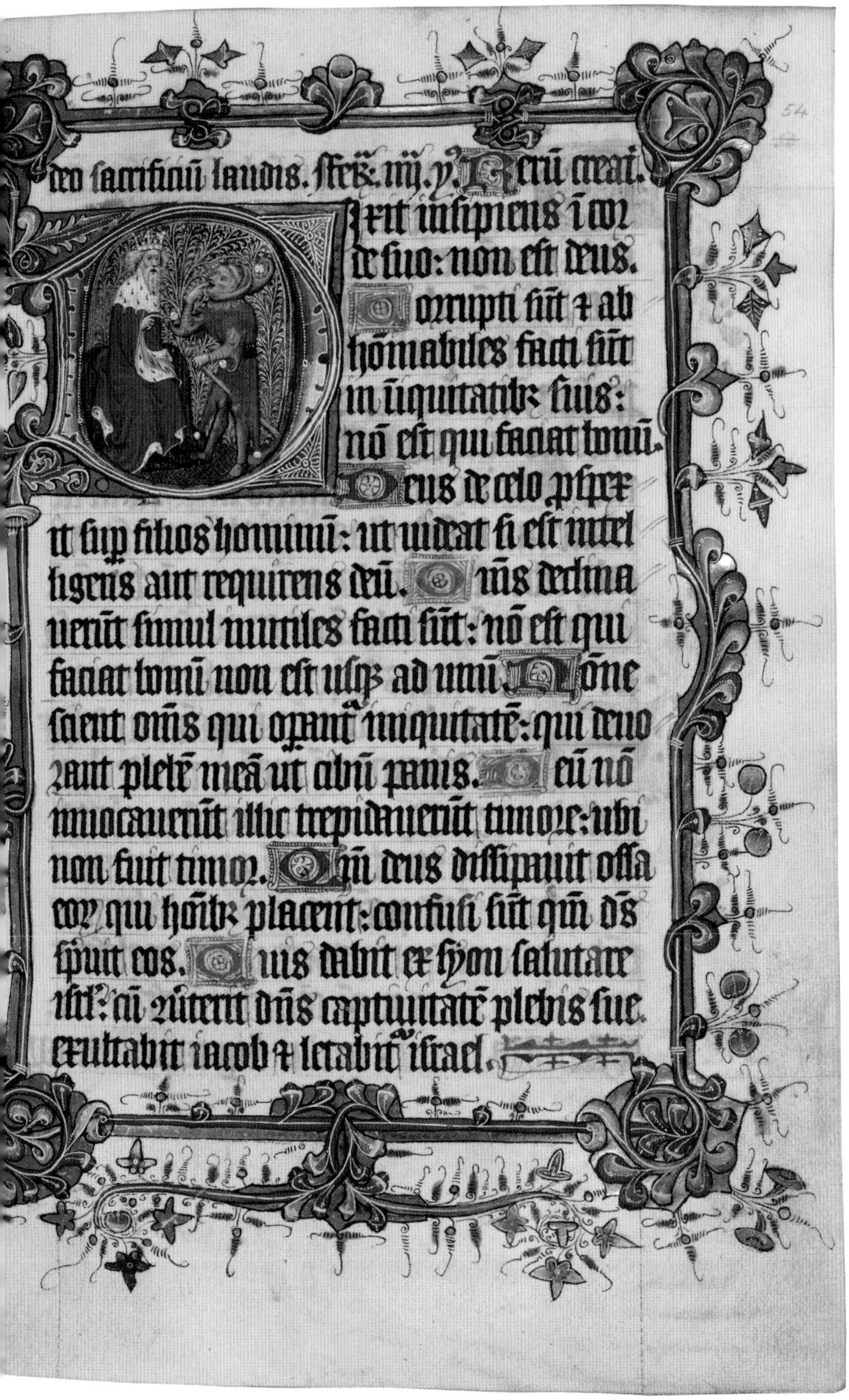

to pray for her soul. This inscription must have been written before 1537, when Mary wed her second husband, Sir Anthony Kingston (d. 1556). It is credible that the manuscript was made for a member of the wealthy Courtenay family. At least one of its members, Richard Courtenay (d. 1415), Bishop of Norwich, is known to have been an avid book collector and purchased numerous luxurious Parisian manuscripts (Rouse and Rouse 2000).

Unfortunately, a later alteration to the volume prevents us from being sure of the identity of its original owner. Unlike most contemporary Psalters that survive, the Princess Joan Psalter now lacks a calendar. This unusual omission is almost certainly the result of the calendar having been removed from the volume at a later date. A significant consequence of this removal is the volume's present lack of such records of family births and deaths as are commonly found in Psalters. Given the commemorative value of such records, it seems unlikely that the calendar was extracted while the manuscript was in the possession of the Courtenay family.

As a replacement for the original calendar, a later owner of the manuscript added to it a copy of John Somer's *Kalendarium.* This copy of the *Kalendarium* may be dated to *c.* 1462, based upon its inclusion of tables that extend Somer's calculations up to 1519 – that is, beyond their original limit of 1463 (Mooney 1998). Because these later calculations would also have been obsolete by the time the *Kalendarium* was probably bound with the Psalter, this text may have been added purely for its textual interest and the royal cachet lent by its dedication to Princess Joan.

The only obit recorded in the appended calendar is for 'Johannes Turk' (f. 9), probably John Turke (d. *c.* 1561), a London bookseller and warden of the Company of Stationers in 1558. With his skills as a stationer, Turke may have been the person responsible for binding this item into the Psalter. It is unknown how or when the manuscript arrived in the Royal collection, but the reference to 'Johanne Principesse Wallie' on its opening page may have recommended it as a suitable gift from a subject eager to earn the favour of the reigning king or queen. *S.D.*

PROVENANCE:

Mary Courtenay (d. 1572), second wife of Sir William Courtenay of Powderham (d. 1535); John Turke (d. *c.* 1561).

22 *Bible historiale*: Genesis to the Apocalypse

Paris, 1356 (vol. 1), 1357 (vol. 2)
390 x 295 mm

BRITISH LIBRARY, ROYAL 17 E. vii

Above:
Sacrifice of Isaac, vol. 1, f. 17v

Opposite:
Solomon, four-part miniature, vol. 2, f. 1

This large book, now bound in two volumes, contains the Bible in French in the version known as the *Bible historiale* or, according to the rubric at the beginning of the first volume, *Histoires escolastres.* It is an example of the *Bible historiale completée moyenne*, in Berger's terminology (Berger 1884; Komada 2000). This work started as a French translation of the Latin *Historia scholastica*, a biblical paraphrase and commentary that was compiled by Petrus Comestor (Pierre 'le Mangeur', d. 1178), so called because of his insatiable appetite for consuming the content of books. The translator, Guyart des Moulins, canon and (from 1297) dean of St Pierre at Aire-sur-la-Lys, Artois, worked from June 1291 to February 1295. Other texts were subsequently added to Guyart's work. Initially, for example, the biblical book of Job was represented in the *Bible historiale* by a short summary (called 'le petit Job'). In volumes like the present one a much longer version ('le grand Job') was added. The most extensive version of the text was termed the *Grande Bible historiale complétée* by Berger. The *Bible historiale* was costly to produce because of its large size and profuse decoration, but popular in the collections of Francophone royal and noble patrons, especially from the middle of the fourteenth century onwards.

Guyart explains the purpose of the *Bible historiale* in his preface as 'pour faire laies personnes entendre les hystoires des escriptures anciennes' (to enable lay people to understand the stories of the ancient Scriptures). This opening text is followed by two further prefaces, derived from the *Historia scholastica*: 'A honnorable pere …' (directed to William, Archbishop of Sens) and 'En palais de roy et d'empereur …' (There are four mansions that appertain to the palace of king and emperor…) – an interesting metaphor. Unlike Latin Bibles, the vast majority of which were unillustrated, most *Bibles historiales* had images throughout. Although Guyart does not mention images explicitly, it is likely that they accompanied his translation from the start.

Each biblical book in this manuscript opens with a one-column miniature, large illuminated initial and partial decorative border. Additionally, unlike any Bible (but compare cat. no. 137), the manuscript begins with a large miniature of the Trinity surrounded by the four Evangelists above the opening of the preface. In the early pages of Genesis the miniatures are numerous – there are eighteen – but they become less common after Cain's murder of Abel (vol. 1, f. 9v). The total in the entire book is eighty-nine. The one-column miniatures are very close in style and technique to the richly gilded and semi-grisaille frontispiece of the Trinity. The text is written throughout by one scribe, it would seem, in 1356 (the date in the first volume) and 1357 (the date in an acrostic poem at the end of the Apocalypse in the second volume).

The only other large miniature marks the beginning of Proverbs and the second volume (pictured). It is organized in four compartments. At the top left Solomon, holding a disciplinary birch, teaches his son Rehoboam (Proverbs teaches wisdom and discipline, according to its opening words). Below, to the left, is the Judgement of Solomon, with the two women kneeling before the King. The third and fourth images seem to read upwards. Below are three sons disputing their father's inheritance before Solomon. Above, two shoot arrows at their father's corpse, while one declines Solomon's command and kneels before him, indicating that this claimant is the true heir. This latter narrative is from a separate medieval compilation, the *Gesta Romanorum*, not the Bible, but is quite frequently found in *Bibles historiales.* The viewing pattern, down in the left column and then up in the right column, is unusual, and the scenes appear to be in disorder. The book's layout in three narrow columns per page is also unusual and seems inconsistent with the layout of this frontispiece, although not that of the Trinity in the first volume.

The miniatures are attributed to the Master of the Bible of Jean de Sy, who worked for both John the Good and Charles V. This *Bible historiale*, seemingly made for Charles V, makes an intriguing comparison with the book made for his father, John the Good, which was captured at Poitiers in 1356 (cat. no. 137). It is not clear how this French royal book found its way to England; probably it was acquired by Thomas Langton, who acted as a royal agent in France for both Edward IV and Richard III, and was promoted by Henry VII. It was three centuries after its manufacture that it became an English Royal book under Charles II. *J.L.*

PROVENANCE:

Charles V of France; Thomas Langton (d. 1501), Bishop of Winchester; John Theyer (d. 1673); Charles II.

23 The 'Great Bible'

London, *c.* 1410–15
630 x 430 mm

BRITISH LIBRARY, ROYAL 1 E. ix

Above:
Jerome giving a book to a boy, f. 2 (detail).

Opposite:
Hannah at prayer blessed by the high priest Eli, and Elkanah accompanied by Peninah and a group of their children, f. 64

Only one Bible is referred to as the *Biblia magna* (Great Bible) in the 1535 list of books at Richmond Palace, the oldest surviving list of manuscripts in the Old Royal library. Very likely this entry describes the present manuscript, the largest Bible in the Royal collection. As Stratford has suggested, the exceptional size of the Royal manuscript may help to trace its earlier provenance. A reference to a *magna Biblia* appears twice in the last will of Henry V, written in June 1421. This manuscript must have had a special value to the King because it was the only book precisely identified in his testament and the only one for which an individual disposition was made. The Big Bible, said to have belonged to Henry IV, the King's father, was given over to the custody of the newly founded Bridgettine monastery at Syon, but meant to be returned to Henry V's unborn successor (Stratford 1994). If the present manuscript was indeed that of Henry IV, its size would have made it an appropriate lectern Bible, first for the Royal Chapel and later for Syon Abbey.

The Great Bible is one of very few biblical manuscripts that are extensively illustrated to survive from the late Middle Ages. Its 143 historiated initials and floral borders mark every important text division. In addition to a biblical cycle at the beginning of the books, each prologue opens with an image of St Jerome, translator of the Bible, surrounded by books in his study, or even preparing for an evening reading in his bedchamber (pictured above).

Stylistically the Great Bible is one of the manuscripts that opened a new chapter in the history of English illumination. The introduction to England of the new, more naturalistic style that emerged in Europe shortly before 1400 and was characterized by soft modelling and elegant figures wearing fluid, three-dimensional robes was the result of foreign influence. In the early research literature this influence was explained in terms of the presence of Bohemian artists in the entourage of Anne of Bohemia, who married Richard II in 1382, and the Great Bible was considered Richard II's commission. More recently the importance of Dutch and Flemish artists working in London has emerged as crucial for the adoption of the new style.

The Great Bible is clearly a collaborative achievement. Between eight and eleven artists are thought to have contributed to its decoration. The iconography and style suggest their origin in the Low Countries, possibly in Bruges (Wright 1986). A combination of French (f. 229) and Low German or perhaps Dutch (ff. 126v, 145) inscriptions seems to confirm this assumption. The best miniatures in the manuscript have been attributed alternatively to Herman Scheerre, an illuminator of German or Netherlandish origin who worked in London *c.* 1405–22 (Kuhn 1940), the Master of the Great Cowchers of the Duchy of Lancaster of 1402–07 (Wright 1986) and the painter (Hand A) of the Carmelite Missal (Scott 1996).

Herman Scheerre's contribution to the illumination of the Great Bible should be reconsidered, on both documentary and artistic grounds. The manuscript is related to him by the inscription *Omnia levia sunt amanti* (All is easy for one who loves) that is written in the background of a miniature of Joel talking to God (f. 229). The same words are inscribed in the manuscript signed with his name (Additional 16998) and in three other books (The Neville Hours, Berkeley Castle; cat. no. 25; and Oxford, Bodleian Library, MS lat. liturg. f. 2). Since the miniatures where the words appear are not all by the same hand, the phrase should be considered a workshop motto of this artist rather than a personal one. Given the scale of the task, it seems plausible that Herman supervised the work on the Great Bible and that only some of the miniatures, such as the opening portrait of Jerome (pictured), were painted by him.

A miniature at the beginning of 1 Kings (1 Samuel), which depicts the story of Elkanah and his two wives, the fertile Peninah and the childless Hannah who comes to the Temple to pray for a son, is a good example of the style of Scheerre's workshop (pictured). Comparable to Herman's autograph paintings in a prayerbook (Additional 16998) and in the Missal of Bishop Henry Chichele (London, Lambeth Palace Library, MS 69), this miniature shows similar slim human figures arranged in a shallow but consistent space. Their pale, oval faces lack the grey-greenish underpaint used by the Carmelite Missal Master. Instead, they are all characterized by a somewhat sad expression that is typical of figures in manuscripts illuminated by Scheerre. *J. F.*

PROVENANCE:

Henry IV (?); Henry V (?); Syon Abbey (?); Henry VI (?); Henry VIII.

liber
regum

24 *Bible historiale*: Genesis to the Psalms

Clairefontaine and Paris, 1411
445 x 340 mm

BRITISH LIBRARY, ROYAL 19 D. iii, vol. 1

This *Grande Bible historiale complétée* is an example of the developed version of the text, as defined by Berger (1884) and Komada (2000) (see also cat. no. 22). It is divided, as is usually the case, into two volumes, with the Psalter ending the first volume and Proverbs beginning the second (see cat. no. 74 for vol. 2 of this book). There are large frontispiece images to both volumes and fifty-four further images in the first volume. Textually this set is of importance for its inclusion of some elements (a Life of Julian the Apostate, *Hystoires apocrifes* of the True Cross, a Life of Pilate, and a Life of Judas) translated with the *Bible historiale* by Guyart des Moulins, but not preserved elsewhere (vol. 2, ff. 552v–558). Another unusual feature of this *Bible historiale* is the inclusion of what is entitled a 'New prologue [to the Psalms, on f. 256] by Brother Jean de Blois of the Augustinian Order, master in theology at Paris'. Its presence may be connected to the fact that the scribe, Thomas du Val, identifies himself in the colophon as an Augustinian, in recording the completion of the writing of the book in 1411 (see cat. no. 74).

After an 'author/translator portrait' of Guyart des Moulins (f. 1) there is a magnificent image of God as Creator (f. 3, pictured). God is clad in a white tunic decorated with gold sunbursts. He wields a pair of dividers, often mistakenly said to be compasses, to measure the cosmos. (Compasses are shown in cat. no. 22, f. 3.) His halo is rendered as long gold rays, with the cruciform rays extending a little further than the rest. Behind God is a red mandorla formed entirely of seraphim. Above is a blue heaven, formed entirely of blue angels, perhaps representing one of the other angelic orders. Between heaven above and earth beneath is a white void. The whole is framed by scrolling acanthus leaves, with very naturalistic plants, especially at the left, and small red and blue medallions formed of red and blue angels. A diminutive cross-nimbed figure (Christ) is located in the upper part of the right-hand border. This highly unusual image is based on the opening words of the accompanying texts, which consist of the biblical quotation, a brief interpretative comment, and its explanatory gloss :

> In the beginning God created heaven, and earth (Genesis 1:1). In the beginning was the Son and the Son was the beginning by whom and with whom God created the world … (Gloss) Theologians say that … there are three heavens of differing colours. The first is the colour of crystal. The second is of white colour like snow. And the third is of red colour like fire …and is the empyrean heaven, and is the highest.

The red and white heavens are conspicuous. Presumably the blue heaven is seen through the crystal. The image shows a knowledge of and interest in Augustinian theology and exegesis, appropriate to the manuscript's production in an Augustinian context. The principal artist has been identified as the Egerton Master (on this artist see cat. no. 144).

The anointing of Solomon (f. 144v), the image that opens 3 Kings (1 Kings in the King James Bible) is treated in contemporary, early fifteenth-century terms, with Zadok the priest, dressed as a bishop, anointing Solomon as King (3 Kings 1:39), in a clear echo of the rite of anointing of the king of France by the archbishop of Reims. Taken together with the possible presence of the Dauphin of France in the opening image of the second volume, it would not be surprising to discover that this was a royal book. Yet it is striking how different it is in its choice of imagery from a royal *Bible historiale* of a generation earlier, for example, in its depiction of God as Creator to open the volume, rather than with an image of the Trinity (compare cat. no. 22). This emphasizes the extent to which variety is present even in situations in which we might expect to find uniformity. *J.L.*

PROVENANCE:
Henry VIII (?); Charles II.

Opposite:
God creates heaven and earth, vol. 1, f. 3

MVSEVM
BRITAN
NICVM

25 The Beaufort/Beauchamp Hours

London, between *c.* 1440 and 1443; (additions) Bruges and London (?), 1401–15
215 x 150 mm

BRITISH LIBRARY, ROYAL 2 A. xviii

This Book of Hours is a complex book. Its core was probably made in a London workshop of William Abell (Alexander 1972) and intended for Margaret Beauchamp, while she was married to her second husband John Beaufort (d. 1444). Although at heart typical of commercially produced manuscripts, Margaret's prayerbook is distinctive on account of several important additions made to it.

The calendar that precedes the prayers and lists the saints' days and major feasts of the year has been transformed into a family chronicle. First, Margaret Beauchamp recorded some important events of her life and of her earlier family history, such as the death of her husband and the birth of her daughter in 1443. Later, two different scribes added notes of numerous events concerning the reign of Henry VII, doubtless at the instigation of Margaret's daughter and the King's mother, Margaret Beaufort. Although an illustrated Primer is listed among the books Margaret bequeathed to her chapel at Westminster Abbey, it is more likely that after her death the Royal manuscript remained in private hands, perhaps with the St John family. Thirty years later further additions were made to the calendar. Apart from royal necrologies, they include the obit of Elisabeth Lucar, daughter of the Bristol merchant Paul Withypoll, connected to the St Johns (Backhouse 2007). The date of the incorporation of the manuscript into the Royal collection is unrecorded.

Artistically, the most spectacular additions to the volume are the twenty-two leaves bearing prayers, images of saints and the *Annunciation* that now form its magnificent opening (pictured). How they came to be incorporated into Margaret Beauchamp's Hours is a complicated tale. It is now generally agreed that they originally formed part of another distinct volume and that this manuscript was commissioned by John Beaufort (d. 1410) and Margaret Holland (d. 1439), the parents of Margaret Beauchamp's husband, John. It is therefore they who are portrayed in adoration of the *Annunciation*. The identity of the original owner as John Beaufort is supported by the prayer to St Christopher (f. 12), which is addressed to the Saint by a man whose name begins with a 'J'. Rickert (1962) identified the core remains of Beaufort's manuscript in a Psalter now in Rennes (Bibliothèque Municipale, MS 22). Later owned by Anne of York (b. 1439, d. 1476), sister of Edward IV, the Rennes Psalter may have come to her from her husband Henry Holland (d. 1475), Duke of Exeter. As Rogers (1982) has demonstrated, an inscription reading 'Huntyngton' in the Rennes Psalter refers to Henry's father John Holland (d. 1447). (John was Margaret Holland's cousin.) It is likely that the original manuscript was dismembered after John Beaufort the elder's death. The core of the Psalter remained with his widow Margaret, who added several prayers in the feminine form (Rennes MS 22, ff. 23–26), while the prefatory prayers and illustrations passed to their son John and were later incorporated in his wife's Book of Hours.

The bifolium on which the *Annunciation* with the donor portraits is included is a separate unit within the Royal manuscript. Smaller in size, and comprising text written by a scribe different from the one responsible for the rest of the prayers and Psalms in both the Royal and the Rennes manuscripts, it was doubtless adapted to fit the Rennes Psalter. The *Annunciation* itself stands out from the rest of the preliminary miniatures of the Royal manuscript in its exceptional beauty. Because the motto *Omnia levia sunt amanti: si quis amat non laborat. de daer* (All is easy for one who loves: he who loves toils not), associated with Herman Scheerre's workshop, is inscribed on the Virgin's *prie-dieu* (see cat. no. 23), the Royal miniature has been attributed by some scholars to this artist (Kuhn 1940). This attribution has, however, been rejected by other researchers who consider the refined execution of the *Annunciation* superior in quality to Scheerre's signed miniatures (see Rickert 1962; Scott 1996).

The series of images of saints that precede the *Annunciation* was painted by a different artist, who is named after this manuscript the Master of the Beaufort Saints. His style and iconography indicate that he was trained in the artistic milieu of Bruges (Smeyers and Vertongen 1992). Each miniature painted by this artist is pasted into the Royal manuscript and faces a prayer addressed to the saint depicted; both texts and images are embellished with typical English border decoration. Like the image of St George, reproduced overleaf, each miniature has inscribed above it the saint's name. These inscriptions were clearly inserted to assist the artists responsible for the completion of the book. All this evidence suggests that the Master of the Beaufort Saints may never have left his homeland and that his illuminations were imported into England as separate leaves. Vertongen (1995) has demonstrated that another work attributed to this artist, a Book of Hours now in Oxford (Bodleian Library, MS lat. liturg. f. 2), was produced in Bruges for export to England, and only adapted there in the workshop of Herman Scheerre for a new English owner. *J.F.*

PROVENANCE:
Margaret Beauchamp (b. 1405/6, d. 1482); Lady Margaret Beaufort (b. 1443, d. 1509).

Opposite:
The Annunciation, f. 23v

St George, ff. 5v–6

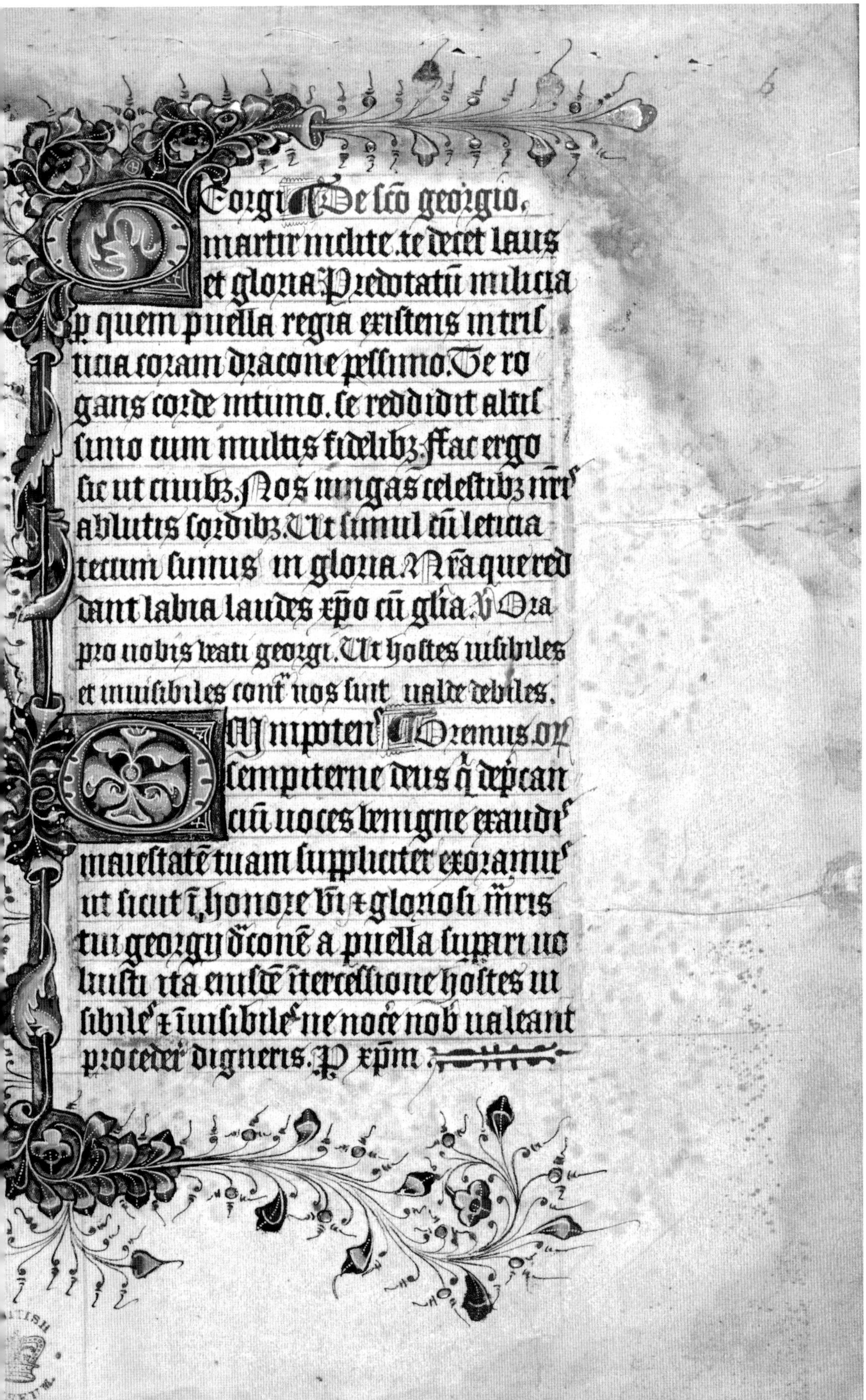
Georgi De sco georgio.
Georgi martir inclite te decet laus
et gloria Predotatu milicia
p quem puella regia existens in tris
ticia coram dracone pessimo Te ro
gans corde intimo se reddidit altis
simo cum multis fidelibz ffac ergo
sic ut ciuibz Nos iungas celestibz nris
ablutis sordibz Ut simul cu leticia
tecum simus in gloria Nra que red
dant labia laudes xpo cu glia V Ora
pro nobis beati georgi. Ut hostes uisibiles
et inuisibiles cont nos sint ualde debiles.
Omnipotens Oremus. Om
nipotens sempiterne deus q deprecan
ciu uoces benigne exaudis
maiestate tuam suppliciter exoramus
ut sicut i honore bi et gloriosi mris
tui georgii dcone a puella superari uo
luisti ita eius tue itercessione hostes ui
sibiles et inuisibiles ne nocere nob ualeant
procedere digneris. P xpm.

26 Bedford Psalter and Hours

London, between 1414 and 1422
450 x 275 mm

BRITISH LIBRARY, ADDITIONAL 42131

Above:
Marriage of David and Michal, f. 151v (detail)
Opposite:
Psalm 1, David anointed by Samuel and assisted by Jesse; and the Tree of Jesse, f. 73

This manuscript, which combines the texts of a Book of Hours with those of a Psalter, is not a typical portable prayerbook intended for private devotion, but a large and impressive object possibly made for display and ostentation during public liturgical celebrations. Its decoration includes eighteen scenes from the lives of Christ and David, each depicted at the beginning of a major division in the Psalms or of a prayer, and more than 280 small initials mostly containing portrait-like heads of kings, queens, monks, ordinary men and saintly figures. Some of the figures are related to the text, and some – like Job, David and apparently the poet John Gower – are identified by inscriptions. The decoration of every page with foliate bar-borders, painted initials and line-fillers further contributes to the book's exceptionally sumptuous appearance. Two inscriptions, 'Herman your meke servant' (f. 124) and 'I am Herman your owne servant' (f. 232v) suggest an association of the manuscript with the London-based artist Herman Scheerre (see cat. nos. 23, 25 and 27). Close examination of the illuminations has, however, revealed them to be the collaborative work of several different artists (Turner 1962, Scott 1996).

The Bedford Psalter and Hours is one of only two extant manuscripts made in England for the third son of Henry IV, John, Duke of Bedford, who is otherwise known for his patronage of several lavish books from Parisian workshops (see cat. no. 142) and the acquisition of the French royal library. (His other English manuscript is a Breviary, now also in the British Library [Additional 74755]). As suggested by the supplication 'I pray god save the Duke of Bedford', which is inscribed in the line-ending on f. 21, the present manuscript must have been illuminated after John had received his ducal title in 1414. Bedford's heraldic arms, motto (*pur souffrir*), crest with the royal leopard, and two badges of an eagle and a black yale are depicted on the first page of the Psalter. The omission from this series of devices of both the tree-root badge, adopted by the Duke after 1422 when he became Regent of France, and the arms of Anne of Burgundy, whom he married in 1423, suggests that the book was completed before these events (Stratford 1987).

Turner (1962) noted that the depiction of the marriage of David and Michal, daughter of Saul, which occurs in the book at the beginning of Psalm 80 (pictured), is uncommon in the illustrative tradition of the Psalms, and he suggested that it might refer to the wedding of Catherine of France and Henry V, Bedford's brother, which took place in 1420. Another unusual scene was placed at the beginning of the Psalter. If included in pictorial cycles, the illustration of Samuel anointing David, son of Jesse, as the King of Israel was almost always associated with Psalm 26. It is noteworthy that a century earlier both these uncommon scenes were included in another English Psalter, now in Munich (Bayerische Staatsbibliothek, cod. gall. 16), which may have been offered to Isabel of France as a gift to commemorate her marriage to Edward II and coronation in 1308.

The imagery of the *Beatus* page in Bedford's manuscript was given a truly royal character (pictured). The border was transformed into the *Tree of Jesse*, which displayed the genealogical line from King David's father to the Virgin Mary, with all the ancestors of the Virgin depicted as kings, in a possible echo of a similar inhabited border in Philippa of Hainault's Psalter (see cat. no. 19). In the right-hand margin, four of these Old Testament monarchs hold sprouting branches that encircle Bedford's arms and badges and visually assimilate the Duke's insignia into the biblical royal imagery. A visual assimilation may have also influenced the choice of the image in the *Beatus* initial. The Anointing of David was considered an archetype of the unction of a king and was referred to as such in the liturgy of French royal coronations. Its illustration in Bedford's Psalter was perhaps intended as another visual allusion to Henry V, whom the Treaty of Troyes (1420) recognized as heir to the French throne. As David was chosen to succeed Saul by Samuel's unction, so Henry was designated by the Treaty to receive the Crown of France after the death of Charles VI, whose daughter he had married.

The arms of William Catesby (d. 1485) that are added to the lower margin of the *Beatus* page and to those of other major divisions of the Hours and Psalter reveal the manuscript's later history. As an executor of the last will of Anthony Woodville, 2nd Earl Rivers, the son of Bedford's second wife Jacquetta of Luxemburg, Catesby must have taken possession of the book after Woodville's execution in 1483. *J.F.*

PROVENANCE:

John, Duke of Bedford (b. 1389, d. 1435); Jacquetta of Luxemburg (b. 1415/16, d. 1472); Anthony Woodville (b. *c.*1440, d. 1483) and Mary Lewis, his wife; William Catesby (b. *c.* 1446, d. 1485); Edward Weld (b. 1741, d. 1775) and Thomas Weld (b. 1750, d. 1810) of Lulworth Castle; purchased for the nation in 1929.

Beatus vir qui
non abiit i con
silio impiorũ:
et in via pecca
torum non ste
tit. et in cathed
pestilencie non
sedit. Sed in
lege domini voluntas eius: et in lege e9
meditabitur die ac nocte. Et erit tan
q̃m lignum quod plantatum est secus
decursus aquarum: quod fructũ suum
dabit in tempore suo. Et folium eius
non defluet: et omnia quecumq3 faciet
prosperabuntur. Non sic impij non
sic: sed tanquam pulvis quem proicit
ventus a facie terre. Ideo non resur
gunt impij in iudicio: neq3 pctores in

27 The Hours of Catherine of France

London (?), between 1421 and 1437
120 x 80 mm

BRITISH LIBRARY, ADDITIONAL 65100

This little Book of Hours belonged to Catherine of France, Queen consort of Henry V and the youngest daughter of Charles VI of France. Four of its pages have her heraldic arms painted in their lower borders. The style of the manuscript's illumination suggests that Catherine's prayerbook must have been made not long after 1421, when the newly-married royal couple arrived in England. Two English artists painted its fifteen miniatures, all but one of which were executed on separate leaves; these miniatures face each of the four Gospel excerpts, each of the eight divisions of the Hours of the Virgin, and the opening texts of the Penitential Psalms, Office of the Dead and Commemoration of the Souls (the sixteenth miniature originally placed at the beginning of the Hours of the Cross has been excised). The principal artist was responsible for only one miniature, the *Annunciation* facing the opening of Matins (f. 27v, pictured). His refined style is characterized by a pale green modelling of human flesh and somewhat serious facial expressions, both features reminiscent of the art of Herman Scheerre (see cat. nos. 23, 25 and 26). The other illuminations were painted by an assistant in a closely related, but slightly cruder style. The same workshop appears to have decorated other manuscripts for patrons from the English royal circle, including a Book of Hours for Sir John Cornwall and his wife Elizabeth (d. 1425), sister of Henry IV (Cambridge, Trinity College, MS B. 11.7; see Rogers 1994), and the *Sanctilogium Salvatoris* given to Henry V's Bridgettine foundation at Syon by his sister-in-law Margaret (d. 1439), Duchess of Clarence (Karlsruhe, Badische Landesbibliothek, MS Skt. Georgen 12; see Scott 1996).

Clearly intended for the private use of the Queen, Catherine's prayerbook is distinctive for its French character, despite having been illuminated by English artists. The calendar was written in French in three alternating colours, red, blue and gold, following the French practice, and was composed for the use of Paris, the liturgical use that was followed by the French royal chapel, as well as in Paris more generally. The selection of antiphons, hymns and readings, which in Books of Hours reflect local devotional habits, is also characteristic of those made in the French capital. The French liturgical content of Catherine's Hours is strengthened by the strikingly French iconography of its illuminations. For example, the Gospel excerpts at the beginning of the book are illustrated by portraits of the four Evangelists, a feature commonly included in Continental books, but unknown in English ones. As Scott (1996) has observed, the illustrations at the beginning of the canonical hours such as the *Annunciation to the Shepherds* (Terce), *Adoration of the Magi* (Sext), *Presentation in the Temple* (None), *Coronation of the Virgin* (Compline), and especially the unusual *Return from the Flight into Egypt* (Vespers), and a peculiar redaction of *David's prayer* in the Penitential Psalms – where the king is emerging from a hole in the ground – seem to follow not only the iconography but also the compositions of the corresponding miniatures in a more lavish Book of Hours illuminated *c.* 1415 in Paris by a follower of the Boucicault Master (Paris, Bibliothèque Mazarine, MS 469; fig. 2.9). The Mazarine Hours includes a motto of Catherine's older brother, Louis of Guyenne (d. 1415), Dauphin of France, and may have been intended as a gift to their father, Charles VI, whose arms were also depicted in the book (Villela-Petit 2001). While still unfinished, the Mazarine manuscript found its way to England, where several leaves were replaced. A prayer to the Holy Face with an image was added at the beginning of the volume; and its decoration was completed with several initials, border details and two miniatures (ff. 126v, 141) that appear to have been painted in the same workshop that illuminated the Hours of Catherine of France. It is possible that the Mazarine Hours was brought to England by Catherine and served as inspiration for the artist who decorated her own prayerbook. Two other manuscripts that formerly belonged to Catherine's brother Louis de Guyenne – his Psalter (cat. no. 141) and perhaps also his *Life of St Louis* (cat. no. 67) – were also brought to England and adapted for the use of Catherine's son, the future Henry VI.

As the Queen's private prayerbook, the Hours of Catherine of France was never incorporated into the royal library. The sixteenth-century ownership inscriptions of two unidentified Welshmen, Robert ap Owen and William Owen, may suggest that the manuscript passed to some Welsh relatives of Owen Tudor (d. 1461), whom Catherine secretly married after the death of Henry V. In the eighteenth century the book was still kept near the Welsh border, in the chapel of Blackbrook in Orell. *J.F.*

PROVENANCE:

Catherine of France (d. 1437); Robert ap Owen; William Owen; Chapel of Blackbrook, Orell; Upholland College, Lancashire; acquired for the nation in 1987.

The Annunciation, ff. 27v–28 (actual size)

28 The Hours of Elizabeth the Queen

London, *c.* 1420–30
210 x 150 mm

BRITISH LIBRARY, ADDITIONAL 50001

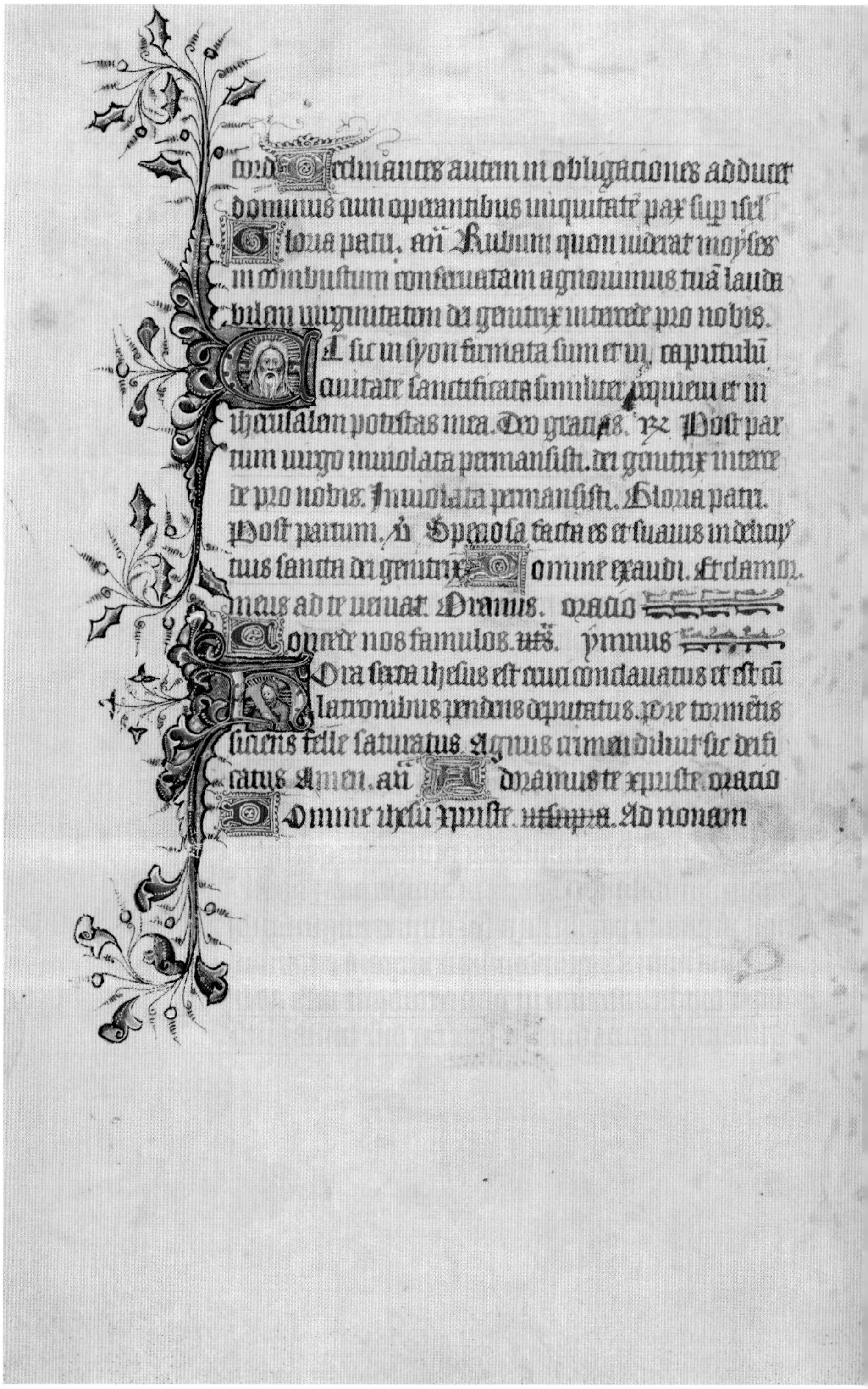

The Crucifixion, ff. 21v–22

In the fifteenth century the increased diversity of devotional books, coupled with the growth of the commercial book trade, meant that lay people had a broad variety of prayerbooks from which to choose. The most popular of these formats was the Book of Hours, or *Horae*, which typically contained a calendar of feast days, a series of prayers to be recited at the eight canonical hours of the day, suffrages (prayers to saints) and additional prayers tailored to the owner's preferences. With its often elaborate pictorial embellishment, the Book of Hours was not only a personalized devotional book but also an object that allowed its owner to exhibit his or her wealth.

This sense of wealth is on show in the Hours of Elizabeth the Queen, a book that has frequently been described as the most lavish Book of Hours produced in fifteenth-century England. The text itself is unusually rich, with the Hours of the Virgin interleaved with the Hours of the Cross, followed by the Penitential Psalms, the Hours of the Passion, the Office of the Dead, the Commendation of Souls, a Gospel Sequence and various prayers to the Virgin. The manuscript also flaunts eighteen half-page miniatures, four small miniatures, a staggering 423 historiated or inhabited initials, and roundels depicting the signs of the zodiac and Labours of the Month to adorn the calendar. Sheer abundance of imagery is not the only reason why this manuscript has been the subject of so much praise; with its saturated hues, dynamic compositions, expressive characters and vividly coloured foliate decoration, the book is alive with technicolor action.

The artists of this illustrative cycle demonstrate that within the standardized programmes required for Books of Hours there was opportunity for experimentation. Marks and Morgan (1981) point to the unique inclusion of a scene depicting the Last Supper before Matins (f. 7). Typically, for a *Horae* containing the Hours of the Virgin illustrated by a Passion cycle, the first two hours would include scenes from Christ's infancy. In the present manuscript, however, the entire pictorial programme accompanying the Hours of the Virgin is given over to a Passion Cycle. Orr (1989) hypothesized that this iconographic deviation might have originated in the patron's personal devotion to Christ's Passion. The three different depictions of the Crucifixion that appear in the volume

seem to support this observation. As in many of the images in this manuscript, the artist of the first *Crucifixion* (f. 22, pictured) heightened its pathos through the addition of narrative detail: Mary is shown as a mourning mother who is comforted by an embrace and the gentle clasp of a hand. This sort of nuance invests iconic images with a delicate sentimentality.

A question frequently asked by scholars who have addressed this manuscript is to what extent it demonstrates foreign influence. Contributions by illuminators from the Low Countries and France have often been surmised in instances where a manuscript produced in England shows aesthetic excellence. For example, Orr (1995) argues convincingly for the involvement of a Netherlandish artist from the Gold Scrolls Group, although this artist contributed only a small fraction of the illumination in this volume, whereas an English artist – possibly Johannes (see cat. no. 21) – provided the majority of its major illustrations. Still, the involvement of a Netherlandish illuminator is typical for a manuscript of this quality and would indicate the desirability of foreign artists amongst patrons willing to spend lavish amounts on luxury books.

Whoever the original owner of this manuscript was, she or he laid out an enormous investment for it to be made. Towards the end of the volume is an erased prayer for the soul of Cecily (d. 1450), Duchess of Warwick (f. 152). Although she may have been too young when the manuscript was made to be its original owner, the book was probably made for a member of her family, one of the most powerful in fifteenth-century England. Her father, Richard Neville (d. 1460), 1st Earl of Salisbury, who was consolidating his power and wealth in the period of the manuscript's production, is a possible candidate. The current name for the volume, however, derives from the most famous person associated with it, Elizabeth of York, daughter of Edward IV and Queen of Henry VII. On the lower margin of the page featuring the manuscript's first depiction of the Crucifixion, Elizabeth inscribed her name, 'Elisabeth the quene' (f. 22). *S.D.*

PROVENANCE:

Cecily, Duchess of Warwick (d. 1450); (?) Elizabeth of York, wife of Henry VII; Edward Stafford (d. 1521), Duke of Buckingham; Bertram, 4th Earl of Ashburnham (d. 1878); Henry Yates Thompson (d. 1928); C.W. Dyson Perrins (d. 1958); acquired for the nation in 1958.

29 Jean Galopes, *Le Livre doré des meditations de la vie de Nostre Seigneur Jésus Christ*

(French translation of Pseudo-Bonaventure, *Meditationes vitae Christi*)

Paris (?), *c.* 1420–22
260 x 185 mm

BRITISH LIBRARY, ROYAL 20 B. iv

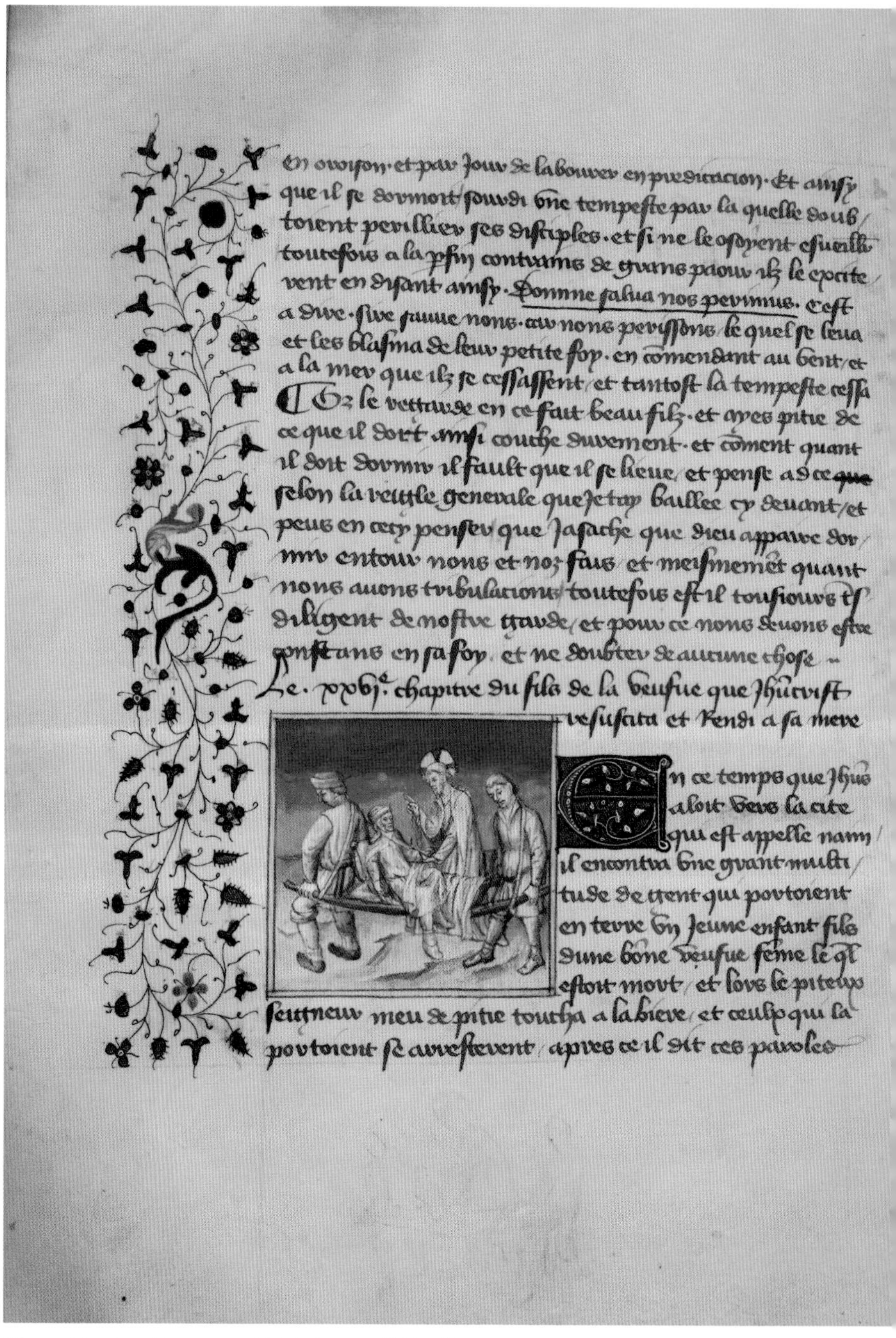

Christ raising the widow's son and Christ healing, ff. 61v–62

The *Meditationes vitae Christi* (Meditations on the Life of Christ) was a popular devotional text of the late Middle Ages. Although attributed to St Bonaventure, the treatise was in fact compiled by another Franciscan author in the fourteenth century who has so far remained unidentified. Its first translation into French was composed by Jean Galopes (d. 1435), Dean of St Louis's of La Saussay (in the diocese of Évreux) and chaplain to Henry V. Galopes must have undertaken the work on his *Livre doré* after the Treaty of Troyes had been signed in 1420 and the English regency in France proclaimed. In his prologue the author addresses Henry V as the heir and Regent of France and specifies that his translation was made at the instigation of the English King.

Henry's choice of this Franciscan text may have been motivated by his personal piety and interest in monastic life. It may also have been prompted by the success of an earlier translation of the *Meditationes* into English by Nicholas Love. Love's text had been used in polemics against the Lollard heresy and recommended in 1410 by Archbishop Thomas Arundel as an alternative to the officially condemned Wycliffite Bible.

Henry's commission of the *Livre doré* appears to have been an act of the ruler of France rather than of England. The King was known for his promotion of the use of English in public documents and his patronage of English vernacular literature (see cat. nos. 64, 65 and 73). As Boulton (2002/2003) has argued, it is possible that, obliged by the Treaty of Troyes to preserve French 'laws, customs, and rights', Henry intended to apply a similar policy regarding the language of his new subjects during his regency in France.

Two copies of the *Livre doré* are contemporary with the composition of the text: the Royal manuscript and Cambridge, Corpus Christi College, MS 213. Both were written by the same French scribe, open with a large presentation scene, and include in their decoration the royal arms of England (the escutcheon in the Royal copy is, however, a later addition). Two added, fifteenth- and sixteenth-century inscriptions in the Cambridge manuscript claim Henry V's ownership of that book and suggest that it was the presentation copy. Whereas the text in both manuscripts is the same, the programme of ninety-eight illustrations in the Royal *Livre* is a significant elaboration of the Cambridge cycle, which includes only three miniatures.

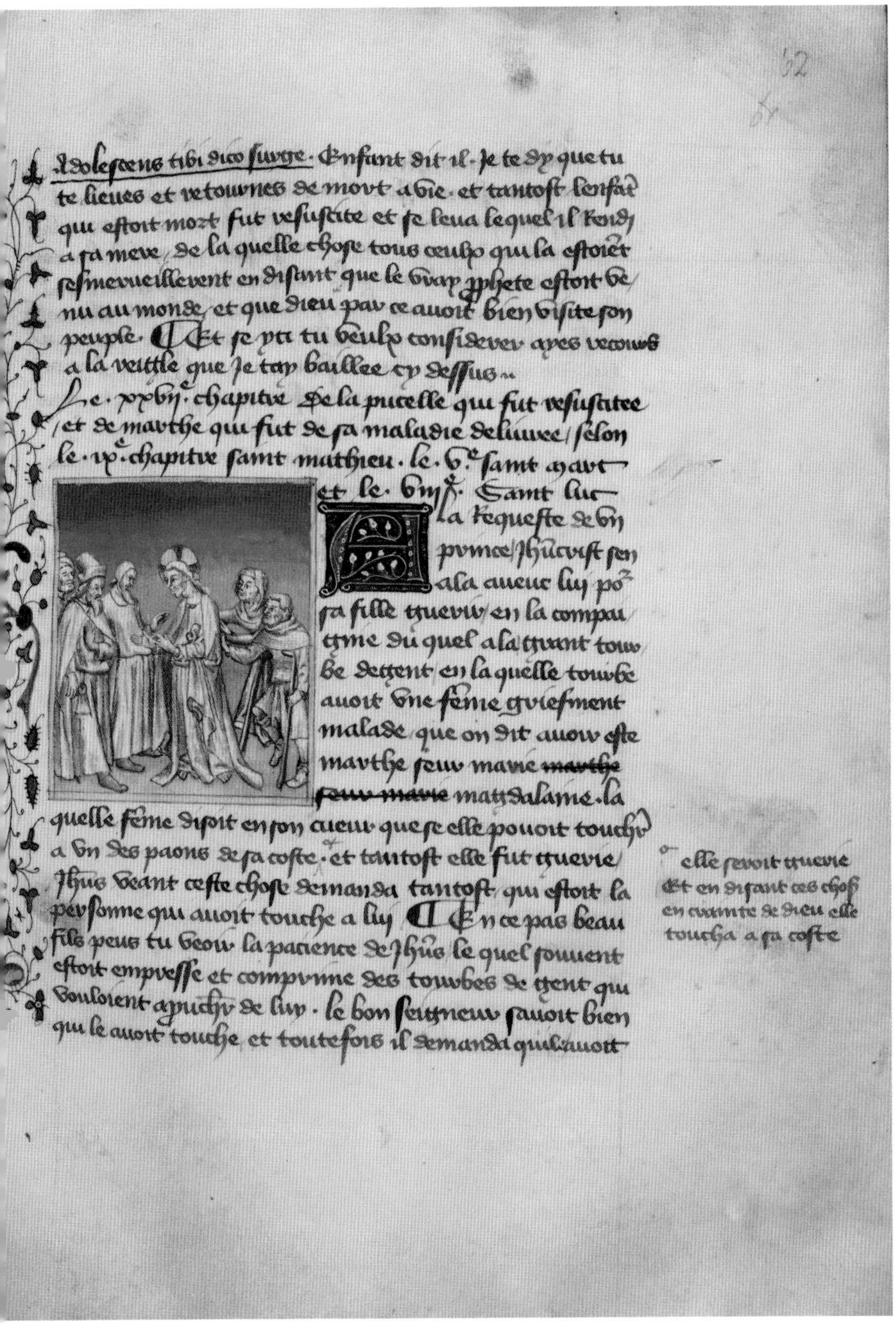

In addition to two opening illustrations in colours and gold that replicate the subjects illustrated in the Cambridge copy, the Royal manuscript marks the beginning of each subsequent chapter with an image in semi-grisaille. Apart from the *Intercession of Angels* at the beginning of the first chapter, which was inspired by the corresponding image in the Cambridge cycle, the semi-grisaille miniatures were probably not based on pre-existing models. They appear instead to have followed preliminary drawings that, in many cases, still survive. In the opening (pictured) a clearly visible sketch in the lower margin of the left-hand page was used by the illuminator as a guide for his image of Christ raising the widow's son.

Henry may have commissioned both manuscripts. The Cambridge *Livre* was perhaps accomplished first as the King's own copy, while the Royal manuscript, in which a place for its owner's arms was initially left blank, was perhaps intended by the King as a gift. This second copy remained, however, in royal possession until after Henry V's death and was probably only then completed with the royal arms of his son, Henry VI. The commissioning of twin manuscripts as gifts was not unusual among aristocracy at the early fifteenth-century French court and seems to have been also practised by Henry V. For example, it has been suggested that twelve copies of books on hunting commissioned from the London scrivener John Robard, a copy of Hoccleve's *Regement of Princes* (see cat. no. 65), and a group of presentation copies of Lydgate's *Troy Book* were all intended as royal gifts (Pearsall 1994).

Jean Galopes, who probably supervised the production of both copies of the *Livre doré,* assigned the illumination of the Royal manuscript to the Parisian workshop of the Master of the Harvard Hannibal (named after Cambridge, MA, Houghton Library, MS Richardson 32; see Meiss 1974), who painted the two full-colour miniatures. A few years later the same artist illustrated another work by Galopes, the Latin translation of the *Pelerinage de l'âme* of Guillaume de Digulleville (London, Lambeth Palace Library, MS 326). This manuscript has been identified as that presented in 1427 to John, Duke of Bedford, by the author, who by then had become chaplain to the new Regent of France. *J.F.*

PROVENANCE:

Charles II.

To alle men/ present/ or in absence
Which to seynt Edmund/ haue deuocion
With hool herte/ and dew reuerence
Seyn this Antephne/ and this Orison
Two hundred dayes/ ys grauntid off pardoun
Write and registred/ afforn his hooly shryne
Which for our feith/ suffrede passion
Blyssyd Edmund/ kyng/ martir/ and virgyne

30 John Lydgate, *The Lives of Sts Edmund and Fremund*

Bury St Edmunds, *c.* 1434–39
250 x 175 mm

BRITISH LIBRARY, HARLEY 2278

In 1433 it was announced that the young Henry VI would sojourn at the abbey of Bury St Edmunds from Christmas of that year through to the following Easter. The occasion promised to be advantageous for both parties involved. For the King's part, the stay was an exercise in thrift over the costly holiday season, as well as a deft show of accord between the monarch and one of England's wealthiest and most influential religious institutions. From the perspective of the abbey, the event offered a chance to showcase its impressive grounds, architecture, significance to the local community and, by extension, its right to self-rule. Just twelve years before, Henry V had summoned the leaders of the Benedictine Order to Westminster, demanded of them a number of reforms and issued an assertion of religious subordination to royal authority. Henry VI's visit presented an opportunity to redress such encroachments on the abbey's independence and impress upon the young King its vital role in the nation's spiritual and political well-being.

In honour of Henry's visit, Abbot William Curteys commissioned John Lydgate, a monk of the abbey and erstwhile poet-propagandist for the Lancastrian court, to compose an English version of the *Life* of the abbey's patron saint. Beginning with a terse entry in the ninth-century *Anglo-Saxon Chronicle*, the story of St Edmund was elaborated over the ensuing centuries as he rose to the status of a national saint. St Fremund's history may be traced to a Latin poem of *c.* 1220; later in the century he was portrayed as Edmund's nephew and avenger. Lydgate was the first to combine the two legends in a single work. Collectively the corpus of legends relating to Edmund shows the abbey's desire to reinforce its own power and independence through the fortification of its patron saint's cult. Lydgate's rendition may be seen as advancing this effort.

The Harley manuscript of the *Lives*, which was probably produced under the supervision of Lydgate, is sensitive to the two main agendas of the poem: it both demonstrates the abbey's support for Henry VI and cultivates his respect for its patron saint – and, by implication, its monastic prerogatives. The manuscript opens with two large illuminations that present Edmund as a model for Henry: the first, an image of the Temptation (f. 1v), and the second, the heraldry of Bury St Edmunds Abbey (a triangular formation of three crowns against an azure ground, f. 3v), are standards under which Edmund was said to have fought his aggressors. The verses on the page opposite each illumination recommend that Henry use such standards as his own. It is even possible that the trigon of crowns was meant to echo propagandistic imagery disseminated by the Lancastrian political machine, imagery that featured the two crowns of England and France united by Henry himself. The subtle resonance between Edmund's arms and Lancastrian publicity, coupled with the explicit recommendations of the adjoining verses, ensured that Henry found in Edmund a viable exemplar for himself.

Like the poem, many of the 118 miniatures adorning this manuscript strengthen an affinity between the saint and the King. The image of Henry kneeling before the sumptuous shrine of Edmund (f. 4v, pictured) – a shrine that had recently been renovated – certainly betrays the abbey's ambitions to foster the monarch's devotion to their patron saint. Furthermore, not only do the two figures resemble one another, but Edmund is also at times shown in activities that Henry himself might have enjoyed, such as watching a hunt (f. 37). The manuscript seems to have contributed to Henry's own saintly self-image, his reputation for deep piety and his later cult.

After its ownership by Henry VI the manuscript left the royal collection. It reappears in the royal library in 1542, when it is mentioned in the inventory of the Upper Library of Westminster Palace. An inscription, 'Audelay baro[n]' (f. 119v), places the manuscript in the hands of John Touchet (d. 1559), 8th Baron Audley, whose signature matches that in a letter to Henry VIII (Stowe 141, f. 19). Carley (2000) postulated that Harley 2278 was a gift from Touchet to the King in appreciation for the restoration of his titles in 1512. With this history of ownership the manuscript presents a compelling narrative of continuity in the politics of gift-giving: whether from the monks of Bury St Edmunds to Henry VI or from a reinstated subject to Henry VIII, the Harley *Lives* was a vivid reminder of a monarch's duty to embody a saintly and equitable ideal. *S.D.*

PROVENANCE:

Henry VI; John Touchet, 8th Baron Audley (d. 1559); Henry VIII; Edward Colston (d. 1721); Robert Harley, 1st Earl of Oxford (b. 1661, d. 1724), by 1720; Edward Harley, 2nd Earl of Oxford (b. 1689, d. 1741); purchased for the nation in 1753.

Opposite:
Henry VI kneeling before the shrine of St Edmund, f. 4v

31 'Salve Regina' Prayer Roll for Margaret of Anjou

London, between 1445 and 1453 (?)
1500 x 225 mm

OXFORD, JESUS COLLEGE, MS 124

This prayer roll is a rare object on three accounts. First, it is one of fewer than twenty prayer rolls known to survive; their scarcity is probably due to their relative fragility as well as the iconoclasm of the Reformation. Such objects were personal aids to devotion, with prayers invoking the intercession of Christ, the Virgin or saints to whom the roll's owner had a particular attachment. Comprising long, narrow strips of parchment that were rolled over a wooden pipe, they were meant to be portable and were even placed upon the body to effect apotropaic powers. As devotional aids, rolls were an alternative to Books of Hours – of which wealthy book-owners such as Margaret of Anjou must have had numerous examples – in that they offered the devotee even greater physical proximity to the text and the flesh on which the words were written.

Secondly, the contents of the Oxford roll are also unusual. The majority of surviving prayer rolls were produced in England and are of the *arma Christi* type – that is, prayers centring on Christ's wounds. However, the present roll is dedicated not to Christ but to his mother. Comprising two long parchment membranes pasted together, it encompasses three successive prayers to the Virgin Mary: the first is the 'Salve sancta mater dei radix'; the second, stanzas 19 to 25 of 'O Virgo Splendens'; and, finally, a series of Aves. Immediately above the first text is the pictorial section of the roll, executed by William Abell, an illuminator who served a royal and elite clientele in mid-fifteenth-century London (Alexander 1972). In this section is a *rota* constructed of prayers to the Virgin, at the centre of which is a depiction of the Virgin and Child (pictured).

The third extraordinary feature of this roll is its depiction of a queen of England, of which very few survive in late medieval manuscripts (see cat. nos. 19, 36 and 122). Just beneath the *rota* is an idealized depiction of the Queen Consort to Henry VI, Margaret of Anjou, kneeling before a *prie-dieu* and an open book. To the right, Margaret is identified by an escutcheon held by two angels that bears her heraldic arms impaled with those of her husband. A similar depiction of her occurs in the Shrewsbury Book (cat. no. 143), while in the Skinners' Company book of the Confraternity of the Assumption of Our Lady (London, Metropolitan Archives, Guildhall MS 31692) Margaret appears in widow's clothing. Together, these images are exceptional in their portrayal of a medieval Queen in three guises: devotee, recipient and widow.

The roll relates to Margaret's two primary functions as queen. When she wed Henry VI in 1445, the hopes of the nation for peace with France and domestic stability were thrust upon her, and specifically upon her ability to produce a son to perpetuate the Lancastrian line. Eight-and-a-half years without issue must have weighed heavily on Margaret, and she is recorded as having visited shrines on at least four separate occasions, one of which, the Shrine of Our Lady of Walsingham, was a popular destination for women with hopes of becoming pregnant. This prayer roll to the Mother of Christ can be seen as an instrument in Margaret's endeavour to succeed in producing an heir.

Additionally, the roll highlights Mary's function as an intercessor, one which Margaret was likewise expected to fulfil as queen, albeit with an earthly rather than heavenly king. The ring surrounding the central depiction of the Virgin and Child contains seven radii made of scrolls that name the people who might pray to her: the 'populus, cler[ic]us, pusillanimes' (people, clerics, knights) and others. An outer series of spokes voices the prayers each group should recite, each beginning alliteratively with the group's name (e.g., the 'cler[ic]us' is to recite 'O clemens'). Sixty-eight surviving letters show Margaret to have pleaded with various temporal powers on behalf of others, a common duty of medieval queens. The image of Margaret gazing up at a crowned, intercessory Virgin may have reinforced to her the obligation she owed to her subjects.

In 1453 Margaret's – and the nation's – hopes were fulfilled when she bore a son, Edward. The prayer roll, with its relevance to a woman's desire to conceive, was probably made before this date. Later, like so many books that were given as gifts from one female to another, it may have been bequeathed by Margaret to a confidante, perhaps before her return to France in 1476. Because the roll was acquired in the middle of the seventeenth century by the antiquary Ralph Sheldon (d. 1684), it almost certainly remained in England from the time of its production. *S.D.*

PROVENANCE:

Margaret of Anjou (d. 1482); bequeathed by Ralph Sheldon (d. 1684) to Jesus College, Oxford.

Opposite:
Margaret of Anjou kneeling beneath a rota with the Virgin and Child.

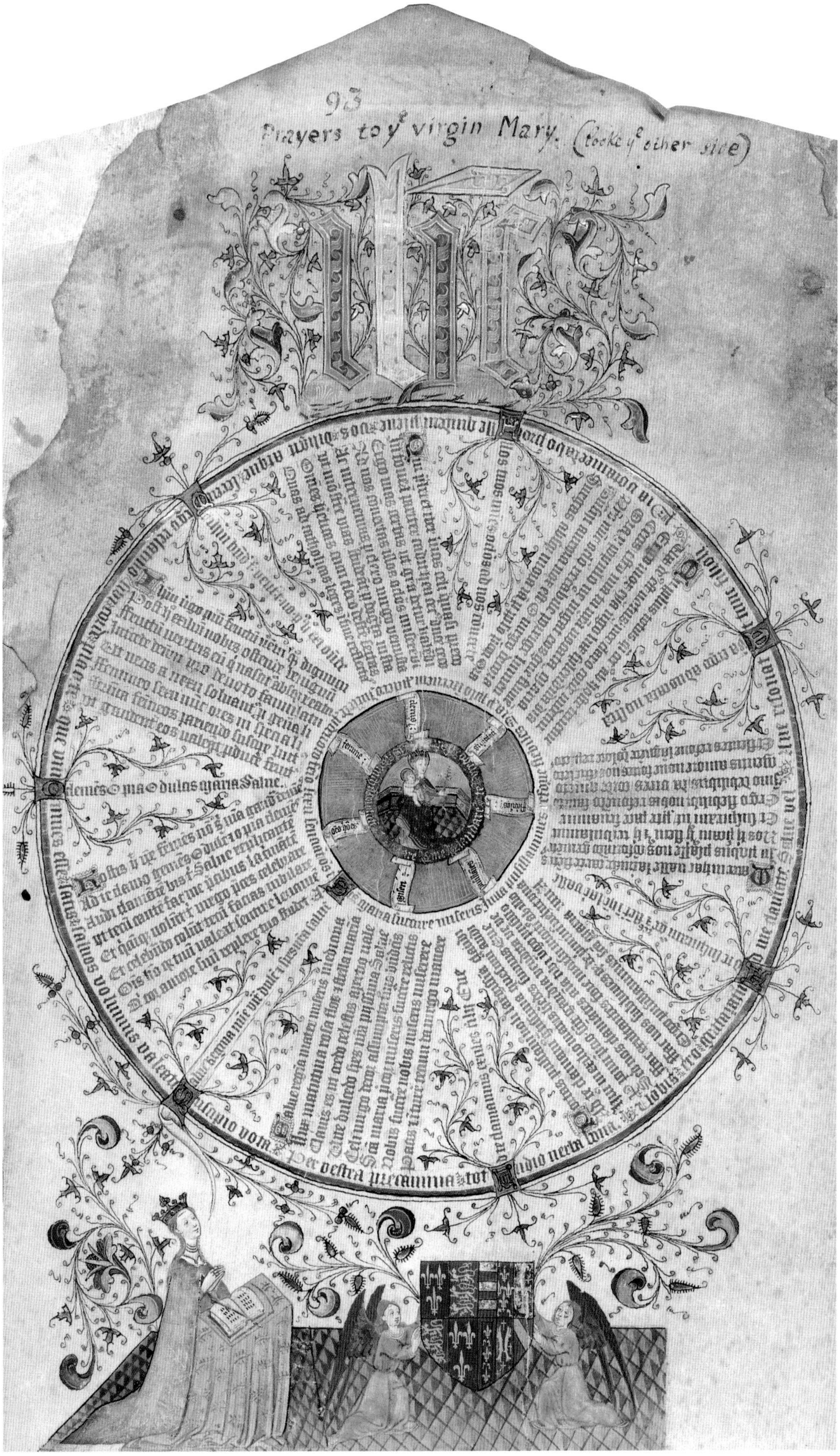
93
Prayers to ye virgin Mary. (looke ye other side)

32 Selection of Psalms, Litanies and Prayers for Humfrey of Gloucester

England, *c.* 1430 – *c.* 1440
245 x 165 mm

ROYAL 2 B. i

Though Humfrey, Duke of Gloucester (d. 1447), was the son of Henry IV, brother to Henry V and uncle to Henry VI, he is remembered mostly as an ardent bibliophile who was at the vanguard of humanistic learning in late medieval England. His personal library has been estimated at over five hundred volumes, and he assumed responsibility for Henry VI's early education. When, in 1447, Humfrey died in mysterious circumstances after being arrested at Bury St Edmunds (to be charged with treason), his vast collection of manuscripts was impounded and disposed of by three servants of the Crown. It is against this background of literary patronage and dispersal that the collection of Psalms produced for Humfrey of Gloucester is best viewed.

Even given the personalized nature of many Psalters, Humfrey's book is remarkable for its idiosyncratic selection of Psalms. The manuscript contains sixty-six Psalms, which do not conform to any particular devotional practice. Instead, the collection is almost entirely Davidic, the only major exceptions being some Psalms from the Gradual sequence (119–133). Additionally, at the centre of the programme are three non-Davidic laments on the national loss of divine favour (77, 85, 88), and a final Psalm of thanksgiving upon its restoration (92).

The illustrative cycle underscores the text's focus on David. Suffusing the manuscript are 115 inhabited initials, including an image of David at his harp and seventy-four 'portrait' heads of David with a white forked beard. The few Psalms not attributable to him, as well as the litanies and prayers, are introduced by forty-one initials that host other Christian images, including Christ of the Passion and the Annunciation. The repetition of David's 'portrait' is unknown in any other Psalter.

Additionally, the volume has a pedagogical inflection, with disproportionate attention given to Psalm 119. This particular Psalm, which includes a stanza for each letter of the Hebrew aleph-bet, has devoted to it twenty-one inhabited initials, one for each stanza. The emphasis on Psalm 119 correlates with the educational use of Psalters, which were sometimes bound with alphabetical primers and poems.

The circumstances of the manuscript's commission have provoked some scholarly debate. On the one hand, the manuscript bears positive marks of Humfrey's ownership. An inscription in French on the final page declares his participation in the manuscript's production, stating, 'this book of Psalms that I selected from the Psalter belongs to me, Humfrey, Duke of Gloucester'. Furthermore, Humfrey's arms (the royal arms of England with a bordure *argent*) appear in a decorated initial and at the foot of the same page prefacing the Psalms (f. 7); the latter emulates a design found in manuscripts illuminated for the Visconti family of Italy by the Master of the *Vitae imperatorum*, who also illuminated Pier Candido Decembrio's presentation copy of the *Republic* for Humfrey (Vatican City, Biblioteca Apostolica Vaticana, MS Vat. lat. 10669). And, featured in the commendation scene is St Alban, a saint to whose abbey Humfrey was a benefactor, and where his tomb remains to this day. Some scholars (Scott 1996; Alexander 1983) have argued that the beardless, youthful figure kneeling in the commendation scene (pictured)may represent Henry VI as Humfrey was at least forty years old at the time of the manuscript's production. However, two contemporary manuscripts depict Humfrey in a similar, beardless guise (Cotton Nero D. vii and Oxford, Bodleian Library, MS Duke Humfrey b.i). Furthermore, the crown on the kneeling figure resembles Humfrey's headgear in the presentation miniature to *In Exodium*, written for him by John Capgrave (Oxford, Bodleian Library, MS Duke Humfrey b.i).

Signs of Humfrey's ownership are strong, but the selection of texts and the pictorial programme suggest he intended to use this volume in his aspirations to influence the early education of Henry VI. The emphasis on David intimates his suitability as a model for Henry, and the non-Davidic Psalms included stress to the King the importance of retaining divine favour for the nation. Seen in this light, the Duke's inscription on the final page advertises his judicious selection of psalms appropriate to his nephew and pupil.

The manuscript probably remained with Humfrey, entering the royal collection shortly after the Duke's death in 1447. Like several other manuscripts owned by him (e.g., cat. nos. 33, 139), part of the inscription has been erased almost beyond legibility – perhaps a hostile reaction to the Duke in the wake of his disgraceful end. Although Henry VI had the majority of Humfrey's books dispersed, Stratford (1999) notes that the King did retain some of the illuminated manuscripts for himself; this volume would have attracted his attention for its embellishment and, perhaps, for its value as a memento from his early education. *S.D.*

PROVENANCE:

Humfrey, Duke of Gloucester (d. 1447); Henry VI.

Opposite:
Commendation Scene, f. 8

Psalmus david gratias agentis deo de li
beracione sua a manibus saulis
audivit me deus iusti
Miserere mei et ex
audi oracionem me
am

Ego autem in innocencia mea ingressus
sum: redime me et miserere mei.
Pes meus stetit in directo: in ecclesiis be
nedicam te domine.
Dominus il
luminacio
mea: et sa
lus mea
quem timebo.
Dominus
protector vi
te mee: a
quo trepidabo.
Dum appropiant super me nocentes: ut
edant carnes meas.
Qui tribulant me inimici mei: ipsi infir
mati sunt et ceciderunt.
Si consistant aduersum me castra: non

33 The St Omer Psalter

Norfolk, *c.* 1330–40; probably Essex, *c.* 1400; London, *c.* 1430–40
335 x 225 mm

BRITISH LIBRARY, YATES THOMPSON 14

Artistic refinement and royal associations combine to make this Psalter a key example of both fourteenth-century English painting and fifteenth-century patronage at court. It was commissioned in the 1330s by a knight of the St Omer family of Mulbarton, Norfolk, who is depicted in heraldic dress on the opening page (f. 7). The first campaign includes four images accompanied by full borders, outstanding witnesses to the Italianate phase in East Anglian illumination, at the divisions for Psalms 1, 52, 68 and 109. However, the campaign remained unfinished. The initials and borders at Psalms 26 and 38 (ff. 29v, 44v) were only drawn in. The illumination of these and the painted decoration of the main text, as well as the calendar text and decoration, and the text of all but three of the last eleven gatherings, were supplied in the fifteenth century. The person usually credited with the manuscript's completion is Humfrey, Duke of Gloucester (d. 1447). The wording of Duke Humfrey's ownership inscription (f. 173), erased as in many of the manuscripts seized after his death (e.g. cat. nos. 32, 139) but legible under ultra-violet light, suggests that he acquired the Psalter after May 1414, when he became Duke of Gloucester and Earl of Pembroke, and before December 1422, when, following Henry V's death, he was made Lord Protector of the young Henry VI.

However, the illumination was not completed within this short period. It was undertaken by at least five artists, one working *c.* 1400 but looking back to the 1380s, the rest working in the 1430s. Unlike the celebrated first campaign, the later contributions have received little attention. Margaret Rickert (1965) perceived them as a single, sustained campaign and dismissed them as 'stiff, awkward', 'coarse', 'overloaded and ugly'. Such a harsh judgement is understandable in the case of the initials and borders for Psalms 80 and 97 (ff. 87, 103), painted in a London workshop in the 1430s. But it overlooks the diversity of styles, English, French and Italianate, that are present on other pages and suggest at least two subsequent attempts to complete the manuscript, first *c.* 1400 and then in the 1430s.

Several large flowers fill the medallions intended for biblical scenes at Psalms 26 and 38, a design found in the Psalter and Hours made for Gloucester's brother, John, Duke of Bedford, in Herman Scheere's atelier *c.* 1420 (cat. no. 26). The exquisite French-style borders confined to two gatherings (ff. 154–167v) may reflect Duke Humfrey's access to French artists. They may also commemorate his participation in the French campaigns or may respond – in a competitive spirit – to the patronage by Bedford of French illuminators that was intimately related to his politics as Regent of France (1422–35). Visual references to Bedford's manuscripts in Gloucester's Psalter could be seen in the light of the brothers' increasingly strained relationship after 1422.

Duke Humfrey's taste also left a mark on the decoration. The border ornament at Psalms 26 and 38 rests against blue or red fields sprinkled with white dots, an early and somewhat hesitant emulation of the standard background of humanistic white vine-scrolls. These motifs feature in manuscripts sent to Duke Humfrey from Italy by his humanist friends, and more accomplished imitations appear in copies made for him in England from the late 1430s onwards. The examples in the St Omer borders belong early in this period, alluding to Gloucester's friendship with scholars and passion for classical texts, the key elements of his reputation as a Renaissance prince.

The main images on these pages, however, were completed *c.* 1400, before Duke Humfrey acquired the manuscript. For Psalms 26 (f. 29v, pictured) and 68 the subject matter and the format – a miniature with the initial in the top right corner – were determined by the original fourteenth-century drawing. But the painting was completed in the early fifteenth century in a style reminiscent of manuscripts made for the Bohun family in the 1380s. The large heads on thin-waisted bodies and the elaborate architecture hark back to works commissioned by Joan Fitzalan (d. 1419), widow of Humphrey de Bohun (b. 1342, d. 1373), 7th Earl of Hereford, Essex and Northampton, and by her daughter, Mary de Bohun, Duke Humfrey's mother. Like another East Anglian manuscript, the Luttrell Psalter (Additional 42130), the unfinished St Omer Psalter may have passed into Bohun ownership via the Fitzalans. Perhaps some of the artists who worked for the Bohuns in the 1380s remained in Joan Fitzalan's service and resumed work on the unfinished St Omer images *c.* 1400. Joan may have then given the Psalter to Humfrey in 1414 to commemorate his elevation to a dukedom. (By 1415 she had given a Missal and Breviary to his brother, Henry V.) Humfrey's attempts to complete the Psalter's decoration produced an experimental composite, a pictorial parallel to the diverse political and cultural trends in fifteenth-century England. *S.P.*

PROVENANCE:

A knight of the St Omer family of Mulbarton, Norfolk; Humfrey, Duke of Gloucester (b. 1390, d. 1447); Egidius Dancel, 17th century; John Wilkes the Elder (d. 1894); Bertram, 4th Earl of Ashburnham (b. 1797, d. 1878); presented to the nation by Henry Yates Thompson (b. 1838, d. 1928) in 1918.

Opposite:
Psalm 26, Anointing and crowning of David, f. 9v

34 The Psalter of Isabel of York

Probably London, between *c.* 1426 and 1458
315 x 210 mm

ROYAL 2 B. xiv

One of the defining features of the Psalter was the many purposes that it could serve. As a devotional collection of relatively brief passages, it afforded the lay person a repertoire of easily remembered prayers for a number of occasions. As a compendium of texts with a simple vocabulary and orthography, it was the foundation of many medieval children's education, and was the primer from which they learned to read. And, with its requisite calendar at the front, it often provided a template for an abbreviated family record of notable events.

All of these functions are represented by the present Psalter, made for Isabel of York (d. 1484), sister to Richard, Duke of York (d. 1460), and aunt to Edward IV. The manuscript, which contains Isabel's arms impaled by those of her husband Henry Bourchier (d. 1483), 1st Earl of Essex (f. 7, pictured), was perhaps a commission by or a gift for her on the occasion of her marriage in 1426. Isabel is known for her devotion and for her literary patronage, having commissioned from Osbern Bokenham (d. after 1463) the *Life of Mary Magdalene* that appears in his *Legendys of Hooly Wummen* (Arundel 327). Isabel's husband Henry was Treasurer of England under Henry VI and subsequently Edward IV – of whom he remained a steadfast supporter, particularly during the Yorkist King's deposition and exile from October 1470 to April 1471. Isabel's heraldic arms are accompanied by the Bourchier knot and Yorkist fetterlock badge. The flanking birds are like that on her brass at Little Easton, Essex.

As a 'starter-volume' for the newly-wed Isabel, the manuscript may have been intended to serve as an aid in educating the children she would have been expected to have. Noblewomen like Isabel were not only assumed to be literate participants in their devotions but were also charged with the tuition of their daughters and even the early education of their sons. Several features support this inference, such as the volume's size, which is large enough to be perused by two people at a time, rather than being of the small dimensions characteristic of more intimate devotional books. Additionally, a fifteenth-century reader has carefully numbered every Psalm in the margin, for ease of reference. Smudges on some folios as well as the occasional droplet of wax also indicate that this volume saw frequent use. It is an elegant book with no figural illustration, but with 'champ' initials throughout and large decorated initials at the liturgical divisions typical of Psalters.

Equal to this volume's significance as a devotional and educational book was its status as a family memorial. In the calendar that precedes the Psalms, nine notices have inscribed next to their respective dates. Among these is a note of the death in 1458 of Isabel's second son, Henry, which has provided the *terminus ante quem* of the manuscript's production. Also noted are the deaths of Isabel's brother Richard and her son Edward (f. 6v), both of whom fell at the Battle of Wakefield (December 1460), as well as the death of her husband Henry (f. 2v). After her own passing, which was also recorded in the calendar (f. 5v), the manuscript passed to Isabel's sixth son, Thomas (d. 1492), who inscribed his name at the back of the volume (f. 135) and added notices of his daughters' births in the calendar (ff. 2, 2v). The inscription of these notes by at least three separate hands further underscores the nature of this book as a family monument in parchment. Also added to the manuscript (ff. 133v–134), in a neat Gothic bookhand of the late fifteenth century, are two prayers that lament the death of an unnamed female and the passing of parents. This practice of adding obits is well attested in later medieval devotional books, and a similar example of Yorkist commemoration appears in a Psalter (Rennes, Bibliothèque Municipale, MS 22), that was once bound with the opening illuminated pages of the Beaufort/Beauchamp Hours (cat. no. 25).

In every sense, then, this is a typical Psalter for a noble lay person of the later Middle Ages. As such, it is a salutary reminder that even members of the royal family owned and prized straightforward devotional volumes alongside their more spectacular commissions. Although its exact date of entrance into the Old Royal library is uncertain, it may have been during the reign of Henry VIII (Carley 2000). Little is known of Thomas Bourchier, but his nephew Henry (d. 1540), 2nd Earl of Essex – who inherited Thomas's lands and possessions upon his death – was extremely close to Henry VIII's court in its early years. It is possible that the manuscript reached the royal collection through Henry Bourchier's hands. *S.D.*

PROVENANCE:

Isabel of York (d. 1484), wife of Henry Bourchier, 1st Earl of Essex (d. 1483); Thomas Bourchier (d. 1492).

Opposite:
Psalms 1–2, f. 7

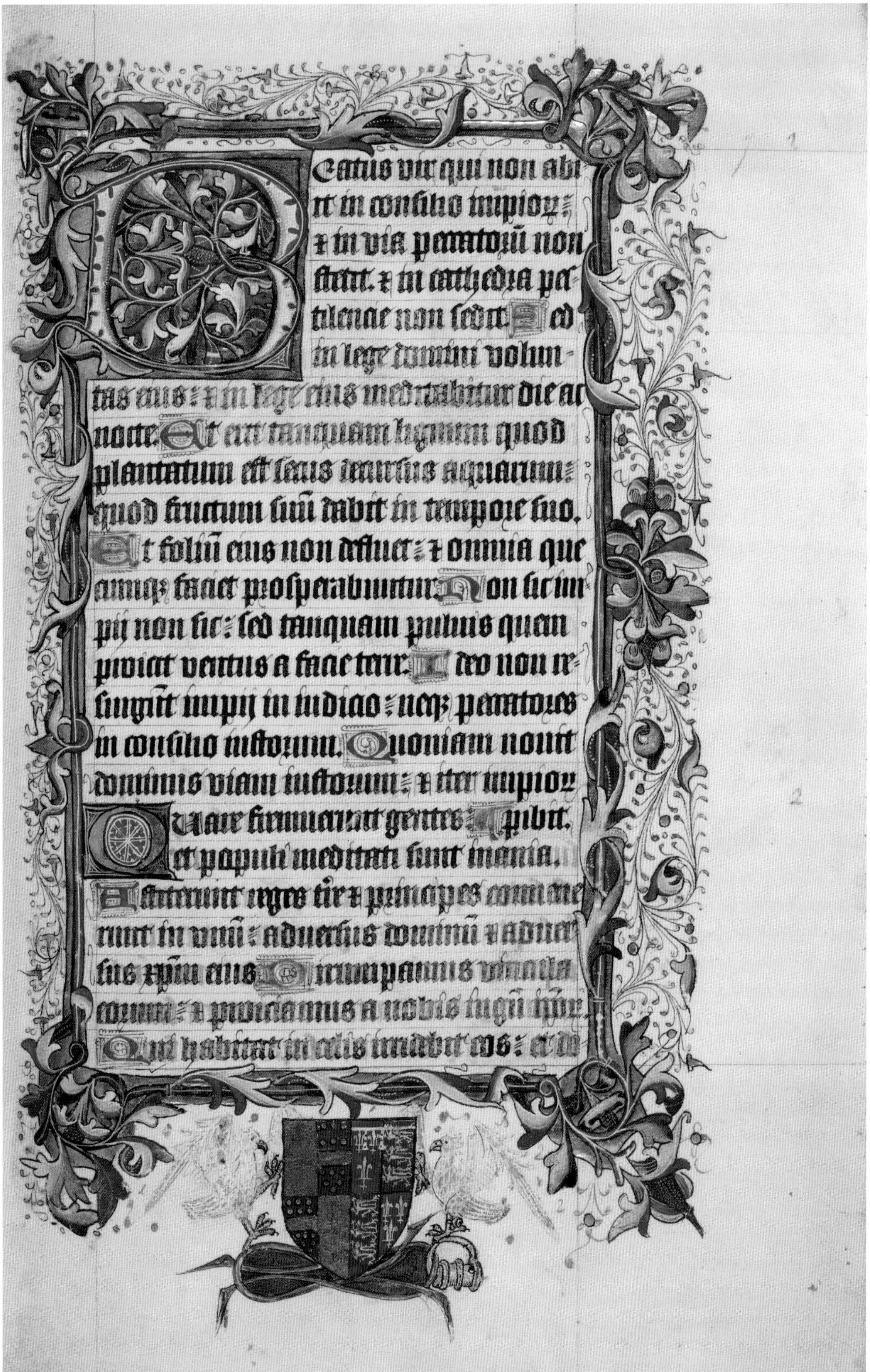
Beatus vir qui non abi-
it in consilio impiorum:
et in via peccatorum non
stetit: et in cathedra pes-
tilencie non sedit. Sed
in lege domini volun-
tas eius: et in lege eius meditabitur die ac
nocte. Et erit tanquam lignum quod
plantatum est secus decursus aquarum:
quod fructum suum dabit in tempore suo.
Et folium eius non defluet: et omnia que-
cumque faciet prosperabuntur. Non sic im-
pii non sic: sed tanquam pulvis quem
proicit ventus a facie terre. Ideo non re-
surgunt impii in iudicio: neque peccatores
in consilio iustorum. Quoniam novit
dominus viam iustorum: et iter impiorum
Quare fremuerunt gentes: peribit.
et populi meditati sunt inania.
Astiterunt reges terre et principes conve-
nerunt in unum: adversus dominum et adver-
sus christum eius. Dirumpamus vincula
eorum: et proiciamus a nobis iugum ipso-
rum. Qui habitat in celis irridebit eos: et do-

35 Nicolas Finet, *Dialogue de la duchesse de Bourgogne à Jésus Christ*

Brussels, *c.* 1468
220 x 140 mm

BRITISH LIBRARY, ADDITIONAL 7970

Margaret of York and the resurrected Christ, ff. 1v–2

During her nine years as Duchess of Burgundy between 1468 and 1477, Margaret of York commissioned several devotional and moral treatises for her private library. By far the most personal of them were two books written specially for her by Nicolas Finet, her almoner, shortly after her marriage to Charles the Bold, the *Benois seront les misericordieux* (Blessed are the Merciful), now in Brussels (KBR, MS 9296) and the *Dialogue de la duchesse de Bourgogne à Jésus Christ* (Dialogue of the Duchess of Burgundy with Jesus Christ). These two texts, preserved only in these two volumes, may have been intended as a guidebook of moral instruction introducing Margaret into her new role of Duchess of Burgundy. They advise respectively on two complementary ways of pious life: the active life of good and charitable deeds and the contemplative life focused on meditation and prayer. The unconventional iconography of their illustrations acts as a mirror in which Margaret could have seen herself exercising Christian virtues. In the opening miniature of the manuscript in Brussels, the Duchess is portrayed performing the seven Acts of Mercy, recommended by Christ in the Gospel of Matthew. She distributes alms, food and clothes to the poor, receives pilgrims, visits prisoners and the infirm and prays for the dead; each time she is accompanied by Christ himself. In the *Dialogue*'s only miniature she experiences an apparition of Jesus Christ in her private chamber (pictured). The intimate and immediate character of this mystical encounter corresponds to the text in which Margaret receives instruction directly from Christ and is urged to contemplate his living presence. The iconography of this miniature recalls images of Christ appearing to his mother, or to Mary Magdalene in the scene known as the *Noli me tangere* (Do not touch me). Perhaps this allusion to the second post-Resurrection appearance of Christ was not a mere re-use of a visual workshop model but an intentional association between Margaret of York and the penitent saint who became a paradigmatic symbol of both the contemplative and the active life.

The two manuscripts of Finet's treatises not only form a complementary pair of texts focused on two aspects of Christian devotion and morality, but they also share a very similar physical appearance. They were written by the same scribe and decorated with similar borders and initials, which feature Margaret's heraldic arms as the Duchess of Burgundy (see also cat. no. 151), her device *Ben en aviegne* (May good come of it) and the initials of the ducal

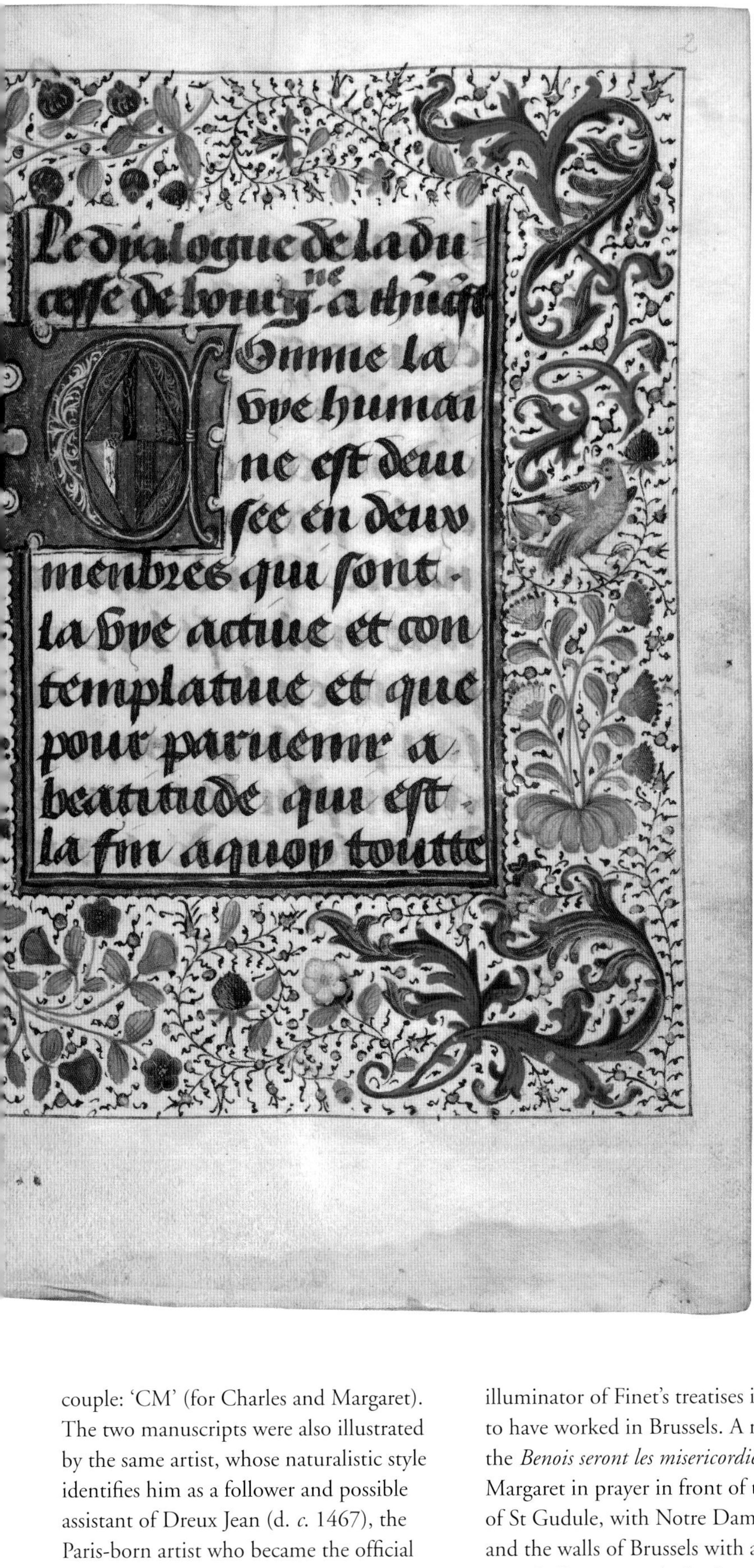

couple: 'CM' (for Charles and Margaret). The two manuscripts were also illustrated by the same artist, whose naturalistic style identifies him as a follower and possible assistant of Dreux Jean (d. *c.* 1467), the Paris-born artist who became the official illuminator and *valet de chambre* to Philip the Good and Charles the Bold (see Kren and McKendrick 2003). Like Jean, the illuminator of Finet's treatises is assumed to have worked in Brussels. A miniature in the *Benois seront les misericordieux* represents Margaret in prayer in front of the Church of St Gudule, with Notre Dame du Sablon and the walls of Brussels with a gate and the town hall tower in the background (Brussels KBR, MS 9296, f. 17). As the Duchess of Burgundy, Margaret often stayed in the ducal residence at the Coudenberg Palace in that city.

The two manuscripts were separated at the end of Margaret's life but, following her wishes, both books were designated to serve for the moral edification of another generation of noble women. Before she died, the dowager Duchess gave the *Dialogue* as a gift to her friend and lady-in-waiting Jeanne de Hallewin (d. 1529), Lady of Wassenaer, and recorded this fact in an autograph dedication at the back of the book (f. 140v). Margaret bequeathed the copy of *Benois seront les misericordieux* with four other manuscripts to her god-daughter Margaret of Austria (b. 1480, d.1530).

The *Dialogue*'s seventeenth-century Brabant binding of white parchment with a gold-tooled panel of the Virgin and Child suggests that at that time the manuscript was still in the southern Netherlands. A virtually identical binding protects a collection of works of Claude Chapuisot, which was printed in Brussels in 1630 and came into the possession of the Jesuit College in Leuven in 1648 (now Brussels, KBR, VH 25.432; see *Exposition de reliures* 1931). It is likely that Margaret's *Dialogue* belonged either to the same institution or to another religious house in Brabant. Following the dissolution of the Jesuit Order in 1773 and the suppression of monasteries in the southern Netherlands in 1796, the book must have entered the antiquarian market. The London bookseller John Cochran, from whom the manuscript was purchased by the British Museum in 1830, states in his sale catalogue that he acquired it from St Petersburg. *J.F.*

PROVENANCE:

Margaret of York (b. 1446, d. 1503), Duchess of Burgundy; Jeanne de Hallewin, Lady of Wassenaer (d. 1529); John Cochran, London; purchased for the nation in 1830.

36 Register of the Fraternity of the Holy Trinity, Luton

Ghent (?) and London, 1475–1546
285 x 205 mm

LUTON, LUTON MUSEUM SERVICES, 1984/127

Although they were a ubiquitous feature of urban life in late medieval England, fraternities have left to posterity relatively few vestiges of their corporate activities. Far fewer remains of them survive than of monastic houses; books associated with fraternities are particularly rare. The present manuscript, therefore, provides important opportunities for historians to learn about the part fraternities played in shaping both local and national life.

Granted a royal licence in May 1474, the Fraternity of the Holy Trinity at Luton was overtly founded to support a chantry at the altar of the Holy Trinity on the south side of the parish church. There, two chaplains were to celebrate the divine office and pray for Edward IV, Queen Elizabeth and the soul of Richard, Duke of York (b. 1411, d. 1460). Elsewhere, at the very centre of commercial and social life in Luton, the Fraternity established its own hall. As has been previously established (Marks 1998), the Fraternity offered a platform upon which the Rotherham family, who held the lordship of the manor of Luton from 1471 to 1614, could consolidate their authority and social standing in the town. It also enabled the Rotherhams and the citizens of Luton to reassert their loyalty to the Yorkist regime and distance themselves from the previous Lord of the Manor, who had sided and fallen with the Lancastrians at the Battle of Tewkesbury.

Edward IV, Queen Elizabeth, Bishop Thomas Rotherham and others at prayer before the Trinity; opening page of the Register, ff. 13v–14

The present manuscript constitutes the most eloquent witness of the motivations behind the establishment and continuing life of the Fraternity. After an opening calendar highlighting key feast days, the volume continues with what now acts as a title-page for the whole volume (f. 13), but explicitly refers only to the following leaf, with which it forms a separate bifolium and on which the names of the founders of the Fraternity are written in gold (f. 14, pictured). Most prominent in this list are Edward IV and Queen Elizabeth; Edward's mother, Cecily, dowager Duchess of York; and his late father Richard, Duke of York, here described as 'the true and indubitable heir to the crown of England'. Immediately after them are Thomas Rotherham (b. 1423, d. 1500), then Bishop of Lincoln; and his brother, Sir John Rotherham, Lord of the Manor of Luton. Other named founder members are gentry, clergy and merchants. Opposite is a visual counterpart to this list, showing the founders in prayer before the Trinity (f. 13v, pictured). Prominently positioned in the centre foreground, Bishop Rotherham leads their entreaties with the couplet 'Blessod lord in trenete / Save all thes fretarnete'. Annual updates made to the Register until the Fraternity's

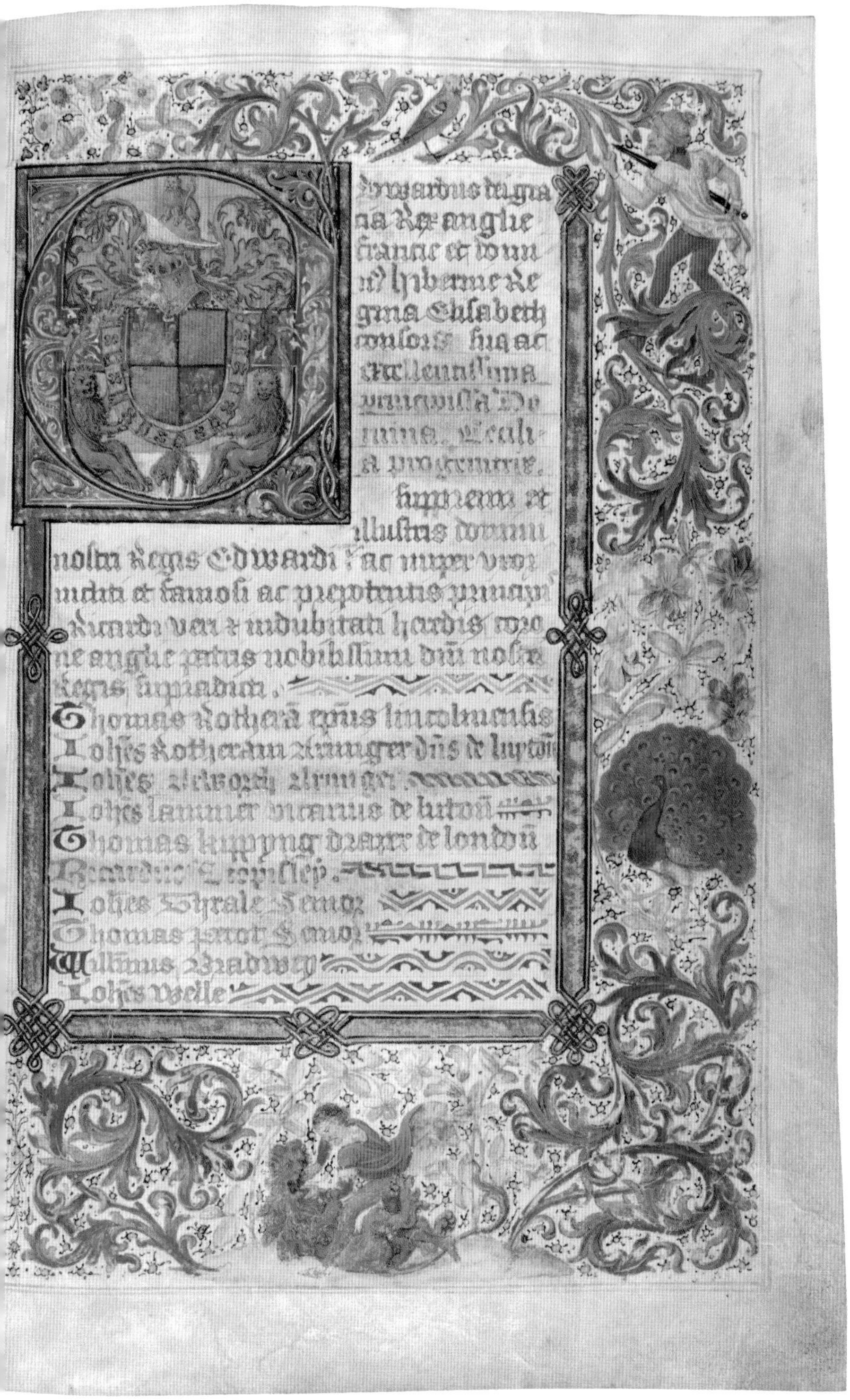

dissolution in 1547 memorialize subsequent members.

Whereas most of the decoration in the Register has been aptly described as of 'splendid vulgarity' (Marks 1998), the principal opening includes illumination of the highest refinement. Previous stylistic assessments of the full-page miniature have rightly placed it within the tradition of south Netherlandish, rather than English, illumination. In the border facing it, the illuminator drew on a new type of marginal decoration adopted in the 1460s by several Netherlandish illuminators, including Lieven van Lathem. In the initial a Netherlandish hand gave greater prominence to the collar of the Burgundian Order of the Golden Fleece than to the Garter. In the miniature the artist drew on a deep knowledge of Netherlandish illumination and panel painting. The central *Seat of Mercy* is based on a pictorial tradition within which the earlier panel of the same subject in St Petersburg attributed to the Master of Flémalle offers a close visual parallel. A further connection with Netherlandish panel painting is provided by the street scene in the upper left, which is – as noted elsewhere (Campbell 1985) – a repetition of the upper left-hand portion of Hugo van der Goes's Monforte *Adoration*. Stylistically the miniature artist is very close to the celebrated Ghent illuminator the Vienna Master of Mary Burgundy (Alexander 1999); in accomplishment he is a worthy follower.

Although previous scholars have cautioned against assigning it a place of production outside England (Marks 1998; Scott 2000), it seems entirely plausible that the entire opening bifolium was commissioned and executed abroad. The miniature and border artists would have had little justification for travelling jointly to England. English hands were capable of adding the heavy gold frames on both pages, the list of the founders and also the title-page text and illumination. If, as seems likely, Rotherham was the prime mover behind the initiation of the Register, his contacts in the Low Countries and intimate knowledge of contemporary court taste for Netherlandish illumination would provide a credible context for such a foreign commission. His aspirations for the Fraternity may also explain why he wished its official record to be an object of display worthy of royal patrons. *S.McK.*

PROVENANCE:

James I; James Matthews; Andrew Ducarel (d. 1785); Thomas Astle (d. 1803); John Stuart, 3rd Earl of Bute (b. 1713, d. 1792); by descent to John Crichton-Stuart, 6th Marquess of Bute (b. 1933, d. 1993); purchased for Luton Museum in 1984.

37 Jean de Meun, *Sept articles de la foy*

Rouen, 1440s
290 x 200 mm

BRITISH LIBRARY, ROYAL 19 A. xxii

In the 1270s Jean de Meun, the Parisian translator and writer, completed the *Roman de la Rose*, an allegorical poem begun about forty years earlier by the courtly poet Guillaume de Lorris (see cat. nos. 129, 130). Jean is best known for this achievement, but his name is also connected with three less celebrated texts: the *Testament* (a satirical treatise) and two religious poems, the *Sept articles de la foy* and the *Codicile*. These texts were often appended to manuscripts of the *Roman de la Rose*, and medieval readers considered them to be by Jean de Meun. Modern scholars, however, are divided on the issue of their authorship and many have rejected the attribution of the religious verses.

The present manuscript of the *Sept articles de la foy* was made in Rouen in the 1440s. Its short text usually circulated with others by, or attributed to, Jean de Meun, but here it is presented on its own as a slim volume. Eight large miniatures of sacred subjects, from the Nativity to the Last Judgement, are framed by borders decorated with strawberries, flowers and ivy. These paintings were made by artists working under the Talbot Master, who headed one of the main workshops active in Rouen when the city was under English rule (1419–49) (see cat. nos. 71, 72, 143). In subject matter and treatment, they strongly resemble those found in Books of Hours made by the same workshop.

The manuscript seems to have been made for an unidentified English knight of the Garter, based in Rouen, whose name once appeared in an inscription (now erased) at the end of the volume (f. 31v). Emblems of the Garter, similar in style to those depicted in several other books made by the same Rouen workshop – including the Shrewsbury Book presented to Margaret of Anjou in 1445 (cat. no. 143), and three Books of Hours made for John Talbot, 1st Earl of Shrewsbury, and his second wife, Margaret Beauchamp – were once visible in the borders of the miniatures, but were later painted over when the manuscript was acquired by Henry VII, who had it altered for his own use.

Not only was the original ownership inscription erased, but so much pressure was applied in the process that a hole was made in the parchment. Scrolls in the borders, presumably bearing the motto of the unknown knight, were similarly effaced and his arms were replaced by the arms of England. In addition, Tudor roses were painted over depictions of the Garter. Although mostly concealed, the Garters may in part be seen behind the stems of the roses and, if one looks carefully at the facing pages, the distinct outlines of the original Garter motifs may be discerned as offsets, prints made inadvertently when the book was closed and the pages were pressed together.

The most radical intrusion is the portrait of a kneeling king, intended to represent Henry VII, which was incorporated into the image of the Trinity (f. 1, pictured). Judging from the asymmetrical position of the throne shared by God the Father and Son, it would seem that another kneeling figure, almost certainly that of the knight who commissioned the manuscript, originally occupied the place usurped by the King. The apparent disregard for this individual and the systematic attempts to abolish signs of his ownership are not as surprising as they may first appear. It was not unusual for people who had acquired manuscripts to efface the names, arms or portraits of previous owners and to substitute their own.

Although the manuscript came to Henry VII, it was earlier associated with at least two other individuals whose names appear in the volume. The name 'L. Galet' is inscribed on the final page (f. 31v). This inscription may allude to Louis Galet of Calais, who served as royal ambassador under Henry VI and Edward IV. In addition, appearing on a blank flyleaf near the end of the manuscript is the name of Jacquetta of Luxemburg (d. 1472), widow of John, Duke of Bedford. She married beneath her rank when she took as her second husband Sir Richard Woodville (d. 1469), 1st Earl Rivers, who himself was elected Knight of the Order of the Garter in 1450. Richard's eldest daughter, Elizabeth, married Edward IV in 1465, and his granddaughter, another Elizabeth, married Henry VII at Westminster Abbey on 18 January 1486. The manuscript probably passed by descent from one Woodville to another until it was customized for the King and entered the Old Royal library.

D.J.

PROVENANCE:

Louis Galet (?); Jacquetta of Luxemburg (d. 1472); Henry VII.

Opposite:
The Trinity with an added portrait of Henry VII, f. 1

38 *Speculum humanae salvationis*

London, *c.* 1500
470 x 345 mm

BRITISH LIBRARY, HARLEY 2838

The Fall of Man; Expulsion from Paradise; Adam digging and Eve spinning; the Flood, ff. 4v–5

As he explains in his prologue, for reasons of modesty the author of the *Speculum humanae salvationis* (Mirror of Human Salvation) kept his name a secret. This was a prudent strategy since the work, a religious treatise in Latin verse, was copied avidly, read widely, and translated into several languages – all of which could have fostered a sense of pride. If he had been more forthcoming, however, he would have spared scholars protracted debate. All agree that the work was written in the first quarter of the fourteenth century, but where or by whom remains uncertain.

The text found favour with low and lofty audiences alike. Crude printed copies thumbed by poor preachers represent one end of the market, and deluxe manuscripts commissioned by affluent nobles, the other. Made for Henry VII, the present manuscript bears the English royal arms enclosed within a Garter and surmounted by a crown (f. 1). Once covered in crimson velvet, a characteristic of Henry VII's books, the manuscript was rebound in the late nineteenth century (Wright and Wright 1966). Although the decorated initials and borders are of English workmanship, the miniatures were painted by a Dutch artist, one of the so-called Masters of the Dark Eyes, who was active in London *c.* 1500 and illustrated several other extant manuscripts (e.g. cat. nos. 39, 42). Instructions to the artist in Dutch are visible below some of the miniatures of the *Speculum*, but most of these notes were painted over by the artist.

The manuscript contains forty-five chapters in rhyming verse. Four miniatures illustrate each one, offering a visual précis of the text inscribed below. In most chapters an episode from the life of Christ or the Virgin Mary is compared with three events drawn from the Old Testament or other sources, an interpretive method known as typology. Christ's Harrowing of Hell, for example, is associated with three 'types': the Israelites' escape from Egypt, the legendary account of Abraham's deliverance from a fire and Lot's flight from Sodom (ff. 33v–34). The book, whose central theme is sin and salvation, begins with a description of the Fall of Man. Having eaten the forbidden fruit, Adam and Eve are exiled from the Garden of Eden (f. 4v, pictured).

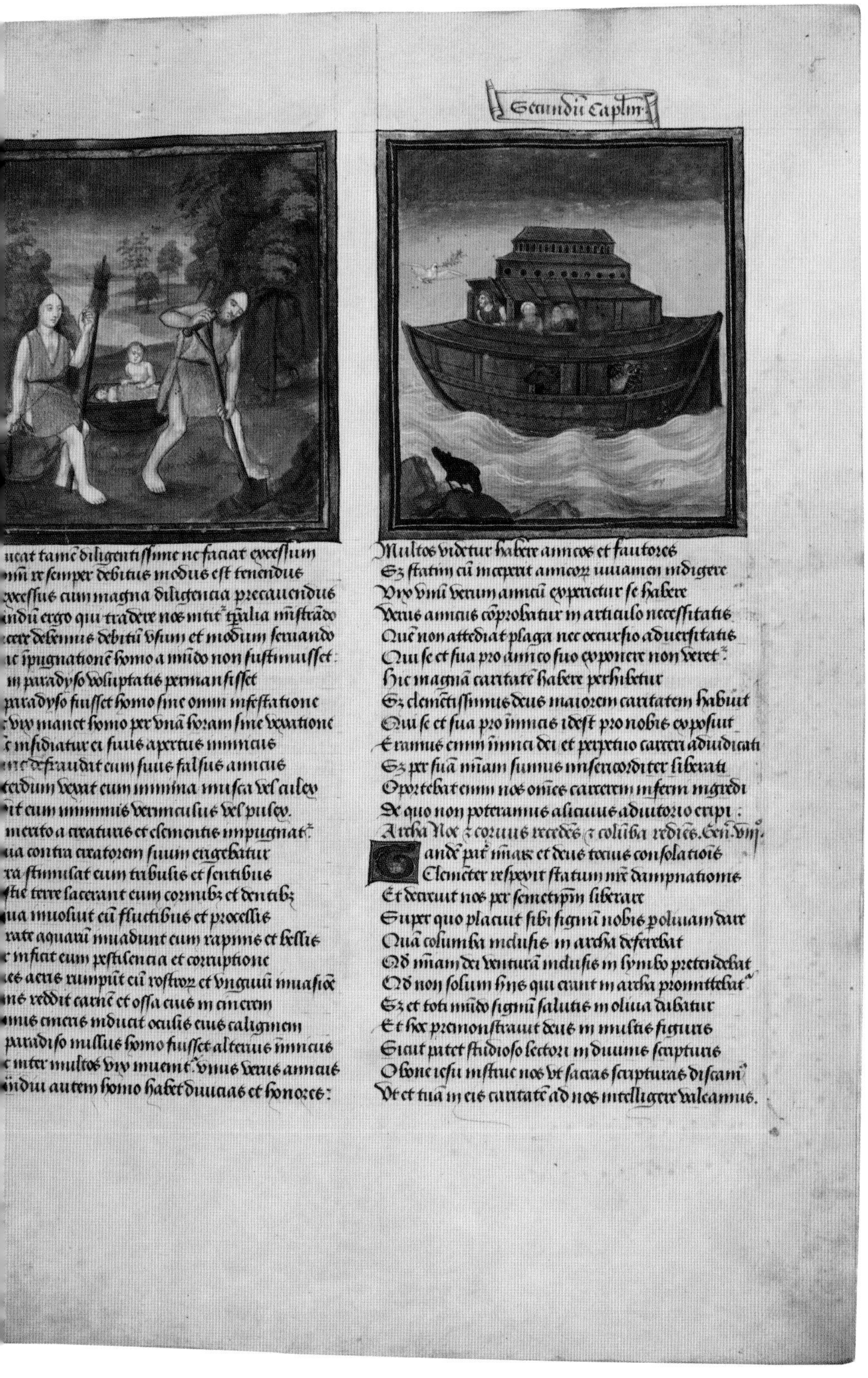

Their disobedience consigns all of humanity to a life of misery. The following miniature depicts Adam digging and Eve spinning, the dull grey of their garments reflecting the sombre mood (f. 5, pictured).

The miniatures generally conform to a standard pictorial programme, but some details reflect the specific circumstances in which the manuscript was made. On f. 44v, for example, which shows Christ enthroned with saints, St George appears front and centre. Since the manuscript was presented to Henry VII this is not surprising: George was England's foremost saint and the main patron of the Order of the Garter. The royal chapel at Windsor, renovated by Henry VII, served as the focus of George's cult and was where the knights of the Garter met to celebrate his feast on 23 April. The King presided over the elite company, a role reflected in the heraldic emblems on the first page of the manuscript: the royal arms with the garter and motto '*Honi soit [qui] mal y pense*' (Shame on him who thinks evil of it), a reference to English claims to the French throne asserted by the order's founder, Edward III.

Most intriguing is the portrait of a bishop kneeling in the miniature of the Coronation of the Virgin (f. 51), the final image in a sequence illustrating the Seven Joys experienced by her, a popular devotional theme. Set apart from the Virgin and the Three Persons of the Trinity, the bishop, a donor figure, is probably the man who commissioned the manuscript and presented it to Henry VII. One of the most likely candidates is Richard Fitzjames (d. 1522), the Oxford-educated theologian who was appointed chaplain to Henry VII in 1489 and bishop of Rochester in 1497, of Chichester in 1503, and finally, of London in 1506. It is possible that Fitzjames gave the manuscript to the King in gratitude for the last appointment. A trusted adviser, Fitzjames was a confidant of the King and, on Henry's death in 1509, served as one of his executors. *D. J.*

PROVENANCE:

Henry VII; Robert Harley, 1st Earl of Oxford (b. 1661, d. 1724), by 1715; Edward Harley, 2nd Earl of Oxford (b. 1689, d. 1741); purchased for the nation in 1753.

39 Ordinances of the Confraternity of the Immaculate Conception

London, 1503–17
330 x 250 mm

OXFORD, CHRIST CHURCH, MS 179

The Confraternity of the Immaculate Conception was established in 1503 at the Dominican conventual church of Blackfriars by a community of French immigrants living in London. This book contains the Confraternity's ordinances, which codified the social and religious practices of its members – ranging from the format of their annual festive meetings to their methods of mutual support, communal worship and provision for masses for dead brethren. Although lay fraternities were numerous in late medieval towns and cities, their foundation documents are relatively rare survivals (see cat. no. 36). Confraternities of foreign residents in London are known to have gathered in mendicant convents rather than in parish churches and thus operated outside the direct jurisdiction of the local bishop. To provide additional protection and legal foundation to their communities, some had their ordinances enrolled in the registers of the Commissary Court; seven records of such documents survive (Colson 2010). The Confraternity of the Immaculate Conception chose a different route to seek official recognition. Using the mediation of a prominent member of the community, the court historian Bernard André (d. 1522), the brethren addressed a petition directly to the King.

The Christ Church manuscript is an official record of this event. The successful petition is integrated as a preamble to the ordinances, and a full-page image of Henry VII, his wife Elizabeth of York and their children – all in adoration of the Immaculate Conception – confirms the King's engagement in the foundation of the Confraternity. The members of the Confraternity clearly aimed to give their foundation document a truly royal character. They commissioned the decoration of the opening pages from the workshop of the Master of the *Speculum humane salvationis* (see cat. no. 38), a Dutch illuminator and one of the so-called Masters of the Dark Eyes, who were active in London *c.* 1500 and illustrated several manuscripts for the royal family and court (Broekhuijsen 2009). The border of the frontispiece to the ordinances – which features the royal arms supported by Tudor heraldic beasts (the red dragon and white greyhound) and Henry VII's badges (the red rose alternating with the Beaufort portcullis) – employs the same design as that used in other books for the King (see cat. no. 41).

Although the iconography of the opening miniature refers directly to the name of the confraternity, it also alludes to one of Henry VII's badges. The image (pictured)depicts the moment of the 'Immaculate Conception' of the Virgin Mary that, according to Church doctrine, occurred without a sexual act and therefore did not transmit the original sin. It happened, according to tradition, when Mary's parents, Anne and Joachim, embraced at the Golden Gate in Jerusalem. The monumental gate with a prominent portcullis that frames the scene being adored by the royal family makes a strong visual link to the Beaufort portcullis depicted in the border. Four additional images painted in the corners of the page complete the story by showing the events that, according to apocryphal writings, surrounded the Virgin's Immaculate Conception: the childlessness of Joachim and Anne, considered a punishment for the couple's unworthiness by a priest who refused their offering; the Annunciations to Anne and Joachim; and Anne with the Virgin in her womb.

Despite the prominent presence of the royal heraldry, it is likely that this copy of the ordinances was commissioned as a record for the Confraternity and was never presented to the King. Although the manuscript consists of only seven leaves, it appears to have been written in two or three phases. Three scribes were responsible for, respectively, the petition, the ordinances and the list of the masters of the Confraternity; each of these parts bears a different date. The earliest, the petition, was probably completed at the beginning of 1503. The recent death of Queen Elizabeth (d. 11 February 1503) is mentioned in the text, but the opening portrait of the royal family disregards the divide between the living and the dead and depicts the Queen alive in an ideal and atemporal adoration with all seven of her children, including the deceased Elizabeth (d. 1492), Arthur (d. 1502) and Catherine (d. February 1503). It is likely that the petition was copied or integrated into the manuscript to complete the ordinances, which, as their introduction states, were composed on 22 March 1503. The last item in the book lists the names of the masters of the Confraternity from 1503 to 1517. It must have been added after these dates and confirms the use of the book by the brethren within the period indicated. As Colson suggested (2010), this lavish copy of the ordinances of the Confraternity of the Immaculate Conception may have been bequeathed to Christ Church by Archbishop William Wake (d. 1737). *J.F.*

PROVENANCE:

Confraternity of the Immaculate Conception, London; (?)William Wake, Archbishop of Canterbury (b. 1657, d. 1737).

Opposite:
Henry VII, Elizabeth of York and their children praying beneath an image of Anne and Joachim embracing at the Golden Gate, f. 1v

40 Proper of the Mass for the Immaculate Conception

London, *c.* 1503–09
215 x 145 mm

BRITISH LIBRARY, ROYAL 2 A. xix

Only a few liturgical manuscripts survive in the Old Royal library; many may have fallen victim to the 1550 Act against Superstitious Books and Images and the 1551 Privy Council edict applying this Act to the royal library at Westminster (see essay, 'The Old Royal Library'). Stored somewhere other than at Westminster, this little volume was spared from the destruction that was supervised at Edward VI's library by its Keeper and confirmed Protestant Bartholomew Traheron.

Royal 2 A. xix is not an ordinary liturgical book. It contains only the Proper of the Mass for the Feast of the Immaculate Conception of the Virgin, which was usually included in the Missal amongst other Eucharistic texts for fixed feast days in the liturgical year (the Proper of Saints). In the Royal manuscript, the service for the Immaculate Conception was selected as a special mass for Henry VII and copied, decorated and bound separately. Three major prayers to be said by a celebrant – the collect, secret and post-communion – contain supplications for the good health and prosperity of Henry VII and for his peaceful and glorious reign. The initial 'G' of the introit of the mass encircles the royal arms of England and the half-page miniature that precedes the text depicts the King in prayer venerating the Virgin in the womb of her mother, St Anne (f. 2, pictured). The shining aureole around Mary's body indicates her sanctification in her mother's womb and her miraculous exemption from original sin at the first instant of her conception.

In the fourteenth and fifteenth centuries, the Franciscans were the principal defenders of the controversial Church doctrine of the Immaculate Conception. Authorized by the Franciscan Pope Sixtus IV, the associated feast was adopted by the entire Latin Church in a decree of 28 February 1476. Henry's devotion to the Virgin has been explained as being stimulated by the piety of the Observant Franciscans whom he vigorously supported during his exile in Brittany and later as king in England (Henderson 2002). Henry may have been introduced to the concept of immaculacy in Brittany (the cult of the Virgin's Immaculate Conception was particularly strong there in the fifteenth century) and he probably remained under the influence of Franciscan devotion throughout his life. However, the commission of the present manuscript appears not to have been directly initiated by the King.

In 1503 a group of French residents of London addressed a formal petition to Henry VII and asked him to authorize a confraternity that they had formed at the conventual church of the Blackfriars and dedicated to the Immaculate Conception of the Virgin (see cat. no 39). In return for royal licence and patronage the brethren obliged themselves in their petition 'more than ever before, to pray especially to sweet Jesus and his Blessed Mother for yours [the King's] safety and long life' (see Colson 2010). Each year, on the Feast of the Immaculate Conception (8 December), members of the confraternity were required to attend a solemn mass in the choir of the Dominican church. One such annual celebration, perhaps the first one after the King's licence had been issued to the community, would have been a perfect occasion to present 'the true founder' of the confraternity with the text of the mass that included special prayers for him.

The illumination of the Royal manuscript may be attributed to a London workshop that is known to have worked on other commissions from the royal court. Although of slightly lower quality and precision than Henry VII's portrait in the Proper, four miniatures illustrating the 1503 indenture for Henry VII's Chapel at Westminster Abbey (cat. no. 41 and London, TNA: PRO, E.33/1) employ the same model for an interior setting, similar facial types and grey tones for human flesh and virtually identical details of border decoration. Scott (2007) has also identified the same artistic style in Henry VII's portrait in a collection of liturgical music presented to the King (Cambridge, University Library, MS Nn.6.46, f. 2). *J.F.*

PROVENANCE:

Henry VII.

Opposite:
Henry VII adoring the Immaculate Conception of the Virgin, f. 2 (actual size)

41 Quadripartite Indenture between Henry VII and John Islip, Abbot of Westminster

London, 1504
370 x 255 mm

BRITISH LIBRARY, HARLEY 1498

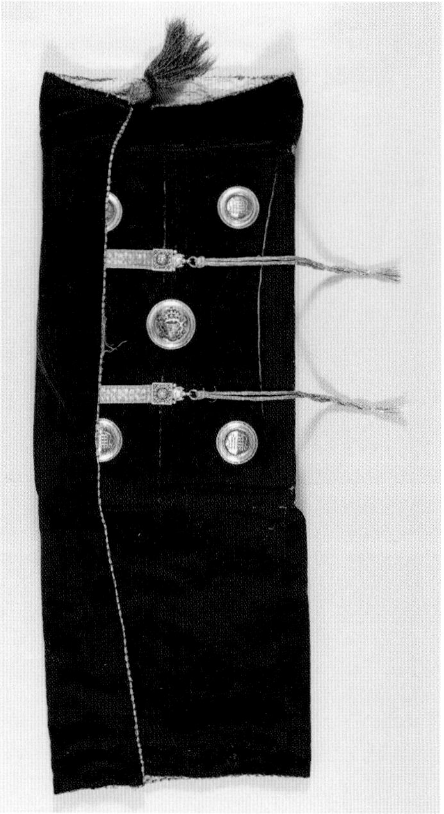

Above:
Velvet chemise binding
Opposite:
Henry VII presenting the indenture to John Islip, Abbot of Westminster, f. 1

One of the most interesting, yet little studied, surviving books commissioned by an English monarch is this quadripartite indenture made for the first Tudor king, Henry VII, and dated 16 July 1504. Both a sumptuous artefact and a legal document, the large volume – resplendent in its original binding – preserves a series of four agreements made between the King and the Abbot and monks of Westminster Abbey, the site chosen, after much deliberation, by Henry VII as his place of burial. The King's intention was to be enshrined near the remains of his saintly uncle, Henry VI, and England's foremost royal saint, Edward the Confessor, in a new chapel that he ordered to be constructed at the east end of the Abbey in place of the thirteenth-century structure built by Henry III. Although the body of Henry VI was never transferred from Windsor Castle to Westminster Abbey, Henry VII's chapel, famous for its pendant fan vaults and among the very finest late Gothic buildings in England, was built in accordance with the King's commands and serves to this day as a testament to his ambition and deep purse.

Few aspects of the building works were left to chance, and the rituals and liturgical ceremonies to be performed by the abbot and monks both in the King's lifetime and posthumously were likewise planned with precision. Henry VII's wishes, which he expected to be fulfilled in perpetuity, included the delivery of sermons and saying of prayers for him, for his beloved and recently deceased consort, Elizabeth of York (d. 1503), and for other family members, both at Westminster and elsewhere. Other instructions concerned, for example, the methods of distributing alms to the poor and the number of tapers to be lit on specified days.

These obligations and many more are outlined in the present manuscript, an unusually grand legal contract comprising four indentures. These indentures were written in duplicate so that each party to the agreement – Henry VII and the Abbot and monks of Westminster – could retain one copy. The present manuscript is the part intended for Westminster Abbey, but the other part, a twin volume made for Henry VII and originally housed in the Exchequer Treasury of Receipt, is also extant (London, TNA: PRO, E.33/1). The pages and boards of both volumes have been cut in a wavy line along their top edges so that the two volumes interlock (hence the term 'indenture' from the French *endenture*, meaning indented or toothed). Although the format is unusual for manuscript books, Henry VII commissioned a series of bound indentures of this type, which mimic ones written on single sheets of parchment and then cut in two along a wavy edge (Condon 2003). To verify the authenticity of the documents interested parties could simply match the two parts.

Each of the four indentures in the present manuscript opens with a lavishly decorated page. In addition to full borders painted with the King's arms, badges and emblems, including Beaufort portcullises and red roses (cf. cat. no. 39), each page features a large initial in which a relevant scene is depicted. The first and fourth initials (ff. 1 [pictured], 98), for example, show the enthroned Henry VII handing the quadripartite indenture to John Islip, Abbot of Westminster (b. 1464, d. 1532), who kneels before him alongside several monks. The second initial (f. 59) is similar in style and composition to the first and final ones, but includes almsmen in addition to the monks. Of particular interest is the third initial (f. 76), which reveals how the indenture was meant to be used in perpetuity. As pictured opposite, annually, the abbot and monks of Westminster were to meet in the Chapter House with the king's representatives to listen to the terms of the agreement being read aloud.

The indenture retains its original crimson velvet chemise binding lined with pink damask (above), the latter of which may have been woven in Italy (Condon 2003). In addition, decorative bosses in silver gilt and enamel, decorated with the King's emblems, adorn both the lower and upper covers. Five original wax seals stored in silver cases are attached to the base of the manuscript. Four bear an image of the enthroned King, and the fifth one of him on horseback. These seals underscore the legal function of the volume and enhance its regal appearance. *D.J.*

PROVENANCE:

Dean and Chapter of Westminster; Henry VIII; Sir Thomas Hoby, 3rd Baronet, of Bisham (b. 1685, d. 1730); Robert Harley, 1st Earl of Oxford (b. 1661, d. 1724); Edward Harley, 2nd Earl of Oxford (b. 1689, d. 1741); purchased for the nation in 1753.

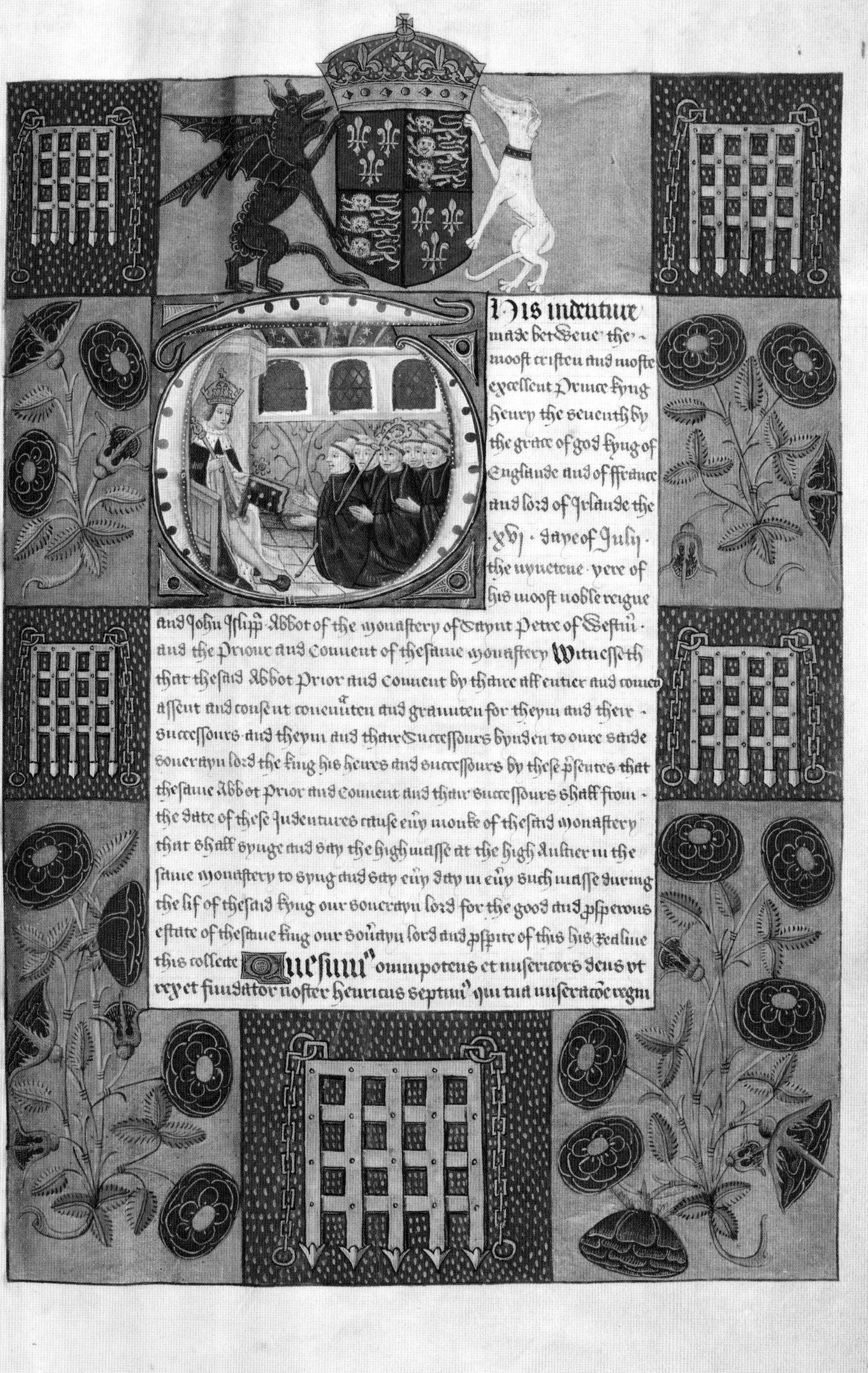
This indenture
made betwene the
moost cristen and moste
excellent Prince kyng
henry the seuenth by
the grace of god kyng of
Englande and of ffrance
and lord of Irlande the
·xvj· daye of July·
the nyntene· yere of
his moost noble reigne
and John Islipp Abbot of the monastery of Saynt Petre of Westm̃·
and the Priour and Couent of the same monastery Witnesseth
that the said Abbot Prior and Couent by thaire all entier and concord
assent and consent concluden and graunten for theym and their·
successours and theym and thaire Successours bynden to oure said
souerayn lord the king his heires and successours by these psentes that
the same Abbot Prior and Couent and thair successours shall from·
the date of these Indentures cause euy monke of the said monastery
that shall synge and say the high masse at the high Aulter in the
same monastery to syng and say euy day in euy such masse during
the lif of the said kyng our souerayn lord for the good and psperous
estate of the same king our souayn lord and psperite of this his Realme
this collecte Quesumus omnipotens et misericors deus vt
rex et fundator noster henricus septimus qui tua miseracione regni

42 Gospel Lectionary

London, 1508
305 x 200 mm

BRITISH LIBRARY, ROYAL 2 B. xiii

Feast of All Saints, with the donors' patron saints, Stephen and Margaret, f. 34 (detail)

Compared to manuscripts employed for public worship in English cathedrals and monasteries, few that belonged to parish churches survive. The total number is estimated to be between sixty and seventy volumes, the earliest of which date to the thirteenth century (Pfaff 2009). Some medieval service books fell apart from constant use, while others were discarded and replaced when outdated. In part, the low rate of survival is due to the reforming zeal of Thomas Cranmer, Archbishop of Canterbury (b. 1489, d. 1556), who championed the Act of Uniformity, passed by Parliament on 21 January 1549. The Act introduced a new liturgy in English, printed in the *Book of Common Prayer*, and it rendered obsolete all existing Latin service books. The 1550 Act against Superstitious Books and Images ensured that thousands of such service books were destroyed.

Two late medieval manuscripts that have come down to us are a pair of lectionaries made for a London parish church (Royal 2 B. xii, 2 B. xiii). These contain excerpts from the New Testament to be read at mass. Slim volumes, they encompass only the lessons for the most important annual feasts, arranged according to the liturgical calendar. Identical in size, written by the same scribe and illuminated by the same artists, they form a handsome pair. Both retain their original bindings: oak boards that once featured decorative panels, now missing. Although they have been stripped of their finery, the manuscripts preserve something equally precious: inscriptions recording when and for whom they were made.

Completed in 1508, the manuscripts were presented to the parish church of St Mary the Virgin, Aldermanbury, in the City of London, by the prosperous merchant Sir Stephen Jenyns (b. 1450, d. 1523) and his wife Margaret. Dedicatory inscriptions, written on the flyleaves of the matching volumes, are surprisingly fulsome. Readers are enjoined to pray not only for the donors, but also for the soul of Margaret's first husband, William Buck, former Master of the Merchant Taylors' Company, a post occupied by Jenyns in 1489, after Buck's death. Sir Stephen Jenyns was born and raised in Wolverhampton, where he later established a grammar school, but the Bucks resided in the parish of Aldermanbury (Clode 1888), and it is likely that Margaret in particular had ties to the local church.

An outstanding philanthropist, Jenyns is referred to in the inscriptions as 'militis et aldermanni Londonie' (knight and alderman of London). In May 1508 he served as alderman of the Lime Street Ward, but he was not knighted until 23 June 1509 (Clode 1888), so the inscription must postdate that event. The final lines reveal that Jenyns was elected Lord Mayor of London in 1508, the same year that he gave the Lectionaries to St Mary's. Gratitude for

John the Baptist flanked by a lion and a unicorn, f. 27 (detail)

this appointment may have prompted his largesse.

Small miniatures in both manuscripts mark the beginning of major feasts. These were painted by a Dutch artist working in England, one of the so-called Masters of the Dark Eyes. One word in Dutch, 'gebort' (birth), written beside the miniature of the Nativity in the Gospel Lectionary (f. 6), suggests that the artist – who produced several manuscripts for the English royal house (see also cat. no. 38) – worked with at least one assistant (Broekhuijsen 2009).

Although it has hitherto been unremarked, the Lectionaries reflect the patron's devotional allegiances. The Feast of St Stephen (26 December) – the donor's name saint – for example, is one of only three lections that feature liturgical music (the others are Christmas and Epiphany) (Warner and Gilson 1921). Aspects of the pictorial programme likewise reveal the couple's concerns, particularly the Feast of All Saints, which depicts the Virgin Mary (the church of Aldermanbury was dedicated to her) being crowned by God the Father and Son (f. 34, pictured). Directly beneath is George, patron saint of England. Stephen and Margaret, the donors' name saints, appear in the foreground on the left and right respectively, alongside Mary Magdalene, who is associated with many hospitals and charities. Beside her stands the patron of the Merchant Taylors' Company, John the Baptist, to whom the couple were especially devoted. Masters of the Company, like Jenyns, were elected on the Vigil of the Feast of the Nativity of the Baptist (24 June) and they demonstrated their loyalty to the saint in tangible ways. In 1512, for example, Jenyns and his wife supplied decorations for the Company's chapel and hall, including a rich cloth on which the patron saint was emblazoned (Furdell 2004, 2010).

A lion and a unicorn flank John the Baptist in the miniature for his feast day in the Gospel Lectionary (f. 27, pictured). Significantly, these animals appear in the same configuration on the seal of the Merchant Taylors' Company, designed in 1502 when it was granted 'a new charter by Henry VII ... [and] first styled itself "The Guild of the Merchant Taylors of the Fraternity of St John the Baptist in the City of London"'(Clode 1888).

Jenyns intended the Lectionaries to remain at St Mary's; how they entered the Royal collection is unknown. The Old Royal library was, however, a fitting home for them. As Lord Mayor of London and Master of one of the most powerful guilds, Jenyns was no stranger to royalty. He attended the funeral of Henry VII and was knighted at Westminster Abbey at Henry VIII's coronation on 23 June 1509, the Vigil of the Feast of the Nativity of his beloved John the Baptist. *D.J.*

PROVENANCE:

Church of St Mary Aldermanbury, London.

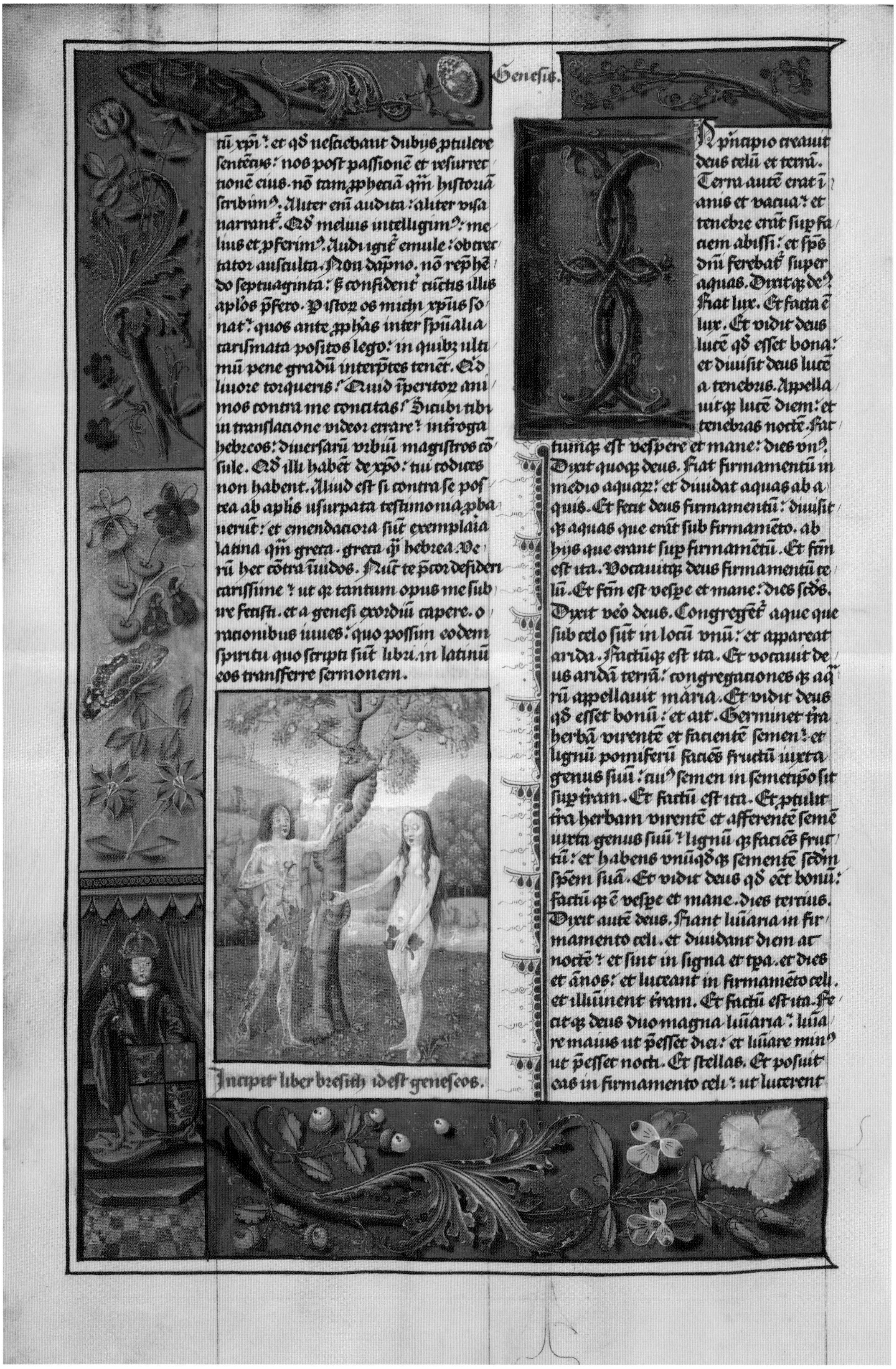
Genesis.

tū xpi: et qd nesciebant dubys ptulere
sententiis: nos post passionē et resurrec
tionē eius nō tam ꝓphetiā q̄m historiā
scribim⁹. Aliter eni audita: aliter visa
narrant. Qd melius intelligim⁹: me
lius et pferim⁹. Audi igit emule: obtrec
tator ausculta. Non dāpno. nō rephēdo
septuaginta: ꝫ confident cūctis illis
aplōs pfero. Per istor os michi xpus so
nat: quos ante ꝓphas inter spūalia
carismata positos lego: in quibꝫ ulti
mū pene gradū interptes tenet. Qd
liuore torqueris? Quid īperitoꝝ ani
mos contra me concitas? Sicubi tibi
in translatione videor errare: interroga
hebreos: diuersarū vrbiū magistros cō
sule. Qd illi habēt de xpo: tui codices
non habent. Aliud est si contra se pos
tea ab aplis usurpata testimonia pba
uerūt: et emendatiora sūt exemplaria
latina q̄m greca. greca q̄ hebrea. Ve
rū hec cōtra īuidos. Nūc te pcor desideri
tissime: ut q̄ tantum opus me sub
ire fecisti. et a genesi exordiū capere. o
rationibus iuues: quo possim eodem
spiritu quo scripti sūt libri in latinū
eos transferre sermonem.

Incipit liber bresith idest geneseos.

In pricipio creauit
deus celū et terrā.
Terra autē erat i
anis et vacua: et
tenebre erāt sup fa
ciem abissi: et sps
dnī ferebat super
aquas. Dixitqꝫ de⁹.
Fiat lux. Et facta ē
lux. Et vidit deus
lucē qd esset bona:
et diuisit deus lucē
a tenebris. Appella
uitqꝫ lucē diem: et
tenebras noctē. Fac
tumqꝫ est vespere et mane: dies vn⁹.
Dixit quoqꝫ deus. Fiat firmamentū in
medio aquaꝝ: et diuidat aquas ab a
quis. Et fecit deus firmamentū: diuisit
qꝫ aquas que erāt sub firmamēto. ab
hys que erant sup firmamētū. Et fcm
est ita. Vocauitqꝫ deus firmamentū ce
lū. Et fcm est vespe et mane: dies scds.
Dixit veo deus. Congregēt aque que
sub celo sūt in locū vnū: et appareat
arida. Factūqꝫ est ita. Et vocauit de
us aridā terrā: congregationesqꝫ aq
rū appellauit maria. Et vidit deus
qd esset bonū: et ait. Germinet tra
herbā virentē et facientē semen: et
lignū pomiferū faciēs fructū iuxta
genus suū: cui⁹ semen in semetipso sit
sup trām. Et factū est ita. Et ptulit
tra herbam virentē et afferentē semē
iuxta genus suū: lignūqꝫ faciēs fruc
tū: et habens vnūqdqꝫ sementē scdm
spēm suā. Et vidit deus qd eēt bonū:
factūqꝫ ē vespe et mane. dies tercius.
Dixit autē deus. Fiant lūiaria in fir
mamento celi. et diuidant diem ac
noctē: et sint in signa et tpa. et dies
et ānos: et luceant in firmamēto celi.
et illūinent trām. Et factū est ita. Fe
citqꝫ deus duo magna lūiaria: lūia
re maius ut pesset diei: et lūiare min⁹
ut pesset nocti. Et stellas. Et posuit
eas in firmamento celi: ut lucerent

43 Bible

Zwolle, 1450–51; Southern Netherlands or England, *c.* 1520
385 x 275 mm

BRITISH LIBRARY, ROYAL 1 C. v

Together with its companion volume (Royal 1 C. vi), this manuscript forms a complete copy of St Jerome's translation of the Bible. Like several other copies of the Vulgate, the two-volume set was produced in the early 1450s at Zwolle by the Brethren of the Common Life, who appended a colophon to each volume (f. 260; Royal 1 C. vi, f. 269). The Brethren practised the *Devotio moderna*, a reformed notion of religion that encouraged the individual to study Scripture independently. The Bibles from Zwolle reflect this ideology by reproducing a text of the Vulgate in which the content is easy to read and not overladen with commentary; these manuscripts strive for uniformity and are laid out in a manner that eases reference, with consistent running headers and rubricated incipits. Likewise, the decoration of the Bibles shows a 'sobriety and cool restraint' (Gumbert 1990) in containing only delicate, penwork initials at the beginning of each book and prologue, the designs of which are unique to the output of the Zwolle Brethren. Like other Zwolle Bibles, the present manuscript was intended for an individual patron, rather than for the Brethren's own use (Obbema 1991).

Whereas the Bible's original destination is unknown, its later history is much clearer. More than half a century after its production it was embellished and modernized, either in the southern Netherlands or in England, for presentation to Henry VIII. Around 1520 the two volumes were enhanced by the addition of seven illuminated borders, as well as seven decorated initials in a south Netherlandish style that were painted over the original, by then less fashionable, initials. The new borders and initials occur, exclusively, at the juncture between Jerome's prefaces to various books of the Bible and the start of each book proper. Some of the borders include flowers and jewels arranged upon backgrounds of saturated hues; others contain figural illustrations, such as on the first page of the book of Job, which shows Jerome (Royal 1 C. vi, f. 1), as well as a pair of monkey paramours serenaded by another simian. In addition to these borders, three miniatures are set into the renovated pages, including a depiction of the Fall at the start of Genesis (f. 4v, pictured). Adjacent to this miniature is an image of Henry VIII himself, sporting his characteristic auburn beard, seated and holding an escutcheon with the royal arms upon it. A further miniature, in the border illumination on the first page of I Kings, captures David wielding a sword over Goliath's fallen body (f. 118v) – surely a deliberate nod to Henry, who modelled himself on King David (see cat. no. 45).

In many ways this Bible corresponds to the kinds of books Henry VIII acquired and collected. However, the date at which it entered the Royal collection may only be surmised. Henry engaged in three major periods of biblical and theological study, during which he sought out books on and of Scripture. First, around 1520, he began his research in preparation for the tract against Martin Luther that was published in 1521; second, later in that decade, the King's appetite for biblical books was inflated by the need to buttress his case for a divorce from Catherine of Aragon; and, finally, during the 1530s, Henry took again to scriptural study in his efforts to break away definitively from Rome. He appears to have developed a particular interest in Bibles, of which he owned numerous copies, collected throughout his reign (Carley 2004).

None of Henry's monastic acquisitions was updated in this way. It is, therefore, unlikely that the present manuscript was plucked from an English monastery for research purposes. The Zwolle Bible appears, rather, to have been a gift from a subject aware of Henry's intellectual leanings and interest in religious reform. One possible donor may be suggested by the 'portrait' of St Jerome in cardinal's garb on the first page of the second volume. Cardinal Wolsey's patronage of Netherlandish art and his dealings with the Low Countries place him in a prime position to have acquired and given this set during his ascendancy in the early 1520s. While the occasion of its presentation is unknown, the nature of Henry's portrait at the beginning of Genesis supports this dating. The earliest known image of Henry with his iconic beard was created *c.*1520; before that date he is represented clean-shaven. The closeness of this portrait to those made in England at the time may also indicate that the volume was refurbished in England by an artist who was trained in the southern Netherlands.

Thus, although the Bible from Zwolle coincides with Henry's studies in the early 1520s, it should also be viewed as formative – that is, as contributing towards the crystallization of his religious ideas as they were ultimately manifested in the Great Bible of 1539. *S.D.*

PROVENANCE:

Henry VIII.

Opposite:
Henry VIII, and the Fall, f. 4v

44 Prayer Roll of Henry VIII

England, between 1485 and 1509
3355 x 120 mm (3rd and 4th membranes 100 mm)

BRITISH LIBRARY, ADDITIONAL 88929

Produced in England during the reign of Henry VII, this is a rare example of a late medieval Prayer Roll. Prayer Rolls of this kind combined devotional and amuletic functions and were typical of late medieval popular piety, but very few survived the Reformation. The number of survivals has been put at a mere sixteen (Stork 2004), of which this is one of the finest.

The roll consists of four narrow strips of parchment that, joined together, measure over three metres in length, and it contains thirteen illuminations juxtaposed with Latin prayers and English rubrics. Visually the roll highlights the interconnectedness of heaven and earth. Its composition and iconography create a clear distinction between the upper half of the roll, devoted to Christ and the Godhead, and the lower half, focused on saints on earth in the time after Christ. A central image of the Virgin and Child provides a transition between the two sections, both structurally and thematically.

The uppermost image establishes the theme for the entire roll and provides a key to its function and form. Within a vertical frame, space is divided into two registers that represent a celestial sphere and an earthly realm. In the lower register a mitred bishop kneels in prayer, gazing upwards to the Trinity, while Christ gazes downwards at him. As a form of visual instruction, this image informs the devotee that by looking upwards towards heaven, both figuratively and literally, one can appeal successfully for the aid and benediction of God. The rest of the upper half of the roll is devoted to the Wounds of Christ and focuses the pious Christian's attention on the Cross and Christ's suffering. The decidedly earthbound nature of the images of the saints on the lower half of the roll emphasizes that Christ's incarnation made it possible for those born after him to transcend the earthly realm by focusing their attention upwards towards God.

As instructed by the rubrics, the reader would scroll down the roll, reading and reciting the prayers while meditating on the images. Other rubrics promised that wearing the roll on the body would bring greater physical proximity to the body of Christ, ward off evil and provide protection from sickness and disease. The amuletic function of this prayer-roll is most explicit in the vernacular instruction that accompanies the image of Christ hanging on a Tau-shaped cross, flanked by two angels, each holding an unfurled scroll that mimics the form of *this* roll. The text explains that the miniature is based on the Measurement of Christ and promises general protection, material prosperity and safe childbirth to those who wear the roll on their bodies:

> This cros, xv tymes moten is the length of our Lord Jesu Criste, and that day that ye bere it upon you ther shal no evyl spirite have power of yow ... and it shal breke your enemys power and encres your worldely goodes, and if a woman be in travell off childe, ley this on her body and she shal be delyverd with oute parel, the childe chrystendom, and the moder purificacyon.

The origin of the roll remains unclear, but it is likely that the bishop, depicted kneeling before the Trinity, represents the original owner or donor. To the left of the bishop an angel bears an escutcheon, the heraldic arms of which have so far resisted identification. What is certain, and makes this prayer-roll particularly important, is its personal association with the young Henry VIII, as evidenced by the inclusion of Henry's royal badges at the head of the roll. These include two Tudor roses and the Prince of Wales's crowned ostrich feather, as well as Catherine of Aragon's emblem of a sheaf of arrows. At some point before his accession in 1509, Henry added an inscription between the images of Christ's Passion and Christ as Man of Sorrows: 'Wylliam thomas I pray yow pray for me your lovyng master Prynce Henry.' Henry's request to Thomas, a Gentleman of his Privy Chamber, indicates that as a young man the Prince practised the devotions characteristic of late medieval popular piety. His prayer-roll thus provides a unique and fascinating insight into his early religious beliefs and the devotional practices that he would later so famously reject. *A.C.* and *S.D.*

PROVENANCE:

Henry VIII; William Thomas (?); presented by Father Bernard O'Reilly (b. 1824, d. 1894) to Ushaw College, Durham, in 1858; purchased for the nation in 2010.

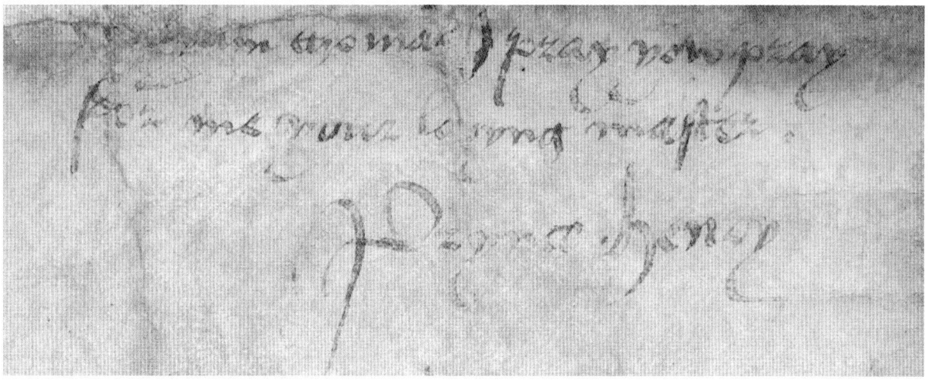

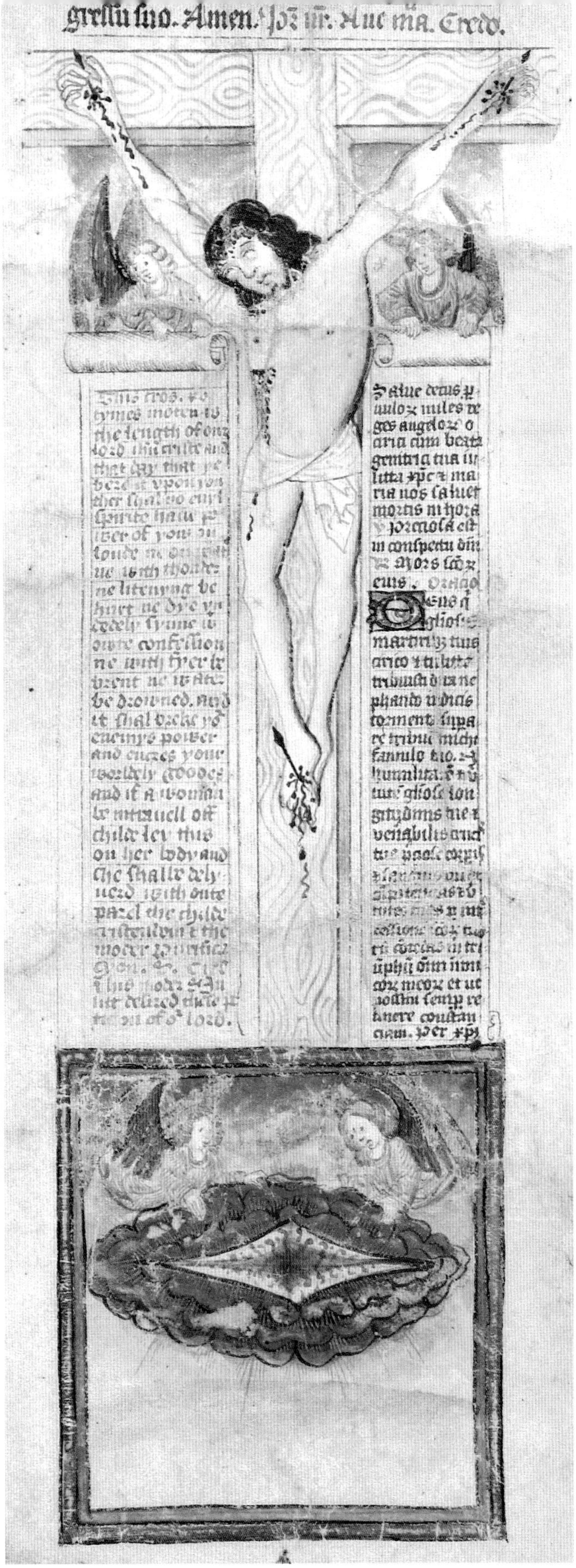

Above:
Praying bishop gazing up at the Trinity

Opposite:
Detail of Prince Henry's inscription

Crucifixion and angels bearing Christ's side-wound

45 The Psalter of Henry VIII

London, *c.* 1540
205 x 140 mm

BRITISH LIBRARY, ROYAL 2 A. xvi

The illustrations that Henry VIII commissioned in a Psalter for his own use *c.* 1540 demonstrate that he saw himself as a Davidic king (on David as a model for medieval kings, see Lowden's essay 'The Royal Manuscript'). In the Psalter's opening self-referential portrait of Henry seated in a chair in his bedchamber holding an open book (pictured), the King looks out at the viewer, who was initially Henry himself. Here he is very probably the blessed man described in the text of the Psalm below the image, 'who hath not walked in the counsel of the ungodly, nor stood in the way of sinners, nor sat in the chair of pestilence' (Psalm 1) (see Carley 2009; Walker 1996). Henry annotated the Psalter liberally with marginal notes, including one to the right of this text, where he comments in Latin 'note who is blessed', referring not only to the text but possibly also to the image of himself. It is not too fanciful to see the open book depicted in the miniature as a representation of this very Psalter, the red velvet binding of which still survives, albeit in a rather worn state (Carley 2009).

This image is, however, multivalent, as it occurs at Psalm 1, the location in a Psalter where an image of David was traditional (cf. cat. no. 12). By this date a manuscript Psalter in Latin rather than the more popular Book of Hours was an unusual choice. Perhaps the opportunity presented for a direct alignment with David accounts, in part, for the commissioning of such a personalized copy of this text (for another late Psalter with a possible portrait of the owner as David see cat. no. 148). Henry's connection with David is made even more directly at the beginning of Psalm 52 in which Henry is pictured with David's traditional attribute of a harp. Similar allusions to David had also been employed in manuscript painting by Henry's rival Francis I of France; he was pictured holding David's harp on two inserted leaves in the Book of Hours now known as the Hours of Catherine of Medici (Paris, BnF, MS n.a. lat. 82, ff. 152, 152v; see Backhouse 1966–67).

Henry commissioned the Psalter from Jean Mallard, who wrote out the Psalms in a beautifully clear Humanistic script and signed his name in the dedicatory preface as the king's poet (*orator regius*). It has never been entirely clear whether Mallard painted the miniatures in the manuscript as well, although it is known that he did illuminate other books, including his *Cosmographie* for Henry (cat. no. 96; on Mallard see Carley 2009). If he did illustrate the miniatures in the Psalter, this may account for the somewhat awkward handling of the perspective and hesitancy in the details in the execution of some of them. For example, Henry's connection to David may have been intended to be made even more explicit in the illustrated miniature prefacing Psalm 26, featuring David and Goliath's famous battle (pictured). In this scene David wears the same black wide-brimmed flat hat with white trim or feathers as Henry wears in Psalm 1 and in portraits at Psalms 52 and 68, as noted by Carley (2009). The lack of modelling in David's facial features makes a positive identification of the figure as a portrait of Henry problematic. Nevertheless, David wears rich contemporary dress against a background scene of elaborate tents, perhaps reminiscent of Tudor encampments such as that of the Field of the Cloth of Gold. Thus it seems likely that this image was intended as a retrospective portrait of a younger Henry as the younger David – the King was forty-nine in 1540 (see also Tudor Craig 1989; Walker 1996).

One puzzling feature of the Psalter is its lack of any miniature to mark the beginning of the last of the major divisions, at Psalm 109. Traditionally an illustration of the Trinity appeared here, interpreting the text 'The Lord said to my Lord: "Sit thou at my right hand"'. The odd omission of any image here may suggest that – notwithstanding his identification with King David, and a recent assessment of Henry's 'sacrialization of himself' as a 'Christic' king (Sharpe 2009) – interposing himself into the Godhead was a step beyond what Henry was prepared to contemplate. *K.D.*

PROVENANCE:
Henry VIII.

Above:
David and Goliath, f. 30 (detail)

Opposite:
Psalm 1, Henry VIII, f. 3 (actual size)

BEATVS vir qui non abiit in consilio impiorum, & in via peccatorum non stetit, & in cathedra pestilentiæ non sedit.

46 The Cotton Genesis

Eastern Mediterranean, *c.* 500
Largest fragment 175 x 150 mm (reduced by shrinkage of some 50%, originally approx. 350 x 300 mm, pages reproduced: 110 x 80 mm, and 145 x 90 mm)

BRITISH LIBRARY, COTTON OTHO B. vi

The fire of 1731 at Ashburnham House, Westminster, reduced the Greek Genesis manuscript, pride of the Cotton collection, to 134 shrunken and charred fragments. Originally it must have comprised some 221 leaves, decorated with some 360 framed illustrative images. Probably never before or since was the book of Genesis so profusely illustrated. Before the fire, however, a quarter of the pages and almost a third of the images were already missing. It is difficult to imagine the original appearance of the book, for even the surviving fragments of the parchment leaves shrank in the fire to about half of their original size. Both script and images were produced very carefully with considerable use of gold in the latter. Fortunately, copies of samples of both the text and one of the miniatures on what was, by the seventeenth century, the book's opening page were made for the French antiquarian Nicholas-Claude Fabri de Peiresc, to whom the book was loaned from 1618 to 1622.

The opening reproduced is from Genesis 18. First, Abraham speaks to God, who is in the form of three angels (Genesis 18:2), and pleads that the people of Sodom be spared destruction if ten just men can be found (Genesis 18:32, ends above the miniature on the left page), and then on the right page we see God (again in the form of three – or two – angels) departing and Abraham returning home (Genesis 18:33, below the miniature on the left page). Although the combination of these two images, just one verse apart, might suggest that the selection of passages to illustrate the text was extraordinarily profuse, this opening follows two pages that contain Genesis 18:16–30, which were without any images.

The book's place of production is uncertain. A focus on representations of Joseph, nilotic landscapes and pyramids has been interpreted (Weitzmann and Kessler 1986) as consistent with an origin in Egypt, but it would be surprising if the late Antique craftsmen had used iconographic details in such a documentary fashion. By the early thirteenth century the manuscript was in Venice, where it was used in a truly astonishing way. In the domical vault at the north-west angle of the ambulatory of the church of San Marco was set a complex mosaic decoration with images of the Creation and Genesis. The unusual iconography means that there can be no doubt that the mosaics are based on drawings copied directly from the manuscript. This connection was first made by the Finnish scholar J.J. Tikkanen in 1888.

The Cotton Genesis was still in Venice in the early sixteenth century, when Markos Bathas copied four images from it into the margins of a Genesis manuscript with catena (a type of multi-author commentary, comparable to the gloss found in some Latin manuscripts; Vienna, ÖNB, cod. theol. gr. 7). It was possibly acquired in the Veneto by Cardinal Reginald Pole in 1526–27. It then passed through the hands of Robert Wakefield (d. 1537), biblical scholar at Oxford, and subsequently of his brother Thomas Wakefield at Cambridge. It has recently been observed (Carley and Tite 2002) that Thomas Wakefield collated the Cotton Genesis, in which he had written his name, against a printed Bible of 1526. He recorded textual variants found in the manuscript, noting that a particular reading was 'in antiquissimo codice additur' (added in the most ancient codex) or 'in antiquissimo exemplari scripto' (written in the most ancient exemplar). The first variant (in the text of Genesis 1:14) was also recorded in a marginal note on one of the Peiresc drawings: 'non concordat cum impresso codice' ([this wording] does not agree with the printed text). Thomas Wakefield was appointed the first Regius Professor of Hebrew by Henry VIII in 1540, and appears to have presented the book to the King. From Henry VIII it passed to Elizabeth I, and from her to Sir John Fortescue (d. 1607). It was in the collection of Sir Robert Cotton by 1611. The story that the Cotton Genesis was presented to Henry VIII by two Greek bishops from Philippi, first recorded in 1624–30, after a note on a flyleaf, appears to be an invention. It is striking that one of the oldest manuscripts to have an English royal provenance shows no indication that it was a royal book before the reign of Henry VIII. *J.L.*

PROVENANCE

Cardinal Reginald Pole (?); Robert Wakefield (d. 1537); Thomas Wakefield; Henry VIII; Elizabeth I; Sir John Fortescue (d. 1607); Sir Robert Cotton (d. 1631); Thomas Howard, Earl of Arundel (on loan, 1630); Howard family (until after 1683); Sir John Cotton; presented to the nation in 1702.

Abraham speaks with God; Abraham returns home, ff. 26v–27

Reconstruction showing shrinkage of leaves as the result of fire damage

Edward IV: Founder of the Old Royal Library

According to a well-travelled Bohemian visitor to England, Gabriel Tetzel, Edward IV had by February 1466 'the most splendid court ... in all Christendom'. Lavish expenditure on clothes, jewels, plate and furnishings preceded his coronation in June 1461 and the marriage of his sister, Margaret of York, to Charles the Bold, Duke of Burgundy, in 1468. Soon after Edward returned from exile in the Netherlands in the winter of 1470–71, such expenditure became established as a relatively consistent feature of his reign.

For many luxury goods, including tapestries and illuminated manuscripts, Edward turned to the Netherlands. Around twenty very large illuminated manuscripts of library texts in French bear signs of having been decorated specifically for Edward at Bruges, mostly *c.* 1479–80. Together with around thirty other Netherlandish manuscripts probably also acquired by him, these books formed the core of the first permanent English royal library. At least two of Edward's manuscripts (cat. nos. 50, 52) support the argument that the King's collecting was influenced by the bibliophile Louis of Gruuthuse (d. 1492), with whom he resided during his exile in the Low Countries. Edward's patronage certainly helped to prolong the production of deluxe manuscripts at a time of political and economic crisis in the Burgundian Netherlands.

Unlike other sections of the present catalogue, this one comprises manuscripts of very similar date, outward appearance and textual content. Edward's collection was very homogeneous. All his manuscripts were the work of commercial book producers active in Bruges. Many of their borders and miniatures were executed by the same artists. The books selected here reflect the overall focus of the collection assembled by Edward; each contains historical or instructional texts. First come parts of lengthy chronicles of England and France that culminated in what was then modern history (cat. nos. 47–49). Next are texts focused on history more distant in time and place that encompasses the stories of ancient Rome and biblical times (cat. nos. 50–57). In some of these works Roman and biblical histories are kept separate; in others, the two are fused to produce a seamless history beginning at Creation. While most of Edward's texts have an instructional aspect, those towards the end of the section (cat. nos. 58–61) are explicit in their didactic purpose. Several draw on historical and other sources for *exempla* to support religious or moral themes. The final work is an important anthology of works on chivalric virtues and military arts (cat. no. 62). These luxurious manuscripts each demonstrate that Edward wished his court to be entertained with appropriate reading matter and his leisure time to be well-spent learning from the experiences of past rulers and their subjects.

A contemporary study (cat. no. 57)

47 Jean de Wavrin, *Recueil des croniques d'Engleterre*, vol. 1

Bruges, *c.* 1475
460 x 345 mm

BRITISH LIBRARY, ROYAL 15 E. iv, vol. 1

Approaching old age and able neither to take up arms nor to undertake long journeys, Jean de Wavrin (b. *c.* 1400, d. *c.* 1472–75), Lord of Le Forestel, turned to writing to avoid idleness, 'the mother of all vices'. His subject was the history of England from legendary times to his own day. His motives were to fill a perceived gap in historical writing, memorialize the high deeds of the kings of England and please his nephew, Waleran de Wavrin. The outcome was a work of monumental proportions that encompassed six huge volumes and took the last twenty-five years of Wavrin's life to complete. Overtly a compositor, Wavrin built up his *Recueil* by editing existing texts; these ranged from contemporary newsletters to the twelfth-century *Historia regum Britanniae* by Geoffrey of Monmouth. The *Chroniques* of Jean Froissart supplied nearly 40 per cent of the content of the *Recueil*. Although Wavrin was aware of the instructional value of historical writing, his overall approach was to provide pleasing entertainment to his fellow aristocratic readers. In this respect the *Recueil* conforms to many other works produced at the Burgundian court of Philip the Good.

Based on the evidence of surviving manuscripts, the *Recueil* achieved limited circulation within its intended audience (Visser-Fuchs 2002). Only one complete set, made for Louis of Gruuthuse between 1470 and 1490, survives (Hans-Collas and Schandel 2009); another near-complete set came to belong to the Nassau library. Both sets are deluxe editions, profusely illustrated by Netherlandish artists. Six separate, illustrated volumes of the *Recueil* were produced in the Low Countries in the 1470s. A further vellum copy of volumes 1 and 2 had spaces for illustrations unfilled. Jean de Wavrin's own unillustrated copy of volume 6 has only recently come to light (Lille, Bibliothèque Municipale, MS E 20). A complete set of six volumes (untraced) was recorded by the Lille scribe and author Jan Du Quesne in 1473/4.

The present manuscript purports to be the first volume of a new edition of the *Recueil*. A new prologue, which replaces the original one addressed to Waleran de Wavrin, dedicates its intended seven volumes to Edward V. Omission of any mention of Wavrin as author suggests that someone else compiled the edition after Wavrin's death. The new prologue's contorted and incoherent language confirms it as the product of commercial piracy. Its reference to Edward V appears to build upon an error in copies of the original prologue which refer to his coronation (which never took place) instead of that of Henry V as the conclusion of the first four volumes of the *Recueil*. Although other pirated versions of Wavrin's text are preserved, no other copy of this new prologue is known to survive, and no further volumes of the purported new edition have been identified.

Twenty-nine large illustrations are the volume's second most notable feature. Other surviving copies of volume 1 have more extensive campaigns of illustration; the present copy contains miniatures of outstanding delicacy and clarity. Compared to his contemporaries, the miniaturist responsible for them, now known after this manuscript as the Master of the London Wavrin (Kren and McKendrick 2003), is remarkable for having treated Wavrin's account of the early history of Britain with consistent freshness and poetic responsiveness to setting and atmosphere. Although he frequently repeated both figure and larger compositional models (Sutton and Visser-Fuchs 1999), the miniaturist made memorable through his artistry episodes ranging from the marriage of Diodicias, father of the legendary Albina, to the historical wedding of Edward II in 1308.

The opening illuminated page (pictured), which marks the beginning of the prologue, seems unambiguously to identify the manuscript as a commission of Edward IV. In the page's lower border the English royal arms are supported by Edward's lions of March. In the miniature the King himself is depicted wearing the collar of the Order of the Golden Fleece that he had received in 1468. Two courtiers in the miniature wear the Garter. Yet no such personalization appears elsewhere in the volume. Moreover, the prologue and its illumination were clearly added to the volume at the same time as its table of contents, undoubtedly after the rest of the manuscript had been completed. The prologue and the table of contents were written by a different scribe from the one responsible for the rest of the volume. Similarly, the border around this prologue was painted by the Master of the London Wavrin – the only border in the manuscript completed by him. Although such divergences are explicable as marking the completion phase of the volume, they may equally suggest that the present copy of the *Recueil* was not begun for Edward IV, but rather transferred to him at a late or later stage when his image and arms were added. *S.McK.*

PROVENANCE:

Edward IV.

Opposite:
The author presenting his book to Edward IV, f. 14

grandement vengiez des cruelez
offences quilz nous ont faites en
france, Nous rauons mainte
nant lor et largent et les ricess
que du temps passe ilz ont porte
de france en engleterre Et auec
ce ancores ilz seront contournez
en captiuoison Et toute leur tre
arse et destruite sans recouurier
Car lors que nous enterons dedes
a lun des costez les escochois y
enteront dautrepart Si ne sau
ront les angloiz ou entendre —
premiers. Ainsi estoient les
angloiz manechiez des francois.
Et donnoient grant marchie de
leurs parolles vanteuses aus
queles oyr il sambloit que tout
feust ia a eulz. Mais les plus
des angloiz nen tenoient compte
Et tout cest apareil de lescluse
Et lesclande quy sen faisoit estoit
pour tirer le duc de lanclastre
et sa route hors de castille
Nous nous souffrirons a parler
de ces besongnes de france Et
parlerons du duc de lanclastre
et du roy de portingal de leurs
acointances et aliances Et comment
Ilz conuindrent ensamble.

Comment le roy de portingal Et le duc de lanclastre se trouuerent ensamble Et de leurs deuises. Chapitre. xliiii.

48 Jean de Wavrin, *Recueil des croniques d'Engleterre*, vol. 3

Lille (?) and Bruges, *c.* 1475–80
460 x 330 mm

BRITISH LIBRARY, ROYAL 14 E. iv

In the third volume of his *Recueil* Jean de Wavrin brings the reader closer to his own times. Beginning with the coronation of Richard II in 1377, his narrative encompasses the ongoing war between England and France, as well as the expedition of John of Gaunt, Duke of Lancaster, in pursuit of his claim to Castile and León and the Duke's alliance with John I, King of Portugal (b. 1357, d. 1433; illustrated). Although of similar length to the first volume (see cat. no. 47), the third volume covers a period of only ten years, ending in 1387. As in the second and fourth volumes, the *Chroniques* of Jean Froissart is Wavrin's main source.

The present copy of Wavrin's third volume is worthy of more detailed study than it has received to date. Not only is it by far the most lavishly illustrated copy of this text, with thirty large and eight small miniatures, but previously unnoticed is the transcription of most of its text by the scribe and translator Jan Du Quesne. Such a scribal identification is important given that it was Du Quesne who first advertised Wavrin's completed work in his own translation of Caesar (see cat. no. 76). Also Du Quesne was based at Lille, a town with which Wavrin had many connections, not least as a celebrated patron of its scribes, illuminators and bookbinders. The principal illuminator of the volume, recently named the Master of the Vienna and Copenhagen *Toison d'Or*, has also been shown to have many historical links to the town of Lille (Hans-Collas and Schandel 2009). He and Du Quesne collaborated on several manuscripts, including a dismembered copy of Wavrin's second volume that appears to have been begun for Anthony, bastard son of the Duke of Burgundy (d. 1504), but was adapted for a set that found its way to the Nassau library (The Hague, KB, MS 133 A 7[1]; Oxford, Bodleian Library, MS Laud misc. 653). Lille also appears to provide a link between the Royal volume and the two other surviving copies of Wavrin's third volume (Paris, BnF, MSS fr. 78–79; The Hague, KB, MS 133 A 7[2]), each of which is illuminated in a distinctive style that reappears in several manuscripts transcribed by Du Quesne and may be the work of a Lille illuminator.

Judged on the style of its other illumination, the Royal manuscript appears to have been completed after Wavrin's death and away from Lille. The majority of its illuminated borders are in a style associated with the Master of the Harley Froissart, six of the miniatures and their associated borders (ff. 81, 98v, 114, 121, 169v, 299) are in the style of the Master of the White Inscriptions and another (f. 293v) is securely attributable to the Master of Edward IV. All of these artists are firmly associated with Bruges and all their contributions appear to date from the second half of the fifteenth century.

This completion phase was undoubtedly undertaken for Edward IV. All the illuminators who contributed to it feature prominently in the other south Netherlandish manuscripts acquired by Edward IV. The two full borders associated with the Master of the Harley Froissart (ff. 10, 71) have fully integrated into them lavish displays of Edward's arms and devices of a kind found in several other manuscripts made for the English King. Most other partial borders in this style and that of the Master of the White Inscriptions also include Edward's devices. On the other hand, the only full borders executed in the style of the Master of the Vienna and Copenhagen *Toison d'Or* (ff. 14v, 281v, 284) do not include Edward's heraldry. Furthermore, only the pages on which the illustrations by the Master of the White Inscriptions occur include written instructions to the illuminator of a type found in other manuscripts made for Edward. In contrast the *Sortie from Nantes* that was executed by the *Toison D'Or* Master for the opening of book 2 (f. 71) was not part of the volume's customization for Edward. Its divergence, therefore, from the illustrative programme that the Royal volume shares with the other two surviving manuscripts for the openings of the other five books and the apparent suppression of their chosen subject, the *Coronation of Charles VI*, cannot be explained as motivated by the producers' wish to please Edward.

As with several other multi-volume works, the *Recueil* may have come to Edward only in part. By 1535 the English royal library at Richmond apparently included only Wavrin's first and third volumes. Much later it nearly lost the third volume to Sir Robert Cotton. At this point it was still bound in its original blue velvet covers. *S.McK.*

PROVENANCE:

Edward IV.

Opposite:
John of Gaunt dining with the King of Portugal, f. 244v

49 Jean Froissart, *Chroniques*, book 4

Bruges, *c.* 1480
475 x 355 mm

BRITISH LIBRARY, ROYAL 18 E. ii

Jean Froissart is now best remembered for writing the monumental *Chroniques*, a key narrative source for the history of western Europe during the fourteenth century. Born at Valenciennes around 1337, Froissart served as court poet, diplomat and functionary in both England and his native Hainault. For almost forty years up to his death he also laboured over his *Chroniques*, drawing on not only earlier historical texts, but also eye-witness accounts. In his work he related the history of his own times. Starting at the beginning of the reign of Edward III and ending with the fall of Richard II, Froissart's text encompassed the origins and progress of the Hundred Years War; insurrections in the Low Countries, England and France; and intrigue and ceremony at the courts of England and France. As a court writer he sought to engage his aristocratic patrons and audience by means of a lively, colourful and dramatic narrative style.

The *Chroniques* were indeed very successful. Over 150 manuscript copies survive of one or more of the four books into which his vast text was divided. Many of these copies are deluxe volumes, lavishly illuminated by French artists and first owned by leading Francophone nobles of the first half of the fifteenth century. The *Chroniques* also enjoyed a spectacular revival at the hands of south Netherlandish miniaturists from the late 1460s to early 1480s (Le Guay 1998). Two complete sets of Froissart's text, each in four folio-sized volumes, were produced for the renowned bibliophiles Anthony of Burgundy (d. 1504) and Louis of Gruuthuse (d. 1492), the first dated 1468 and the second from the mid-1470s. A third set came to belong to the Burgundian ducal library sometime before 1487, and a fourth, this time arrayed in five volumes, to Edward IV's Chancellor of the Exchequer, Sir Thomas Thwaytes (see cat. no. 120). A separate copy of book 4 of the *Chroniques* was made for the chronicler and noble Philippe de Commynes (b. 1447, d. 1511). Each of these Netherlandish copies rivalled the earlier French volumes in their lavish decoration and illustration.

The present volume provides further evidence of the success of the *Chroniques* around seventy-five years after the death of its author. Outdone only by Commynes's volume, the Royal manuscript is the second most profusely illustrated copy of book 4 of the *Chroniques*, comprising twenty-three large and thirty-one small illuminated miniatures. Most of these illustrations are executed in a style that draws on the inventions of the Netherlandish illuminator Loyset Liédet. Recently they have been proposed as the collaborative work of two other Bruges artists, the Master of the Chattering Hands and the Master of the Harley Froissart (Wijsman 2008, 2010). Two of the large miniatures (ff. 7, 206) were, however, clearly painted by a different hand, capable of more subtle handling of light, space and colour than his collaborators. Known as the Master of the Getty Froissart after his extended contribution to the illustration of a copy of book 3 of the *Chroniques* now in Los Angeles (Kren and McKendrick 2003), this artist produced a particularly fine frontispiece to the present volume. In it he treated what had become the conventional subject for the opening illustration, Isabel of Bavaria's state entry into Paris (pictured), with typical artistic independence, defining the narrative by means of complex spatial relationships between human figures, landscape and architectural setting.

Whereas the copy of book 4 of the *Chroniques* owned by Philippe de Commynes appears to have been produced as a separate volume, the Royal manuscript was almost certainly part of a set. A copy of book 2, also in the Royal collection (Royal 18 E. i), and the copy of book 3 now in Los Angeles (J. Paul Getty Museum, MS Ludwig XIII 7) are both very similar to the present volume in overall dimensions and page layout and also include contributions from the same artists. Moreover, since it still bears the corresponding Old Royal library shelfmark, the present volume was undoubtedly part of the set of three volumes of the *Chroniques* that was recorded at St James's Palace in 1666. Given the inclusion of the arms of Edward IV on its first illuminated opening (f. 7), this copy of book 4 had been in continuous English royal ownership. The Getty copy of book 3 may have been that recorded at Richmond Palace in 1535. The drawn arms of William, Lord Hastings, in the Royal copy of book 2 may also indicate only his intended rather than actual ownership. Despite its later ownership by John, Lord Lumley, it too may have been owned by Edward IV. Book 1 of Edward's set is so far untraced. *S.McK.*

PROVENANCE:

Edward IV.

Opposite:
The entry of Isabel of Bavaria into Paris, f. 7

MVSEVM
BRITAN
NICVM

50 *La Grande histoire César*

Bruges, 1479
480 x 380 mm

BRITISH LIBRARY, ROYAL 17 F. ii

Above:
Murder of Julius Caesar, f. 344 (detail)

Opposite:
Birth of Julius Caesar, with arms of Edward IV, f. 9

In the prologue to his text, the anonymous thirteenth-century author of the *Faits des Romains* explains his intentions: 'We have written here the ancient history of the Romans, who on account of their reason and their prowess conquered most of the world, so that in their deeds one can learn to do good and avoid evil.' Yet, despite initial plans to provide a broad account of the twelve Caesars – based on the histories of Lucan, Suetonius, Sallust and other classical Roman writers – the author managed to complete only the history of Julius Caesar (d. 44 BC). Subsequently, editors and scribes in the fourteenth and early fifteenth centuries often paired the *Faits* with complementary histories, such as the *Histoire ancienne jusqu'à César* and extracts from the *Chronicle of Baldwin of Avesnes* (see cat. nos. 135, 55 and 56). After the first quarter of the fifteenth century, the popularity of the *Faits* declined significantly until the 1470s, when a renewed interest in Roman history – and the life of Julius Caesar in particular – spread amongst nobles at the Burgundian court and their close associates (Guenée 1976). Dated by its colophon to 1479, Edward IV's manuscript participates in this final moment of the manuscript tradition, yet stands apart in several respects.

Unlike other examples of the *Faits* dating to the 1470s, Edward's copy contains passages from the *Chronicle of Baldwin of Avesnes* covering the reign of Augustus, Julius Caesar's nephew, up to the closing of the temple of Janus (29 BC). To this were added further sections from the chronicle treating the 'meurs et condicions' of Julius Caesar. Marking the end of this section, the manuscript's colophon reads: 'icy fine la grande histoire Cesar … faicte a Bruges du commandement de treshault, tres excellent et tres victorieux prince le roy Edouard quatrieme de ce nom lan de grace mil cccclxxix' (Here ends the *Grande histoire César* … made in Bruges on the order of … King Edward the fourth … 1479). Following the colophon, there appears a summary of the emperors and their reigns up to Frederick II (d. 1250), versions of which can be found in other manuscripts of the *Faits*. The particular selection of texts, along with the presence of the colophon before the summary list of emperors, suggests that the *Grande histoire César* ought to be understood as a revision of the *Faits des Romains* made specifically for Edward IV (McKendrick 1990). A modest, unillustrated copy of the *Faits* now in Paris (BnF, MS n.a. fr. 11673), which has a text that is nearly identical to that of the Royal manuscript – including the colophon mentioning Edward IV – perhaps descends directly from the fair copy used by the scribe of Edward's volume. The presence of the drawn arms of Louis of Gruuthuse in the Royal volume (f. 9) is evidence of the Bruges nobleman's role in its production.

Accompanying only the text of the *Faits* proper, a frontispiece and thirty-nine one-column miniatures depict events from the life of Caesar, extending from his birth to his death. In terms of their placement, composition and style, the miniatures differ from those in near-contemporary manuscripts of the *Faits* produced for such patrons as Louis of Gruuthuse (Paris, BnF, MS fr. 40), Anthony of Burgundy (Pommersfelden, Schlossbibliothek, MS 310), Wolfart van Borselen (Paris, BnF, MS fr. 20312 bis) and Antoine de Chourses (Chantilly, Musée Condé, MS 770). Compared with these examples, the Royal manuscript's rate of illumination of approximately one miniature per gathering results in a longer programme of illustration, despite the relatively modest scale of the single-column miniatures. Whereas, though varying in quality, the majority of the miniatures have been attributed to the Master of Edward IV (pictured above), the opening miniature of the Birth of Julius Caesar (pictured opposite) has so far resisted a firm attribution. Nevertheless, the recognition of the same artistic hand in a two-column miniature of Edward IV's *Bible historiale* (see cat. no. 53) further links this anonymous illuminator to the group of manuscripts produced for the King (Brinkmann 1997).

As the only manuscript with an original colophon referring specifically to Edward's involvement, the *Faits des Romains* bears special witness to the monarch's engagement with illuminated manuscripts. Though grounded in the contemporary interests of his Burgundian counterparts, Edward's patronage of books emphasized ancient history – particularly that of imperial Rome – to a greater extent than that of his fellow collectors. The King's fascination with this period may be understood in the broader context of his attempts to recast his return from exile (1471) as a time of peace and prosperity: a golden age, with Edward as England's Augustus. *J.O'D.*

PROVENANCE:
Edward IV.

51 *Romuléon*

(Benvenuto da Imola, *Romuleon*, translated into French by Jean Miélot)

Bruges, 1480
475 x 335 mm

BRITISH LIBRARY, ROYAL 19 E. v

Above:
Trajan enthroned, f. 367v (detail)

Opposite:
Romulus and Remus being suckled by a wolf, f. 32

Spanning the history of Rome from its legendary foundation to the reign of Emperor Constantine, the *Romuléon* offers a broad overview of key events in Roman history; it thus distinguishes itself from more focused historical texts such as the *Faits des Romains* (see cat. no. 50). Unlike the *Faits*, the *Romuléon* is not an original French compilation, but rather the translation of a Latin text that dates from between 1361 and 1364, and is most likely attributable to the Florentine scholar Benvenuto da Imola (d. 1388), who drew heavily upon the writings of ancient historians such as Livy and Suetonius in creating his work. Surviving copies of Benvenuto's compilation almost all have an Italian provenance, and it is not until Philip the Good, Duke of Burgundy, commissioned Jean Miélot to provide a translation of the *Romuleon* into French that copies of the text began to be produced north of the Alps. Yet the translation seems never to have achieved popularity beyond a small, elite group of Burgundian nobility; apart from the Royal manuscript, only five complete copies survive. As one of a select group, Edward IV's copy of the *Romuléon* offers particular insight into the development of the monarch's library and his qualities as a collector.

A brief sketch of the chronology of the group reveals that Edward's acquisition of the manuscript occurred several years after his Burgundian contemporaries' initial interest in the text. According to the prologue found in the manuscript made for Philip the Good (Florence, Biblioteca Medicea Laurenziana, MSS Med. Pal. 156^1,156^2), Miélot began his translation in 1460 and finished it in 1462. By 1464 the well-known Burgundian scribe David Aubert had completed Philip's manuscript and several copies followed quickly thereafter. In 1467 Philip acquired a second copy (Besançon, Bibliothèque Municipale, MS 850), and in the following year, 1468, his illegitimate son Anthony of Burgundy had another copy made (Brussels, KBR, MS 9055). The remaining two manuscripts – one belonging to Jean de Wavrin (Brussels, KBR, MS 10173–4) and the other to Louis of Gruuthuse (Turin, Biblioteca nazionale universitaria, MSS $L.I.4^1$, $L.I.4^2$) – date to the end of the 1460s and the beginning of the 1470s. In contrast, the Royal manuscript was made only in 1480, according to a dated inscription in the miniature prefacing book 10 (f. 367v, pictured right). This time-lag, along with the limited popularity of the text, suggests that by 1480 the acquisition of a *Romuléon* manuscript was a deliberate choice on the part of the English monarch (McKendrick 1994).

One can gain some sense of the possible motivations for Edward's acquisition of the *Romuléon* by considering further the reception of Philip's manuscript now in Florence. After Philip's death in 1467, the Florence *Romuléon* almost certainly passed into the possession of his son, Charles the Bold, who – as we know from documentary evidence – was fond of having passages of Roman history read aloud to him and a small group of intimates while away on military campaigns (McKendrick forthcoming). Around the same time, Edward and Charles began negotiations that would lead ultimately to the marriage of Edward's sister, Margaret of York, to Charles in 1468. The resulting ties between England and Burgundy would have important consequences after the untimely death of Charles at the Battle of Nancy (1477), when Margaret turned to her brother Edward for military support against the French. Seen in this context, Edward's acquisition of the *Romuléon* – a text closely associated with the leading figures of the Burgundian nobility – becomes particularly remarkable in that it occurs during a period of such instability.

Apart from its script, which may be attributed to a close follower of David Aubert (see cat. no. 152), the Royal manuscript demonstrates the close stylistic links shared among the manuscripts produced for Edward in 1479–80. The manuscript's nine two-column and two one-column miniatures are predominately the work of the Master of the White Inscriptions, an artist named after his conspicuous use of inscriptions in the *Romuléon* and other manuscripts made for Edward. Furthermore, the fully decorated borders surrounding the manuscript's two frontispieces (ff. 32 [pictured], 196) prove nearly identical to ones in several of the King's other manuscripts. The decorative and stylistic affinities lend a sense of coherence to the collection – no matter how remarkable an individual commission may be. *J.O'D.*

PROVENANCE:
Edward IV.

MVSEVM
BRITAN
NICVM

52 *Antiquités judaïques et la guerre des Juifs*, vol. 2

(Flavius Josephus, *Jewish Antiquities* and *Jewish War*, in an anonymous French translation)

Bruges, *c.* 1478–80
490 x 350 mm

LONDON, SIR JOHN SOANE'S MUSEUM, vol. 135

Sometime during the reign of Charles VI of France, an unknown author compiled French translations of both the *Jewish Antiquities* and the *Jewish War* by Flavius Josephus (b. AD 37/8). Combined into one long text in twenty-seven books, these translations transmitted to late medieval nobles a detailed account of the history of the Jews from Creation to Josephus's own times. Whereas the very small number of surviving manuscripts suggests that few nobles obtained or read copies of this text, the consistently high ambitions of their illustrations mark it as one in which some important bibliophiles and miniaturists of the fifteenth century took considerable interest (Deutsch 1986). Distinguished early owners include John, Duke of Berry (b. 1340, d. 1416), John the Fearless, Duke of Burgundy, and Louis, Duke of Guyenne (b. 1397, d. 1415); one extant copy includes a contemporary attribution of nine of its miniatures to the renowned French court painter and illuminator Jean Fouquet.

The present volume is one of only five volumes written and illustrated in the southern Netherlands that preserve the translation of Josephus. Whereas the other four form two complete texts, each in two volumes, the Soane manuscript contains just the second half of the translation. Its narrative therefore begins in book 15 with Herod the Great's ascent to the throne of Judaea in 37 BC. Twelve large miniatures accompanied by full decorated borders mark the openings of books 15–26. One principal artist, known from this manuscript as the Master of the Soane Josephus (see also cat. no. 53, 55), worked together with three assistants on the twelve large miniatures. The Master of the Froissart of Philippe de Commynes, recently identified as the immigrant French illuminator Philippe de Mazerolles (Hans-Collas and Schandel 2009), may have been responsible for the border decoration.

The Soane manuscript is probably the earliest of the south Netherlandish copies of the Josephus translation. Almost without doubt it can be identified with the 'booke of Josephus' for the 'dressing' of which the London stationer Piers Bauduyn was paid by Edward IV in 1480. The heraldic and subsidiary decoration is certainly consistent with such a date, as is the evidence of costume in the miniatures. The manuscript is also best explained as belonging to Edward's intense period of collecting around 1479. Its focus on ancient history is in line with that of other volumes that the King acquired at this time.

The present volume provides critical evidence that Edward IV's collecting of books was directly connected with that of the Bruges bibliophile Louis of Gruuthuse. At its two principal openings (ff. 11, 150) the heraldic arms of Gruuthuse have been overpainted and replaced by those of the King. In the escutcheon at the centre of the lower border of the second of these pages, a saltire cross that once formed part of Gruuthuse's arms is visible underneath the royal leopards of Edward's arms. On a scroll held by a bird in the right-hand border of the same page it is still possible to discern under the white overpaint an inscription bearing Gruuthuse's motto *Plus est en vous.* To the right and left of the escutcheon on each of these pages additions to the border decoration obscure, but do not entirely conceal, Gruuthuse's emblem of the 'bombard'. The outline of the wings of Gruuthuse's peacock crest may also be seen underneath the paint of the central border decoration. At the very least we must conclude that this volume had originally been intended by its producers for Gruuthuse's collection (McKendrick 1992). Its diversion to Edward must have been undertaken with Gruuthuse's approval. Gruuthuse seems to have been quick in ordering a replacement. An even grander copy of the text was commissioned by him in 1480 and completed in 1483 (Paris, BnF, MSS fr. 11–16; Hans-Collas and Schandel 2009).

As with several other texts that he acquired (see cat. nos. 48, 49, 57, 58), Edward may have secured only the part of it that was of particular interest to him. The second part of the French translation of Josephus's works certainly would have provided a good supplement to his reading about Roman history. In that respect it had much more to offer Edward than the first part. Comparison with other entries in the 1535 Richmond inventory suggests that the 'Josephus' mentioned there was a solitary volume. By 1666 the Old Royal library definitely included only 'Volume 2de de Josephus' (Royal Appendix 71, f. 13).

S.McK.

PROVENANCE:

Edward IV; Thomas Noel Hill, 2nd Baron Berwick (b. 1784, d. 1832); Sir John Soane (b. 1753, d. 1837).

Above:
Arms of Edward IV, f. 11 (detail)

Opposite:
Antiochus Epiphanes besieging Jerusalem, f. 150

53 *Bible historiale*: Tobit to Acts

Bruges, 1470 (script) and 1479 (large miniatures)
435 x 320 mm

BRITISH LIBRARY, ROYAL 15 D. i

The scholar responsible for the textual classifications of *Bibles historiales* considered this copy to be the most beautiful French Bible ever made (Berger 1884). It is the fourth volume of a *petite Bible historiale*: the first and second volumes of this made-up set are cat. no. 54 and Royal 18 D. x (dated 1479). There is no record of a third volume. This fourth volume, which extends from Tobit to the end of Acts, was made as the final part of a *Bible historiale* that omitted the Apocalypse (contrast, for example, cat. no. 74). It has seventy-seven miniatures, of which eleven are large, extending across both columns of text, and of high quality craftsmanship. The remainder are squareish single-column illustrations executed in partial grisaille and all but one of them (f. 346) of much less impressive artistry.

The large number of miniatures, which illustrate not just the incipits of the biblical books, is unusual for a *Bible historiale.* There are, for example, thirty-one scenes from the Life of Christ, including (f. 353) a large image of the Crucifixion between thieves. Another of the large miniatures is the depiction of Belshazzar's Feast (f. 45, pictured). The story is told in Daniel 5, especially verses 1–5. We see King Belshazzar presiding over the great feast to a thousand of his lords. The table is laden with the gold and silver vessels, taken, we are told, by Nebuchadnezzar from the Temple at Jerusalem, but they do not look specifically liturgical. Above the diners the disembodied hand inscribes the warning on the wall. Like this one, the other ten large images have the English royal arms in the borders that accompany them.

The history of the book's production is complex. The volume was written by a single scribe, who identifies himself at the end of Acts (f. 439v): 'Escript par moy J[ean or Jan] Du Ries.' Du Ries is known to have written two other books for Edward IV: Royal 14 E. vi, and 15 E. ii–iii (the latter dated 1482; see cat. no. 93). At the end of the preliminary rubrics (ff. 1–17v) Du Ries describes this book as the 'fourth' volume of the 'Istoire scolastique', but the word 'quart' was written over an erasure. He then continues: 'Lequel livre fut fait a Bruges par le commandement et voulenté de [then over an erasure] tres hault tres excellent et tres victorieux prince Edouard le quart de ce nom Roy d'Angleterre et cet. [then in the original hand] L'an de grace mil CCCC LXX.' (The which book was made at Bruges by order and wish of [his] highness the most excellent and victorious Prince Edward, fourth of this name, King of England etc., in the year of grace 1470.) Originally, therefore, the book was intended for someone other than Edward IV. Although the date has not been changed, there is no likelihood that the book was adapted for Edward IV as early as 1470, and it seems probable that this manuscript was finished at the same time as Royal 18 D. x – in 1479. Careful examination of the miniatures and borders suggests the book was produced in two distinct phases of work. It was indeed written in 1470, but only the small miniatures were completed at that stage, when the original patron withdrew from the commission (perhaps he or she died). The book was then completed for Edward IV in 1479 by a small group of artists led by the so-called Master of Edward IV, along with two newly commissioned parts of the *Bible historiale* (Royal 18 D. ix and 18 D. x). This involved supplying the eleven large miniatures, two small miniatures that had been overlooked in phase 1 (ff. 346, 425v), plus the borders to all the miniatures. The first of these miniatures appears at the beginning of Tobit (f. 18) with a border decorated with the coat of arms of England, within the Garter inscribed 'Honi soit qui mal y pense' and surmounted by a helm and crown. The outer border has the arms of England on a banner, and a long red pennant with the motto 'Dieu et mon droit' and a gold Yorkist rose. There are no signs of changes in the border, and the arms have not been altered or added. The method by which the three-volume set was assembled gives a valuable insight into the collecting practices and methods of Edward IV. *J.L.*

PROVENANCE

Edward IV.

Opposite:
Belshazzar's Feast, f. 45

xxviii.

45

Mane thechel phares

Apres ensieult la vi.e vision quy est la quarte en daniel Mais Jheromes lappelle seote en abacuc. Il advint que Daires et cyrus assigerent en babilonne baltasar le roy de babilonne et des assiriens de quy nous avons parle ou chapitre dessusdit des roys de babilonne Et fut cestuy baltasar filz de eutlamorada et quy fut filz nabugodonosor le grant. Ce balthasar fist ung grant mengier a mille de ses princes Si commanda quon apportast les vaisseaulx dor et dargent que nabugo

54 *Bible historiale*: Genesis to Ruth

Bruges, 1479
425 x 310 mm

BRITISH LIBRARY, ROYAL 18 D. ix

Above:
Unfinished border, f. 195v (detail)

Opposite:
God's Creation before he created man, f. 5

This manuscript and its companion volume (Royal 18 D. x) were made for Edward IV as parts of a multi-volume *Bible historiale.* The present manuscript bears the date 1479, which can reasonably be applied to the completion of the whole enterprise. The third volume, described in the rubric as the 'fourth', came from a different multi-volume set that had been left unfinished in 1470 (cat. no. 53) but was also completed, it would seem, in 1479, and adapted for Edward IV. It appears that there is no missing volume. A principal artist of all three was the Master of Edward IV, who was first identified by Winkler in 1913 (Kren and McKendrick 2003).

The illustration in this opening volume of the set is quite sparse: seven large miniatures are located at the incipits of the biblical books; a further six small miniatures occupy a single column's width. In contrast, other luxury copies of the text typically include many more illustrations. The manuscript begins with a small image of the translator, Guyart des Moulins, at work (f. 1). Edward's arms and those of his sons are prominent in the lower border, which includes three escutcheons bearing the English royal arms, the central shield crowned (for the King), and the flanking shields bearing silver labels with three points (for his sons). The right-hand border repeats the royal arms, and the initial 'P' contains the white Yorkist rose. This heraldic identification of a single escutcheon with the royal arms is repeated in the borders at the beginning of the other six biblical books, except in two cases. At the beginning of Numbers the left border is unfinished (f. 195v, reproduced), and at the opening of Judges (f. 291v), a border of inferior craftsmanship was supplied on only one side. The upper part of the standard border design for Numbers has also been left partially finished. That these elements were left entirely blank show that specialists were employed for certain details, birds and beasts in this case, while most of the border was executed formulaically by a less adept hand. Heraldry was also presumably supplied by a specialist, especially in cases where it was complex, as here.

The Creation miniature (reproduced) accompanies the preface 'En pallais de roy et d'empereur …' (see cat. no. 22), and is most unusual in content. God, wearing a triple crown and wielding a sceptre, kneels within a red and yellow mandorla, and creates with his sceptre a group of animals including a lion, horse, stag and camel, and a remarkably naturalistic cow seen from behind. The whole is set within a delicately painted paradisiacal landscape. God is framed by tall slender trees, the upper branches of which create a pattern strongly reminiscent of Gothic tracery. At the left the lower parts of all but two of the trees have been overpainted by a rocky outcrop. There appear to be two horizons, or perhaps the intermediate sky represents a gleaming lake or seascape. This artist, despite his obvious skill, and the recognition of his talent implied by allotting him the first major image in the book, has yet to be identified. McKendrick (Kren and McKendrick 2003) has suggested 'circle of the Master of the London Wavrin' (on this artist see cat. nos. 47, 56, 76).

Although there are only thirteen miniatures, McKendrick (as above) proposed that five or possibly six artists were involved in the production of the manuscript. This could be seen as a necessary outcome of the demand of Edward IV for numerous high-quality books to be completed within a short period, which sometimes led to surprising results. Whereas it was perfectly understandable that God's Creation (f. 5) should take place in a landscape reminiscent of Flanders, it is harder to see why God's appearance to Moses in the tabernacle of the congregation in the desert of Sinai in the pictured scene at the beginning of Numbers should also call to mind a late medieval stone structure and a northern woodland. *J.L.*

PROVENANCE:
Edward IV.

n palaiz
de roy et
dempere
appertient
avoir trois
mansions. Cest assavoir
auditoire ouquel il fait
ses jugemens & donne a
chascun son droit. Cham
bre en la quelle il repose.
MVSEVM BRITANNICVM
et cenacle ou sale en la
quelle il donne ses mengiers
En ceste maniere nre
empereur au commande
aux vens et a la mer a le
monde pour auditoire ou
quel toutes choses sont fetes
a son commandement et a
sa voulente. Dequoy il est
escript. Je empliz le ciel et

Les hebrieux a
prez ce oublierent
nostreseigneur
et se prindrent
a mal faire si comme ilz auoi
ent accoustume quant ilz ne
auoient point de prince. Dont
vindrent les madianiens
et les amalechiens et les a
rabiens. Et leur coururent
sus a grant puissance. Ceulx
qui eschapperent fuirent aux
montaignes et se muchoient
es fossez et la ou ilz pouoient
mieulx. En telle doulour fu
rent les filz disrael vii. ans
Apres ce nostreseigneur e
ut mercy deulx quant il vit
leur repentance. et inspira
ceur de gedeon qui estoit de
la lignee manasse et filz ja
ab / sy grant hardement. Il
entreprint les filz disrael
a deffendre. En ce temps les

55 *Histoire tripartite*

Bruges, 1473 and before 1480
465 x 325 mm

According to the anonymous compiler of the vast historical compendium from which the *Histoire tripartite* was adapted, 'readers are lazy and do not like to study'. With this in mind, the compiler undertook a revision of numerous lengthy books on ancient and biblical history so that his readers might understand and retain the wealth of knowledge that the books contain more easily. The result of his endeavour is a work known today as the *Chronicle of Baldwin of Avesnes*, a text compiled *c.* 1278 for, or under the supervision of, Baldwin of Avesnes (d. 1289), Lord of Beaumont and a member of the nobility of Flanders and Hainault. Baldwin's chronicle may be characterized as an ambitious universal history encompassing the entire span of time, from Creation to contemporary events. To this were added philosophical and ethical digressions taken from ancient writers such as Aristotle, Seneca and Cato. Judging from the more than fifty manuscripts of the chronicle that survive from the fourteenth and fifteenth centuries, the efforts of its unknown compiler met with great success.

In fact the popularity of the chronicle has made it difficult for scholars to determine its history – a challenge due in large part to the broad nature of the text, which lends itself well to being adapted and reworked. For instance, the dates covered by surviving copies of the chronicle vary widely: many include contemporary events, while others end at different moments in the history of Rome. This is the case for the Royal manuscript, which concludes with the reign of the Emperor Hadrian. Furthermore, the thirteenth-century text appears to have been left untitled. As a result, later editors began to supply their own titles, such as the *Trésor de sapience* or the *Trésor des histoires* (see cat. no. 56). Therefore the presence of the title *Histoire tripartite* in the Royal manuscript – one found in no other copy of the chronicle – is most likely to be considered an addition by the scribe or editor of the text.

As is the case with all versions of the chronicle, the text of the Royal manuscript lacks internal divisions into books. Instead, the various histories are presented essentially as one narrative, with a list of headings only – in nineteen leaves at the beginning of the manuscript – serving as a guide to the reader. The resulting structure of the text is such that a section on the Old Testament story of Gideon, represented here, is followed by an account of the Greek story of Troy; the story of Alexander is followed by the teachings of Aristotle; and so on. This interweaving of various histories into a single text constitutes a distinguishing characteristic of the chronicle.

Such a distinctive approach to narrative ought to be kept in mind when considering the manuscript's illumination. The twelve two-column miniatures and forty-two one-column miniatures appear to constitute a hierarchical programme of illumination, with the larger miniatures marking major breaks in the text. Yet, rather than corresponding to the peculiar nature of the narrative, the miniatures apply a much more common organizational structure – in effect giving the manuscript the appearance of being divided into various books and chapters.

It is not yet clear whether the scenes for the miniatures were selected arbitrarily, or if in fact they work to emphasize particular aspects of the narrative. The parts of the text that are illustrated cover the Old Testament, the history of Rome and, to a much lesser extent, the histories of Thebes and Troy. Compared with its closest relation, a near-contemporary south Netherlandish copy of the chronicle now in Baltimore (Walters Art Museum, MS W. 307), the miniatures of the *Histoire tripartite* depict more scenes drawn from Old Testament history – often deriving, however, from apocryphal sources. Furthermore, the subject matter of the illuminations tends towards battle scenes, murders and other such violent events, which may reflect the interests of the manuscript's intended recipient.

Although the colophon of the manuscript clearly states that the writing of the text was completed in the year 1473, the style of the illumination suggests that the manuscript was not finished until later in the decade, when the manuscript was almost certainly acquired by Edward IV. The attribution of the large miniatures to the Master of the Soane Josephus (see cat. no. 52), further strengthens the case for the ownership of Edward IV. As one of a number of illuminated historical manuscripts from Edward's library, the *Histoire tripartite* attests to the lively interest among fifteenth-century royalty in what they surely saw as their own history. *J.O'D.*

PROVENANCE:
Edward IV (?); Henry VIII.

Opposite:
Gideon's battle with the Midianites, f. 54v

est la cite de tieus. Femce a par
devers orient arrabe. Par devs
midi la rouge mer. Par devers
occident la grant mer. Et p devs
septemtrion la montaigne du
liban. Femce est tres bonne terre
en arbres et en bledz en lait et
en miel et huille et est pleine de
montaignes de fontaines et
de rivieres et es montaignes
on treuve les metaulx de plu
sieurs manieres. Ceste hystoi
re demonstre et parle de la terre
de flandres. Chap. iiii.c et lxxj.

Flandres est une
province de france
assise sur la rive
de la mer. Si a allemaigne
vers orient. Angleterre vers
septemtrion. La mer de france
devers occident. Et france et bo
urgongne par devers midi. Fla
dres combien quelle soit petite
quant a siege toutesvoyes est
ce bonne terre et pleine de biens
moult singulieres. Car elle est
pleine de toutes bonnes pastu
res de buefz de brebis et dautres
bestes. Et y a moult de bonnes
villes dont les principalles sont
gand et brughes. Il y a plus(ieur)s
grans pors de mer si comme
lescluse le dam et autres. Il y a
bonnes rivieres si come lescaut
et le liz. Flandres est grandement
peuplee et armee. Il y a belles
gens et fors qui font grant
generation et sont riches et

56 *Trésor des histoires*

Bruges, c. 1475–80
480 x 355 mm

BRITISH LIBRARY, COTTON AUGUSTUS A. V

The *Trésor des histoires*, formerly in the Cotton Library, is one of the most remarkable manuscripts of a secular text to have been produced in the last quarter of the fifteenth century. The fifty-five large miniatures of the volume are of the very highest visual sophistication in the illustration of such a text. A refined and ambitious treatment of light and landscape defines the unique contribution of the artists who painted these miniatures.

In outline, the text that the Cotton manuscript contains is far from unusual. The *Trésor des histoires*, as it is described in the volume's closing text, or the *Chronicle of Baldwin of Avesnes*, as it is now commonly known, is one of several vernacular world chronicles that were repeatedly copied for and read by French-speaking nobles from the thirteenth century onwards. Redaction A of the *Chronicle* was compiled shortly after 1278 for Baldwin of Avesnes (d. 1289), son of Bouchard of Avesnes and Margaret of Flanders, Countess of Hainault (see cat. no. 55). No fewer than fifty-seven manuscripts and fragments preserve this redaction, the slightly later redaction B or various interpolated versions of the chronicle. Throughout their long narrative of the past, 'the idea of the ethical value of history is implicitly present' (Noirfalise 2009).

The particular version of the *Chronicle* text that the Cotton manuscript contains is, however, rare and worthy of note. Within its 763 chapters, which relate the history of the world from Creation to the papacy of Clement VI (r. 1342–52), material has been interpolated from instructional works that were written earlier for the French royal court. Included among these are the so-called *Manuel d'histoire de Philippe VI de Valois*, compiled around 1326–30; Jean de Vignay's *Jeu des échecs*, compiled shortly before 1350; Jean Corbechon's *Livre des proprietez des choses*, completed in 1372 (see cat. no. 93); and Guillaume de Tignonville's *Dits moraux des philosophes*, completed sometime before 1402. One of these interpolations – a passage of text that compares Athens to Paris as the mother of the arts and sciences (f. 345) – suggests that the Cotton version of the *Chronicle* was put together at Paris in 1416 (Ross 1969). Although several other manuscripts of the *Chronicle* were produced in the Low Countries, none contains this version. It therefore seems likely that the text of the Cotton manuscript was copied directly from a much earlier manuscript, probably of Parisian origin and dating from the first quarter of the fifteenth century.

Although some dependence on earlier models has been discerned (Ross 1969), the illustrations of the Cotton manuscript are largely the result of a new and independent response to the text. They were clearly planned with much care. The miniatures, which punctuate the text in a strikingly regular manner throughout the volume, work together to form an impressive visual summary of the narrative of the *Chronicle*. Within that campaign their faithful illustration of the interpolated texts proves that all the miniatures were devised for this uncommon version of the *Chronicle*. To facilitate this, detailed instructions to the miniaturists outlining the principal elements of each illustration were written in the lower margins of each page on which an image was to be painted.

Most of the illustrations are stylistically linked to the work of two particularly innovative south Netherlandish artists, the Master of the London Wavrin (see cat. nos. 47, 76) and the Master of the Getty Froissart (see cat. nos. 49, 61). The reproduced image is one of the most beautiful of those undertaken by them (f. 345v, pictured), and has been recognized as one of the earliest independent views of the Flemish countryside and thereby an important landmark in the development of northern European painting (Pächt 1978, Kren 2007). Only two miniatures are painted in the much weaker style of a follower of the Bruges illuminator Loyset Liédet (ff. 22, 30v).

Although the present volume does not now include any marks of royal ownership, it is recorded as part of an exchange in 1616 between the then royal librarian, Patrick Young, and the English antiquary Sir Robert Cotton. As recorded by Cotton in his list of books that he wanted from Young, the *Trésor* was then 'fair bound in blew velvet' (Carley 2000). The manuscript is also identifiable in the 1535 Richmond inventory. Given that it is related closely in its date of production, type of text and style of decoration to other manuscripts acquired by Edward IV, the Cotton *Trésor* very probably came into royal possession during his reign. *S.McK.*

PROVENANCE:

Edward IV (?); Henry VIII; Sir Robert Cotton (d. 1631) in 1616; bequeathed to the nation by Sir John Cotton, 1702.

Opposite:
View of Flanders, f. 345v

57 *Miroir historial*, vol. 1

(Vincent of Beauvais, *Speculum historiale*, translated into French by Jean de Vignay)

Bruges, *c.* 1478–80
470 x 340 mm

BRITISH LIBRARY, ROYAL 14 E. i, vol. 1

The *Miroir historial* is one of a remarkable sequence of translations that were undertaken in the second quarter of the fourteenth century by the French Hospitaller and writer Jean de Vignay. Like many of his other works, the *Miroir* was dedicated to Jeanne de Bourgogne (d. 1349), wife of Philip VI of France. Through it de Vignay opened up to an aristocratic readership part of Vincent of Beauvais's monumental work of scholarship, the *Speculum maius*, and introduced to them a wealth of encyclopaedic knowledge set within a historical framework. The broad historical canvas of the *Miroir* stretches from the Creation and the Fall of Man to Vincent's own times. Volume 1 alone encompasses the Marvels of the East, the Old Testament, ancient Greek history and legend, Roman history, the New Testament and the miracles of the Virgin.

To judge from surviving manuscripts, the transmission and reception of the *Miroir* was relatively restricted. Fewer than forty volumes of de Vignay's text are now extant. Although four lavishly illustrated volumes were produced in the translator's own time, most surviving copies of the *Miroir* were produced in Paris in the late fourteenth or early fifteenth century. Of these later manuscripts, the set made for John, Duke of Berry (b. 1340, d. 1416), appears to have spawned most fifteenth-century copies. One route by which it did so was through three early fifteenth-century volumes that Louis of Gruuthuse (d. 1492) acquired sometime before 1455 (Paris, BnF, MSS fr. 308–310). Unfinished at the point when he acquired them, these volumes were fully illustrated for Gruuthuse at Bruges; a fourth volume (fr. 311) was also made after he acquired the first three to complete the set (Hans-Collas and Schandel 2009).

Together with a companion volume (Royal 14 E. i, vol. 2), the present manuscript is one of only six volumes of the *Miroir* to have been produced in the southern Netherlands. In addition to Gruuthuse's volume 4, one is another copy of volume 1 (Los Angeles, J. Paul Getty Museum, Ludwig MS XIII 5), in which the producers clearly followed not only their exemplar's text, but also the placement of its 132 illustrations. In sharp contrast the artists of the Royal volume restricted themselves to eight illustrations. These miniatures mark the beginning of each of the nine books of de Vignay's text, except book 2. Very similar in their illustrative restraint are the three other Netherlandish volumes, each of which omits to illustrate one of the books that they contain (The Hague, KB, 128 C 1[1–3]). Although these manuscripts appear to have been completed at a later date than the Royal volume and to have had a different first owner, it has been argued persuasively that these copies of volumes 2, 3 and 4 were conceived as part of the same set as the Royal copy of volume 1 and intended to form part of a set with it (Chavannes-Mazel 1988).

As is evident from the illuminated border that marks the opening of de Vignay's prologue (pictured), the Royal volume was first owned by Edward IV. In the right-hand border the Yorkist badge of the *rose-en-soleil* features prominently between two angels supporting banners with the English royal arms. In the lower border the central arms of Edward are flanked by those of his two sons, the celebrated Princes in the Tower. All these features conform to a template that was drawn up for the use of the Netherlandish artists who illuminated Edward's manuscripts (McKendrick 1994). At the expense of heraldic accuracy these artists sought symmetry of design in the lower border, inverting the position of the quarters of the royal arms in the left-hand escutcheon.

The artists who undertook the decoration of Edward's copy of volume 1 of the *Miroir* were those responsible for many of his other manuscripts (Kren and McKendrick 2003). The Master of the White Inscriptions, who painted the opening large miniature (pictured), imbued its author portrait with both a monumentality and a brooding atmosphere in characteristic fashion. Eschewing his model's rather generic depictions of both de Vignay and Vincent (Paris, BnF, MS fr. 308, ff. 1, 2), he chose to depict the Dominican author of the original Latin text, Vincent of Beauvais, in a lavishly appointed study in which several volumes of similarly huge proportions to Edward's own manuscript are on display. The volume's one-column miniatures were executed by the Master of Edward IV, a Bruges illuminator named after part of Edward's *Bible historiale* (cat. no. 54). Strikingly similar in execution are the one-column miniatures in Edward's *Grande histoire César* (cat. no. 50). The illuminated borders in the *Miroir* are in a style now associated with the Master of the Harley Froissart (see cat. nos. 49, 52, 56). *S.McK.*

PROVENANCE:

Edward IV.

Opposite:
Vincent of Beauvais at work in his study, f. 3

De la cause de leuure emprinse.
Premier chapitre.
Pour ce que la multi
tude des liures et la
briefuete du temps et
la foiblesse du mëore
ne seuffrent pas les
choses qui sont escriptes estre com
prinses ensemble en vng courage
ce m'est aduis a moy qui suis le
moindre de tous mes freres en sciece.
Et ce puis ie scauoir en moy mesmes
qui ay veu leu et retourne plusieurs
liures p moult long temps assiduele
ment et curieusement. Et neatmois
par le conseil daulcüs de mes pl' sou
uerains et greigneurs aulcües fle
que iay esleues p mon petit engin
A bien pou de tous les liures de nře
foy catholique ou des liures payens

58 St Augustine, *La Cité de Dieu*

(*De civitate dei* translated into French by Raoul de Praelles)

Bruges, *c.* 1480
480 x 330 mm

BRITISH LIBRARY, ROYAL 17 F. iii, vol. 2

In 1371 Charles V of France commissioned Raoul de Praelles to provide a French translation of, and commentary on, St Augustine's *City of God*, a fifth-century text comprising twenty-two books that treat human history and Christian theology. According to a passage from the commission of the text, the King ordered the translation for the 'public utility' of the kingdom and for all of Christianity. The theme of the public appeal of the translation is taken up time and time again in the author's prologue, in which de Praelles frequently praises the King's love of learning and his widely recognized interest in texts and translations. The repeated emphasis on a wider public interest appears not to have been an empty promise since de Praelles's translation and commentary met with huge success in the late fourteenth and early fifteenth centuries. As a measure of the magnitude of his success, one scholar has noted that only four illuminated manuscripts of the *City of God* survive from before de Praelles's translation, whereas from 1376 to 1503 there exist fifty-seven illuminated copies, over half of which date from before 1410 (de Laborde 1909). Produced around 1480, the manuscript of the *City of God* made for Edward IV – his arms and those of his sons appear twice in the manuscript – belongs to the end of that tradition.

An important aspect of this manuscript is its structure and division into two volumes. Together the two volumes include only the first ten books of Augustine's *City of God*: the first volume containing books 1 to 3 ends rather abruptly; the second starting immediately with the end of book 3 and the beginning of book 4. The sharp break in the text of book 3 suggests that the division into two parts occurred at some point later in the manuscript's history – perhaps in an effort to make what must have been an unwieldy tome somewhat more manageable. The presence of a large double-column miniature at the beginning of book 6 (pictured), decorated with a full border bearing the arms of Edward IV, suggests that the manuscript originally marked an internal division of the text into two sections of five books each. Near-contemporary examples – one in Paris, commissioned by Louis of Gruuthuse, another in London, commissioned by an unidentified patron (Paris, BnF, MS fr. 17; and Royal 14 D. i) – attest to the existence of other single-volume manuscripts containing the first ten books of Augustine's text.

A comparison of the manuscripts produced for Edward IV and Louis of Gruuthuse reveals the difficulties in establishing a south Netherlandish tradition of the *City of God*. Both Gruuthuse's manuscript – illuminated by the Master of Margaret of York – and Edward's manuscript – by the Master of the White Inscriptions – comprise eleven miniatures: a large presentation scene of Charles V receiving the manuscript from Raoul de Praelles, followed by ten miniatures marking the beginning of each book. However, with the exception of the miniature prefacing book 6, the illumination of Edward's manuscript consists primarily of one-column miniatures depicting a highly simplified subject matter. Seemingly avoiding any detailed images of landscape, the artist prefers to place his scenes within narrowly delimited interior settings – often with figures that appear too large for the space they inhabit. The drastic simplification of both composition and narrative makes any meaningful identification of the scenes difficult. The miniature prefacing book 8 (f. 212), for example, shows the discussion of a group of philosophers set against a background of a grey stone wall. In contrast, the corresponding miniature in Gruuthuse's manuscript depicts Augustine lecturing before an assembly on the nature of demons, examples of which fill the surrounding sky. The drastic simplification of the miniatures in Edward's manuscript gives little indication that the artist drew upon the models available for the illumination of Augustine's text.

The generic motif of a group of philosophers in discussion recurs throughout Edward's manuscript, making the large miniature opening book 6 all the more remarkable (f. 120, pictured). Set in a vast, if nondescript landscape, the illumination clearly establishes a contrast between pagan idolatry on the left and Christian worship on the right. The composition of the scene – with the pagans placed prominently in the lower left-hand corner separated by a dividing wall from the Christians on the right – further nuances the juxtaposition by implying a chronological succession from the errant ways of the past to the future promised by the Christian faith. Thus the artist of Edward's manuscript successfully distils a major theme of Augustine's *City of God* – a text that relates the history and religion of ancient Rome, if only to point the way to its ultimate successor. *J.O'D.*

PROVENANCE:
Edward IV.

Opposite:
Pagan and Christian worship, f. 120

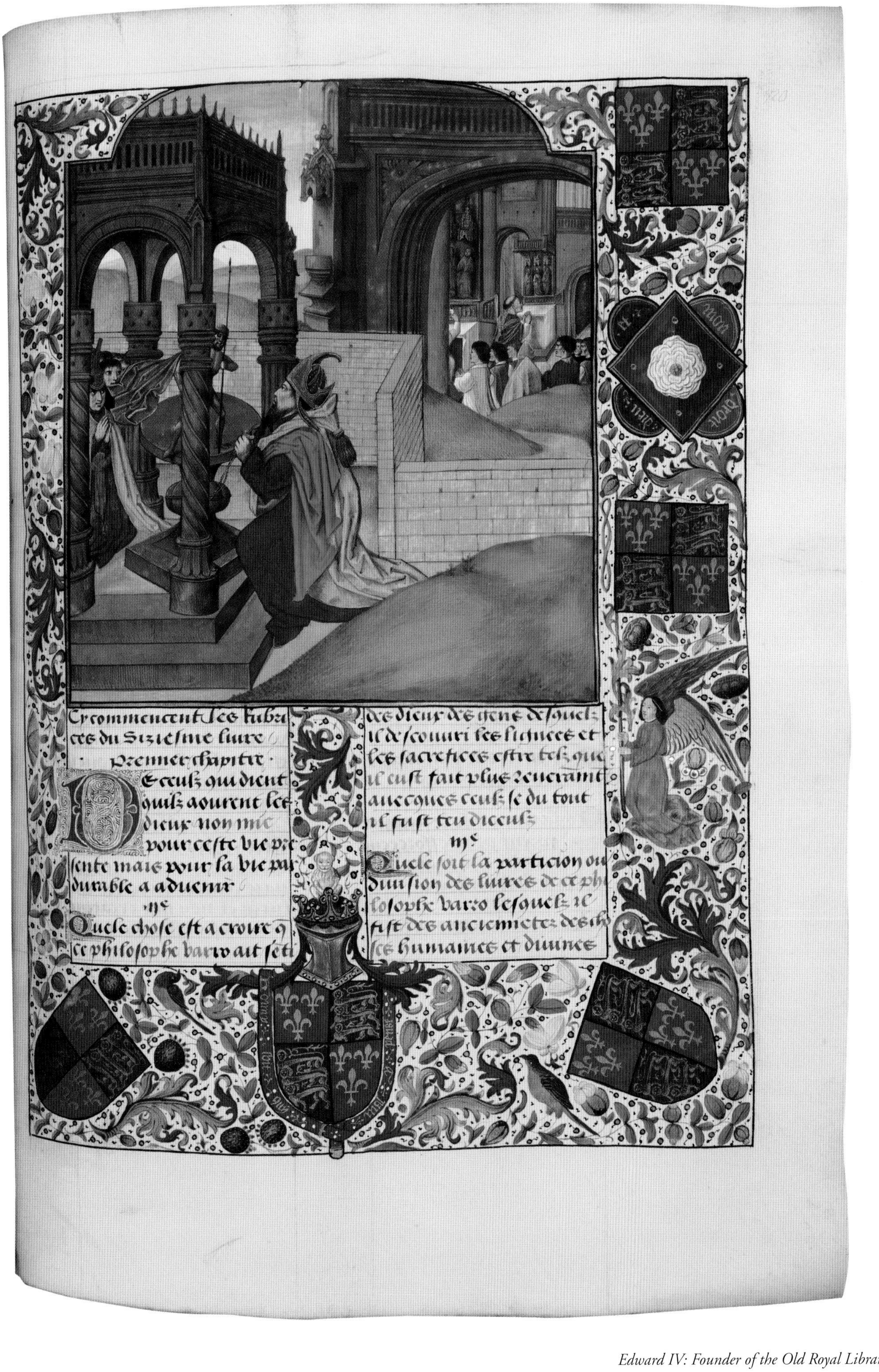
Cy commencent les rubri
ces du Sixiesme livre
Premier chapitre.
De ceulz qui dient
qu'ilz aourent les
dieux non mie
pour ceste vie pre
sente mais pour la vie par
durable a advenir
ij.e
Quele chose est a croire q
ce philosophe varro ait seti
des dieux des gens desquelz
il descouvri les signes et
les sacrefices estre telz que
il eust fait plus reveramment
avecques ceulz se du tout
il fust teu diceulz
iij.e
Quele soit la particion ou
division des livres de ce phi
losophe varro lesquelz il
fist des ancienetez des cho
ses humaines et divines

59 St Gregory the Great, *Homilies* and *Dialogues* in French Translation

Bruges, *c.* 1480
430 x 320 mm

BRITISH LIBRARY, ROYAL 15 D. v

A miniature found towards the beginning of the present manuscript represents a well-dressed man, perched precariously atop a barren tree, who seems unaware that Death is about to swing a final blow and fell the tree – a coffin waiting in the lower left corner suggests the ultimate outcome of the scene (f. 26, pictured). Illustrating a passage from the Gospel of Luke (3:9), 'For now the axe is laid to the root of the trees. Every tree therefore that bringeth not forth good fruit, shall be cut down and cast into the fire', the image serves as a fitting characterization of a manuscript that can best be described as a moral compendium. The book comprises French translations of the *Homilies on the Gospels* and the *Dialogues* – two works by the sixth-century Pope Gregory the Great (d. 604) – as well as a translation of the anonymous Latin collection of moralizing anecdotes known as the *Alphabetum narrationum.* Although somewhat unusual as a grouping, the three texts are related in at least one important respect. The idea of the *exemplum,* or story, is a pervasive motif of the texts and thus constitutes a unifying feature of the compilation. That being said, the manuscript accords special prominence through both its layout and illumination to the *Homilies.*

The text of the *Homilies,* which probably derives from the fourteenth-century French translation of Pierre de Hangest, Provost of Amiens, accounts for more than two-thirds of the entire manuscript. Its contents consist of forty Gospel extracts, each followed by the corresponding commentary of Gregory. Further elucidating the divisions of the text, a partial border and a one-column miniature mark the beginning of each homily – with the exception of the first, which lacks a miniature, and the fourth, which has three miniatures. As one would expect with a homily – that is, a text read aloud for the purpose of providing an explanation of Scripture suitable for a general audience – the nature of the commentary is more anecdotal and allegorical than scholarly.

In contrast to the *Homilies,* both the *Dialogues* and the *Alphabetum narrationum* lack one-column miniatures and border decoration. Furthermore, the latter two texts appear to have been regarded as one group since the manuscript marks a clear break between the *Homilies* and the *Dialogues* through a large double-column miniature representing Gregory in dialogue with Peter the Deacon (f. 218, pictured). No such break occurs between the *Dialogues* and the final text. This can be explained on that basis that the *Dialogues* and the *Alphabetum narrationum* are in fact a large extract taken from book 3 of Jean Mansel's fifteenth-century encyclopaedic compilation, the *Fleur des histories,* as De Poerck (1935) noted. Yet the absence of a programme of miniatures for this section of the manuscript cannot be accounted for by the lack of any illustrated tradition; illuminated examples of both the *Fleur des histoires* and Gregory's *Dialogues* exist from this period. Louis of Gruuthuse, for example, owned a manuscript of the *Dialogues* illuminated by Loyset Liédet around 1470 (Paris, BnF, MS fr. 911).

Within the miniatures accompanying the *Homilies* in the Royal manuscript, four hands may be distinguished. The difference between two of them is not only in terms of style and quality, but also of technique, with the stronger hand preferring to work in semi-grisaille, as seen, for example, in the detail from f. 26 (pictured). Also responsible for the two two-column miniatures prefacing the *Homilies* and the *Dialogues,* this artist has been identified as the Master of Edward IV. Some of the one-column miniatures in a near-contemporary manuscript containing book 4 of Mansel's *Fleur* (Copenhagen, Kongelige Bibliotek, MS Thott 568 2°) bear a striking resemblance in both style and technique to the Master of Edward IV's miniatures in the Royal manuscript. The lesser hand, characterized by a rough handling of colour (e.g., ff. 33v, 44), has been identified as the Master of St Omer 421, who was perhaps an apprentice of the Master of Edward IV (Brinkmann 1997).

The illuminations of the *Homilies* serve on the one hand as visual rubrics allowing for a quick identification and summary of the lesson presented. On the other, their focus on parables, miracles and preaching underscores the moralizing aspects of the subject matter. The moral or didactic function of the manuscript makes it an appropriate complement to the several examples of historical texts among the manuscript associated with Edward IV.

J.O'D.

PROVENANCE:

Edward IV (?); Henry VIII.

Above:
Death chopping down a barren tree, f. 26 (detail)

Opposite:
Gregory seated at a desk, in dialogue with Peter the Deacon, f. 218

ccx
Dyalogue cest a dire parolle de deux hommes et le liure qui a a nom dyalogue que saint gregoire pape fist fut ainsy appelle pource que le dyacre
de monseigneur saint gregoire lequel auoit nom pierre luy dist ung iour comme par admiracion quil se donnoit grant merueille quil y auoit eu sy peu de saintes gens en ytalie au regart des autres nacions du monde

60 Simon de Hesdin and Nicolas de Gonesse, *Faits et dits mémorables des romains*

(French translation of Valerius Maximus, *Facta et dicta memorabilia*)

Bruges, 1479
480 x 340 mm

BRITISH LIBRARY, ROYAL 18 E. iv

Medieval readers derived information about ancient Rome from diverse sources. One of the most important was Valerius Maximus's *Facta et dicta memorabilia* (Memorable Deeds and Sayings), composed *c.* AD 31. Preserved in Carolingian copies, the *Facta et dicta* was consulted throughout the Middle Ages. According to Bloomer (1992), more manuscripts of the work survive 'than of any other Latin prose text, save the Bible'. The *Facta et dicta* is divided into nine books with chapters devoted to specific subjects ranging from religion to unseemly conduct. As Valerius explains in the preface, he gleaned the anecdotes from various authors and arranged his material thematically to make the book easy to use. Because the narratives are brief – many a single sentence – the work was popular with orators who mined it for telling anecdotes.

Vernacular translations introduced the text to an even wider readership. Among the most influential was the *Faits et dits mémorables des romains*, a French translation begun in 1375 for Charles V by the Hospitaller Simon de Hesdin, but left unfinished until 1401 when a second translator, Nicholas de Gonesse, resumed the work for John, Duke of Berry (b. 1340, d. 1416). In dedicating his *Faits et dits* to the King of France, Simon de Hesdin followed the precedent set by Valerius himself, who dedicated his book to the Emperor Tiberius (r. AD 14–37). Simon de Hesdin's work is an expansion of Valerius's original text with much added new material, rather than a translation in the strict sense.

At least sixty-five manuscripts of the *Faits et dits* survive, including lavishly illustrated copies made in the southern Netherlands in the late fifteenth century (Schullian 1981). The present manuscript, made in Bruges in 1479, is the second of a two-volume set of the *Faits et dits* made for Edward IV (the first is Royal 18 E. iii). The borders of the miniatures in both volumes are emblazoned with his royal arms and those of his two sons. Like several other copies of the work made in Bruges, this one contains nine large miniatures, one at the beginning of each book. The first volume opens with an image of the translator, Simon de Hesdin, at his desk (fig. 2.16). An inscription on the wall behind him records the year in which the manuscript was made – 1479 – and bears the motto of the main artist, the so-called Master of the White Inscriptions, who illustrated several manuscripts commissioned by the English monarch (see cat. nos. 48, 51, 57, 58, 61, 62, 77). A single image in the second volume (f. 19), a depiction of clemency by a military leader, was painted by another illuminator, now known as the Master of the Flemish Boethius (Kren and McKendrick 2003; see also cat. no. 152).

Some manuscripts of the *Faits et dits* have illustrations that show Valerius explaining to the Emperor Tiberius various incidents mentioned in the text, but the Master of the White Inscriptions, who invariably broke with tradition, dispensed with this motif and devoted his compositions to the anecdotes themselves. The miniature at the beginning of the final book (f. 229, pictured), for example, features a group of noblewomen clothed in the high-waisted gowns and conical headdresses fashionable in France and Flanders in the 1470s (Scott 2007). For aristocratic and royal readers, illustrations showing people dressed in contemporary courtly fashions would have added a new dimension to the ancient tales. Velvet, ermine and cloth of gold were much in evidence at the court of Edward IV, and both he and his sister Margaret of York (see cat. no. 35), wife of Charles the Bold, spent considerable sums on luxurious fabrics, which reflected their high status.

As explained by Valerius, the women depicted presented themselves to the tribunes, Marcus Junius Brutus and his brother Publius, to protest against the *Lex Oppia*. Created in 215 BC, during the Second Punic War, this law prevented women from wearing multi-coloured clothes, owning significant sums of money or travelling by carriage. The Master of the White Inscriptions set the women's protest in a narrow chamber. The creases in the red cloth of honour behind the tribunes, and the receding lines of the floor tiles, draw the eye to the doorway through which the women enter. Despite being described in the text as vacuous and vain, the women, with their demure expressions and downcast eyes, are models of decorum. Valerius, who denounces women's obsession with appearances and obedience to the fickle dictates of fashion, concedes that men can be equally self-indulgent. *D.J.*

PROVENANCE

Edward IV.

Opposite:
Roman women protesting against the *Lex Oppia*, f. 229

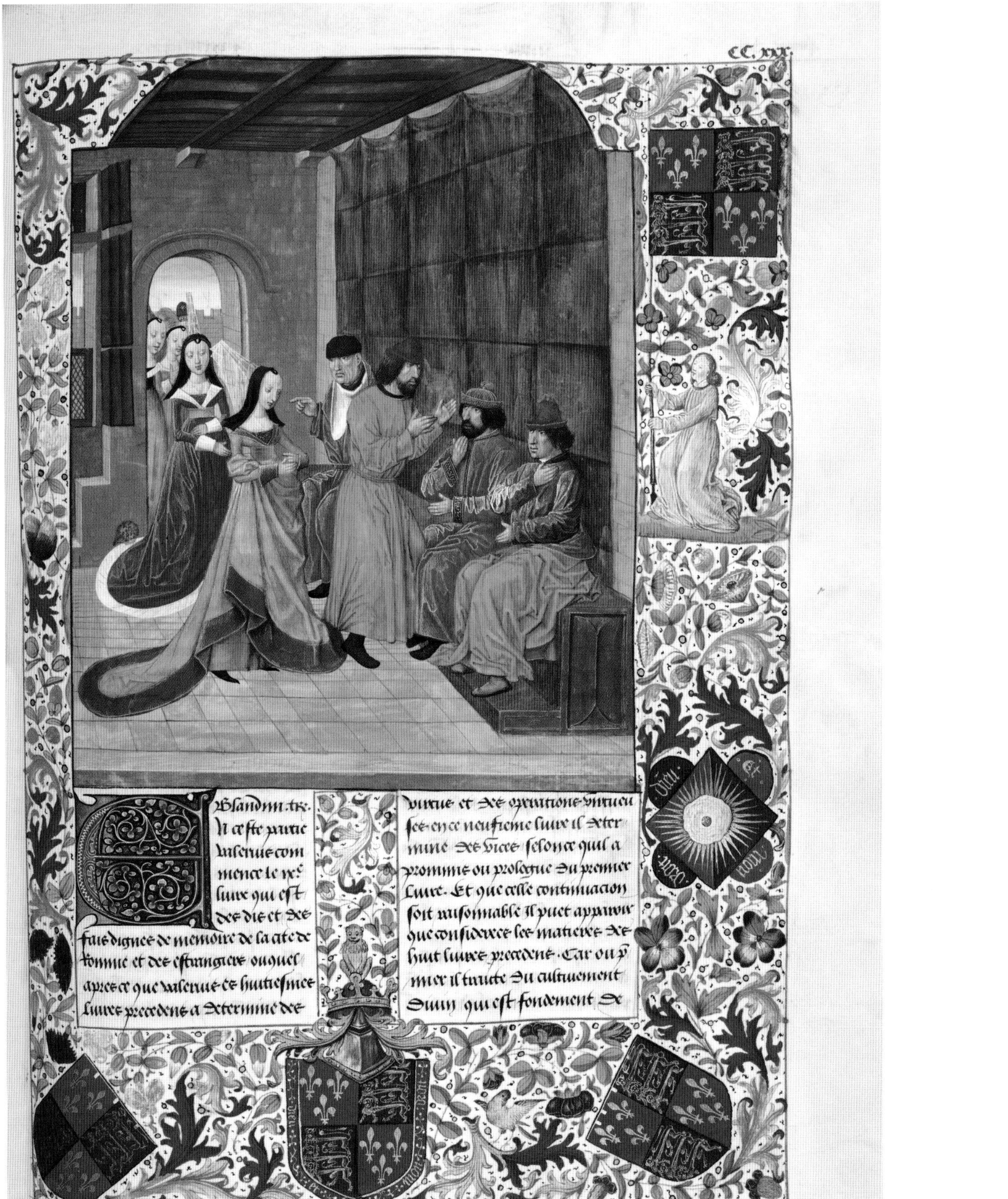
Il ceste partie
Valerius com
mence le ix.e
livre qui est
des dis et des
fais dignes de memoire de la cite de
Romme et des estrangiers ouquel
apres ce que Valerius es huitiesmes
livres precedens a determine des
vertus et des operations vertueu
ses en ce neufieme livre il deter
mine des vices selon ce quil a
promis ou prologue du premier
livre. Et que ceste continuacion
soit raisonnable il puet apparoir
que considerees les matieres des
huit livres precedens. Car ou p
mier il traicte du cultivement
divin qui est fondement de

61 *Des Cas des nobles hommes et femmes*

(Giovanni Boccaccio, *De casibus virorum illustrium*, translated into French by Laurent de Premierfait)

Bruges, *c.* 1480
480 x 340 mm

BRITISH LIBRARY, ROYAL 14 E. v

In many respects the present volume, made in Bruges *c.* 1480, resembles the fifty or so other Netherlandish manuscripts made for Edward IV around the same time; it is a large volume, contains a secular text in French written in a formal cursive script, has an extensive cycle of illustrations and bears the English royal arms. Despite these typical features, it is an unusual book that stands apart from other manuscripts made in Bruges in the final decades of the fifteenth century.

The text is a copy of Laurent de Premierfait's second, amplified translation of Boccaccio's *De casibus virorum illustrium*, which Premierfait completed in 1409 and dedicated to his patron, John, Duke of Berry (b. 1340, d. 1416). Although Premierfait's second translation survives in over fifty illuminated manuscripts (Bozzolo 1973), very few were produced in the southern Netherlands and none of these was as lavishly illustrated as the present volume (Kren and McKendrick 2003). Edward IV and members of his court circle may well have been more familiar with Premierfait's work than was the Flemish scribe who copied this manuscript because illuminated volumes of Premierfait's second French translation had made their way into the libraries of English aristocrats (see cat. no. 72), and an English version of the text had been made in the 1430s by Lydgate for Humfrey, Duke of Gloucester. No surviving copy of *Des Cas* from the library of the dukes of Burgundy or from that of the Flemish bibliophile Louis of Gruuthuse, who sheltered Edward IV during his exile in Bruges in 1470–71, resembles this one (Reynolds 2005). Edward IV's decision to commission a copy of *Des Cas* from Bruges craftsmen, despite their unfamiliarity with the text, reflects his preference for Netherlandish miniatures and his desire to stock his library with books of uniform appearance. Unlike many of his royal and aristocratic contemporaries on the Continent, Edward IV very rarely acquired luxury books at second hand, consistently preferring custom-made volumes.

Like the scribe who copied the text, the Netherlandish artists who executed the miniatures were probably unfamiliar with Premierfait's work (Reynolds 2005). Nine large miniatures mark the beginning of each book and sixty-nine smaller ones signal the beginning of select chapters. Not all of the 165 chapters were distinguished in this way – approximately 42% are illustrated. Reynolds (2005) has posited that the illuminators were aware of some visual models since the miniatures sometimes deviate from the text and cannot, therefore, be based on it alone. No single visual source has been identified, however, and the divergence between the placement and content of the miniatures in Edward's *Des Cas* and those of other surviving manuscripts is noteworthy.

The large miniature reproduced here depicts Fortune, characterized as a courtly lady, appearing to Boccaccio. The illustration is a respite from the violent images featured on other pages, but despite the placid setting of Boccaccio's studio, which overlooks a quiet Flemish town, Fortune is a disturbing presence. Although she lacks her customary wings and blindfold, she is endowed with six hands, ready to mete out good and bad luck, and to prevent anyone from escaping her grasp. Light enters the chamber by an open door and from a window, at which a spectator sits, absorbed by the view. This figure at the window, with his back turned to the viewer, evokes similar motifs in contemporary Netherlandish panel paintings and was probably inspired by such a source.

McKendrick has attributed all nine large miniatures to a single artist whom he christened the Master of the Getty Froissart because the artist also illuminated for an aristocratic or royal patron (probably Edward IV) a copy of Jean Froissart's *Chroniques* book 3 (Los Angeles, J. Paul Getty Museum, MS Ludwig XIII 7; Kren and McKendrick 2003). These miniatures were previously attributed to the Master of the White Inscriptions, who is thought to have worked on some of the smaller miniatures in the present manuscript.

Entertaining passages notwithstanding, Premierfait's *Des Cas* was primarily didactic – a moralizing work, cautioning against the abuse of power by the elite and illustrating, in the most horrific ways, the punishments of evil despots. Like several manuscripts made for Edward IV this one includes both his arms and those of his elder son (e.g. f. 174). This suggests that Edward conceived of his library as a repository of knowledge to be consulted by his heirs. He could not, of course, have predicted that his ten-year old son and namesake, who met his fate in the Tower of London in 1483 alongside his younger brother, would have few opportunities to do so. *D.J.*

PROVENANCE:

Edward IV.

Opposite:
Fortune appearing to Boccaccio, f. 291

Cy commence le sixieme liure des
neuf liures de Jehan bocace Con
tenant en soy quinse chappitres
Duquel liure le premier chappitre
contient le parlemẽt de fortune
et de lacteur de ce liure. Et racõte
en brief le cas daucũs maleureux
nobles hões. Et comence ou latin.
Fortune qui est vn
hideux monstre et
qui comme cham
beriere donne et depart aux hões
et aux femmes les bieneurtez mõ
dames Suiuant de nat moy
depuis que je mestoie vn petit repo
se. Prenoie ma plume apres la
fin du cinquiesme liure pour recõ
mencier le sixieme liure. Je qui fuz
esbahiz de lymage de fortune mes
criay a dieu qui est le donneur
des vrais biens Et se aucũs
me demandent quele fut ma sen
tence apres ce que jeus auise la

62 Jean de Courcy, *Le Chemin de vaillance*

Bruges, between *c.* 1479 and 1483
470 x 345 mm

BRITISH LIBRARY, ROYAL 14 E. ii

Among the manuscripts of historical and didactic interest that were commissioned by Edward IV in Bruges towards the end of his reign is this anthology of moral works on chivalric virtues and military art. The volume starts with the only extant copy of the allegorical poem *Le Chemin de vaillance* (the Road of Valiance), written in *c.* 1424–26 by the Norman knight Jean de Courcy of Bourg-Achard (see Dubuc 1994). Four shorter texts follow this poetic guide to knightly conduct. The *Epistre d'Othéa* by Christine de Pizan (d. *c.* 1434) is a collection of didactic stories addressed by the Goddess of Wisdom Othea to the young Hector of Troy, who was perceived throughout the Middle Ages as a model of chivalric prowess. The praise of the twelve virtues that define nobility is the subject of the next poem in the volume, *Le Breviaire des nobles*, composed in *c.* 1422–26 by Alain Chartier. Following this the short, anonymous work entitled *Les Complaintes des IX malheureux et des IX malheureuses* is a variation on the theme of the Nine Worthies and consists of poetic expositions by nine heroes and nine heroines of the Bible, ancient history and mythology on the instability of Fortune. The final text in the volume is a French translation of the *Order of Chivalry* by Ramon Lull (d. 1315), a treatise widely read in the Middle Ages. In this work an old knight-hermit instructs a young squire on the obligations of knighthood.

The texts included in the Royal manuscript form a coherent collection focused on moral virtue and replete with examples of chivalrous deeds through which a nobleman might achieve honour and good renown. In this respect they conform to the literary culture of the Burgundian court that Edward's other commissions also emulated. Although the *Chemin de vaillance* is the only known copy of this text and its inclusion in Edward's anthology might suggest an originality of choice on the King's part, it is possible that the entire contents of the Royal manuscript merely reproduce those of an earlier manuscript (untraced). All the texts included in it had been composed or translated in France at least two generations earlier, and by the last quarter of the fifteenth century they may have been available in Bruges as a ready-made collection. The appending of three of them – the poems of Christine de Pizan and Alain Chartier, and the *Complaintes* – to a copy of the *Ovide moralisé*, a French version of Ovid's *Metamorphoses*, in another manuscript produced in Bruges (Royal 17 E. iv) suggests a wide circulation of similar anthologies.

Given the didactic character of its contents, the Royal manuscript might have been intended for Edward's sons, Edward, Prince of Wales (b. 1470), and Richard, Duke of York (b. 1473). The arms of both Princes are included in the splendid heraldic display of the opening page of the book together with the royal arms of their father and the arms of two patron saints of the kingdom, Edmund and Edward the Confessor. In the 'ordenaunces concerning the welfare of Edward, Prince of Wales' addressed to the prince's tutor Anthony Woodville, the King asked him to 'read before the Prince such noble Stories' and instruct the prince in 'vertue, honour, connynge, wisdome, and dedys of worship' (see Kekewich 1971).

Le Chemin de vaillance, the main text in the Royal manuscript, is richly illuminated. A series of twelve miniatures (two more mark the beginning of the poems of Christine de Pizan and Alain Chartier) illustrates the key episodes of the imaginary journey which the Author undertakes to meet the Goddess Valiance. The miniature reproduced here depicts him on horseback accompanied by Seven Virtues who are showing him the right path. The Author has just left the Forest of Temptation, where he had encountered and combated the Seven Deadly Sins.

The miniature is a good example of the style of the Master of the White Inscriptions with its oversized figures and repetitive facial types. Apart from the opening image (f. 1), all of the miniatures in the volume have been attributed to the same Master (Kren and McKendrick 2003). This commercial Bruges artist seems to have worked exclusively for the English market. He contributed to the illumination of seven other manuscripts acquired by Edward IV, one of which bears a date of 1479 (see cat. no. 60) and another a date of 1480 (cat. no. 51). These dates coincide with a record of payment for books made to the merchant Philip Maisertuell in 1479 and with another mention of books in the Great Wardrobe Accounts of 1480 (see fig. 2. 17). The present manuscript was probably dispatched to England during this short and intense period of Edward's acquisitions. *J.F.*

PROVENANCE:

Edward IV.

Opposite:
The author accompanied by Seven Virtues leaving the Forest of Temptation, f. 194

How to be a King: Works of Instruction and Advice

From an early age royal princes were introduced to their future roles and responsibilities as monarchs. Books composed specifically for that purpose were used in their education from as early as the Carolingian period, but it was not until the Capetian courts of St Louis and his descendants that the so-called 'mirrors for princes' flourished. In England the *Secretum secretorum*, fashioned as a letter Aristotle sent to his pupil Alexander the Great, proved the most popular text of this type, and influenced one of the first texts of royal instruction written there (see cat. no. 63). At the turn of the fifteenth century a series of 'mirrors' in verse composed by the poets Gower, Hoccleve (cat. nos. 64, 65) and Lydgate filled the gap in English educational and advisory literature.

The Aristotelian idea that, to rule successfully, a prince should first learn how to govern himself was a commonplace of these texts. 'Mirrors of princes', therefore, stressed the importance of Christian values and chivalric virtues in the upbringing of a future king. These concerns explain the popularity within royal and aristocratic circles of vernacular compendia of Christian faith and morality, such as the *Somme le roi* (cat. no. 66) and the Anglo-Norman *La Lumiere as lais* (cat. no. 87). Chivalric treatises were also dedicated to the instruction of young princes, such as the *Enseignement de la vraie noblesse*, which was commissioned by Henry VII, doubtless with his elder son Arthur in mind (cat. no. 69).

It was, however, knowledge of history that was recommended as the true lesson of wisdom, virtue and knightly conduct. The present section, therefore, also includes a wide range of historical and legendary texts featuring heroes and heroines from the Bible, Christian hagiography, ancient mythology and Greek and Roman history and legend (cat. nos. 70–79). Several heroes from the past gained special esteem as models to emulate: Solomon for his wisdom (cat. no. 74), Alexander (cat. no. 75) and Caesar (cat. no. 76) for their military accomplishments, and Hercules for his chivalric virtues (cat. no. 77). The prefatory pictorial cycle of the Old Testament stories in the Queen Mary Psalter may have played a similar role by displaying models and anti-models of biblical kingship (cat. no. 85). Other moral lessons were conveyed in bestiaries featuring animals as exemplars of virtues and vices. Although these texts were mostly read in monasteries, the existence of highly illuminated copies (cat. nos. 80, 81) and the inclusion of a bestiary cycle in the Queen Mary Psalter suggests their reception also in aristocratic and royal circles. Finally, morally correct conduct was stimulated in aristocratic readers by vividly depicted visions of the end of times in illustrated Apocalypses, such as the one owned by Cecily Welles, daughter of Edward IV (cat. no. 87).

King Solomon instructing his son (cat. no. 74)

63 Pseudo-Aristotle, *Secretum secretorum*

London, 1326–27
240 x 160 mm

BRITISH LIBRARY, ADDITIONAL 47680

Alexander the Great receiving the book from Aristotle's messenger, ff. 10v–11

This copy of the *Secretum secretorum* was conceived by Walter of Milemete (fl. 1326–73) as a companion volume to his own treatise, *De nobilitatibus sapientiis et prudentiis regum* (Oxford, Christ Church, MS 92). As he explained in the prologue to the latter text, both books were written for presentation to Edward III at the beginning of his reign. Milemete's intention was to supplement the general knowledge of the *Secretum*, which extended from rhetoric to medicine and astrology, with more focused instruction on the office of the king. His choice of the *Secretum* reflects its growing popularity in England. Edward also received a copy of the *Secretum* in French, bound with other advisory texts as a betrothal gift from his future wife Philippa of Hainault (Paris, BnF, MS fr. 571). Later, the text would inspire Gower, Hoccleve, and Lydgate, and result in numerous French and English translations.

The *Secretum*, which was partially translated from Arabic by Johannes Hispaniensis in the middle of the twelfth century and in full by Philip of Tripoli almost one hundred years later, was believed in the Middle Ages to be a genuine work of Aristotle, composed for the instruction of Alexander the Great. The relationship between the ancient Greek king and the philosopher was perceived as a model for that between a medieval prince and his tutor. The miniature reproduced here (f. 10v) depicts the critical moment when Alexander received Aristotle's text from a messenger sent by the philosopher. In its contracted narrative Aristotle is shown standing behind his envoy. An escutcheon on the messenger's girdle bearing the arms used by the future Edward III as Earl of Chester permitted the young prince to recognize himself in the role of Alexander. The same arms, supported by two angels, are repeated in the upper margin and once again in the *bas-de-page* beside the arms of Edward II.

A series of heraldic devices in the lower margins of the manuscript reveals the complicated historical context of its production. The page opposite the illumination (f. 11, pictured) hosts the arms of Edward's uncles, Thomas Brotherton, Earl of Norfolk, and Edmund of Woodstock, Earl of Kent – both of whom joined Edward's mother, Isabel of France, and her lover, Roger Mortimer, against Edward II. Both Earls were present at the baronial council in Bristol that on 26 October 1326 declared Prince Edward keeper of the realm; after his coronation both sat on the regency council presided over by Henry of Lancaster. Henry's arms are also represented in the book, together with those of his brother, Thomas of

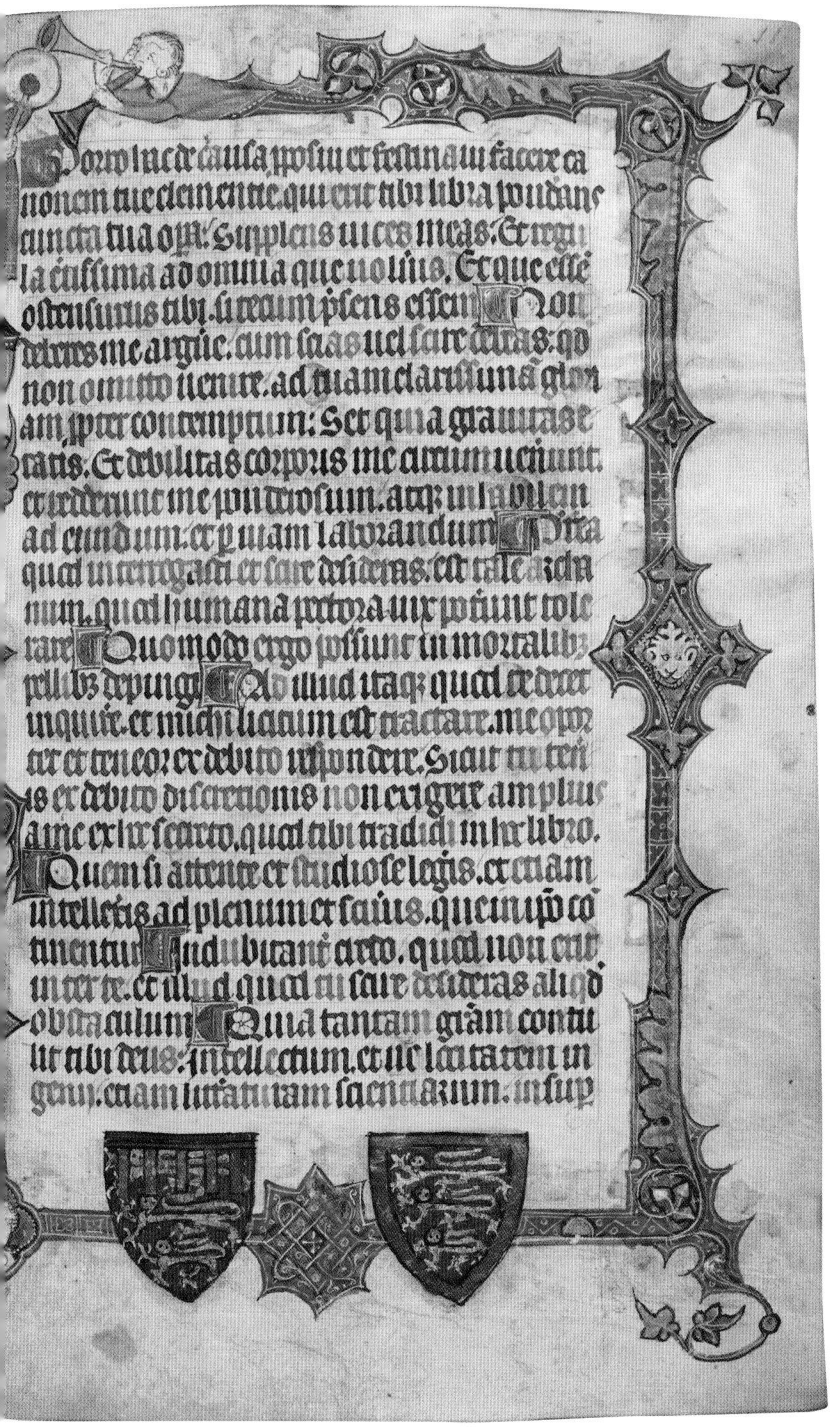

Lancaster, who was beheaded in 1322 as the leader of the baronial opposition to Edward II. This configuration of heraldry suggests that the manuscript was produced after the queen's party had come to power.

Further evidence suggests that Milemete composed his treatise and work began on both the Royal and the Oxford manuscripts when Prince Edward was declared keeper of the realm; corrections to Milemete's text appear to have been made after his coronation and the deposition or death of his father. Although the prologue to Milemete's treatise in the Oxford manuscript addresses Edward III as king, this text was written by a different scribe from the one responsible for the rest of the manuscript and seems to be a later amendment. Similarly, whereas in a prayer closing the first chapter of the same treatise Edward is named Duke of Aquitaine, and Earl of Chester and Ponthieu, one invocation to him has been altered by a different hand to 'Duke and King'. His father is twice referred to as the 'King of England', and only the second reference is refined with the word '*nuper*' (formerly) (f. 10).

It is uncertain whether Milemete's volumes were ever presented to the King. Work on them was certainly never fully accomplished. The two manuscripts were written – probably simultaneously – by two different scribes, but the pictorial decoration was completed only in Milemete's own treatise. (The series of full-page underdrawings at the end of the Oxford volume is a later addition.) The miniatures and borders of the *Secretum,* to which three of Milemete's five artists had contributed, either remained unfinished or were completed by a group of illuminators working twenty-five years later (see Sandler 1986). Furthermore, the Royal and Oxford manuscripts do not share a common, later provenance. From the sixteenth century the *Secretum* was in the possession of the Coke family of Norfolk, who later acquired the earldom of Leicester and founded the Holkham Library. Milemete's treatise was given in 1707 to Christ Church by William Carpenter, rector of Stanton. Nevertheless, since all of Edward III's manuscripts were dispersed before the creation of the Royal library, the early history of this pair of volumes remains obscure. *J.F.*

PROVENANCE:

Edward III (?); Sir Edward Coke (b. 1552, d. 1634); Carey Coke (b. 1680, d. 1707); Thomas William Coke, 1st Earl of Leicester of Holkham (b. 1754, d. 1842); Thomas William Coke, 4th Earl of Leicester of Holkham (b. 1880, d. 1949); Holkham Hall Library, MS 458; purchased for the nation in 1952.

64 Thomas Hoccleve, *Regement of Princes*

England, *c.* 1430–38
265 x 175 mm

BRITISH LIBRARY, ROYAL 17 D. vi

65 Thomas Hoccleve, *Regement of Princes*

London *c.* 1411–13
290 x 185 mm

BRITISH LIBRARY, ARUNDEL 38

Thomas Hoccleve wrote the *Regement of Princes* in 1410–11 and addressed it to Henry, Prince of Wales, who was soon to ascend to the throne of England as Henry V. Hoccleve's English poem was inspired by the three classics of the 'mirror for princes' genre, the pseudo-Aristotelian *Secretum secretorum*, Giles of Rome's *De regimine principum*, and the *De ludo scaccorum* of Jacobus de Cessolis. The text also followed the interests of the Ricardian poets in works on political advice. Hoccleve's initiative conformed to Henry's policy of encouraging the use of English, as demonstrated in his commissioning of Lydgate's *Troy Book* in 1412 (see cat. no. 73) and later in its promotion in government documents.

The *Regement* was composed at a very important historical moment. In December 1409 Prince Henry took formal control of the Council – which ruled during the serious illness of his father – from the hands of the Chancellor, Thomas Arundel. Until 1411, when Henry IV regained his power, the young Prince was in charge of the government and sought to pursue a programme of *bone governance* (good government) to which he had pledged himself in the Parliament of January 1410.

The *Regement* survives in three illuminated copies. One (cat. no. 64) was acquired by William FitzAlan, Earl of Arundel, probably soon after his marriage to Joan Neville in 1438 (their impaled arms are added on f. 4). Its presentation scene shows Henry receiving the book from Thomas Hoccleve (pictured). The image interacts closely with the text. It is not placed at the beginning of the poem, but follows a long prefatory dialogue between the author and an old man, in which Hoccleve describes his miserable condition as a clerk of the Privy Seal and is advised to write a poem for Prince Henry and seek his patronage. In consequence the presentation scene appears only at the beginning of the text in which Hoccleve addresses the Prince directly.

Seymour (1974, 1982) portrayed Hoccleve as one of the earliest 'publishers' in England who supervised the production of a series of presentation copies of his texts. Even if the author's personal engagement with the production of manuscripts for royal patrons was not as straightforward as this, two verse dedications of the *Regement* to Edward, Duke of York, and John, Duke of Bedford – which survive in Hoccleve's autograph miscellany (San Marino, Huntington Library, HM 111) – are suggestive of his strategy of self-promotion. None of the extant copies of the *Regement* can be identified with the books he presented to the three Princes. Harley 4866, usually evoked in this context, has the 'dedication' miniature excised and its 'twin' (cat. no. 65), attributed to the London workshop of Herman Scheerre, seems to tell a different story.

As Scott (1996) has noted, the Arundel manuscript was indeed a gift copy but not necessarily from Hoccleve. The sequence of figures depicted in the Arundel presentation miniature starts on the left-hand side with Prince Henry, who therefore may be the donor rather than the receiver of the book. The man kneeling before the Prince and dressed in a long, high-collar gown of an aristocrat does not reflect the image of a humble author that is given in the poem. Perhaps he may be identified as John Mowbray (b. 1392, d. 1432), 2nd Duke of Norfolk and Lord Mowbray and Segrave, by the inclusion in the manuscript of his arms. England ancient with a label of three points argent (f. 2) was used by his ancestor, Thomas of Brotherton (d. 1338), Earl of Norfolk and fifth son of Edward I, but are sometimes wrongly associated with Prince Henry. Later in the manuscript appear the arms of Mowbray (f. 37, pictured overleaf) and Segrave (f. 71). Mowbray was the heir of a family that had opposed the Lancastrian usurpation of Henry IV. The royal gift of this manuscript may have been intended to mark the final restoration of Mowbray's lands and lost titles of Earl Marshal and Lord Mowbray and Segrave, which occurred upon his coming of age in 1413, the year of Henry's coronation. Such a gesture would have been consistent with Henry's policy of reconciliation with the families of former rebels.

As a royal gift Arundel 38 did not form part of the royal collection. The manuscript stayed in the hands of the Mowbray family and later, through Henry Howard, Duke of Norfolk, passed to the Royal Society. Ironically, the Royal copy of the *Regement,* which had been owned at an early date by a member of the Arundel family, came into the Old Royal library in the early seventeenth century as part of the Lumley collection acquired by Prince Henry Frederick.

J.F.

PROVENANCE:

64) Royal 17 D. vi
William FitzAlan, 9th Earl of Arundel (b. 1417, d. 1487), and Joan Neville (b. 1400, d. 1460); John, 1st Baron Lumley (d. 1609); Henry Frederick, Prince of Wales (d. 1612).

65) Arundel 38
John Mowbray, 2nd Duke of Norfolk, Lord Mowbray and Segrave (b. 1392, d. 1432); Henry Howard, 6th Duke of Norfolk (b. 1628, d. 1684); Royal Society, London, 1667; purchased for the nation in 1831.

Opposite:
Hoccleve presenting the book to Prince Henry, Royal 17 D. vi, f. 40

Hye and noble prince excellent
My lord the prince my lord gracious
I humble servaunt and obedient
Unto your estate hye and glorious
Of whiche I am full tendir and full ielous
Me recommaunde unto your worthynesse
With hert entier and spirite of mekenesse

Prince Henry offering the book to John Mowbray, Arundel 38, f. 36v–37

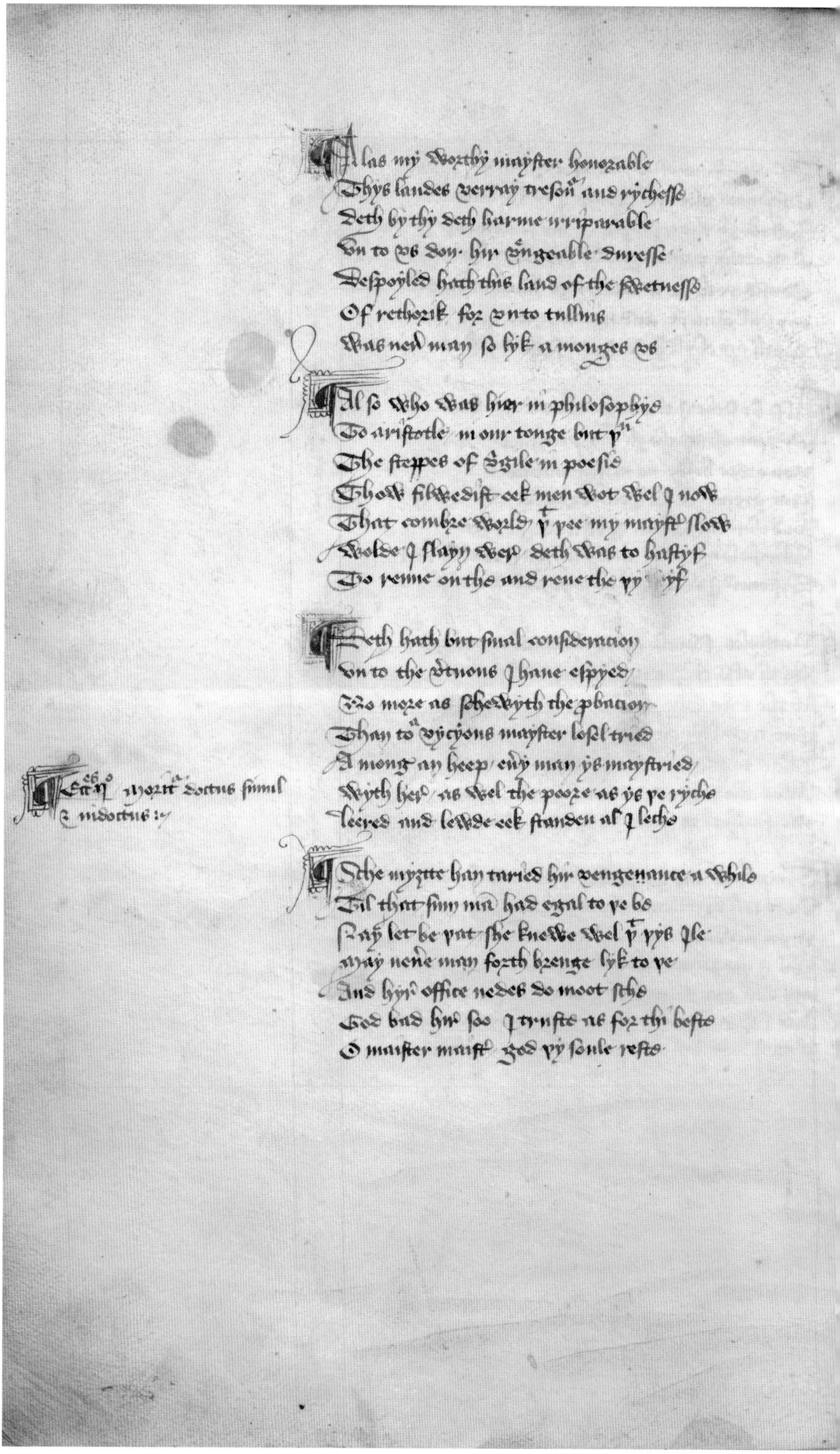
Alas my worthy mayster honorable
Thys landes verray tresor and rychesse
Deth by thy deth harme irreparable
Vn to vs doon hir vengeable duresse
Despoyled hath this land of the swetnesse
Of rethorik for vnto Tullius
Was neuer man so lyk amonges vs

Al so who was hier in philosophye
To aristotle in our tonge but thou
The steppes of Virgile in poesie
Thow filwedist eek men wot wel ynow
That combre world that the my mayster slow
Wolde I slayn were deth was to hastyf
To renne on the and reue the thy lyf

Deth hath but smal consideracion
Vn to the vertuous I haue espyed
No more as schewyth the probacion
Than to a vycyous mayster losel tried
A mong an heep euery man ys maystried
With her as wel the poore as ys the ryche
Leered and lewde eek standen al y liche

Mors necat doctus simul & indoctus

She myghte han taried hir vengeaunce a whyle
Til that sum man had egal to the be
Nay let be that she knewe wel that this yle
May neuere man forth brynge lyk to the
And hyr office nedes do moot she
God bad hir so I truste as for thi beste
O maister maister god thy soule reste

ye noble and myzty Prince excellent
My lord the Prince . o my lord gracious
I humble servant and obedient
Un to zour estate hye and glorious
Of whiche I am ful tendre and ful gelous
Me recommaunde unto zour worthynesse
With herte enter and spirit of meekenesse

66 Friar Laurent, *La Somme le roi*

Paris *c.* 1340–50
315 x 220 mm

BRITISH LIBRARY, ROYAL 19 C. ii

Prudence, Temperance and Fortitude, ff. 48v–49

In 1279 Friar Laurent, former Prior of the Dominican convent of St Jacques in Paris, confessor to the king and tutor to the royal children, completed a treatise on the vices and virtues at the request of Philip III of France. Because of this royal commission, the text would soon be known as the *Somme le roi* (Survey for the King).

Laurent's work was not a typical 'mirror' for a prince. The task of compiling such a 'mirror' text was entrusted by the King to another friar, the Augustinian Giles of Rome, who wrote *De regimine principum,* and dedicated it to the future Philip IV. In contrast, the King's confessor provided a comprehensive manual on a moral life and penitence. His book summarized the principles of the Christian faith, beginning with the Ten Commandments and the Creed, and included tracts on the Seven Deadly Sins and the virtues correlated with the articles of the *Pater Noster* and the Gifts of the Holy Spirit. The Royal manuscript also includes the Gospels and a devotional text entitled *La Plainte de la Vierge*.

All three of the texts in the Royal manuscript are in French because, as Laurent explains, 'cist livre est plus fez pour les lais que por les clers, car ils savent les Escriptures' (this book is made for lay people rather than for clerics, for they know the Scriptures). Although Laurent's remark implied a broad lay audience, the early circulation of the *Somme le roi* was limited to members of the French royal family and the entourage of Philip IV. Seven luxurious and closely related manuscripts of his text date from this period; each is decorated with fifteen full-page miniatures, including Philip's own copy, now perhaps Additional 54180 (Rouse and Rouse 2000).

The *Somme le roi* became a medieval 'best-seller', and survives in more than ninety manuscripts. It was still an obligatory item in the library of a king or a prince in the late fourteenth and fifteenth centuries. Ten copies were included in the inventories of Charles V and Charles VI, and at least four were in the library of the dukes of Burgundy. Clemence of Hungary, Queen of France, is known to have had a copy that was subsequently owned by Jeanne d'Évreux and Blanche of France. Blanche of Navarre, Queen of France, bequeathed a copy to Louis, Duke of Orleans, and Jean Gerson recommended the *Somme le roi* as useful reading to Louis, Duke of Guyenne, Dauphin of France. In 1484 William Caxton translated the text

into English under the suggestive title *The Royal Book*.

It is not known when the Royal copy of the *Somme le roi* entered the English royal collection, although it has a characteristic late 'Westminster inventory' number indicating that it was in the library at Westminster Palace by the middle of the sixteenth century. On stylistic grounds it is clear that the Royal copy is a Parisian manuscript of the second quarter of the fourteenth century. Its illuminations were painted by a recognizable Parisian artist (see cat. 91) who also illustrated a copy of the *Golden Legend* that includes a mention of the Parisian *libraire* Richard de Montbaston of the rue Neuve Notre Dame and a date of 1348 (Paris, BnF, MS fr. 241). In the Royal *Somme le roi* the de Montbaston artist continued the work of another slightly better-trained illuminator whose style is closer to the early 'royal' copies of the *Somme*.

In comparison to the manuscripts produced for the entourage of Philip IV, the present manuscript represents a modest version of the iconographical cycle. Fifteen full-page miniatures are replaced in the Royal copy by nineteen one-column illuminations. Only one half-page miniature echoes the splendours of the earlier copies.

The *Somme le roi* was intended to function visually as a model of the moral Christian life, and all early versions contain captions explaining the subjects depicted. In the Royal manuscript not only did the captions disappear, but the artist seems to have misunderstood some aspects of the original iconography. The opening (pictured) shows three of the four Cardinal Virtues located at the beginning of the *Traité des vertus,* the most densely illustrated part of the text, with fourteen miniatures. Prudence, associated with wisdom and knowledge, and represented as a teacher in the classroom in other manuscripts of the *Somme,* is depicted in the Royal copy as a scribe. Similarly, Temperance, the virtue of moderation – instead of refusing a cup offered to her by a young man – is deep in a conversation while the man is having the drink! Only Fortitude, holding a disc decorated with a lion, follows the established iconography. *J.F*

PROVENANCE:

Henry VIII.

67 Guillaume de Nangis, *Gesta S. Ludovici et Regis Philippi*

Paris, *c.* 1401–15

270 x 185 mm

BRITISH LIBRARY, ROYAL 13 B. iii

The *Gesta S. Ludovici et Regis Philippi* was composed *c.* 1289–96 by Guillaume de Nangis, archivist and keeper of books at the abbey of St-Denis, and addressed by him to Philip IV, King of France. In his prologue the author clearly explained the purpose of his work as an 'exemplum virtutis quasi speculum' (an example of virtue, as if it were a mirror). This example was provided by the lives of St Louis and his son, Philip III.

In the Royal manuscript, Guillaume's dedication to Philip IV is replaced by a miniature painted in the Parisian style of *c.* 1400. It represents Louis, Duke of Guyenne, Dauphin of France (b. 1397, d. 1415), receiving instruction from his sainted ancestor and namesake (pictured). The Dauphin is identified by the arms of his mother, Isabel of Bavaria, and his own arms of France ancient quartered with or a dolphin azure. In front of him St Louis is shown in the full splendour of his holy kingship, with the royal arms of France decorating the walls behind and the canopy above his chair.

In Guillaume's text St Louis embodied all the qualities of a fearless knight, just sovereign, peacemaker and humble saint. In the Royal manuscript his life is designed as a model for Louis of Guyenne as the future 'most Christian king'. Another manuscript, the Dauphin's personal Breviary (Châteauroux, Bibliothèque Municipale, MS 2), seems to have appropriated this image. There, St Louis is represented wearing a gown decorated with three stripes on each shoulder, a distinctive sign of French kings' sons (f. 298v). In the Breviary portrait, as in a mirror, the Dauphin could have identified himself with his patron saint.

Louis of Guyenne became the official heir to the throne in 1401, and because of the illness of his father he soon played an important role in government. In 1409, at the age of only twelve, he was removed from the guardianship of his mother and called upon to preside over the royal Council in the 'absence' of the King. The heraldic programme of the miniature highlights his dynastic mission and, by linking him directly to his venerated ancestor, reinforces his place in the royal lineage. Since the Capetian dynasty had died out in 1328, it was their genealogical descent from St Louis that was used to legitimize the new Valois dynasty's claim to the throne. It has been suggested that Louis de Guyenne may have received the Royal *Gesta Ludovici* during this period of political initiation (*Paris 1400* 2004). The prominence of the Bavarian arms of Isabel, however, implies the Dauphin's subordination to the Queen's guardianship, and hence possibly dates the manuscript to 1409 or earlier.

The commission of the *Gesta* belongs to a larger programme for the education of the young Prince undertaken by contemporary intellectuals. The manuscript may have been one of the 'chosen books' recommended for the Dauphin's library in the *Opusculum de considerationibus quas debet habere princeps* (1408) that Jean Gerson composed for Louis's tutor Jean d'Arsonval. Gerson saw books as a mean of nourishing Louis's knowledge and engaging him in 'colloquia sancta' (holy conversations) with God and the saints. The volume may also be placed in the context of Jean de Montreuil's appeal to the Dauphin in his *Regali ex progenie* (1408) to imitate his ancestors and defend the title of king of France.

Louis of Guyenne died in 1415. His mother, Isabel of Bavaria, and uncle, John, Duke of Berry, were executors of his will. The inventory they had prepared in 1416 remains silent about his books (Pannier 1874). Some of Louis's manuscripts were probably integrated into the library of Charles VI; others were perhaps appropriated directly by Louis's executors or other family members. The Royal *Gesta Ludovici* is not mentioned in either the inventories of the French royal library or the catalogues of the Duke of Berry's collection. Perhaps the manuscript was brought to England by Catherine of France, Louis's younger sister, who in 1420 married Henry V. Just as Louis's Psalter (cat. no. 141) was adapted for Henry VI, Catherine's son, to assist his devotions, so the *Gesta* may have been selected for the young English King whose education had become a matter of no less concern than that of the Dauphin over two decades earlier. As a result of the Treaty of Troyes, Henry VI became the King of France after the death of Charles VI. At this time literary and visual propaganda in support of the dual monarchy, focused on the legitimacy of Henry's royal lineage in both realms and genealogical descent from St Louis, was once again used to support a claim to the French throne (see cat. no. 143). *J.F.*

PROVENANCE:

Louis, Duke of Guyenne (b. 1397, d. 1415); Henry VIII.

Opposite:
Louis of Guyenne receiving instruction from St Louis, f. 2

Gesta sancti ludouici. et Regis philippi eius primogeniti.

68 *Miroir des dames*

(Durand de Champagne, *Speculum dominarum,* in an anonymous French translation)

Northern France (?Normandy), 1428; England, *c.* 1485–1509
305 x 225 mm

BRITISH LIBRARY, ROYAL 19 B. xvi

The arms of Henry VII with his crown in the hawthorn bush, f. 1v

Manuals of moral instruction addressed specifically to women were far less numerous than similar texts written for men. The new tradition was initiated at the Capetian court by the *Miroir de l'âme* (Mirror of the Soul) dedicated to Blanche of Castile (d. 1252) and the *Instructions* composed by St Louis for his daughter Isabel, later Queen of Navarre (*c.* 1267–70). The *Speculum dominarum* was addressed to a member of the French royal family of the next generation, Joan of Navarre (b. *c.* 1271, d. 1305), wife of Philip IV of France, and written by her Franciscan confessor Durand de Champagne towards the end of the thirteenth century. Shortly after its composition, the treatise was translated into French at the Queen's request as the *Miroir des dames* (Mirror of Women). The miniature reproduced shows Jeanne accompanied by her ladies-in-waiting, and the author offering her his work; a mirror in the background metaphorically evokes the title of the book.

Durand's text focuses entirely on the spiritual and moral life, discussing virtues such as pity, humility and moderation, which should complete and reflect the royal dignity of a queen. As the image of feminine perfection granted special divine grace, the Queen is portrayed as the 'mirror' for other women. The instructions in moral edification given to Joan remained popular for succeeding generations, and the *Miroir des dames* was frequently included in princely libraries. Several queens and princesses owned a copy of the text, among them Jeanne d'Evreux, Blanche of Navarre, and Valentine Visconti, Duchess of Orleans. A new translation was made by Ysamberd de St-Léger for Margaret of Valois as late as *c.* 1526–31.

The manuscript reproduced was completed – as its colophon records – on 9 July 1428, and illuminated in a provincial northern French atelier. The presentation scene that originally formed its opening illustration is now faced by a visually prominent addition. A full-page heraldic composition painted by an English heraldic artist during the reign of Henry VII depicts a shield bearing the royal arms of England, which hangs from the branch of a crowned hawthorn bush (pictured). The arms are supported by two beasts first adapted as royal badges by Henry VII at the beginning of his reign: a red dragon indicating his descent from Cadwaladr, the supposed last king of the Britons (see cat. no. 99), and the white greyhound of his Lancastrian ancestors. The acclamation inscrip-

Durand de Champagne presenting his book to Joan of Navarre, f. 2

tion below reads *VIVE LE NOBLE ROY HENRY* (Long live the noble King Henry).

Although it is clear that the crowned hawthorn bush became a device for Henry VII (for example, it appears in a stained-glass window in Henry VII's chapel at Westminster Abbey and on his tomb there), the meaning of this imagery is uncertain. According to legend, after the Battle of Bosworth (1485) Richard III's crown, misplaced in the combat, was found in a hawthorn bush and placed on the head of Henry Tudor. However, the absence of this episode in any contemporary or sixteenth-century account of the battlefield coronation suggests a probable later origin. Both the continuator of the *Croyland Chronicle* (1486) and Polydore Vergil, Henry VII's court historian, state only that the crown was found amongst the spoils of battle. A link between the hawthorn bush and the Bosworth coronation was not established until the early seventeenth century, when Sir William Segar (d. 1633), Garter King of Arms under James I, commented on Henry's emblem. The hawthorn was, however, in use as a decorative motif before the Tudors. The accounts of Margaret of Anjou's manor of Pleasance at Greenwich (1453) record a window decoration that incorporated the hawthorn, describing it as 'the king's flower' and referring it to Henry VI (Siddons 2009).

Henry VII had many opportunities to take possession of this French manuscript. He may have acquired it during his fourteen-year exile in Brittany and had his arms added later in England, or received it from a loyal subject – perhaps a companion in the French exile – after he came to power. The inclusion of the acclamation inscription in the added frontispiece seems to suggest a date early in his reign for this adaptation. Perhaps the addition dates from the time of Henry's marriage to Elizabeth of York, which was announced at Christmas 1485 and accomplished after his accession to the throne on 18 January 1486. The choice of this particular mirror for the queen, written by a Franciscan author, may also reflect Henry's support of the Observant Franciscans. He supported the Order during his sojourn in Vannes (1483–84) and later endowed a Franciscan convent in Greenwich. (see cat. nos. 40 and 151). *J.F.*

PROVENANCE:

Henry VII.

69 Hugues de Lannoy, *Enseignement de la vraie noblesse*

Sheen (Surrey), 1496; Bruges, *c.* 1496–97
310 x 215 mm

BRITISH LIBRARY, ROYAL 19 C. viii

In the fourteenth and fifteenth centuries the moral education of a young prince or knight was not the monopoly of clerics. Instructions and precepts on how to lead a noble life were written by noble laymen and addressed to other members of the same social group (see cat. nos. 62 and 143). The *Enseignement* or *Imagination de la vraie noblesse* composed in 1440 is one of such knightly 'mirrors'. It focuses on the definition of true nobility, a subject that particularly animated literary discussions at the Burgundian court of Philip the Good. The author of the text has been identified as Hugues de Lannoy, Lord of Santes, near Lille, a knight of the Order of the Golden Fleece and a member of a family closely related to the ducal court (Visser-Fuchs 2006).

However, Lannoy's name does not appear in the text copied in the present manuscript. Instead, the manuscript's colophon informs us that the book was 'finished at the manor of Shene on the last day of June 1496 by Q. Poulet'. Quentin Poulet was appointed Keeper of Henry VII's library by 1492 and is also recorded as a scribe working for the King. In a short prologue to the Royal *Enseignement* he addresses the book to Henry VII and presents himself as the original author of the text. Poulet's Lillois origin helped him to fashion this literary conceit. The narrative of the *Enseignement* consists of a story told by a knight from Lille, who describes how on his way to the sanctuary of Our Virgin in Halle he met Lady Imagination. Her instructions concerning how to lead a noble and virtuous life constitute the core of the text, and her appeal that her message be communicated to all the knights and princes of Christendom is consistent with Poulet's royal dedication.

The manuscript is embellished by six large miniatures illustrating the author's dialogue with Lady Imagination and highlighting the major points of their conversation. The illumination reproduced introduces the main subject of the book, the definition of true nobility. It shows the knight and Imagination accompanied by three young women who are reminiscent of personifications of the four Cardinal Virtues mentioned in the text as pillars of morality. Yet the miniature appears to be a literal equivalent of the rubric, which reads 'Immaginacion demonstre au chevalier quelle chose est vraye noblesse et la comprent en trois partie' (Imagination shows the knight what the true nobility is and encompasses it in three parts). The three ladies therefore personify the three aspects of nobility that may be summarized as the love of God, the love of justice and the desire for good renown.

In his influential monograph, Kipling (1977) adduced this manuscript as key evidence of the critical importance of Henry VII for English patronage of south Netherlandish art and reception of Burgundian court culture. More recent research has revealed the earlier and more significant role of Edward IV in this endeavour. The Royal *Enseignement* is in fact an exceptional example of Henry VII's patronage. It is better explained as an initiative of Henry's librarian, who may have used his personal connections to organize the commission of the book. The choice of the Bruges artist known as the Master of the Prayer Books of around 1500 may certainly be explained by Poulet's links to the town where he had registered as an apprentice of the Confraternity of St John in 1477/8. Indeed, Poulet may also have collaborated with the same artist in another manuscript (cat. no. 133) that was completed and adapted for Henry VII. Perhaps Poulet also advised the painter of the *Enseignement* on the subjects of illuminations, or at least required him to include a personal, visual reference to Poulet's own name. A chicken emerging from a shell represented in the lower decorated border of one page (f. 32v) seems to be a rebus for *poulet* (the French word for 'chicken').

The Royal manuscript must have been ready and presented to Henry VII by 1497, if the record of a sum of 23 pounds sterling for a book and a reward of 10 marks received by Poulet on 26 July of that year refers to this commission (Backhouse 1987). Although its addressee was Henry VII and his arms are represented in the border of the opening page (f. 3), it is very likely that this manual of knightly life was intended by the King for his son, the ten-year-old Prince Arthur. *J.F.*

PROVENANCE:
Henry VII.

Opposite:
Lady Imagination introduces the author to the three aspects of nobility, f. 11

T pour poursuir mon propos
Je te veul premieremēt monstrer
et enseigner quelle chose est
vraye noblesse a en parler se
lon nr̄e foy xp̄ienne qui est
la fondacion principale de ce
livre. Et pour le bien entendre je te dis q̄ vraye

70 *Des Cleres et nobles femmes*

(Giovanni Boccaccio, *De mulieribus claris*, in an anonymous French translation) Paris, *c.* 1410

390 x 280 mm

BRITISH LIBRARY, ROYAL 20 C. V

Today Boccaccio's fame rests primarily on the *Decameron*, but in his lifetime he was equally, if not more, acclaimed for works in Latin on the history and mythology of ancient Greece and Rome. Among these is *De mulieribus claris*, a compilation of biographical sketches of famous women, begun in 1361 and revised several times before his death in 1375. Replete with moralizing messages, the work contains both 'exhortations to virtue' and 'incentives for avoiding and detesting wickedness' (Brown 2001). Crimes are chronicled alongside heroic deeds – sometimes performed by the same women.

Over one hundred manuscripts of *De mulieribus* survive, including a copy in Boccaccio's hand. The success of the work is further attested by Italian translations made in the final decades of the fourteenth century and by an anonymous French version, *Des Cleres et nobles femmes*, completed at the beginning of the fifteenth. None of the manuscripts in which Boccaccio's Latin text is preserved has an extensive cycle of miniatures. When the work was translated into French, however, it was transformed. The nobles for whom the first French copies were produced – Philip the Bold, Duke of Burgundy, and his brother John, Duke of Berry – expected their books to be beautiful as well as instructive. Their copies of *Des Cleres et nobles femmes,* dating from 1402 and 1403, contain 109 and 107 miniatures respectively, at least one for each biography.

The present manuscript belongs to a small group containing the oldest redaction of the French translation. It was made in Paris *c.* 1410, and illustrated by an artist active there, now known as the Boethius Master because he illuminated a copy of Boethius dated 1414 (Paris, BnF, MS fr. 12459). Since there was no established iconographic programme for *Des cleres et nobles femmes*, he was relatively free from constraints when he designed its 106 miniatures. Intriguingly, some miniatures contain details that are not included in the accompanying text. For example, Camilla, Queen of the Volscians, is shown killing a stag and a goat (f. 59v). The relevant passage (f. 60) mentions the stag, but contains no reference to the goat. If we consult Boccaccio's *De mulieribus*, however, we read that Camilla used to chase and catch deer and wild goats ('cursu cervos capreasque silvestres insequi atque superare'), and the goats are mentioned in some copies of the French translation – including the earliest extant manuscript, made for Philip the Bold (Paris, BnF, MS fr. 12420). It is likely that the Boethius Master, when designing the pictorial programme of the present manuscript, had access to a more accurate copy of the text, to a set of comprehensive written instructions or to visual models based on such a text. It is not necessary to insist on a single source; several could have been employed.

Evidently, the miniatures in the present manuscript were not based directly on the earlier Parisian manuscripts of *Des Cleres et nobles femmes* made for the Dukes of Burgundy and Berry since these differ from each other and from it in both composition and style. It is clear, therefore, that the artists who illuminated these manuscripts did not rely on the same visual models. Nevertheless, barring the odd exception, the same episodes are depicted in all three. Since each manuscript contains over one hundred miniatures, the correspondence of subject matter is significant. Reynolds (1988) has suggested that 'all three copies could perhaps derive from the same list of verbal instructions', and this would explain why the same incidents from the biographies were chosen to be illustrated while others were ignored.

The miniature reproduced shows, among other scenes, the author presenting his work to Andrea Acciaiuoli, Countess of Altavilla. Boccaccio had considered dedicating the book to Queen Joanna I of Naples (r. 1343–82), but elected instead to dedicate it to one of her courtiers. Andrea was the sister of his friend Niccolò Accaiuoli, Grand Seneschal of the kingdom of Naples, whom Boccaccio visited in 1362. Although he had started the book before travelling to Naples, Boccaccio added a final chapter in praise of Joanna and a dedication to Andrea in which he expressed his hope that the women of antiquity would inspire her.

The identity of the original owner of the present manuscript is unknown. That it came to England in the fifteenth century and ultimately the Old Royal library is, however, clear since the English inscription, 'The booke of the noble ladyes in French', written in a late fifteenth-century hand, occurs on a flyleaf at the beginning of the book, and the Beaufort badge, surmounted by a coronet, has been added to the initial 'D'(e) on the first folio, probably to signal ownership of the volume by Lady Margaret Beaufort. *D. J.*

PROVENANCE:

Member of the Beaufort family, probably Lady Margaret Beaufort (d. 1509); Henry VIII.

Overleaf right:
Boccaccio reading a book; Boccaccio presenting the book to Andrea Acciaiuoli; a messenger presenting a letter to Semiramis; and a queen with four musicians, f. 5

71 *Des Cleres et nobles femmes*

(*Giovanni Boccaccio, De mulieribus claris*, in an anonymous French translation)

Rouen, *c.* 1440
410 x 270 mm

BRITISH LIBRARY, ROYAL 16 G. v

In almost every respect this copy of *Des Cleres et nobles femmes*, made in Rouen *c.* 1440, resembles Royal 20 C. v (cat. no. 70), which was produced in a Parisian workshop at least two decades earlier. A plausible explanation for this correspondence is that the Parisian manuscript served as the direct model for the present one. Shared textual anomalies strongly suggest a model–copy relationship. Strikingly similar miniatures and peculiarities of layout also point to this conclusion.

The two books are similar in size and have comparable spaces devoted to text and images. The Parisian model contains 106 miniatures while the Rouen copy has 103, but this discrepancy is easily explained. In the latter, a single folio is missing after f. 13. This would have contained two miniatures, one each for chapters nine and ten. In addition, owing to an oversight or miscalculation of space, one other miniature, on f. 79, was never executed (Reynolds 1988).

Though dissimilar in style, individual miniatures in the twin manuscripts share the same subject matter and compositions, down to the smallest details. Colour schemes also frequently match. In both manuscripts, the image of the witch Medea, for example, features a child in a purple tunic and red socks, Jason on horseback in red with a green turban and reins, and a knight in a green surcoat whose sword extends beyond the frame.

Not surprisingly since they are 'twin' manuscripts, the same errors sometimes occur in the two books, including the omission of words. The following example elucidates this point. According to Boccaccio, the painter Irene was famous for four portraits: 'a girl seen on a panel painting at Eleusis, the aged Calypso, Theodorus the gladiator and Alcisthenes, a celebrated dancer in his day'. All four paintings are mentioned in the earliest manuscript of the French translation (Paris, BnF, MS fr. 12420), although Theodore is described as a 'maker of swords and knives' rather than a gladiator, a change also reflected in the two Royal manuscripts. In the latter, however, the name of the dancer, Alcisthenes, has been omitted and as a result Theodore is described as a dancer as well as a knife maker: 'theodore le noble [faiseur] de glaivus et de couteaux et en son temps tres noble sailleur' (Theodore a celebrated maker of swords and knives and in his day a very celebrated dancer). Since the accompanying miniatures show Irene painting the boy dancer, Alcisthenes, they present a different and more accurate version than the text.

One of the most compelling arguments to suggest that the Rouen *Des Cleres et nobles femmes* is a direct copy of the Parisian manuscript was articulated by Reynolds (1988), who noticed that the size and arrangement of the miniatures in the former often imitated the latter. Additionally, both books feature near-identical four-part frontispieces showing Boccaccio reading at a lectern and presenting his book to Andrea Acciaiuoli, Countess of Altavilla, to whom it is dedicated (pictured). The two remaining panels depict a queen being serenaded by female musicians and the Assyrian Queen Semiramis combing her hair. Informed by a messenger that Babylon had rebelled against her rule, she abandoned her toilette and rushed into battle. Semiramis is the first 'pagan' woman to be described by Boccaccio, which would explain why she is depicted in the frontispiece. Furthermore, her biography comes directly after the first chapter in the book, which is dedicated to Eve.

Rouen, capital of the duchy of Normandy and centre of the English occupation, which lasted from 1419 to 1449, was a haven for artists who sought the patronage of the English elite. The distinctive style of the Rouen-based Talbot Master and his assistants, who painted the miniatures in the present manuscript, is conspicuous in four other Royal manuscripts: the Shrewsbury Book (cat. no. 143), *Les quatre fils aimon* (Royal 16 G. ii), a copy of Laurent de Premierfait's French translation of Boccaccio's *De casibus virorum illustrium* (cat. no. 72) and Jean de Meun's *Sept articles de la foy* (cat. no. 37). Most of the miniatures of the Rouen *Des Cleres et nobles femmes* are probably the work of assistants. Having provided them with a model – the Parisian manuscript – the Talbot Master perhaps chose to devote himself to more challenging commissions. Copying manuscripts illuminated decades earlier enabled these illuminators to work quickly to meet commercial demands. As Dubois has shown, at least one other manuscript was likewise copied by the Talbot workshop from a Parisian exemplar (Dubois 2009).

No information concerning the early provenance of the Rouen *Des Cleres et nobles femmes* has survived, but the manuscript and its model are both listed in the Royal Catalogue of 1666. Whether or not these twin manuscripts stayed together from the moment the Talbot artists completed their copy has yet to be determined. *D.J.*

PROVENANCE:

Charles II.

Overleaf left:
Boccaccio reading a book; Boccaccio presenting the book to Andrea Acciaiuoli; a messenger presenting a letter to Semiramis; and a queen with four musicians, f. 3v

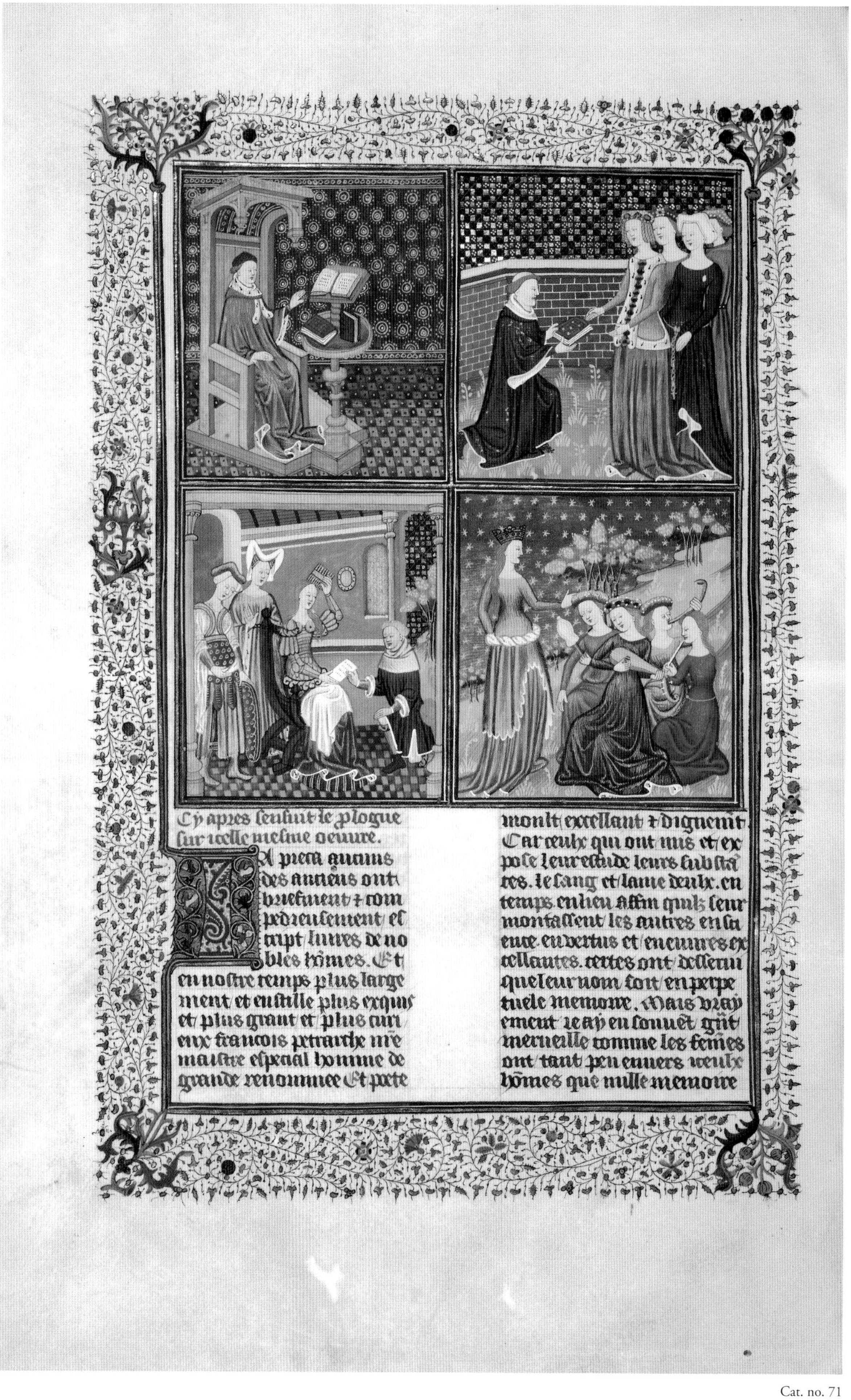

Cat. no. 71

Cy apres sensuit le plogue
sur ycelle meisme oeuvre.
el pieca aucuns
des anciens ont
briefment et
compendieuse
ment escript
liures des no
bles hommes. Et en nostre
temps plus largement et en
stille plus exquis et plus gnt
et plus curieux francois pe
trarche nostre maistre especial
homme de grande renommee
Et poete moult excellant et
dignement. Car ceulz qui

Cat. no. 70

72 *Des Cas des nobles hommes et femmes*

(Giovanni Boccaccio, *De casibus virorum illustrium*, translated into French by Laurent de Premierfait)

Rouen, *c.* 1440
430 x 320 mm

BRITISH LIBRARY, ROYAL 18 D. vii

Boccaccio's *De casibus virorum illustrium*, completed *c.* 1358, is a series of cautionary tales about famous individuals. As stated in the preface, Boccaccio intended his readers, particularly princes and rulers, to contemplate the power of God, their own frailty and the vagaries of fortune. In 1400 Laurent de Premierfait translated the work from Latin into French; in 1409 he completed another, amplified version which he dedicated to John, Duke of Berry. Premierfait's second translation was embraced by the French nobility and survives in over fifty illuminated manuscripts (Bozzolo 1973).

The earliest of these – presented in 1411 to the Duke of Berry by his counsellor, Martin Gouge – and a twin manuscript made for the Duke's nephew, John the Fearless, Duke of Burgundy, contain vast pictorial cycles (Hedeman 2008). Not long after these volumes were completed, another manuscript of Premierfait's second translation was produced with a less elaborate set of illustrations: a frontispiece and nine miniatures – one for each chapter. Painted in Paris by the workshop of the Master of the Cité des Dames, the manuscript (Paris, BnF, MS fr. 131) was made for Premierfait's friend and colleague Gontier Col, a scholar who served as secretary to Charles VI and to John of Berry. Evidently Col esteemed Boccaccio: he also owned Latin copies of *De casibus* and the *Genealogia deorum*, a work that had not yet achieved wide circulation in France (Meiss, Smith and Beatson 1974).

Col was killed during political violence in Paris in 1418 and his library must have been dispersed shortly afterwards because his copy of *Des Cas* served as the direct model for two other manuscripts: one illuminated by a Parisian workshop, *c.* 1420 (Oxford, Bodleian Library, MS Bodley 265); and the present manuscript, painted in Rouen by the Talbot Master in the 1440s. Proof that the Royal manuscript was based directly on Col's is supplied by an identical set of verses in praise of Boccaccio that occur at the end of both, but are not found in the Oxford volume (Gathercole 1963). The inclusion of Col's *Des Cas* in a sixteenth-century inventory of books owned by Rouen's city council provides independent evidence of the manuscript's presence there.

Col's *Des Cas* and the two manuscripts copied from it (Oxford and Royal) have the same number of illustrations (nine, in addition to the frontispiece). Although the miniatures in the three manuscripts differ in style, they occur at the same points in the text and share the same iconography. Furthermore, all three books open with an identical quadripartite frontispiece which depicts the three estates of man – the clergy, nobility and labourers – and shows Premierfait presenting his book to John of Berry (pictured). Hedeman (2008) has argued that Boccaccio is the man dressed in academic robes standing behind Premierfait, but the individual depicted may well be Martin Gouge, John of Berry's functionary, later Bishop of Chartres and Chancellor of France, who has also been identified as the cleric seated at the duke's table in the famous January calendar scene in the *Très Riches Heures* (for the latter, see Longnon and Cazelles 1969).

The presentation scene in the Royal manuscript is based directly on the one in the copy made for Col, who moved in the same circles as Premierfait and Gouge. Col may well have requested that his copy of *Des Cas* include their portraits to record the fact that on New Year's Day 1411, Gouge had given the duke a copy of *Des Cas* that Premierfait had translated for this very purpose.

As stated above, Col's *Des Cas* was taken to Rouen, where it served as the model for the Royal manuscript. We know nothing of its original owners, but the Royal copy bears the name of Marie Rivieres (Mary Rivers) who became, in 1480, the second wife of Anthony Woodville, 2nd Earl Rivers (d. 1483). Woodville was the brother-in-law of Edward IV, and uncle, guardian and tutor to Edward, Prince of Wales, the future Edward V. A scholarly and religious man, Woodville was the author of verses on the fickleness of fortune, and he translated from French into English the *Dictes and Sayings of the Philosophers* (1477), the first dated book printed by Caxton in England. It is possible that Woodville bequeathed the Royal *Des Cas* to his wife, Mary, having perhaps inherited it from his mother, Jacquetta of Luxemburg. Woodville was executed by Richard III in 1483 shortly before the incarceration and suspicious disappearance of the young Edward V. It is not clear how or when the manuscript entered the royal collection, but it may have been at Richmond Castle by 1535. Other Woodville manuscripts incorporated in the Old Royal library include another Rouen book (cat. no. 37). *D.J.*

PROVENANCE:

Mary Lewis, 2nd wife of Anthony Woodville, 2nd Earl Rivers; Henry VIII(?).

Opposite:
The Clergy, Nobility and Labourers; and Laurent Premierfait presenting his book to John of Berry, f. 2

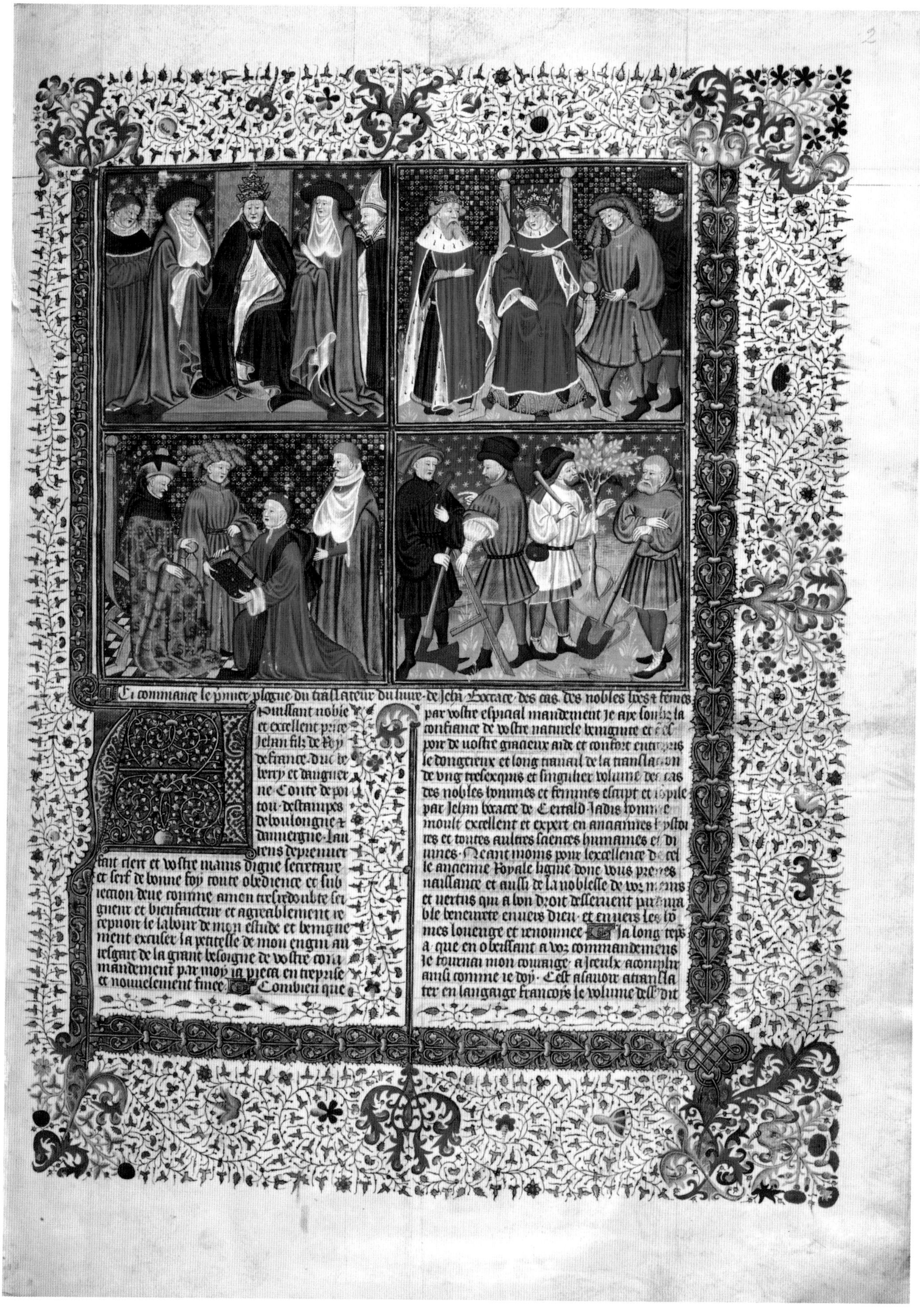

73 John Lydgate, *Troy Book* and *Siege of Thebes*, with verses by William Cornish, John Skelton, William Peeris and others

England, *c.* 1457–60; (additions) *c.* 1490–1530
395 x 280 mm

BRITISH LIBRARY, ROYAL 18 D. ii

The legends of Troy and Thebes, in their various versions, were favoured reading among the European nobility from the twelfth century. Troy, in particular, held a significant place in the royal imagination because it showcased the exploits of Trojan heroes from whom the ruling families of Europe traced their descent (see cat. no. 135). The romances of Thebes, on the other hand, recounted the downfalls of tyrants and flawed kings. When John Lydgate (d. *c.* 1451) added his English rendition of both stories to the existing body of romance, he was serving both Henry V's interest in contributing towards a native literary culture on a par with its Continental counterparts, and enlisting the famed legends into his own preferred genre of the *exemplum*. The tales of Troy and Thebes that form the core of this manuscript thus provide a catalogue of royal models to emulate and eschew.

The opening illustration in this manuscript suggests that it was commissioned with a royal destination in mind. Set at the beginning of the *Troy Book*, the miniature depicts not a presentation scene but rather Sir William Herbert (d. 1469) and his wife Anne Devereux (d. *c.* 1486) kneeling before an enthroned king. Their posture and raised hands seem to indicate that they are offering themselves up as loyal subjects, and their prominent family arms and mottoes stand for an enduring, faithful lineage. Although previous studies have favoured Edward IV as the king depicted here, it is more likely that the manuscript was intended as a gift to Henry VI, who pardoned Herbert in June 1457 for his assistance to Yorkists in Wales. Lydgate's poetry declares ardent support for the Lancastrian cause, and the prologue to the *Troy Book*, with its praise of Henry V, remains unredacted here. Consequently this manuscript would have provided a convincing token of renewed fealty to the Lancastrian dynasty that Herbert had lately betrayed. Furthermore, the incomplete state of the illustrative programme in the fifteenth century suggests a short period of time between the volume's conception and the halting of its production. It is therefore probable that the manuscript was commissioned shortly before 1460, when Herbert committed decisively to the Yorkists.

The miniatures that were completed during the first campaign highlight the instructional nature of this book for a royal pupil. Of the five miniatures, four represent an enthroned king, nearly identical to that in the opening illustration. Although book 2 opens with verses on the rotation of Fortune's wheel, the Royal volume's miniature of a king enthroned atop it (pictured) is unique among the seven extant illustrated manuscripts of Lydgate's *Troy Book* (Lawton 1983). The emblem of a king poised at the apex of Fortune's wheel was a traditional reminder of the vagaries of power (see fig. 3.2). Looking at this image and the other royal figures represented throughout this book as if at his own reflection, the intended recipient of this volume would have been made aware of the insecurity of his position.

This icon proved prescient. The deposition of Henry VI in 1461 ensured that the manuscript never reached its intended recipient. Instead it passed into the Percy family with the marriage of William Herbert's daughter Maud to Henry Percy (d. 1489), 4th Earl of Northumberland. A second pictorial campaign resulting in three further miniatures was initiated in the last decade of the fifteenth century, perhaps with the intention of presenting the completed volume to Henry VII. This presentation, too, never came to pass; and the planned pictorial cycle for the manuscript, including the entire programme for the *Siege of Thebes*, was completed only in the first quarter of the sixteenth century, probably by members of the Horenbout family of artists (Kren and McKendrick 2003).

Despite its many accretions, this manuscript remained coherent in its consistent assertion of alliance between family and monarchy. Alongside such texts as a versified register of the kings of England and an ekphrasis on the royal arms throughout history are the Percy family's own quasi-dynastic chronicle, an elaborate family crest lit by the luminous image of a king within the Tudor rose, and the motto, *esperance*, recalling Henry 'Hotspur' Percy's legendary cry as he charged into battle against Scottish forces in 1378. With such elaborate marks of family identity, it is not surprising that the manuscript remained with the Percys for three more generations. The manuscript then passed into the Old Royal library when Lord Lumley's collection – he had married into the Percy family – passed to Prince Henry Frederick, the eldest son of James I in 1609. It is fitting that these books, and perhaps this copy of Lydgate specifically, were intended for the tuition of another young prince. *S.D.*

PROVENANCE:

Sir William Herbert, 1st Earl of Pembroke (d. 1469), and his wife Anne Devereux (d. *c.* 1486); Henry Percy, 4th Earl of Northumberland (d. 1489); Henry Algernon Percy, 5th Earl of Northumberland (d. 1527), and his wife Katherine (d. 1542); Henry Fitzalan, 19th Earl of Arundel (b. 1512, d. 1580); John, 1st Baron Lumley (d. 1609); Henry Frederick, Prince of Wales (d. 1612).

Opposite:
Wheel of Fortune, f. 30v

74 *Bible historiale*: Proverbs to the Apocalypse

Clairefontaine and Paris, 1411
445 x 340 mm

BRITISH LIBRARY, ROYAL 19 D. iii, vol. 2

This is the second volume of a *Bible historiale* of the most developed type (for the first volume see cat. no. 24). It opens with Proverbs and a large frontispiece within a rich acanthus border with remarkably naturalistic flowers (f. 289, pictured). The miniature focuses on only the first of the usual four images of Solomon: the King instructing his son, Rehoboam (contrast cat. no. 22). Solomon with long grey hair and beard is enthroned under a textile canopy woven in blue and gold with the French royal arms. The King is identified by crown and sceptre. He wears a gown of oriental silk and instructs his son with the gesture of his left hand. The son is in the process of kneeling before the King. A group of three courtiers stand to either side behind the throne. They wear exotic hats of a type seemingly influenced by the Parisian visit of the Byzantine Emperor Manuel II in 1402–04. (Pisanello popularized the headgear in his medallion of Emperor John VIII, who attended the church council of Ferrara/Florence in 1438.) The floor is tiled, and the back wall is decorated with swans and bears(?), perhaps intended to call to mind John, Duke of Berry. Berry's sons were all dead by 1412, but the representation of Rehoboam bears a resemblance to images of the Dauphin, Louis of Guyenne (d. 1415), son of Charles VI, as portrayed, for example, in Louis's *Gesta S. Ludovici* (cat. no. 67). The focus on Solomon teaching his son, together with the decision to overlook the usual narrative scenes of Solomon's wisdom, makes the possible link between monarch and biblical model all the more powerful.

The book has ninety-one images in this second volume, including a large miniature of the Tree of Jesse at the start of the Gospels (f. 458) and a very unusual and extensive Apocalypse cycle, comprising fifty-two scenes. The pages of the Apocalypse (ff. 594v–604) look quite unlike any other part of this – or any other – *Bible historiale* owing to the large size and frequent occurrence of the miniatures. There are as many as five separate images on a single page (e.g. f. 597v), and one image may have multiple scenes: the first miniature on f. 597v (pictured) illustrates the Giving of the Trumpets, the angel censing the altar in heaven, and the incense cast upon the Earth (Apocalypse/Revelation 8:1–5). The cycle appears to be adapted from a type of illuminated Apocalypse manuscript, without, however, being closely based on any surviving example. The principal artist has been identified as the Egerton Master (on this artist see cat. no. 144).

At the end of this volume the scribe identifies himself and comments that it was 'escript et parfait par les mains de frere Thomas du Val prestre et chanoine profes de l'abbaye Nostre Dame de Clerefontaine ou dyocese de Chartres' (written and completed by the hands of Brother Thomas du Val, priest and professed canon of the abbey of Notre Dame de Clerefontaine, in the diocese of Chartres) and dates this Friday 20 February 1411 (f. 604). A puzzle is why Thomas says he has written and completed the book by his 'hands' (in the plural).

This manuscript appears to be unique in containing several short additional texts, translated along with the *Bible historiale* by Guyart des Moulins, namely a Life of Julian the Aspostate, *Hystoires apocrifes* of the True Cross (the very idea of such apocryphal stories is intriguing), a Life of Pilate, and a Life of Judas, all found in sequence on ff. 552v–558. This suggests an unusual textual transmission, according to which, despite its popularity, the *Bible historiale* had to wait an entire century before this otherwise unknown group of short narratives was passed on. It is, therefore, disappointing that the first even plausible mention of the book in a royal context is no earlier than the Richmond Palace list of 1535, when it may be identifiable with a book simply termed 'la grant Bible'.

J.L.

Above:
Scenes from the Apocalypse, f. 597v (detail)
Opposite:
King Solomon, f. 289

PROVENANCE:
Henry VIII (?).

Cy cõmence la seconde partie principale de la bible qui parle de sapience, et des propheties de lincarnacion
de ihesucrist. Et premierement les paraboles
salemon. Des queles ou premier chapitre sapi
ence deffant a son filz quil ne suive ne ne se cõ
sente aux paroles des flateurs. et quil ne voise
avec les pecheurs ne avec les herites. J.
es paraboles salomon filz de
david roy disrael. a savoir
sapience et discipline. a en
tendre paraboles et pruden
ce et recevoir enseignemēt
de doctrine. et iustice. et iu
gement. et loiaute. et droitture. afin que sen
soit donnee aux petiz. cest a dire aux humbles
ignorans. Et que science soit donnee aux iouen
nes. et entendement a ceulx qui en ont mestier.
Les sages seront plus sages de louir. et celui q̄
bien entent en saura mieulx gouverner soi
et autri. Et apperceura paraboles et interpre
tacions. et les figures. et les paraboles des sages.
La paour de nostre seigneur est cõmence
ment de sapience. Les fols despisent sapience
et doctrine. Filz oi la discipline de ton pere. et
ne delaisse point la loi de ta mere. afin q̄ grace
soit aioustee a ton chief. et fermeil dor a ton
col. Mon filz se les pecheurs talechent. ne les
croi mye. cest a dire se les flateurs te flatent

75 *Le livre et la vraye hystoire du bon roy Alixandre*

Paris, *c.* 1420–25
285 x 195 mm

BRITISH LIBRARY, ROYAL 20 B. xx

Winning battle after battle, Alexander the Great, son of Philip II of Macedon and Olympias of Epirus, conquered vast territories stretching from Egypt to India. Besides his mastery of military strategy, the young commander was known for his political acumen and interest in science and philosophy, which were fostered by his tutor, Aristotle. Alexander's rise to power was swift, but was cut short by his death from fever at the age of thirty-two in 323 BC. Recognizing his genius, several of his contemporaries wrote accounts of his life. Only a few fragments of these works have been preserved, but historians writing in the first and second centuries AD – including Plutarch and Quintus Curtius Rufus – drew on these ancient sources, composed their own accounts of Alexander's deeds and kept his memory alive.

A biography of Alexander, erroneously attributed to his official historian, Callisthenes of Olynthus, was among the most influential texts. Referred to by scholars as the *Romance of Alexander* or 'Pseudo-Callisthenes', this Greek work, written by an unknown author in the third century AD, was introduced to the West via Latin translations. Most popular among these were the *Res gestae Alexandri Magni*, composed by the North African Julius Valerius in the fourth century, and the *Historia de preliis Alexandri Magni* (History of the Battles of Alexander the Great) written by Leo of Naples in the tenth. These two Latin works served as the basis for translations into numerous vernacular languages. An anonymous thirteenth-century French translation of the *Historia de preliis*, entitled *La vraye hystoire du bon roy Alixandre*, has been preserved in at least eighteen manuscripts; eleven are illustrated, and four have spaces left for miniatures that were never executed (Ross and Stones 2002).

Made in Paris *c.* 1420–25, this splendid copy of *La vraye hystoire* contains eighty-six miniatures, most of which were painted by a single illuminator. Meiss (1974) attributed all but eight of the miniatures to an artist he christened the Master of the Harvard Hannibal, but they are now thought to have been painted by a different person who is known after this important manuscript as the Master of the Royal Alexander (Reynolds 1994). The page reproduced opposite (f. 49v), which depicts Alexander battling dragons, is typical of the Master's style. Each element, from the undulating terrain to the dragons' scales, has been painstakingly rendered with layers of paint applied in tiny brushstrokes. The vigorous gestures and varied expressions of the combatants hold the viewer's interest, and there is no mistaking the hero. Placed at the centre of the composition, Alexander is distinguished by the gold crown perched on his helm, and by his red surcoat and shield. Curiously, both of the latter are emblazoned with the arms of King Arthur: gules, three crowns or.

Alexander's strength and courage earned him a place on the list of the Nine Worthies compiled by the French writer Jacques de Longuyon in his fourteenth-century poem, *Les voeux de paon* (The Vows of the Peacock). Like the other eight heroes (Hector, Julius Caesar, Joshua, David, Judas Maccabeus, King Arthur, Charlemagne and Godfrey de Bouillon), Alexander provided an ideal role model for male members of the aristocracy and royalty throughout medieval Europe; 'not only did they hope to be, like Alexander, mighty conquerors ... they also wanted to share his independence and sense of self-worth' (McKendrick 1996).

Illustrated copies of *La vraye hystoire du bon roy Alixandre* are also found in three other volumes from the Old Royal library: Royal 20 A. v, a manuscript with tinted drawings made in France or Flanders, *c.* 1310; Royal 19. D. i (cat. no. 91), a mid-fourteenth-century compendium of travel accounts and other texts; and Royal 15 E. vi (cat. no. 143), a miscellany made for Margaret of Anjou on the occasion of her marriage to Henry VI in 1445. The present volume differs from these other manuscripts because it was designed primarily as a small-format picture book. Generous spaces were reserved for each image, and all are placed in a privileged position at the top of each page – perhaps as a concession to a young reader, like the ones depicted in the exquisite miniature at the beginning of the volume, which shows Aristotle tutoring Alexander (f. 10v, pictured). The manuscript contains no evidence of its original owners or early provenance, but the monogram 'HR' (for *Henricus rex*), referring to Henry VIII, appears on a parchment flyleaf at the beginning of the book (Carley 1997 and 2000). *D.J.*

Above:
Aristotle tutors the young Alexander the Great, f. 10v (detail)

Opposite:
Alexander the Great slays dragons, f. 49v

PROVENANCE:
Henry VIII.

76 Jan Du Quesne, *Les Commentaires de César*

(French Translation of Julius Caesar, *Bellum Gallicum*)

Lille and Bruges, between 1473 and 1476
395 x 285 mm

BRITISH LIBRARY, ROYAL 16 G. viii

In Lille in 1473 Jan Du Quesne (or Duchesne) completed a new French adaptation of Julius Caesar's *Gallic Wars* and dedicated his text to Charles the Bold (d. 1477), Duke of Burgundy. A comparison of the script in the Royal manuscript with other works signed by Du Quesne suggests that this is an autograph copy (see also cat. no. 48). Lavishly illuminated with twenty-three miniatures, the Royal *Commentaires de César* is the earliest manuscript of this text to survive and may have been the one the translator presented to the Duke. Another copy of the *Commentaires* – which was transcribed in 1476 by Hellin de Burchgrave for Jacques Douche, one of Charles's counsellors, and illustrated with a series of miniatures closely replicating the images in the Royal manuscript (New Haven CT, Yale University Library, MS 226) – includes a scribal note stating that it was copied from the Duke's original. Although a collation of the two texts confirms their close relationship, it is uncertain whether the contents of the Yale *Commentaires* derive directly from those of the Royal copy, or the two manuscripts had a common model.

Charles the Bold, who owned several books on ancient history, seems to have been fascinated by Roman history, and by Caesar in particular (see McKendrick forthcoming). According to Olivier de la Marche, his courtier, before going to bed the Duke used to listen to 'the sublime stories of Rome and took very great pleasure in the deeds of the Romans'. He owned several copies of the *Faits de Romains*, a historical compilation that included the first medieval translation of Caesar's *Gallic Wars* (see cat. no. 50). Within Du Quesne's work Caesar's conduct was designed as examples and counter-examples for the Duke to inform him on military virtues and prowess, and on the dangers of vain ambition and abuse of power. The author also intended to provide a companion volume covering the period up to the time of Charles the Bold and secure the Duke a place in imperial history (an abbreviated version of this text survives in former Longleat, Marquess of Bath, Botfield MS 2).

Caesar's account of his Gallic campaign was featured by Du Quesne as part of a national history of the Burgundian Netherlands. Not only did Du Quesne provide the contemporary names for towns and places mentioned in Caesar's book to update the historical narrative for an audience in the Low Countries, but he stressed the independence of the Belgian Gauls and their extraordinary courage and bravery. For Du Quesne writing at the beginning of the war with France, the territory of the Belgian Gauls as described by Caesar corresponded to the boundaries of the Burgundian Netherlands projected by Charles the Bold in 1472 against the territorial claims of Louis XI (Schmidt-Chazan 1980).

Du Quesne's strategy of shaping history according to current political needs was echoed in the illustrations of the Royal *Commentaires*. In several of these, battles of the Roman army are set in extended landscapes scattered with familiar-looking towns and castles that include Flemish architectural features. The miniature reproduced here depicts Caesar receiving a group of citizens of a surrendered Gallic town. The scene is dominated by a vast panorama comprising a fortified city shaded in a pale rose and violet sunset light, with an airy mountainous landscape behind. Such a subtle setting for a narrative was a 'trademark' of the distinctive Bruges artist who illustrated the Royal *Commentaires*, the Master of the London Wavrin (named after cat. no. 47; see Kren and McKendrick 2003).

Appealing to a very local identity, Du Quesne's translation did not share the popularity of either the previous adaptation of the *Gallic Wars* in the *Faits des Romains*, or the later translation completed in 1485 by Robert Gaguin for Charles VIII of France. All eight extant copies of the *Commentaires* were produced in the Low Countries within a short period of time. The Yale and Royal manuscripts date from Charles the Bold's lifetime. Two copies (ex-Botfield MS 2 and Copenhagen, Kongelige Bibliotek, MS Thott 544 2°) were made shortly after the Duke's death and both were owned by two members of the Burgundian court, André de Haraucourt (d. 1484), one of Charles the Bold's former captains, and Pierre de Luxemburg (d. 1482), one of the great nobles faithful to the Burgundian cause after Charles's death. The four remaining manuscripts, including a copy owned by Louis of Gruthuuse (d. 1492) (Paris, BnF, MS fr. 38), date from the period of renewed 'nationalism' within the Burgundian Netherlands after the death of Mary of Burgundy in 1482 (Egerton 1065; Oxford, Bodleian Library, MS Douce 208; Paris, BnF, MS fr. 280).

The present manuscript was first listed in the English Old Royal library in 1535. It seems likely that after Charles's death it was given to Edward IV, who continued to maintain contact with the Burgundian court. The English King may have expressed some interest in Du Quesne's translation since its companion, the abbreviated chronicle in the Botfield manuscript that ends with Edward's reign, may have been originally intended for him (Montigny 2007). *J.F.*

PROVENANCE:

Edward IV (?); Henry VIII.

Opposite:
Surrender of a city of Gaul, f. 225

Cy cōmence le .xe. livre cōtinue par Jullius celsus cōe il apert par son prologue q̄ contient en soy .xxvi. chapitres Du premier il traite coment les gaullois p nouveau cō seil recōmencerent murmure de guerre Et comment cesar

Nam gallia devicta erat Toute gaule le vaincue et subiuguie comme cesar neust en leste superiore

de ce adverti les chastia- moult rudement. .I. nul tempz cesse de guerroier moult asprement pour quoy il auoit en propos mettre tous ses gēs a leur aise

77 Raoul Lefèvre, *Le Recueil des histoires de Troyes*

Bruges, *c.* 1475–83
400 x 280 mm

BRITISH LIBRARY, ROYAL 17 E. ii

Long after the destruction of Troy by the Greeks, the city continued to be celebrated in literature and works of art. The story of Troy retained its appeal partly because almost all the royal families of medieval Europe traced their ancestry back to Trojan progenitors who had abandoned the city after its fall (see cat. no. 49). In the Middle Ages, Homer's *Iliad*, describing episodes in the Trojan War, was inaccessible to readers in western Europe because it was in Greek, a language mastered by few. Readers relied instead on chronicles of Troy in Latin and vernacular languages by a wide range of authors.

One of the most original contributions to the canon of Trojan legend was made in the fifteenth century by Raoul Lefèvre, who dedicated his French prose version, *Le Recueil des histoires de Troyes*, to Philip the Good, Duke of Burgundy, whom he claimed to have served as chaplain. Although Lefèvre drew on several sources, notably Giovanni Boccaccio's *Genealogia deorum gentilium* (On the Genealogy of the Pagan Gods) and the Sicilian writer Guido delle Colonne's late thirteenth-century *Historia destructionis Troiae* (History of the Destruction of Troy), he radically reshaped the narrative. Instead of concentrating on the deeds of the defeated Trojans, as previous authors had done, he focused on the victorious Greeks – and on one individual in particular: Hercules.

Lefèvre's text is divided into three books, which describe four successive destructions of Troy, two inflicted by Hercules. Lefèvre presents the Greek hero and demigod as a noble knight who is humiliated and unjustly treated by Laomedon, King of Troy, and is therefore justified in razing the city. After Hercules has rescued Laomedon's daughter from a sea monster, the King reneges on his promise to reward the hero with a pair of supernatural steeds, an event that precipitates Hercules' first attack on Troy. Laomedon's refusal to allow Jason, Hercules and the Argonauts to anchor at Troy to provision their ships leads to Hercules' second assault on the city and the obdurate King's death.

Lefèvre's success lay in his ability to make ancient history relevant. By presenting figures of the distant past as individuals who overcame obstacles and experienced emotions, Lefèvre captured the imagination of his readers. Infusing ancient characters with chivalric values, he attempted to modernize them and make them more believable.

Made in Bruges for Edward IV, who furnished his library with books made in the southern Netherlands (see section 'Edward IV', pp. 192–225), this copy of Lefèvre's *Recueil* contains sixty-five miniatures that have been attributed to an artist now known as the Master of the White Inscriptions. Based in Bruges, this artist devoted himself exclusively to the illustration of secular texts, and illuminated several other books for Edward IV (cat. nos. 48, 51, 57, 58, 60, 61, 62). Although many of the works illuminated by him had a long illustrative tradition, he generally invented new compositions (Kren and McKendrick 2003).

The manuscript is divided into three books, each of which begins with a large miniature. The one at the beginning of the second book (f. 148, pictured), shows Hercules battling not one, but three Nemean lions. Sent by Juno to kill the lions, Hercules acts like a knight seeking to win his lady's favour; he overcomes the animals through his exemplary courage and strength and presents their skins to the goddess. Throughout the ordeal Hercules acts with valour, preferring to die rather than to behave dishonourably. He refuses, for example, to be dissuaded from his mission by his beloved, Megara, daughter of King Creon of Thebes, or by a herdsman who has taken refuge from the lions in a tree (a detail not depicted in the miniature). Although he is a model of chivalry, the hero, as portrayed by Lefèvre, is not invincible. Like any battered knight Hercules is susceptible to pain, and he suffers a sleepless night as a result of the suppurating wounds inflicted by the lions' claws.

Descriptions of battles on blood-soaked fields littered with severed heads and limbs, of tender embraces exchanged by lovers, and of extremes of behaviour: treachery and loyalty, cowardice and courage, generosity and greed, made Lefèvre's *Recueil* popular with aristocratic and royal audiences. Twenty-four other manuscripts of the work survive, as well as five editions printed before 1500. William Caxton's English translation, dedicated to Margaret of York, wife of Charles the Bold, was printed in Bruges in 1474. The first book ever printed in English, Caxton's translation, a copy of which was owned by Elizabeth Woodville, consort of Edward IV, gave Lefèvre's work an even larger readership (Kekewich 1971).

D.J.

PROVENANCE:
Edward IV.

Opposite:
Hercules slays three lions of Nemea, f. 148

Comme doncqz la vieille Juno par sa mauuaise enuie se donna a ymaginer et songier comment elle pourroit faire mourir hercules nouuelles vindrent en certe que
en la forest de Nemee estoyent plusieurs lyons. Et q entre les autres vng en y auoit grant de seize paulmes plus que les autres qui destruisoit et gastoit le pays. Celle Juno enuoya querir hercules et soubz

en saiue. einz estoient a des freschés. ⁊ ouerte.
⁊ si en i auoit aucune si parfonde. que tu i
poisses boter le plus lonc doit de ta mein.
iusqu a la paume. Et quant il voit au
cune ioene eneantie ou fere desordeneement
aucune chose. il li disoit. Ha. se tu sauoies
com grant peine il te couendra soffrir por
ce que tu fez tu nen feroies riens. Et ie me
ismes vi les plaies. ⁊ les senti meintes forz.
⁊ graces ⁊ merciz rent ie a nostre seigneur.
de ce que ie l enseueli a mes meins.

sseiz de genz ont souent doute qui fu li premi
ers hermites qui premierement habita es
forez. Car li aucun dient que seinz helyes
⁊ seinz iohans furent chief ⁊ comencement
de tel maniere dordre. Dece z. ii. nos semble il
que seinz helyes fu plus que hermites ⁊ seiz
iohanz propheiza ancois quil fust nez. Li
autre tesmoignent que seinz antoines fu
chies de tel maniere dordre. ⁊ a cels se consent
toz li pueples ⁊ ce est uoirs en une maniere.
Il ne fu pas del tot li premiers qui entra es
deserz. mes il dona premierement essample
au monde de mener tel maniere dordre. Ama
thas ⁊ machaires li deciple antoine cil qui
son cors enseuelirent tesmoignent ⁊ affermẽt
que uns princes de thebee qui out non poux
fu chies ⁊ comencement de ceste ordre. ⁊ la
leur opinion prouons nos en ceste maniere.
Au tens decien ⁊ ualerien en icel tens
que cornelius fu martiriez a ro
me. ⁊ cypriens en cartage. sostint
seinte eglise en egypte. ⁊ en thebaida molt
griés persecution. Et pres que tuit li crestien
ne desierroient a ce tens nule rien tant come
morir por amor ihu crist. Mes por ce que li
deables desierre toz iorz plus a ocierre les ames
que les cors. si controua une maniere de no
uiax tormenz tardis a la mort des cors. ⁊ has
tis a la mort des ames. si quen ne lessoit uenir
a martyre tele ente estoit ceuls qui por deu
desierroient amorir. Si come seinz cypriens
meismes qui a ce tens fu martyriez le tesmoig
ne. Et por ce que la cruaute de lenemi soit pl⁹
coneue. si uos dirons. ii. manieres des tormenz
quil controua por espargnier as cors ⁊ por de
ceuoir les ames.
Quant li deuant dit cypriens out seur
monte totes les manieres de tormenz
que len li pout fere. si li fist li a
nemis oindre tot le cors. ⁊ puis metre tot nu
a lardant soleil. les meins liees derriere le
dos. por ce que cil qui auoit seurmontez
les tormenz del feu ⁊ dautre chose. fust uei
cuz par les pointures des mosches. Une au
tre foiz auint que li menistre a lenemi pris
trent. i. ioene bacheler. ⁊ le uouldrent con
treindre a renier la foi ihu crist. ⁊ por ce ql
ueoient quil estoit appareilliez a totes ma
nieres de tormenz soffrir. si se penserent
quil ne le tormenteroient mie en cors mes
en esperit. Lors le menerent en un iardin
qui mol estoit beax ⁊ delitables ⁊ solatable
a humeine nature. En cel iardin li firent
il un lit molt tres bel de boene coute de plu
me. ⁊ cointement acesmez de toz les aor
nemenz qui a biau lit apartienent. Li
bachelers fu en celit couchiez en tel manie
re quil pooit ueoir dune part les lis

78 Legendary

Paris, between *c.* 1240 and 1250
330 x 220 mm

BRITISH LIBRARY, ROYAL 20 D. vi

A legendary (*legendarium*), or collection of saints' lives, derives its name from the Latin word *legenda*, 'things to be read'. Following the recommendations of the Rule of St Benedict (d. *c.* 547), hagiographical collections were prescribed throughout the Middle Ages as communal monastic readings for the moral edification of monks. However, first in verse and by the turn of the thirteenth century also in prose, French translations of Latin legendaries began to target a new, secular audience. Although they never reached the popularity of vernacular versions of the *Golden Legend* (see cat. no. 79), over thirty French prose legendaries, written mainly in the thirteenth and fourteenth centuries, survive.

The Royal legendary, comprising fifty-seven saints' lives, represents an early stage in the evolution of the French prose legendary. It was grouped (Meyer 1906) with two other surviving copies of the same text (Paris, BnF, MSS lat. 411 and 412) under the name of the prose legendary C. As has been demonstrated elsewhere (Thompson 1998, 1999), these three manuscripts incorporate parts of an older collection that was compiled and translated by Wauchier de Denain for Philip, Margrave of Namur (b. 1175, d. 1212). Wauchier's legendary was entitled *Li saint confessor* (The Saints Confessor) and appears to have included the lives of four French and four Italian saints (Martin, Briccius, Giles, Martial, Nicholas, Jerome, Benedict and Alexis), the largest and the most coherent addition in the C legendary. The translator, who revealed his name in the lives of Sts Martin and Martial, also dedicated to Philip of Namur another hagiographical collection, the *Vie des sainz peres* (Lives of the Holy Fathers), that survives in the unique manuscript now in Carpentras (Bibliothèque Municipale, MS 473). Although Wauchier followed his Latin sources closely, he clearly intended his collections of legends to be a source of good examples for his patron, incorporating in them several versified moralizations.

The Royal collection of saints' lives is the oldest surviving copy of the legendary C. Its sixty miniatures were painted by four or five artists who shared the commission by dividing between them gatherings of the manuscript and providing work in their individual styles. Following Robert Branner's (1977) suggestions, the illuminations of three of them may be attributed to Parisian workshops that emerged in the second quarter of the thirteenth century under the influence of the production of the *Bibles moralisées*. The majority of initials in the Royal legendary were illuminated in two styles close to those of the Psalter and Hours for the use of Soissons, now in New York (Pierpont Morgan Library, MS M. 92) and the so-called Potocki Psalter, now in Warsaw (Biblioteka Narodowa, MS 8003 I). The third major contributor, whose miniature of St Paul the Hermit is reproduced here, elaborated the very refined style of the Sainte Chapelle Evangeliary (Paris, BnF, MS lat. 8892) and the Psalter now in Philadelphia (Free Library, MS Lewis E 185), both produced in *c.* 1225–30. While the work of his collaborators is characterized by striated, fluid draperies forming hairpin-like loops, this artist shifts towards larger, triangular, more 'Gothic' folds that would later prevail in Parisian art of the second half of the thirteenth century (see ff. 92v and 178v). This stylistic innovation suggests that the Royal legendary was probably illuminated in *c.* 1240–50.

It is not known for whom this lavishly illustrated manuscript was originally made. A colophon that states that the book was written by a certain Bonaventure may have been copied from an earlier model as the same phrase is also included in one of the legendaries C in Paris (BnF, MS lat. 412). The Paris manuscript – which was written in the Picard dialect, probably at Mons, and dates from 1285 – is, according to Thompson (1999), the version closest to the original model. Because the two manuscripts share a strikingly similar iconography, the legendary C that served as a source for both the Royal and the Parisian copies was probably also illustrated.

The date of the Royal legendary's incorporation into the royal collection is uncertain. The inscription on a flyleaf reading 'God save kyngge Harre and kyenne Ellessabet 'suggests that the manuscript must have been in England during the reign of Henry VII, before the death of Elizabeth of York in 1503. A large number '63' on the same flyleaf identifies the book as one of the early possessions of Henry VIII (see Carley 1997). A fifteenth-century shelfmark '3° y' (f. 1) of an unidentified library suggests an earlier monastic provenance. Clearly intended for an aristocratic reader, the Royal legendary would, though, 'return' to a secular ownership by its inclusion into the Old Royal library. *J.F.*

PROVENANCE:
Henry VIII.

Opposite:
St Paul the Hermit, f. 195v

79 *La Légende dorée*

(Jacobus de Voragine, *Legenda aurea*, translated into French by Jean de Vignay)

Paris, 1382
305 x 215 mm

BRITISH LIBRARY, ROYAL 19 B. xvii

Severed limbs, shattered skulls and buckets of blood were the stock-in-trade of Jacobus de Voragine, whose compendium of saints' lives, replete with ingenious tortures and martyrdoms, was enormously popular. Written in Latin by the Dominican friar *c.* 1260, the *Legenda aurea* (Golden Legend) was translated into every major western European language and survives in over 1000 manuscripts and countless printed books. As captivating as any tale of chivalry, the *Golden Legend* describes the lives of exemplary men and women who did not flinch when their faith was tested. For medieval Christians these righteous models – holy heroes and heroines – were not remote figures but ever-present allies.

Veneration for the saints cut across class boundaries. It was believed that they would respond with equal alacrity to the prayers of the destitute and disenfranchised and the rich and powerful. But wealthy aristocrats and members of the royal family had a major advantage: the material means to express their gratitude to, and interest in, the saints. Some built chapels dedicated to their favourites; others founded hospitals or commissioned artworks and books, including lavish editions of the *Golden Legend.* The French King Charles V (r. 1364–80), for example, owned at least seven copies (Delisle, *Recherches* [1907], 2).

In 1333 the cleric and author Jean de Vignay, who translated several works for Jeanne de Bourgogne, wife of Philip VI (see cat. nos. 57, 91), completed the first French translation of the *Legenda aurea.* Thirty-four manuscripts of de Vignay's text survive and almost all are deluxe, illustrated volumes made for royalty and nobles of the French and Burgundian courts (Maddocks 1986, 1991). The present copy of the *Légende dorée*, which was completed in 1382, contains the earliest version of de Vignay's translation, designated by scholars 'Type A'. Eighteen other manuscripts are in this group, including five earlier ones ranging in date from 1348 to 1375 (Hamer and Russell 1989).

Each chapter in the present manuscript opens with a small image. Most are pleasant but pedestrian. On f. 109, for example, St George rescues a princess from a deflated dragon. Only the two prefatory miniatures and the one illustrating the first chapter, which were painted by a master craftsman, are studies in elegance. Although his name has been lost to history, this artist is known as Pseudo-Jacquemart de Hesdin because of his close association with Jacquemart de Hesdin, the Flemish artist who illuminated manuscripts for John, Duke of Berry. The two painters often worked together on the same books. The miniatures in the present manuscript are the earliest securely dated works by Pseudo-Jacquemart (Meiss 1967). Especially striking is his frontispiece, comprising four separate scenes: the *Coronation of the Virgin*, the *Last Judgement*, and groups of male and female saints (f. 5, pictured).

In the lower margin, below the frontispiece, appears the motto 'My tryst ys' and the name 'Arundell', inscribed by a later owner, William Fitzalan (b. 1417, d. 1487), who became the 9th Earl of Arundel in 1438. His interest in the *Legenda aurea* is attested not only by his possession of this particular manuscript, but also by his patronage of the printer, William Caxton, who was struggling to translate the work from French and Latin into English and would have abandoned the task had it not been for the Earl's encouragement. As Caxton explains in his dedicatory prologue, Arundel pledged to buy a 'reasonable quantity' of the copies that were printed in 1483, and to grant Caxton 'a yearly fee, that is to wit, a buck in summer and a doe in winter'. Arundel's motto is included in the woodcut that precedes Caxton's prologue in this printed edition.

It is not clear when the present manuscript left Arundel's collection, but it is not recorded among the books owned by his great-grandson, Henry Fitzalan (d. 1580). Instead it passed to a member of the Beaufort family, probably Henry VII's mother, Lady Margaret Beaufort (b. 1443, d. 1509). Red roses of Lancaster and the Beaufort portcullis and arms appear on a flyleaf added to the manuscript (f. 1v). The design also incorporates four scrolls bearing the motto *Me sovent sovant* (I remember often) and blue flowers with four petals, probably speedwells (*Veronica chamaedrys*), intended to reinforce the message of the motto; speedwells, like forget-me-nots, signified remembrance (Fisher 2007). Lady Margaret's household accounts for 4 August 1503 include the record of a payment made to a certain 'Lenard of the vestry for byndyng of Legenda Auria' (Powell 1998). If this manuscript is the copy in question, the folio with the Beaufort arms may have been added at that time. One thing is certain: this copy of the most widely read collection of saints' *Lives* held the interest of aristocratic and royal readers for over one hundred years. *D.J.*

PROVENANCE:

William Fitzalan, 9th Earl of Arundel (b. 1417, d. 1487); a member of the Beaufort family, probably Lady Margaret Beaufort (b. 1443, d. 1509); Henry VIII.

Opposite:
The Coronation of the Virgin; male and female saints; the Last Judgement, f. 5

80 Bestiary with Theological Texts

Central or northern England, *c.* 1200–10
220 x 160 mm

BRITISH LIBRARY, ROYAL 12 C. xix

Above:
Deer, f. 23 (detail)

Opposite:
Lions breathing life into their newborn cubs, f. 6

Animals painted with admirable skill and set against brilliant gold grounds are featured in this early thirteenth-century bestiary (Book of Beasts), which is among the very first to include full-colour illustrations rather than simple line drawings. A near-identical book, the Worksop Bestiary, written *c.* 1187 (New York, Pierpont Morgan Library, MS M.81), served as the direct model for the present one. Possibly made in Lincoln or York, the Worksop Bestiary was given in 1187 by Philip, a canon of Lincoln, to the monks of the Augustinian priory of Radford (now Worksop), Nottinghamshire. 'Not only do the two [manuscripts] coincide in every word of text, and in the compositions of their miniatures, [but] they are also ruled with the same number of lines per page (twenty-four), and for the first ninety-seven leaves of Bestiary text … [have] exactly the same words on every page, and almost on every line' (Baxter 1998).

Like its model, the Royal bestiary opens with the lion, 'ruler of all beasts'. Described as regal, merciful and courageous, the animals are also characterized as benevolent parents. 'When the lioness gives birth to her cubs', explains the author, 'she brings them forth dead, and watches over them for three days, until their sire ... breathes in their faces and gives them life' (Clark 2006). The cubs' transformation, depicted in the miniature reproduced here, is compared with God the Father's resurrection of Jesus Christ.

Miniatures, showcasing different creatures, occur at the beginning of each chapter. Roman numerals, written in plummet, are visible beside some of these. 'VIII', for example, appears beside a picture of a hyena gnawing on a corpse (f. 11v); and 'IX' follows next to an image of a crocodile being disembowelled by a hydrus, a serpent-like creature native to the Nile (f. 12v). Seemingly inconsequential, and overlooked by scholars more concerned with the problems raised by the text, these numbers – which correspond to the order of pictures in the Worksop Bestiary – served as guides for the artists of the Royal bestiary, enabling them to depict the right animals in the appropriate places. Sequences of numbers are discernible (e.g. Unicorn–VI, Beaver–VII, Hyena–VIII, Hydrus–IX, Hydra–X), but there are gaps that point to missing folios – eighteen have been lost (Baxter 1998).

Judging from the pictorial programme of the Worksop Bestiary, the Royal volume lacks twenty-six miniatures. The total, however, is slightly higher because the Worksop Bestiary has also lost some of its miniatures. To assess the lacunae fully it is necessary to consult a third manuscript (Los Angeles, J. Paul Getty Museum, MS 100), which was copied directly from the Royal bestiary *c.* 1250, possibly in London, but is known as the Northumberland Bestiary because it was formerly owned by the dukes of Northumberland. A consideration of its contents reveals that both the Worksop and the Royal bestiaries probably had four more illustrations each: two depicted various kinds of fish, one depicted a whale, and another the mythical Peridexion tree said to attract doves and repel dragons.

Although all elements of the page are seamlessly integrated in the Royal bestiary, it is obvious that the scribes copied the text before the artists supplied the images. On f. 23, for example, there is a series of unwarranted spaces between words. This odd arrangement is explained by recourse to the Worksop manuscript, whose scribe left gaps so that the artist who painted the picture of a stag directly beneath the text (pictured) could extend its antlers into the space above (Morgan MS M.81, f. 30). Deviating from the model by portraying the stag in a different pose, with its head inclined towards the ground, the artist of the Royal bestiary chose to ignore the spaces left by his fellow scribe. Other miniatures likewise reveal the artists' creative engagement with, and liberal departure from, their models.

The Royal bestiary may have been copied at or near Radford priory, home of its model. Some scholars, however, observing the similarity in style between the miniatures in the Royal manuscript and others produced in Durham – such as the resplendent *Life of St Cuthbert* (Yates Thompson 26) – point to that northern city as the place of production. Regardless of where the Royal manuscript was made, the Northumberland Bestiary, which was copied from it, proves that it exerted an influence on at least one group of artists who may have been based in London. The later history of the Royal manuscript is as obscure as its origins. We know nothing of its owners until it was purchased by the antiquary John Theyer in the seventeenth century. On his death it was acquired with the rest of his collection by Charles II. *D.J.*

PROVENANCE:

John Theyer (d. 1673), antiquary; Charles II.

12 C xix · p. 204 · 6

Incipit lib' de naturis bestiarꝫ. & earum significa-
tionib;. Bestiarũ uocabulum ꝓprie ɔuenit leonib; pardis & tigrib; lupis & uulpib;. canibus & simiis. ursib; & ceteris que uł ore uł unguib; seuiunt exceptis serpentib;. Bestie autẽ dicte a ui q̄ seuiunt. fere appellate eo q'd naturali utunt᷑ libertate. & desiderio suo ferant᷑. Sunt enĩ libere eoꝝ uoluntates & huc atq; illuc uagant᷑. Et quo animus duxerit: eo ferantur. De naturis leonum.

81 Bestiary and Lapidary ('The Rochester Bestiary')

South-east England (?Rochester), *c.* 1230
300 x 215 mm

BRITISH LIBRARY, ROYAL 12 F. xiii

Animals of all shapes and sizes are represented in medieval bestiaries. Despite appearances these are not works of natural history, but serve instead as guides for moral conduct; each animal exemplifies virtues to be emulated or vices to be avoided. Anecdotes about animal behaviour, often lacking basis in fact, are not recounted for their own sake, but to convey religious truths. Not surprisingly, given their didactic emphasis, bestiary manuscripts could be found in many medieval monastic libraries, particularly in England. No convincing reason for their particular appeal to British readers has yet been advanced, but the fact remains that far more bestiaries were produced in England in the twelfth and thirteenth centuries than elsewhere, and many of these were lavishly illuminated.

Bestiaries vary from one another in terms of content, illustrations and the order of material. Scholars have divided surviving Latin examples into various groups according to their principal texts. The present manuscript, which was once owned by the Benedictine monks of the cathedral priory of St Andrew, Rochester, and may have been made there, falls into M.R. James's 'Second Family', the largest one of all, represented by over forty manuscripts.

Despite the family resemblance, the Rochester manuscript departs from the norm: it is unique in terms of both text and pictorial programme. Unlike any other surviving bestiary, it includes lengthy excerpts from the *Pantheologus*, a book of animal lore by Peter of Aldgate, an Augustinian canon, and later Prior (1197–1221) of Christ Church within Aldgate, London. Only one complete copy of this work has survived (Clark 2006). Written in the early thirteenth century and now in three volumes in the British Library (Royal 7 E. viii, and 7 C. xiii–xiv), it too was once owned by the Benedictines of Rochester, and may have been employed as a source text by the author of the Rochester Bestiary.

Painted by an English artist whose work is also found in two Bibles, a Psalter and a medical miscellany, the miniatures offer a fresh interpretation of the text. They are bespoke creations designed for this particular book. Notes, written in plummet, describing the subjects to be depicted, are visible in the margins beside many of the miniatures. The note on f. 29v, for example, begins, 'Mastins a garder la faude' (Mastiffs guarding the [sheep] fold), which is what the artist has represented in the adjacent scene. Similar annotations also occur near spaces allocated for miniatures that remain blank. The fact that these instructions are in French suggests that the artist was a professional craftsman, rather than a monk, and that he was working under the direction of an individual who could read the Latin text.

Rarely depicted subjects include a small elephant with its trunk tucked under the chin of one of its fallen comrades, attempting to hoist him aloft (f. 11v, pictured). The courteous pachyderm represents Christ who humbled himself in order to elevate mankind. The sixty miniatures include four dedicated to the king of beasts. Curiously, the lion represented on f. 4 cowering under a tree is virtually identical to the one on f. 5v, which shows the animal cringing before a white cockerel. The idea that lions are afraid of white roosters was derived by the authors of medieval bestiaries from Pliny the Elder's *Natural History*, but the image is a medieval innovation. Another notion advanced by Pliny is that the lion is capable of compassion and will spare suppliants. This, too, was repeated in the bestiary and is illustrated in the upper register of f. 5v. An ideal model for human monarchs, the lion – incorporated into the arms of England in the twelfth century – symbolized not only majesty and might, but also justice and mercy.

The manuscript bears a fourteenth-century ownership inscription from the cathedral priory of Rochester and a note explaining that it was returned to the monks by one John of Malling, who seems to have borrowed or stolen it. After passing through the hands of various individuals, it came into the Upper Library at Westminster Palace by 1542, together with many other manuscripts from Rochester priory. *D.J.*

PROVENANCE:

Cathedral priory of St Andrew, Rochester; Brother John of Malling, 14th century; William Grybbons and Thomas Aston, 15th century; Henry VIII.

Opposite:
An elephant with a castle strapped to its back lumbers into battle; a small elephant hoists aloft its fallen companion, f. 11v

32 Psalter

Bruges, 2nd or 3rd quarter of the 13th century
255 x 185 mm

BRITISH LIBRARY, ROYAL 2 B. iii

As more people learned to read, the demand for devotional books increased. Manuscripts continued to be made in provincial scriptoria and monasteries, but by the middle of the thirteenth century, workshops staffed by professional scribes and artists could be found in many European cities. Bruges is now famous for the innumerable Books of Hours produced there in the fifteenth and sixteenth centuries, but two hundred years earlier the city had already emerged as one of the most important sites of production of devotional books in the prosperous county of Flanders. Luxurious Psalters, in particular, were a speciality of Bruges workshops, the artists of which responded to models from France and England. Flemish artists also developed new approaches, as attested by surviving Psalters from the region. These take four forms: the first and rarest, which follows foreign models, contains initials with portraits of King David; the second and third types, invented in Flanders, have initials with portraits of the Apostles and saints respectively; and the fourth, popular in the region, has initials with scenes from the life of Christ.

The Psalter featured, of the fourth type, was made in Bruges for an unknown patron. Several local saints are mentioned in the calendar – including Donatian, whose feast on 14 June is highlighted in red. Seven full-page miniatures, devoted to Christ's infancy, are clustered at the beginning of the book, and the first Psalm opens with an initial depicting King David, which occupies an entire folio (f. 15v). In addition, six full-page miniatures – illustrating Christ's ministry, death, and triumph over Satan – are interspersed throughout the volume. To streamline production, the full-page miniatures were painted on separate leaves and not inserted in the book until it was bound. Located at the main liturgical divisions of the Psalter, these pictures face the texts of Psalms 26, 38, 52, 68, 97 and 109 (the miniatures for Psalms 80 and 101 are missing). The liturgical divisions are also distinguished by historiated initials. At Psalm 26, for example, the full-page miniature depicts Christ's triumphal entry into Jerusalem (pictured left), while the initial '*D*' (*ominus*) on the facing page shows him being tested by the Devil, who challenges him to turn stones into bread (ff. 36v–37, pictured).

The First Temptation is an appropriate choice of subject matter since Psalm 26, a call to courage in face of adversity, begins, 'The Lord is my light and my salvation, whom shall I fear? The Lord is the protector of my life: of whom shall I be afraid?' Believed by medieval Christians to be the author of accidents, illness and sin, and, ultimately, the soul's destruction, the Devil was a source of terror. Reading the Psalms was an antidote, a way of rendering powerless the venom of the Serpent.

Carlvant, who examined the Psalter in the context of others produced in Bruges, has attributed its decoration to a single artist, and posited that he came from Germany. However, the handling of certain details – notably the eyes – points to at least two, if not three, different individuals working side by side, sometimes on the same illustrations. The hand of the main artist is also found in a closely related Psalter now in Cambridge (Magdalene College, MS F.4.7) and in a slightly later one (Aschaffenburg, Hofbibliothek, MS 5) (Carlvant 1987).

In the sixteenth century the Psalter came into the possession of a professor or scholar at the University of Cambridge, who amended the calendar. Among the dates added are the *exequiae* of prominent local men, including William Bateman, founder of Trinity Hall, Cambridge, and

Above:
The First Temptation of *Christ*, f. 37 (detail)
Opposite:
Psalm 26, entry into Jerusalem, f. 36v

Bishop of Norwich (d. 1355); and the judge Sir Robert Rede (d. 1519), founder of three Cambridge lectureships. The next owner of the Psalter, Ralph Pryne (or Prynne), grocer of London, left an even more conspicuous mark on the manuscript in the form of a verse dedication (f. 1v). Addressed to Mary I, it reads in part: 'God save the Quene / Be me your humbull and poore orytur Rafe Pryne.' The grocer is mentioned in one other document: a record of court proceedings in which he accused an apothecary of selling him sub-standard rhubarb. As unlikely as it may seem, Pryne – whose surname provided a convenient rhyme for 'queen' – may have given the Psalter to Mary, which would explain its presence in the Old Royal library. If so, he was not the only subject to curry favour in this fashion. A more prestigious manuscript, the Queen Mary Psalter (cat. no. 85) was likewise presented to the Catholic monarch by one of her subjects, the customs officer Baldwin Smith, who prevented its export abroad. *D.J.*

PROVENANCE:

Unknown Flemish patron; probably owned by a Cambridge scholar or professor in the first half of the 16th century; Ralph Pryne, grocer of London, *c.* 1550; Mary I.

2
2 mathewe
2 mathew

83 Psalter with Prefatory Miniatures

Oxford, 1st quarter of the 13th century
350 x 240 mm

BRITISH LIBRARY, ROYAL 1 D. x

Top:
A bishop, f. 21v (detail)

Above:
The Virgin and Child, f. 86 (detail)

Opposite:
The Magi before Herod, and the Adoration of the Magi, f. 2

More medieval English paintings are preserved on parchment than in any other media. Manuscripts like this Psalter, with sixteen full-page prefatory miniatures, give us some idea of the riches of monumental paintings that have been lost. The first northern European Psalters with prefatory images date from the twelfth century and they continued to be produced throughout the thirteenth. These pictures were intended to inspire devotion, to help people focus on key episodes of sacred history and to model their conduct according to the examples set by Christ and the saints. The prefatory cycle in this Psalter is devoted to the life of Christ. It opens with Gabriel's *Annunciation to Mary* and ends with a depiction of *Christ in Majesty*.

Miniatures in the calendar and gilded initials further enhance its luxurious appearance. Whereas Parisian Psalters, such as cat. no. 13, are generally divided into eight sections, this Psalter – which conforms to the preferred English scheme – has ten large initials, marking the liturgical divisions at Psalms 1, 26, 38, 51, 52, 68, 80, 97, 101 and 109. By dividing the text into groups of Psalms to be read at specific times over the course of the day, the entire Psalter could be read in one week. This venerable practice, first followed by nuns, monks and priests, was imitated by the laity.

Although its original owner is unknown, the manuscript appears to have been made in Oxford. The calendar lists the feasts (12 February and 19 October) of the city's patron saint, the seventh-century virgin martyr Frideswide, who is said to have founded a priory on the present site of Christ Church. She is also invoked in the Litany. The omission from the calendar of the translation of the relics of Thomas Becket suggests that the Psalter was made before this feast was established in 1220.

As has long been recognized by scholars, the Psalter belongs to a group of manuscripts made in the same workshop (Rickert 1965, Morgan 1982). Since these craftsmen shared pictorial models and techniques, it is sometimes difficult to distinguish their work. One artist, however, left an unmistakable mark on the miniatures he painted. Vertical columns of discs, resembling vertebrae, define the throats of his figures (see detail, *Virgin and Child*, f. 86). His hand can be detected in the full-page miniature of the *Annunciation* and the *Visitation* (f. 1), the enthroned Virgin in the *Adoration of the Magi* (f. 2), the *Virgin and Christ at Cana* (f. 3v), *Christ in Majesty* (f. 8v), a man cutting corn on the August calendar page (f. 12v), a bishop in a historiated initial (f. 21v, pictured), and in nine other historiated initials (ff. 32, 42v, 52, 52v, 62, 74v, 86, 87v and 98). The same artist also painted some of the initials in another Psalter produced in Oxford (Imola, Biblioteca Comunale, MS 100) (Rickert 1965). Evidently he excelled at sacred subjects. His rendering of the *Virgin and Child* in this manuscript, an appropriate but unusual subject for Psalm 97, 'Cantate domino' (Sing to the Lord), is exquisite (f. 86, pictured). A second artist painted the other miniatures in the prefatory cycle and it is probable that assistants executed most of the decorated initials.

The *Nativity* (f. 1v), painted almost exclusively by the second artist, shows the Virgin suckling the newborn Christ, and Joseph adjusting her pillow. Below, an angel, announcing the good tidings, stands in a field beside the shepherds instead of assuming his usual position in the heavens above. The similar pose of an angel in the Imola Psalter suggests that the composition was one favoured by the Oxford workshop. On the facing page (f. 2, pictured) the Magi consult Herod and pay homage to the Christ Child seated on his Mother's lap. Of these figures, only the enthroned Virgin was painted by the first artist, whose treatment of the throat is so distinctive. The prayer 'Deus misereatur nostri et benedicat nobis' (God have mercy on us and bless us) and the monogram 'E.H.' were written on f. 15v by a sixteenth-century owner who has yet to be identified. *D.J.*

PROVENANCE:

Inscribed (f. 15v) 'Deus misereatur nostri et benedicat nobis E.H.', 16th century.

84 The Psalter of John of Dalling

St Albans, middle of the 13th century (after 1246)
280 x 195 mm

BRITISH LIBRARY, ROYAL 2 B. vi

The martyrdom of Sts Alban and Amphibalus; Sts John the Baptist, John the Evangelist, and two bishops, ff. 10v–11

Alban, a Christian convert who was executed by order of the Roman emperor in the third century, is regarded as the first English martyr. A modest shrine first marked the place where he was beheaded, but later, according to tradition, King Offa of Mercia founded a Benedictine monastery near the site in 793. Until its dissolution in 1539 St Albans was one of the wealthiest abbeys in Britain. Far from retreating from the world, the monks kept abreast of political and intellectual developments through frequent visits from high-ranking and royal guests. Pilgrims seeking cures or favours from Alban also travelled to the abbey to venerate his relics and those of his friend and mentor, Amphibalus.

The present Psalter was given to the Benedictine monastery of St Albans by one of the monks, John of Dalling, about whom nothing else is known. According to an inscription in the volume (f. 1v), the monk asked John of Hereford (abbot 1235–63), to permit him to keep the book until he died. The manuscript opens with a series of drawings of the life of Christ and the saints, rendered in brown ink with transparent washes of colour, a technique favoured by artists working at St Albans *c.* 1250. Prefatory images of saints began to appear in Psalters in the middle of the thirteenth century, and the present manuscript is one of the earliest surviving examples of the type (Brieger 1957).

One opening (ff. 10v–11, pictured) depicts the martyrdoms of Alban and Amphibalus, whose final moments are rendered in vivid detail. As Alban's head is severed, the eyes of his executioner are torn from their sockets – divine punishment for his wickedness. In the panel below this scene Amphibalus's torturers plunge their knives into his skull and wind his entrails around a tree. Although these tinted drawings recall the more famous ones in Matthew Paris's *Life of St Alban* (Dublin, Trinity College, MS 177), the compositions in the two manuscripts differ, and the figures in the Psalter, while competent, lack Matthew's verve (cf. cat. no. 114).

John of Dalling's name saints, John the Baptist and John the Evangelist, are depicted on the facing page (f. 11), as are two saintly bishops who have not been identified but must have had special significance for Dalling. Thomas Becket is a likely candidate for the one on the left, and the one on the right may be Edmund of Abingdon (b. 1175, d. 1240), also Archbishop of Canterbury, whose name appears in both the calendar and the Litany

and who was canonized in 1246 (evidently, the present Psalter was made after that year). Matthew Paris wrote biographies of both Thomas and Edmund, and links between St Albans and Christ Church, Canterbury – both leading Benedictine foundations – were close. When a new shrine was ordered for Thomas Becket in 1220, for example, the commission was entrusted to Master Walter of Colchester, monk and sacristan of St Albans.

Some other saints represented in the Psalter remain to be identified, including the youthful king seated beside Edward the Confessor (f. 11v). He may be Oswin of Deira, who was murdered in 651 by his rival Oswiu of Bernicia and whose feasts are inscribed in gold in the calendar. King Oswin was the patron saint of the Benedictine abbey at Tynemouth, Northumberland, a cell of St Albans. Furthermore, a chapel at St Albans was dedicated to him and Edmund of Bury, and around 1247 Master Richard, the foremost artist at the abbey, made a new altarpiece and altar frontal. St Catherine is depicted in the lower panel of the miniature, beneath the enthroned monarchs, with another female martyr seated beside her, possibly Margaret of Antioch – although she lacks her customary attribute: a dragon. Catherine and Margaret, who was whipped and beheaded after spurning the advances of a Roman governor, were the most popular female saints in England; their feasts are also noted in the calendar of the present Psalter and their names appear in succession in the Litany. The prefatory cycle ends with an image of the *Virgin and Child* by a different artist (f. 12v). Some scholars have speculated that it is a late work by Matthew Paris or a close associate, and this is possible (Lewis 1987).

Like other books from St Albans, the Psalter was probably removed during the Reformation, perhaps as early as 1521 when Cardinal Thomas Wolsey (d. 1530) began to plunder the abbey in order to finance the building of Cardinal College, Oxford (refounded as Christ Church by Henry VIII in 1546). The remaining monks surrendered the abbey's seal to the Crown in 1539, and the glorious shrine of Britain's first martyr fell into neglect. *D.J.*

PROVENANCE:

John of Dalling, monk; the Benedictine abbey of St Albans; Robert Gylles, 16th century; John Theyer (d. 1673), antiquary; Charles II.

85 The Queen Mary Psalter

London (?), *c.* 1310–20
275 x 175 mm

BRITISH LIBRARY, ROYAL 2 B. vii

No other manuscript approximates to this one, a magnificent Psalter preceded by a French summary of Old Testament narratives, and featuring an unrivalled pictorial programme. The statistics speak for themselves: 319 leaves containing 223 prefatory images, 24 calendar scenes, 104 half- or full-page miniatures, 23 historiated initials and 464 marginal drawings. This precious manuscript is one of the most extensively illustrated Psalters ever produced in western Europe – the result of innumerable hours of painstaking labour. The volume is, moreover, not the hurried product of multiple craftsmen, but a tour de force whose illustrations were executed by a single artist of exceptional talent. Because the hand of this anonymous artist is apparent on every page, the manuscript has a remarkably homogeneous appearance. Working closely with one main scribe, the artist controlled every aspect of the design, from the layout of each page to the size and form of every illustration.

All of the underlying sketches and marginal scenes were completed before the more heavily painted elements of the decorative programme. This is especially apparent in the sequence of twenty-two marginal scenes relating to Thomas Becket. For example, the tail of the initial 'Q'(*uicumque*), the first word of the Athanasian Creed, was painted on top of the tinted drawing of the entombed Becket (f. 298v). The primacy assigned to the marginal scenes proves that they were not conceived as an afterthought, but as an integral part of the design. Rare features of the pictorial programme include large miniatures of saints mentioned in the litany (ff. 302v–309). Warner (1912) failed to identify those saints lacking attributes, but their names are listed directly beneath the miniatures, proof of the close collaboration between scribe and artist that is evident throughout the volume.

The correlation between the text and images of the Old Testament prefatory cycle in particular suggests that the scribe and the artist worked closely together. Many of the images comprise several scenes, and each scene has its own caption – an arrangement demanding close cooperation between the two craftsmen. In an illustration of Samuel's life (f. 49), for example, the caption of the scene on the left has not been inserted, but in an earlier illustration depicting Jerubbaal (Gideon) (f. 37, pictured), the reverse is true: the caption, 'Coment Jeroboal les envoyast quere les aneles qe estoyent de denz les orayles occis' (How Jerubbaal sent them to seek the rings that were in the ears of the slain) is present, but the episode has yet to be illustrated. Significantly, the French text of the captions and of longer unillustrated passages occurs in no other manuscript and may well have been composed for this one (Stanton 2001). Could the anonymous author of the text have liaised with the artist and scribe, creating, as a result, new interpretations of the ancient narratives? Obscure episodes from the Old Testament and Apocrypha are depicted in the manuscript, and traditional motifs are often rendered in novel ways. Did learned advisers of the patron, possibly Edward II or his consort, Isabel of France (Warner 1912; Stanton 2001), foster the relationship between author and craftsmen?

Scholars agree that the Psalter was made for a high-born, probably royal, patron, but its original owner has not been identified definitively and the volume derives its name from a later one, the Tudor Queen Mary, to whom it was presented in 1553, the year she succeeded to the throne. Confusingly, although the artist who illustrated the Psalter flourished two hundred years before she was born, he is now known as the Queen Mary Master. Surviving works from the period suggest that his illustrations were esteemed by other artists who emulated his style and by privileged patrons who sought his work.

Many questions regarding the Queen Mary Master remain to be answered. Where did he train? What were his influences? Where was he based? It is obvious that the Queen Mary Master, while cultivating a distinctive style, was receptive to many different ideas, and drew on an unusually wide range of models. Copying compositions that captured his attention and inventing others, he built up an encyclopaedic repertoire of subjects. The range of his interests points to a cosmopolitan setting for his activities and to a patron (with a coterie of spiritual advisers) who was the catalyst for this extraordinary work. In London, specifically within the context of the royal court at Westminster, the Queen Mary Master would have had access to wall-paintings, altarpieces and sculptures, as well as manuscripts, and found a prestigious patron wanting a devotional book unlike any previously produced.

D.J.

PROVENANCE:

Henry Manners, 2nd Earl of Rutland (b. 1526, d. 1563); Mary I.

Opposite:
Scenes from the life of Jerubbaal (Gideon), f. 37

Palm 38, Angel appearing to the Magi, and Massacre of the Innocents, ff. 131v–132

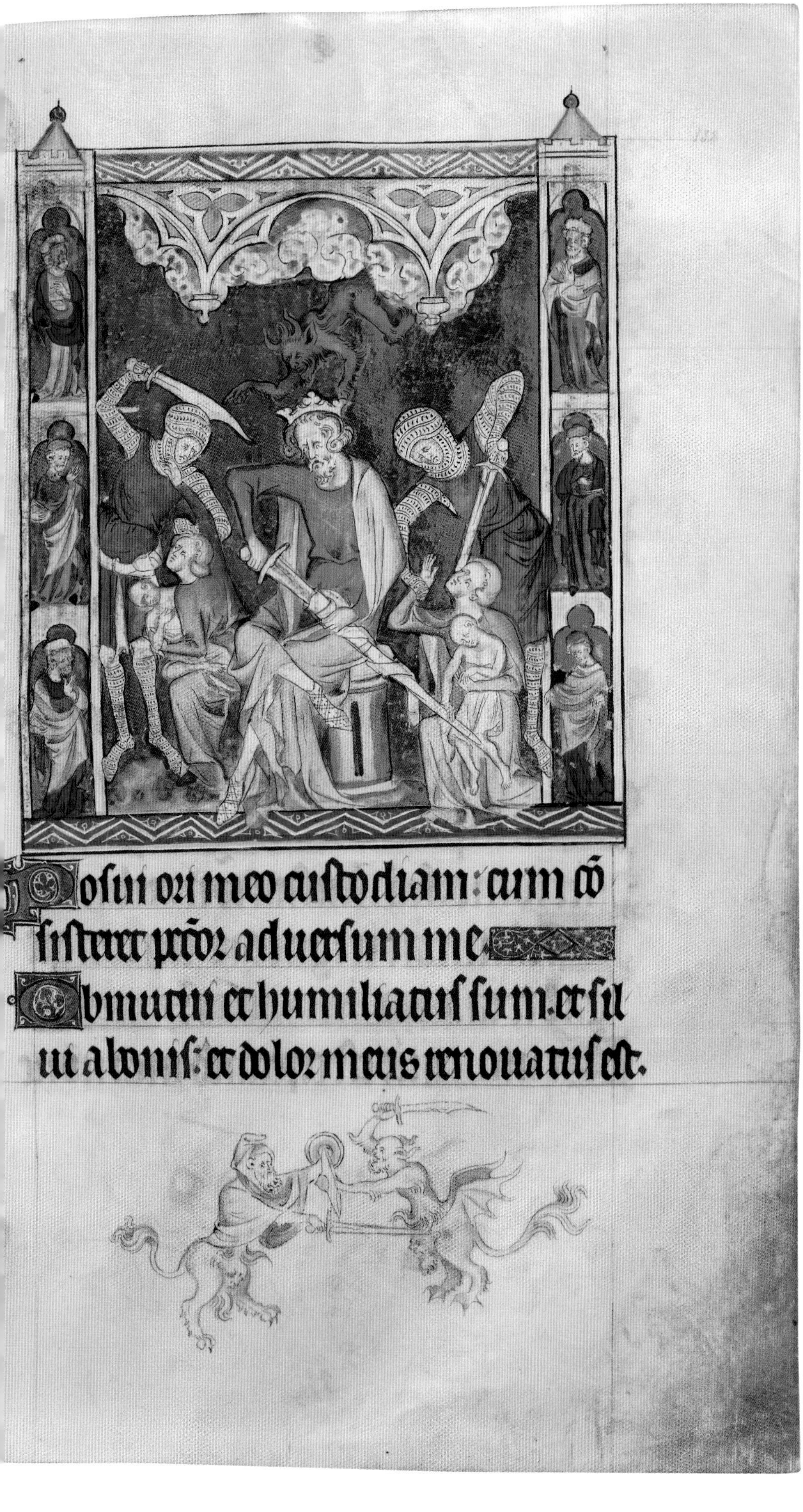
Posui ori meo custodiam: cum cõ
sisteret pccõr aduersum me.
Obmutui et humiliatus sum et si
lui a bonis: et dolor meus renouatus est.

Sextum

Ceo vi les aigneus out ouert vn des seals · e oi qe le quatre bestes me dit ·· au
si come voiz de tonerre · venez veer · Et ieo vi vn blanc cheual issir · e al
qi seet sure ·· out ark · e corone lui est done ·
Par le cheual blanc est signifie seint · e il issit en veinquant pur veintre eglise
qest nette de peche par baptesme · pur la mort ihesu crist · Cil qi seet
sure signifie le fiz dieu · Par le ark ·· est signifie seint escripture qe manace les
maufesantz par le iugement · Par la corone qe lui est done ·· signifie le peple
de paens qe se est conuertez a lui · Ceo qil issit en veinquant pur veintre ·· signifie
qe il conuertera les suens par ceux qil enuerra vers la fyn del mounde

86 The Queen Mary Apocalypse

London or East Anglia, *c.* 1310–25
305 x 210 mm

BRITISH LIBRARY, ROYAL 19 B. xv

Above:
An angel speaks to the sleeping St John while he is exiled on Patmos, f. 2v

Opposite:
Two horsemen, portents of pestilence and war, seen in a vision by St John, f. 9v

Illustrated copies of the Apocalypse (Book of Revelation), which describes the destruction of the world and the creation of a new heaven and earth, were among the most popular books produced in England from *c.* 1250 to 1280, and then again, after a brief hiatus, from *c.* 1300 to 1340 (Morgan 2006). The Italian abbot Joachim of Fiore (d. 1202) predicted that the world would end in 1260. Although he was proved wrong, his prophecy only served to enhance interest in the Apocalypse, the final book of the Bible, purported to have been written by John the Evangelist.

Artists working in a wide range of styles met the demand for illustrated copies, which survive in large numbers. Undoubtedly the appeal of these manuscripts lay largely in the dramatic images that graced their pages – images representing terrifying spectres and cosmic battles between good and evil. Evocative descriptions of strange beings – including locusts with long tresses, lions' teeth and scorpions' tails – lent themselves to illustration.

One of a group of twenty-six lavishly illustrated Apocalypses in French prose (James 1931), the present manuscript was written in cursive script by a single scribe. Scholars have posited that three different artists were responsible for its seventy-three illustrations, which are executed in three different styles (Warner 1912). Generally speaking, the first artist concentrated on the first part, the second on the middle of the manuscript and the third artist on the final section. One of the pages depicting horsemen seen by the visionary St John showcases the work of the first artist (f. 9v, pictured). The subtle tones of the tall, slim figures contrast with the strident red and blue grounds. John's vigorous gestures and the implied movement of the horses (which are about to exit the stage) make the illustrations dynamic.

Because this miniature and others in the first part of the present manuscript resemble the illustrations of the Queen Mary Psalter (cat. no. 85), it was long held that they were by the same artist, now known as the Queen Mary Master. Elements of the miniatures in the two manuscripts are undeniably similar. The horse depicted on f. 10 of the Apocalypse, for example, is identical in pose to the one on f. 20 of the Queen Mary Psalter, as are two men among the crowds on f. 1v (Apocalypse) and f. 50 (Psalter). Furthermore, in the image of St John (f. 2v, pictured), the treatment of the ground with its mottled patches of brown, the distinctive vegetation and the winsome hares all resemble the handiwork of the Queen Mary Master. Whether the same artist was responsible for both manuscripts has, nevertheless, been questioned.

Dennison, for example, has argued that the Apocalypse illuminations are not by the Queen Mary Master, but by a less capable artist who copied a manuscript or model book by him (Dennison 1994). It seems possible, however, that the Queen Mary Master drew most of the miniatures on the initial pages of the Apocalypse, but an assistant executed some elements of the designs, and outlined in a thicker, darker line some of the figures drawn by the Master. This would explain the divergence in quality between the elegant figures drawn by a sure hand and the awkward ones by a less confident one, both of which occur in the first sixteen leaves of the manuscript. Once the chief artists (whether the Queen Mary Master or not) had sketched the composition in plummet, the figures were outlined in darker ink, details were gilded, pigment was applied and finally black contour lines were drawn to redefine elements such as haloes. Close examination of the Queen Mary Psalter reveals similar disparities in the quality of the draughtsmanship; almost certainly at least one assistant also helped to complete its vast pictorial programme.

The artists who illustrated the rest of the Apocalypse have not been identified and attempts by some art historians to link them with other manuscripts are not entirely convincing. The fact that three main artists with divergent styles illustrated the Queen Mary Apocalypse suggests that its original owner did not expect the manuscript to have a uniform appearance, but was satisfied with a book that, to modern eyes, is stylistically discordant. Who that owner was, and where the manuscript was made, remain to be determined. *D.J.*

PROVENANCE:
Henry VIII.

87 The Welles Apocalypse

England, 1st quarter of the 14th century
450 x 300 mm

BRITISH LIBRARY, ROYAL 15 D. ii

Christ enthroned with the twenty-four elders and John ascending a ladder into heaven, ff. 117v–118

With its large, clear script and vibrant illustrations, this manuscript may be viewed easily by more than one person at a time. Given its generous dimensions, it was probably placed on a lectern and perused by its original owner, who is unknown, perhaps in the company of a cleric or friar who helped him or her interpret its contents. Since the text is in French, the language spoken by the English elite, rather than Latin, the language of the Church, a literate lay person could have read it with relative ease. The didactic function of the manuscript is underscored by five initials showing a student in discussion with his master. These initials appear in the first part of the manuscript, a lengthy religious treatise in verse, *La Lumiere as lais*, composed, *c.* 1270, by the English writer Peter of Fetcham – about whom almost nothing is known. Most chapters of this text begin with a question posed by the student and answered by the master. A full-page illustration of Christ instructing his disciples to say the prayer *Pater Noster* (Our Father) reiterates the pedagogical theme (f. 64v).

The *Lumiere as lais*, the most lavishly illustrated surviving copy of the text, is followed by the Apocalypse in French prose with a prologue and commentary. Both parts of the present manuscript were written by a single scribe and illustrated by a single artist (Sandler 1986). Figures are outlined in stiff, black lines and white pigment is used throughout to represent flesh tones. In addition, the Apocalypse illustrations feature large expanses of white owing to the colour's importance as a symbol of purity. One of the pages for example, shows twenty-four elders wearing gold crowns and white robes, who are gathered around the throne of God (f. 117v, pictured). The pale figures lack volume, but provide a striking contrast to the multi-coloured grounds. Also depicted are four creatures with six wings that sing God's praises and guard his throne, and John the Evangelist, the purported author of the book, who climbs a ladder to heaven.

Despite the close correspondence between text and illustrations, the artist almost certainly drew his inspiration from another Apocalypse manuscript or a model book, rather than the text itself. Illustrated Apocalypses, first produced in England *c.* 1250, maintained their popularity for about a hundred years, and there would have been no shortage of suitable prototypes. In the case of the *Lumiere as lais*, a text that was not as frequently

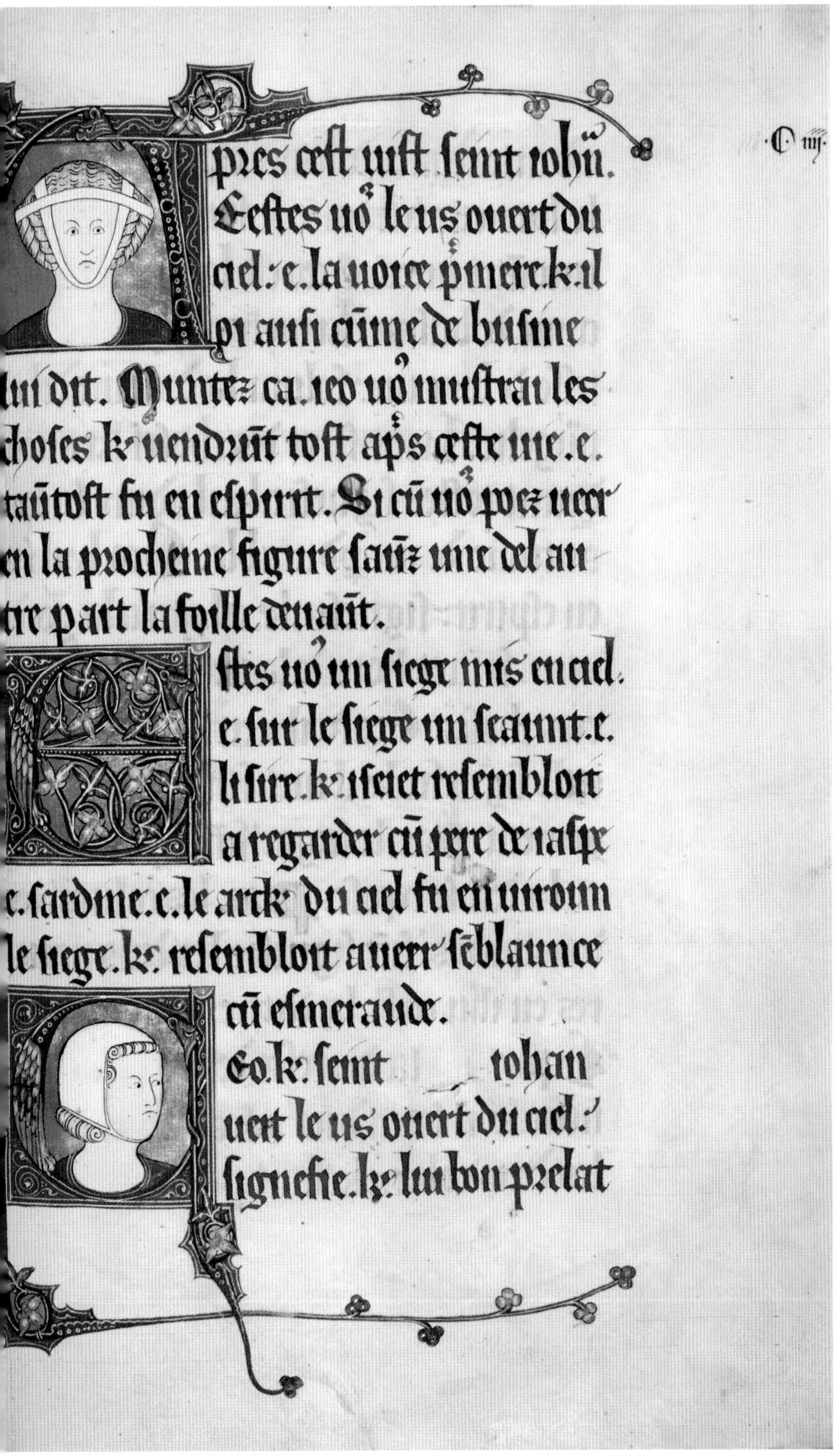

illustrated, the artist probably designed the pictorial programme. Certain compositions are, however, based on existing miniatures. The image of the Annunciation (f. 3), for example, is similar in style to the one in the Clifford-Pabenham Hours (Cambridge, Fitzwilliam Museum, MS 242, f. 2) (Egbert 1940).

Numerous initials in the present manuscript are decorated with heads of men and women, the latter often dressed in the latest fashions with their hair artfully arranged (f. 118, pictured). Like the knights in chainmail, riding into battle in the Apocalypse illustrations, the ordinary men and women depicted in these initials must have lent an immediacy and contemporary relevance to the cataclysmic events described in the text. As noted by Egbert, the initials featuring heads share stylistic affinities with those occurring in several other English manuscripts of comparable date, notably the Clifford-Pabenham Hours and the Bardolf-Vaux Psalter (London, Lambeth Palace Library, MS 233), but the precise relationship between these manuscripts and the present one is not clear.

The Apocalypse is listed in an inventory, dated 1430, of twelve books owned by Leo, 6th Baron Welles (b. 1406, d. 1461). In addition, two lists written on blank flyleaves in the manuscript relate to Leo's son, John, Viscount Welles (d. 1499). The first list records the purchase of trees from properties owned by John in or near Well, Lincolnshire, and the second comprises a list of his books, including the present volume, which he obviously valued and kept close to hand. Traces of the name of his wife, Cecily Welles (d. 1507), daughter of Edward IV, appear on the first folio of the manuscript (Egbert 1940). In 1502, three years after John's death, Cecily remarried, provoking the wrath of Henry VII, her brother-in-law, who coveted the Welles estates and seized them for himself. The manuscript presumably came into the royal collection at this time. Certainly, after the volume had left the Welles family, Cecily's name was erased from the first leaf and the monogram 'HR', probably a reference to Henry VIII (see essay 'The Old Royal Library'), was inscribed in the lower margin.

D.J.

PROVENANCE:

Leo, 6th Baron Welles (b. 1406, d. 1461); John, Viscount Welles (d. 1499); Cecily Welles (d. 1507); ?Henry VII; Henry VIII.

The World's Knowledge

'Rex illiteratus est quasi asinus coronatus' (An illiterate king is like a crowned ass) states one of the first political treatises on rulership, John of Salisbury's *Policraticus* (1159). Medieval works of princely instruction stressed the importance of the intellectual formation of kings and encouraged an appetite for knowledge. This section features manuscripts intended for, presented to or appropriated by English kings as books of reference and learning.

Several such manuscripts share a monastic provenance and attest to monastic scholarly interests. These volumes all came late into royal possession in the early modern period. Removed from monastic libraries by Henry VIII's agents or appropriated in the aftermath of the Act of Supremacy, these and other monastic books formed a major part of the Old Royal library, as explained in the third essay in this volume. This section starts with the two pillars of medieval knowledge of the world, Isidore of Seville's *Etymologiae* and Rabanus Maurus's *De universo* (cat. nos. 88, 89). Biblical texts and commentaries, which served as the foundation for much medieval learning, are also featured, such as Peter Lombard's *Glossed Epistles* (cat. nos. 103–105) and collections of canon law (cat. nos. 106–108), compiled and read at medieval universities.

The group of manuscripts central to this section features the texts and cycles of illustrations that transmitted knowledge considered particularly valuable for a king. The *Livre des proprietez des choses* was advertised by its translator Jean Corbechon in his dedication to Charles V of France as a handy digest of information about the natural and spiritual world for a busy monarch. This recommendation clearly still appealed to Edward IV when he acquired his copy of Corbechon's text (cat. no. 93). Geographical knowledge appears as an important subject in royal education, doubtless for its practical value. Gerald of Wales dedicated his *Topographia Hibernica* to Henry II to encourage the King to progress his conquest of that country (cat. no. 90). The anthology that combines texts on Alexander the Great's conquests and Marco Polo's travels with the itinerary to the Holy Land was probably compiled for Philip VI of France when he was preparing for a crusade (cat. no. 91). Nearly two centuries later, works by Jean Rotz and Jean Mallard were designed to inform Henry VIII about new geographical discoveries, perhaps as a response to the King's personal interests (cat. nos. 95, 96). Personal interests or courtly fashion also prompted some princes and monarchs to collect books on divination and astrology, which were studied exclusively at the universities and royal courts (cat. nos. 97–99). A final group of manuscripts shows Humfrey of Gloucester, Henry VII and Henry VIII to have been receptive to new humanistic currents in the world's knowledge (cat. nos. 109–111).

Study and War at the gateway to Virtue (cat. no. 110)

Æternitas
Gloria
VIRTUS
Studiũ
Mars

88 Isidore of Seville, *Etymologiae*

England (?Canterbury), last quarter of the 11th century
310 x 235 mm

BRITISH LIBRARY, ROYAL 6 C. i

Any discussion of the traditions of medieval scholarship must begin with Isidore of Seville (*c.* 560–636). Born into a noble Visigothic family, Isidore served as Archbishop of Seville for more than three decades, and was a prolific and versatile writer. His masterwork was the enormously influential *Etymologiae*, which has been described as the first encyclopaedia and as the 'basic book' of the Middle Ages, second only to the Bible in cultural significance. The text of the *Etymologiae* covers a vast range of topics, including grammar, logic and rhetoric, arithmetic, geometry, geography, zoology, medicine, agriculture and theology, to name but a few. Writing during a time of great social and cultural chaos, Isidore had the ambitious goal of creating a comprehensive anthology of all the world's knowledge, that would serve as an epistemological bridge between the classical world and Christian scholarship. To create his compendium of knowledge, he drew on hundreds of authors from both of these spheres. Isidore's method, as his title suggests, is based on the practice of etymology. Isidore believed that an examination of a word's history was the key to comprehending its meaning: 'When we know the origins of a word we understand its power all the more quickly' (Lindsay 1911).

The present manuscript dates from the last quarter of the eleventh century. Written by three scribes in nearly uniform Caroline minuscule, it was probably the product of a monastic scriptorium. It was almost certainly designed for inclusion in an ecclesiastical library, the typical destination for copies of the *Etymologiae* at this time. A shelfmark and ownership inscription place this copy in the library of the Benedictine abbey of St Augustine, Canterbury, in the fourteenth century, and internal evidence suggests that it was probably produced there as well. Although the manuscript survives in a relatively pristine condition, it appears to have been a working copy. Chapter numberings and occasional marginal notes in later medieval hands certainly indicate that it remained in use for several centuries.

This copy of the *Etymologiae*, like most of its era, includes few illuminations, but several pages contain diagrams and other *figurae*. Two such figures are reproduced here, from Book 3, *De Mathematica*, which contains all those subjects considered by Isidore to be related to mathematics. As may be expected, dialogues on arithmetic and geometry open the text, followed perhaps less obviously by dissertations on music and astronomy. On f. 30 two diagrams complement Isidore's writings on the sun and the moon. In the upper right corner of the page a circular diagram illustrates the journey of the sun through the sky, a schematic extrapolation of the chapter that appears in virtually every copy of the text. Interestingly, the second set of illustrations on this page is called for by Isidore's text itself. Beginning with 'Lunae prima figura bicornis est' (the first figure of the moon is two-horned), Isidore explains the eight phases of the lunar cycle with the use of these drawings, describing how our view of the moon changes as a result of its position in relation to the Earth and the sun.

The *Etymologiae*'s sections on astronomy in particular are good examples of Isidore's unique style of intellectual synthesis. As a bishop and Christian scholar, he believed implicitly in the words of Scripture as the final arbiter of truth, but in borrowing extensively, and uncritically, from the works of pagan writers on astronomy he showed a greater tolerance of classical scholarship than might be expected. Among his many statements that were potentially heretical, for example, are his assertions that the sun lies at the centre of the universe, and that Earth is round, illustrated by his famous diagram of the world, the tripartite (or 'T–O') map (see f. 108v, detail above).

Above:
Diagram of a 'T–O' map of the inhabited world, f. 108v (detail)

Opposite:
Diagram and coloured drawings of the positions and phases of the moon, f. 30

The profound influence that Isidore of Seville and his *Etymologiae* exercised on later medieval scholarship should not be underestimated. The text survives in nearly a thousand copies from this period, an indication of the importance with which it was viewed by thinkers of the time. The *Etymologiae* also served as a significant primary source for later medieval scholars, particularly on subjects encompassed by what we would today refer to as the natural sciences. Isidore was an authority relied upon by the compilers of bestiaries, lapidaries, medical miscellanies, cartographies and astronomical treatises, and his crucial influence can be traced in the work of later authors such as Rabanus Maurus, Orosius, Bartholomaeus Anglicus and Vincent of Beauvais. *S.J.B.*

PROVENANCE:

St Augustine's Abbey, Canterbury, by the 14th century; Charles II.

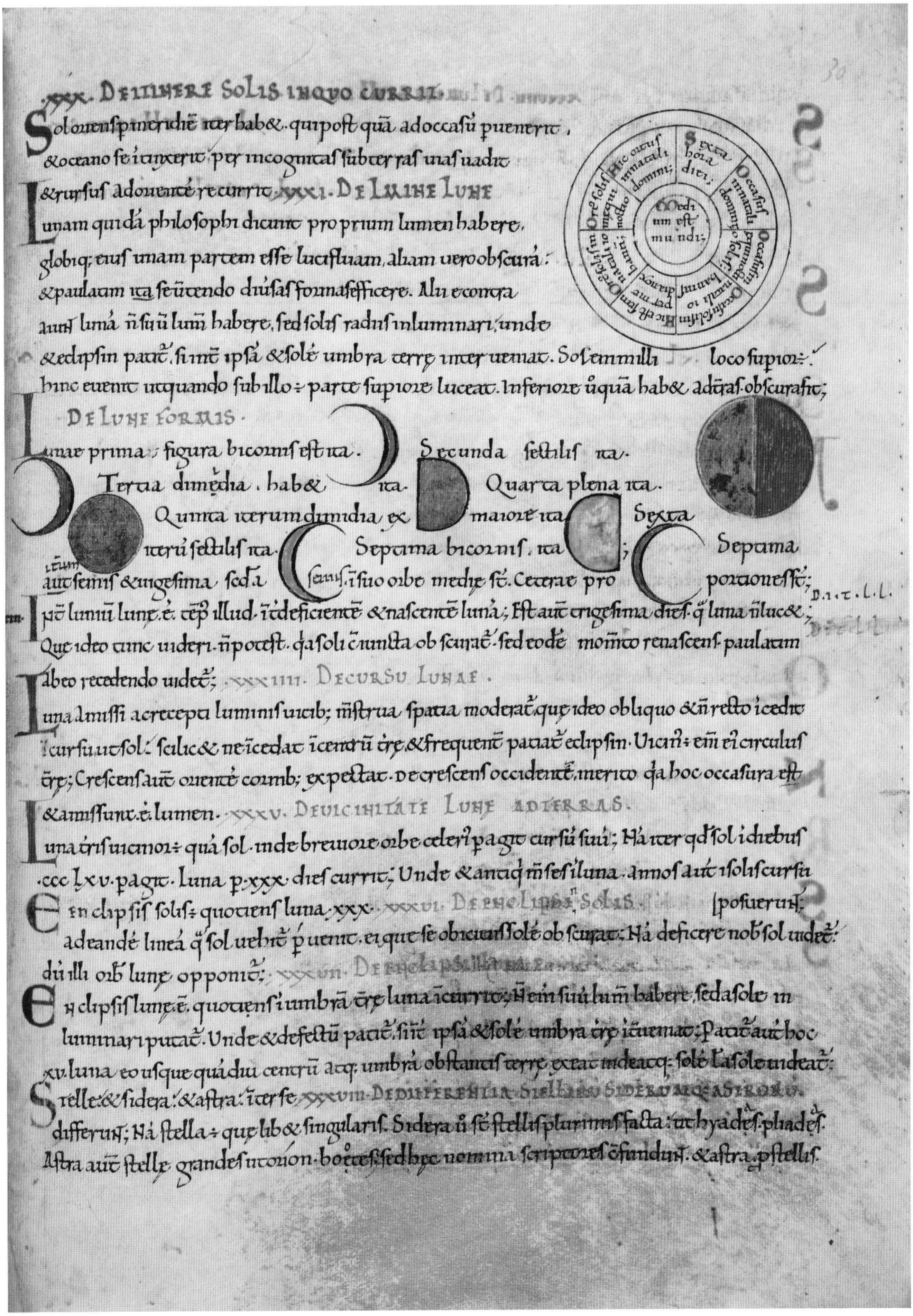

xxx. De itinere solis in quo currit.
Sol oriens per meridiem iter habet. qui postquam ad occasum pervenerit,
et oceano se intinxerit, per incognitas sub terras vias vadit
et rursus ad orientem recurrit. xxxi. De lumine lunae
Lunam quidam philosophi dicunt proprium lumen habere,
globique eius unam partem esse lucifluam, aliam vero obscuram:
et paulatim ita se vertendo diversas formas efficere. Alii e contra
autem lunam non suum lumen habere, sed solis radiis inluminari. unde
et eclipsin patitur, si inter ipsam et solem umbra terrae interveniat. Sol enim illi loco superior est.
hinc evenit ut quando sub illo est parte superiore luceat. inferiore vero quam habet ad terras obscura sit.
De lunae formis.
Lunae prima figura bicornis est ita. Secunda sectilis ita.
Tertia dimedia habet ita. Quarta plena ita.
Quinta iterum dimidia ex maiore ita. Sexta
iterum sectilis ita. Septima bicornis ita. Septima
autem semis et vicesima secunda semis in suo orbe media est. Ceterae pro portione sunt.
Interlunium lunae est tempus illud inter deficientem et nascentem lunam; Est autem trigesima dies quo luna non lucet;
Quae ideo tunc videri non potest quia soli coniuncta obscuratur. sed eodem momento renascens paulatim
ab eo recedendo videtur; xxxiiii. De cursu lunae.
Luna amissi ac recepti luminis vicibus menstrua spatia moderatur. quae ideo obliquo et non recto incedit
in cursu ut sol. scilicet ne incedat in centrum terrae et frequenter patiatur eclipsin. Vicinus enim ei circulus
terrae est; Crescens autem orientem cornibus expectat. decrescens occidentem. merito quia hoc occasura est
et amissura est lumen. xxxv. De vicinitate lunae ad terras.
Luna terris vicinior quam sol. inde breviore orbe celerius peragit cursum suum; Nam iter quod sol in diebus
ccclxv peragit. luna per xxx dies currit; Unde et antiqui menses in luna. annos autem in solis cursu posuerunt;
Eclipsis solis est quotiens luna xxx. xxxvi. De eclipsi solis
ad eandem lineam qua sol vehitur pervenit. eique sese obiciens solem obscurat; Nam deficere nobis sol videtur
dum illi orbis lunae opponitur; xxxvii. De eclipsi lunae.
Eclipsis lunae est quotiens in umbram terrae luna incurrit; Non enim suum lumen habere sed a sole inluminari putatur. Unde et defectum patitur si inter ipsam et solem umbra terrae interveniat; Patitur autem hoc
xv luna eo usque quamdiu centrum atque umbram obstantis terrae exeat videatque solem vel a sole videatur.
Stellae et sidera et astra inter se xxxviii. De differentia stellarum siderum atque astrorum.
differunt; Nam stella est quaelibet singularis. Sidera vero sunt stellis plurimis facta. ut hyades. pliades.
Astra autem stellae grandes ut orion. bootes. sed haec nomina scriptores confundunt. et astra pro stellis.

89 Rabanus Maurus, *De rerum naturis*

St Albans, 2nd or 3rd quarter of the 12th century
420 x 285 mm

BRITISH LIBRARY, ROYAL 12 G. xiv

Rabanus Maurus (*c.* 780–856) was, like Isidore of Seville (see cat. no. 88), a scion of an aristocratic family who devoted himself to a life of scholarship and religious enquiry. Born in Mainz, he took holy orders as a youth. In 802 Rabanus was sent to Tours to study under the noted Alcuin of York, who granted him the surname Maurus after a favoured disciple of St Benedict, in recognition of his scholarship and diligence. After his studies Rabanus returned to Fulda, where he was later appointed Abbot. There he set about transforming the abbey into a centre of learning, eventually developing its monastic school into one of the most famous in the Carolingian Empire.

As one of the pre-eminent thinkers of his day, Rabanus was also honoured with the title *Praeceptor Germaniae* (teacher of Germany). He was the author of many theological texts, mostly commentaries on Scripture, along with treatises on grammar, numbers, the calendar and pedagogy. Arguably his greatest achievement was the encyclopaedia *De rerum naturis* (On the Nature of Things, otherwise called *De universo*), which he compiled between 842 and 847. Drawing on his experiences as both student and teacher, Rabanus intended this text to be a useful reference source for preachers and other religious instructors, and a tool for scriptural interpretation. He relied heavily on Isidore's *Etymologiae*, adding his own allegorical and mystical commentary and dramatically reorganizing the structure of the earlier work.

Despite the importance of Rabanus Maurus as both a writer and a teacher, copies of *De rerum naturis* were not broadly disseminated until the twelfth century; only five or six copies can be dated to before 1100 (Schipper 1997). Shortly after this time there was a relative explosion in the creation of versions of the text, with surviving copies, fragments, extracts and references in library catalogues attesting to the prevalence of the encyclopaedia through the later medieval era. The production of nearly a third of the extant copies of *De rerum naturis* by monastic scriptoria in England suggests that the text had particular significance to ecclesiastical thinkers of this region.

Most of the English copies of *De rerum naturis*, including the present volume, show evidence of use of the text as a pedagogical tool, as Rabanus had intended. A sumptuous product of the St Albans scriptorium under abbot Ralph Gubiun (1146–51), the Royal manuscript is written throughout in an even hand characteristic of that institution. It includes hundreds of notations, both interlinear and marginal, which seem to be original to this Royal copy of the text (as may be seen on the page reproduced). The scribe also included several 'boxed' notes in the margins of the pages, which contain further commentary and unique textual variants; their ultimate source, though much investigated, has not yet been traced. The evenness of all these notations and their similarity to the elegant Protogothic script throughout the volume imply that they were part of the original plan of the manuscript, rather than later additions. As Schipper notes, further evidence that these annotations were intended as part of a whole comes from the fact that the Royal manuscript appears to have served as a template for at least two other copies of the text (Oxford, St John's College, MS 5, originally from Reading; and Cambridge, University Library, MS Dd.8.13, from Kirkstead Abbey). As well as sharing nearly identical versions of the interlinear notes found in the Royal *De rerum naturis*, these two later copies repeat the Royal manuscript's anomalous divisions of chapters and text and also include the 'boxed' marginal annotations. This suggests that the twelfth-century interest in *De rerum naturis* had motivated a scholar, possibly a St Albans scribe, to create a critical recension of the work, which in turn became the model for later copyists.

Rabanus Maurus's *De rerum naturis* was an essential element of any significant monastic or ecclesiastical library. The present manuscript probably remained in the scriptorium at St Albans for several centuries. A monogram 'TC' (for 'Thomas Cardinalis') that was added in the sixteenth century suggests that by then the volume had probably come into the possession of Cardinal Thomas Wolsey (d. 1530), the Abbot of St Albans from 1521. It later passed from him to Henry VIII's library (Carley 2000). *S.J.B.*

PROVENANCE:

Benedictine abbey of St Albans, 13th century; Cardinal Thomas Wolsey; Henry VIII.

Opposite:
Inhabited initial with human figures and animals, at the beginning of Book 1, f. 6

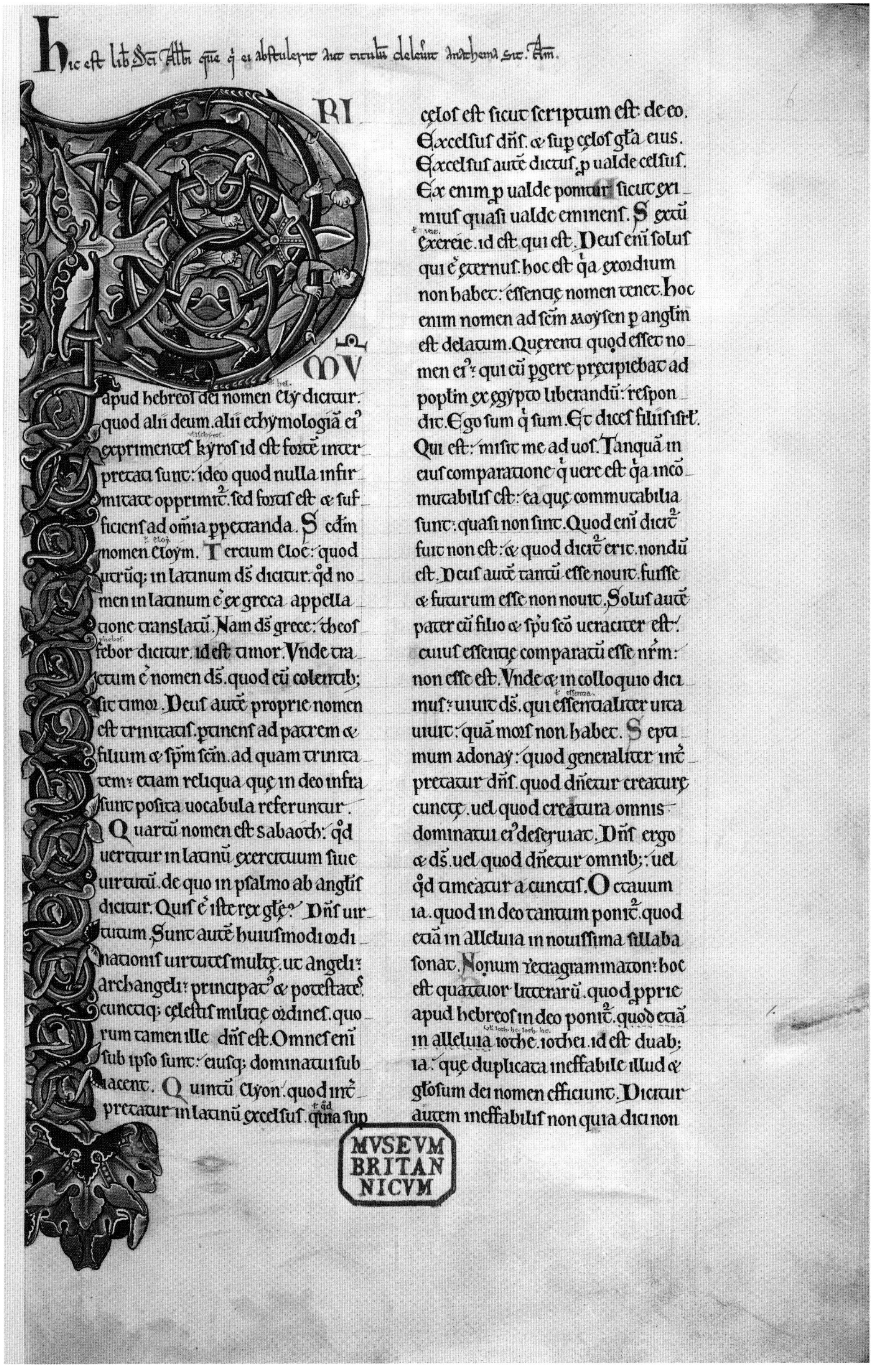
Hic est liber Sancti Albani quem qui ei abstulerit aut titulum deleverit anathema sit. Amen.

PRIMUM apud hebreos dei nomen Ely dicitur. quod alii deum. alii ethymologiam eius exprimentes kyros id est fortem interpretati sunt: ideo quod nulla infirmitate opprimitur. sed fortis est et sufficiens ad omnia perpetranda. Secundum nomen Eloym. Tercium Eloe: quod utrumque in latinum deus dicitur. quod nomen in latinum est ex greca appellatione translatum. Nam deus grece: theos febor dicitur. id est timor. Unde tractum est nomen deus. quod eum colentibus sit timor. Deus autem proprie nomen est trinitatis. pertinens ad patrem et filium et spiritum sanctum. ad quam trinitatem: etiam reliqua que in deo infra sunt posita uocabula referuntur. Quartum nomen est sabaoth: quod uertitur in latinum exercituum siue uirtutum. de quo in psalmo ab angelis dicitur. Quis est iste rex glorie? Dominus uirtutum. Sunt autem huiusmodi ordinationis uirtutes multe. ut angeli: archangeli: principatus et potestates. cunctique celestis milicie ordines. quorum tamen ille dominus est. Omnes enim sub ipso sunt: eiusque dominatui subiacent. Quintum Elyon. quod interpretatur in latinum excelsus. quia supra celos est sicut scriptum est: de eo. Excelsus dominus. et super celos gloria eius. Excelsus autem dictus. per ualde celsus. Ex enim pro ualde ponitur. sicut eximius quasi ualde eminens. Sextum Exereie. id est qui est. Deus enim solus qui est eternus. hoc est quia exordium non habet: essentie nomen tenet. Hoc enim nomen ad sanctum Moysen per angelum est delatum. Querenti quod esset nomen eius: qui eum pergere precipiebat ad populum ex egypto liberandum: respondit. Ego sum qui sum. Et dices filiis israel. Qui est: misit me ad uos. Tanquam in eius comparatione qui uere est quia incommutabilis est: ea que commutabilia sunt: quasi non sint. Quod enim dicitur fuit non est: et quod dicitur erit. nondum est. Deus autem tantum esse nouit. fuisse et futurum esse non nouit. Solus autem pater cum filio et spiritu sancto ueraciter est. cuius essentie comparatum esse nostrum: non esse est. Unde et in colloquio dicimus: uiuit deus. qui essentialiter uita uiuit: quam mors non habet. Septimum adonay: quod generaliter interpretatur dominus. quod dominetur creature cuncte. uel quod creatura omnis dominatui eius deseruiat. Dominus ergo et deus. uel quod dominetur omnibus: uel quod timeatur a cunctis. Octauum ia. quod in deo tantum ponitur. quod etiam in alleluia in nouissima sillaba sonat. Nonum tetragrammaton: hoc est quattuor litterarum. quod proprie apud hebreos in deo ponitur. quod etiam in alleluia ioth he. ioth ei. id est duabus ia: que duplicata ineffabile illud et gloriosum dei nomen efficiunt. Dicitur autem ineffabilis non quia dici non

MVSEVM BRITANNICVM

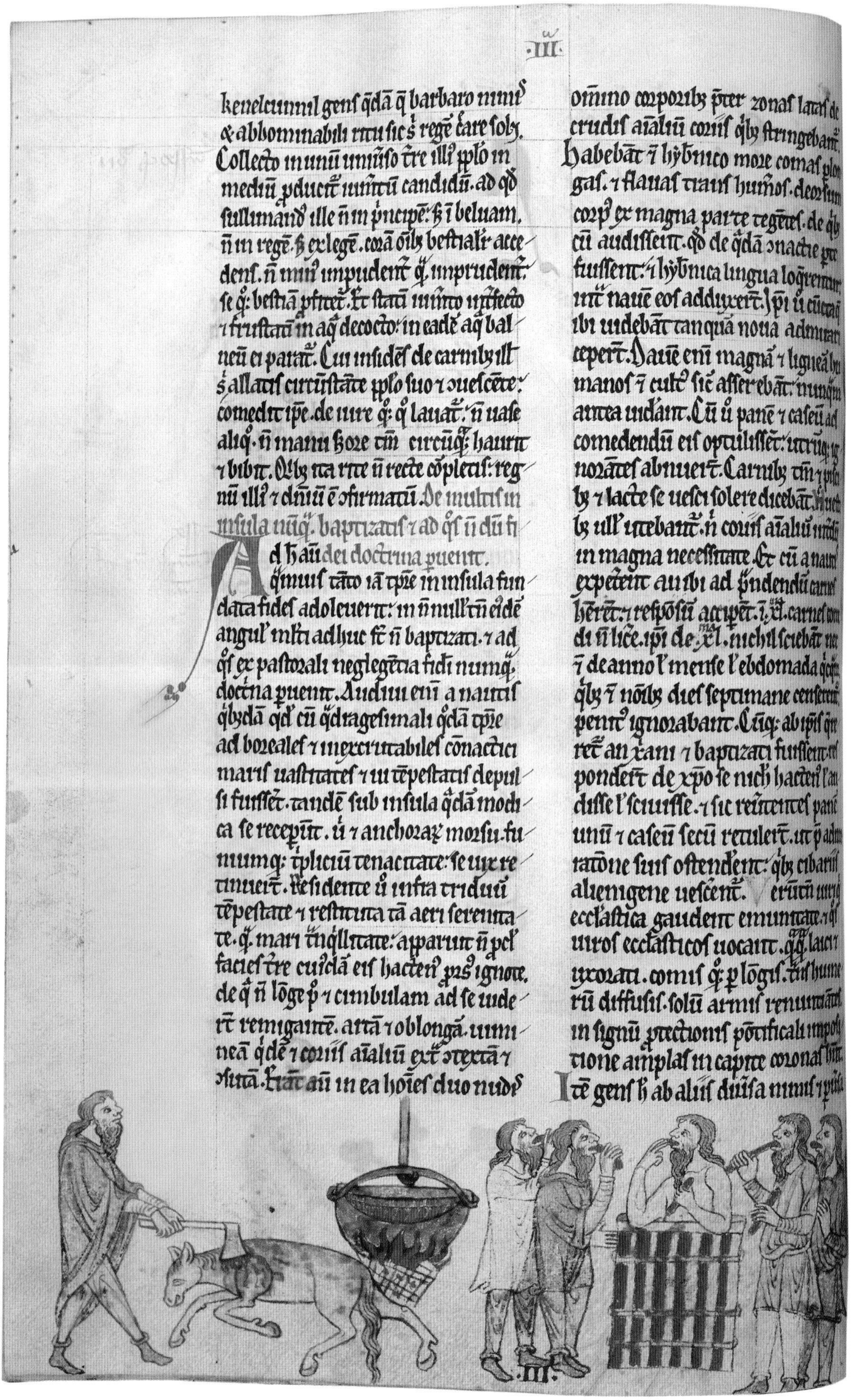

90 Gerald of Wales, *Topographica Hibernica*

Lincoln (?), *c.* 1196–1223
275 x 190 mm

BRITISH LIBRARY, ROYAL 13 B. viii

This manuscript is an anthology containing descriptions of the topography, history and marvels of the world centred on the western border region of twelfth-century Christianity: Ireland and Wales. It comprises three works by Gerald of Wales (b. 1146, d. 1223), an ecclesiastical author of half-Welsh, half-Anglo-Norman origin (the *Topographia Hibernica, Expugnatio Hibernica* and *Itinerarium Kambriae*), Henry of Saltrey's *Treatise on St Patrick's Purgatory*, and excerpts from the writings of Eusebius of Caesarea on various marvels and miracles. Later in the thirteenth century the manuscript was supplemented by Alain of Lille's *Anticlaudianus*, an allegorical poem inspired by the naturalism of the school of Chartres. Only the *Topographia Hibernica* is illustrated.

Gerald composed the *Topographia* between 1186 and 1188, immediately after his second journey to Ireland with Prince John in 1185. Gerald considered himself a historian, as 'historia' was the only term available to categorize his proto-ethnographic descriptions of the contemporary world and its societies. He was an observer eager to discover 'things not found in other countries and entirely unknown, and at the same time worthy of some wonder because of their novelty'. His descriptions of Irish topography, climate, beasts and birds, people and their customs and finally of all the marvels that, in his words, could equal the wonders of the East, reflected the revival of interest in nature during the twelfth century.

Because Gerald believed that 'things imparted through the ears enliven the mind more slowly than things placed before our trustworthy eyes', it is very likely that from the beginning he envisaged that his text be illustrated, and he may even have been involved personally in providing the first cycle of images (see Brown 2002). In the four extant illuminated copies, of which the London volume is the oldest, a series of tinted drawings placed in the margins follows Gerald's narrative. The almost informal character of these images, quickly sketched and modelled with light colour washes, make them look like ad hoc authorial annotations. Marginal drawings juxtaposed with the subjects they illustrate were occasionally included in chronicles (see cat. no. 114) and in scientific and legal texts as a method of explaining unfamiliar information. Here, they could have helped to familiarize an English audience with the otherwise unknown wonders of Ireland.

Gerald's naturalism was not mere curiosity. He dedicated the *Topographia* to Henry II. Calling the Angevin king 'our western Alexander' and praising his victories, Gerald aimed to stimulate royal interest in the conquest of Ireland. The choice of images formed part of this plan. Apart from the depiction of natural wonders (such as a leaping salmon, f. 23) and unnatural marvels (such as the man-ox of Wicklow, f. 19), many pictures show examples of bestiality, ferocity or immorality. The illustration reproduced displays a ritual to confirm kingship practised in Kenelcunill (Tirconnell), north Ulster. The king-to-be, after having had intercourse with a white mare and then slaughtered it, is shown having a bath in the mare's broth and, surrounded by his people, sharing with them the mare's meat. The evidence of Irish sexual vices, virtual paganism and alleged inadequate religious practices of the Irish Church was used in Pope Alexander III's letter to Henry II of 1172 to support the Anglo-Norman invasion of Ireland.

As Brown (2002) has demonstrated, stylistic and palaeographical evidence suggests that the Royal *Topographia* was made in Lincoln. The manuscript also contains some local additions, such as an image and description of a deer with golden teeth, allegedly captured in Dunholm wood, a forest close to that city. Lincoln might have been the place where the pictorial programme of the *Topographia* was elaborated, possibly under Gerald's supervision during his sojourn in the abbey in 1196–98, or after 1207/8 when he retired there definitively.

The existence of four closely related illustrated copies – but of very different provenance – two of which date from the author's lifetime (Royal 13 B. viii and Dublin, National Library of Ireland, MS 700), seems to relate to Gerald's strategy of presentation and distribution of his works. Aiming for patronage and promotion, he addressed the *Topographia* to Henry II and later offered a presentation copy to Richard I. He is also known to have presented works to other men of power, such as William Longchamp, Bishop of Ely; Hugh, Bishop of Lincoln; and Hubert Walter and Stephen Langton, both Archbishops of Canterbury. While the original recipient of the Royal manuscript is unknown, from at least the fifteenth century it belonged to St Augustine's Abbey, Canterbury. It may therefore have also been one of Gerald's 'political' gifts. *J.F.*

PROVENANCE:

St Augustine's Abbey, Canterbury; John Twyne (?) (b. *c.* 1505, d. 1581); Henry VIII.

Opposite:
Ritual of confirming kingship in Tirconnell, f. 28v

91 *Roman d'Alexandre en prose* and Other Texts

Paris, *c.* 1340
425 x 310 mm

BRITISH LIBRARY, ROYAL 19 D. i

Made in Paris *c.* 1340, this compendium contains eight works in French, united by the theme of travel to the East. No other manuscript has this particular combination of texts. The *Roman d'Alexandre en prose* (an anonymous translation into French prose of Leo of Naples's *Historia de preliis* [see cat. no. 75]) is followed by *La vengeance d'Alexandre* and the *Travels* of Marco Polo. Various works about the Holy Land ensue, among them a chronicle of Louis IX's final crusade. Richard and Mary Rouse (2000) have suggested that the manuscript was designed as a handbook for Philip VI of France, who aspired to lead a crusade to Jerusalem. Of the eight texts, three are unique examples of French translations by Jean de Vignay (b. 1280, d. *c.* 1340), who worked for Philip VI and Jeanne de Bourgogne (see cat. nos. 57, 79), and one of these – *Le Directoire a faire le passage de la Terre Sainte*, a treatise on routes to the Holy Land – is dedicated to the King.

Although the compendium was copied by five different scribes, the illustrations, which are characteristic of a particular Parisian workshop, give it a unified appearance. Located on the rue Neuve Notre-Dame, the workshop was owned by Richard de Montbaston whose wife, Jeanne, an illuminator, worked alongside him and ran the business when he died *c.* 1352 (see cat. no. 66). Whether the present volume was illuminated largely by Jeanne, as stated by the Rouses, is impossible to prove. Fifty-one manuscripts have been attributed to the de Montbastons (Rouse and Rouse 2002).

The miniatures are not evenly distributed throughout the volume: 102 of the 164 occur in the first work in the compendium, the *Roman d'Alexandre*, but three of the other texts have only a frontispiece. The uneven distribution of the illustrations is easily explained; for the miniatures of the *Roman d'Alexandre* the artists took as their model a lavishly illustrated manuscript, but for texts without a long pictorial tradition they had no such guide. For Marco Polo's *Travels*, for example, the artists did not follow a visual model but took their cues from the summary of the story provided by the rubrics (Dutschke 1998). Most of the miniatures of the *Roman d'Alexandre* were painted by a single artist, but a second intervened in twenty-five miniatures (gathering 4; ff. 25–32); and a third executed the following thirty-one scenes (gatherings 5–6; ff. 33–45), including an image of Alexander being lowered into the sea in a submarine (f. 37v, pictured). Ungainly, yet appealing figures set against vibrant backdrops are typical of the de Montbaston workshop.

One hundred and twenty-four sketches in lead point – an unusually large number – are visible in the margins of the manuscript (Ross 'Book Production' 1952). These were drawn by the master who designed the pictorial programme – whether one of the de Montbastons is impossible to say – and would have been consulted by the illuminators. When the master drew the sketches in the margins, he or she took as a model an illuminated copy of the life of Alexander in French prose. Now lost, the model almost certainly resembled a copy of Leo of Naples's tenth-century *Historia de preliis* made in Italy *c.* 1300 (Paris, BnF, MS lat. 8501), which contains illustrations based on an earlier French prose manuscript (Ross 1963). The illustrations in the Italian *Historia de preliis* are stylistically remote, but compositionally close to those in the present volume and offer instructive comparisons.

Although the direct model has been lost, it is possible to prove that the master responsible for the marginal sketches in the present manuscript followed his archetype more faithfully than the illuminators working under his direction. This is evident if one compares the sketches in the present compendium with the illustrations in the Italian *Historia de preliis*. In the marginal sketch of the death of Alexander, for example, which conforms to the depiction in the Italian *Historia de preliis*, Iobas hands Alexander a poisoned feather, which he unwittingly sticks down his throat, but the feather was omitted from the finished miniature (f. 41v). Evidently the master who drew the sketches had a better understanding of the story of Alexander and followed his model more scrupulously than did his fellow illuminators.

The Royal compendium had come to England by *c.* 1360–70, when an extract from Jean de Vignay's *Miroir historial* was copied by an English scribe into a manuscript associated with the Fitzalan and Bohun families (Oxford, Bodleian Library, MS Bodley 761). The text of Marco Polo's *Travels* was also copied from the Royal volume into another manuscript *c.* 1410 (Oxford, Bodleian Library, MS Bodley 264). This manuscript had belonged, *c.* 1397, to Thomas, Duke of Gloucester, the youngest son of Edward III, but by the time the *Travels* were added it had passed to an unknown individual, probably someone with close ties to the court, who commissioned English scribes and artists to augment the volume. Probably he or she borrowed the compendium from an aristocratic or royal owner, whose identity, unfortunately, remains unknown. *D.J.*

PROVENANCE:

Philip VI of France (?); Henry VIII (?).

Opposite:
Alexander in a submarine, f. 37v

92 James le Palmer, *Omne bonum*

London, *c.* 1360–75
455 x 310 mm

BRITISH LIBRARY, ROYAL 6 E. vi

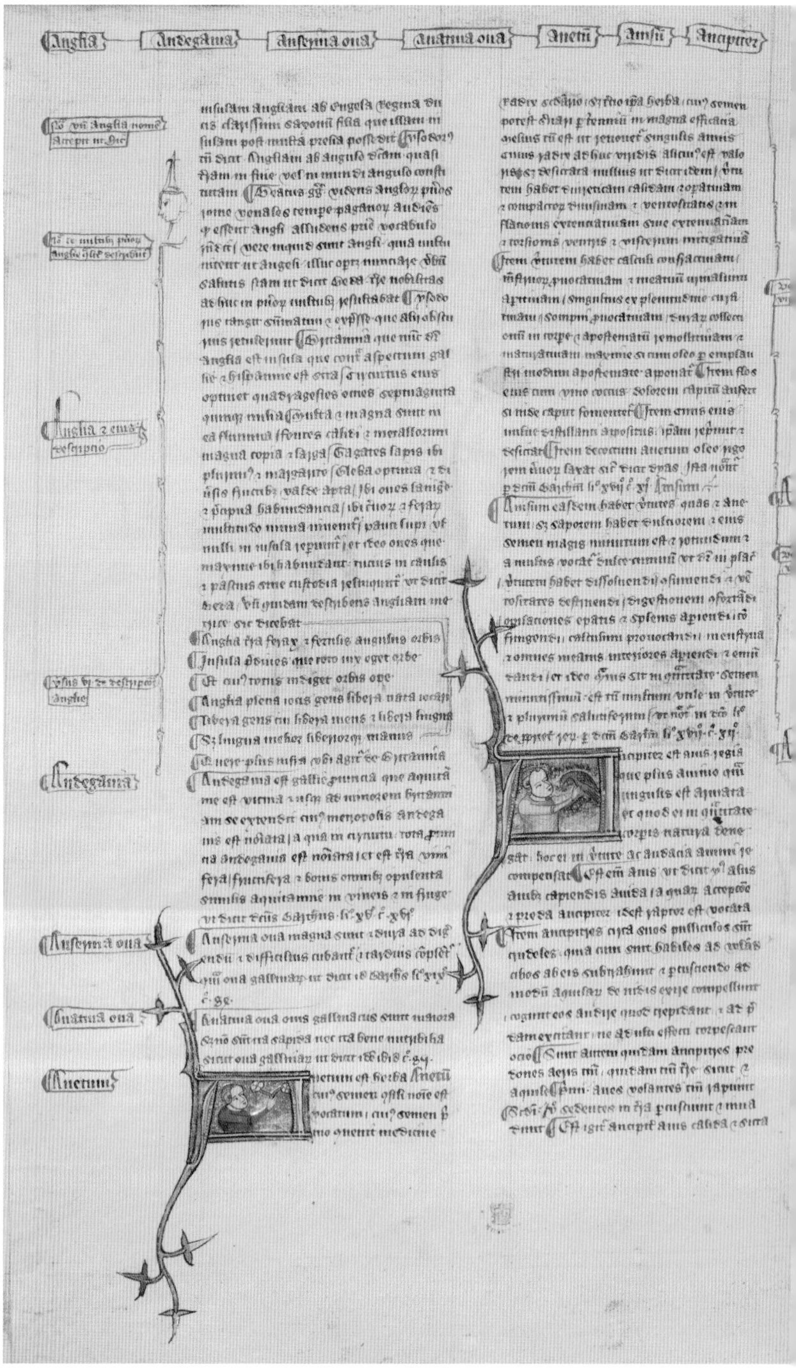

Anise, bird of prey and written appeal, ff. 107v–108

'Since virtually all good things are in one way or another contained herein, I thought it fitting to name this little work *Omne bonum* – all good things.' As this statement of James le Palmer, the author of the text, suggests, his work aspired to be a universal collection of knowledge. Written on large pages and now bound in two volumes, each of which is divided in two parts (Royal 6 E.vi and Royal 6 E. vii), the *Omne bonum* contains more than 1350 entries, even though James's text remains unfinished. If it had been completed, it would have been the equal of the *Speculum maius* by Vincent of Beauvais, the most extensive of medieval encyclopaedias (see cat. no. 57).

The range of topics covered in this unique autograph copy is unparalleled. The content selected and edited from a wide variety of sources (115 of them are listed in the preface) includes entries on canon law extracted from the *Decretum*, the *Decretals,* and numerous legal commentaries; on natural history, quoted mainly from Bartholomaeus Anglicus's *De proprietatibus rerum* and the Pseudo-Aristotelian *Secretum secretorum;* on theology based on various general compendia, such as the *Summa summarum* by William of Pagula; and finally information on biblical history, hagiography, and moral instruction. As Sandler (1996) has pointed out, the *Omne bonum* constitutes a landmark in the development of the universal encyclopaedia because its heterogeneous material is organized not hierarchically or topically, as in earlier compilations of this type, but alphabetically, anticipating a mode of organization followed to the present day. Entries are arranged under the twenty-three letters of the medieval Latin alphabet, each letter beginning a new book. Over 750 entries are illustrated by historiated initials. An additional prefatory series, at the beginning of the volume, is dedicated to the Bible.

The pages reproduced are representative in both textual content and illustration. The ordering of topics alphabetically led to the juxtaposition of entries referring to natural history: *Anetum* (dill), *Anisum* (anise), *Ancipiter* (bird of prey); grammar: *Anphorismus* (aphorism); and law: *Appellacio* (written appeal). The three images accompanying these terms follow a strategy widely adopted in this book by illustrating the general subject of the entry rather than a particular phrase in the text. The dill plant and the bird are simply held by two men, while the written appeal is shown as a courtroom hearing, doubtless adapted from a standard image in a legal text. An exceptional illustration was provided for the entry for England (*Anglia*). Unlike other images of geographical terms, which were usually limited to isolated buildings, it depicts a king with his herald presenting the royal insignia (pictured). The

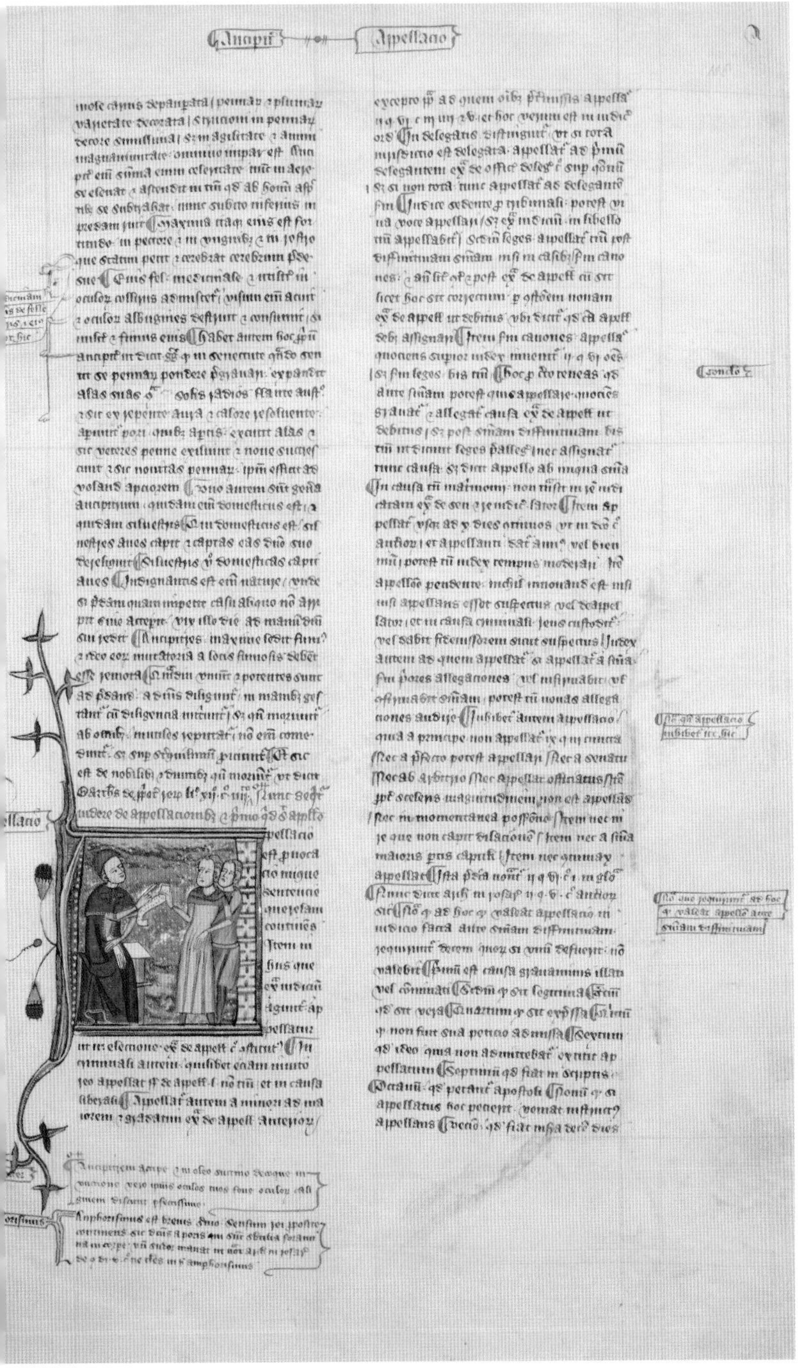

King of England, illustrating *Anglia*, f. 107 (detail)

insignia include a sceptre and the arms of England quartered with France, in a version first adopted by Edward III in 1340.

The identity of the author of the *Omne bonum*, who called himself James in the preface, was unknown to scholars until Sandler identified the scribe of the Royal manuscript with the hand of the *Gospel Commentary* of William of Nottingham (Oxford, Bodleian Library, MS Laud misc. 165) written by a certain James le Palmer for his own use. Le Palmer (b. 1327) was appointed king's clerk in the Exchequer by 1359 and is mentioned in numerous documents until 1375, when he was granted a pension by Edward III. He must have been working on his text while he held the Exchequer office in London. His numerous notes inserted in the margins of the Royal manuscript refer to his colleagues, as well as to other local issues concerning merchants of London, canons of St Paul's or monks of Westminster. Whereas a later owner made an attempt to complete the illustrative programme by employing two new artists in *c.*1380, no writer completed James's text. James's failure to finish his ambitious work may explain why the *Omne bonum* was never disseminated.

The *Omne bonum* was never dedicated to a king or intended for a royal audience. James le Palmer addressed it 'for the instruction of whichever simple individuals who wish to seek out the precious pearls of learning' (f. 18v), and the book found its way into the royal library only under Henry VIII. The 'TC' monogram added on the first page and read by Carley (1997) as 'Thomas Cardinalis' suggests that the manuscript belonged to Cardinal Thomas Wolsey (d. 1530), who might have acquired it from one of the religious houses in or around London.

J.F.

PROVENANCE:

Cardinal Thomas Wolsey (b. 1470/1, d. 1530); Henry VIII.

asia
affrica
europa
Playde de nostre seigneur nous dirons briefment aulcunes choses generalement des pties de la terre par lesquelles est le monde divise non mie toutesfois de chascune mais seulement de celles dont la sainte escripture fait mension. Le monde est divise en trois parties comme dist ysidore ou xv.e livre Car une partie est appellee asie lautre europe et la m.e affriq Lesquelles trois parties les
anciens nont point divise equalement Car asie vient de midi par orient jusques en septentrion Europe de septentrion en occident Mais affrique doccident par midi sestend Seule asie contient une partie de nostre habitable cest ass la moitie affrique et europe sortissent lautre partie. Entre ces parties la grande mer progresse yelles doccean car il est entrefeable Pourquoy se tu divises le mōde en deux parties dorient et occident En une partie

93 *Livre des proprietez des choses*

(Bartholomaeus Anglicus, *De proprietatibus rerum*, translated into French by Jean Corbechon)

Bruges, 1482
470 x 330 mm

BRITISH LIBRARY, ROYAL 15 E. iii

Bartholomaeus Anglicus (b. *c.* 1203, d. 1272) wrote his encyclopaedia of theology, natural history and science, *De proprietatibus rerum* (On the Properties of Things) *c.* 1245, while he was a lector in the Franciscan convent at Magdeburg. His work soon became a 'bestseller' among preachers and in 1284 was included in the list of books on offer from university stationers in Paris. A century later, in 1372, Jean Corbechon, Parisian scholar and chaplain to the King, translated Bartholomaeus's encyclopaedia into French and dedicated it to Charles V of France, who was famous for his love of knowledge, his impressive library and the number of translations he commissioned. As Corbechon explained in his prologue, this book 'which is like a general *summa* of all matters' was designed as a digest of all accessible knowledge for the King, whose duties did not allow him to spend enough time studying.

In contrast to its rarely illustrated Latin source, the *Livre des proprietez des choses* was often illuminated with a pictorial cycle. As in the present manuscript and its companion volume (Royal 15 E. ii), the miniatures announce the subject of each text division. The page reproduced here (f. 67v) includes the illustration for book fifteen, 'On the provinces and countries'. It illustrates Isidore of Seville's division of the world into three parts, Asia, Europe and Africa, which is discussed in the first chapter. Instead of a simple 'T–O' map that traditionally illustrated Isidore's description (see cat. no. 88), a tripartite miniature depicts each continent as a complex mountainous landscape with numerous castles; only Africa is differentiated, by its black inhabitants.

The Royal manuscript is a late copy of Corbechon's translation. It probably belonged to Edward IV, although the royal arms of England included in the frontispiece of its first volume are not augmented by any other heraldic device of the Yorkist King. The book was copied in Bruges in 1482 by Jean Du Ries, a scribe who also wrote two other manuscripts for Edward (Royal 14 E. vi and cat. no. 53), and responded well to the King's taste for deluxe Flemish manuscripts.

Edward was focused mainly on acquiring historical works, but he also owned a few books of instruction and general knowledge – such as the *Secretum secretorum* acquired at an early age (Royal 12 E. xv), the *Rustican* of Petrus de Crescentiis also copied by Du Ries (Royal 14 E. vi) and the *Speculum historiale* of Vincent of Beauvais in the French translation of Jean de Vignay (cat. no. 57). The choice of the *Livre des proprietez des choses* may have been inspired by the example of the Burgundian court, where translations once commissioned by Charles V circulated widely. Philip the Good, Duke of Burgundy, inherited a copy of Corbechon's translation from his grandfather, Philip the Bold (Brussels, KBR, MS 9094), and owned two manuscripts of Bartholomaeus's Latin text (one is now Brussels, KBR, MS 9743). Also Louis of Gruuthuse (d. 1492), a Burgundian courtier and bibliophile who played a role in shaping Edward's taste and guiding his acquisitions of manuscripts, acquired a lavishly illuminated copy of the *Livre* (Paris, BnF, MS fr. 134) a decade earlier than the English king.

As in several other manuscripts made for Edward IV, work on the illumination of the Royal *Livre* was shared by a group of subcontracted artists. At least two painters, the Master of Edward IV (Royal 15 E. iii, ff. 200, 269) and a follower of the Master of the Flemish Boethius, who worked with an assistant and contributed to the majority of illustrations, are recognizable in other books for Edward (respectively cat. no. 54 and Royal 15 E. i). Another illuminator is close in style to the Master of the White Inscriptions (vol. 1, f. 7), a craftsman involved in a number of commissions of the English King (see cat. nos. 48, 51, 57, 58, 60–62, 77). Such collaboration appears to reflect an effort by the volume's producers to bring it to a quick completion.

The most puzzling aspect of the Royal *Livre* is the contribution of the artist of the opening miniature of the second volume (Royal 15 E. iii, f. 11), whom Winkler (1925) named the Bruges Master of 1482 after the present manuscript. His works, including several books for Louis of Gruuthuse, date from the last two decades of the fifteenth century (Hans-Collas and Schandel 2009). The Master of 1482's intervention might, therefore, have postdated Edward's death. The leaf that bears the miniature painted by him appears not to have originally formed part of the book, but probably replaced one that was previously excised. It was pasted into the first quire of book twelve and its text was supplied by a different scribe. It is difficult to determine when and why this alteration occurred as its decoration does not include any heraldic device or reference to the owner of the book.

J.F.

PROVENANCE:

Edward IV (?); Henry VIII.

Opposite:
Map of the world, f. 67v

94 Maps of an Itinerary from London to Apulia in Italy, and Maps of the Holy Land and Britain

St Albans, *c.* 1250
360 x 245 mm

BRITISH LIBRARY, ROYAL 14 C. vii, ff. 2–5v

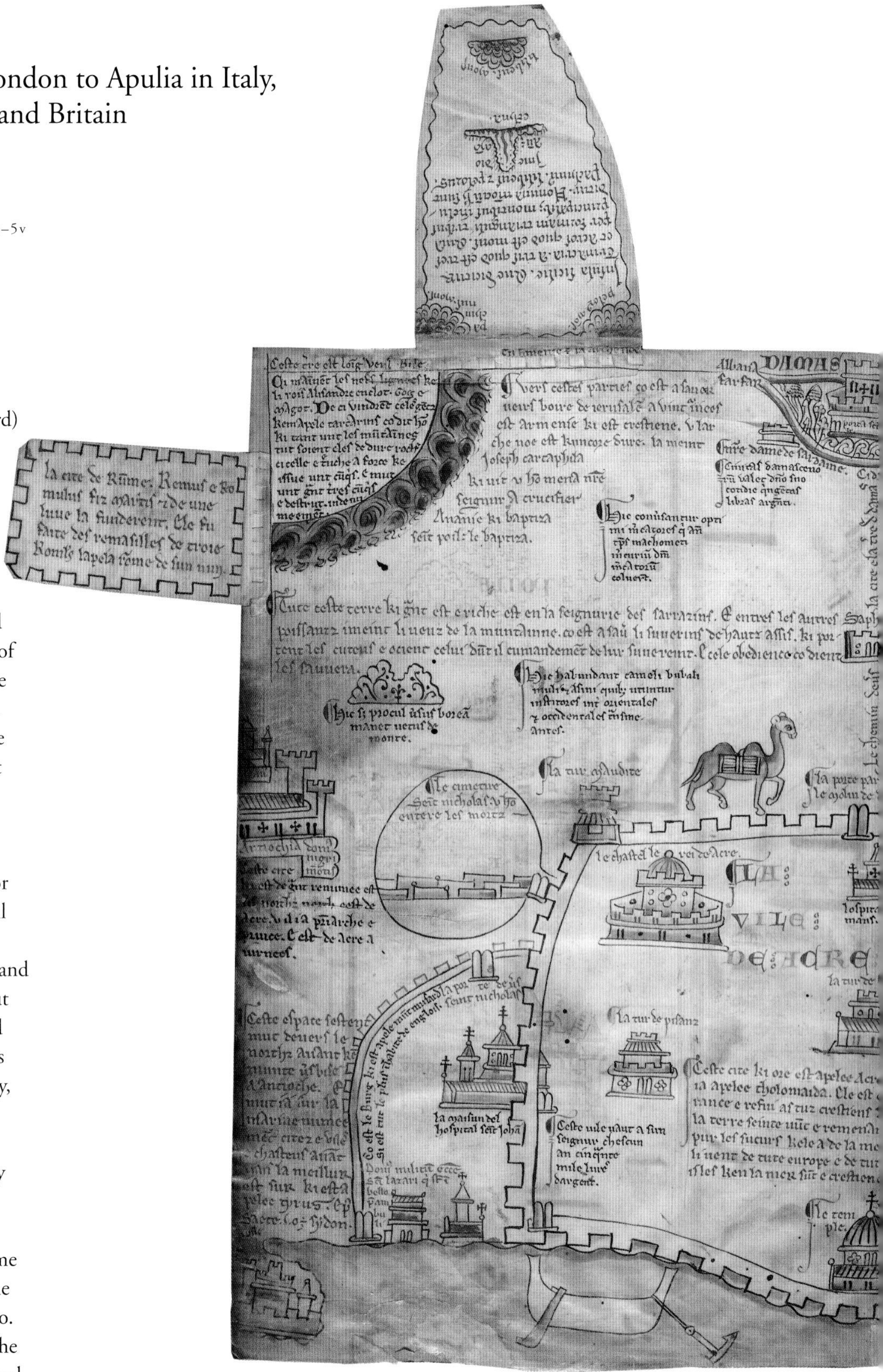

Map of the Holy land, ff. 4v–5

Matthew Paris is one of only two thirteenth-century English illuminators (the other is William de Brailes of Oxford) whose works survive and whose life can be sketched out. Although the date of Matthew's birth is unknown, evidence indicates that he joined the Benedictine monastery of St Albans in 1217, assumed the role of historian and writer in residence during the 1230s and went on to produce an impressive body of work – much of which, unusually for the time, he personally wrote and illustrated – before his death in, or shortly after, the summer of 1259 (Vaughan 1958). Apart from several journeys within England, he seems to have left the kingdom only once, when he visited Norway in 1248; otherwise he resided in the monastery for all of his adult life. In this context it is all the more remarkable that Matthew was responsible for not only several detailed and surprisingly accurate maps of Britain, but also a series of remarkably well-informed itineraries showing the route for pilgrims travelling from London to Apulia in Italy, which culminate in a map of the Holy Land.

Of the several versions of the itinerary that survive (Lewis 1987), the one reproduced here – which until recently was bound at the beginning of the volume containing the *Historia Anglorum* and the third part of the *Chronica maiora (*cat. no. 114) – is arguably the finest. Although the itinerary becomes increasingly complicated as it progresses, its overall design is relatively straightforward. Two parallel columns that need to be read from lower to top left, then from lower to top right, show a series of towns and cities connected by a vertical line of colour, with notes in red concerning the number of days required to complete each section (typically given as 'jurnee', meaning one day). Clustered around the drawings of the various staging posts, Matthew also inserted a number of informative comments dealing with topics such as history and topography. The map of Palestine, however, is in a more conventional medieval form, consisting of a bird's-eye view of the principal sights spread over a double opening, with buildings, animals and other objects in elevation, and orientated so as to show east at the top (pictured). On the back of the last leaf is a globular and rather sketchy map of 'Britannia', which seems to have been added as an afterthought and is a poor example of his map-making skills.

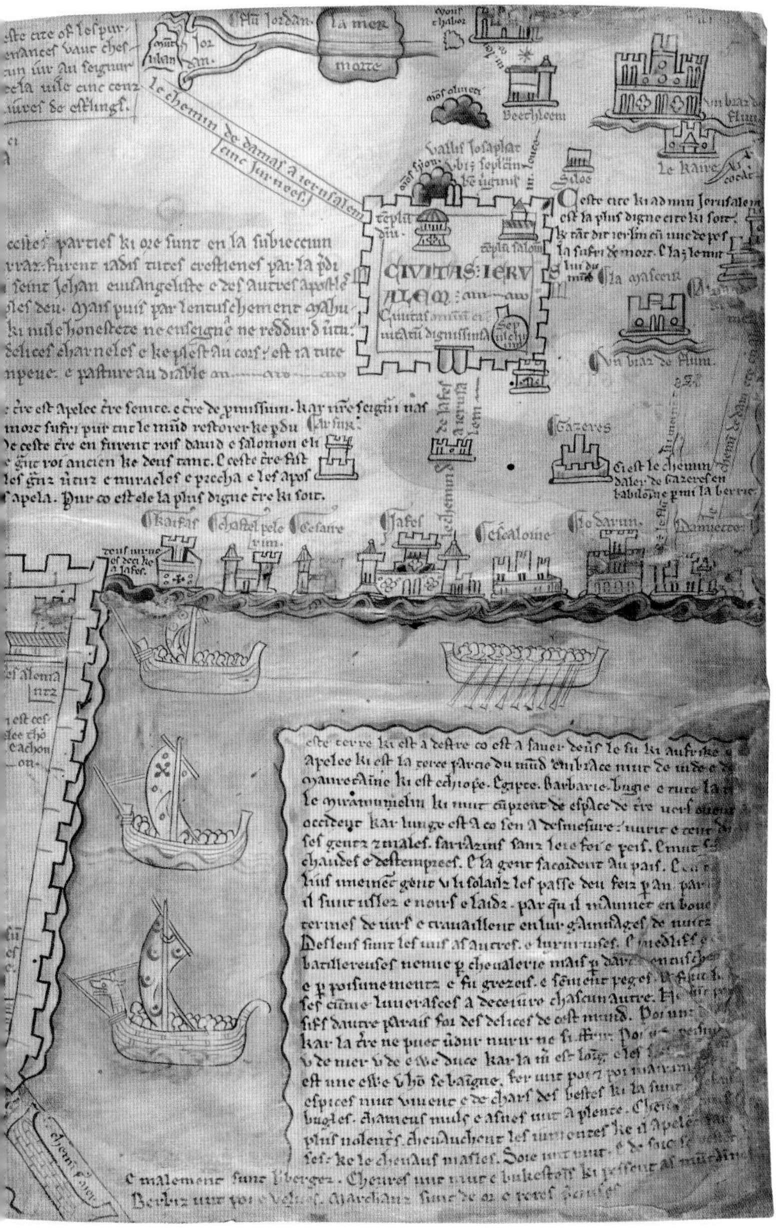

A recent study has emphasized the itinerary's function as a tool for the monks of St Albans to visualize a spiritually rewarding journey to Jerusalem that they were unable to undertake owing to their monastic vows and commitments (Connolly 2009). Although this may have been one of the primary ways in which the monks of St Albans made use of the itinerary, considerable prominence is afforded to the Crusader Kingdom of Acre – in the centre of the Palestine map – whereas Jerusalem, the more obvious focus for an imaginary pilgrim, occupies a smaller space in the upper portion of the right-hand side. Such a balance suggests that Matthew may have been inspired as much by the political realities of the mid-thirteenth century as by biblical events when he created his itineraries. Indeed, because one complete copy of the itinerary and Palestine map, and a fragment of another, preface the two volumes of Matthew's *Chronica maiora* now in Cambridge (Corpus Christi College, MSS 26 and 16), it is tempting to conclude that Matthew designed them as historical, rather than predominantly spiritual, itineraries.

It is clear that a Benedictine monk, who mainly lived his life within the confines of the monastery at St Albans, was capable of drawing a detailed set of maps that reveals a remarkable knowledge of the world beyond his personal experience. The places and journey times recorded in the itinerary are generally accurate, and details such as the stork perching on the building representing the Italian town of Sutri suggest an origin in personal observation. When one considers that St Albans was part of an order with houses throughout Europe, and that Matthew reveals in his writings that he was acquainted with visitors who had knowledge of Armenia, Palestine, Germany, Flanders and Castile, the accuracy of his maps becomes more understandable. Even so, they bear remarkable witness to the way in which accurate information could be transferred and recorded during the Middle Ages. *J.C.*

PROVENANCE:

Humfrey, Duke of Gloucester (b. 1391, d. 1447); John Russell, Bishop of Lincoln (d. 1494); Henry VIII; lent to Henry Fitzalan, 12th Earl of Arundel (b. 1511, d. 1580); John, 1st Baron Lumley (d. 1609); Henry Frederick, Prince of Wales (d. 1612).

95 Jean Rotz, *Boke of Idrography* ('The Rotz Atlas')

Dieppe and England, *c.* 1535–42
570 x 380 mm

BRITISH LIBRARY, ROYAL 20 E. ix

Chart of the coast of Brazil with a village of the Tupinambá tribe, ff. 27v–28

Some time between 1536 and 1540 Jean Rotz, a hydrographer and navigator from Dieppe, started work on a maritime atlas of the known world that he intended to present to Francis I. However, when the French King appointed Rotz's Portuguese rival, João Pacheco, as a royal hydrographer, the disappointed Rotz decided to offer his services to Henry VIII instead. He was doubtless attracted by the high salaries that Henry was ready to pay to foreign naval experts. In 1542 Rotz presented the English King with an instrument of his own invention, the 'differential quadrant', and a treatise describing its use (Royal 20 B. vii). His gift was accepted and when in the same year he offered to Henry his newly accomplished atlas, now entitled the *Boke of Idrography* and supplied with Tudor badges and legends in English, he could already call himself a servant to the King.

The Rotz Atlas is made of large sheets of parchment folded centrally to form double-page openings on which eleven regional charts and a hemispheric map of the world are depicted. The charts are preceded by explanations and diagrams on how to use a compass, calculate the elevation of the North Pole and determine latitude. Rotz copied his atlas from a large map of the world because, as he argued, such a book was 'more convenient to handle and to look at than a single chart four or five yards in length'. The names of numerous geographical places included in Rotz's book suggest that his model was in Portuguese. Portuguese and Spanish hydrographers, more experienced in navigation than the French, built on the medieval tradition of portolan charts (from the Italian *portolano* – relating to a port) which depicted coastlines and harbours of the Mediterranean, by including geographical discoveries of the fifteenth and sixteenth centuries. Although such maps were considered secret documents of state in Portugal and Spain, several charts may have made their way to Dieppe, one of the most important maritime ports in Europe in Rotz's times. There is also evidence of Portuguese hydrographers working in the Norman town. Among six extant portolan atlases produced there, two were made by anonymous Portuguese hydrographers, one for Henry, Dauphin of France (1536–47) (The Hague, KB, MS 129 A 24) and the other for Nicolas Vallard of Dieppe in 1547 (San Marino, Huntington Library, MS HM 29). Several similarities between them and the Rotz Atlas suggest common sources. The Portuguese influence was a distinctive

feature of what became known as the Dieppe school of cartography, of which the Rotz Atlas is the earliest surviving work.

Rotz hoped his gift to Henry VIII would provide a 'recreation of the king's mind' and a tool to learn some principles of navigation and to discover the countries of the world and their inhabitants. The inscriptions of geographical names and depictions of coastlines incorporate the most recent additions to geographical knowledge resulting from Portuguese and Norman voyages, but what is most remarkable about the atlas is the profusion of illustrations related to each continent. Although the insertion of pictures of geographical places and their inhabitants was a common feature of medieval *mappae mundi*, Rotz's images with their ethnographical accuracy were, like their Portuguese models, shaped by a new Renaissance spirit of observation. The images illustrate curiosities and local habits reported by maritime sailors, such as a rajah's procession in Sumatra, the story of three members of the Parmentier brothers' expedition of 1529 killed in Madagascar, Hottentots of southern Africa wearing lion skins and the native North Americans and their *tipi*s.

The map reproduced here depicts the coast of Brazil from the Strait of Magellan in the south to the Cape of St Augustine in the north (south is represented at the top, according to the common practice of the time). A vivid image incorporated in the chart records the gathering of the main object of European trade in Brazil: brazilwood, used to produce a red dye for the cloth industry in France and the Netherlands. The map also depicts with ethnographical precision a fortified village and several activities of the Tupinambá tribe: a ritual dance, battle and killing of a captive – who is subsequently dismembered, grilled and eaten. It is possible that some details of Rotz's illustration were based on his experiences during a voyage to Brazil in 1539.

At the time of Rotz's arrival in England, English exploration of the New World had not yet begun. Although included in the Old Royal library by the middle of the sixteenth century, the *Boke of Idrography* was overlooked by Elizabethan geographers and explorers and never influenced English plans for overseas ventures. *J.F.*

PROVENANCE:

Henry VIII.

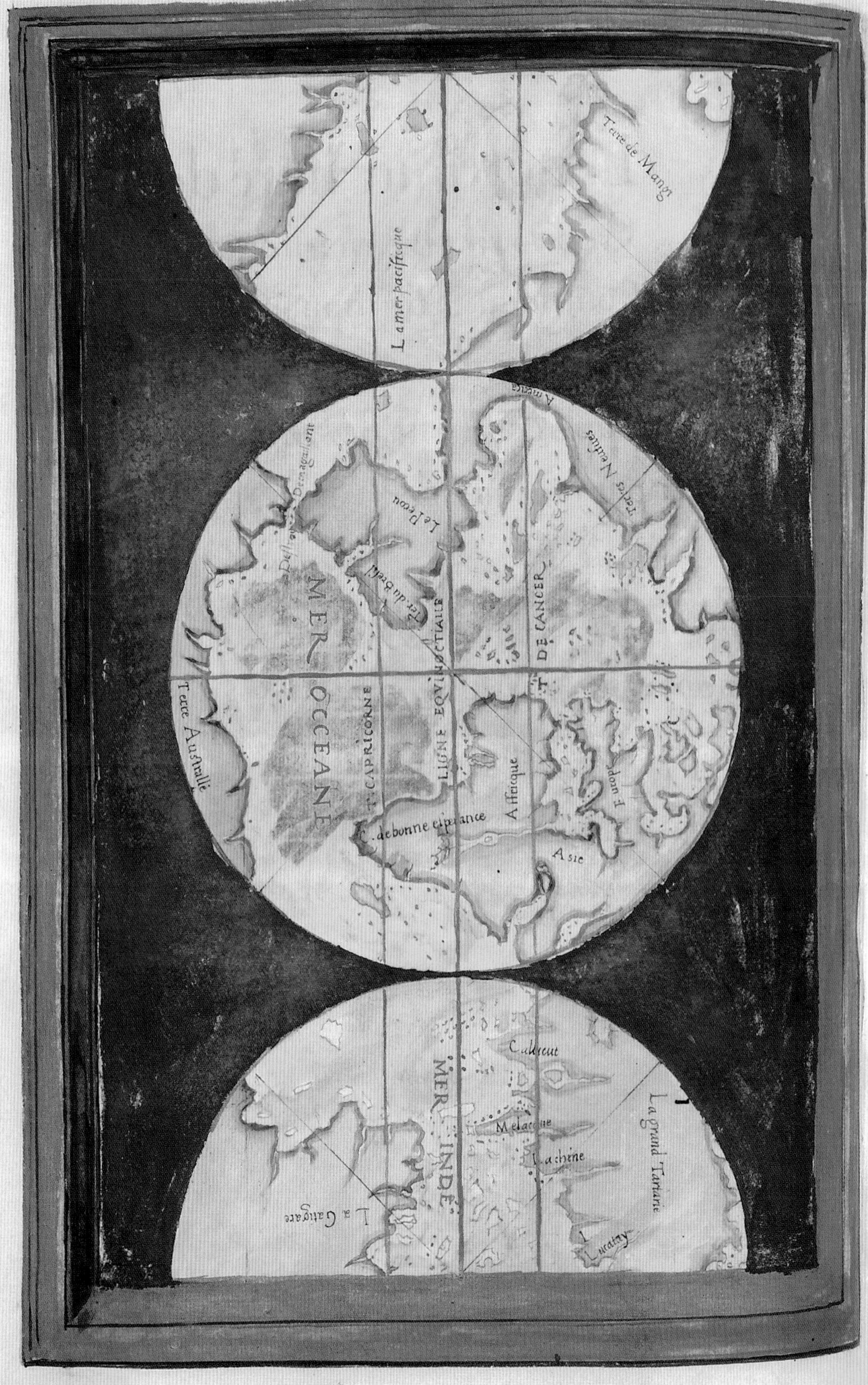
Terre de Mangi
La mer pacifique
MER OCCEANE
LIGNE EQUINOCTIALE
DE CANCER
CAPRICORNE
Terre Australle
Affrique
Asie
MER INDE
La grand Tartarie

96 Jean Mallard, *Le Premier Livre de la cosmograpphie en rhetorique francoyse*

London, *c.* 1540
265 x 180 mm

BRITISH LIBRARY, ROYAL 20 B. xii

Like his personalized Psalter (cat. no. 45), this manuscript was written and illuminated for Henry VIII by the Frenchman Jean Mallard (b. *c.* 1515). Unlike in the Psalter, Mallard was also the author of this text in verse, a 'recycled' poem on cosmography and navigation that Mallard had previously presented to Francis I of France (Cooper 2003; Carley 2009). Although Mallard's poem was an original work, he based it on a pilot's guide or portolan by Jean Alfonce de Saintonge, itself a French version of the *Suma de Geographia* (Taylor 1930; on portalans see cat. no. 95). Mallard's book, the only one completed of a projected four volumes, describes the coasts of Spain, France, Britain, northern Germany and South America to the Strait of Magellan (Cooper 2003; Taylor 1930).

Mallard included an original and intriguing map of the hemispheres to illustrate his text, which encompasses a much greater area than that discussed in the poem. Running through the central and two half-spheres are three vertical gold lines, identified as the Tropic of Capricorn to the left, the Equator in the centre, and the Tropic of Cancer to the right. Although not labelled, the single horizontal line must be the Prime Meridian, identifying zero degrees longitude and dividing the world into the eastern (below the line) and western (above the line) hemispheres. The map is oriented with west at the top, rather than north, perhaps to fit this extended view on the page. The eastern hemisphere contains large land masses labelled Africa, Asia and Europe, with *C. de bonne esperance* (Cape of Good Hope) also noted prominently. In the western hemisphere Brazil and Peru are identified in South America, with *America* just visible at the top of the central map, as well as the Strait of Magellan, mentioned in the text. The continent at the far left of this central sphere is the fabled great *Terra Australle* (southern land). The half-sphere at the top is a continuation of the western hemisphere (the Pacific Ocean is included), and the lower half map continues with the Indian Ocean, with Asia marked as *La grand Tartarie.*

In the dedicatory preface and on the title-page Mallard explicitly identifies both the script and the illumination as his own work. He states that he has written the work 'avec ma main qui peult escrire & paindre comme voyez dedans ce livre ouvert' (with my hand which can write and paint as you see in this open book) (f. 2). On the title-page he identifies himself as an 'Escripvain, Cosmographe et Mathematicien' and notes that he has 'apres reduyt par luy mesmes en figure' (f. 4), the figure presumably being the map itself. The King was sufficiently satisfied with the gift and Mallard's work to appoint him as an 'an orator or [blank] in the Frenche tongue' at a salary of £10 a year from Christmas 1539 to March 1541 (Carley 2009). At the end of his preface Mallard states that he, a Frenchman, would like to become English to serve Henry: 'Et vous servir dont ie qui fuys Francoys Pour y entrer ie me souhaitte Angloys' (f. 3). As happened with the hydrographer Jean Rotz (see cat. no. 95), Mallard's disappointment at the French court enriched Henry's and in turn the scientific collections of the Old Royal library. *K.D.*

PROVENANCE:
Henry VIII.

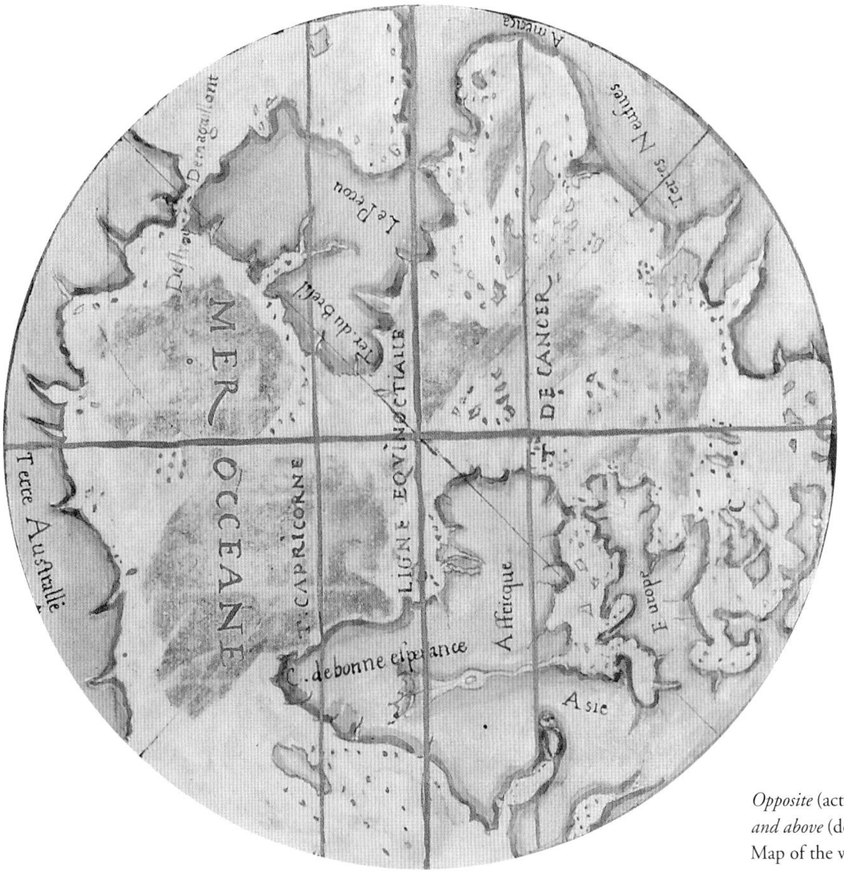

Opposite (actual size) *and above* (detail): Map of the world, f. 4v

97 *Liber iudiciorum*

London (?), *c.* 1391–1410
220 x 150 mm

BRITISH LIBRARY, ROYAL 12 C. v

Geomantic figures, *Rubeus* and *Tristicia*, with a table of their natures and properties, ff. 21v–22

The *Liber iudiciorum,* which was composed in 1391 for Richard II, is a handbook of geomancy. This Arabic 'scientific' technique of divination, the name of which means literally 'foresight by earth', involved drawing, originally in sand, and interpreting a series of dots arranged in sixteen figures. Richard may have had a particular interest in 'occult' sciences; his opponents, such as the chronicler Thomas Walsingham, recorded that he used to surround himself with 'pseudo-prophets' and 'sorcerers'. On the other hand, Richard may have simply followed an international courtly fashion. Several of his contemporaries owned books on the art of geomancy, amongst them the Holy Roman Emperor Wenceslaus II and Charles V of France.

Richard's handbook of geomancy is an anonymous compilation based on a treatise by William of Moerbeke (d. 1286). What makes it exceptional is a series of personified representations of the geomantic figures, which form a visual index to the tables used for specific predictions. The illustrations are arranged in pairs and depict the 'Table of figural images with their nature and properties'. Each image includes one of the sixteen combinations of dots and a man whose clothes, attributes, or gestures are linked to a name traditionally given to a relevant figure, or to an extended signification derived from the interpretation of that name in geomantic practice. In the miniature reproduced a man in red corresponds to the geomantic name *Rubeus* (red), but the knife he points at his throat reveals murder as a secondary meaning of this figure. *Rubeus* is paired with *Tristicia* (Sadness), a man in blue who makes a gesture usually associated with fear and refers perhaps to death and misery, also symbolized by this geomantic figure.

Each image is correlated with a table listing its name, governing planet, corresponding sign of the zodiac, element, humour and season, quality, colour, etc. This illustrated index is followed by tables deriving from the work of the Arabic writer Abdallah (d. 1265). Abdallah's tables show possible combinations of the figures used to answer the twenty-five general questions that may be asked by a geomancer, such as whether a traveller will return from his journey, or a pregnant woman will give birth to a son, together with around 3200 possible answers to these questions.

The only reference in the Royal manuscript to Richard II as the commissioner of the *Liber iudiciorum* is a Latin

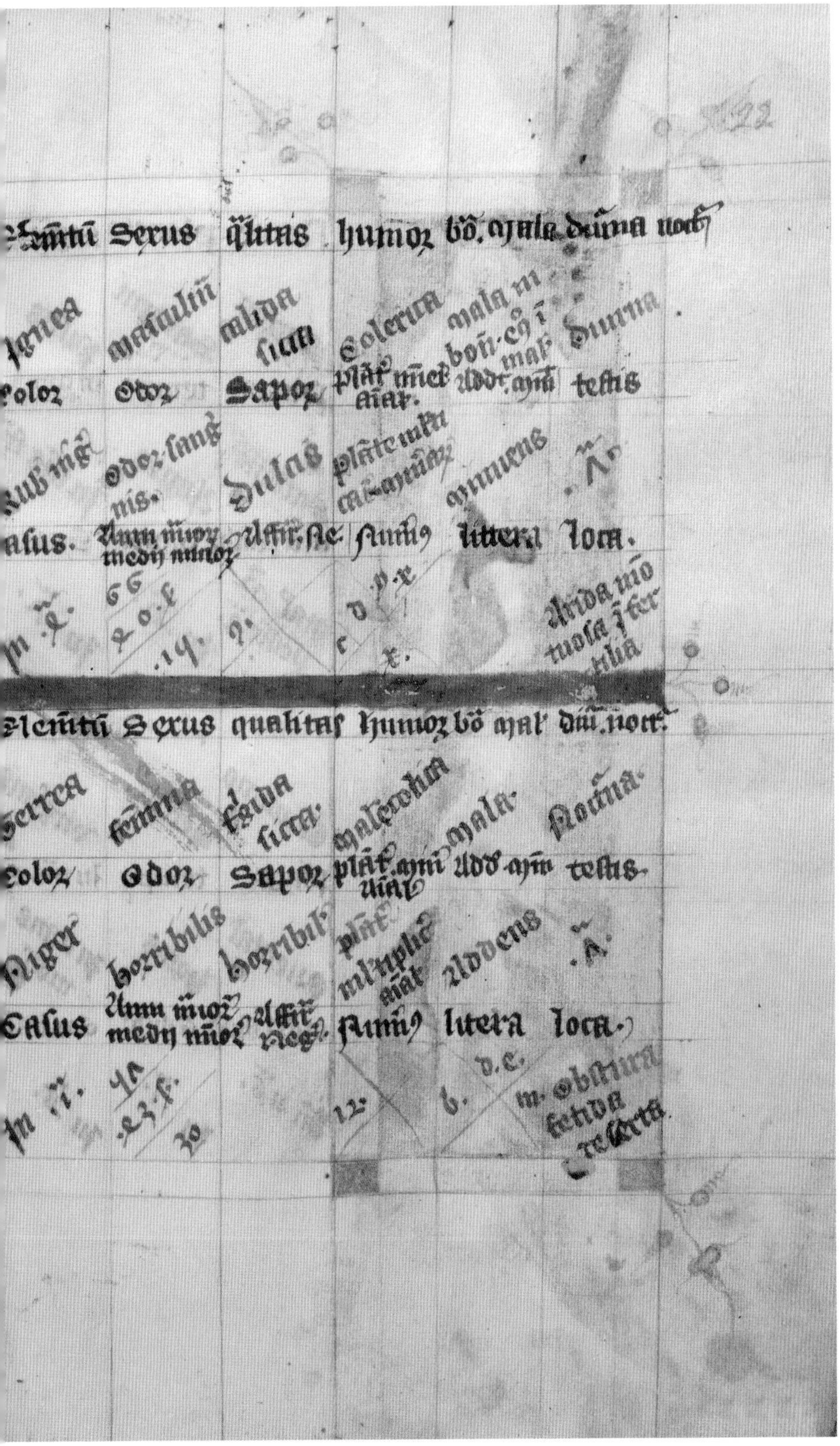

note, contemporary to the text, added on a flyleaf, reading 'the book of King Richard II that he had made at his personal instigation in the fourteenth year of his reign in England and France'. It is unlikely, however, that the note records the context of production of this book as all other references to Richard have been deliberately omitted from its prologue. This alteration becomes clear when the text of the Royal copy is compared with the only other extant version (Oxford, Bodleian Library, MS Bodley 581).

The Oxford manuscript is a higher quality book, illuminated by the artist, who also illustrated a compilation of royal documents that includes a description of Richard II's coronation (cat. no. 121). The Oxford *Liber iudiciorum* constitutes only a part of a larger collection of texts. It starts with the *De quadripartite regis specie,* an abridged version of the *Secretum secretorum,* addressed to Richard II by an anonymous Irish clerk, and continues with the *Physionomia Aristotelis* and the *Sompniale Danielis.* The Oxford *Liber*, dated and dedicated to the King, is illustrated by Richard's portrait and a series of geomantic figures closely resembling the illustrations of the Royal copy. Finally, this book has appended another text of a clear Ricardian reference, the *Rosarium regis Ricardi de signis.* It has been suggested that the Oxford manuscript was the King's presentation copy (Sandler 1986, Eberle 1999). If so, the Royal *Liber* may be its direct or indirect descendant. The omission of the dedication to Richard in the Royal manuscript may have resulted from an attempt to adapt the book for another reader or, even more likely, to obliterate any record of the King after his deposition in 1399.

We do not know for whom the manuscript was originally intended. The earliest evidence of its provenance is a fifteenth-century monogram 'HVP' with a Franco-Flemish motto 'Ich byn dyn. Tout pour le meuz'. A request for prayer inscribed by William Meddleton suggests that he may have been its late fifteenth-century owner. The manuscript came to the Royal collection through Lord Lumley, who obtained it from his brother-in-law, the antiquary Humphrey Lloyd. *J.F.*

PROVENANCE:

William Meddleton (?), late 15th century; Humphrey Lloyd (b. *c.* 1527, d. 1568); John, 1st Baron Lumley (d. 1609); Henry Frederick, Prince of Wales (d. 1612).

98 William Parron, *Liber de optimo fato Henrici Eboraci ducis et optimorum ipsius parentum*

London (?), 1502–03
190 x 130 mm

BRITISH LIBRARY, ROYAL 12 B. vi

The *Liber de optimo fato Henrici Eboraci ducis et optimorum ipsius parentum* (the Book on the High Good Fortune awaiting Henry, Duke of York, and likewise his parents) was written in 1502 by William Parron. It is likely that the author presented his text to Henry VII on New Year's Day, to console them for the death of Prince Arthur (2 April 1502). William Parron of Piacenza (b. *c.* 1461, d. *c.* 1503) was a professional astrologer who introduced to England the continental fashion for printed almanacs, or *prognosticones*, containing general predictions for an incoming year, and 'democratized' the formerly exclusive royal art of astrology by addressing them to a wider public. At the same time, with his special manuscript publications addressed to Henry VII, he attempted to secure the long-term patronage of the King, whose interests in astrology must have been widely known and are still particularly well documented (see cat. no. 99).

The *Liber de optimo fato* followed Parron's first publication, the *De astrorum vi fatali*, which was presented to Henry in 1499 (now Oxford, Bodleian Library, MS Selden supra 77) but did not share its success. Parron knew that predicting the future to a monarch was a dangerous undertaking, and chose in his new book to tell his patron what the latter wished to hear. However, he went too far. His revelations of a bright future for Prince Henry, the King's younger son and the new successor to the throne – as a devoted servant of the Church, victorious monarch, and happily married father to a large number of sons – may have comforted the grieving parents. Yet, his prediction that Henry VII's consort, Elizabeth of York, would live to the age of at least eighty cost him his position at the court when the thirty-seven-year-old Queen died within less than a year of Parron's predictions on 11 February 1503.

The Royal copy of Parron's book of prognostications opens with a full-page miniature laid out like a horoscope in the traditional square format. An identical image was depicted by the same artist in a twin copy of the same text addressed to Henry, Duke of York (Paris, BnF, MS lat. 6276). The Paris copy contains a note explaining this unusual iconography: first, there is the horoscope, or picture of the sky at the moment of the creation of the world, in the form of an astrological chart divided into twelve fixed places or 'houses', with the signs of the zodiac and planets in their relevant positions on that day. Second, a series of scenes indicates the significance of each house in the sky for a specific area of life on Earth. This sequence is indebted to the classical Greek theory of *Dodecatropos* (twelve-direction), and starts on the left with the house of life (*vita*), illustrated by a nativity scene. It then moves counter-clockwise to the house of wealth and commerce (*lucrum*), brothers (*fratres*), parents and family (*parentes*), children or guests (*filii, hospites*), health (*valitudo*), marriage or danger (*nuptiae* or *pericula*), death (*mors*), travel and religion (*peregrinationes*), honours (*honores*), friends (*amici*), and enemies (*inimici*). The third component is a map of the world with personifications of the four winds, depicted in the middle of the chart, where astrologers traditionally put the name and the date of birth of the person for whom the horoscope was intended. The imposing image of a monarch illustrating the house of Honours at the top of the diagram suggests the influence exercised by royal power over the future of the world, and could have been related by a contemporary reader to the anticipated role of the future King Henry VIII. A similar image of royal majesty appears at the beginning of the preface that faces the dedication to Henry VII; this time it portrays the reigning King.

Despite his rather average skills, the artist who illuminated both presentation copies of the *Liber de optimo fato* must have been well regarded by Parron for his ability to capture in illustrative form the complicated astrological concepts of the text. He also decorated the dedication copy of Parron's *De astrorum vi fatali* in Oxford. Scott (1996) named him the 'Placentius Master' after the author of the three volumes ('Placentius' means 'of Piacenza' and refers to Parron's possible place of birth). The Master's flat, simplistic and rather crude style, close to a group of commercially produced manuscripts of the *Statuta nova* (see cat. no. 124), is typical of Henry VII's books, which seem to have been collected more to gratify his personal interests than for display. *J.F.*

PROVENANCE:

Henry VII.

Opposite:
Horoscope diagram: Aspects of life associated with the twelve astrological houses, f. 1 (actual size)

12 B vi. p. 199.
MVSEVM
BRITAN
NICVM

99 Collection of Astrological Treatises

London (?), 1490
440 x 300 mm

BRITISH LIBRARY, ARUNDEL 66

Above:
Constellation Draco, f. 33v (detail)

Opposite:
Henry VII and his courtiers discussing a book of astrology with a French ambassador, f. 201

This manuscript is one of the most exceptional and sophisticated collections of astrological texts composed for an English monarch. It combines works of so-called judicial astrology, based on calculations of movements of the planets and stars, with political prophecies popular in England since at least the time of Geoffrey of Monmouth (d. 1154/5). Each major part of the manuscript was written by a different scribe and illuminated by a different artist, but the uniform layout and the use of the same pen-flourished pattern throughout the volume suggest that from the beginning it was designed as one collection.

The main text included in the manuscript is a popular compilation on astrological practice, the *Liber astronomiae* (Book of Astronomy) by Guido Bonatti of Forlì (b. *c.* 1207, d. *c.* 1296). An informal note at the end of this text informs us that Bonatti's treatise was 'compositus et renovatus' (assembled and brought up to date) by John Wellys on 30 June 1490 (f. 249). Wellys is perhaps identifiable as John Willis, doctor of medicine, who was noted in the Cambridge Grace Book between 1456 and 1480 and whose works were quoted by the royal physician John Argentine (d. 1508) (see Talbot and Hammond 1965). The *Liber astronomiae* is preceded by two sets of astronomical tables composed for astrological use. The first work, the planetary tables by John Killingworth (d. 1445), astronomer and mathematician of Merton College, Oxford, is an adaptation of the tables completed under the patronage of Alfonso X, King of Castile and León (b. 1221, d. 1284). The second work consists of illustrated tables of constellations that, according to its colophon, were verified in 1449 by astrologers of both Alfonso, King of Aragon and Naples (b. 1396, d. 1458) and Humfrey, Duke of Gloucester. The manuscript also contains another item associated with Duke Humfrey's name: the geomantic tables appended to the *Liber arenalis*, a Latin translation of the geomancy of Alpharinus by Plato of Tivoli (*c.* 1138). The volume ends with a collection of prophecies concerning English monarchs.

The manuscript was almost certainly intended for Henry VII. Several initials decorated with either red or red-and-white roses refer to the union of the houses of Lancaster and York under the Tudor King. Even the constellation of Draco in the astronomical tables (f. 33v, pictured) is depicted as the Red Dragon, symbol of Cadwaladr ap Cadwallon (d. 664/82), the supposed 'last king of the Britons', set on a ground of the Tudor livery colours of green and white, as was used on Henry's standard at the Battle of Bosworth. The motif of the dragon also appears in three of the volume's decorated initials, and in two prophecies of Merlin Ambrosius and Merlin Silvestris that are included at the end of the manuscript. These ancient prophecies of the Red Dragon, symbol of the Britons, overturning the White Dragon of the Saxons were fulfilled in the person of Henry VII, according to the King's official historian Bernard André.

A further political message is included in a portrait of the King (f. 201, pictured) painted by a skilful follower of the Bruges Master of 1482 who also illuminated the first volume of the *Grandes chroniques de France* designed as a gift for Henry VII (cat. no. 120). This frontispiece-type image is inserted at the beginning of the treatise 'On the Revolutions of the Year of the World' of the *Liber astronomiae*, where Bonatti explains the influence of the stars on worldly rulers, rather than at the beginning of the volume itself where it might have been expected. The image depicts Henry assisted by members of his court, including Archbishop John Morton, Lord Chancellor, and probably the Lord Great Chamberlain, John de Vere, 13th Earl of Oxford – distinguished by the collar of SS around his neck and the Sword of State in his hand. The King and another courtier, perhaps John Wellys, are showing a book to a French ambassador who holds an escutcheon bearing the royal arms of France as a sign of his mission. Given the date of the production of the manuscript, the image may refer to the negotiations for a perpetual peace between France and England initiated by the embassy of Charles de Marigny and Robert Gaguin in 1489 and broken off only in August 1490. The same concern for peace between the two kingdoms is echoed in the volume's inclusion of a pertinent vision of St Bridget of Sweden.

If the book was ever presented to the King to satisfy his astrological passion and contribute to his image as a peace-maker, it probably left the royal collection at an early date. It was not included in the 1542 inventory of Henry VIII's Upper Library at Westminster Palace. By 1667 it was among the books donated by the Duke of Norfolk to the Royal Society. *J.F.*

PROVENANCE:

Henry VII (?); Henry Howard), 6th Duke of Norfolk (b. 1628, d. 1684); Royal Society, London, 1667; purchased for the nation in 1831.

19 A v. p. 295
Jehan · chabot ·
COME IAI DIT

00 Aldobrandino of Siena, *Livre de physique* (*Régime du corps*)

Southern Netherlands, between 1494 and 1496
285 x 200 mm

BRITISH LIBRARY, ROYAL 19 A. v

The *Livre de physique* (Book of Medicine) was composed in the middle of the thirteenth century by Aldobrandino of Siena (d. *c.* 1296), an Italian physician active in the French city of Troyes. A treatise on hygiene and diet, it was compiled from several tracts of earlier Arabic authors. A prologue that was added to Aldobrandino's text between 1257 and 1261 and is preserved in six manuscripts claims that the *Livre* was originally intended for Beatrice of Savoy (d. 1267), Countess of Provence; other copies of the *Livre* attribute the patronage of the treatise to Louis IX of France, his mother Blanche or even the Emperor Frederick II (Féry-Hue 1987). Although Aldobrandino's royal connections may be apocryphal, his wish to achieve wider dissemination of medical knowledge to an extended lay audience is clear. His book, which was entitled the *Régime du corps* or *Régime de senté* by later scribes, was the first vernacular contribution to a Latin literary genre, the *regimina sanitatis* or rules for the preservation of health, that began to flourish in the thirteenth century. The four parts of Aldobrandino's work are devoted in sequence to general hygiene, specific care of particular organs, diet and physiognomy.

Extant in over seventy manuscripts, the *Livre de physique* is known from several abbreviated or modified versions. The Royal copy belongs to a group of seven manuscripts containing a version of the text that seems to have originated in the Low Countries. Five of these volumes date from *c.* 1470–80 (Royal 16 F. viii; Royal 20 B. ix; Royal 19 B. x; Additional 8863; and Oxford, St John's College, MS 68), and all – except the modest, unillustrated Additional manuscript – were illuminated in Bruges. The sixth manuscript (Sloane 3152), which was copied in Mechelen in 1492 and omits the last book of the *Livre,* is the closest in its textual and codicological features to the present copy of Aldobrandino's text.

The Royal *Livre de physique* is a paper manuscript of modest quality. A coloured drawing at the beginning of the text suggests, however, that the book was intended as a gift for a king. It depicts a knight wearing his heraldic tabard and identified by an inscription as 'Jehan Chabot, chevalier seigneur d'Eymalle' (Jean Chabot, knight, lord of Emæl) and by the motto 'comme j'ai dit' (as I said). The knight hands over the manuscript to a monarch whose throne is decorated with the royal arms of England. Given the date of production of the manuscript and the fact that the knight wears the Lancastrian livery collar of SS, the king is doubtless Henry VII. Henry, who asserted his descent from the house of Lancaster, reintroduced the collar after his accession as a badge for his supporters. Jean Chabot, the third son of Jean Chabot (d. 1454), alderman of Liège, must have presented his gift to the King after 1494 when he had inherited the estate of Emæl and before 1496 when he died. A member of a family involved in the political life of his country, Jean may have come to England on a diplomatic mission. Unfortunately no record of his visit at the English court has so far been identified.

Aldobrandino's treatise appears to have been a popular text in the circles of the Yorkist and Tudor royal courts. A copy was owned by a member of the Tunstall family, perhaps Thomas, a squire of the body to Richard III, or his son Cuthbert (Manchester, John Rylands University Library, MS French 7); and another manuscript that was made in Bruges in *c.* 1475–80 and entered the royal library at Westminster later passed to the Tudor courtier Thomas Boleyn (Lisbon, Biblioteca de Ajuda, MS 52.XIII.26). Three of the six manuscripts that are textually related to Henry VII's own copy were also eventually incorporated into Henry VIII's library. They were all illuminated by Bruges artists who worked on Edward IV's commissions and two of them (Royal 16 F. viii and Royal 19 B. x) were previously owned by members of the Tudor court – respectively Charles Somerset (d. 1526), Earl of Worcester, Henry VII's cousin and Vice-Chamberlain; and probably Henry Lovel (d. 1489), 8th Baron Morley, whose nephew Henry Parker was a protégé of Lady Margaret Beaufort. Henry VII, who also owned another copy of Aldobrandino's work (Cambridge, University Library, MS Ii.5.11), may have played a role in creating a fashion for this text in England. Judging from their extant books, Henry VII and his mother shared an interest in texts related to health. A handy collection of *regimina sanitatis* and tracts on the plague includes the arms of Lady Margaret Beaufort (Cambridge, Fitzwilliam Museum, MS 261), and Thomas Forestier's treatise on pestilence of 1485 is dedicated to Henry VII (see Additional 27582). Chabot's choice of gift appears to have corresponded well with the King's reading preferences. *J.F.*

PROVENANCE:

Henry VII.

Opposite:
Jean Chabot presenting the book to Henry VII, f. 1v

101 Smaragdus of St Mihiel, *Expositio in regulam S. Benedicti*

Canterbury (Christ Church), *c.* 1170–80
245 x 175 mm

BRITISH LIBRARY, ROYAL 10 A. xiii

This manuscript, a copy of a commentary on the Rule of St Benedict, composed *c.* 817 by Smaragdus, abbot of St-Mihiel-sur-Meuse, was written at the Benedictine cathedral priory of Christ Church, Canterbury, *c.* 1170. A single leaf, once detached from the volume, but presented here in its original position, bears a portrait of St Dunstan. Adviser to kings, Abbot of Glastonbury, and later Archbishop of Canterbury, Dunstan (d. 988) led the revival of Benedictine monasticism in tenth-century England; he was also a gifted artist and author. He is depicted at a lectern, writing the words: 'Obsculta, o fili, praecepta magistri' (Listen, my son, to the precepts of the master), the first line of the Benedictine Rule and Smaragdus's commentary alike. Now detached from the manuscript, the portrait was originally bound into the book so that it faced the first page of text, which is similarly inscribed 'Obsculta'. Whether by accident or design, the miniature creates the impression that Dunstan, not Smaragdus, is the author of the text.

By chance a mid-tenth-century copy of Smaragdus's commentary, with annotations in Dunstan's own hand, has survived (Cambridge, University Library, MS Ee.2.4; and Oxford, Bodleian Library, MS lat. th. c. 3, ff. 1, 1* and 2). This manuscript is so close in content to the one reproduced that it may well have served as its exemplar. If the scribe of the Royal manuscript had used as a model Dunstan's own copy of the commentary, complete with his annotations, he could have mistakenly assumed that Dunstan, not Smaragdus, was the author of the text. This misattribution may explain the frontispiece.

There was confusion regarding Dunstan's literary output. Anselm of Canterbury (d. 1109), for example, while still Prior at Bec in Normandy, thought that Dunstan had written a Rule of the monastic life. Anselm almost certainly had in mind the *Regularis concordia*, a guide for English monastic observance, which reflected Dunstan's ideas but was compiled, *c.* 970, by Bishop Æthelwold of Winchester (see cat. no. 6). Since the *Regularis concordia* was sometimes referred to by the same title as Smaragdus's commentary, *Expositio in regulam S. Benedicti*, it is not surprising that people were perplexed (see Barker-Benfield 2008). A fourteenth-century inscription on the flyleaf of the present manuscript is evidence of ongoing confusion regarding Dunstan's oeuvre. Still visible in the early twentieth century, but now faded, it read:

St Dunstan, ff. 2v–3

'Expo[s]it[i]o s[anc]ti du[n]stani sup[er] regula[m] s[anc]ti B[e]n[e]d[ic]ti', to which is added, 'quidam vero dicunt quod est exp[ositio] Smara[g]di monachi, alii dicunt quod est expositio Eligii et ita est' (St Dunstan's commentary on the Rule of St Benedict ... some say that it is the commentary of the monk Smaragdus, others say that it is the commentary of Eligius, and thus it is).

Like many of the oldest surviving manuscripts from Christ Church, the present one has a distinctive mark at he top right corner of the first text page (f. 3). Resembling runic characters, these marks correspond to matching ones in a catalogue of Christ Church books made *c.* 1170, which survives in a fragmentary state: Cambridge, University Library, MS Ii.3.12 (ff. 74–75v). Significantly an identical mark also appears on f. 2 – the back of the leaf containing the portrait of Dunstan (pictured). This raises two possibilities: first, that the leaf with the miniature was in place when the catalogue was compiled *c.* 1170; and, second and more likely, that the leaf was added to the manuscript subsequently and a second 'runic' mark, corresponding to the first on f. 3, was inserted so that the manuscript could still be identified by users of the catalogue. If not created when the manuscript was written, the frontispiece was added relatively soon afterwards, possibly to commemorate the transfer of Dunstan's body to a new shrine near the high altar on 16 April 1180 after extensive rebuilding of Christ Church cathedral.

A later catalogue of Christ Church manuscripts was compiled during the priorate of Henry de Eastry (1285–1331) (Gameson 2008). Two copies of Smaragdus's commentary are listed in it: nos. 138 and 139. It is possible that no. 138 in Eastry's catalogue is Dunstan's own copy, which served as the model for the Royal manuscript, identified as no. 139 by M.R. James (1903). The word 'nova' (new) is appended to the late twelfth-century title written on f. 2 of the present manuscript, as if to distinguish it from its precursor. Like ten other Christ Church manuscripts, this one was appropriated by Thomas Cranmer (b. 1489, d. 1556), champion of the Reformation and Archbishop of Canterbury, who had unrestricted access to the spoils at the Dissolution. *D.J.*

PROVENANCE:

Christ Church, Canterbury; Thomas Cranmer, Archbishop of Canterbury; John, 1st Baron Lumley (d. 1609); Henry Frederick, Prince of Wales (d. 1612).

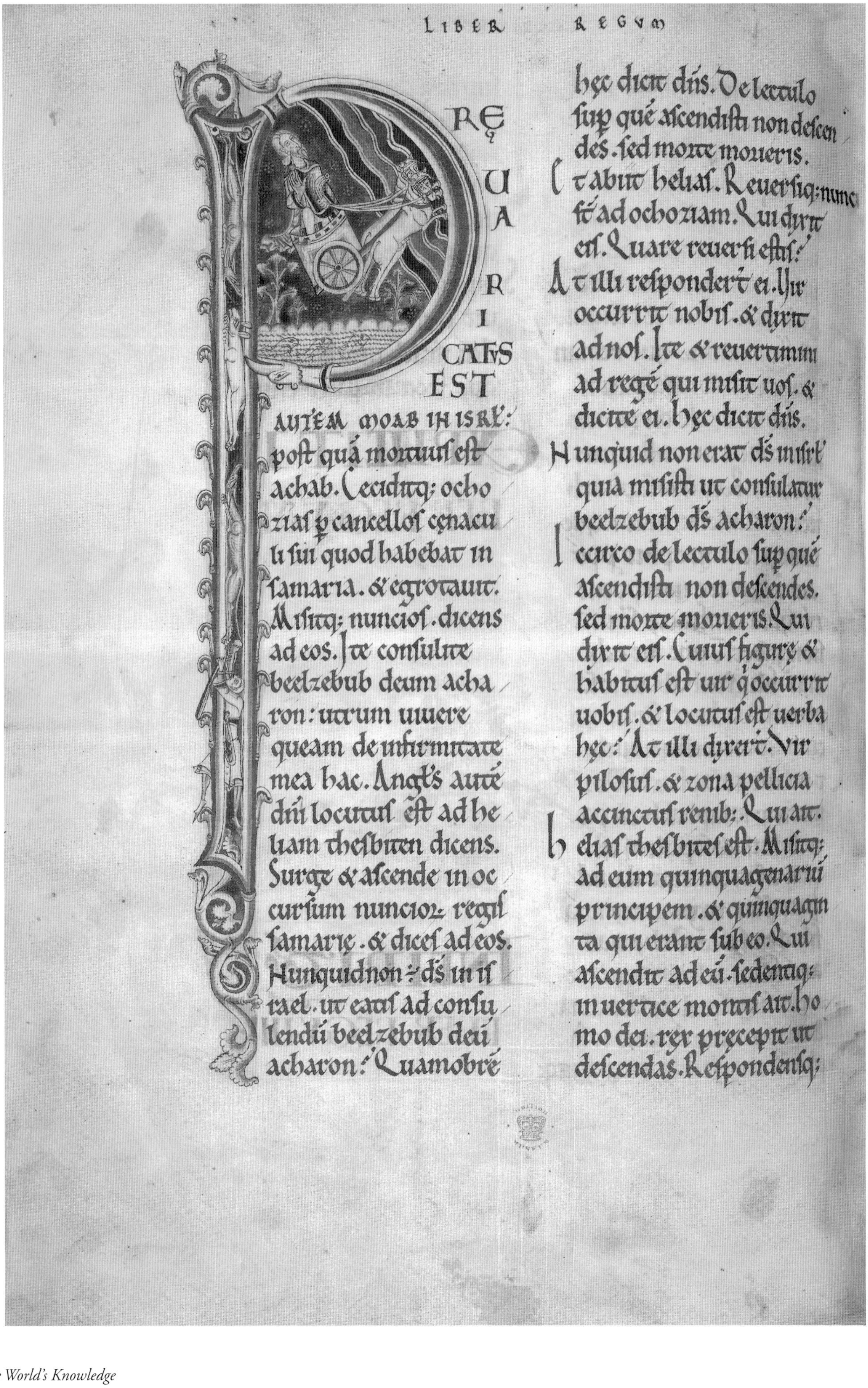
LIBER REGUM

PREUARICATUS EST
AUTEM MOAB IN ISRL:
post quã mortuus est
achab. Ceciditq; ocho
zias p cancellos cenacu
li sui quod habebat in
samaria. & egrotauit.
Misitq; nuncios. dicens
ad eos. Ite consulite
beelzebub deum acha
ron: utrum uiuere
queam de infirmitate
mea hac. Angls autẽ
dñi locutus ẽ ad he
liam thesbiten dicens.
Surge & ascende in oc
cursum nunciorũ regis
samarie. & dices ad eos.
Numquid non ÷ ds in is
rael. ut eatis ad consu
lendũ beelzebub deũ
acharon? Quamobrẽ
hec dicit dñs. De lectulo
sup quẽ ascendisti non descen
des. sed morte morieris.
Et abiit helias. Reuersiq; nunc
ii ad ochoziam. Qui dixit
eis. Quare reuersi estis?
At illi responderũt ei. Uir
occurrit nobis. & dixit
ad nos. Ite & reuertimini
ad regẽ qui misit uos. &
dicite ei. Hec dicit dñs.
Numquid non erat ds in isrl
quia misisti ut consulatur
beelzebub ds acharon?
Iccirco de lectulo sup quẽ
ascendisti non descendes.
sed morte morieris. Qui
dixit eis. Cuius figure &
habitus est uir q occurrit
nobis. & locutus est uerba
hec? At illi dixert. Uir
pilosus. & zona pellicia
accinctus renib;. Qui ait.
Helias thesbites est. Misitq;
ad eum quinquagenariũ
principem. & quinquagin
ta qui erant sub eo. Qui
ascendit ad eũ. sedentiq;
in uertice montis ait. Ho
mo dei. rex precepit ut
descendas. Respondensq;

102 The Rochester Bible

Rochester, 1st half of the 12th century
395 x 265 mm

BRITISH LIBRARY, ROYAL 1 C. vii

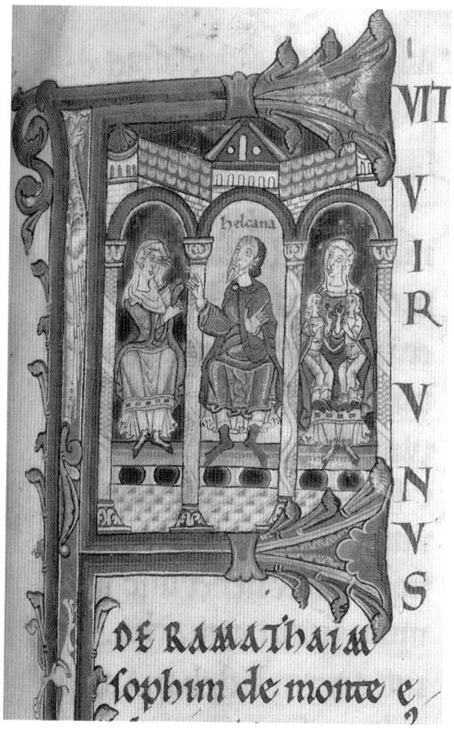

Elkanah and his wives, f. 58 (detail)

Moses and Joshua, f. 2v (detail)

By far the largest group of monastic manuscripts in the Old Royal library – comprising around one hundred volumes – comes from the former cathedral priory of St Andrew, Rochester. This collection includes particularly fine examples of twelfth-century and thirteenth-century illumination, including the Rochester Bestiary (cat. no. 81). One of the most important of these books is the Royal portion of the Rochester Bible (the New Testament from this manuscript is now Baltimore, Walters Art Museum, MS W. 18). The Royal portion includes only the books of Joshua, Judges, Ruth and 1–4 Kings (1–2 Samuel and 1–2 Kings); the rest of the Old Testament from this set has not survived.

The Royal portion of the Bible is now one of the best known of the Rochester manuscripts on the basis of the rarity of its format and the importance of its initials. It is one of only twelve known extant English Romanesque display Bibles, and the earliest of these to include narrative scenes (Cahn 1982; Kauffmann 1975). Interestingly, these historiated initials occur only in the Royal portion of the Bible, and at the beginning of only four of its seven books (Joshua and 1, 2 and 4 Kings).

In one of these historiated initials the choice of imagery is relatively straight-forward. 1 Kings begins with a discussion of Elkanah and his two wives, who are included in the initial, helpfully labelled with their names above (f. 58, pictured). In other initials, however, the choice of subject is less straightforward. At the beginning of Joshua, which describes the death of Moses and God's choice of Joshua as leader, for example, the artist has used the space of the letter 'E' creatively by including a sideways view of an older man handing a younger man a book, presumably Moses passing the book of the law to Joshua (see Richards 1981; f. 2v, pictured). Similarly, the initial at the beginning of 4 Kings (f. 154v, pictured) illustrates not the first, but the second chapter of the text, which describes how, after seeing 'a fiery chariot', Elijah went up to heaven (4 Kings 2:11). Kauffmann (2003) has argued that the choice of this text as the illustration rather than something from the first chapter of the book indicates the typological significance of the event as a prefiguration of Christ's Ascension.

The initials at the beginning of each of the other books – which include creatures such as dragons, hybrid lion-birds, and white lions or dogs – are more difficult to connect with any illustration of the biblical text. These sorts of figures are present in the initial for 4 Kings as well, with a huntsman blowing a horn, and two dogs chasing a hare in the long descender of the letter 'P'. The apparently random selection of various textual and non-textual images and elements suggests that at this early point a programme of illustration had not been developed. The artist may even have been free to determine the content of the initials to be decorated, as with other 'giant' Bibles of the period, which often included decorated initials only.

The Royal portion of the Rochester Bible has an early Westminster inventory number (507), indicating that it was in the Upper Library at Westminster Palace by 1542. Unlike the glossed biblical texts and commentaries that entered the Old Royal library during Henry's reign to be searched for support for the Great Question, this portion of a large-scale lectern Bible may have been selected as an elegant and handsome 'ancient' book as part of the King's assemblage of Vulgate Bibles (see cat. no. 43).

K.D.

PROVENANCE:

Cathedral priory of St Andrew, Rochester; 'Thomas Greyburn' (?), 15th century; William Barrow (d. 1429), Bishop of Bangor (1418) and Carlisle (1423); Henry VIII.

Opposite:
Ascension of Elijah, f. 154v

a d p h i l i p p e n s e s .

03 Peter Lombard, Gloss on the Pauline Epistles

Chester, 2nd half of the 12th century
445 x 310 mm

BRITISH LIBRARY, ROYAL 4 E. viii

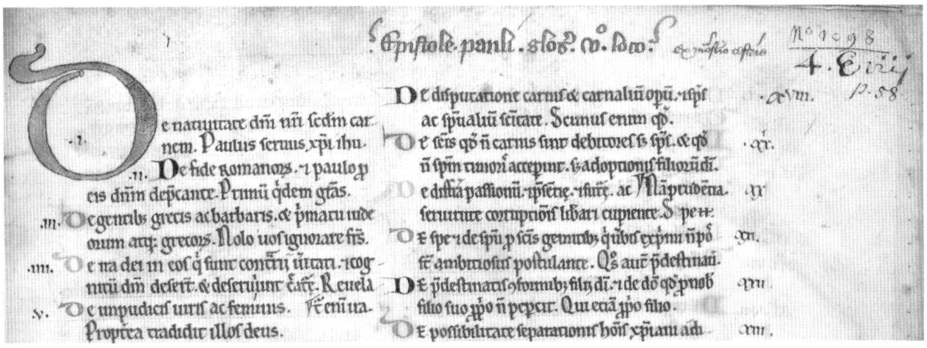

Opposite:
Philippians, capitula and incipit, f. 182v

Above:
Westminster inventory number and Chester ownership inscription, f. 1 (detail)

Henry VIII's search of monastic and collegiate collections resulted in what has been characterized as an 'eccentric collection' (Ker 1985), particularly strong in glossed books and commentaries on the books of the Bible. That this elegant copy of the Pauline Epistles was part of that collection is clear because it has the distinctive inventory number in the form of an Arabic number preceded by 'No' (here No 1098), indicating that it was once in the library at Westminster Palace (pictured as a detail). However, the point at which it entered the Old Royal library is unclear. The manuscript was not included in the 1542 inventory of the Upper Library, which ends with the number 908. Instead, it is one of the nearly three hundred surviving manuscripts and printed books that have numbers greater than this and must have entered the library at a later date.

Other inscriptions on this first page indicate the contents of the work, and that the manuscript was once in the Benedictine abbey of St Werburgh, Chester (*Ex monasterio Cestrie*). Monastic manuscripts like this one that include these later Westminster numbers may have been moved there after 1542 from another of the royal libraries, perhaps from Greenwich or Hampton Court, the two other principal libraries John Leland (d. 1552) identified as repositories of Henry's monastic books (see essay in this volume 'The Old Royal Library'; Carley 2000). The other added references on the first page are the eighteenth-century shelfmark of the manuscript ('4. E viij'), which was retained after the transfer of the Old Royal library to the British Museum, and the page number ('p. 58') on which the description of the manuscript appears in the first printed catalogue of the royal collection, published by the Deputy Librarian David Casley in 1734.

A complete set of glossed biblical texts was an essential reference and study tool for monastic centres; it has been estimated that copies would have been present in 'practically every library in Europe' by the end of the thirteenth century (De Hamel 1984). In this very large-scale copy of the Epistles the biblical text and the gloss are written continuously in the same column, distinguished by colour: the biblical text is written in red, with the commentary following it written in black. This layout is an early or 'old style' format of glossing, to be distinguished from the parallel column Parisian format that rapidly replaced it (see cat. no. 105). An unusual refinement is the colour of the *lemmata*, which are also written in red. These marginal abbreviated references and their corresponding signs of two dots over words in the text are visible on the illustrated page in the right column and in the inner margin. The first marginal inscription, the number '1', corresponds to the *capitulum* or chapter heading. The next abbreviations of 'aimo' and 'ams' refer to the supposed authors of the works on which Lombard's commentary was based, in this case Haymo, Bishop of Halberstadt (d. 853), and Ambrose, Bishop of Milan (d. 397). That this page layout is old fashioned for the date of the manuscript supports its attribution to a provincial centre. (The ownership inscription identifying the abbey at Chester is a later, fourteenth-century addition.)

Functionally, the handsome, large decorated initials assist the reader in finding textual divisions, although they are not as helpful as the running titles as finding aids. Throughout the volume these initials are composed solely of non-figurative, stylized leaves, flowers and geometric patterns. As a result, they are resistant to what Cahn (2008) has called the modern 'quest for meaning' so often applied to Romanesque art. In this manuscript it is reasonable to conclude that the primary purpose of these attractive initials is as decoration and ornamentation to a carefully planned and written text. By extension, the apparent lack of any more patent meaning may suggest that other, potentially more multivalent iconography – such as the portraits of St Paul in another illustrated copy of Lombard's *Magna glossatura* on the Epistles from the Old Royal library (cat. no. 105), and other monastic books – may also be primarily decorative in function. *K.D.*

PROVENANCE:

The Benedictine abbey of St Werburgh, Chester; Henry VIII.

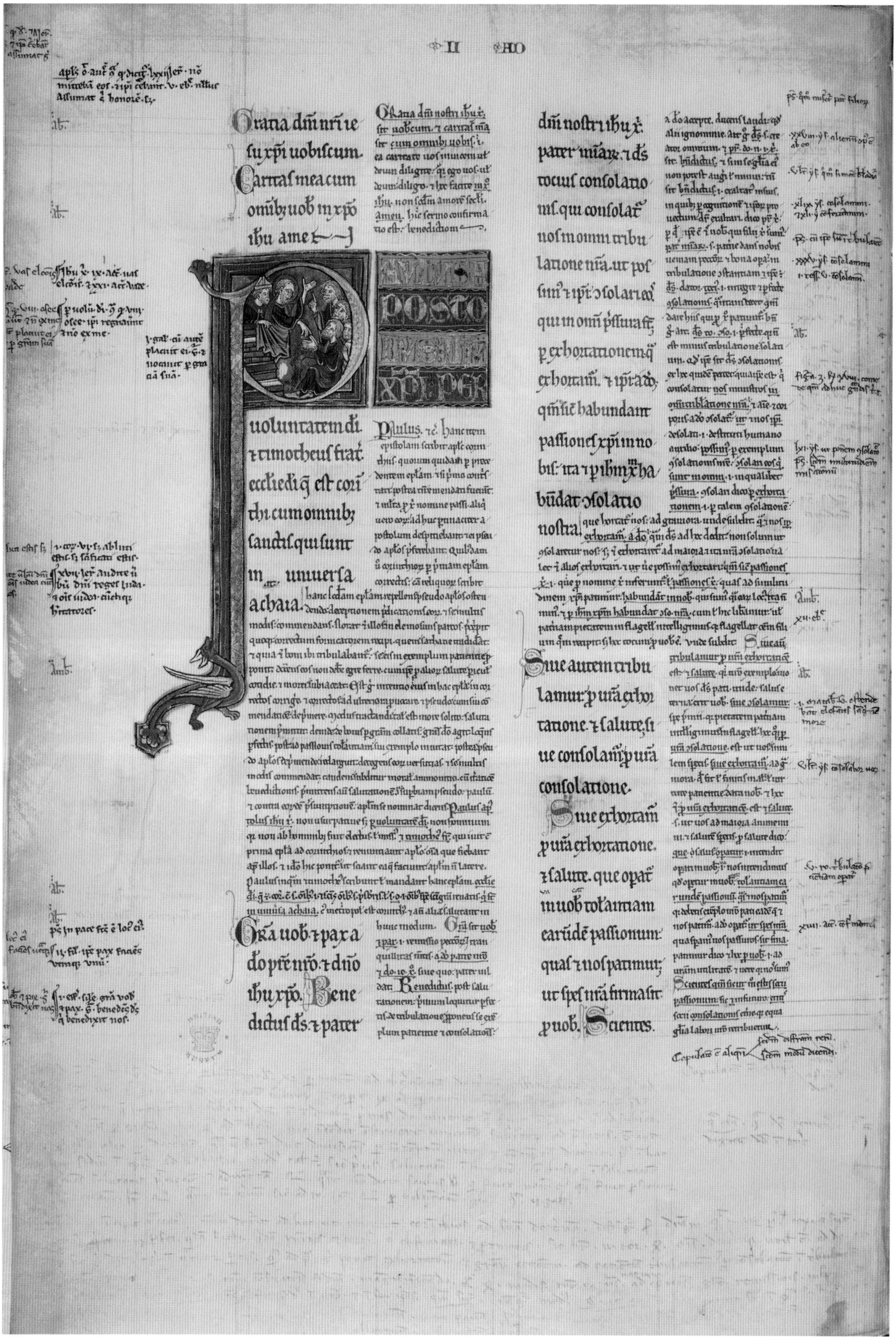

104 Peter Lombard, Gloss on the Pauline Epistles (*Magna glossatura*)

Paris, *c.* 1210–20
390 x 270 mm

BRITISH LIBRARY, ROYAL 4 D. viii

By the last quarter of the twelfth century Peter Lombard's *Magna glossatura*, his gloss on the Psalms and on the Epistles of St Paul, had largely replaced the respective parts of the *Glossa ordinaria* in complete sets of glossed Bibles, and had become a major tool for the scholastic exegesis of Scripture. Although illuminated with gold and colours, the present book is an example of a working copy of this famous text. The manuscript implements the alternate-line system that was introduced by early Parisian publishers of the *Magna glossatura*, and integrates in the same column Lombard's commentary written in a small script and the biblical text written on every second line in a large Gothic textualis (see cat. no. 105). *Lemmata* are underlined in red to direct a reader to the relevant explanation in the gloss section of the selected terms or portion of the biblical text. In the outer and inner margins, the abbreviated names of Augustine, Cassiodorus, Jerome and other authorities on whose writings Lombard's commentary was based are provided in red. On the page reproduced here, this is illustrated by the abbreviations 'Ab' or 'Amb' for Ambrose, Bishop of Milan (d. 397), as in cat. no. 103. Pairs of similar *sigla* mark the length of citations in the margins, and corresponding double dot signs signal the same quotations within the text of the gloss. Occasionally the marginal reference is highlighted by a red vertical line. This handy system of references to sources, clearly differentiating between earlier writings and the glossator's own commentary, was explained by Herbert of Bosham (d. *c.* 1194), Peter Lombard's former student, in the preface to his revised edition of the *Gloss* on the Psalms (Cambridge, Trinity College, MS B.5.4, f. 1v). Herbert used this system in his revisions of both the Glossed Psalms and the Glossed Epistles, which he prepared at the request of Thomas Becket. Finally, the margins of the Royal manuscript are supplemented by numerous glosses arranged in two or three columns and squeezed in between the ruling lines. These annotations, which must have been added in at least three campaigns shortly after the book was completed, reflect its continued scholarly use.

The Royal manuscript was produced in Paris, the very centre of scholastic education, and illuminated by one of the most distinctive Parisian artists of the first quarter of the thirteenth century, the Almagest Master. His easily recognizable style is characterized by soft, looping drapery worked in a series of tight folds decorated with wavy, 'turbulent' white ornaments at the lower edges of robes and around the necks of persons depicted. The Almagest Master was first identified by Avril (1976), and placed within the first generation of professional secular illuminators working in the French capital. Avril named the artist after a copy of Ptolemy's *Almagest* (Paris, BnF, MS lat. 16200), which was copied in 1213 from an exemplar kept in the abbey of St-Victor in Paris. The Parisian location of the artist's workshop is confirmed by the early provenance from St-Germain-des-Prés of two volumes of a Bible also illuminated by the Master (Paris, BnF, MSS lat. 11558, 11559) and by the artist's involvement in the decoration of a multi-volume Bible (Paris, Bibliothèque Mazarine, MSS 131–144), which was probably commissioned by Jacques de Rome, Prior of St-Victor (1219–37), and later given to the abbey by Pierre de Châteauroux (see Rouse and Rouse 2000).

Throughout his career the Almagest Master seems to have been occupied primarily with biblical illustration. Despite their standard and repetitive subjects, his biblical miniatures display a wide variety of compositions, as is evident in the Royal manuscript. All of the manuscript's twelve surviving historiated initials (one is missing) show St Paul preaching or addressing the recipients of his letters, but none repeats the same configuration of persons.

This manuscript was a late arrival in the royal library. It was bought by Charles II, together with around 330 other volumes, from the collection of the antiquary John Theyer (d. 1673). The presence of numerous names of patristic authorities, written in the margins in Theyer's hand, shows that Peter Lombard's commentary was being used by him as a reference tool. By the time Theyer had acquired the manuscript it had fallen out of use and suffered substantial damage. It probably had been exploited as a stock of material for new bindings. Some leaves have disappeared; others are misbound and now mounted on paper slips and reintegrated in the modern binding. Theyer may have acquired the manuscript from a religious house. Although no evidence remains in the Royal volume, it is possible that he inherited it from his great uncle, Richard Hart, the last Prior of Llanthony Secunda in Gloucestershire. *J.F.*

PROVENANCE:

John Theyer (d. 1673), antiquary; Charles II.

Opposite:
2 Corinthians, St Paul preaching, f. 71v

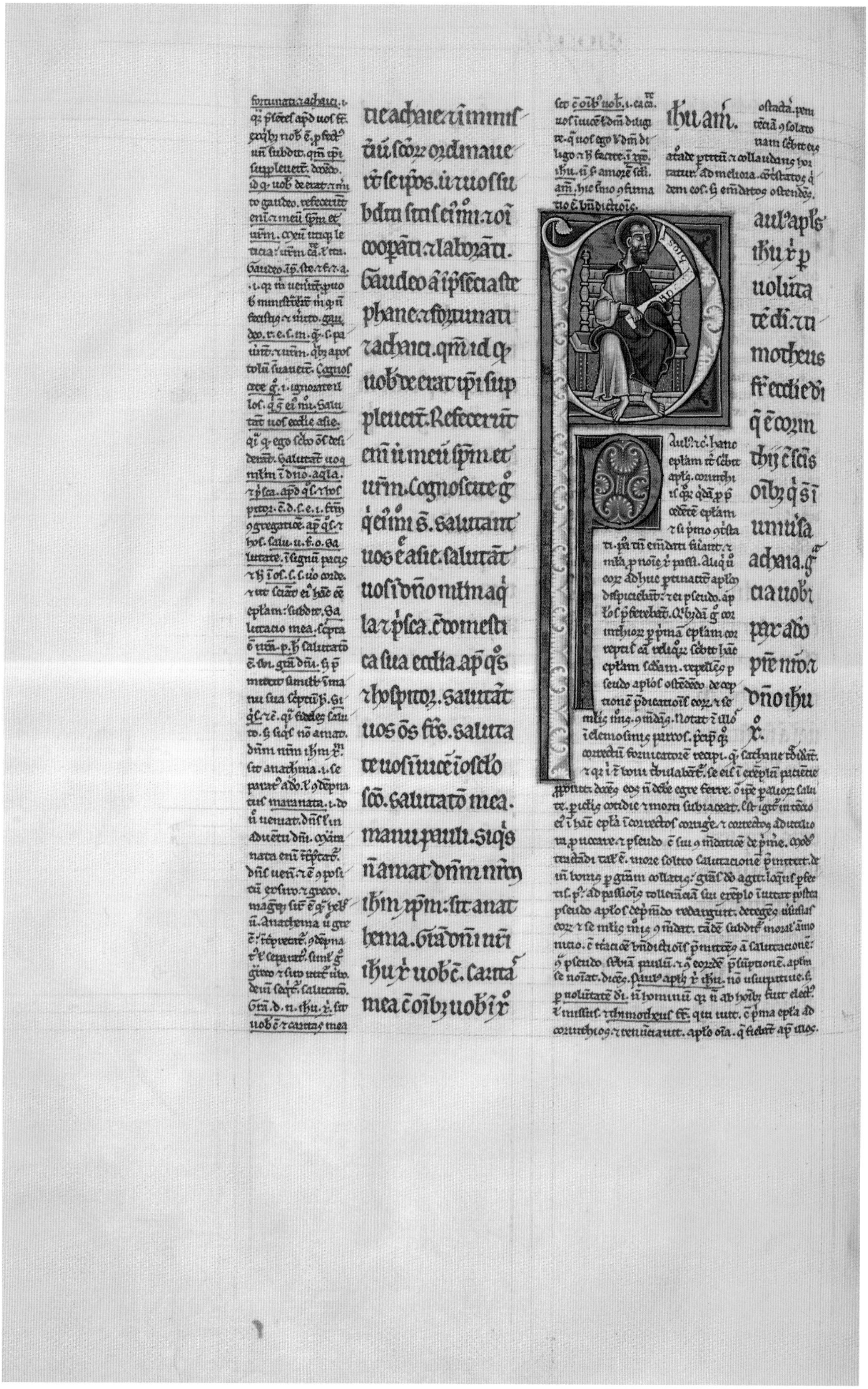

05 Peter Lombard, Gloss on the Pauline Epistles (*Magna glossatura*)

Northern France, *c.* 1200
445 x 290 mm

Peter Lombard's commentary on the Epistles of St Paul, known as the *Magna glossatura* (Great Gloss), is one of the most representative texts of twelfth-century scholastic exegesis of Christian Scripture. The product of his teaching activity at the University of Paris, Lombard's gloss was completed and released by 1159, spread quickly, and soon achieved great popularity amongst western European scholars. By the mid-1160s his commentary was already perceived as the authoritative interpretation of the Epistles, and had eclipsed the previous exegetical achievements of Anselm of Laon and Gilbert de la Porée.

One of the reasons for this success was undoubtedly the new physical format of Lombard's commentary. As in the reproduction opposite, every page of his work includes both biblical text and its explanation, each running in parallel from page to page. On f. 84v (pictured) a portrait of St Paul holding a scroll inscribed with the title of his Second Epistle 'Ad Corinthos' introduces the words of Scripture. Similar pictures are painted within the initials of the other twelve Pauline Epistles. A smaller decorated letter in gold marks the beginning of the gloss. Both texts are written in two columns on the same ruling, but the text of the Epistles is copied on alternate lines. As de Hamel (1984) has demonstrated, this innovative layout – which was introduced by Parisian scribes who first 'published' Peter Lombard's *Magna glossatura* – allows readers to distinguish the large Gothic book script of the biblical text from the slightly smaller Gothic characters of the commentary. To ensure easy orientation within the running commentary on each subdivision, the gloss mirrors the articulation of the main text by introducing the same initial letters at the beginning of passages corresponding to each biblical verse. Individual words or phrases of the biblical text are underlined in red and explained in the commentary section.

This format was designed for scholarly use of the biblical text, yet the Royal manuscript does not appear to have been commissioned by an ordinary student. Neatly written on high quality parchment and lavishly illuminated, it may well have belonged to a wealthy abbot or bishop. Unfortunately no ownership inscription is present to enable its provenance to be traced.

Brown (1990) suggested that the manuscript might have been written by an English scribe, and the 'Channel Style' decoration of a large foliate initial inhabited with small white lions, at the beginning of the prologue (f. 1), does not contradict this hypothesis. However, the figural style of the historiated initials and the rest of the ornamental design suggest that it is a French production. According to Avril (1975) the Royal Lombard was illuminated in Paris by the second artist of a manuscript miscellany of classical authors (Paris, BnF, MS lat. 7936). Although the Royal and Paris manuscripts share similar decorated initials consisting of quasi-geometric figures interlaced with highly stylized foliate motifs, their historiated initials cannot be ascribed to the same hand. A closer relative to the Royal Lombard is a Bible now in Berlin (Staatsbibliothek Preussischer Kulturbesitz, MS theol. lat. fol. 9), another Parisian product of *c.* 1200 (see Ayres 1982). The volumetric, almost monumental human figures in the Berlin Bible, especially striking for its numerous portraits of St Paul and the Prophets, recall the same classicizing style of Byzantine inspiration that characterizes the historiated initials of the Royal manuscript, and suggest that both cycles might have issued from the workshop of the same painter.

The Royal manuscript is not definitively identifiable in the Old Royal library catalogues. The catalogue of 1666 (Royal Appendix 71) mentions glossed Epistles three times (ff. 2, 3, 17) and the 1698 printed catalogue of the library of St James's Palace includes four entries entitled 'Pauli epistolae glossatae' or 'Commentarium in S. Pauli Epistolas' (CMA 7732, 7734, 7782, 7980), but none of them may be linked definitively to Royal 4 E. ix. Since the manuscript includes the ownership inscription of neither John Lumley nor John Theyer, it seems likely that it entered the royal collection at the time of the Dissolution, or slightly earlier, when royal agents were selecting a working library for Henry VIII. Two of the four glossed Pauline Epistles with later Westminster inventory numbers have secure monastic provenances (no. 1030, Royal 4 D. vi, belonged to the Franciscan convent in London, and no. 1098, [cat. no. 103], to the abbey of St Werburgh, Chester). As it does not have a 1542 or later Westminster inventory number, Royal 4 E. ix may have been kept in a different location, most likely at Hampton Court or Greenwich. *J.F.*

PROVENANCE:

Henry VIII (?).

Opposite:
2 Corinthians, St Paul, f. 84v

106 Gratian, *Decretum*; Bartholomew of Brescia, *Glossa ordinaria*

Paris, *c.* 1260–70
440 x 260 mm

BRITISH LIBRARY, ROYAL 10 D. viii

The *Decretum* is a comprehensive compilation of canon law that includes decisions of Church councils, papal bulls and excerpts from the Fathers of the Church. It was composed by Gratian, a legal scholar working probably in Bologna, in at least two recensions between 1139 and 1158. Gratian's own title – *Concordia discordantium canonum* (the Concord of Discordant Canons) – reveals his intention to reconcile the contradictory opinions found in the existing body of canon law, through dialectical method of reasoning and systematic argumentation. The success and rapid dissemination of Gratian's text was almost immediate. During the twelfth century the *Decretum* became a major university textbook, first in Bologna, then in other European law faculties including Montpellier, Paris, and Oxford.

The Royal *Decretum Gratiani* is a high-quality legal textbook produced under the supervision of a university stationer, whose correction notes are preserved at the end of each gathering. The layout of its pages is typical of a university law book. In addition to the text of the *Decretum*, it contains the *Glossa ordinaria*, a systematic commentary in the form of marginal glosses that was composed by the Italian canonist Bartholomew of Brescia (d. 1258). Both text and gloss of the Royal *Decretum* are written in regular round characters emulating the *Littera bononiensis*, a characteristic Italian legal script. The system of cross-reference between text and gloss, however, does not include the letters of the alphabet as was common in Italy, but adheres to scribal practices often used in France, such as graphic signs and underlined *lemmata*.

The manuscript was almost certainly illuminated in Paris, one of the major centres for canon law studies. Its thirty-eight miniatures at the beginning of the three parts (*Distinctiones*, *Causae* and *De consecratione*) and of the individual cases of part three can be identified as works of the illuminator of a Missal for the use of Paris (Paris, BnF, MS lat. 830). Branner (1977) attributed the Missal's illuminations to a Parisian workshop active in the third quarter of the thirteenth century which he named the 'Bari Atelier'. The artist of the Royal *Decretum* might have specialized in the illustration of legal books; his other works include a *Decretales* (Luxemburg, Bibliothèque Nationale, MS 140) and Justinian's *Codex* in French (Giessen, Universitätsbibliothek, Cod. 945). The Giessen *Codex* contains a publicity notice for the bookseller Herneis le Romanceeur, who owned a shop in front of Notre-Dame in Paris.

The opening miniature of the Royal *Decretum,* reproduced here, provides a powerful image of the process of law-making. A king assisted by his counsellors addresses a scribe with a clear gesture of command. This image, which focuses exclusively on royal legislative activity, replaced an earlier iconography of the co-active powers of the pope and the secular monarch. Such earlier imagery represented the distinction between natural law, which was of divine origin (*lex naturale*) and the law decreed by people (*lex humana*), and often reserved a dominant place for the ecclesiastical ruler. The new iconography, of which the Royal *Decretum* is an early example, was widely disseminated in French – especially Parisian – copies of Gratian's text (see Nordenfalk 1980). It seems, however, that the illustration was not original to canon law books but adapted the opening image of the constitution *De novo codice componendo* (On the Composition of the New Code) of Justinian's *Codex*, which is known from at least two mid-thirteenth-century French copies in Paris (Paris, BnF MSS fr. 496 and 20120). This new iconographic formula was invented at the same time as new concepts of sovereignty were emerging. The concept of the French king as the 'emperor in his own reign' with independent legislative and judicial power was first defined under Louis IX and Philip III by both civil and canon lawyers, such as Jean de Blanot and Guillaume Durand.

The Royal manuscript was not originally made for an English patron, but several marginal glosses in *Anglicana* script suggest that it had arrived in England by the fourteenth century. Before its integration into the Old Royal library, the book belonged to Howel Kyffin, Dean of St Asaph in northern Wales (from 1381). A later ownership note of a certain Cowley, who also owned a *Moralia in Job* of Rochester Priory provenance (Royal 6 D. vii), might date from the time of Dissolution. A fifteenth-century letter of a prior of Belvoir to the prior of St Albans concerning a quittance for a parson of Great Rissington (now Royal 14 B. li) was once inserted in the Royal *Decretum* as a detached leaf, and may also suggest a monastic provenance for the manuscript.

J.F.

PROVENANCE:

Howel Kyffin, Dean of St Asaph (1381–84); Henry VIII.

Opposite:
King dictating the law, f. 1

107 Gregory IX, *Decretals*; Bernard of Parma, *Glossa ordinaria*

435 x 370 mm
Paris, after *c.* 1281; England, *c.* 1300–20

BRITISH LIBRARY, ROYAL 10 D. vii

In 1234 Pope Gregory IX promulgated a new collection of decretals, the first official compilation of canon law to be issued since the monumental work of Gratian nearly a hundred years earlier. Compiled by the Catalonian canonist Raymond of Penyafort (d. 1275), the *Decretals* were addressed and sent to two major universities of medieval Europe, Paris and Bologna, as the authoritative text to be taught in the law faculties. The Royal copy, addressed to the University of Paris, represents an expanded version of this papal collection. The *Decretals* of Gregory IX with the *glossa ordinaria* of Bernard of Parma are incorporated here with the *Novellae* of Innocent IV (1243–54), glossed by Bernard of Compostella Modernus; and followed by the *Constitutions of the Second Council of Lyon* (1274), promulgated by Gregory X (1271–76) and accompanied by the ordinary gloss of the Spanish scholar Garsias Hispanus (see Linehan 1998). Two different but contemporary scribes added further decretals, one of Nicholas III (1277–80), and the other of Alexander IV (1254–61), Clement IV (1265–68) and Urban IV (1261–64), and the *Constitutions of the Council of Bourges* of 1276.

The text in the Royal *Decretals* was probably copied not long after Garsias Hispanus completed his apparatus on the *Constitutions of the Council of Lyon* in *c.* 1281and his commentary on the decretal *Cupientes* of Nicholas III, written presumably by the same time. Such an early date for the Royal copy is also suggested by the fact that Simon de Brie, the future Pope Martin IV (1281–85) and the author of the *Constitutions of the Council of Bourges*, is named in the Royal manuscript as a papal Legate, former Cardinal of France and priest of the titular church of St Cecilia in Rome; no reference is made to his accession to the Holy See in 1281. The style of illumination in the Royal manuscript confirms this dating. Six miniatures at the beginning of the *Decretals* of Gregory IX and Nicholas III were painted by a Parisian artist who illuminated the *Grandes chroniques de France* that Matthew of Vendôme commissioned for presentation to Philip III of France soon after the composition and translation of this work by Primat of St-Denis in 1274 (Paris, Bibliothèque Ste-Geneviève, MS 782; see *Rois maudis* 1998).

Further evidence suggests that the Royal copy of the *Decretals* was in England in the fourteenth century. Numerous glosses in a characteristic *Anglicana* script were added throughout the book and an extract from Edward III's statute of 1372 was copied at the end of the volume. By far the most spectacular addition, however, was that of two large images of the Trees of Consanguinity and Affinity. These diagrams, showing two types of kinship, by descent and by marriage, that were crucial for establishing inheritance rights and matrimonial alliances, were two of the earliest pictorial tools to be introduced into legal manuscripts. Both had already been included in the collection of canons of Burchard of Worms (d. 1025) and in the *Decretum Gratiani*. In thirteenth-century copies of the *Decretals*, the trees illustrate the treatise *Quia tractare intendimus* that was attributed to Raymond of Penyafort and included, at the end of book 4, *On Betrothal and Marriage*. In the Royal manuscript the text of this treatise was copied on a separate bifolium, but spaces for the diagrams were originally left blank. At the beginning of the fourteenth century an English artist completed the decoration, but roundels in both diagrams were never filled in with relevant information. The images in the Royal *Decretals* follow the standard iconography of the subject as it was canonized in French Gothic art. A monumental figure of Adam, father of all humankind – represented here as a king – accompanies the unfinished diagram of consanguinity. An image of a man and a woman on either side of an ivy tree introduces the degrees of affinity which were calculated backwards in time from the couple that intended to marry.

The tree-diagram illustrations of the Royal *Decretals* were painted by an illuminator whose very refined style, emulating the best achievements of Parisian art from the circle of Master Honoré, is difficult to locate. The only parallel to his miniatures in English illumination that has so far been noted is the Trees of Consanguinity and Affinity in the *Decretum Gratiani* in Cambridge (Fitzwilliam Museum, MS 262). The Royal illustrations seem, however, closer in style to East Anglian works of *c.* 1300–10 such as the Ormesby Psalter (Oxford, Bodleian Library, MS Douce 366). *J.F.*

PROVENANCE:
Henry VIII.

Opposite:
Marriage ceremony, f. 233

Trees of Consanguinity and Affinity, ff. 257v–258

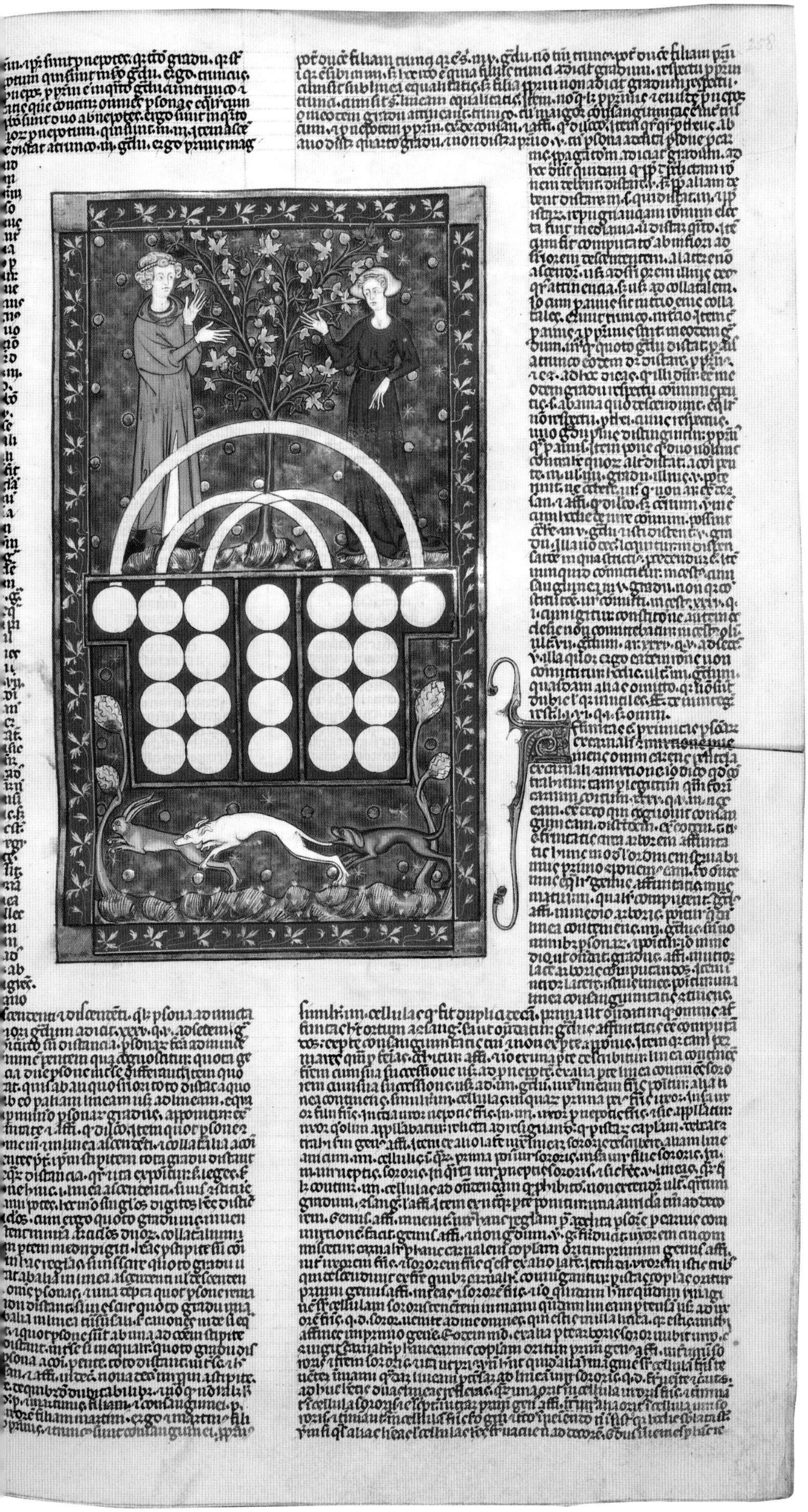

108 The Smithfield Decretals

Toulouse (?), *c.* 1300; London, *c.* 1340s
455 x 285 mm

BRITISH LIBRARY, ROYAL 10 E. iv

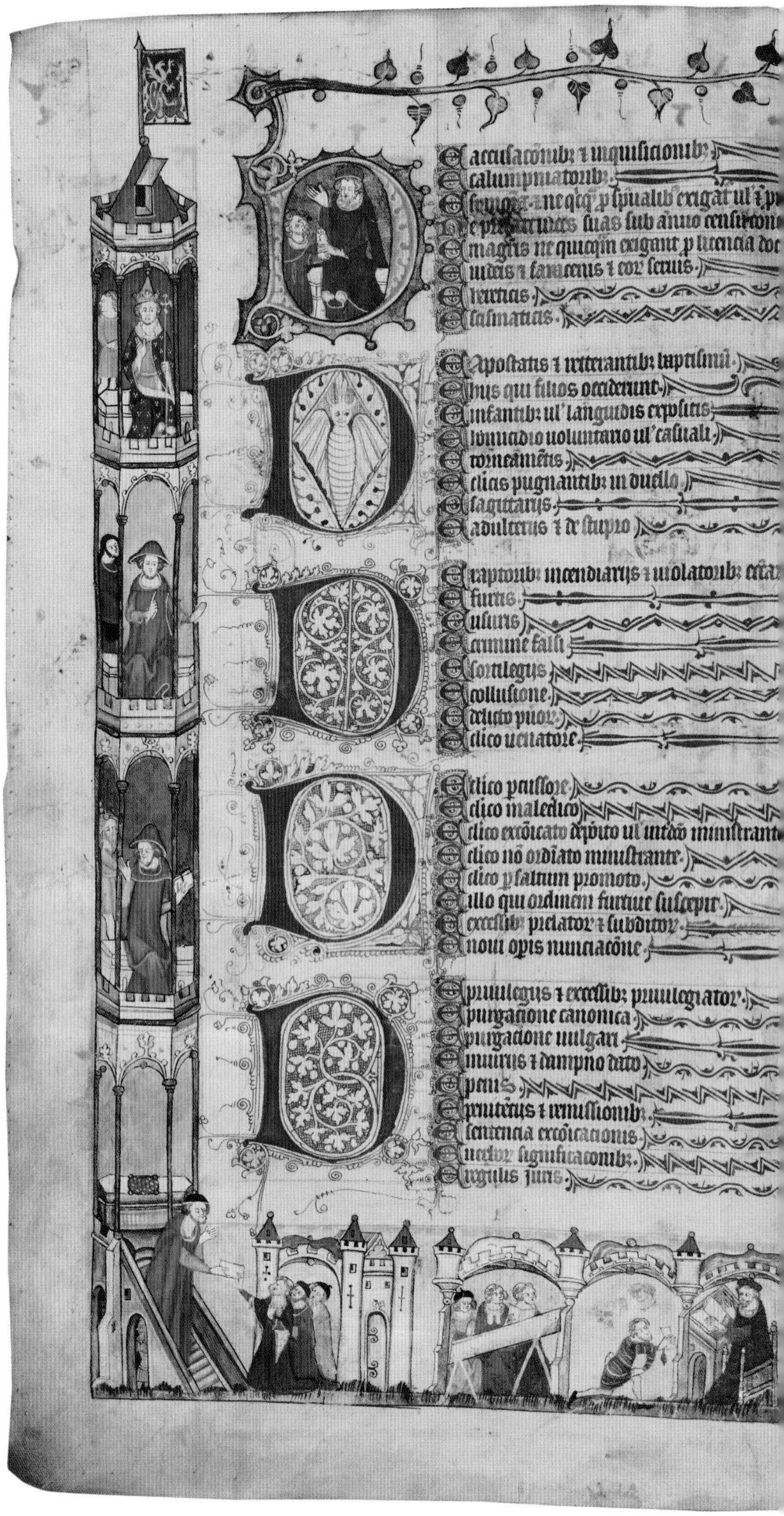

The promulgation of the *Decretals* by Gregory IX, ff. 3v–4

The Smithfield Decretals is an exceptionally important copy of the glossed *Decretals* of Gregory IX, not on account of its texts (in almost every respect they are standard), but because of its extraordinary programme of marginal illumination. Approximately 675 manuscripts survive of the *Decretals*, which was an essential work for legal study, practice and reference from the time of its promulgation in 1234. Within this large group, the Smithfield Decretals is by far the most extensively illuminated copy, with every one of its 626 pages of text embellished with imagery.

The Smithfield Decretals was copied in the south of France, probably in or near Toulouse, at the turn of the fourteenth century. There it was furnished with miniatures that mark the beginning of each of the text's five books. By *c.* 1340 the manuscript was in London, where its owner commissioned a group of local illuminators to add an illuminated list of the topics covered in the *Decretals* to the beginning of the book (the final page of this list, f. 3v, is pictured), and to fill its wide, bare margins with narrative images and decorative motifs. The coat of arms of the Batayle family of Essex is repeated twenty-five times in the manuscript and shown twice in the book's most magnificent opening (ff. 3v–4). The manuscript's patron was probably John Batayle, a canon of the Augustinian priory of St Bartholomew at Smithfield, located just outside London's medieval walls. The ownership mark of St Bartholomew's was inscribed on the manuscript's first leaf by a fifteenth-century hand.

The London illuminators charged with the immense task of embellishing Batayle's book painted two sets of borders on each page, one around the main text and another around the gloss; placed monsters, grotesques and other motifs in the gaps between the columns of text; and filled the lower margins with scenes, most of which recount stories that unfold over many pages. These narrative sequences relate tales drawn from an astonishing variety of sources, including the Bible, saints' lives and miracles, romances, bawdy tales, moral fables and parodies. This programme of images has an entertaining yet sharply didactic flavour, and may have been devised as a tool for instructing lay people. No other medieval law book contains a scheme like that of the Smithfield Decretals, but

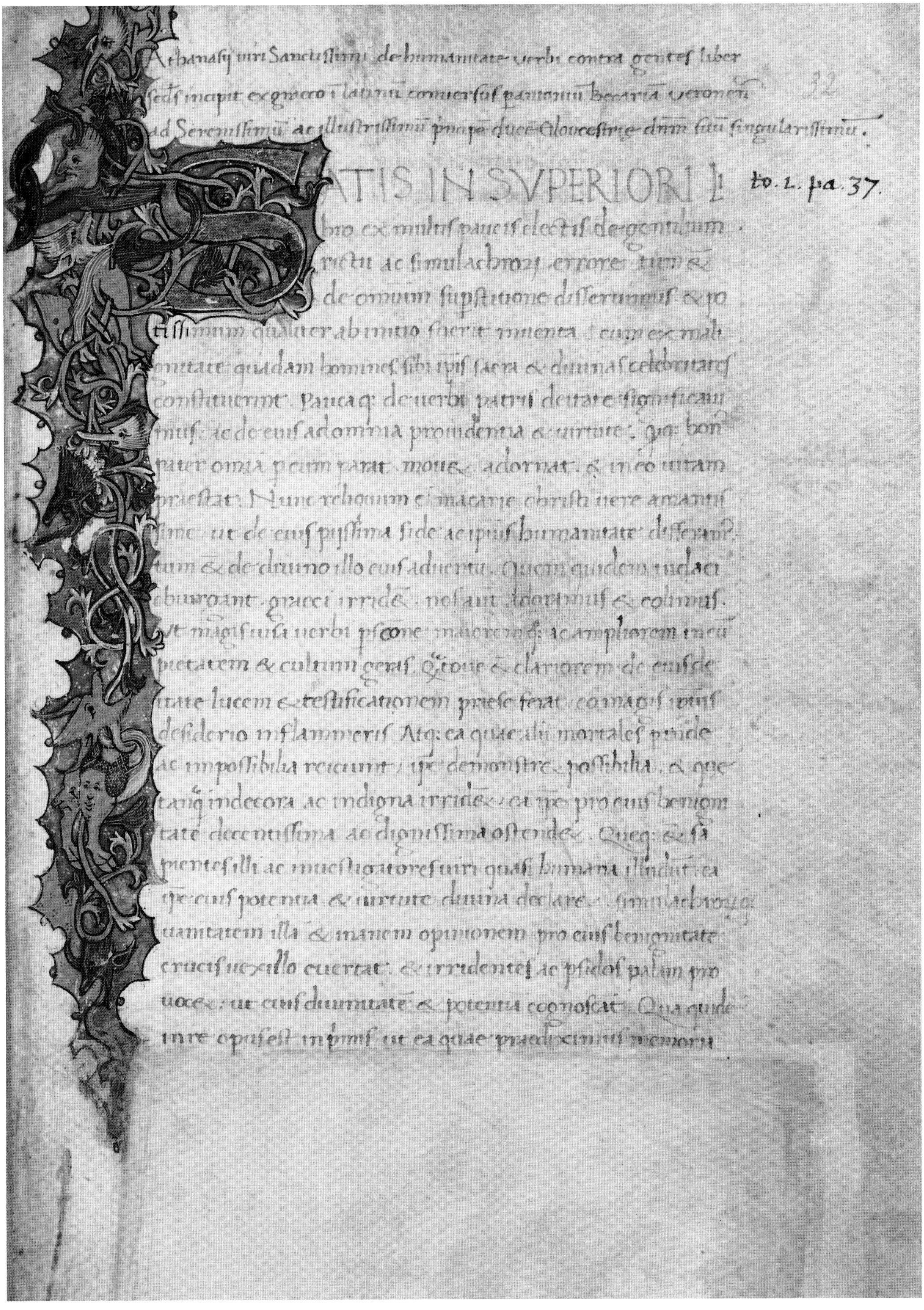

Æternitas
Gloria
VIRTUS
Mars.

10 Filippo Alberici, *Tabula cebetis*, *De mortis effectibus* and Other Poems

Paris, 1507; Cambridge, after 1507
205 x 140 mm

BRITISH LIBRARY, ARUNDEL 317

In Henry VII emerging humanist poets and scholars found a reliable patron. French and Italian *literati* such as Bernard André, Pietro Carmeliano and Polydore Vergil sought an international reputation for themselves through employment at Henry VII's court. But however much Henry welcomed their services as resident scholars and poet-propagandists, it was not always easy for aspiring humanists to attract the King's patronage. The present manuscript is a fascinating example of the risks involved in attempting to establish for oneself a literary reputation.

This volume is a rare object for its combination of traditional and avant-garde elements, which were brought together to attract the King's attention. The manuscript contains *Tabula cebetis* (Cebes' Tablet), translated from Greek into Latin by the little-known Mantuan friar Filippo Alberici (d. 1531) (see also cat. no. 111) and written in his own hand during a visit to Paris early in 1507. The Greek text, erroneously believed to have been written by Socrates' pupil Cebes, had been a popular pedagogical tract since its printed publication by Laurentius di Alopa in 1496. It tells how Cebes, entering the temple of Saturn, espies an enigmatic painted tablet on the wall. A wise person – noting Cebes' confusion – describes the tablet, which depicts the three circles of human life, each one a different struggle between vice and virtue. With its resemblance to wisdom literature and its Christianized allegorical content, the *Tabula cebetis* is in many ways conventional.

What is extraordinary about this manuscript is its unprecedented cycle of illustrations. Sider (1990) has referred to it as 'proto-emblematic' because it anticipates by twenty-four years the first emblem book, Andres Alciati's *Emblemata*. An extended ekphrasis, the manuscript contains six full-page miniatures, each opposite a descriptive text; each miniature depicts a circle of Cebes' tablet and is itself, in its rectangular, framed form, a tablet for the viewer to 'read'. The last of these (f. 20v, pictured), depicting Alberici's greatest departure from the original Greek text, advances an ideal of kingship that he and his contemporary humanists wished to promote: the triumph of Virtue by way of *Studium* and *Mars*, Scholarship and Might.

An important aspect of this manuscript's history is that it was intended to be a presentation copy for the King, but that it may never have been given to him. In search of a patron, Alberici had composed this volume and had it illuminated in Paris by an artist whose style resembles that identified with Jean Coene IV. Alberici subsequently travelled to Cambridge, where he hoped to present the book to Henry VII upon the latter's visit there in July 1507. However, as Rundle has argued (2005), Henry appears not to have received this manuscript. A text at the end of the volume, *De mortis effectibus*, was evidently written at a later date, and is introduced by a full-page miniature (f. 25, pictured) produced by an artist who was probably working in Cambridge. To this text Alberici added a rededication to Joachim Bretoner, seneschal of King's Hall. The erased escutcheon at the foot of the page containing the dedication to Henry VII (f. 3) further suggests that Alberici had redesignated this book for a different recipient, one who was not ennobled.

Given Henry's known receptiveness to humanistic literature and learning, it seems likely that, *pace* Carlson (1993), he did not reject this book outright. The vision of monarchic virtue it advocates is entirely in line with other poetry Henry commissioned, and its illustrations, though novel, were not so outlandish as to

Above:
Death, f. 25

Opposite:
The Seat of Virtue, f. 20v (actual size)

provoke a negative response; they include personifications and allegorical figures that had been well established in visual imagery for centuries. Rather, Alberici appears to have suffered the unfortunate fate of simply never having had the opportunity to present his lavishly illustrated volume to the King. After its ownership by Bretoner, the book made its way back into and out of the royal collection. It was presented by Princess Elizabeth, daughter of James I, to George Carew (d. 1629) in 1608. Eventually, in 1667, the book reached the Royal Society and, in 1831, the British Museum. *S.D.*

PROVENANCE:

Joachim Bretoner, seneschal of King's Hall; Elizabeth Stuart (d. 1662), daughter of James I; George Carew, Earl of Totnes (d. 1629); Thomas Howard, 2nd Earl of Arundel (d. 1646); Henry Howard, 6th Duke of Norfolk (d. 1684); Royal Society, London, 1667; purchased for the nation in 1831.

111 Filippo Alberici (?), *Hieroglyphica* and Emblematic Inscriptions

Paris, *c.* 1507
220 x 145 mm

BRITISH LIBRARY, ROYAL 12 C. iii

In 1419 a manuscript called the *Hieroglyphica* was discovered by the Florentine priest Christoforo Buondelmonti on the Greek island of Andros. By the early 1420s the manuscript was in Florence, where scholars believed its contents – definitions of 189 hieroglyphs attributed to one Horapollo – to be an ancient Greek translation of an Egyptian text. Copies of the Greek manuscript proliferated in Italy throughout the fifteenth century, fuelling enthusiasm for iconology and strengthening the belief in the existence of an eternal and universal language of symbols.

The present manuscript is extraordinary as a virtually unknown, abbreviated translation into Latin of the *Hieroglyphica*, and as the earliest illustrated copy of the text. (Modern scholarship considers the earliest illustrated version of the *Hieroglyphica* to be a manuscript of *c.* 1512, with a translation by Pirckheimer and images by Dürer.) The manuscript opens with an 'index rerum quae ab Egytiis [sic] quondam hierogliphis scribebantur' (an index of things that were written by ancient Egyptians in hieroglyphs). Each of the fifty-seven items or concepts listed in the index is described in the text proper and accompanied by a marginal illustration of the related hieroglyph. The exceptions to this schema are four full-page miniatures, each of which illustrates one of the seasons, and a half-page miniature that depicts the mythological origins of the cornucopia. After the symbols have been described and illustrated, eight full-page miniatures combine groupings of these symbols into a series of emblematic pictures, which are explained in adjoining inscriptions. For example, a combination of hieroglyphs that includes a crown and the sword of justice (f. 20, pictured) is spelled out in a caption, which begins 'Vivat rex p[er] eterna seculei' (Long live the king, for all time) and goes on to praise the monarch as the preserver of justice and the guardian of peace. This manuscript evokes an aura of mystery that would be even greater were it not for the existence of another volume in the British Library.

In 1507 the Mantuan friar Filippo Alberici journeyed to England, via Paris, in search of a literary patron. While in Paris he produced an elaborate copy of the *Tabula cebetis* (cat. no. 110), which he had intended to present to Henry VII. Features shared by the *Tabula cebetis* and the present manuscript suggest that the latter too was produced by Alberici for presentation to the King. Alberici himself was the scribe of at least one portion of the *Tabula cebetis* (ff. 24v and following), and characteristics of the script in the *Hieroglyphica* intimate that it was executed by the same hand. The images in this manuscript are not as accomplished as those in the *Tabula cebetis*, but they were clearly produced by an artist trained to work in the same style. It is even possible that the two manuscripts were once bound together as their pages are close in size, colour and texture, and their contents are similar in length, at twenty-eight leaves for the Arundel manuscript and twenty-five for the Royal. Many of the emblematic inscriptions in the *Hieroglyphica* relate to monarchic success, but the volume lacks a dedication, further suggesting that it was bound together with the *Tabula cebetis*. This hypothesis is also supported by a significant detail that lends a sense of coherence to the pictorial programmes of the two volumes: a writing tablet is suspended by a bow from various surfaces in full-page miniatures in both manuscripts.

Although the illustrative cycle of this manuscript is unprecedented, Alberici and the illuminator he contracted may have taken inspiration from the Venetian printer Aldus Manutius. Not only was Manutius responsible for the *editio princeps* of the *Hieroglyphica* in 1505, but in 1499 he published the *Hypnerotomachia*, an extravaganza of symbolic pageantry. Some of the so-called hieroglyphs featured in the *Hypnerotomachia*'s woodcut illustrations are imitated in the present manuscript, and one in particular – a dolphin wrapped around an anchor with the caption 'tarde festina' (hasten slowly) – is similar to the imprint of Manutius's shop.

Like its probable companion volume, this manuscript was never presented to Henry VII. If the two manuscripts were indeed once bound together, then Alberici's *Hieroglyphica* would have been presented to Joachim Bretoner, who left it in Cambridge upon his departure for Italy in 1511. Subsequently disbound and separated from its companion, this portion of the manuscript was acquired by Henry Fitzalan (d. 1580), 19th Earl of Arundel. Like his other manuscripts, this book almost certainly made its way into the Old Royal library through Prince Henry Frederick's acquisition of the Arundel-Lumley collection in 1609. *S.D.*

PROVENANCE:

Henry Fitzalan, 19th Earl of Arundel (d. 1580); John Lumley, 1st Baron Lumley (d. 1609); Henry Frederick, Prince of Wales (d. 1612).

Opposite:
Hieroglyphic emblems, f. 20

Viuat rex p eterna secula. mundi ornamentum. pacis
seruator malorz cedes. iustitie conseruator. liberalis
rerũ copiã suppeditãs et celeri prudẽtia agens

112 Pauline and Catholic Epistles

London, 1506 (Vulgate) and after 1516 (Erasmian version)
450 x 305 mm

BRITISH LIBRARY, ROYAL 1 E. v, vol. 2

During the late fifteenth and early sixteenth centuries, learned Englishmen, inspired by Continental scholars, devoted themselves to interpreting classical texts and refining their knowledge of Latin. Among such early English humanists was John Colet (b. 1467, d. 1519), Dean of St Paul's, London, and friend of Sir Thomas More. Colet's contribution to knowledge is attested by his correspondence with Erasmus, his surviving religious writings and his founding – in *c.* 1511 – of a new school, which still exists, at St Paul's Cathedral. Students at St Paul's learned Latin, Greek and biblical precepts. Having served as a core text for medieval scholars, the Bible retained its importance for Tudor intellectuals, who developed new translations and glosses.

The present volume is one of a set of three large manuscripts of the New Testament written for John Colet by Pieter Meghen, a one-eyed Brabantine scribe who worked in England from at least 1502 until his death in 1540 at the age of seventy-four. Each of the three New Testament manuscripts written by him for Colet ends with an inscription providing the names of the patron and scribe and the date it was produced, and explaining that Colet commissioned them as a memorial to his father, Henry Colet (d. 1505). The present volume, containing the Pauline and Catholic Epistles, was completed on 1 November 1506; that containing the Gospels of Matthew and Mark (Cambridge University Library, MS Dd.7.3) on 8 May 1509; and a third, with the Gospels of Luke and John (Royal 1 E. v, vol. 1), on 7 September of the same year.

Jerome's fourth-century Latin translation of the New Testament appears in the central columns of the parchment leaves of each volume. A second translation of the New Testament, made by Erasmus, occupies the outer margins. First published in 1516, Erasmus's translation was added by Meghen long after the Vulgate text had been transcribed by him and almost certainly after Colet's death in 1519, when the set was acquired by a new owner, Henry VIII (Warner and Gilson 1921; Brown 1984). When the three manuscripts came to the King, Meghen produced a fourth one (Hatfield House, Marquess of Salisbury, Cecil Papers MS 324). Adorned with the initials of Henry VIII and Catherine of Aragon, this final volume – made in *c.* 1528–33 and containing the Acts of the Apostles and the Apocalypse – completed the set. Shortly afterwards, Meghen was appointed Writer of the King's Books, a post he occupied until his death in 1540.

It is unlikely that Colet planned from the start to include Erasmus's translation since the latter had not completed it when Colet commissioned the volumes. Colet undoubtedly instructed Meghen to leave generous margins and large spaces between lines for a commentary and interlinear gloss, possibly of his own authorship (Brown 1984). A manuscript of the Psalms (Royal 1 E. iii) written by Meghen provides some idea of how Colet's New Testament manuscripts might have looked had they been completed.

Significantly, Meghen did not copy the New Testament books in the order in which they appear in the Bible but began, in 1506, with the Pauline and Catholic Epistles, books on which Colet had lectured and written. The frontispiece of the Epistles shows Paul writing his letter to the Romans while a herald waits to deliver it. The sword, tucked into the herald's belt, is probably an allusion to Paul's martyrdom. Despite the Roman setting, the landscape and buildings reflect the artist's northern origins, as does the border enlivened by naturalistic flowers, insects and birds. Images of Paul composing and dispatching his Epistle occur in hundreds of biblical manuscripts, but in f.5 (pictured) the motif is enhanced by the inclusion of the patron, John Colet, who is shown kneeling before Paul – to whom Colet, as Dean of St Paul's, was particularly devoted. Curiously, the second volume in the set, containing the Gospels of Matthew and Mark, also opens with a frontispiece in which Colet is depicted, in this case kneeling before St Matthew. This suggests that, in 1506, Colet may have conceived of the Pauline manuscript as an independent volume, deciding only afterwards, in 1508 or 1509, to commission the matching Gospel manuscripts. All three volumes made for Colet feature frontispieces by Netherlandish artists, as does the later Hatfield volume made for Henry VIII. The opening words of the books are incorporated in the frontispieces and continue on the back, which proves that Meghen worked in close consultation with the artists who executed the miniatures. Whether they were based in England or the Low Countries is uncertain.

Throughout his life, Colet maintained connections with the Crown; he often preached at court and he served on Henry VIII's council in 1517 and 1518. Shortly afterwards, he retired to the Carthusian priory of Sheen, Richmond, which had been founded by Henry V in 1414. On Colet's death on 16 September 1519, he was buried at St Paul's and his possessions were dispersed by his executors. Given the close proximity of the priory to Richmond Palace, it is probable that Colet's three volumes made their way directly from the priory to the royal residence. *D.J.*

PROVENANCE:

John Colet (b. *c.* 1456, d. 1519); Henry VIII.

Opposite:
John Colet kneeling before St Paul who writes his Epistle to the Romans, vol. 2, f. 5

AVLVS
SERVVS
Epistola Diui Pauli ad Romanos

113 Pandolfo Collenuccio, *Apologues*; Lucian of Samosata, *Dialogues*

Rome and Florence, *c.* 1509–17
320 x 225 mm

BRITISH LIBRARY, ROYAL 12 C. viii

Made in Italy and imported to England, this slim volume contains satirical dialogues by Lucian of Samosata (*c.* AD 120 – *c.* 180) and Pandolfo Collenuccio of Pesaro (b. 1444, d. 1504). Lucian's dialogues, rediscovered by Italian humanists in the first quarter of the fifteenth century, were originally published in part in Latin translation in Rome in 1470. In the first decade of the sixteenth century the profile of Lucian's writings in England was raised significantly by translations of specific dialogues by Erasmus and Thomas More, who dedicated these to English patrons, including prominent Cambridge academics and Richard Foxe, Bishop of Winchester (Rummel 1985).

This manuscript was commissioned by Geoffrey Chamber for presentation to Henry VIII. A functionary of the English court, Chamber held a variety of posts over the course of his career, including Gentleman Usher of the Chamber and Surveyor-General (Wolpe 1958). Evidently Chamber, who ordered the manuscript during a sojourn in Italy in the first part of the sixteenth century, wished to offer Henry VIII a gift worthy of a king because he engaged some of the finest Italian craftsmen of the day. The volume was copied by Ludovico Vicentino degli Arrighi (b. 1475, d. 1527), a scribe of the papal chancery in Rome, who is famous for his contribution to the development of Humanistic cursive script. Extraordinarily lucid, this script was employed by Arrighi and his contemporaries for both manuscripts and chancery documents, and was also adopted for printed books. It has continued to be used up to the present day.

The beauty of Arrighi's hand is matched by the decorative borders and initials painted by one of the leading miniaturists of the period, Attavante degli Attavanti (b. 1452, d. *c.* 1520–25), based in Florence, who numbered among his patrons Manuel I of Portugal, Matthias Corvinus, King of Hungary, and the Medici. On the opening page (f. 4, pictured), which exemplifies the opulence of the artist's style, more space has been devoted to the border than to the opening lines of the text. Putti and intertwined flowers and strands of foliage stand out against the brilliant gold background of the border, as do the two angels in the lower margin, who hold aloft the emblem of the Garter that encircles the arms of the dedicatee, Henry VIII.

The title of the first text in the manucript, the *Agenoria*, one of four works by Collenuccio included in the volume, is written in gold capitals on a rich, red ground. Beneath, in a medallion surrounded by a laurel wreath, is an image of the author. Despite the small scale of the image, Attavante rendered every detail with care, using, for example, tiny brushstrokes to represent the texture of Collenuccio's beard. Ostensibly the miniature is a portrait of the author, but in fact it is a generic type frequently employed by Attavante (Kren 1983) and bears, for example, a strong resemblance in terms of facial type and clothing to one of the men depicted in the frontispiece of an eight-volume Bible made by him, *c.* 1494–97, for Prince Manuel of Portugal (Lisbon, Arquivos Nacionais, Torre do Tombo, MS 161/2, 4, vol. 2, f. 1v).

Interestingly, our manuscript was not the first associated with Attavante to enter the Old Royal library. An earlier volume (Oxford, Bodleian Library, MS Bodley 488), a copy of the statutes of the Hospital of Santa Maria Nuova, Florence – probably decorated by members of his workshop in the early sixteenth century – 'was sent as a gift from Francesco Portinari to Henry VII in connection with his plans to found a similar hospital in London' (Alexander 1999; see also Kren 1983).

Whether Henry VIII read the present manuscript is unknown since it bears no annotations in his hand, but in the mid- or late sixteenth century it came into the possession of Nicholas Bond (b. 1540, d. 1608), doctor of theology and President of Magdalen College, Oxford. Evidently, desiring to return the book to a royal reader, Bond presented it to Henry Frederick (b. 1594, d. 1612), Prince of Wales and son of James I, on the occasion of his matriculation from Magdalen College, Oxford, 29 August 1605 (Wolpe 1958). Around this time the manuscript acquired a new cover of English workmanship. Now stored separately from the volume, which is bound in its original red leather, this rare chemise of crimson velvet, decorated with seed pearls and silver and gold thread, bears the Prince's badge and motto. *D.J.*

PROVENANCE:

Henry VIII; Nicholas Bond (b. 1540, d. 1608); Henry Frederick, Prince of Wales (d. 1612).

Opposite:
Pandolfo Collenuccio, and the arms of Henry VIII, f. 4

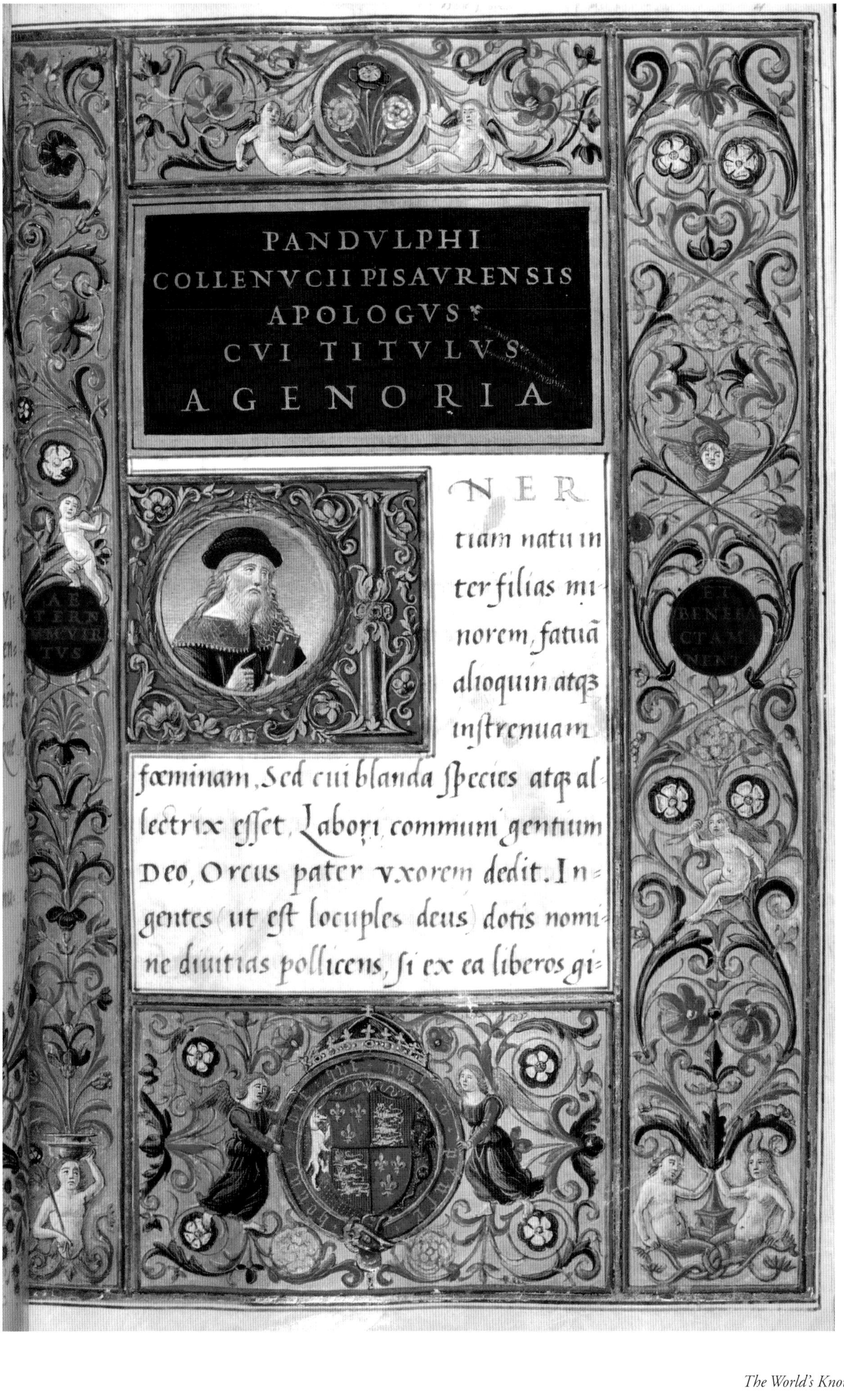

PANDVLPHI
COLLENVCII PISAVRENSIS
APOLOGVS
CVI TITVLVS
AGENORIA

INER
tiam natu in
ter filias mi
norem, fatuā
alioquin atq3
instrenuam
fœminam, Sed cui blanda species atq3 al
lectrix esset. Labori commum gentium
Deo, Orcus pater vxorem dedit. In
gentes (ut est locuples deus) dotis nomi
ne diuitias pollicens, si ex ea liberos gi

Royal Identity

For many centuries writings about the past have proved a powerful tool for shaping the identity of rulers and nations. In the Middle Ages chronicles, in which historical material was usually organized according to the regnal years of kings, constituted a rich repository of royal iconography, and also provided an important record of royal ideology and propaganda. The first group of manuscripts in the present section explores the use of history in the legitimization and promotion of royal power and as a persuasive medium of instruction. Viking invasions, the Norman Conquest, Lancastrian and Yorkist usurpations and the Tudors' victory in the Wars of the Roses all disrupted dynastic continuity in England. Genealogy, heraldry, legend and political prophecy were used to sanction these shifts of power. Searching for continuity in royal succession, Peter of Langtoft placed King Arthur's crown on William the Conqueror's head and his sword in the hand of Richard the Lionheart (cat. no. 116); genealogical roll chronicles featured the Plantagenets as the heirs of both Anglo-Saxon kings and Norman dukes (cat. nos. 117, 118); and Henry VII used as his badge the red dragon of Cadwaladr ap Cadwallon, the supposed last King of the Britons (cat. no. 120). The examples of monarchs from the past were also used as influential models of kingship. The Benedictine monk Matthew Paris created a portrait gallery of kings as founders of religious institutions (cat. no. 114) and John Capgrave presented biographies of 'illustrious Henrys' for Henry VI to imitate (cat. no. 119).

Royal status and identity were expressed and sustained by rituals and ceremonies. Of these, the coronation was the most critical. The Westminster *Liber regalis* that codified the liturgy of royal investiture was perhaps owned by Richard II and his successors (cat. no. 122). Innumerable images of coronations were included in chronicles and royal documents, not only to commemorate particular events (cat. no. 121) but equally as symbols of royal power (cat. no. 115). The use of the king's image in books owned by his subjects could also represent an expression of their loyalty or allegiance to the monarchy (cat. nos. 121, 124). In the case of legal compilations, these images provided confirmation of royal authority over the law (cat. nos. 123, 124).

The king's role as the military leader was also a part of his royal identity. English monarchs shared with the rest of the nobility the chivalric values and concepts of courtesy that were both shaped by the literature of knightly instruction (cat. nos. 125–127) and by romances in French, the elitist language of the court (cat. nos. 129–133), and embodied in the foundation of the elite chivalric order, the Order of the Garter (cat. no. 128).

The Coronation (cat. no. 115)

Jon regna Henry le terz sun fiz. lvi. aunz.

114 Matthew Paris, *Historia Anglorum*

St Albans, *c.* 1250
360 x 245 mm

BRITISH LIBRARY, ROYAL 14 C. vii

Portraits of English kings from William I to Henry III, ff. 8v–9

The chronicles written by Matthew Paris are amongst the most fascinating to have survived from the Middle Ages. Forthright in his opinions and engaging in his style of delivery, Matthew combined an obvious talent for writing with skills as an artist to produce a series of works that captivated his contemporaries and exercised an increasingly strong appeal in the centuries after his death in 1259 or 1260. Thomas Walsingham, for example – who, like Matthew, was a monk in the Benedictine monastery of St Albans – was still praising him in the late fourteenth century as an 'incomparable chronicler and excellent painter', since unequalled in the Latin world (Vaughan 1958). More recent scholarship has bolstered this opinion by proving that he variously acted as author, translator, illustrator and scribe on an impressive number of works ranging from historiography through to biography and cartography, the vast majority of which survive (Vaughan 1953, Lewis 1987).

Principal amongst Matthew's chronicles is the large *Chronica maiora*, or *majora*, covering world history from the Creation. The third and last part, with annals from 1254 to 1259, and brief later entries by others to 1272, occupies the last third of the present volume. Internal evidence clearly indicates that Matthew intended the third part of the *Chronica* to form a separate volume, similar in form to the two other surviving parts (Cambridge, Corpus Christi College, MSS 26 and 16). However, it somehow became bound up with the most significant of his shorter histories, the *Historia Anglorum*, along with a small section of material consisting of tables, diagrams, maps, and other illustrations that now forms a preface to the present volume. The relationship between this prefatory material and Matthew's chronicles is not entirely clear (see cat. no. 94). Recent studies have favoured the opinion that the scenes showing the kings of England from William I to Henry III (pictured) were designed to introduce the *Historia*, partly because of their current placement in the present manuscript and also because the kings Matthew chose to portray correspond to the chronological range of the shorter chronicle, which begins with the Norman conquest of England and ends with the year 1253.

What remains a bigger mystery is the intended audience for such a gallery. It is certainly fit for a king, and Henry III

visited the abbey of St Albans on a number of occasions and was personally familiar with Matthew. Yet the *Historia* contains a number of comments highly critical of the King – many of which Matthew himself subsequently highlighted with marginal comments noting that they were potentially offensive and needed to be revised (Vaughan 1958). It seems, therefore, that even Matthew questioned whether the *Historia Anglorum* was suitable for a royal audience.

If Matthew did originally design the portraits with the King in mind, the image of royalty that Matthew chose to present is somewhat unusual. Each of the kings is seated regally upon a throne, and each holds a symbol representative of his reign. But instead of choosing a symbol to represent a political or military act or event, Matthew showed the kings holding buildings, all but one of which represent religious foundations. Thus, William I is shown as though holding a model of Battle Abbey, which he founded; Henry I clasps his foundation of Reading Abbey; Stephen presents his abbey of Faversham; Henry II cradles Waltham Abbey, which he reformed; Richard I holds the church of St Thomas of Canterbury that he established at Acre; John shows us the Cistercian abbey at Beaulieu; and Henry III is associated with the newly established Westminster Abbey. The single exception to the theme of religious establishments is William II, who is shown holding a model of Westminster Hall. As a result the overall impression given by the images is of the king as patron, especially as patron of religious foundations. However, it is no coincidence that the seven religious foundations are monasteries and that four represent Benedictine houses; Matthew was a shamelessly partisan supporter of monasticism in general, and of his Order in particular. It therefore seems that Matthew may have designed the gallery in the hope that the pious actions of the King and his royal forebears, especially in support of the Benedictines, might inspire Henry III in his Christian duties as ruler.

J.C.

PROVENANCE:

Humfrey, Duke of Gloucester (b. 1391, d. 1447); John Russell, Bishop of Lincoln (d. 1494); Henry VIII; lent to Henry Fitzalan, 12th Earl of Arundel (b. 1511, d. 1580); John, 1st Baron Lumley (d. 1609); Henry Frederick, Prince of Wales (d. 1612).

115 Images of English Kings, from Edward the Confessor to Edward I

England, *c.* 1280–1300
200 × 140 mm (maximum size of original parchment as preserved)

BRITISH LIBRARY, COTTON VITELLIUS A. xiii, ff. 3–6v

King John offered a cup of poison by a monk of Swineshead; Coronation of Henry III, ff. 5v–6

Images of kings are common throughout the arts of the Middle Ages, yet the ideals of kingship that they project are not constant. Depending upon the patron of a given image, they could inform the king of the ideal his subjects hoped he would embody, serve as the medium through which the king projected an idealized image of himself or assist in the formation of future rulers. The present four leaves, of obscure origins, are remarkable for the complex ideas about monarchy that they convey.

Within these eight pages a sequence of large illustrations reveals ten successive kings of England in various settings and activities. Each page features one or two miniatures showing a king, below which is text in Anglo-Norman French that details the length of that king's reign, one or two notable events from his life and, finally, where his remains are kept. Six of the kings each have devoted to them a three-quarter-page miniature illustrating episodes from their lives. The remaining four kings, about whom the author or illustrator presumably knew little, are accorded half that space and shown only as standing or seated figures. Taken together, these images present the various activities in which any king would be expected to participate: coping with domestic threats from upstart noblemen (f. 3), waging war against foreign leaders (f. 3v), hawking at leisure (f. 4v) and balancing his power with that of the Church (ff. 5v, 6). A lingering question about this short sequence of illustrations is whether it was intended for the king, or whether the king intended it for his subjects.

Because these leaves were preserved as part of a seventeenth-century compilation of historical texts drawn from several earlier volumes (only since 1939 have they been kept separately from the rest of the compilation), the original context for which they were intended may now only be surmised. An introductory text (f. 3) proclaims 'here are the kings of England from the time of Edward the Confessor to the time of Edward, son of King Henry III', and thus refers only to the pictorial cycle itself. However, independent cycles of illustration like this are unknown; rather, most such cycles formed prefatory matter to larger texts, usually genealogies or chronicles on the history of England (see cat. nos. 114, 116). These literary genres were common in the thirteenth and fourteenth centuries, and many illustrated

examples survive (Dean and Boulton 1999).

It is probable that these leaves were produced during the reign of Edward I. Sandler (1986) dated the images to the last two decades of the thirteenth century on the basis of the style of the miniatures as well as the absence of text (save the letter 'A') from the final depiction of Edward I. The image that illustrates his reign is generic (f. 6v), showing him enthroned before courtiers, clergy and scribes (Michael 1994), an open ending that was common in genealogical rolls. In its subject matter, this gallery of monarchs seems to have been informed by the many large-scale images of kings commissioned by Edward's father, Henry III, such as on his throne at Windsor and in the hall of Dublin Castle. At the same time, the small size of the leaves indicates that the manuscript for which they were destined was of modest dimensions. By transforming a monumental and imposing subject into something more intimate, perhaps this sequence was appropriate only for possession by the King himself. In 1301 the King purchased for his eldest son, Edward, a *De gestis regum Anglie* (Cavanaugh 1988), an enticing match for the present leaves.

Still, the aims of this cycle remain difficult to determine, as exemplified by the juxtaposition of two leaves that once faced one another, showing King John and Henry III (pictured). On the page devoted to John (f. 5v), monks look on as one from their group offers a chalice filled with poison to John. The text below specifies that a six-year long interdict had been imposed upon England by the pope when John refused to accept Stephen Langton as Archbishop of Canterbury. But is this image glorifying or vilifying the monk who poisoned him? In contrast, the opposite page (f. 6) shows Church and State in perfect harmony. Henry III appears at his coronation, flanked by clergy who place the crown upon his head, while he holds a model of Westminster Abbey before his chest. These and the other miniatures in this sequence tell the story of England's monarchy as one of constant negotiation. Whether Edward I was poised to follow the successful model of his father remained an open question in this unfinished programme. *S.D.*

PROVENANCE:

Sir Robert Cotton (d. 1631); bequeathed to the nation by Sir John Cotton, 1702.

116 Peter of Langtoft's *Chronicle, the Lament of Edward II*, fragments of Romances, and a letter attributed to Joanna, Queen of Sicily

Northern England, *c.* 1307–27
230 x 150 mm

BRITISH LIBRARY, ROYAL 20 A. ii

Peter of Langtoft's French verse chronicle, written *c.* 1307, traces the history of Britain from its legendary foundation by Brutus, whose ancestors had been exiled from Troy, to the reign of Edward I. The complete text survives in nine manuscripts made in northern England. Six, including the present volume, were copied before 1350 (Summerfield 1998). Little is known about Langtoft except that he was a canon at Bridlington, an Augustinian priory in Yorkshire.

This manuscript of Langtoft's *Chronicle*, made during the reign of Edward II, opens with a series of full-page tinted drawings of kings, arranged in chronological order. No other copy of the *Chronicle* has a comparable visual preface. Two artists, whose style is easily distinguished, drew the images of kings on the first ten leaves of the manuscript, which forms an independent gathering. Later, a third artist sketched images of the Creation of the World and of the Fall of Troy on a blank flyleaf (ff. 1–1v). Though not part of the original pictorial programme, these later images are based on Langtoft's text, which opens with a cursory account of the Creation of the World, and a description of the Fall of Troy and the flight of the Trojan exiles, which led to Brutus's discovery of Britain.

The first ten images of kings, from Brutus to Edward the Confessor (ff. 2–5), were executed by an artist who framed his compositions in black. Sketched with stiff strokes of the pen, his figures have angular features, large hands and quizzical expressions. King Arthur, for example (f. 4, pictured), is shown with his fabled sword Excalibur and his shield emblazoned with an image of the Virgin and Child (rather than the three crowns of the French tradition). The shield with the Virgin's likeness is described in an anonymous ninth-century chronicle, composed in Wales, the *Historia Brittonum* (History of the Britons), and is also mentioned by Geoffrey of Monmouth, whose *Historia regum Britanniae* (History of the Kings of Britain), written *c.* 1136, was one of the many sources consulted by Langtoft. Thirty crowns, arrayed in rows beneath Arthur's feet, represent kingdoms under his subjection. Since few images of Arthur occur in extant English manuscripts, this one is noteworthy (Loomis and Loomis 1938; Stones 1991, 2006).

In his chronicle Langtoft links subsequent kings with Arthur, the most illustrious British model of Christian kingship (Summerfield 1998). He states, for example, that on Christmas Day 1066, Arthur's crown was placed on the head of William the Conqueror, and that Richard I wielded Arthur's sword. Edward I's disregard for the nobles who fought in his campaigns against the Scots, and his failure to reward them, are contrasted with Arthur's largesse and ability to inspire loyalty. Reluctance to accept that such an ideal king could die gave rise to the myth that Arthur was immortal and would one day return.

A second artist executed the last ten images of kings (ff. 5v–10), beginning with William the Conqueror. The change of artist and shift from Anglo-Saxon to Norman rulers heralded a new approach. In this final section, images of enthroned kings appear at the top of the pages, with genealogical tables and/or Latin verses in the spaces beneath. The artist probably based the tables on royal genealogical rolls, first produced in England in the middle of the thirteenth century (e.g. cat. nos. 117, 118). Vines and oaks sprout from or flank the thrones of all the Norman monarchs portrayed, as if to stress the robustness of the royal line. A pragmatist, this second artist did not hesitate to trace his 'portrait' of William Rufus (f. 6) in order to complete his 'portrait' of Henry I on the back of the same leaf. Undeterred by a small hole in the parchment, he used it to represent decorative apertures in their thrones.

The final image depicts Edward II, who is identified in the caption as a prince. Originally a Latin poem praising him was written beneath the image, but after Edward's deposition or death, *c.* 1327, this text was effaced and a lament in French verse, allegedly written by the King himself and including the memorable lines 'Home m'appele roys abatu, / E tout le secle me va gabaunt' (I am called the tumble-down king, and all the world mocks me) was inserted in its place. It is apt that the present manuscript, which opens with images of English monarchs and chronicles their deeds, came into the royal library, but how and when it was acquired is unknown. It was among the volumes in the Upper Library at Westminster Palace by around the middle of the sixteenth century. *D. J.*

PROVENANCE:

Henry VIII.

Opposite:
King Arthur armed for battle, f. 4

117 Genealogical Chronicle of the English Kings

England, 1274 – *c.* 1300
3935 x 240 mm

BRITISH LIBRARY, ROYAL 14 B. v

118 Genealogical Chronicle of the English Kings

England (?East Anglia), *c.* 1300–07; (addition) *c.* 1340–42
4750 x 275 mm

BRITISH LIBRARY, ROYAL 14 B. vi

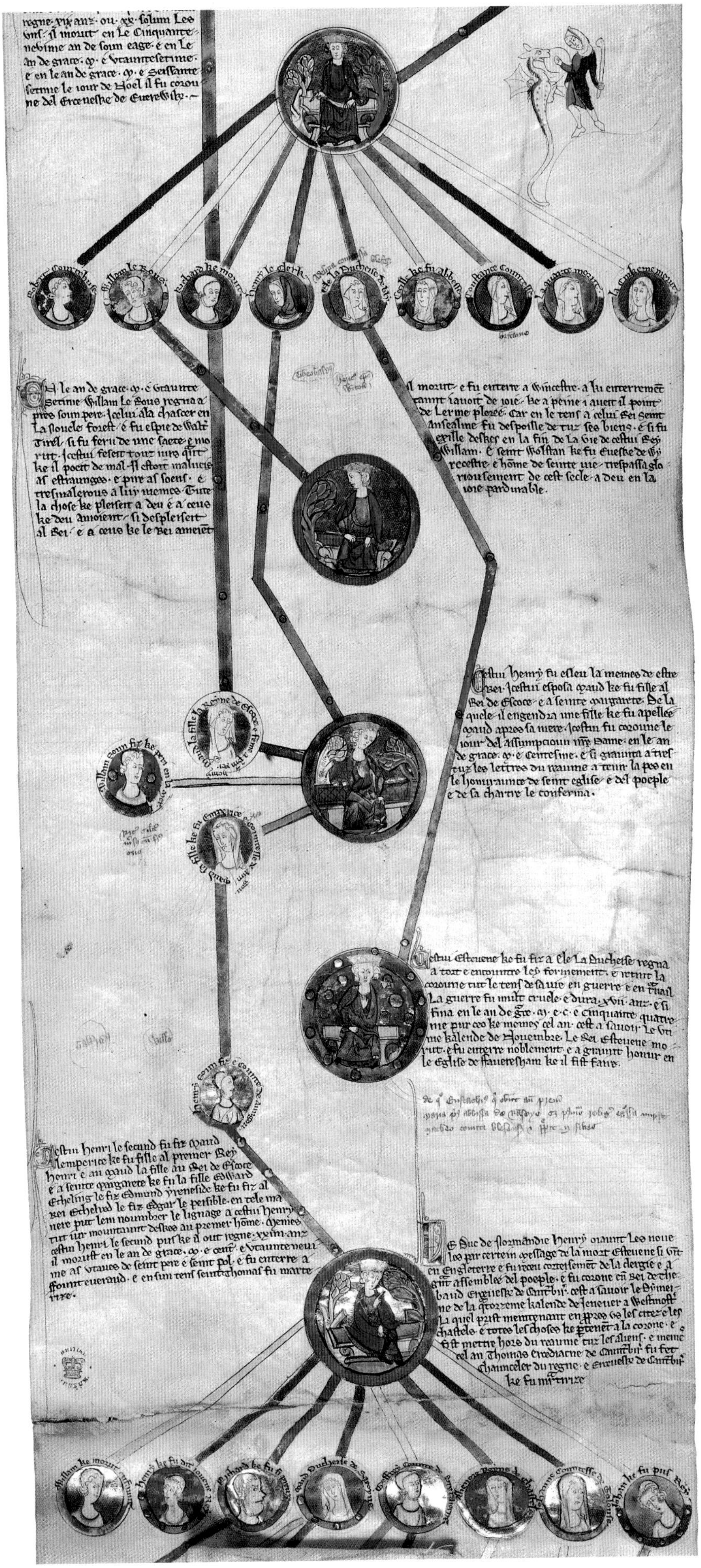

The presentation of history in the form of an illustrated genealogical diagram of royal descent depicted on long rolls (often several metres in extent) gained considerable popularity in medieval England. Forty such genealogical chronicles of English kings survive from the period between Edward I's accession to the throne (1272) and the death of Henry V (1422); the peak of their popularity occurred during the reigns of Edward I and Edward II. Most of these rolls contain variants of the same anonymous Anglo-Norman text, which is displayed in short captions and provides a commentary on the royal portraits in the interconnected roundels. The roll format of the chronicle was probably adopted from the *Compendium historiae in genealogia Christi* of the late twelfth-century Parisian scholar Peter of Poitiers. However, the use of a royal genealogy in diagrammatic form to tell the history of English monarchy was the invention of Matthew Paris, the Benedictine monk and historian from St Albans (d. 1259). Four drafts of royal pedigrees with illustrations and inscriptions arranged in roundels around a vertical line survive in three of Matthew's autograph manuscripts (Cambridge, Corpus Christi College, MSS. 16 and 26, and Cotton Claudius D. vi). Matthew's historical writings (see cat. no. 114) also constituted a major textual source for the roll chronicles' commentary. De Laborderie (2002) has suggested that the chronicler from

St Albans may have written the original royal genealogy (now lost) as a companion to the Anglo-Norman life of Edward the Confessor, *La Estoire de Seint Aedward le Rei*, which Matthew probably wrote and dedicated to Eleanor of Provence, Henry III's Queen.

Both rolls from the Old Royal library date from the reign of Edward I and both represent the most common variant of the genealogical chronicle. Their historical narrative begins with a large round diagram known as the Heptarchy representing the seven Anglo-Saxon kingdoms (Northumbria, Mercia, East Anglia, Essex, Kent, Sussex and Wessex), which are arranged geographically and provide a schematic map of England. The royal line starts below with 'Ecgberht' (Egbert, d. 839), the King of Wessex who united the Anglo-Saxon kingdoms, and ends with a portrait of Edward I. In Royal 14 B. vi, the royal line was later extended to include a series of portraits drawn in pen of Edward I's descendants to Edward III. The text of the accompanying commentary, which is unique to this roll, helps to date the additions. It mentions Edward III's claim to the French throne, first expressed in 1340, and the Black Prince's creation as Duke of Cornwall in 1337 – without referring to his title as the Prince of Wales, which was granted to him in 1343.

Unlike their later counterparts of the Yorkist and Tudor periods, the genealogical rolls produced during the reign of Edward I did not arise from any dynastic crisis.

Left:
Genealogical descent of the dukes of Normandy, Royal 14 B. vi (detail)

Opposite:
Genealogical descent of the English kings from Henry I to Henry II, Royal 14 B. v (detail)

Instead of proving the legitimacy of a new royal regime, they were fashioned to shape the past of the English monarchy and promote the image of Plantagenet dynastic identity. Following a genealogical argument first established by Ailred of Rievaulx in 1154 and repeated by Matthew Paris, the rolls emphasized the Anglo-Saxon descent of the Plantagenet dynasty through Henry I's wife Matilda, grandmother of Henry II and great-granddaughter of Edmund Ironside, the half-brother of Edward the Confessor. In both Royal rolls a line nearly a metre long links St Margaret, Edmund's granddaughter, to Queen Matilda, reuniting the Anglo-Saxon kings with the descendants of the Norman dukes to whom the Plantagenets owed the English throne.

The inclusion of the Norman ancestors of William the Conqueror was an innovation of Anglo-Norman roll chronicles, and never appears in their less numerous Latin counterparts (de Laborderie 2003). The Norman lineage from Rollo, 1st Duke of Normandy (d. *c.* 932), to Duke Richard I the Fearless (d. 996) was included between the roundels of Harold II (Godwineson) and William the Conqueror and is prominent visually. In Royal 14 B. v, the dukes are portrayed with all the attributes of royal authority; they are crowned and sit on thrones. In Royal 14 B. vi images of two green trees, an oak and a maple (or a chestnut), single out the Norman line and highlight it clearly within the genealogical diagram (pictured overleaf). Similar depictions of a tree and a rosebush flank the portrait of Edward I in the last roundel of the roll (pictured opposite). It is uncertain whether these images refer to royal fertility (de Laborderie 2002), allude to the general idea of genealogy as a tree, or play on associations with Edward the Confessor's prophecy of the green tree which – according to Matthew Paris's interpretation – flourished when the Norman trunk was reunited with the Anglo-Saxon roots. Despite the ambiguous status of William the Conqueror as both an illegitimate child and a usurper of the English throne – both are acknowledged in the roll chronicles – the inclusion of the Norman origins of the Plantagenet dynasty must have responded to the Anglo-Norman identity that the ruling house shared with the English aristocracy (de Laborderie 2003).

Although only restricted information about the original owners of such rolls survives, the translations of genealogical chronicles into Anglo-Norman that they include were probably intended primarily for a lay aristocratic audience. It is also likely that presentation copies were made for royal patrons. Not only does the concise and often anecdotal text of the roll chronicles give a memorable account of English history, but its praise of military prowess and condemnation of treachery, immorality and weak rulers expresses basic chivalric values and may have informed models and anti-models for reigning kings.

Both Royal rolls are lavish copies of the genealogical chronicle and were doubtless intended for wealthy patrons. Royal 14 B. v was probably accomplished before 1300 and, as de Laborderie (2002) has suggested, may have served as a model for Royal 14 B. vi and two other rolls illuminated at Westminster (Cotton Rolls xv. 7 and Oxford, Bodleian Library, MS Broxbourne 112.3). The style of its decoration, which combines painted portraits of the English kings with drolleries elegantly executed in tinted drawing, is difficult to localise. An almost illegible note at the end of the roll that apparently contains excuses concerning the illuminator's work (Warner and Gilson 1921) includes no information about the original owner.

Royal 14 B. vi, which contains illuminations stylistically close to the work of the East Anglian artists of the Ramsey Psalter (St Paul im Lavanttal, Stiftsbibliothek, Cod. XXV/2,19, and New York, Pierpont Morgan Library, M. 302; *c.* 1300–10), must have been owned by 1340 by someone who was well informed on current politics at the royal court, so detailed is the addition explaining Edward III's rights to the French throne. The decoration of the roll also includes an intriguing depiction of a red rosebush next to the portrait of Edward I (pictured opposite). The red rose is said to have been a badge of Edward's brother Edmund Crouchback, founder of the earldom of Lancaster (Siddons 2009), but as no other contemporary image of this device survives the meaning of the Royal illumination is uncertain, and no conclusions about early royal ownership can be made on this basis. It is, however, possible that Royal 14 B. vi is the *Role des roys dAngleterre* that was listed amongst the books kept at Richmond Palace in 1535 and described by several seventeenth-century travellers (see Carley 2000). It is likely that a roll that came into the Old Royal library from Lord Lumley, described in the catalogue of the Lumley collection as containing the royal genealogy until Edward I, can be identified with Royal 14 B. v. *J.F.*

PROVENANCE:

117: John, 1st Baron Lumley (d. 1609); Henry Frederick, Prince of Wales (d. 1612).
118: Henry VIII.

Opposite:
Genealogical descent from Henry III to Edward I, Royal 14 B. vi (detail)

Edward son fiz.
Edward.
Henry
Joan.
Amphous.
Edward roy.

119 John Capgrave, *Liber de illustribus Henricis*

England (?East Anglia), *c.* 1447
205 x 140 mm (maximum size of original parchment as preserved)

BRITISH LIBRARY, COTTON TIBERIUS A. viii

John Capgrave (d. 1464), an Augustinian friar with a prolific literary output, is remarkable for his involvement in the production of manuscripts containing his works. Like John Lydgate, Capgrave tailored his oeuvre to the intellectual interests of his patrons and dedicatees. He wrote saints' lives for leaders of religious houses; scholarly commentaries on biblical texts for the self-styled humanist, Humfrey, Duke of Gloucester; a chronicle for Edward IV; and the *Liber de illustribus Henricis* (The Book of Illustrious Henrys) for Henry VI. While these last two works have been mustered as evidence of Capgrave's sycophancy, they instead reflect an acute mind employing flattering language to influence kings' behaviour.

De illustribus Henricis, as its title indicates, compiles exemplary narratives of renowned Henrys throughout history. Composed between *c.* 1440 and early 1447, it is dedicated to Henry VI, 'so that thou who art crowned with this name, mayest also imitate the virtue of the name'. The work is divided into three parts: the first concerns the Holy Roman emperors, the second treats the kings of England, and the third profiles sundry famous Henrys who preceded Henry VI. A working copy of this text, written in Capgrave's own hand (Cambridge, Corpus Christi College, MS 408), provides evidence for the occasion of the text's completion: on 1 August 1446 Henry VI visited Capgrave's priory at Lynn, and it is in his account of this visit that Capgrave wrote in the margin '*data compilatoris*' (information of the compiler). The chapter devoted to the life of Henry VI, unlike the surrounding biographies, does not record the memorable deeds of the King, but praises only his piety and expresses the hope that he will follow the more active examples of his namesakes and forebears.

This hope is underscored by the pictorial programme of the manuscript reproduced, the only other extant copy of *De illustribus Henricis*. Each of the twenty-four chapters opens with an inhabited initial depicting the Henry whose biography it begins. In the first part each Holy Roman emperor is identical to the rest, portrayed as a standing figure with a white beard and triple-crown, holding a sword and orb. The figures in the second part are similar, but the artist has replaced the imperial crown with the royal crown, substituted a sceptre for the sword, and introduced nuances that give each figure a hint of individuality. Finally, the various Henrys of the third part are shown only in bust and are entirely different from one another, each wearing headgear that reflects his respective status. Their appearance as busts and accompaniment by less elaborate marginal sprays than in the first and second parts diminish the significance of the notables of the third.

Several subtle features focus the recipient's attention on the central portion of the volume, that is, the biographies of the most immediate succession: Henry IV, Henry V and Henry VI. While the first eight figures face to the left, Henry IV gazes to the right, looking forward in the direction of the text and, by implication, towards his son and grandson. This alteration in the nearly uniform procession of emperors and kings is striking enough to arrest the viewer's notice. Similarly there are only two instances of marginal *notae* in the manuscript: one marks Henry IV's dying exhortation to his son; the other highlights the praise of England sung by Emperor Sigismund's subjects as they departed from the successful diplomatic encounter with Henry V. Perhaps, in heeding these marks, Henry VI would find the impetus to commit his own deeds worthy of such *notae*.

Although some doubt has been cast upon the identity of the original recipient of this manuscript (Lucas 1997), it is probable that it was the presentation copy made for Henry VI. The deluxe nature of the manuscript itself indicates an exalted destination, but it is a mention in the earliest extant royal inventory, that of the partial list of the library at Richmond Palace that points more persuasively towards its royal ownership. Among the items listed in French is a book of *Les roys Henry empereurs* (Carley 2000). This volume's subsequent incorporation into the Cotton collection suggests that the book passed into Sir Robert Cotton's hands as part of the dispersal of many royal manuscripts under the tenure of James I's librarian, Patrick Young. Unfortunately the 1731 fire that damaged and destroyed so many Cotton manuscripts consumed the opening pages of the present volume. Consequently we do not know whether it, like three other manuscripts of Capgrave's works, once contained an initial depicting the presentation of its text to the king whom Capgrave hoped would become another illustrious Henry. *S.D.*

PROVENANCE:

Henry VI; Henry VIII; Sir Robert Cotton (d. 1631); bequeathed to the nation by Sir John Cotton, 1702.

Opposite top:
Henry V, f. 58v (detail)

Opposite below:
Henry VI, f. 67 (detail)

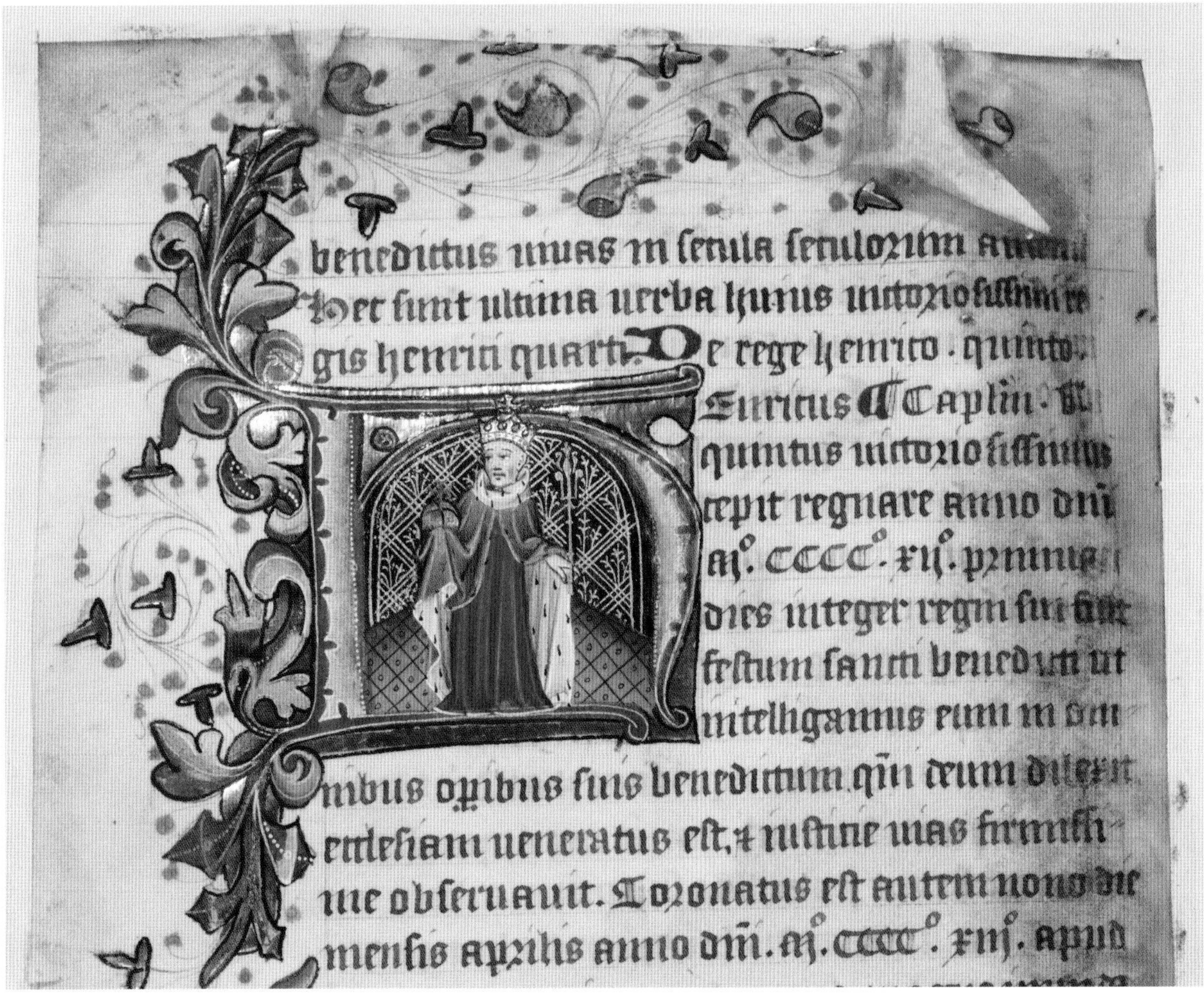

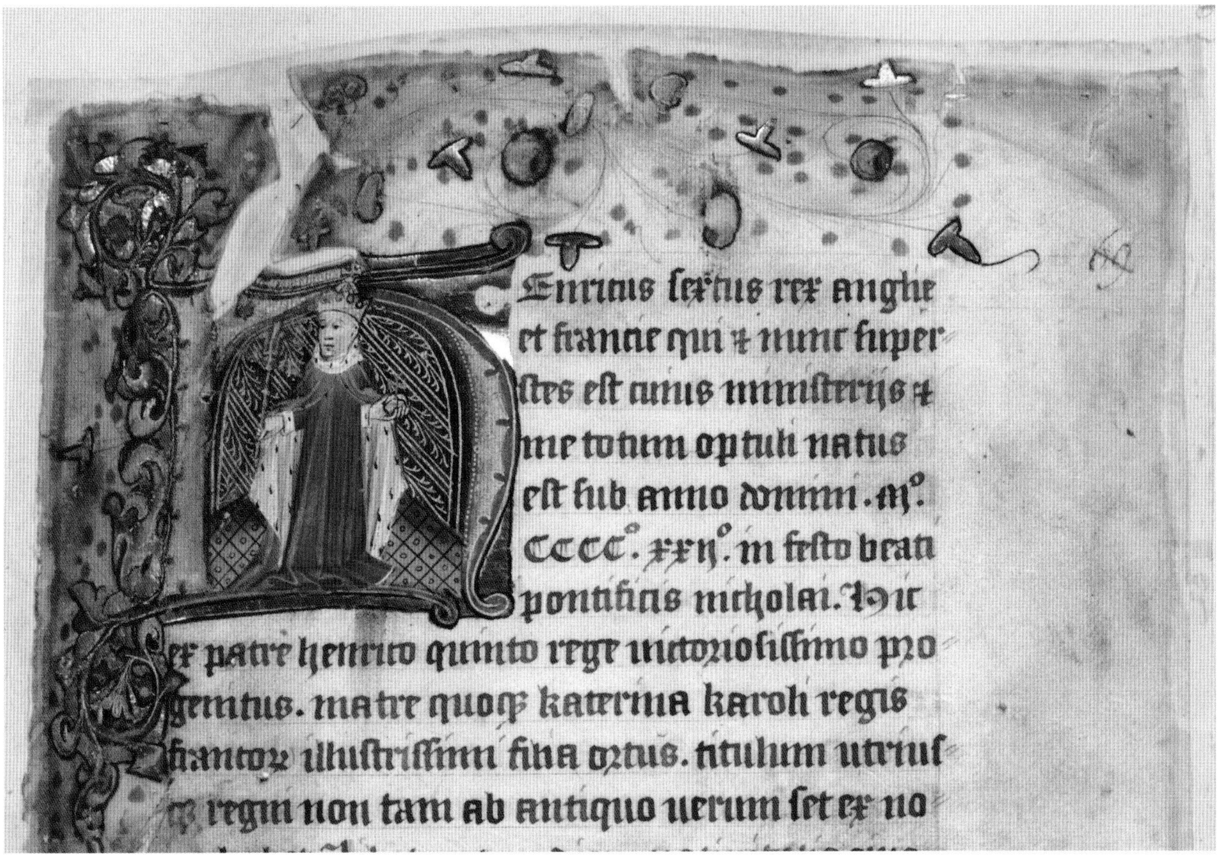

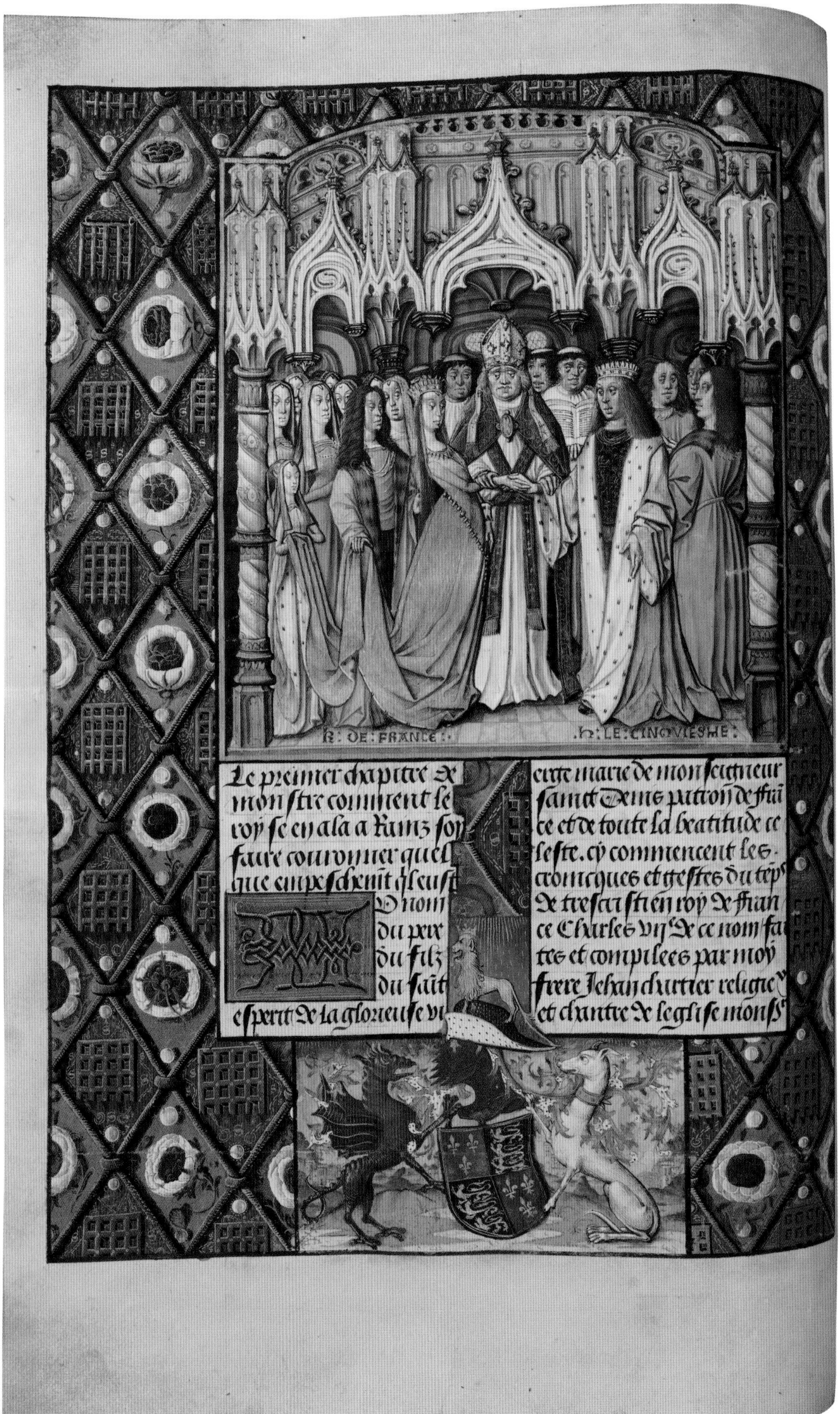
H: DE: FRANCE:
.H: LE: CINQUIESME:

20 Jean Chartier, *Chronique de Charles VII*

(Continuation of the *Grandes chroniques de France*)

Calais, 1487; Southern Netherlands and England, between 1487 and 1494
535 x 335 mm

BRITISH LIBRARY, ROYAL 20 E. vi

This massive manuscript – the last of a set now bound in six volumes (Royal 20 E. i–vi) – contains Jean Chartier's continuation of the *Grandes chroniques de France,* a French translation of the history of the French monarchs (see cat. no. 136), and covers the reign of Charles VII. The Royal *Grandes chroniques* is one of the very few deluxe copies of this historiographical work that were made at the end of the fifteenth century.

The six volumes were copied in a large angular formal bastard script by Hugh de Lembourg, a native of Paris in the service of Sir Thomas Thwaytes, Treasurer of the Pale of Calais. Hugh's colophon at the end of what originally was the first volume of the set (now Royal 20 E. iii, f. 94v) provides the date of completion of the first portion of the text on 13 October 1487. Thwaytes, a former servant to both Edward IV and Richard III, who retained his office under the new Tudor regime, doubtless designed the manuscripts as a political gift to Henry VII. Although neither a formal dedication to the King nor a presentation miniature survives, a number of Henry's badges, mottos and arms clearly define the intended recipient of the book. The border of the miniature reproduced here is a good example of the overwhelming presence of the King's emblems and devices of the new dynasty. The margins are divided into lozenge-shaped compartments and decorated alternately with a Tudor rose and a golden portcullis. The red-and-white rose refers to the union between the houses of York and Lancaster, which was reaffirmed by the marriage between Henry and Elizabeth of York. The portcullis, a badge of the Beauforts, was adopted by Henry to highlight his royal lineage through his mother, Lady Margaret Beaufort, a great-granddaughter of John of Gaunt, Duke of Lancaster, third son of Edward III. In the lower margin the supporters of the royal arms, the white greyhound and the red dragon of Cadwaladr, mark Henry's descent from the Lancastrians and legendary kings of Britain (see cat. nos. 68, 99).

Work on the decoration of the Royal *Grandes chroniques* probably started in Calais where the text was written, and may have been disturbed by Thwaytes's departure from the city in 1490. Initials and ivy-stem borders introduced only in the first quire of the first volume suggest such a break in production. The second campaign began shortly thereafter, with miniatures, borders and initials executed by more than six different artists working simultaneously on all volumes of the set. The quality of their illumination varies, from the high standards of a Flemish-trained follower of the Bruges Master of 1482 (Royal 20 E. i, f. 47) to – as in the case of the miniature reproduced – rather crude imitations of Flemish work by artists whose English origins are suggested by two extant instructions to them in their mother tongue that still accompany their illustrations (Royal 20 E. iv, ff. 30v, 71v).

The full programme of illumination is now impossible to reconstruct. Only thirty-nine out of 203 planned miniatures were completed, and substantial portions of the text covering the reigns of Philip VI and Charles V are now missing. Several existing miniatures, however, that depict episodes rarely or never illustrated in other copies of the *Grandes chroniques* seem designed specifically for an English audience. These include scenes from the history of pre-conquest Normandy, such as the baptism of Rollo (Royal 20 E. ii, f. 233) and the fleet of Æthelred II attacking the Normans at the Cotentin Peninsula (Royal 20 E. ii, f. 258v), or from the Hundred Years War, such as the English victory at the battle of St James in 1426 (Royal 20 E. vi, f. 20). The miniature of the marriage between Henry V and Catherine of France in 1420, which guaranteed the English succession in France, must have had a special meaning for Henry VII's own royal identity (pictured). His paternal grandfather, Owen Tudor, Henry V's squire, secretly married Queen Catherine after the King's death and thereby secured for his progeny a place in the French royal lineage.

Thwaytes's project remained unfinished. In 1494 he was arrested for treason as a supporter of the royal pretender Perkin Warbeck, and only avoided a death sentence by paying a heavy fine to the King. His books may have been confiscated and passed into the Old Royal library either on his detention or just after his death in 1503. Two other deluxe manuscripts bearing Thwaytes's arms, a five-volume Froissart (Royal 14 D. ii–vi) and Xenophon's *Cyropaedia* bound with Vegetius's *De re militari* (Royal 17 E. v), may also have been incorporated into the royal collection at the same time. *J.F.*

PROVENANCE:

Sir Thomas Thwaytes (d. 1503); Henry VII.

Opposite:
Marriage ceremony of Henry V and Catherine of France, f. 9v

121 Documents on Royal Politics, Legislation and Ceremony (Edward III to Richard II)

London, *c.* 1386–99
360 x 240 mm

BRITISH LIBRARY, COTTON NERO D. vi

The present manuscript contains a collection of historical documents concerning royal politics, legislation and ceremonies. The first group of texts relates to the reign of Edward III and English affairs in France (the Treaty of Brétigny in 1360, the grant of Aquitaine to the Black Prince, Alfonso of Castile's renouncement of Gascony in favour of Henry III and its ratification in 1362) and in Scotland (the truce at Berwick-upon-Tweed in 1357). The second group of documents concerns the reign of Richard II. It contains a description of his coronation, two tracts on the King's presidency over Parliament and a duel at the royal court, a short chronicle from the time of Noah to the accession of Richard II, texts related to the office of the earl marshal, and several statutes and ordinances promulgated by Richard II.

The principal documents within this collection are illustrated by images of kings or their officers exercising their prerogatives as guarantors of rights and sources of power. The illustrations show them confirming peace treaties, granting charters, receiving homage, appointing officials, holding parliament and presiding over a judicial duel. The historiated initial reproduced here depicts the fundamental ritual of kingship – the royal coronation. The image shows the crucial moment of the ceremony when the crown is placed on the king's head by two bishops. The illustration in the Cotton manuscript is clearly a reduction of a more complex composition that illustrates the coronation order for an English king in the Litlyngton Missal (London, Westminster Abbey, MS 37). Commissioned in *c.* 1383–84 by Nicholas Litlyngton, Abbot of Westminster, the Missal was illuminated by the artist who decorated the Cotton collection and several other manuscripts associated with the patronage of either Richard II or Westminster, namely the *Liber geomantiae* (Oxford, Bodleian Library, MS Bodley 581), an Apocalypse (Cambridge, Trinity College, MS B. 10.2) and the Life of the Black Prince (London, University Library, MS 1) (see Sandler 1986).

The Cotton *Coronation* marks the beginning of a description of Richard II's coronation of 1377 that was appended to an account of the proceedings of the Court of Claims that John of Gaunt, the Lord Steward, held before the coronation ceremony. This text, which was copied from the official record of the coronation enrolled in Chancery (see London, TNA: PRO, CR I Ric. II. mem. 45), lists the claims of various magnates to the right to serve the King at his coronation, together with the decisions of the court. The arms of each participant of the ceremony are inserted beside the description of their offices and duties. Together they create an armorial of the nobility loyal to the King.

It has been suggested that the Cotton manuscript may have been commissioned by Richard II (Scattergood 1983). Textual evidence suggests, however, that it is more likely that the compilation was made for Thomas Mowbray (b. 1366, d. 1399), Earl Marshal. A herald wearing Mowbray's arms is depicted receiving a letter from Richard II that appoints Mowbray to the office of marshal (f. 85), and Mowbray's arms are repeated at the beginning of the chapter listing the marshal's duties in time of peace (f. 86). Three further documents – a description of the marshal's office held by Thomas of Brotherton (d. 1338), Mowbray's great-grandfather, the *Modus tenendi parliamentum* and the Durham ordinances – also relate to the marshal's privileges and duties (Archer 1995). The Mowbray arms also highlight the participation of Thomas's brother John in Richard II's coronation and add to the Marshal's image as a loyal servant of the King.

The manuscript may have been copied in or just after 1386, when Thomas Mowbray received the title of Earl Marshal and still enjoyed the King's favour, or after 1389 when he was granted the wardenship of the East March at the Scottish border. The second context would explain the inclusion in the collection of several documents concerning Scotland, such as Richard II's war ordinances of 1385 and an account of Edward I's invasion of that country in 1296. The addition to the beginning of the volume of a list of 'seigneurs de Mowbray' that initially ended with Thomas (d. 1405), 2nd Duke of Norfolk, and was later supplemented with the names of his brother John (d. 1432) and nephew John (d. 1461), certainly suggests that the manuscript was in the possession of the Mowbray family during the first half of the fifteenth century.

Mowbray's compilation survives in several manuscripts of the late fourteenth and early fifteenth century (e.g. Additional 32097, Cotton Vitellius C. iv, and Paris, BnF, MS lat. 6049). One of them, a contemporary copy that was later listed in the royal library at Richmond (Royal 20 D. x), closely replicates the text, iconography and even the layout of the section of the Cotton compilation that relates to Edward III's reign. It is, however, unclear whether this Royal manuscript served as a model for the Cotton manuscript or was copied from it after Richard II's deposition and any record of the King intentionally omitted.

J.F.

PROVENANCE:

Mowbray family; Sir Gilbert Dethick (b. 1499/1500, d. 1584); Sir William Dethick (b. 1543, d. 1612); Sir Robert Cotton (b. 1571, d. 1631); bequeathed to the nation by Sir John Cotton, 1702.

Opposite:
The coronation of Richard II, f. 70

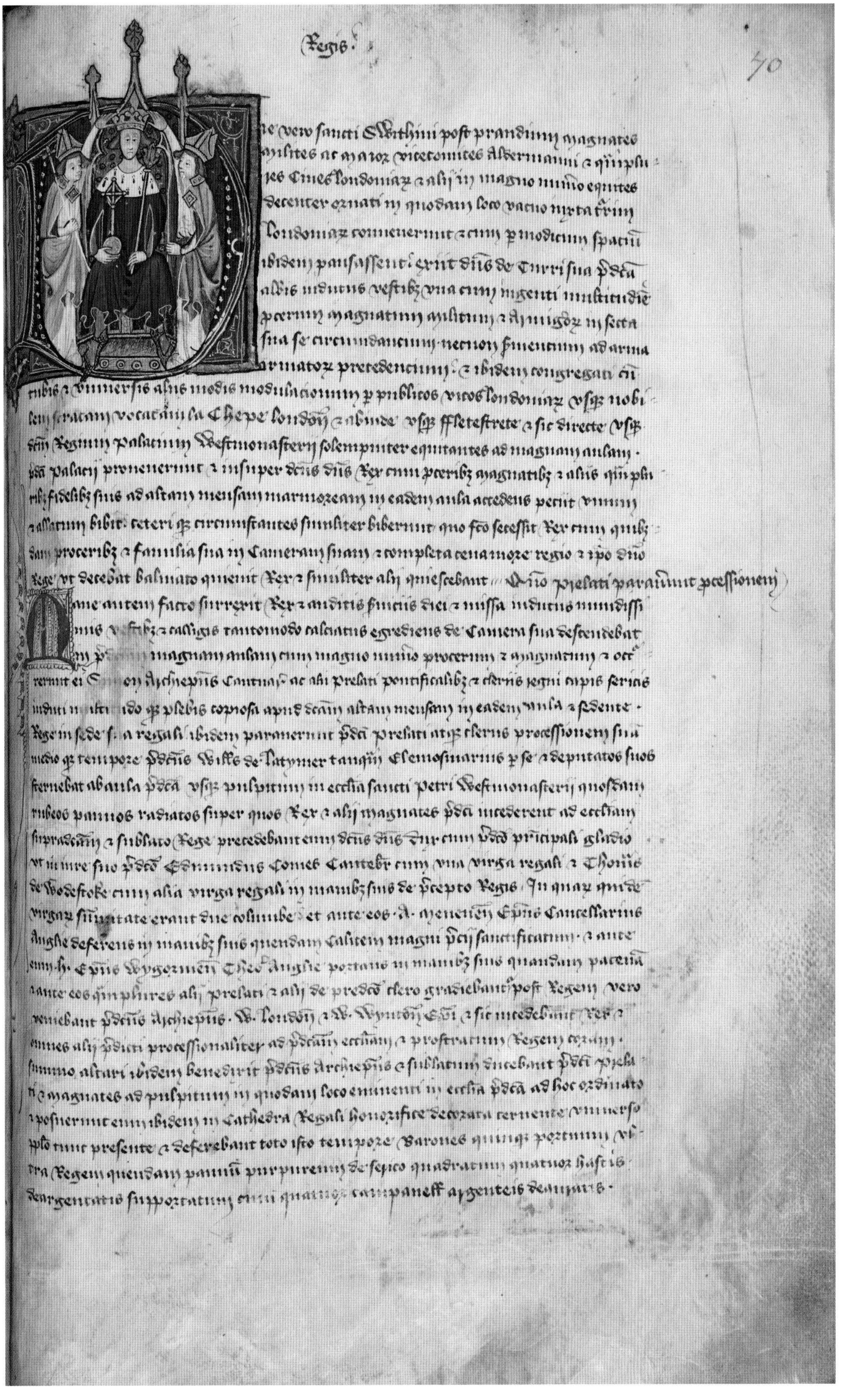

122 *Liber regalis* (Coronation order of English kings)

Westminster, between *c.* 1380 and 1400
255 x 175 mm

LONDON, WESTMINSTER ABBEY, MS 38

Westminster Abbey was recognized from at least the Norman Conquest as the traditional site of English royal coronations. The Abbey was also the place where specialist knowledge on the liturgy of the coronation was generated and stored. The two extant inventories of books at Westminster Abbey, dated 1388 and 1540, mention several manuscripts containing coronation orders. None, however, can be identified with the *Liber regalis*, the most splendid surviving English coronation book, now in the Abbey's possession.

The *Liber regalis* contains the fourth and final recension of the English medieval coronation order, which was first used for the coronation of Edward II in 1308. As it appears in the *Liber*, this recension was supplemented by several additions highlighting the role of Westminster Abbey in the ritual. These additions include references to the Abbey's custodial rights over coronation regalia, and to a privilege of the abbot of Westminster to guide the king through the ceremony. Because the same text, with only minor variants, also occurs in the Missal made in *c.* 1383–84 for Nicholas Litlyngton, Abbot of Westminster (1362–86) (Westminster Abbey, MS 37), and in the coronation order now in Pamplona (Archivo General de Navarra, MS 197) which was copied from the Missal, this variant of the order has been associated with Abbot Litlyngton (Ullmann 1961). This so-called 'Litlyngton' revision was probably elaborated *c.* 1377 as its directions match a description of Richard II's coronation. The text in the three manuscripts, however, seems also to have taken account of the coronation of Richard's wife, Anne of Bohemia, in 1382. All three books contain the same addition of the order for the coronation of a queen alone, which is included together with the directions for the coronation of a king, a king and his queen consort, and the liturgy of a royal funeral.

In addition to its common textual recension, the *Liber regalis* shares with the other two manuscripts a similar iconography of royal rituals depicted at the beginning of each liturgical section. It is, however, the only one to include an image of a king and queen crowned together. With the exception of the detail that shows the queen's throne placed a step lower than that of the king in the double coronation miniature, the images do not provide a literal illustration of the coronation liturgy. They repeat instead the same concise and symbolic image of the ritual in which a king or a queen, assisted by their peers, is crowned by two bishops (see cat. nos. 115, 121). The same formula is used twice in the miniature of the double coronation. Although several bishops took part in the ceremony, only the archbishop of Canterbury anointed and crowned the king. It is likely that this iconography – which was inspired by coronation images in English chronicles, such as the mid-thirteenth-century Westminster copy of the *Flores historiarum* (Manchester, Chetham's Library, MS A.6.89) – echoed the coronation of Edward the Confessor, who is known to have been crowned jointly by the Archbishops of York and Canterbury.

The similarities between the illuminations of the *Liber regalis* and those of the Litlyngton Missal and Pamplona coronation book end with their iconography. The figural style of the miniatures in the *Liber* – distinctive for large faces with high cheekbones, pointed noses and heavy, half-drawn eyelids; their technique of subtle shades mixing pinks, greens and whites in flesh tones; and their way of building pictorial space with architectonic structures – stand apart from the mainstream of the English illumination of the late fourteenth century. These stylistic features were once believed to result from the influence of Bohemian art transmitted to England via the entourage of Richard II's Queen, Anne of Bohemia (Rickert 1952). Still a subject of debate (see Simpson 1984), the origins of the style that the *Liber regalis* shares with two other manuscripts illuminated in England between 1388 and 1397, the English Statutes now in Cambridge (St John's College, MS A.7) and the Bergavenny Missal (Oxford, Trinity College, MS 8), have been more recently put in the context of Bohemian illumination of the time of King Wenceslas IV (b. 1361, d. 1410) (Binski 1995, 1997).

No evidence in the *Liber regalis* links its production to any specific event, such as the coronations of Anne of Bohemia (1382) or Isabel of France (1396). It is possible that the book was originally intended for the Palace of Westminster rather than the Abbey. As Ullmann (1961) has demonstrated, in *c.* 1446–48 the text of the coronation order from the *Liber* was copied by the Dean of the royal chapel, William Say, into the *Liber regie capelle* (Book of the Royal Chapel) at the request of the Portuguese Count and Knight of the Garter Alvaro Vaz d'Almada (Evora, Biblioteca Pública, CV I-36 d). There is no evidence of the *Liber regalis* being in Westminster Abbey before it was annotated by Archbishop Sancroft (1678–90) in the late seventeenth century.

J.F.

PROVENANCE:

Richard II (?); Westminster Abbey.

Opposite:
Coronation of a king and queen, f. 20

47

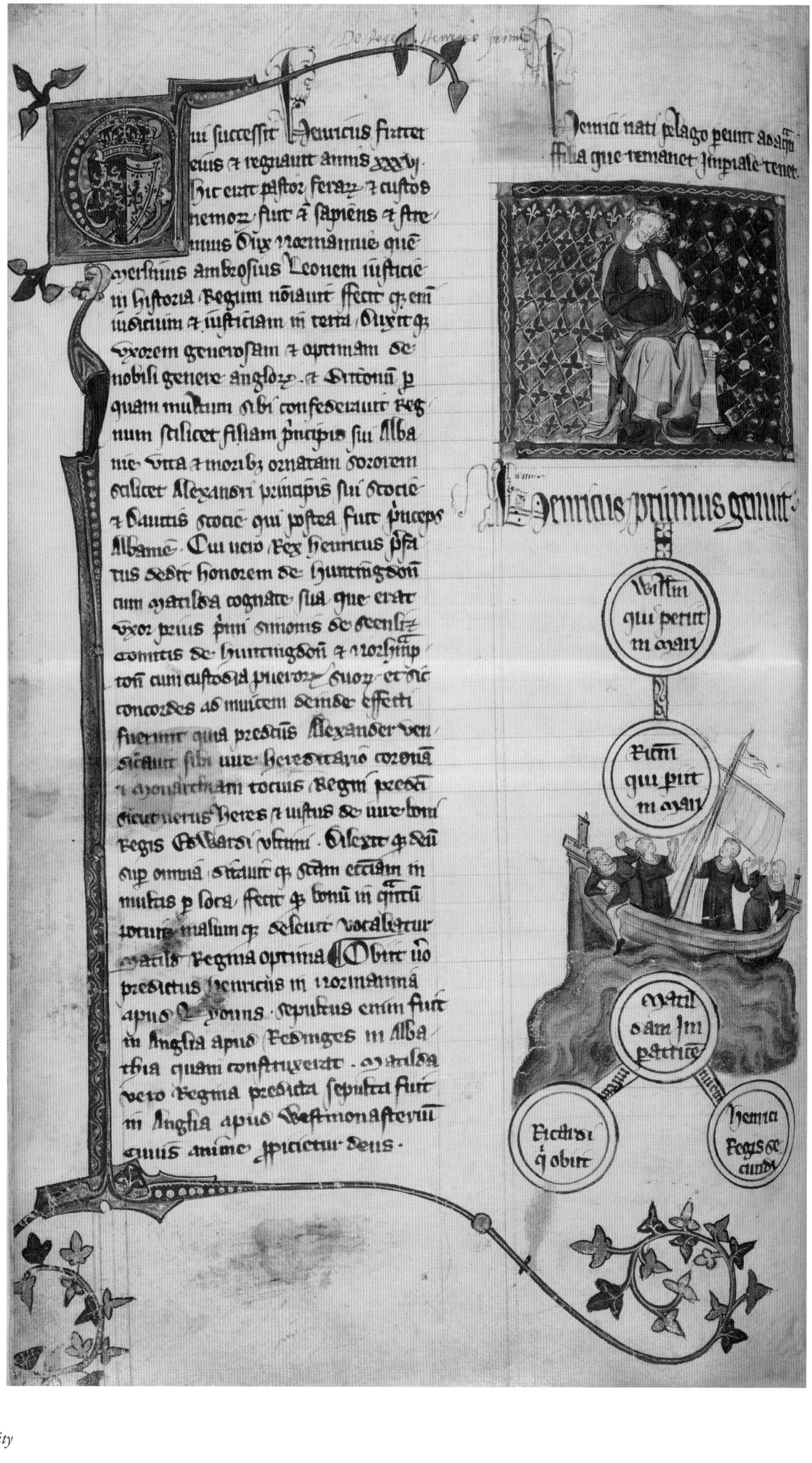
Cui successit Henricus frater
eius et regnavit annis xxxvj.
Hic erat pastor ferarum et custos
nemorum fuit et sapiens et stre-
nuus dux Normannie quem
Merlinus ambrosius Leonem iusticie
in historia Regum nominavit. Fecit quia enim
iudicium et iusticiam in terra. Duxit quia
uxorem generosam et optimam de
nobili genere anglorum et Britonum per
quam multum sibi confederavit reg-
num scilicet filiam principis sui Alba-
nie vita et moribus ornatam sororem
scilicet Alexandri principis sui Scocie
et David Scocie qui postea fuit princeps
Albanie. Cui vero Rex Henricus prefa-
tus dedit honorem de Huntingdon
cum Matilda cognata sua que erat
uxor prius primi Simonis de Seenliz
comitis de Huntingdon et Northamp-
ton cum custodia puerorum suorum et sic
concordes ad invicem deinde effecti
fuerunt quia predictus Alexander ven-
dicavit sibi iure hereditario coronam
et monarchiam totius Regni predicti
sicut verus heres et iustus de iure boni
Regis Edwardi ultimi. Dilexit quia deum
super omnia statuit quia [illegible] etiam in
multis per loca fecit quia bonum in circuitu
totum malum quia deseruit vocabatur
Matilda Regina optima. Obiit vero
predictus Henricus in Normannia
apud Lyons. sepultus enim fuit
in Anglia apud Redinges in Abba-
thia quam construxerat. Matilda
vero Regina predicta sepulta fuit
in Anglia apud Westmonasterium
cuius anime propicietur deus.

Henrici nati pelago periunt [illegible]
Filia que remanet imperiale tenet.

Henricus primus genuit
Willelmum qui periit in mari
Ricardum qui periit in mari
Matildam imperatricem
Ricardum qui obiit
Henrici Regis secundi

23 *Liber legum antiquorum regum*

London, *c.* 1321
320 x 210 mm

BRITISH LIBRARY, COTTON CLAUDIUS D. ii

The *Liber legum regum antiquorum* (Book of the Laws of Ancient Kings) was a collection of royal statutes and London ordinances compiled for the use of Guildhall of London. Carefully written in a small but neat *Anglicana* script and elegantly illuminated, the book was doubtless intended as a formal record. Only one part of the *Liber legum* is preserved in the Cotton volume. A victim of antiquarian interest, the original manuscript was removed from Guildhall by William Fleetwood, Recorder of London, and passed to Sir Robert Cotton, probably through the antiquary Sir Francis Tate (d. 1616). Cotton dismembered the book, embellished it with his own coat of arms (see image opposite), and bound its first portion together with parts of the *Liber custumarum*, a separate Guildhall compilation of laws, and also with other English legal records. The second portion of the *Liber legum*, together with parts of the *Liber custumarum*, was given by Sir Francis Tate to Oriel College, Oxford (MS 46). Only the third portion was returned to Guildhall (now London Metropolitan Archives, MS *Liber custumarum*).

A fifteenth-century table of contents in the Oxford volume informs us of the original composition of the *Liber legum*. It contained the *Leges Anglorum*, a London compilation of *c.* 1200 incorporating the laws and charters of English kings from Ine, King of Wessex (b. 688, d. 726), to Henry II; followed by a collection of royal charters from William the Conqueror to Henry III, a collection of London ordinances, the statutes of Henry III and Edward I, a fragmentary *Registrum brevium*, and various London documents, including a list of mayors and other London officials from 1276 to 1321. The last date in this list suggests an approximate date for the compilation of this unique collection of texts.

The illuminated portraits of kings that precede the text of the laws promulgated during their reigns provide visually strong allusions to royal authority over the law, and echo the king's Great Seal that authenticated royal charters and statutes in their original form of letters patent. As on the page reproduced here, each king is placed within a broader chronology, and the names of his descendants are listed in separate roundels similar to those in genealogical rolls illustrating the dynastic lineage of English monarchs (see cat. nos. 117, 118). The line of descent from Henry I (pictured) is divided by an image of a ship in a stormy sea. It illustrates the wreck of the White Ship in 1120, a tragedy disastrous for the Plantagenet dynastic succession, in which both William Ætheling, Henry's only legitimate successor, and Richard, his natural son, died. The royal line continues with Henry's daughter Matilda (widow of the Holy Roman Emperor Henry V) and two of her sons, including the future Henry II. The roundels with the names of the Empress Matilda and Henry II anticipate the next two collections of laws copied in the manuscript.

The artist responsible for the illumination of the *Liber legum* worked in a style close to that of the Queen Mary Psalter (cat. no. 85). He has been called the Subsidiary Queen Mary Artist (Dennison 1990). An assistant was responsible for several historiated initials, and another artist – of East Anglian origin – painted the bar-borders decorated with hybrids and ivy leaves.

The *Liber legum regum antiquorum* must have been one of the finest books in the possession of Guildhall. Catto (1981) suggested its identification with 'one great book of the history of the English, in which are contained many things of utility' that Andrew Horn (b. *c.* 1275, d. 1328), a fishmonger of Bridge Street and chamberlain of London from 1320, bequeathed to Guildhall in his last will. Catto also argued that in the fourteenth century the manuscript encompassed the *Annales Londonienses*, a chronicle attributed to Horn, and that therefore it may be identified with the *Greater Liber Horn*, known from a reference in another city custumal, the *Liber albus* of 1419. As early as 1311 Andrew Horn was involved in making collections of legal records that he wished would 'always remain in the Chamber of the Guildhall'. They included the *Liber Horn* (now London Metropolitan Archives, MS *Liber Horn*); a volume containing the *Leges Anglorum*, the *Mirror of Justices* and *Britton* (Cambridge, Corpus Christi College, MSS 70 and 258); and the *Liber custumarum*. Within the *Liber legum* and other compilations bequeathed to Guildhall civic customs were combined with old laws of English kings on which, according to Horn, the fundamental liberties of the city of London reposed. *J.F.*

PROVENANCE:

Guildhall of London; William Fleetwood (b. *c.* 1525, d. 1594); Sir Francis Tate (b. 1560, d. 1616); Sir Robert Cotton (b. 1571, d. 1631); bequeathed to the nation by Sir John Cotton, 1702.

Opposite:
Henry I and the wreck of the White Ship, f. 45v

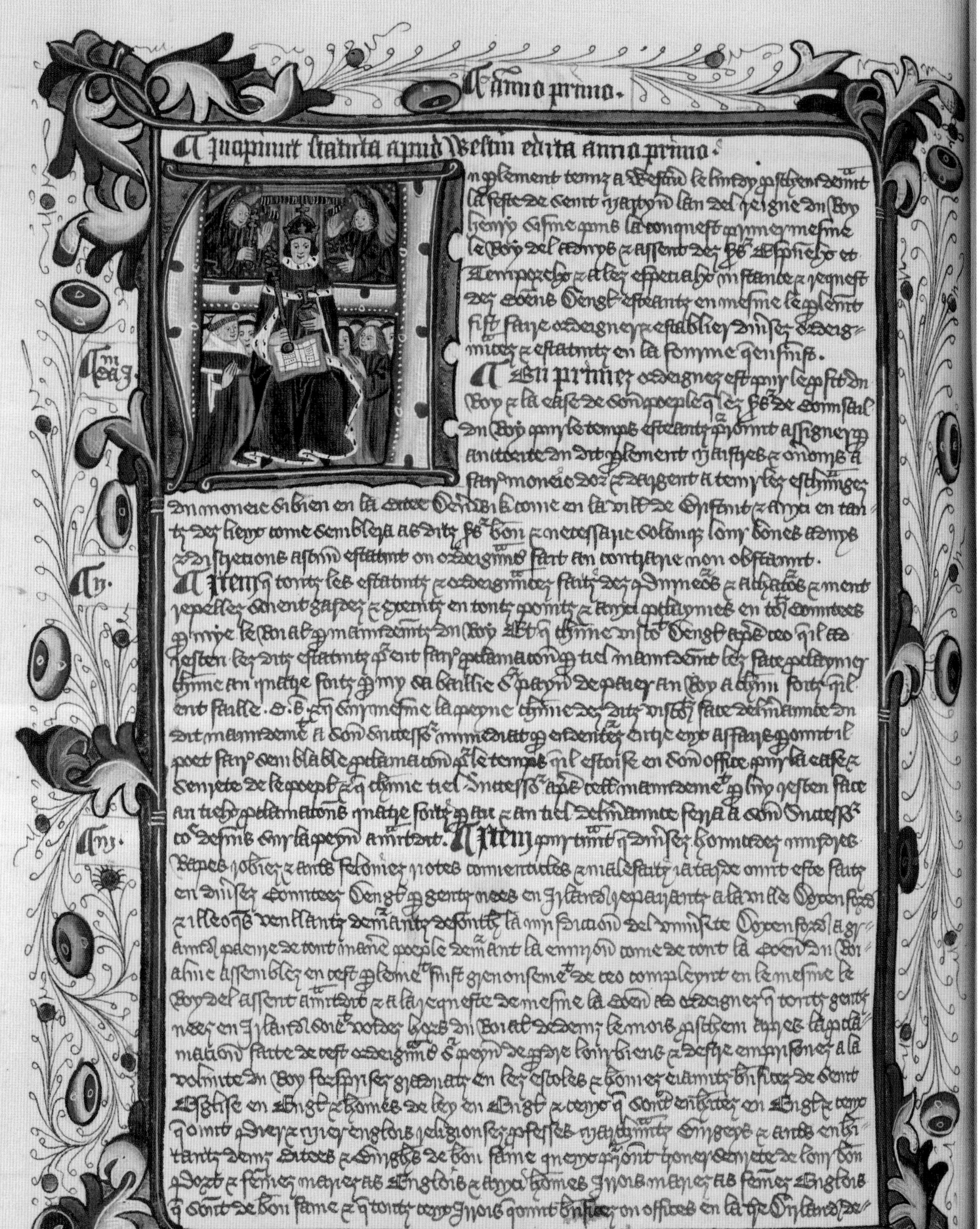
Anno primo.
Incipiunt statuta apud Westm edita anno primo.

24 *Nova Statuta Angliae*

London, 1488 or 1489
310 x 210 mm

BRITISH LIBRARY, HARGRAVE 274

The *Statuta Angliae* (Statutes of England) emerged at the end of the thirteenth century as a compilation of statutes of English kings and Acts of Parliament. The collection came to be divided into two parts: *Vetera statuta* (Old Statutes), comprising documents from *Magna carta* to the reign of Edward II; and *Nova statuta* (New Statutes), covering the reigns from Edward III's onwards. Copies of it usually ended with the last statute available to the scribe. The *Statuta* responded to the needs of common lawyers and public officials, but was also used by large landholders, both lay and ecclesiastical. This widespread interest contributed to a growth in the production of statute books during the fourteenth and fifteenth centuries: over four hundred copies of the *Statuta Angliae* survive.

The present manuscript contains the *Nova statuta* up to August 1488, or the end of the third year of the reign of Henry VII, suggesting that the book was written and decorated shortly thereafter. The text is preceded by an alphabetical index of legal terms (from 'Accusations' to 'Worsted'), which replaced earlier tables of contents. At the end, following widespread practice, three ruled leaves were left blank for further additions.

The Hargrave manuscript is a typical commercial product. As Scott (1996) has demonstrated, it belongs to an interrelated group of illuminated statute books that were produced during the 1480s and 1490s by artists and scribes of specialist London workshops. Each volume within this group contains texts in Anglo-Norman French, the language used for professional legal literature until the late fifteenth century; is written in a very similar formal *Anglicana* script; and shares the same format, page layout, and iconography of royal portraits at the beginning of the statutes for each reign. Two illuminators were responsible for the figural decoration in the Hargrave manuscript. One painted the first five images of kings up to Henry VI, and the other the remaining three images starting from the portrait of Edward IV. Despite the rather mediocre quality of his art, the first artist was a prolific painter who contributed to at least three other copies of the *Nova statuta* (Holkham Hall, MS 232; London, TNA: PRO, E 164/11; and Oxford, Bodleian Library, MS Hatton 10), and can perhaps be identified with the illuminator of two copies of the *Liber de optimo fato* that were presented to Henry VII and his son, the future Henry VIII, by William Parron (see cat. no. 98).

All *Statuta Angliae* manuscripts of the late fifteenth-century London group use the same emblematic image of a king seated under a canopy and flanked by lay and ecclesiastical advisers, which presented a clear appreciation of the advisory role of the royal council in the formation of the law. This repetitive iconography was altered in the Hargrave manuscript at the beginning of the statutes promulgated during the reign of Henry VI. In that image (f. 204v, pictured) the King is surrounded by his counsellors, kneeling in a gesture of prayer, while an open book on the King's lap refers more to his piety than to his role as a law-giver. Henry is also assisted by two angels holding a sceptre and a crown, symbols of the heavenly reward for his saintly life.

The Hargrave image is an allusion to the cult of the Lancastrian king that was initiated under Edward IV and flourished during the reign of Richard III in opposition to Yorkist rule. Soon after the accession of Henry VII in 1485, and around the time of the production of the manuscript, the cult of Henry VI was invested with a new political meaning. According to tradition, Henry VI designated Henry Tudor as his successor to the throne. The sanctification of his Lancastrian uncle could, therefore, assist in the legitimization of Henry VII's new regime. Despite repeated attempts, however, Henry failed to secure the formal canonization of his royal ancestor.

The inclusion of an image of Henry VI that directly referred to his saintliness must have been a partisan choice of the patron of the present volume, reflecting his support for the Lancastrian–Tudor party. The arms inserted in the lower border of each page at the beginning of a new regnal year identify the owner of the Hargrave *Statuta* as a member of the Gylle (or Gill) family of Buckland, Hertfordshire – possibly John Gylle (d. 1499). Political pro-Tudor sympathies of the family from Buckland may be inferred from the fact that Henry VIII granted John Gylle's grandson, also John (d. 1546), the manor of Wyddial, which had previously been confiscated by Richard III after the execution of Sir Anthony Woodville. *J.F.*

PROVENANCE:

John Gylle (or Gill) (b. *c.* 1430, d. 1499), of Buckland, Hertfordshire; Francis Hargrave (b. 1740/1, d. 1821); purchased for the nation in 1813.

Opposite:
Henry VI worshipped by his court, counsellors and angels, f. 204v

25 Flavius Vegetius Renatus, *De re militari* (in Anglo-Norman French and Latin)

England or (?) Acre, between *c.* 1265 and 1272
200 x 140 mm

CAMBRIDGE, FITZWILLIAM MUSEUM, MS MARLAY ADD. 1

In the Middle Ages few classical texts enjoyed the popularity of Flavius Vegetius Renatus's *De re militari.* Composed in the late fourth or early fifth century to support the military reform of a late Roman emperor, perhaps Theodosius I the Great (r. 379–395), the treatise survives in over two hundred copies of the Latin text, all written between the ninth and fifteenth centuries, and in over sixty manuscripts containing translations into French, Italian, English, Catalan, Spanish, German and Czech. Vegetius's focus on both the practical and theoretical aspects of warfare; his comments on the selection and training of individual soldiers, organization of the army, military strategy and skills of the commanders – together with his Christian faith and his belief in the use of arms in defence of the common good – concurred with medieval chivalric ideals. To judge from surviving manuscripts, the popularity of the treatise increased during the thirteenth century, when the first translations were commissioned (see cat. no. 126).

The earliest known vernacular translation of Vegetius's text rendered it into Anglo-Norman French. Accompanied by a Latin version, it survives in only one copy. The opening miniature of this unique manuscript (f. 2v, pictured) highlights the didactic purpose of the work and reveals its intended readers. It depicts a grey-haired Vegetius, identified in an inscription on the arch above him as *Vegetius Philosophus,* who addresses a young prince and his companions with words inscribed on a scroll: 'Venez a moy, senurs chevalers qui volez aver honur de chevalerie' (Come to me lord knights who wish to have the honour of chivalry). Two further inscriptions on the arch identify the young men respectively as *Dominus Edwardus* (Lord Edward) and *Milites Domini Edwardi* (Lord Edward's knights), and the image shows Prince Edward committing himself to Vegetius's teaching by placing his hand in that of the 'philosopher' in a gesture evocative of the rite of vassalage.

As Thorpe (1952) was the first to suggest, the Prince depicted in this opening illustration is the future King Edward I of England. Before his coronation in 1272, Edward was usually referred to in documents as *Dominus Edwardus*; the miniature must therefore have been painted before he became King. The first rubric of the text introduces the *De re militari* as 'the book every prince of the world has to have' and echoes Vegetius's belief, fully adopted by medieval didactic writers such as John of Salisbury and Giles of Rome, that rulers, as those responsible for the defence of their realms, should be well informed on military matters. It is very likely that Vegetius's treatise was specially translated for the heir to the English throne. A reference to Edward's surprise attack on the younger Simon de Montfort's forces at Kenilworth that took place in 1265 and led to the victory of Evesham is the translator's only interpolation and was doubtless included to please the Prince. Previous scholars have suggested that the translation was commissioned for the future King by his wife Eleanor of Castile in Acre, in the Crusader Kingdom of Jerusalem, where the couple spent several months in 1271–72. A flyleaf at the back of the manuscript contains a short dedicatory poem in Anglo-Norman in which a certain Master Richard claims to have written the book for a patroness in France while doing his penance in Acre in the Holy Land. It is, however, uncertain whether Richard was the translator of the *De re militari,* the scribe of the Marlay manuscript or neither. The proposed identification of the addressee of his verses with Eleanor (Thorpe 1952) is not entirely convincing.

The Marlay manuscript is a composite book and not easy to interpret. It is formed of two parts, containing respectively the Anglo-Norman and Latin text, each written by a different, but contemporary English scribe. Although the translation includes some passages omitted in the Latin version, both texts are very similar and, as Reeve (2000) has argued, the Latin text may be a copy of the translator's exemplar. The two miniatures that illustrate the translation, the introductory scene of Vegetius receiving Prince Edward and an image of a naval battle at the beginning of the final chapters of book 4, were painted separately by two different illuminators and added to the manuscript on a separate bifolium (ff. 1–2) and a separate piece of parchment pasted into the book (f. 86). Although isolated in their style from surviving contemporary illumination, both miniatures have been associated by Morgan (1988) with the figure style of the Oscott Psalter (Additional 50000). It remains, however, uncertain whether the manuscript was produced in England and presented to Prince Edward before he set off on crusade (*c.* 1265–70) or, as the presence of the above-mentioned poem implies, completed for him in Acre by English scribes, possibly with the use of prefabricated miniatures. *J.F.*

PROVENANCE:

(?) Prince Edward, later Edward I; purchased for the Fitzwilliam Museum in 1916.

Opposite:
Prince Edward and his companion knights receiving instruction from Vegetius, f. 2v (actual size)

126 Jean de Meun, *Les establissemens de chevalerie*

(French translation of Flavius Vegetius Renatus, *De re militari*)

Paris, *c.* 1300
260 x 165 mm

Les Establissemens de chevalerie (Institutions of Knighthood) is a French adaptation of the treatise on Roman warfare *De re militari* of Flavius Vegetius Renatus (fl. *c.* 383–450). It was completed in 1284 by Jean de Meun and dedicated to Jean I de Brienne, Count of Eu (b. *c.* 1230, d. 1294). Jean's translation was accomplished shortly after a similar adaptation into Anglo-Norman French had been composed in *c.* 1265–72 for the future Edward I of England (cat. no. 125). Both translations of Vegetius's text have their origins in an increased interest in military practice during the later crusades when the values, discipline and efficiency of Roman soldiers on a battlefield served as models for Christian knights. Jean de Brienne, who like Prince Edward took part in an expedition *outremer* in his youth, descended from a family of crusaders. His grandfather, also Jean (d. 1237), had been King of Jerusalem and his father, Alphonse de Brienne, died in 1270 at the Battle of Tunis during the Eighth Crusade.

The Royal copy of the *Etablissemens de chevalerie* was made within a generation of the composition of Jean de Meun's translation. The elegant style of its illumination is distinctive for its supple draperies; refined, three-dimensional modelling; bright, nuanced palette of blues, reds and pinks; and graceful gestures and poses. In this respect the Royal manuscript is closely related to works associated with the distinguished Parisian workshop of Master Honoré (fl. 1288–1312), such as the Breviary of Philip IV of France (Paris, BnF, MS lat. 1023) and the *Somme le Roi*, now in London (Additional 54180); and with the later style of Honoré's contemporary artist, the Méliacin Master (fl. *c.* 1280–1310) (see Burney 275).

The volume's only miniature was inserted between the prologue and the beginning of book 1. It depicts two episodes. The first refers to a Roman custom, described in the prologue, of authors presenting their newly written works to a prince for his instruction, and shows an emperor surrounded by his counsellors receiving the book from Vegetius. The composition of the image clearly draws on a model similar to Master Honoré's miniature at the beginning of the *Decretum Gratiani,* now in Tours (Bibliothèque Municipale, MS 558, f. 1), which also depicts a monarch and his council. The second episode is an illustration of two military exercises recommended by the *De re militari*: a fight at the 'pile' (or 'pale'), a wooden pole used for training with sword and shield, and the task of mounting a horse in full armour. The picture updates Vegetius's text. As in Jean de Meun's adaptation, the Roman *tirones* (recruits) are represented as *chevaliers* (knights). In addition, the training depicted seems to correspond better with medieval than with Roman practice. Whereas the use of war horses was marginalized by Vegetius in favour of infantry, the core of the Roman legions, it was crucial to the cavalry of mounted knights formed by medieval nobles.

The Royal manuscript belongs to a larger iconographic family. Four other contemporary French copies of Jean de Meun's translation of the *De re militari* share very similar opening illustrations (Carpentras, Bibliothèque Municipale, MS 332; Vatican City, Biblioteca Apostolica Vaticana, MS Reg. lat. 1628; Dresden, Staatsbibliothek, MS Oc 57; and Sloane 2430). The miniature in the Vatican manuscript not only combines a virtually identical depiction of the exercising knights with a similar dedication scene in a historiated initial, but also shows a close stylistic affinity with the Royal Vegetius. The two manuscripts may have been illuminated in the same Parisian workshop. The distinctive iconography was probably created in Paris especially for Jean de Meun's translation as it differs considerably from miniatures in manuscripts of Vegetius's Latin text and other vernacular versions of his treatise. The inclusion of an image of the same military training in Jean Priorat's versified adaptation of *Les Establissemens de chevalerie* of *c.* 1300 (Paris, BnF, MS fr. 1604) appears to constitute a reuse of what had become the standard iconography for Jean de Meun's translation.

It is not possible to determine when this Parisian manuscript entered the Old Royal library. By 1542 it was already listed as one of six copies of Vegetius, in both Latin and vernacular versions, that were included in Henry VIII's Upper Library at Westminster Palace. *J.F.*

PROVENANCE:

Henry VIII.

Opposite:
Vegetius presenting his book to an emperor; two military exercises, f. 3

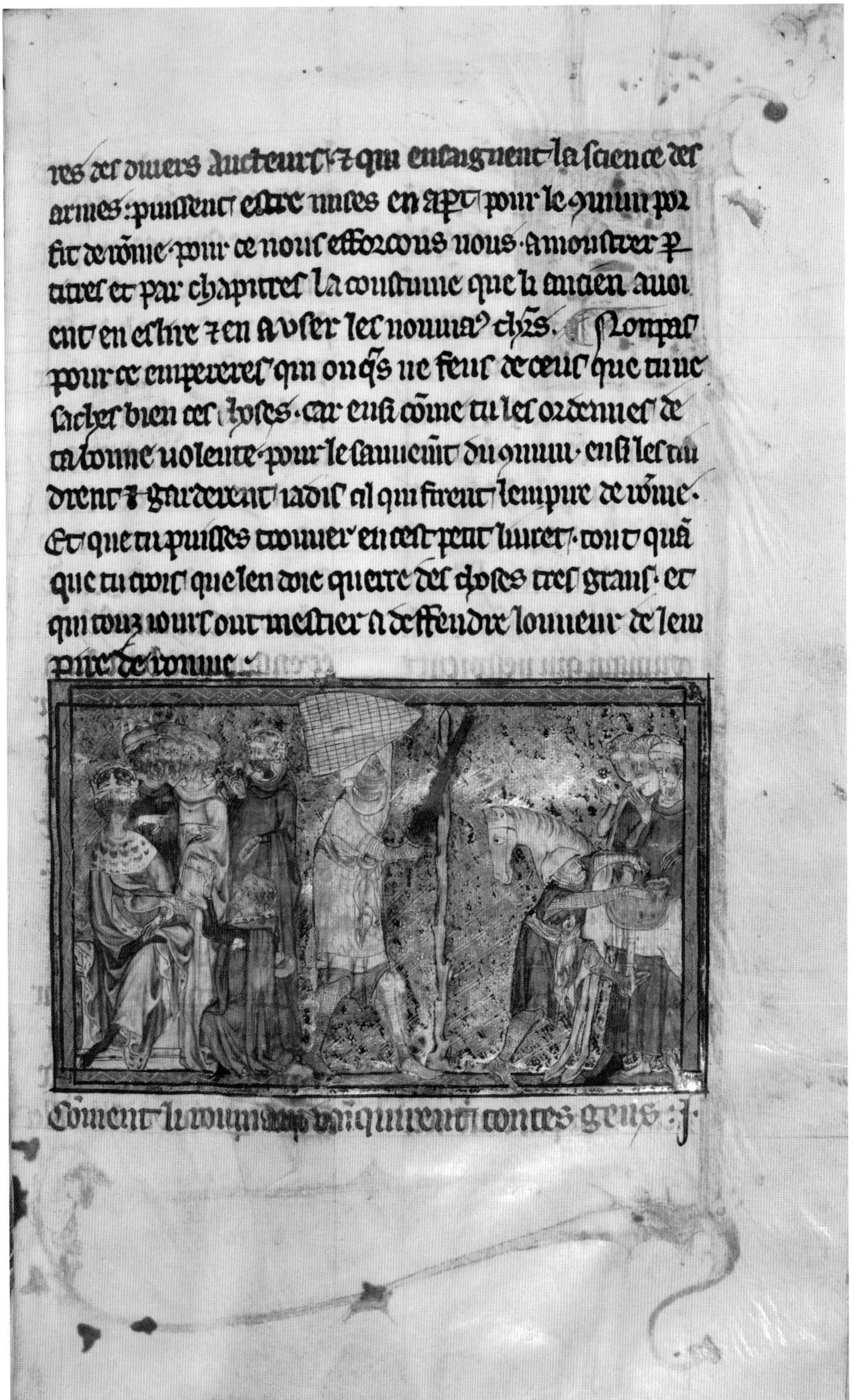
res de divers aucteurs · et qui enseignent la science des
armes : puissent estre unies en .i. pour le commun pro-
fit de rome · pour ce nous efforcons nous a moustrer par
titres et par chapitres la coustume que li ancien avoi-
ent en eslire et en user les nouviaus chevaliers. Non pas
pour ce emperieres qui onques ne feus de ceus que tu ne
sachez bien ces choses · car ensi comme tu les ordennes de
ta bonne volente · pour le sauvement du commun · ensi les tin-
drent et garderent jadis cil qui firent lempire de rome ·
Et que tu puisses trouver en cest petit livret · tout quan-
que tu croiz que len doie querre des choses tres grans · et
qui touz jours ont mestier a deffendre lonneur de lem-
pire de romme ·
Coment li chevalier vainquirent toutes gens : I.

127 *The Book of Vegecye of Dedes of Knyghthode*

(Flavius Vegetius Renatus, *De re militari*, translated into English by (?) John Walton)

London, *c.* 1483–85
240 x 155 mm

BRITISH LIBRARY, ROYAL 18 A. xii

An English adaptation of the *De re militari,* a popular manual of warfare composed by the late Roman author Flavius Vegetius Renatus (fl. *c.* 383–450), was not undertaken until the early fifteenth century, when English began to replace Anglo-Norman French as the language spoken in aristocratic circles. The translation was addressed to all knights to provide instruction on the use of arms and chivalry for young students of the art of warfare, and as entertainment 'to grete disport and daliaunce' for old, experienced warriors. The text itself was commissioned by a veteran soldier. As the colophon of the Royal manuscript states, the treatise was translated in 1408 'at the ordenaunce and bidding of the worthy and worshipfull lord Sire Thomas of Berkeley' (f. 123v). Sir Thomas (b. 1352, d. 1417), of Berkeley Castle, Gloucestershire, was a magnate active in affairs of state and military campaigns in France and Scotland, but is also known for his impressive patronage of literary translations. Disappointed with Richard II's policies and retired from the court, he commissioned his chaplain, John Trevisa (d. 1402), to translate into English three works of instruction and knowledge: Ranulf Higden's *Polychronicon* (1387), Bartholomeus Anglicus's *De proprietatibus rerum* (1398) and Giles of Rome's *De regimine principum.* The adaptation of the *De re militari* was work of a different translator, identified by Science (1927) with John Walton, who in 1410 translated into English the *De consolatione philosophiae* of Boethius for Elizabeth Berkeley, Sir Thomas's daughter. This attribution, however, has not been universally accepted and the identity of the translator of Vegetius's text is still the subject of research.

The Royal manuscript is a work of relatively modest quality, decorated only with foliate borders and initials typical of London work of the second half of the fifteenth century. It is, however, one of the few books that can be firmly associated with Richard III, during his short reign (1483–85). The royal arms of England surmounted by a crown and supported by two silver boars, Richard's badges, are included in the first initial of the opening page (pictured), and the arms of Richard's wife, Anne Neville (d. 1485), appear at the beginning of book three of the translation (f. 49). A large golden griffin, a heraldic badge of the earldom of Salisbury, is depicted in the lower margin of the frontispiece page. Richard's consort, who was the younger daughter of Richard Neville (b. 1428, d. 1471), 16th Earl of Warwick and 6th Earl of Salisbury, may have used her father's badge. More plausibly the griffin relates to Edward of Middleham (b. *c.* 1474–76, d. 1484), the royal couple's only child, who received the earldom of Salisbury at an early age in 1478.

The *De re militari* would have been an appropriate gift for a young prince and presumed future military leader. Recommended as a text of chivalric instruction by its English translator, Vegetius's treatise was at times even bound in one volume with proper 'mirrors for princes' texts. Such practice seems particularly common in the case of its English adaptation, preserved in several manuscripts owned by members of both the gentry and the aristocracy. Two extant copies of *The Book of Vegecye of Dedes of Knyghthode* are bound with the Pseudo-Aristotelian *Secretum secretorum* in the English translation of John Lydgate and Benedict Burgh (Additional 14408 and New York, Pierpont Morgan Library, MS M.775); one accompanies John Trevisa's adaptation of the *De regimine principium* (Oxford, Bodleian Library, MS Digby 233); and others, as in Sir John Paston's 'Grete Booke' (Lansdowne 285), form volumes with texts on tournaments and jousts. Together with chivalric epic stories that praised the prowess of an individual hero of Troy or King Arthur's court, Vegetius's text was meant to contribute to the formal education of a knight, but it also shaped his idea of the group identity in a different way. Rather than a romantic figure, the knight of the *Book of Vegecye* was a prudent and well-trained warrior, loyal to his ruler, obliged to defend his country and serve for 'the helthe and profight of the comynalte'.

The use of English in this military manual probably intended for the young Yorkist Prince is symptomatic of literature in the last quarter of the fifteenth century, when translations of texts of history and instruction proliferated. The choice of language in the Royal manuscript may have had a didactic purpose to ensure that its text was understood by the Prince, as in the case of three English adaptations of *Dictes of the Philosophers,* the *Cordyale* and the *Moral Proverbs* of Christine de Pizan, made only slightly earlier for another Yorkist Prince, Edward, Prince of Wales, by his tutor Anthony Woodville. *J.F.*

PROVENANCE:
Richard III.

Opposite:
Royal arms of Richard III, f. 1

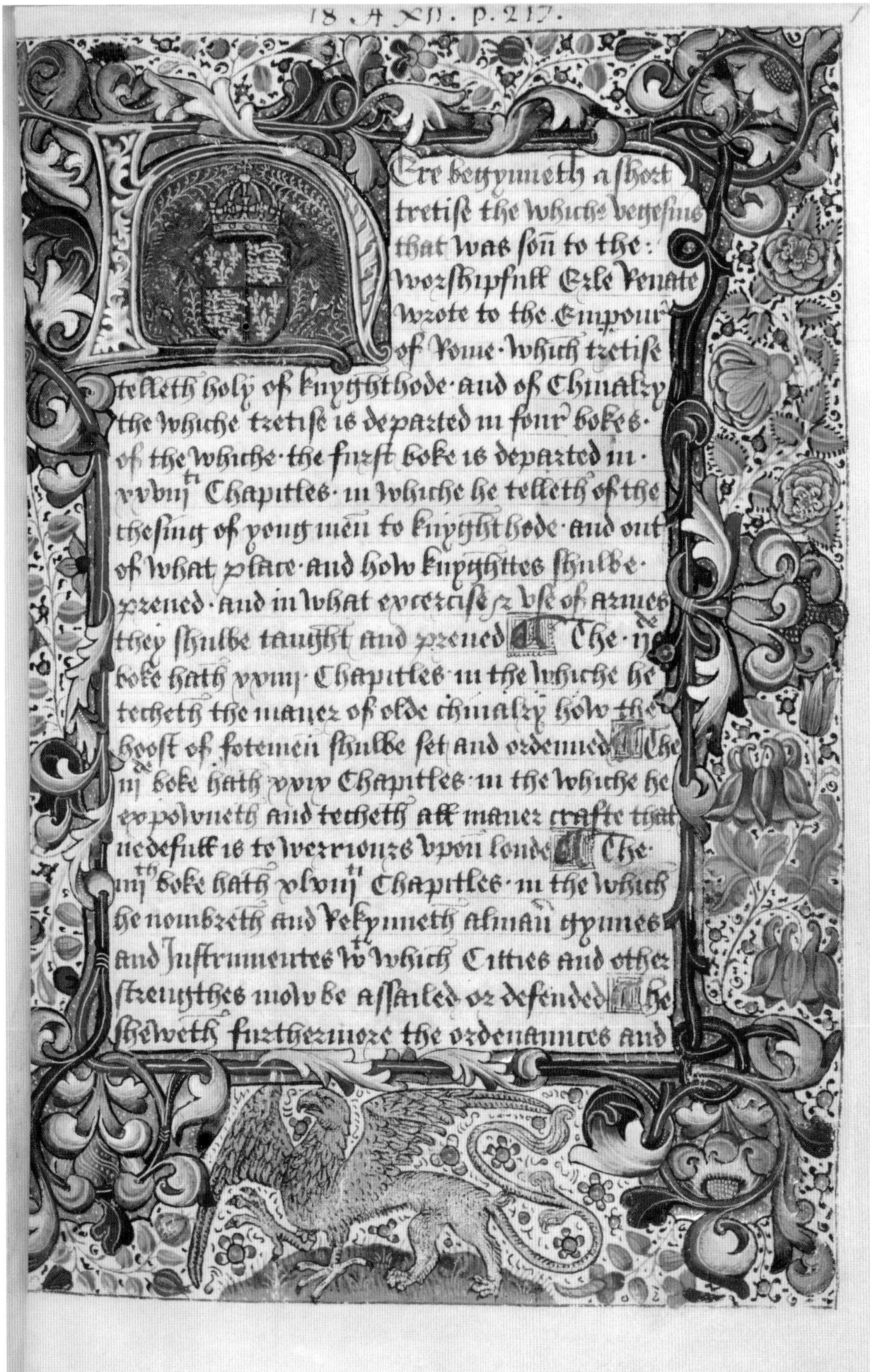
18 A XII. f. 217.

Here begynneth a short tretise the whiche Vegesius that was son to the: worshipfull Erle Renate wrote to the Emperour of Rome. whiche tretise telleth holy of knyghthode and of Chivalry the whiche tretise is departed in four bokes. of the whiche the first boke is departed in. xviii.ti Chapitles. in whiche he telleth of the chesing of yong men to knyghthode. and out of what place. and how knyghttes shulbe. preved. and in what exercise & use of armes they shulbe taught and preved. The .ii.de boke hath xxviii. Chapitles in the whiche he techeth the maner of olde chivalry how the hoost of fotemen shulbe set and ordeyned. The iii.de boke hath xxiv Chapitles. in the whiche he expowneth and techeth all maner crafte that nedefull is to werriours upon londe. The iiii.th boke hath xlviii.ti Chapitles. in the which he nombreth and rekynneth all man thynges and instrumentes wt whiche Cities and other strengthes mow be assailed or defended. The shewith furthermore the ordenaunces and

Roy :
dward :

28 William Bruges's Garter Book

London, *c.* 1430–45
385 x 285 mm

BRITISH LIBRARY, STOWE 594

Above:
William Bruges adoring St George, f. 5v

Opposite:
Edward III, founder of the Order of the Garter, f. 7v

The earliest known armorial of the Order of the Garter was almost certainly made for William Bruges (d. 1450), who was appointed to the newly created office of Garter King of Arms by Henry V in 1417. Bruges is depicted on the opening page wearing a tabard of the royal arms, as well as a large crown, the symbol of his office. He kneels before St George, the patron saint of the order (f. 5v, right). The remaining thirteen pages of the manuscript probably retain their original arrangement. They display full-page 'portraits' of Edward III, founder of the Order, and his first twenty-five Knights Companion. The order of the portraits corresponds to that of the Garter knights in their stalls at St George's Chapel, Windsor. In his portrait each knight wears plate armour and a surcoat with his personal arms beneath a blue mantle embroidered with St George's cross encircled by the Garter; each supports a framed tablet bearing the arms of his successors in his stall at Windsor.

Edward III founded the Order of the Garter as a chivalric confraternity in 1348, soon after he had abandoned his plans to renew King Arthur's brotherhood of the Knights of the Round Table. The spiritual and ceremonial centre of the new Order was established in the chapel at Windsor, thereupon rededicated to St George and the Virgin. The adoption of St George as the patron of the Order completed the assimilation of this warrior saint as the patron saint of England. The motives behind the selection of the Order's emblem, a garter with the motto *Honi soit qui mal y pense* (Shame upon him who thinks evil of it), remain unclear. The story that links the device with words allegedly pronounced by Edward III at a ball, while retrieving a garter lost by the countess of Salisbury, is a later legend. A more plausible explanation situates the origin of the badge during the celebration of victory at Crécy in 1346, when it was first used. Rather than an item of female underwear, the Garter resembles a belt of arming equipment tied in a knot and may symbolize the ties of loyalty within the brotherhood (Vale 1982). All of the founder-knights were Edward's companions in arms from his campaigns in Flanders and France. The institution of the Order was intended to consolidate their loyalty to the King and support for the French war.

The Garter armorial was composed nearly a hundred years after the establishment of the Order and followed the revision of its statutes by Henry V in 1421. As the Garter Herald, William Bruges must have supervised the compilation of the book. According to the Order's statutes, his duties encompassed recording the arms of successive knights on the metal plates in their stalls at St George's. The restoration of those Garter plates in 1421 may have inspired Bruges to undertake the armorial. The Garter Book belongs to a tradition of rolls of arms that display heraldic shields or written blazons, but is one of the earliest to include 'portraits' of the arms' holders as substitutes for such shields. Judging from the size of the book, it was probably not only an official register of the arms and names of the Garter knights, but also a commemorative record of the founders of the Order, intended for display.

Three artists were responsible for the pictures of the Garter knights. Each followed the same figural model and worked in a similar, almost two-dimensional, heraldic style close to that of two other armorials, the *Alderman of London Roll* (London Metropolitan Archives, formerly Guildhall Library, Print Room, s.n.) and the *Military Roll of Arms* (Harley 4205), which were compiled in *c.* 1446–47 and between 1431 and 1448, respectively (Scott 1996). Work on the Garter Book may have started as early as *c.* 1430, but the arms of the successors of the founder-knights were added over a longer period of time. The last shield painted in Bruges's lifetime belongs to Sir Thomas Hoo, who was installed as a Garter knight in 1445. Some arms were added later and the names of the knights were annotated by John Writhe, 3rd Garter, and completed by other hands including Thomas Wriothesley, Writhe's son and successor in the office (Wagner 1950). These additions suggest that before it appeared on the antiquarian market the armorial had passed from one Garter king of arms to another for nearly a hundred years. *J.F.*

PROVENANCE:

William Bruges (d. 1450); John Writhe (d. 1504); Sir Thomas Wriothesley (formerly Writhe) (d. 1534); Elias Ashmole (b. 1617, d. 1692); John Anstis (b. 1669, d. 1744); William Bayntun, F.S.A. (d. 1785); John Meyrick (d. 1805); John Towneley (d. 1816); 1st and 2nd Dukes of Buckingham and Chandos; 4th and 5th Earls of Ashburnham; purchased for the nation in 1883.

129 Guillaume de Lorris and Jean de Meun, *Roman de la Rose*

Probably Paris, *c.* 1320–40
310 x 210 mm

BRITISH LIBRARY, ROYAL 19 B. xiii

Men and women wounded by the God of Love, ff. 3v–4

Love's pitfalls and pleasures are the theme of one of the most famous of all medieval poems, the *Roman de la Rose*, begun by Guillaume de Lorris *c.* 1230 and completed by a second author, Jean de Meun, about forty years later. Written in French verse, the poem describes the attempts of the Lover to win his Beloved: the Rose. The appeal of the poem was immediate and widespread; the text is preserved in an estimated 310 manuscripts dating from the thirteenth to the sixteenth centuries; approximately 230 of these are illustrated (Blamires and Holian 2002).

The present copy, made in France *c.* 1320–40, opens, most unusually, with two striking full-page miniatures, which serve as a visual preface (ff. 3v–4, pictured). Each miniature is divided into two parts. On the left-hand page in the upper compartment is the winged God of Love wearing a crown and a fur-lined cloak. He aims his arrow at the wounded Lover, who kneels before him with another arrow protruding from his heart. Arrows have also struck the hearts of all but one of the implausibly tall figures, depicted in the lower compartment of the miniature and on the facing page, who clasp scrolls bearing amorous phrases. Even nuns, monks and friars are not immune to love's power. Twenty-two smaller miniatures illustrate the poem proper, beginning with a picture of the Lover, dreaming of the Rose (f. 5). A portent of future difficulties, *Dangier*, the guardian of the rose bush, keeps vigil, ready to rebuff the Lover's attempts to pick the most beautiful bud.

Neither the makers of the manuscript nor its original owner have been identified, but an inscription at the front of the volume states that it was once owned by Sir Richard Stury (b. *c.* 1327, d. 1395), soldier and privy councillor to Edward III and Richard II. One of the elite household knights, Stury was a trusted adviser to both Kings, a loyal servant and an expert on France – where he was often sent on diplomatic missions and probably acquired the manuscript. Born into the lower gentry, Stury rose to the ranks of the nobility through his close association with the monarch and his marriage in 1374 to Alice, daughter of Sir John Blount and widow of Sir Richard Stafford. The favour in which he was held by Edward III enriched and protected him; properties granted to him by the King included extensive holdings in Wales, and his alleged Lollard sympathies

did not tarnish his reputation. A cultured man, Stury counted among his friends Geoffrey Chaucer, who translated, in part, the *Roman de la Rose*, and Jean Froissart, court poet, chronicler and compatriot of Edward III's consort, Philippa of Hainault (see cat. nos. 19, 49).

It is easy to understand the appeal of the *Roman de la Rose* for a man of Stury's rank, particularly a diplomat, who was equally adept in the art of conversation as in the art of war. 'Be reasonable ... and just toward men of both high and low rank', advises the God of Love; 'cultivate the habit, when you go along the streets, of being the first to greet other people; if someone greets you first ... take care to return his greeting without delay' (Dahlberg 1995). Aimed at an elite audience, the text touches on appropriate conduct for noblemen. Riding, jousting, singing, playing musical instruments and dancing are deemed worthy pastimes, and courtesy reigns. Stury's taste in books was shared by the kings he served. A list of fourteen manuscripts, probably inherited by Richard II from his grandfather, Edward III, includes a copy of the *Roman de la Rose* (Green 1976). Furthermore, in 1395 Froissart presented Richard II with an illuminated treatise on love. Delighted with the book, the King began to read it immediately, impressing Froissart with his mastery of French, the preferred language of the English elite.

On Stury's death in 1395, the present copy of the *Roman de la Rose* was sold by his executors to Edward III's youngest son, Thomas of Woodstock, Duke of Gloucester, uncle of Richard II. Thomas's passion for books matched that of his wife, Eleanor Bohun, whose family members were active patrons of illuminators and avid bibliophiles (see cat. nos. 20, 131). Accused of treason, the Duke was imprisoned in Calais, where he was murdered in 1397 by order of his nephew, the King. An inventory of books dated 1397, when his goods were seized by the Crown, survives to this day. The present copy of the *Roman de la Rose* is listed among the 123 books kept at Pleshey in Essex, his wife's family seat.

D.J.

PROVENANCE:

Sir Richard Stury (b. *c.* 1327, d. 1395); Thomas of Woodstock, Duke of Gloucester (b. 1355, d. 1397); Henry VIII (?).

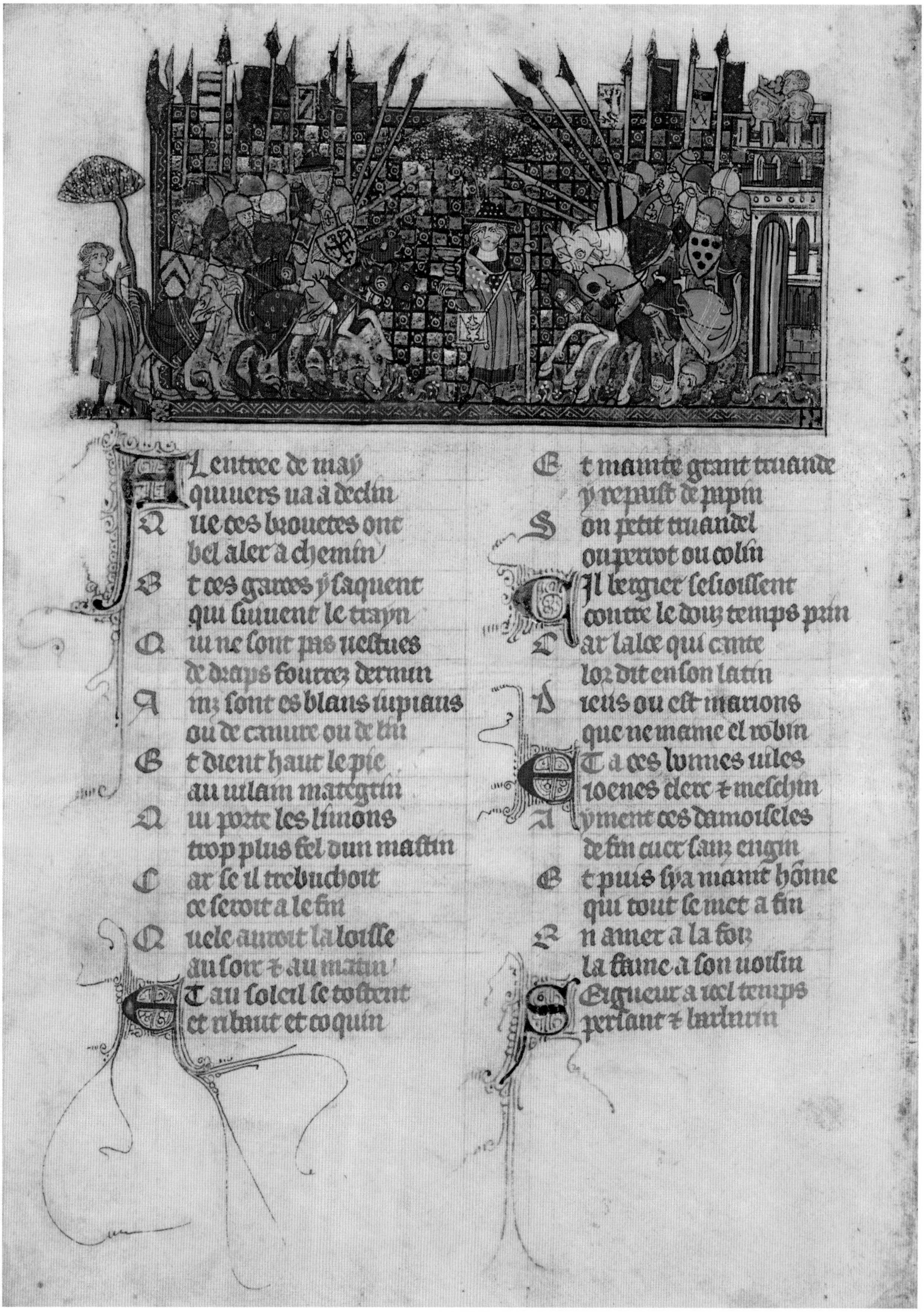
A lentree de may
Quiuiers ua a declin
Que ces brouetes ont
bel aler a chemin
Et ces garces y saquent
qui siuuent le trayn
Qui ne sont pas uestues
de draps fourrez dermin
Ainz sont es blans supiaus
ou de canure ou de lin
Et dient haut le pie
au uilain mategtin
Qui porte les limons
trop plus fel dun mastin
Car se il trebuchoit
ce seroit a le fin
Quele auroit la loisse
au soir ⁊ au matin
Et au soleil se tostent
et ribaut et coquin
Et mainte grant truande
y repaist de pepin
Son petit truandel
ou perrot ou colin
Cil bergier sesioissent
contre le douz temps prin
Car laloe qui cante
lor dit en son latin
Dieus ou est marions
que ne maine el robin
Et a ces bonnes uiles
ioenes clerc ⁊ meschin
Ayment ces damoiseles
de fin cuer sanz engin
Et puis si a maint hōme
qui tout se met a fin
En amer a la foy
la fame a son uoisin
Seigneur a icel temps
perlant ⁊ larlurin

30 Guillaume de Lorris and Jean de Meun, *Roman de la Rose*; and *La Bataille d'Annezin*

Northern France (Artois or Picardy), *c.* 1340–50
230 x 170 mm

BRITISH LIBRARY, ROYAL 20 A. xvii

The *Roman de la Rose* chronicles a young man's quest for love. As the title of the poem suggests, the object of his desire is a flower that he discovers in an enclosed garden. Captivated by the Rose, and wounded by arrows shot by the God of Love, the Lover embarks on an obsessive quest to pluck the Rose and attain true love. Reason, Hope, Jealousy and Abstinence are among the characters he meets along the way who offer him advice or impede his progress. Begun in *c.* 1230 by Guillaume de Lorris, the *Roman de la Rose* was left incomplete on his death. Nothing is known of the author apart from his name, which is mentioned by Jean de Meun, the writer who completed and greatly expanded the allegorical poem in *c.* 1270. Approximately 20,000 lines of verse, many devoted to philosophical musings and advice on courtly behaviour, precede the plucking of the Rose. In Guillaume's text, which is infused with chivalric values, the love object is unattainable, but in the longer section composed by Jean de Meun – which presents a far less idealized view of women and is critical of courtly conventions and the social order – the Lover consummates his passion.

The original readers of the work, drawn from the upper echelons of society, probably identified with the Lover's quest. Although the text may have been perused by a sole reader, it is more likely to have been read aloud to a group of people who had time to devote to leisure. An estimated 310 manuscripts and fragments of the work have been preserved, the earliest of which date to the 1280s. Of these, 230 have miniatures or, in the case of unfinished manuscripts, spaces reserved for them (Blamires and Holian 2002). The pictorial programme of each *Roman de la Rose* manuscript is distinctive, but the same subjects are generally represented.

Made in France around 1340–50, the present manuscript was copied by two scribes and features an extensive cycle of pictures. Forty-three miniatures illustrate the Lover's quest. A miniature showing the Lover entering the garden is typical of the anonymous artist's unrefined yet lively style (f. 7v, pictured, right). Encouraged by Idleness, an attractive woman who points the way, the Lover passes through the gate, which is surmounted by birds that sing love's sweet song. The rapidly sketched figures are outlined in black, and the background is a riot of pattern in alternating squares of bright blue and gold.

All but one of the miniatures illustrate the poem. The exception is the miniature, showing knights arrayed for battle, which occurs towards the end of the manuscript (f. 176v, pictured). Although painted by the same artist as the preceding images, it illustrates a different text, *La Bataille d'Annezin* (The Battle of Annezin), a verse epic about a pilgrim who made peace between warring factions of Christians and Saracens. The importance of this short text cannot be overstated: for it is a rare survival, one of only three *chansons de geste* with partial musical notation (Langlois 1910) and the sole illustrated example. It has been argued convincingly that the brief melody jotted down at the end of the epic is 'a form of scribal shorthand for singers doubtless familiar with the conventions for the performance of this kind of poetry' (Duncan 1988).

The combination of the *Roman de la Rose* and *La Bataille d'Annezin*, though unique to this manuscript, has an underlying logic. Near the beginning of the *Roman de la Rose*, Joy, another character encountered by the Lover, sings a carol of love that inspires dancers (f. 9). In addition, in the course of the narrative the God of Love advises the Lover to cultivate the art of music, stating: 'If you have a clear, sound voice and are urged to sing, you should not try to excuse yourself, for a beautiful song is very pleasing' (Dahlberg 1995). None of the manuscript's owners has been identified and how it came to be in the Old Royal library remains a mystery. Given the grimy appearance of numerous pages and the worn surfaces of many miniatures, it is clear, however, that the manuscript was well thumbed and well read. *D.J.*

Above:
Idleness encourages the Lover to enter the garden, f. 7v (detail)

Opposite:
A pilgrim makes peace between battling Christians and Saracens, f. 176v

PROVENANCE:
Charles II.

moisiele fait il car il ne vous auen
ra mie tant de maus comme vous
cuidies se dieu plaist. Dieus le
vous otroit sire fait elle. Car si
mait dieus jou n'auroie ke boi
ne aventure vous avenist.
Quant il sont .j. poi eslongiet
si dist li varles a lans. ha si
re pour dieu car crees conseil &
aies merchi de vous meismes
retournes dont naves vous oy
ke ceste damoisiele vous dist ke vous
ales a vostre mort. mout empe
sera a tax ki vous counoisseront
a tax ki onques mais ne vous vi
rent empoise. Pour dieu retour
nes tant comme vous en aves le loisir
Et iou por vous retournerai & vous fe
rai compaignie tant ke vous se
res hors de ceste forest. Et il dist
ke il ne le feroit en nule maniere
mais taisent sent. Et il dist ke il
n'en plera mais puis ke ses cuers
l'est atournes.

Et dist li contes ke tant
ont aler ke il vinrent
en une praerie desous
une tour ou il avoit
bien tendus .xxx. pavellons les pl'
riches kil onkes mais eust veus
Et enmi les pavellons avoit
.iiij. pins grans & par teus & es
toit li uns contre l'autre tout
ausi comme a la reonde. Et enmi
lieu avoit une caiere d'ivoire co
uerte d'un viermeil. Et desus le
samin avoit une caiere tor dre
chie sour une verge d'arget. Tout
entour les pins avoit dames &
damoisieles & chrs. dusk'es a .c.
dont li un estoient arme & li au
tre des arme. Et chevauchier
i avoit les heaumes laces ausi
com se chou fussent fremailles. Et
tens i avoit ki caroloient enco
tes & en mantiaus & tenoient les
damoisieles par les mains. Car
il y avoit plus ke de damoisiel

Chest chi ensi comment lans. chevauchoit par mi une forest & il vint en
une praerie. Et comment il carola a le carole ki estoit faite par encante
ment. Et comment il akieva chelle aventure & comment on l'asist en une caiere.

131 *Lancelot du Lac*

Northern France (?Arras), *c.* 1300–15; and England (Pleshey Castle), *c.* 1370–80 (after 1374?)
340 x 240 mm

BRITISH LIBRARY, ROYAL 20 D. iv

Left:
Royal banquet at King Arthur's court, f. 1 (detail)
Opposite:
Lancelot taking part in the enchanted dance, f. 237v

The *Lancelot du lac* (Lancelot of the Lake) or the *Lancelot proper* is the third and longest part of the *Lancelot-Grail* cycle (see cat. no. 132). It recounts Lancelot's adventures, from his upbringing by the Lady of the Lake to his arrival at King Arthur's court and his adulterous love for Queen Guinevere, which inspired him to become the bravest of the knights of the Round Table. The Royal manuscript begins in the middle of the story, with a banquet held by King Arthur to celebrate his reconciliation with Lancelot and the return of the Queen, and ends abruptly with Lancelot's dream of the Perilous Forest. It is possible that this volume was originally preceded by another volume, now lost, containing the first part of the story, but more probably its text simply reflects an imperfect model. Nevertheless the Royal *Lancelot* is a high-quality book designed to please the eyes of a noble patron. It was illuminated by an artist who was named the *Maître au menton fuyant* (Master of the Weak Chin) (fl. *c.* 1290–1325) because of the characteristic style of his figures; their faces, often drawn in three-quarter profile, lack a prominent chin. Stones (2002) identified his hand in several manuscripts made for patrons who resided mainly in the diocese of Arras, and in the Psalter probably made for Guillaume de Termonde (d. 1312), the son of Guy de Dampierre, Count of Flanders (Tournai, Cathedral Treasury, MS Scaldis H. 12/2).

The page reproduced here (f. 237v), provides a sample of the artist's fanciful style. The two-column miniature depicts Lancelot who, after having wandered into the 'Forest Perdue', joins an enchanted dance. At the same time the picture anticipates another magical episode, recounted only a few pages later: Lancelot is invited to sit on a throne to receive the crown of his father, King Ban, and to lift the enchantment from the dancers. The surrounding border is animated by a half-human archer shooting at a dragon, a bear, a drum player and a dancing horse – a humorous continuation of the theme in the miniature, doubtlessly designed to enrich the experience of an entertaining pastime.

The Royal *Lancelot* came into English hands at an early date and may even have been made for an English patron. Several initials in the manuscript are decorated with heraldic arms (some, perhaps only decorative, with incorrect tinctures) including England and France ancient, and León and Castile. Once in England a major pictorial addition was made. The opening miniature of Arthur feasting with his court (f. 1, pictured) and another image further in the text (f. 202v) were painted by one of the artists working for the Bohun family in the second half of the fourteenth century. Both images are accompanied by the family arms, overpainted on two original initials. In the first initial the arms of Bohun are paired with the old arms of England. As in other manuscripts associated with the Bohuns, the old royal arms, not in use since 1340, were introduced to underline the long connection between the family and the royal dynasty initiated by Humphrey de Bohun's marriage to Princess Elizabeth in 1302 (Sandler 2003).

The Royal manuscript was probably adapted for Humphrey de Bohun (d. 1373) or for his daughter Eleanor (d. 1399). In 1374 Eleanor married Thomas of Woodstock (b. 1355, d. 1397), the youngest son of Edward III, and inherited a part of her father's estates including Pleshey Castle, where an 'in-house' team of artists worked for the family until at least 1384 (see cat. no. 20). The inventory of Thomas of Woodstock's possessions seized at Pleshey by Richard II after Thomas's arrest and murder lists among nineteen other romances 'un large livre en Frannceis appellez le Romance de Lancelot', which may be the Royal manuscript. The value placed on Thomas's *Lancelot* in the inventory, 13 shillings 4 pence – twice that of a *Roman de la Rose*, another illuminated book from his collection preserved in the Old Royal library (cat. no. 129) – strengthens its identification with the sumptuously decorated Royal Lancelot. A *Lancelot du Lac* that is listed at Richmond Palace in 1535 may also refer to the present manuscript. However, it is only the 1666 catalogue of books in the royal library that clearly identifies the volume as 'le second volume de Lancelot', a title repeated in the manuscript. *J.F.*

PROVENANCE:

(?) Humphrey de Bohun, 7th Earl of Hereford, Essex and Northampton (b. 1343, d. 1373); Henry VIII (?).

132 Lancelot-Grail Cycle

Northern France or Flanders (St-Omer or Tournai), *c.* 1315–25
485 x 335 mm

BRITISH LIBRARY, ROYAL 14 E. iii

The *Lancelot-Grail* Cycle is a collection of epic stories inspired by legends of King Arthur and the knights of the Round Table. It was composed in stages between *c.* 1210 and 1230, using older sources. The Royal manuscript contains only three of the five parts of the cycle. It begins with the *Estoire del Saint Graal*, which recounts the story of the Grail – that is, the chalice in which Joseph of Arimathea collected the blood of Christ after the Crucifixion. The story continues with the *Queste del Saint Graal*, in which the attempts of the knights of the Round Table to find the Grail culminate in its eventual recovery by Lancelot's son Galahad. The cycle concludes in the *Mort Artu* with Arthur's death.

The Royal manuscript was produced in the same workshop as two other *Lancelot-Grail* cycles (Additional 10292–10294, and the volume now divided in three parts: former Amsterdam, Bibliotheca Philosophica Hermetica, MS 1; Manchester, John Rylands University Library, MS French 1; and Oxford, Bodleian Library, MS Douce 215). The date of 12 February 1316, which is inscribed in the Additional manuscript (Additional 10292, f. 55v), gives an approximate period for the activity of the workshop. All three of these copies of the *Lancelot-Grail* cycle include works by the same painter, whom Stones (1987) has identified as the artist of a donor portrait in a Psalter for the use of Tournai that Gilbert de Ste-Aldegonde presented in 1323 to the Chartreuse of Longuenesse near St-Omer (St-Omer, Bibliothèque Municipale, MS 270). This historical connection situates the production of all the manuscripts in the group in the Franco-Flemish border region of Artois, Hainault, and Flanders, the location of the most prolific workshops disseminating Arthurian romances at that time. Despite their stylistic affinity, the three pictorial cycles differ significantly in iconography and choice of episodes illustrated. In each case the artists followed a separate set of instructions, still partially visible in the margins of the illustrated pages.

Large in format, profusely illustrated, and lavished with gold, the Royal *Lancelot* was evidently an expensive aristocratic commission. The layout of its text in three columns is characteristic of fourteenth-century vernacular *romans*. Each of the three parts of the cycle opens with a large miniature, and the story continues in smaller pictures illustrating selected episodes. The page reproduced here (f. 89) contains the beginning of the *Queste del Saint Graal*. The first illustration on it shows the moment when the Pentecost banquet at Camelot presided over by Arthur and Guinevere was disturbed by the arrival of a lady who asked Lancelot to leave the court and knight his son Galahad. The second illustration represents Lancelot knighting Galahad in front of the nunnery where the latter was raised. The columns of the text are accompanied by a bar border which provides a setting for further chivalric themes and pictorial jokes.

Text and images in the Arthurian cycles were sources of entertainment often criticized by contemporaries as vain pleasures. On the other hand, these chivalric romances offered models of behaviour, manners and customs to the medieval princes and aristocrats. Although the original owner of the Royal *Lancelot* remains unknown, the manuscript soon made its way into the French royal library. 'Un livre du saint Graal et de la Table ronde, bien escript et enluminé, à iii coulombes et en grant volume' is identified with the Royal volume by references to its second and last folios in all inventories of the Louvre library founded by Charles V and acquired by John, Duke of Bedford, after Charles VI's death (Middleton 2006). The manuscript did not, however, remain in possession of the English royal family. It passed to the soldier and poet Sir Richard Roos (d. 1482), perhaps when he was serving in Normandy in 1436. In his will Roos bequeathed his 'grete booke called saint Grall' to his niece Eleanor Haute.

It was probably thanks to Eleanor's royal connections that the book finally entered the royal library. The manuscript has inscribed on it four names of the members of the Woodville family who were related to the Hautes by marriage: 'E. Wydevyll', perhaps the autograph of Elizabeth Woodville, wife of Edward IV, or her brother Edward; 'Jane Grey', Elizabeth's sister Joan; and the names of the Queen's two daughters, Cecily and Elizabeth. Unless this collection of signatures is merely an *album amicorum* of Eleanor Haute, the manuscript may have been a gift to Queen Elizabeth or to her brother, and later passed to the Queen's daughters. It may also be identifiable as *le Saint Gral, donne a la royne* (given to a queen) recorded in the list of books at Richmond Palace in 1535. By that date the reference to a queen would seem to point to Catherine of Aragon or Anne Boleyn, rather than to Elizabeth Woodville. However, because the Richmond list may have been copied from an earlier inventory of Henry VII's collection (Carley 2000), the reference may have been to an earlier gift to Elizabeth of York, Henry's wife and Elizabeth Woodville's daughter. *J.F.*

PROVENANCE:

Charles V of France; Charles VI of France; John, Duke of Bedford (b. 1389, d. 1435); Sir Richard Roos (b. *c.* 1410, d. 1482); Eleanor Haute (d. *c.* 1486); Henry VIII.

Opposite:
Pentecost feast at King Arthur's Court, and Lancelot knighting Galahad, f. 89

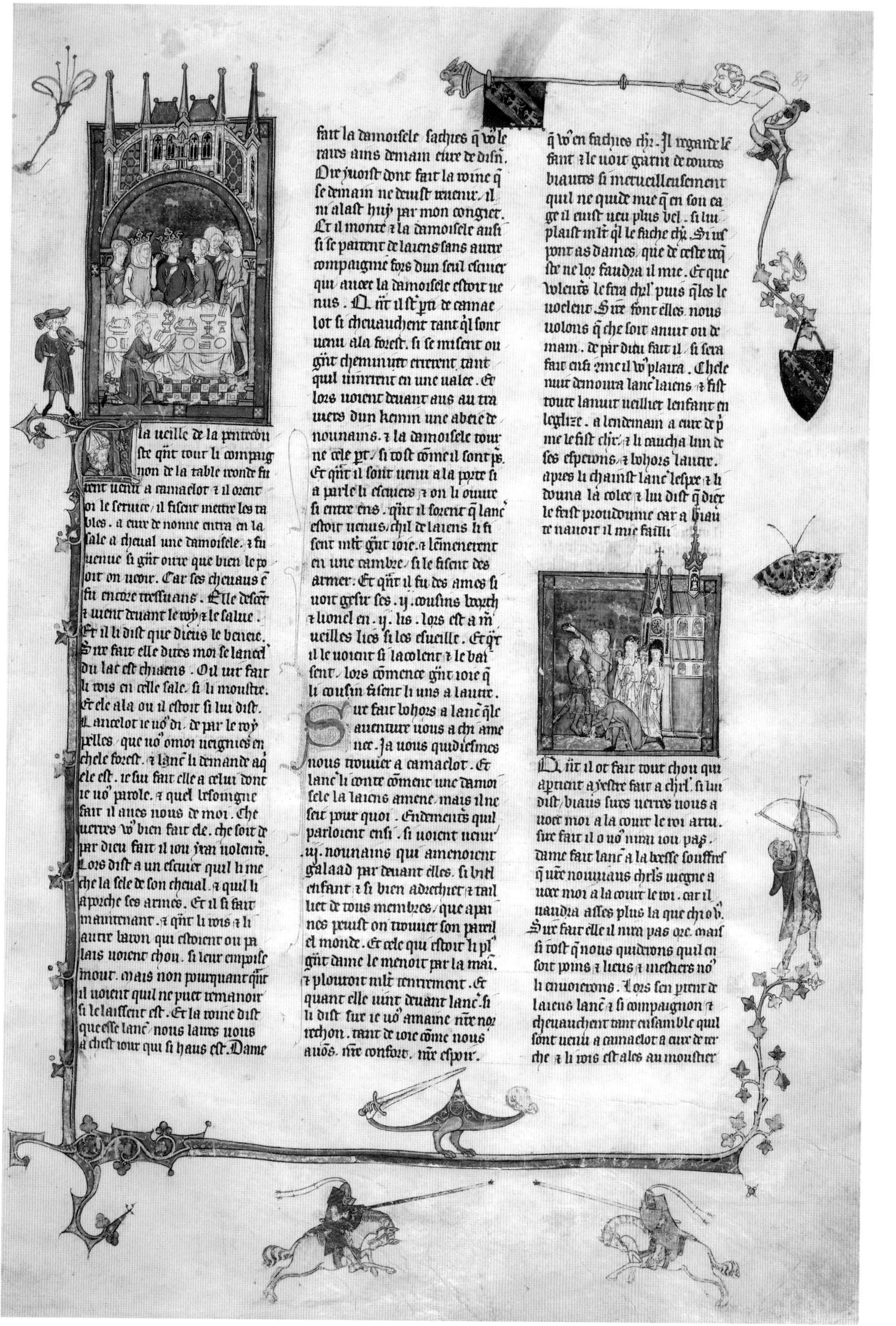

133 Charles of Orleans, Poems; with other Texts relating to Love and Princely Instruction

Bruges and London (?), *c.* 1483; *c.* 1492 – *c.* 1500
370 x 260 mm

BRITISH LIBRARY, ROYAL 16 F. ii

The poetry that Charles, Duke of Orleans (d. 1465) composed during his twenty-five-year captivity in England enjoyed relatively wide dissemination in manuscript and print during the second half of the fifteenth century. Unique to the present manuscript is its luxurious cycle of illumination, comprising six three-quarter-page miniatures, elaborate borders and hundreds of decorated initials. The selection of 166 poems by Charles contained here might be seen as guiding the theme of the volume; those chosen for inclusion are exclusively amorous or political in content (Champion 1923–27), as are the succeeding texts in the ensemble.

Because of the staggered nature of this manuscript's production, scholars have largely concentrated on reconstructing the history of its patronage. Its first two miniatures were executed in the early 1480s, while the last four were painted some time during the subsequent decade. Backhouse (2000) noted numerous badges and motifs that point to Edward IV as its original intended recipient; these include the white rose in splendour (f. 1), the royal arms supported by silver lions (f. 73, pictured) and lions that appear frequently in the decorated initials and line-fillers that were completed during the first campaign of illumination. Sutton and Visser-Fuchs (1997) have also noted the presence in one illuminated border (f. 73, pictured) of a gillyflower, a flower that may have been an emblem of Elizabeth Woodville. Additionally, Marian prayers that the scribe wrote into ornate ascenders (e.g., 'Ave Maria gratia plena d[omi]n[us] tecu[m]', f. 96v) are also present in a manuscript believed to have been made for Elizabeth (New York, Pierpont Morgan Library, MS M.126). Due to Edward's untimely death in 1483, production on the manuscript halted abruptly, leaving the illumination incomplete. The book was recovered, probably by Henry VII's librarian Quentin Poulet (fl. 1492–1506), who appears to have recopied three leaves that replaced earlier ones with unfinished illumination. The illumination was subsequently completed by the Master of the Prayer Books of around 1500 (Kren and McKendrick 2003; see fig. 2.18), and the heraldry around the first miniature repurposed for Henry VII and his family. After its presentation to Henry, the manuscript remained in the royal collection.

Questions about this manuscript remain. The content of this volume sets it apart from the books that were ordered by Edward IV from Bruges (see essay 'Edward IV'). Edward's library comprised mostly books relating to history and contained neither lyric poetry nor instructive texts on love. If this volume had been intended as a gift, why would the donor have commissioned a work so out of touch with the King's known interests?

Furthermore, the present volume's appearance differs from the consistent style seen throughout Edward's books. In contrast to the unadorned script used in the books ordered by Edward, the script in this volume is bold and calligraphic. Even more unusual are the blue and gold line-fillers, which do not appear in Netherlandish illumination. Perhaps the patron had requested that the illuminator provide line-fillers in imitation of the English practice, complete with the devices of the King of England. Even more extraordinary is the panorama of London (f. 73) that heads the poem, *Des Nouvelles d'Albyon.* This portrayal of the city – including the Tower of London in the foreground with Charles of Orleans within – is the earliest known topographically accurate depiction of London. Despite the artist's obvious virtuosity, his hand has not been detected in other extant works. But whoever commissioned this volume must have sought out an artist who could reliably offer an impressive tribute to the monuments and landscape of England's first city.

This and the other miniature produced during the earlier campaign – each by a different artist – characterize the volume as one intended for the education of a prince of England. In the opening miniature a prince is introduced to the Court of Love by the personification of Youth. However, the follies and allures of Love's Court are tempered by the only figure in the scene to make eye contact with the viewer: a fool, whose mouth is drawn back into a menacing smile, admonishes the audience to approach love with caution. And the miniature of London, which shows Charles of Orleans composing a letter to his brother requesting aid in his liberation, is not in actuality a celebration of the poet. Rather, it is a celebration of Charles of Orleans's captivity and the conquest of him and his poetic corpus by the English. With the Tower of London and the urban skyline showcased, the metropolis emerges as a centrepiece of England's power and splendour. *S.D.*

PROVENANCE:

Edward IV and Queen Elizabeth (?); Henry VII.

Opposite:
Charles of Orleans in the Tower of London, f. 73

England and the Continent: Affinity and Appropriation

Many of the most lavish illuminated manuscripts once owned by English royalty were made not in England itself, but in France or the Burgundian Netherlands. Through several outstanding volumes this last section explores some of the contexts in which this collecting took place during the late medieval and Tudor periods. Some manuscripts were acquired as a result of the close dynastic relations between English kings and their relatives at the courts of France and Burgundy. Other acquisitions stemmed from the fact that, for much of the medieval period, large parts of France were claimed or occupied by English kings. As a result English patrons commissioned manuscripts from local artists and scribes, such as the Book of Hours acquired and modified by Henry V's brother John, Duke of Bedford, while he was Regent of France (cat. no. 142). Another example is the collection of texts made in Rouen that was given by the English commander John Talbot, 1st Earl of Shrewsbury, to Margaret of Anjou on her wedding to Henry VI in 1445 (cat. no. 143). This grand manuscript also vividly illustrates English claims to the French throne in an elaborate genealogy setting out Henry's allegedly superior rights, as derived from a closer descent from St Louis than that of the French Charles VII, who is judiciously omitted from the French royal line altogether.

The section focuses on two main political centres, but starts with two manuscripts from Angevin Italy ruled by a cadet branch of the French royal family. The first manuscript was presented to the King of Naples, Robert of Anjou (d. 1343), by the citizens of Prato (cat. no. 134). In this large volume the artist included an almost iconic image of the power of the enthroned King against a background of repeated fleurs-de-lis emphasizing his French lineage. French manuscripts follow, highlighting the Lancastrians' affinity for and appropriation of French royal books (cat. nos. 136–143) and the Tudors' taste for the French style of book decoration (cat. nos. 144–148). One of the most important of these is the Coronation Book of Charles V, which depicts in detail Charles's coronation ceremony and that of his Queen (cat. no. 138). English engagement with Burgundian bibliophilia and Netherlandish artistic styles is demonstrated in several manuscripts, including some connected with Edward IV's sister, Margaret of York, wife of Charles the Bold, Duke of Burgundy (cat. nos. 149, 151, 152). The continued patronage of Continental artists by the English court is illustrated by two music manuscripts made for Henry VIII (cat. nos. 153, 154), the last with a fitting image of the Tudor rose melding the white and red elements of the houses of York and Lancaster.

The English claim to France (cat. no. 143)

Mere edward:
Secund degre:
Tiers degre:
Quint degre:
Roy henry

134 Carmina regia: Address of the City of Prato to Robert of Anjou

Tuscany, *c.* 1335
480 x 340 mm

BRITISH LIBRARY, ROYAL 6 E. ix

Robert of Anjou enthroned, addressed by a personification of Italy, ff. 10v–11

Before the enthroned monumental figure of Robert of Anjou, King of Naples (r. 1309–43), a personification of Italy bows in supplication (ff. 10v–11, pictured). The King, shown in profile and set against an azure ground patterned with fleurs-de-lis, looks out across the page, but does not meet the woman's lowered gaze. This dramatic staging of king and supplicant forms the focal point of a manuscript of the *Carmina regia* – a text attributable perhaps to Convenevole da Prato (d. 1338), a professor of grammar who is known today chiefly as Petrarch's teacher. In the guise of a panegyric, the florid Latin text presents in effect a petition to the King on behalf of the city of Prato, beseeching him to unite the peninsula under his rule and restore the papacy to Rome from Avignon, where the popes had been in residence since 1309. Ultimately, the plea left Robert unmoved; he lacked the means of fulfilling such imperial ambitions; Prato's dream of a unified Italy would take another five hundred years to become reality.

Nevertheless, in crafting this appeal the artist of the *Carmina regia* produced an iconic royal portrait unmatched in the history of western art. The magnificence of the opening derives in large part from the most characteristic features of the manuscript: the monumentality of its figures, and its daring combinations of text and image. For example, the text of a poem referring explicitly to the portrait has been embedded piecemeal within each of the lilies' petals – thus giving voice to the heraldic emblem of the French kings and, through dynastic ties, of the house of Anjou, which had ruled the kingdom of Naples since its conquest by Robert's grandfather, Charles of Anjou (r. 1266–85). The text on the facing page, which surrounds the personification of Italy and conforms to her deferential pose, is a lament wherein Italy despairs of the misdeeds done against her. Taken as a whole, the combination of word and image conjures up a procession of sorts as one turns the pages of the manuscript. After the figure of Italy there follows a series of similarly monumental personifications (such as Rome and Florence), each of whom turns towards the King and presents his or her own petition (see fig. 1.17).

Understanding the sequential nature of the miniatures helps to explain the position of Robert's portrait within the manuscript. Unlike more common depictions of royal

figures, such as presentation scenes and donor portraits, the portrait of Robert enthroned does not occur at the beginning of the manuscript. Instead, the opening miniature is a representation of the throne of God (f. 1v), with a depiction of paradise (f. 2v), and then a double opening with Christ enthroned facing a kneeling Virgin Mary (ff. 4v–5), followed by a procession of angels, saints and martyrs (ff. 6–8). Thus the heavenly court mirrors the earthly court and, in so doing, provides a religious precedent for an otherwise political request.

A comparison of the London manuscript with the illumination of the only other extant manuscripts of the text (Vienna, ÖNB, cod. s.n. 2639; Florence, Biblioteca nazionale centrale, MS Banco rari 38) reveals a nearly identical programme of illumination. Yet unlike the other two manuscripts, the style of the London exemplar, in both the monumentality and the expressive quality of its figures, points to the milieu of early trecento Florence. In turn, scholars have attributed the miniatures of the *Carmina regia* to Pacino di Bonaguida (fl. 1303–40), a leading follower of Giotto. Furthermore, on the basis of these stylistic differences, as well as the presence of textual variants among the three manuscripts, they have come to consider the London manuscript as the presentation copy given to Robert himself on behalf of the city of Prato.

The high quality of the painting together with the unprecedented combinations of text and image make it clear that both the poet and the artist exploited the full potential of the illuminated manuscript to catch the eye of their royal reader. Robert was renowned for his learning and love of books, and under his patronage culture at the Angevin court of Naples flourished. Dynastic ties between the Angevins and French royalty ensured a lively cultural exchange between the two kingdoms, resulting in several Neapolitan manuscripts entering the libraries of both Charles V of France, and John, Duke of Berry (see cat. no. 135). Although exactly how and when the manuscript came to England remains unknown, there can be no doubt that such a book – designed specifically to appeal to a king – would have been a prized addition to the English Old Royal library.

J.O'D.

PROVENANCE:

Robert of Anjou, King of Naples (b. 1277, d. 1343).

135 *Histoire ancienne jusqu'à César*

Naples, *c.* 1330–40
335 x 235 mm

BRITISH LIBRARY, ROYAL 20 D. i

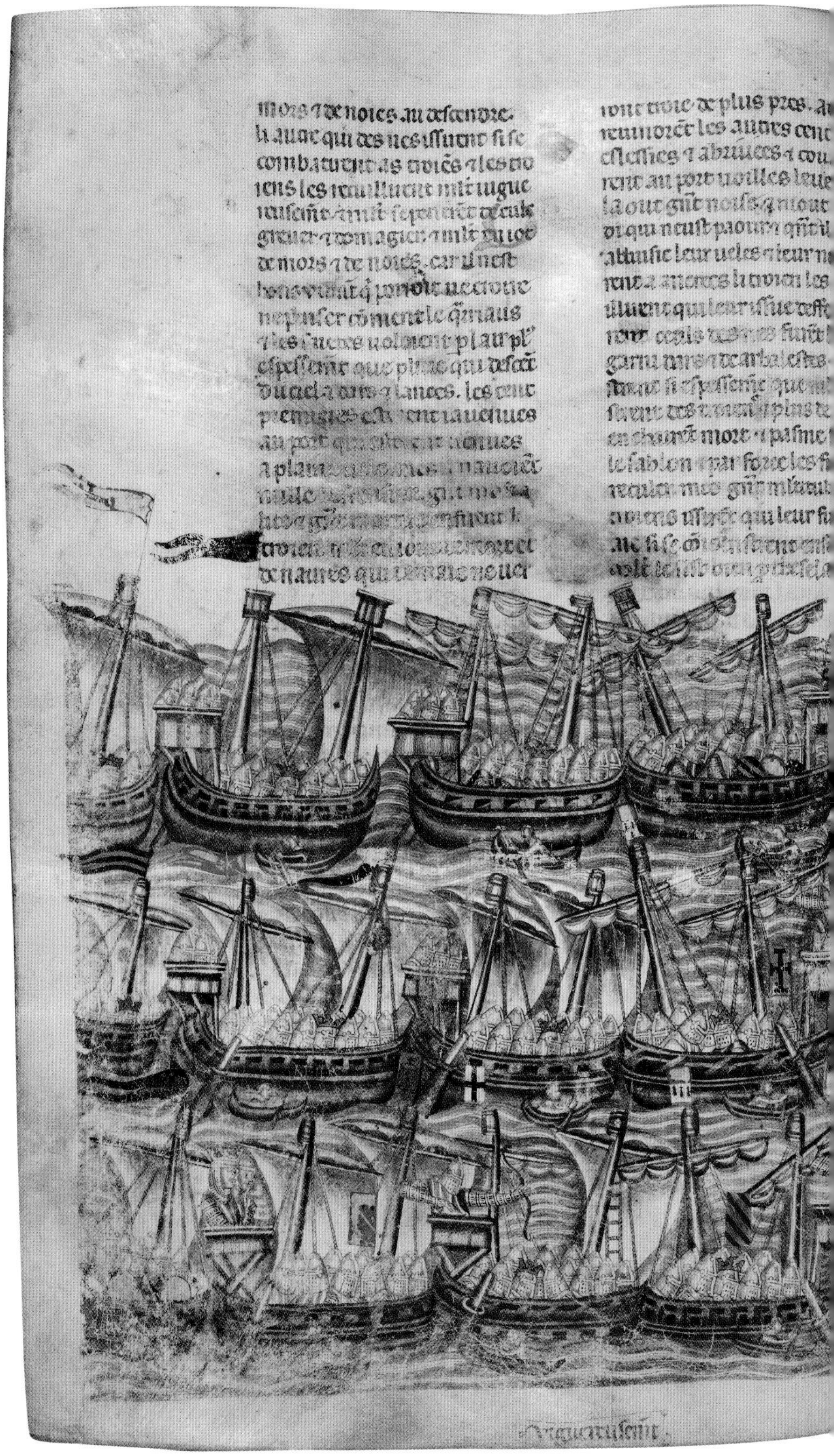

The arrival of the Greeks at Troy, ff. 66v–67

Reflecting the sophistication of the French monarchs who ruled over Naples and much of southern Italy from 1266 to 1435, this manuscript, commissioned by a member of the house of Anjou, whose arms are featured on its pages, is unusual in both content and appearance. The lengthy text in French prose, copied by several scribes in a round Italian script, is a compilation of ancient history composed in the fourteenth century. Although the text is based, in part, on the *Histoire ancienne jusqu'à César* written *c.* 1208–13, this second version diverges from its precursor. Much greater emphasis, for example, is placed on Troy (Williams 1984). Over three hundred pages of this manuscript are devoted to the fate of that famous city, while shorter passages cover episodes of Greek, Roman, Theban and Persian lore and legend.

No earlier example of the text survives, and it may well have been composed for the French ruler for whom the volume was made, probably Robert of Anjou (r. 1309–43) (Avril 1969). Robert was a patron of some of the finest writers and artists of his day – including Giotto, who decorated the King's palace of Castel Nuovo with paintings of illustrious men, among them heroes of the Trojan War. The illustrations in this manuscript owe little to Giotto, although both the manuscript, and the wall-paintings completed by the Florentine master between 1328 and 1334 attest to the high value assigned to historical narrative at the Neapolitan court. Foreign ambassadors are said to have been greatly impressed by Robert's knowledge of their native lands, which was based, primarily, on his study of history.

More famous for his sermons than his swordplay, Robert nevertheless immersed himself in military affairs. Between 1330 and 1343 he made six attempts to wrest from Frederick III the rich island of Sicily to which the latter was entitled. Robert's goal of conquering the island kingdom was intended as a prelude to an even greater challenge: the conquest of Jerusalem. This manuscript could not have failed to appeal to such a ruler, who would have viewed the heroes and warriors of classical Antiquity as models of chivalry and moral exemplars. Some of the Greek heroes depicted in the manuscript, including Hercules and Theseus, bear the arms of Anjou (Warner and Gilson 1921).

Like the text itself, probably composed for this manuscript, the 297 tinted drawings, which decorate the lower margins of almost every page, were created

for this particular book. Saggese (2001) has suggested that the miniaturists drew inspiration from frescoes in the Neapolitan church of Santa Maria Donna Regina, dated *c.* 1320 (Elliott and Warr 2004). These have been attributed to various artists, some of whom may have trained with the Roman master Pietro Cavallini (b. *c.* 1250, d. *c.* 1330). Also included in the volume are four full-page images devoted to the story of Troy and thought to have been painted by the Neapolitan native Christophoro Orimina, who worked for the Angevin court (Saggese 2010). Paint has been more heavily applied to these leaves (ff. 26v, 67, 154, 172) and gold and silver pigments used more liberally. The opening, for example, shows Greek ships approaching the city, and warriors clashing outside the walls (ff. 66v–67, pictured). The urban scene is divided into separate registers like contemporary wall-paintings and has a monumentality that belies its relatively small scale. No earlier manuscript contains a comparable cycle, which suggests that the artists invented the pictorial programme for their Angevin patron. Among the visual sources employed by the artists were earlier illustrated historical chronicles produced in both France and Italy (Saxl 1957).

By 1373 the manuscript was in the library of Charles V of France, who bequeathed it to his son, Charles VI. The latter was so attached to the volume that he took it with him on pilgrimage to Mont-St-Michel in 1394 (Avril 1969). Around 1400 a leading Parisian workshop made a copy of the manuscript for its then owner, Charles V's brother, John, Duke of Berry, and another copy, featuring miniatures by a Netherlandish artist, was made in Paris about the same time (Paris 2004). These manuscripts and the well-worn appearance of the present one are ample proof of the work's popularity with the French elite. How and when the manuscript came to the English Old Royal library is unknown. On a front flyleaf (f. i), inscribed in a fifteenth-century hand, is the exhortation: 'Vive le roy noble Henry. O misericordia of the Taxe!' This addition suggests that the volume was presented by someone hoping to receive a tax concession – possibly from Henry VII, who introduced changes to the management of royal revenues. *D.J.*

PROVENANCE:

(?) Robert of Anjou, King of Naples (b. 1277, d. 1343); Charles V of France; Charles VI of France; John, Duke of Berry (b. 1340, d. 1416); Henry VIII.

136 *Les Grandes chroniques de France*

Paris, *c.* 1332–40
390 x 280 mm

BRITISH LIBRARY, ROYAL 16 G. vi

The conflict now known as the Hundred Years War originated with the death of Charles IV, the last direct descendant of the Capetian line. While the ensuing contest for the throne of France was waged in battle, it was also fought out in culture: subsequent monarchs of France and England, each with legitimate Capetian hereditary links, sought control over the representation of history in order to strengthen their respective claims to the throne. Both French and English efforts in this dynastic struggle have left their mark on the present manuscript.

The *Grandes chroniques de France* was the most ambitious campaign by the kings of France to shape reception of the past. It is a history of France told through the biographies of its kings from legendary times to Louis IX. The present manuscript is a revised edition that was commissioned by John II before his assumption of the throne. The revisions clarify content such as place-names, while marginal additions throughout the manuscript comprise a second set of emendations that were executed later in John's life. These notes add further detail to the events described, or offer improved translations of the original Latin texts from which the *Chroniques* was compiled.

Evidence of John's commitment to this project goes far beyond the adjustments to the text that he commissioned. Intensive labour was also devoted to the manuscript itself—its 418 miniatures make it one of the most heavily illustrated manuscripts produced in fourteenth-century France. Six artists were responsible for this pictorial programme, which includes, at the start of almost every chapter, a one-column miniature or nearly half-page picture. Hedeman (1991) has shown that the images in this cycle often centre on the theme of monarchic succession and betray an attempt to thwart propaganda decrying John's hereditary claim. The miniature that introduces the prologue epitomizes this aim, depicting a gallery of kings whose just succession is not through blood (f. 3, pictured). Rather, the image articulates a more deterministic view of legitimacy: that is, it is conferred by the very fact that the figures occupy the office – or, in the image, pedestal – of the king.

When John was taken hostage and brought to England in 1356 and again in 1364, he lived in a regal captivity that would have allowed for his *Grandes chroniques* to accompany him. Yet neither the inventory of his effects in England at the time of his death, nor the 1363 inventory of the Dauphin's treasures, mentions this book, and nothing is known of its whereabouts until the middle of the fifteenth century. An inscription written at the end of the manuscript by Humfrey, Duke of Gloucester (d. 1447), tells us that in 1443 it was given to him by the executors of Sir John Cornwall, Baron Fanhope (d. 1443) (Rundle 2004). If the manuscript was not brought to England by John, it is possible that Fanhope acquired it on one of his many military campaigns in France or through his wife, Elizabeth, Henry IV's sister. Whatever Fanhope's means of acquiring the volume, his executor's gift was an astute choice in congruence with Humfrey's advocacy of resuming the war with France. The volume's numerous gory images of mounted combat between the rival nations would have presented visual justification for his hawkish ambitions.

The continued political and artistic significance of this manuscript to its later owners is evinced by several additions and repairs they commissioned. In the late fourteenth century a table of contents was added at the beginning of the manuscript that lists the names of the French kings, ending with Charles V; studiously added to these names is the place of death of John II, 'en Engleterre' (in England). Further repairs to the manuscript intimate the lengths to which a custodian of the English royal library went to maintain the beauty of its display: ff. 99 and 243 are replacement pages for damaged folios, their script in careful imitation of the original but probably produced in the late fifteenth century. Additionally their two miniatures and accompanying decorated initials are carefully preserved vestiges of the damaged pages that were excised and affixed to the replacement pages.

It is not known how the manuscript entered the Old Royal library between Humfrey's death and the later fifteenth century. Given Henry VI's apathy towards acquisitions more generally, perhaps one of the recipients of Humfrey's confiscated books presented this volume to him, hoping to encourage the English King's pursuit for the throne of France: the 'inheritance' of this dynastic volume would have reinforced Henry's image as true heir to the French crown. *S.D.*

PROVENANCE:

John II of France; Sir John Cornwall, Baron Fanhope (d. 1443); Humfrey, Duke of Gloucester (d. 1447); Henry VI (?); Henry VIII.

Opposite:
Coronation of Pharamond, f. 3

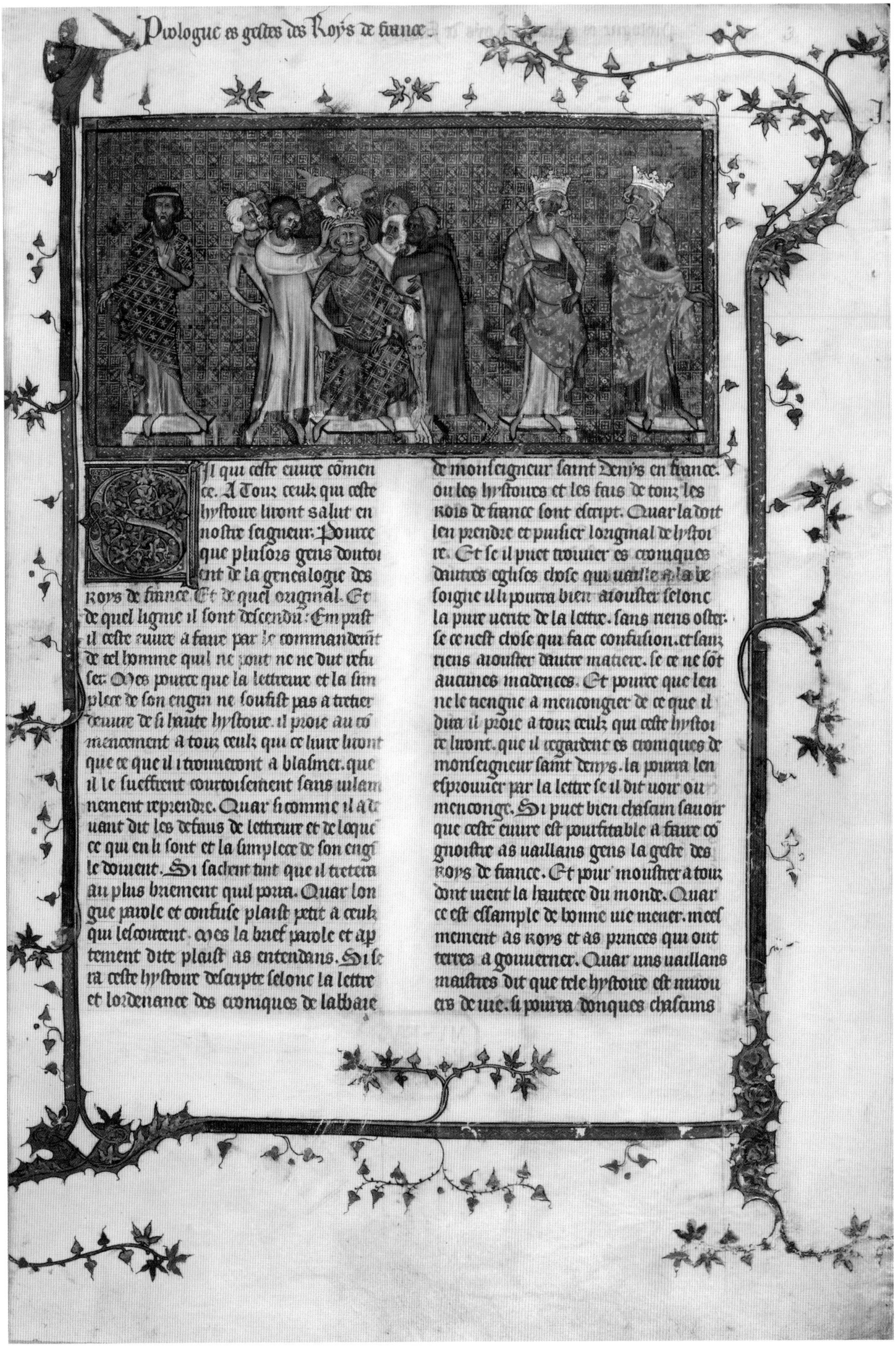
Prologue es gestes des Roys de france
Cil qui ceste euvre comence. A touz ceulz qui ceste hystoire liront salut en nostre seigneur. Pource que plusors gens doutoient de la genealogie des Roys de france. Et de quel original. Et de quel ligne il sont descendu. Emprist il ceste euvre a faire par le commandement de tel homme quil ne pout ne ne dut refuser. Mes pource que la lettreure et la simplece de son engin ne soufist pas a tretier oeuvre de si haute hystoire. il proie au commencement a touz ceulz qui ce livre liront que ce que il i trouveront a blasmer. que il le sueffrent courtoisement sans vilainement reprendre. Quar si comme il a devant dit les defaus de lettreure et de loquence qui en li sont et la simplece de son engin le doivent. Si sachent tuit que il tretera au plus briement quil porra. Quar longue parole et confuse plaist petit a ceulz qui lescoutent. Mes la brief parole et aptement dite plaist as entendans. Si sera ceste hystoire descripte selonc la lettre et lordenance des croniques de labbaie
de monseigneur saint Denys en france. ou les hystoires et les fais de touz les Rois de france sont escript. Quar la doit len prendre et puisier loriginal de lhystoire. Et se il puet trouver es croniques dautres eglises chose qui vaille a la besoigne il li pourra bien aiouster selonc la pure verite de la lettre. sans riens oster. se ce nest chose qui face confusion. et sanz riens aiouster dautre matiere. se ce ne sont aucunes mauvaises. Et pource que len ne le tiengne a mencongier de ce que il dira il proie a touz ceulz qui ceste hystoire liront. que il regardent es croniques de monseigneur saint Denys. la pourra len esprouver par la lettre se il dit voir ou mencongne. Si puet bien chascun savoir que ceste euvre est pourfitable a faire cognoistre as vaillans gens la geste des Roys de france. Et pour moustrer a touz dont vient la hautece du monde. Quar ce est essample de bonne vie mener. mesmement as Roys et as princes qui ont terres a gouverner. Quar uns vaillans maistres dit que tele hystoire est mirouers de vie. si pourra donques chascuns

137 Bible historiale: Genesis to the Apocalypse

Paris, *c.* 1350 (before 1356)
420 x 285 mm

BRITISH LIBRARY, ROYAL 19 D. ii

This book is a dramatic and explicit witness to links between French and English royal volumes. Its text, the *Bible historiale*, was especially popular among the Valois monarchs and their closest relatives, and the present volume was made for John II *c.* 1350, hence possibly before he ascended the throne that same year. It begins with a frontispiece image, not to the start of Genesis, which begins later (f. 3v), but to the preface of the translator, Guyart des Moulins, which begins (f. 1) 'Pour ce qe li diables…' (Because the devil who every day disturbs and sullies the hearts of men through idleness…). Surprisingly, this text has nothing to do with the image above it. God is enthroned. Above his head two angels support a gold triple crown. Numerous red angels flank the throne as though represented in a textile. Set within a complex gold architectural frame are the four Evangelists. In the wider margins vine tendrils spring from the bars and support a range of naturalistic birds, one of which is shot at by an archer. Taking the lower bar border as a base line, we see Samson carrying the gates of Gaza (Judges 16:3), with the city behind him at the left, and Solomon instructing three sons to shoot arrows into the swathed corpse of their father (see below, and compare cat. no. 22).

The book contains ninety-three miniatures, only two of which are of large size: the frontispiece (f. 1) and an image to Proverbs (f. 273), the latter probably intended as the frontispiece of a second volume had the book been bound in two parts (compare cat. nos. 22, 24, 74). Instructions to the artists appear in several of the borders. For example, at the start of the Epistle to the Hebrews (f. 499v) we see two bishops seated in a crowd and can read in the margin: '[L'] apostre qi presche la parole de dieu as evesques et as autres gens' (The apostle who preaches the word of God to bishops and other people). It is interesting that instructions are given in verbal form, rather than as sketches. This implies that the person giving the instructions was not an artist. It also implies that the artists of this *Bible historiale* were not simply copying its images from another, in which case a simple numbering would have sufficed. The principal artist has been identified as the Master of the Coronation Book of Charles V (see cat. no. 138). Apparently it was written by more than one scribe: the second part of the book (ff. 309–526) has been recognized in *Fastes du Gothique* (1981) as the work of Henri de Trévou, écrivain du roi (royal scribe).

On 19 September 1356 the book suffered a grave misadventure, together with King John, as recorded in an inscription at the beginning of the book:

> Cest livre fust pris ove le Roy de Fraunce a la bataille de Peyters et le bon counte de Saresbirs William Montagu la achata pur cent mars et le dona a sa compaigne Elisabeth la bone countesse qe Dieux assoile et est continus dedeins le Bible entier ove text et glose le mestre de histoires et incident tout en memes le volym laquele lyvre la dite countesse assigna a ces executours de le vendre pur xl livres. (This book was taken with the King of France at the Battle of Poitiers, and the good Count of Salisbury, William Montagu, bought it for 100 marks and gave it to his wife Elisabeth, the good Countess, whom God forgive, and there is contained within it the entire Bible with text and gloss, the Master of the Histories, and events, all in the same volume, the which book the said Countess assigned to her executors to be sold for 40 pounds [i.e. 60 marks].)

Thus the book did not go directly from one royal library to another; it became a Royal book much later, possibly under Henry VIII. It is perhaps to be identified with 'La Bible' included in the list of principally French books at Richmond Palace in 1535.

J.L.

PROVENANCE:

John II of France; William Montagu, 2nd Earl of Salisbury (d. 1397); Elizabeth, Countess of Salisbury (d. 1415); Henry VIII (?).

Left:
Solomon instructing three sons to shoot at their father, f. 1 (detail)

Opposite:
God with the Evangelists, f. 1

19 D II. p. 299.

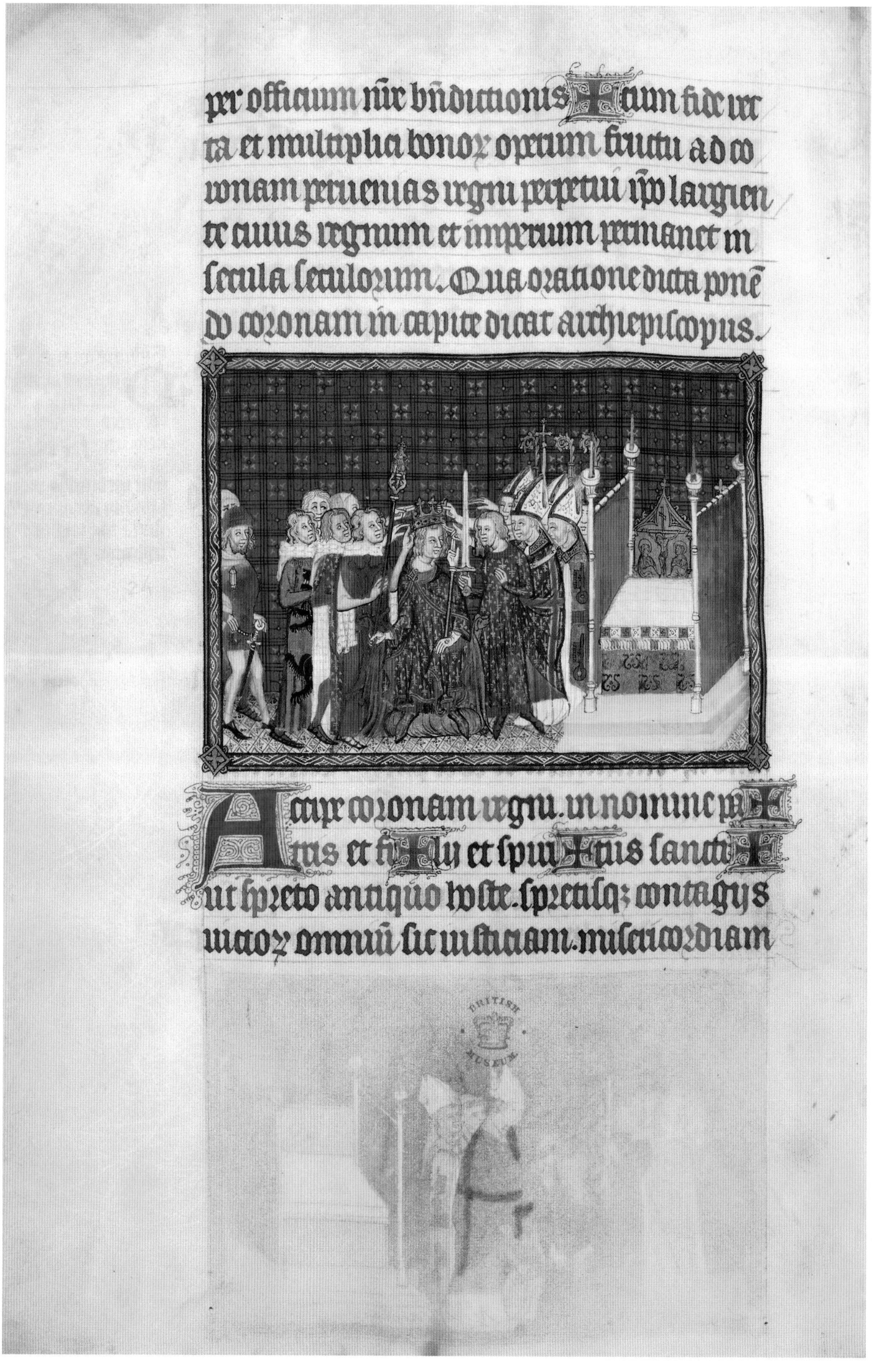

38 Coronation Book of Charles V (*Livre du sacre des rois de France*)

Paris, 1365
280 x 190 mm

BRITISH LIBRARY, COTTON TIBERIUS B. viii, ff. 35–80

The Coronation Book of Charles V was completed in 1365, only a year after the King's coronation at Reims Cathedral. Its directory of the coronation order, selection of liturgical texts and extraordinary cycle of illustrations constitute an ample account of this ceremony, structured in the way Charles wanted it to be remembered. The King's autograph inscription (f. 74v) stresses his personal engagement with arranging, writing, correcting and illustrating the text. By referring there to the book as the 'livre du sacre des rois de France' (Coronation book of the kings of France), Charles also implied its programmatic role as the model for future ceremonies. The manuscript played that role at least once. A marginal note in the inventory of the Louvre library records that in 1380 Charles VI took the Coronation Book to Reims for his coronation (Jackson 2001).

In the *Livre du sacre*, the king's *ordo*, which is paired with that of the queen's, reflects historical fact. Jeanne de Bourbon was crowned at Reims together with Charles V as the last French Queen to join her husband in the coronation ceremony. Both orders were expanded for this occasion and in both cases the liturgical additions reflect vital political concerns. In the aftermath of the destructive war with England over the disputed succession to the French throne and the Treaty of Brétigny that left a large part of France in English hands, the liturgical emphasis on triumph over the enemy, peace and God-given kingship with its quasi-sacerdotal character was coupled with new prayers that stressed the fecundity of the still childless Queen and highlighted her role in providing continuity for the royal line (Jackson 1984).

The most striking innovation of the Coronation Book, however, was its programme of illustrations. Thirty-eight (originally over forty) miniatures, painted by one of Charles's favourite artists – named after the present volume as the Master of the Coronation Book – depict successive steps of the ceremony and act as visual equivalents to the directions given in the rubrics of the accompanying text. Although the descriptive illustration of coronation *ordines* was not unprecedented in France, the cycle in Charles's book surpasses the programmes of two earlier extant manuscripts (the *Ordo of 1250*, Paris, BnF, MS lat. 1246, and the *Last Capetian ordo*, University of Illinois, Urbana-Champaign) in the number of images, their extraordinary attention to detail and their personal character, achieved by the inclusion of portraits of Charles.

The images, which are placed either in the ruled space for the text, or in the lower margins, form a continuous cycle with only a few gaps where pages or parts of them were excised. It is likely, however, that the original design of the book was modified at an early stage of its production (see Sherman 1977). Only nine miniatures (including two missing images) were originally planned in the body of the text to illustrate crucial moments of the rite. The programme was then extended, probably at the King's special request, by a series of marginal scenes.

The expanded programme combines two cycles, illustrating both the King's and the Queen's *ordines*. Although considerably shorter, the Queen's cycle mirrors the King's ceremony, but it also emphasizes crucial differences between them. The Queen is not anointed with the heavenly balm that was believed to have been brought by the Holy Spirit for the baptism of Clovis to ensure the special, quasi-religious status of the French kings. Her regalia are smaller and, as the miniatures reproduced here display, instead of the *main de justice* and the sceptre of Charlemagne, she receives a short rod and the so-called sceptre of Dagobert. Her crown is sustained by the barons, not by the peers of France as for the King. The Queen's cycle highlights her high social status, but at the same time, anticipating Jean Golein's interpretation of the royal unction, it points out her inability to rule.

After the death of Charles VI in 1422, the Coronation Book was acquired with the rest of the Louvre library by John, Duke of Bedford, who became the Regent of France during Henry VI's minority. Although the chronicler Enguerrand de Monstrelet (b. *c.* 1400, d. 1453) reports that the coronation of Henry VI as King of France that took place in Paris in 1431 was performed 'more after the English than the French mode', the present volume may have been consulted at that time. The inclusion of an oath of a bishop's allegiance to the king of England that was added at the end of the volume sometime after that date may also suggest an interest in English appropriation of the Coronation Book of French kings.

Acquired by Sir Robert Cotton, the manuscript was listed as a separate volume in the first catalogue of his collection (Harley 6018, *c.* 1621), before being used by him to supplement a twelfth-century pontifical. *J.F.*

PROVENANCE:

Charles V of France; Charles VI of France; John, Duke of Bedford; Sir Robert Cotton (b. 1571, d. 1631); presented to the nation by Sir John Cotton in 1702.

Opposite:
The peers of France sustaining the King's crown, f. 59v

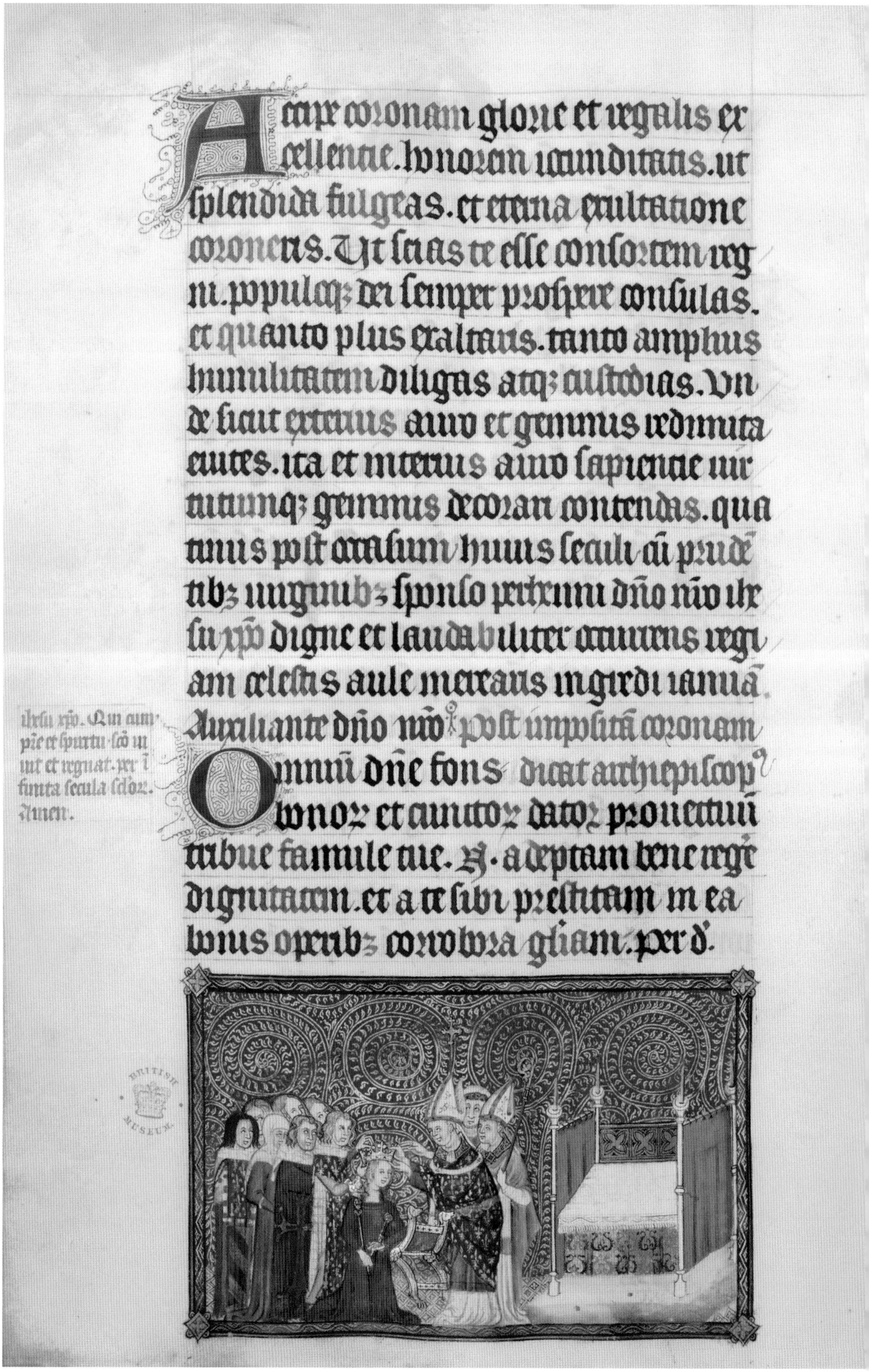

The coronation of the Queen and sustaining of the Queen's crown, ff. 69v–70

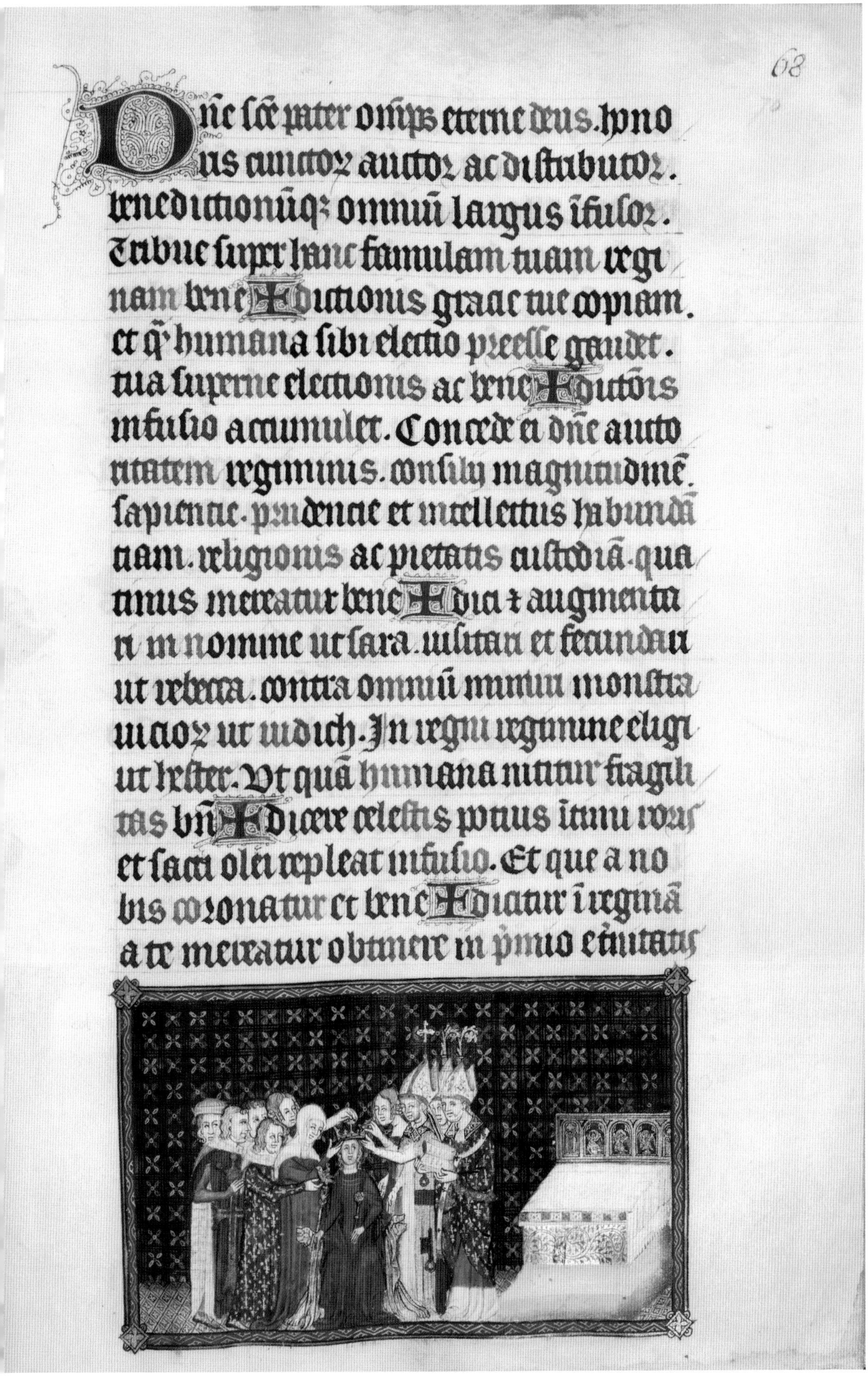

68

Dne scē pater omps eterne deus. hono
rus cunctor auctor ac distributor.
benedictionūq; omniū largus īfusor.
Tribue super hanc famulam tuam regi
nam bene✠dictionis gratie tue copiam.
et q̄ humana sibi electio preesse gaudet.
tua superne electionis ac bene✠dictōis
infusio accumulet. Concede ei dn̄e aucto
ritatem regiminis. consilii magnitudinē.
sapientie. prudencie et intellectus habundā
ciam. religionis ac pietatis custodiā. qua
tinus mereatur bene✠dici ✠ augmenta
ri in nomine ut sara. visitari et fecundari
ut rebecca. contra omniū muniri monstra
uiciorum ut iudith. In regni regimine eligi
ut hester. Ut quā humana nititur fragili
tas bn̄✠dicere celestis potius irrigui roris
et sacri olei repleat infusio. Et que a no
bis coronatur et bene✠dicatur ī reginā
a te mereatur obtinere in pmio eternitatis

139 *Le Songe du Vergier*

Paris, 1378
325 x 245 mm

BRITISH LIBRARY, ROYAl 19 C. iv

In 1374 a councillor to Charles V of France, identified as Evrart de Trémaugon, Professor of Canon Law at the University of Paris and *maître des requêtes* (Master of Requests) of the Royal Household, was commissioned by the King to write a treatise that defined the relationship between secular and ecclesiastical power (see Schnerb-Lièvre 1980, 1982). Four years later this Latin text, called the *Somnium viridari*, was revised and translated into French as *Le Songe du Vergier* (The Dream of the Orchard) at the special request of the King. The present manuscript is Charles's presentation copy and includes his autograph ownership note.

The full-page miniature at the beginning of the Royal manuscript (pictured) provides a pictorial introduction to Trémaugon's treatise. The narrative of the *Songe* is styled as the account of a dream the author had when he fell asleep in an orchard, and the image depicts him sleeping while his vision unfolds above. Set in a large garden and structured as a legal debate in front of the King, it features Charles V as supreme judge being addressed by two crowned women, the Spiritual and the Secular Power, and their advocates, the Cleric and the Knight. The theme of a dispute between a knight and a priest, which had flavoured French polemical literature since the quarrel between Boniface VIII and Philip IV at the turn of the fourteenth century, constitutes a frame for Trémaugon's work and a pretext for the affirmation of the sovereignty of the French King. The opening image of the *Songe* seems also to update the text by referring to the political events of 1378 that started the Great Schism. The Spiritual Power wears the Franciscan habit of Clement VII, the Pope elected that year with the support of Charles V against the previously designated Pope Urban IV (*Paris 1400* 2004).

The author's vision of the dispute between the spiritual and secular power; presentation of the book to Charles V, ff. 1v–2

The miniature on the opposite page gives a different image of the King. Dressed as a university scholar, Charles receives the book from Evrart de Trémaugon in his private chamber while his courtiers gaze from behind the curtain and his son – perhaps the ten-year-old Charles – observes the event from behind the King's back. The intimate character of this scene evokes Charles's very personal engagement with the intellectuals that he appointed to compose and translate books for him, and reveals the King's taste for learning.

The *Songe du Vergier* is one of several texts of political and legal interest that the King incorporated into his library at the Louvre and that had a clear advisory purpose for royal government. In addition,

the book belongs to a vast programme of translations of over thirty moral, political and historical works that were accomplished at Charles's instigation and, as Christine de Pizan stated in her biography of the King, aimed to provide instruction in all the arts and sciences for the benefit of the whole kingdom and future generations (Sherman 1971).

Charles's literary enterprise required the well-organized production of manuscripts for the royal library. A team of over a dozen scribes and illuminators are recognized to have worked for the King on a regular basis. The illustrator of the *Songe,* named the Master of Jean de Sy after a Bible now in Paris (BnF, MS fr. 15397; *Fastes du Gothique* 1981), was one of them. Employed previously by Charles's father, John II, he illuminated in his elegant and naturalistic style several other books for the King, including two presentation copies of Nicole Oresme's translations of Aristotle's *Ethics* (Brussels, KBR, MS 9505–06) and *Politics* (private collection). The debate miniature in the *Songe* is distinctive among his work as one of the earliest depictions of a landscape.

Charles's library of over one thousand volumes was gradually dispersed after the death of his son Charles VI and the acquisition of his collection by John, Duke of Bedford (1389–1435). Unlike many other manuscripts from the Louvre library, the subsequent whereabouts of Charles's copy of the *Songe* is relatively well known. A now-erased inscription at the back of the book states that it was owned by Bedford's brother and committed bibliophile Humfrey, Duke of Gloucester (d. 1447). It is likely that Humfrey received the manuscript from his brother. A record of Bedford's gift to Humfrey of a manuscript that had previously also belonged to Charles V survives in a copy of Livy's *History of Rome*, now in Paris (Bibliothèque Ste-Geneviève, MS 777; fig. 2.3). Accused of treason in 1447, Gloucester is said to have died without leaving a will; his lands reverted to the Crown and his books were confiscated by order of Henry VI (see cat. no. 32). Although the majority of Humfrey's manuscripts were dispersed, this book that had once belonged to the King's great-grandfather may have attracted Henry VI's attention and been incorporated into his library. *J.F.*

PROVENANCE:

Charles V of France; Charles VI of France; John, Duke of Bedford (b. 1389, d. 1435); Humfrey, Duke of Gloucester (d. 1447); Henry VI (?); Henry VIII.

140 Philip de Mézières, *Epistre au Roi Richart*

Paris, 1395
260 x 180 mm

BRITISH LIBRARY, ROYAL 20 B. vi

The Crown of Thorns and the union of the crowns of England and France; and Philip de Mézières presenting the book to Richard II, ff. 1v–2

Expressions of unity and peace between England and France were rare during the many years in which they were engaged in fierce political rivalry and military conflict. This unusual manuscript is the fruit of over a decade of diplomatic rapprochement between the two kingdoms. Written in support of Charles VI's policy of reconciliation with the King of England, the *Epistre au Roi Richart* (Letter to King Richard) is the work of Philip de Mézières (b. *c.* 1327, d. 1405), a former tutor to Charles and counsellor to Charles V, the King's father. Despite his retirement to the Celestine convent in Paris after Charles V's death in 1380, this former Chancellor of Cyprus and crusader continued to play an active role in public affairs; indeed most of his political writings date from this period.

The *Epistre* addresses Richard II with the major concerns that animated Anglo–French politics at the time. It focuses on the peace between the two kingdoms that, confirmed through Richard's proposed marriage to Charles's infant daughter Isabel, would help to end the schism in the Church and bring about a joint crusade against the Turks, who were menacing the south-eastern confines of Europe. Although the author states clearly that the letter was composed at the 'express command' of Charles, King of France (f. 82v), he does not hesitate to use it to promote his own life-long project for the new crusading order, the Order of the Passion of Jesus Christ. Philip claimed to have received the constitutions of the Order directly from God in the Church of the Holy Sepulchre when, in 1347, as a young man, he was on pilgrimage in Jerusalem. During his long life, he composed three versions of the Order's rule. Recruited from all European nations, the Order of the Passion was designed to restore peace amongst Christians and liberate the Holy Land. Philip's project might never have succeeded, but at the time he was writing the *Epistre* it was well received by some members of the European elite. Between 1390 and 1395 over eighty knights either enrolled in his Order or promised their support, including such prominent figures as the Dukes of Berry, Bourbon and Orleans in France, and the Dukes of Lancaster and Gloucester, and John Holland – Richard II's half-brother – in England (Palmer 1972).

The painted diagram that precedes the text in Richard's presentation copy conveys the central message of the *Epistre*: that the reconciliation between the kingdoms of England and France is achieved through the peace of Christ. The colours of the

two realms and the crowns, identified by inscriptions and the devices of Charles VI and Richard II, are united by the Crown of Thorns and Christ's monogram of YHS, and Christ's words *pax vobis* (peace be with you) are addressed to both monarchs. At the same time, the monogram with a cross and the Crown of Thorns were also emblems of the Order of the Passion and referred to the idea of the projected crusade. On the opposite page the author, who presents the book to Richard II with the banner of the Order in his hand, is portrayed directly as an envoy preaching the crusade.

However, Philip de Mézières never crossed the Channel. The frontispiece scene of him handing the book to the King of England refers more to the *topos* of authorial dedications than to any historical event. According to the most likely scenario, the *Epistre* was presented to Richard II in May 1395, together with Charles VI's official letters, by Robert le Mennot (Robert the Hermit), Philip's associate, who was closely involved in his crusading project. Taking into account the currency of its contents, the *Epistre* must have been completed shortly before that date (see Palmer 1972).

Philip commissioned the decoration of the manuscript in a Parisian workshop that has been associated with the illuminator Perrin Remiet (Avril 1969). The name of Remiet appears in two manuscripts, a *Pèlerinage de la vie humaine*, dated 1393 (Paris, BnF, MS fr. 823), and a much earlier *Histoire ancienne* (cat. no. 135). In the second he is referred to as the artist who illustrated a copy of this manuscript, identified with a book now in Paris (Paris, BnF, MS fr. 301). Remiet is known to have worked for Louis, Duke of Orleans (1372–1407), Philip's intimate friend, and to have painted a *tableau* for the chapel that the Duke endowed at the Celestine convent only a year after the *Epistre* was illuminated. More recently, however, the identification of Remiet's hand has been disputed (Camille 1996), and miniatures in both Paris manuscripts have been attributed to Jean de Nizières, whose documented work in the *Livre des propriétez des choses* (Paris, Bibliothèque Ste-Geneviève, MS 1028) strikingly resembles the images of the *Epistre*.

It is possible that after Richard's deposition and death the manuscript remained in royal possession. In 1535 it was listed amongst the books at Richmond Palace. *J.F.*

PROVENANCE:

Richard II.

141 The Psalter of Henry VI

Paris, *c.* 1405–10 and (tables) *c.* 1420; (added miniatures) Paris or Rouen, *c.* 1430
195 x 140 mm

BRITISH LIBRARY, COTTON DOMITIAN A. xvii

Produced at a time when the Book of Hours was the principal prayerbook on which aristocrats lavished their wealth and illuminators created their finest works, the present deluxe Psalter is an important survival. Within it almost every page is ornamented with a full border of gold ivy leaves. Although the calendar is unillustrated, seven of the eight liturgical divisions of the Psalter (on the Psalter divisions see cat. no. 13) open with two illustrations, one filling the whole of the left-hand page and the other a large part of the right-hand one. Executed in the refined style of painting developed in Paris in the first quarter of the fifteenth century, these miniatures add to the volume's overall luxurious appearance.

As is common with many high-status manuscripts, the decoration of the Psalter was not all undertaken at the same time. Instead, it appears that the calendar, the text of the Psalms, all the marginal decoration that accompanies them and all the miniatures that head the opening pages of the eight liturgical sections were executed together at an earlier date than the full-page illustrations facing them. Largely neglected by previous scholars who have lingered over the later campaign, these earlier illustrations deserve greater attention for their exquisite painting. Meiss (1974) cursorily attributed them to an illuminator related to the artist he named the Master of Berry's *Cleres Femmes*. Pächt's (1963) attribution of the first campaign to the 'youthful' Bedford Master was rejected by Spencer (1966) who nevertheless thought it, like the frontispiece of a finely illustrated copy of Gaston Phébus's *Livre de la chasse* (Paris, BnF, MS fr. 616), the work of 'an independent illuminator of equal distinction'. Further study is required to determine the place of the Psalter miniatures in relation to the *Cleres Femmes* illuminators and the so-called 'Bedford trend' corpus.

Within this initial campaign six of the miniatures each includes the portrait of a young boy engaged in a devout conversation with the Virgin and Christ; in two he is supported respectively by St Louis (reproduced) and St Catherine (fig. 2.8). Wearing a crown and accompanied by the quartered arms of England and France ancient, this boy is generally now recognized as the young Henry VI. Yet, as is evident from close examination, the arms of England are a later addition. Originally the arms sported by the boy were those of France ancient alone. Given his apparent age, royal status and attendance by St Louis, he has been repeatedly identified as the Dauphin Louis, Duke of Guyenne (b. 1397, d. 1415). This identification, together with the style of border and miniature illumination and square format of the miniatures, suggests a dating of the first campaign to *c.* 1405–10. At this very time Louis's mother, Isabel of Bavaria, is recorded as having devotional manuscripts made for her other children.

The later campaign differs from the first in several important respects. First, the artists responsible for it had to accommodate their miniatures into whatever space was left at the end of each division of the Psalter. Apparently they did not have the option of disbinding the volume and adding further leaves. Second, the subjects that they chose to illustrate were very different from their predecessors' choices, namely a sequence of different religious orders at communal worship culminating in David, the supposed author of the Psalms, engaged in song with eight musicians. Third, the complex architectural settings of these illustrations point to artists who had access to models used by the famous Limbourg brothers. Most notably two (ff. 150v, 177v) employ architectural settings also used by the Limbourgs in the *Très Riches Heures*. Whereas to earlier scholars this dependency suggested the hand of either one of the Limbourg brothers or a member of their workshop, more recent studies have seen it as another instance of the influence of the *Très Riches Heures* on illuminators working in Paris in the 1410s and 1420s. The attribution of at least part of the second campaign of the Psalter to the Master of the Royal Alexander (see Reynolds 1994; also cat. no. 75) is consistent with this explanation, given his use elsewhere of the same Limbourg patterns.

Setting aside questions of attribution, a key unresolved question is when and why this second campaign was undertaken. Since the volume must have been disbound to make the addition (ff. 8–11) of a set of computistical tables that run from 1420 to 1462, the failure at this point to insert further leaves for the second campaign suggests that it was undertaken at a later date. Given that, it is tempting to see it and the addition of the arms of England as painted at the same time, *c.* 1430, on the eve of Henry's coronation in France. Whereas the tables may have been added to the Psalter at the request of Louis's sister, Catherine of France (d. 1437), in the very year that she married Henry V, the second campaign may have been undertaken to enhance the volume's role in the education of Catherine's young son Henry VI and his induction into the cultural and religious values appropriate to the King of France (see also cat. nos. 67, 74, 142). *S.McK.*

PROVENANCE:

Louis, Duke of Guyenne (d. 1415); Catherine of France (?); Henry VI; Sir Robert Cotton (d. 1631); bequeathed to the nation by Sir John Cotton, 1702.

Opposite:
The young Prince presented by St Louis to the Virgin and Child, f. 50

Dominus illuminaci
o mea: et salus mea
quem timebo
Dominus protector uite mee:

142 The Bedford Hours

Paris, *c.* 1410–30
265 x 185 mm

BRITISH LIBRARY, ADDITIONAL 18850

John, Duke of Bedford, at prayer before St George, ff. 256v–257

On Christmas Eve 1430 Anne of Burgundy, the wife of John, Duke of Bedford, presented this lavish Book of Hours of the use of Paris to her nine-year-old nephew, Henry VI. At that time Henry was residing with the Duke and Duchess at Rouen, awaiting his coronation as King of France. In the event it was almost a year later when he was crowned at Notre Dame in Paris. The following year, in November 1432, Anne died, ending an important personal dimension of the political alliance between England and Philip the Good, Duke of Burgundy.

At its presentation to Henry VI, the manuscript included several particularly prominent reminders of the Duke and Duchess. First, their joint heraldic arms, devices and mottoes feature at various key points within the book. Second and most importantly, separate, full-length portraits of the Duke and the Duchess were placed before prayers to St George and St Anne, respectively. The first image includes a remarkable life-like representation of the Duke's head in profile (pictured). A record of the gift to Henry VI was inscribed by the young King's personal tutor and physician, Dr John Somerset (d. 1454), on the reverse of the Duke's portrait.

Yet, as was first noted almost fifty years ago (Spencer 1965), these personal markers of the Duke and Duchess form later additions to the volume. Unlike in other manuscripts associated with them (see cat. no. 26), none of their heraldry was part of its original decorative programme; instead most were inserted in spaces that the original producers had left blank. Moreover, as was recorded by Gough (1794), the two portraits and their accompanying prayers once formed part of a cluster of additions inserted at the front of the manuscript, after its calendar. These additions included a remarkable sequence of four full-page illustrations of the stories of Adam and Eve, Noah and the Tower of Babel. On the reverse of one of these miniatures a large heraldic display, now overpainted with the arms of Henry II of France, formerly included those of the Duke and Duchess. Only in the nineteenth century were the portraits moved to their present location, before the book's suffrages. Some scholars have argued persuasively that all these additions, together with the final miniature of Clovis (fig. 2.1), its accompanying legend of the fleur-de-lis written in alternate lines of blue and gold and all the explanatory inscriptions that accompany the principal illustrations, were undertaken in 1430 for the Duke and Duchess to enhance their Christmas gift. Thus adapted, the Bedford Hours may have served a similar didactic purpose to that of the Psalter of Henry VI (cat. no. 141).

Questions still remain about the original

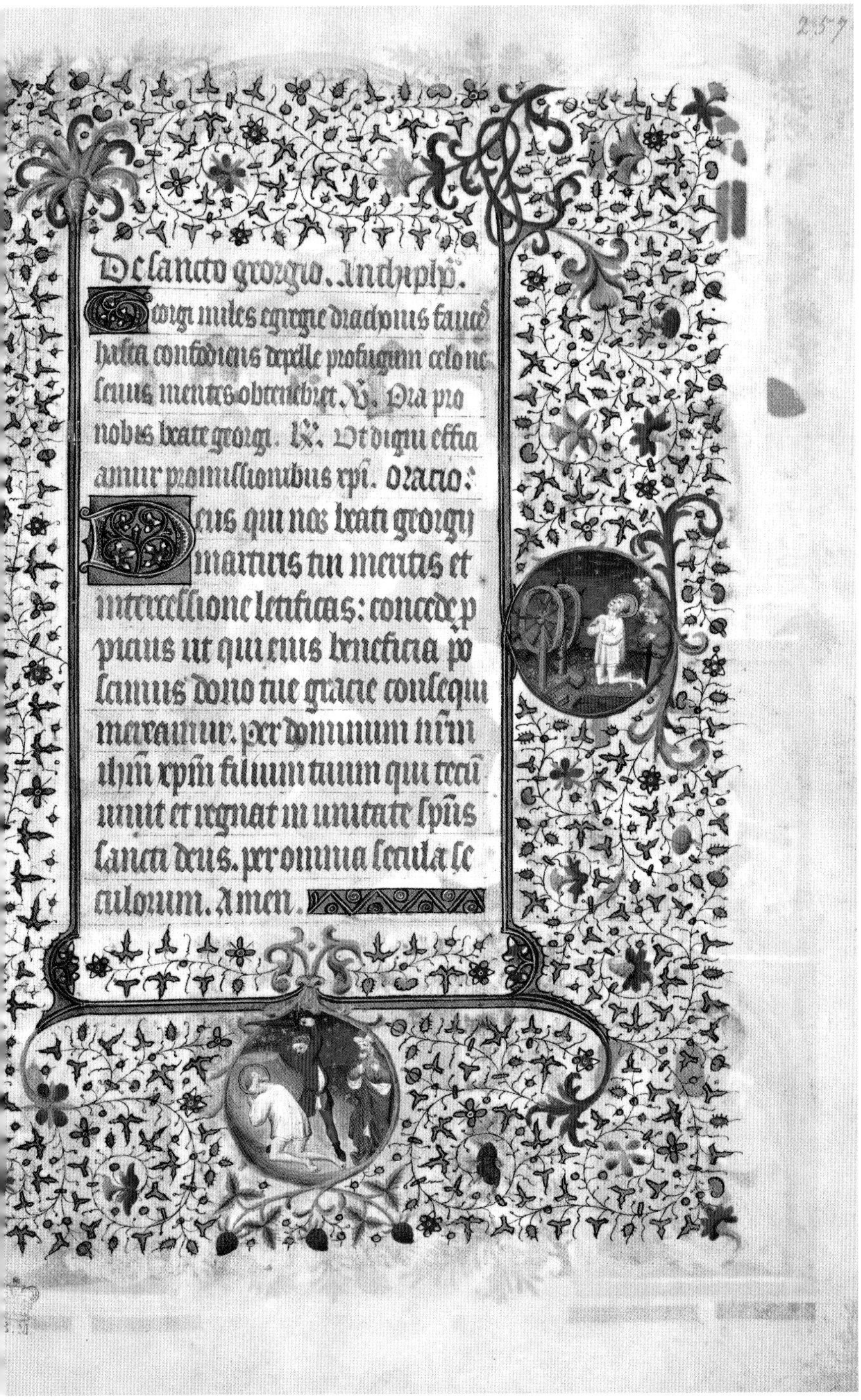

starting date of the book's production. The Bedford portraits and, if one accepts them as contemporaneous, the Genesis miniatures must date from between 1423 (the year of Anne's marriage to the Duke) and 1430. The remainder of the manuscript, with its thirty-one large miniatures marking the main divisions of the book and around 1200 marginal roundels providing a complementary narrative of and commentary on the New Testament, has proved less easy to date. Recent scholarly discussion on this point has revolved around the relationship of the Bedford Hours to the famous *Très Riches Heures*, left incomplete on the death of John, Duke of Berry, in 1416. Close compositional similarities between several miniatures in the Bedford Hours and their counterparts in the *Très Riches Heures* clearly suggest that the artists responsible for the former had first-hand knowledge of at least part of the latter (Reynolds 2005). However, what are we to make of the further observation of similar artists having contributed to the marginal decoration of the *Très Riches Heures*? For Stirnemann and Rabel (2005), knowledge of the Limbourgs' compositions was gained by the Bedford artists before work for Berry ceased on his manuscript and was quickly reused by them in the present volume for a member of the French royal family, possibly the Dauphin, Louis, Duke of Guyenne (d. 1415). For Reynolds (2005) and König (2007), the transfer of knowledge occurred later, after Berry's death, in the early 1420s. For them only parts of the manuscript's decorative borders are datable to the 1410s (see Reynolds 2006), and the identity of its original patron remains unproven.

Whatever its historical origins may have been, the Bedford Hours remains one of the most outstanding illuminated manuscripts ever produced. The artists now recognized as responsible for it – most scholars now accept that the name artist, the Bedford Master, worked on it with accomplished assistants and associates – formed one of the most influential artistic workshops in Paris during the first half of the fifteenth century. Their work for the Duke of Bedford on this and several other manuscripts exemplifies the active engagement of English royalty with the leading illuminators of their French domain. *S.McK.*

PROVENANCE:

John, Duke of Bedford, and his wife, Anne of Burgundy (d. 1432); Henry VI; Henry II of France; Sir Robert Worsley, 4th Baronet, of Appuldurcombe (b. 1669, d. 1747); Edward Harley, 2nd Earl of Oxford (b. 1689, d. 1741); Margaret Cavendish, Duchess of Portland (b. 1715, d. 1785); James Edwards (d. 1816); George Spencer-Churchill, 5th Duke of Marlborough (b. 1766, d. 1840); John Milner; Sir John Tobin (b. 1763, d. 1851); Rev. John Tobin; William Boone, bookseller, of London; purchased for the nation in 1852.

143 The Shrewsbury Book

Rouen, 1444–45
470 x 370 mm

BRITISH LIBRARY, ROYAL 15 E. vi

The Shrewsbury Book is one of the most remarkable manuscripts to have been preserved in the Old Royal library. Although typical in its overall appearance of deluxe books produced at Rouen around the middle of the fifteenth century, the volume is strikingly distinctive in almost every other respect. Most notably it comprises a unique collection of fifteen texts in French that encompasses *chansons de geste*, chivalric romances and treatises on warfare and chivalry. *Chansons de geste* and romances make up the first two-thirds of the volume, beginning with Alexander the Great and moving forwards in time to Carolingian heroes and medieval knights, such as Guy of Warwick and the Swan Knight. The remaining one-third comprises a thirteenth-century and three fifteenth-century instructional texts, combined with a *Chroniques de Normandie* and ending with the Statutes of the Order of the Garter. The underlying theme of the collection is the theory and the past and present practice of chivalry.

Equally remarkable is the volume's lavish illumination. Embellished with richly decorated borders, two monumental miniatures occupy the whole of two of the volume's folio-sized pages and form part of its two magnificent frontispieces (ff. 2v–4). Thereafter eighty-one further miniatures are dedicated to the opening text, the *Roman d'Alexandre en prose*, nine miniatures to the romance *Quatre fils Aymon* and thirty-six to the romance *Ponthus et Sidoine*. A single miniature marks the beginning of each of the other texts. Just as no other surviving volume contains the same selection of texts as the Shrewsbury Book, no other has the same overall campaign of illustration. The more extensive illustrative treatment of three of the texts may reflect such factors as the preference of the patron, the experience of the artists or the illustrative content of the textual exemplars. Although each text was transcribed as a separate booklet, the images are presented as a single, integrated campaign led by one artist, named after this manuscript the Talbot Master, who was responsible for most of the illumination (see cat. nos. 37, 71, 72). The miniature of Babylon (f. 4v, pictured) was executed by an illuminator working in a style close to that of the Bedford Master (see cat. no. 142).

Undoubtedly the most celebrated part of the book is the first grand opening (ff. 2–3, pictured overleaf). Here – on the left-hand page – text, image and decorative border work together to clarify the context for which the volume had been made. From them we learn that the manuscript was a gift to Margaret of Anjou from the renowned military commander John Talbot, 1st Earl of Shrewsbury (d. 1453), shown wearing his Garter robes. Yet, as has been elsewhere demonstrated (Reynolds 1993), only the presentation verses record real time. Although the image represents Margaret hand-in-hand with her husband Henry VI and bearing the sceptre and crown of the Queen of England, Talbot's presentation probably took place before her departure from France, marriage and coronation in England. In the verses she is described merely as affianced. The book may have been begun almost one year earlier, upon the finalization of the marriage agreement in May 1444. Thereafter Talbot, who had taken part in the marriage negotiations in Anjou, would have had several months at Rouen to arrange for the manuscript to be made before setting out later that same year to conduct Margaret from Anjou to England. His best opportunity to present the book would have been on Margaret's arrival in Rouen in March 1445.

The image on the right-hand page is visually more complex, but straightforward in its aims: it presents the genealogical claim of Henry VI to be the rightful King of France. Preserved elsewhere in more schematic form, this vehicle for Henry's claim may have been widely promulgated in English-held France. Despite its beautification, the genealogy retained a potency of meaning at the moment of its incorporation in the Shrewsbury Book. English military fortunes in the Hundred Years War were waning and about to plummet; the dual monarchy was under severe threat.

Although the opening text and image appear to make clear the intended audience for the Shrewsbury Book, there remains some ambiguity on this point. The apparent male focus of the chivalric treatises has variously been interpreted as evidence of the volume having been first conceived for Talbot or ultimately intended for the hoped-for heir of the royal union. The legendary connections of Guy of Warwick and the Swan Knight with Talbot's wife's family, the Beauchamps, have similarly been explained in terms of either Talbot's intended ownership or his wish to achieve a presence in the volume beyond his repeated heraldry and to reassert to its recipients his chivalric values and accomplishments. Although the opening verses aspire to peace and unity between England and France, the Hundred Years War was still a present reality.

S.McK.

PROVENANCE:

Margaret of Anjou; Henry VI.

Opposite:
Nectanebus at Babylon, f. 4v

The Earl of Shrewsbury presents his book to Margaret of Anjou; the genealogical descent of Henry VI from St Louis, ff. 2v–3

144 The Egerton Hours

Paris, *c.* 1405–10; (additions) Provence, *c.* 1440
220 x 165 mm

BRITISH LIBRARY, EGERTON 1070

Painted by some of the finest Parisian artists of the early fifteenth century, this remarkable Book of Hours was made for a French aristocratic or royal patron. Some scholars have suggested that it was started for Louis, Duke of Orleans (d. 1407), and completed for Charles of Blois, father of Mary of Blois, wife of Louis I of Anjou (Avril and Reynaud 1993; *Splendeur* 2009). Eight full-page miniatures introduce the Offices of the Virgin (devotional readings to be recited at set times of day). These miniatures include a striking *Visitation* (fig. 2.5). Historiated initials on the facing pages contain subsidiary scenes relating to the subjects of the full-page miniatures.

Copious images of saints illustrate intercessory prayers known as suffrages. More exceptional still is the border decoration, which is unique to this Book of Hours and features pairs of angels, floating serenely in the margins and holding aloft branches of acanthus. The volume was painted by at least four people whose work has been identified in other important manuscripts. All but two miniatures of the original cycle were completed by an artist known from this manuscript as the Master of Egerton 1070 (see also cat. nos. 24, 74), and by his close associate, the so-called Mazarine Master (*Splendeur* 2009).

Around 1440 the manuscript came into the possession of the great bibliophile and author, René I (b. 1409, d. 1480), King of Naples and Duke of Anjou, who customized it for his own use. A frontispiece with his arms was added to the volume, and billowing sails, inscribed with his motto, *En Dieu en soit*, were placed in the hands of the border angels on several leaves. Material added at René's behest was thoughtfully integrated into the manuscript. Prayers, for example, in which he is named, were inscribed on the pages directly preceding an existing image of the penitent King David (f. 44v) – an arrangement that encourages readers to draw parallels between the biblical monarch and René. More spectacular are five added full-page miniatures. These too were slotted in at key points in the book. An allegorical image of Death, for example, shown as a putrefying corpse wearing a golden crown, was inserted immediately before the Office of the Dead (f. 53, pictured).

The macabre figure functions both as a specific 'portrait' of René and as a general portrait of Death, ruling over all people for all time. Although the corpse clasps a scroll inscribed, 'Memento homo quod sinis es et in sinere [*sic*] reverteris' (Remember, man, that you are dust and to dust you will return), it was not intended to evoke despair, but to encourage René to live wisely. This very sentiment is articulated in an excerpt from a poem of uncertain authorship, the *Rythmus de contemptu mundi*, added to the facing page, which reads in part, 'O food for worms, O pile of dust, / O dew, O vanity, why are you so extolled? / You do not know if you will be alive tomorrow, / Do good to all for as long as you are able.'

Most recent scholars have attributed the five added miniatures to Barthélemy d'Eyck, a Netherlandish artist who worked for René in the middle of the fifteenth century. Although Barthélemy's style is strikingly different from that of the artists who painted the original campaign, he may have borrowed from them at least one feature. The textile bearing René's arms, stretched across the foreground of the miniature of Death, is analogous to the rich cloths similarly arranged in many of the images of saints painted by the Egerton Master (e.g. f. 105v, pictured). René's preoccupation with Death personified is attested by a similar figure added, *c.* 1446, to another Book of Hours owned by him (Paris, BnF, MS lat. 1156A, f. 113v), and by the design of his tomb in the cathedral in Angers (*Splendeur* 2009).

Above:
St Quintinus, f. 105v (detail)

Opposite:
Death personified, f. 53

Backhouse (1995) plausibly suggested that the present manuscript came to England with Rene's daughter, Margaret of Anjou, who married Henry VI in 1445. Between 1505 and 1509 it was presented to Henry VII by his chaplain George Strangeways, Archdeacon of Coventry. Henry VI's association with Coventry is well documented, and a spectacular tapestry of Netherlandish manufacture, associated with the King, still hangs in St Mary's Hall there (Campbell 2007). *D.J.*

PROVENANCE:

(?) Louis, Duke of Orleans (b. 1372, d. 1407); (?) Charles of Blois, father of Mary of Blois, wife of Louis I, Duke of Anjou; René, King of Naples and Duke of Anjou (b. 1409, d. 1480); presented to Henry VII by his chaplain George Strangeways, Archdeacon of Coventry from 1505; Jesuit College, Cracow, by 1630; purchased for the nation from H. Ruschewagh in 1844.

145 Xenophon, *Anabasis*

(French translation by Claude de Seyssel)

Bourges, *c.* 1506
320 x 225 mm

BRITISH LIBRARY, ROYAL 19 C. vi

The royal arms of England; Claude de Seyssel presenting the manuscript to Henry VII, ff. 16v–17

Xenophon's *Anabasis* tells the story of ten thousand Greek mercenaries conscripted by Cyrus the Younger, who rebelled against his brother, King Artaxerxes II, and sought to usurp the Persian throne. At the Battle of Cunaxa, north of Babylon (401 BC), disaster struck: Cyrus was killed and the Greeks, surrounded by their enemies, had to fight their way home. Xenophon, an eyewitness, who took command of the retreating troops, presents his readers with a tale of adventure and exemplary leadership.

This manuscript of Xenophon's *Anabasis* in French translation has two prefaces. The first explains that Xenophon's original Greek text was translated *c.* 1504–05 for Louis XII of France by Claude de Seyssel (d. 1520), a counsellor and ambassador in the King's service. De Seyssel had discovered in the royal library at Blois a copy of the work, brought by Charles VIII from Naples. Since de Seyssel did not know Greek, he persuaded his fellow diplomat, the humanist Janus Lascaris, to translate the text from Greek into Latin. It was this Latin version that de Seyssel used as his source text.

The second preface explains how de Seyssel, having been sent on a diplomatic mission to England in 1506 (Dionisotti 1995), met Henry VII and was impressed by his learning and his newly constructed library (probably located, though not explicitly stated here, at Richmond Palace). De Seyssel describes this library as 'tres belle et tres bien acoustree' (very beautiful and very well appointed) and observes that Henry VII was fond of 'histoires at aultres chouses apartenant à ung noble et saige prinpce [*sic*]' (stories and other matters appropriate for a noble and wise prince).

On his return to France, de Seyssel sent Henry VII the present copy of his French translation of Xenophon's *Anabasis*. The manuscript was illustrated by an illuminator of Bourges, who was active *c.* 1490–1510 and is now known as the Master of Spencer 6 after a Book of Hours illuminated by him (New York Public Library, Spencer 6). The Master of Spencer 6 took as his model the illustrations painted by the so-called Master of Philippa of Guelders in the earliest copy of the text, which was commissioned *c.* 1505 by de Seyssel for presentation to Louis XII (Paris, BnF, MS fr. 702). De Seyssel's gift would have been a welcome addition to Henry VII's library, which was filled with French works, some inherited from Edward IV and others acquired by him along with

printed books – notably those published by the Parisian printer Anthoine Vérard (Carley 2000; fig. 2.13).

Seven of the miniatures in Henry VII's volume illustrate Xenophon's text, showing, for example, Greek soldiers waging war. More interesting are the ones preceding the two prefaces. The first (f. 9v) depicts de Seyssel offering his translation to Louis XII, who is surrounded by his counsellors, courtiers and an armed guard. The second prefatory image (f. 17, pictured), which reiterates and reinforces the royal dedication of the first, depicts Henry VII enthroned beneath a canopy, inscribed with the motto *Dieu Est* [sic] *Mon Droit*. An image of God is situated directly above Henry VII's head, and the rays emanating from the Divine flow down to the King, a sign that he is God's earthly representative. An obeisant de Seyssel is shown once again, this time presenting his book to the English monarch. This image closely resembles the presentation scene in the manuscript that de Seyssel offered to Louis XII (see Scheller 1983); the French and English kings are virtually interchangeable.

Curiously, in the rubric inscribed beneath the image the King is referred to as 'Henry VI' rather than 'Henry VII', an error that also occurs in the verse dedication on the facing page (f. 16v). Above the verses are emblazoned the arms of England and, in the lower margin, the arms of de Seyssel: girony or and azure. Although the lack of care exemplified by the reference to the wrong English king and the incorrect wording of the royal motto suggest ignorance or inattention, the intensity of the red and blue pigments employed contributes to the overall impression of regal splendour.

Evidently de Seyssel anticipated that his gifts would be well received. Besides the copies he presented to Louis XII and Henry VII, a virtual twin of the latter manuscript, with modified prefatory text and images, was made by the Master of Spencer 6 for de Seyssel, a Savoyard born in Aix-les-Bains, to present to Charles II, Duke of Savoy (Avril and Reynaud 1993). De Seyssel's translation of the *Anabasis* was not printed before his death in 1520, but was published shortly afterwards, in 1529, by order of another royal reader – Francis I (Boone 2000). *D.J.*

PROVENANCE:
Henry VII.

146 Martin de Brion, *Tresample description de toute la Terre Saincte*

Paris, *c.* 1540
230 x 160 mm

BRITISH LIBRARY, ROYAL 20 A. iv

As rivals in artistic and literary patronage Henry VIII of England and Francis I of France were occasionally abetted by the artists and authors who vied for their attention. The French author Martin de Brion presented this copy of his *Tresample description de toute la Terre Saincte* to Henry, and another of the same text to Francis I (Paris, BnF, MS fr. 5638). He also published in Paris, in 1540, a printed edition of a Latin version of the *Tresample description*, with a dedication to Francis. A manuscript copy of this Latin version was given by de Brion to Pope Paul III (Vatican City, Biblioteca Apostolica Vaticana, MS Vat. lat. 5536). Because nothing is known of Martin de Brion's life, he can only be gauged by his literary output (Karrow 1993). A Latin translation of Ecclesiastes and the Song of Songs that he presented to Edward VI (Royal 2 D. iii) suggests that he received some positive response from the Tudor court. Moreover, his presentations of the *Tresample description* to three heads of western Christendom intimates astonishingly lofty ambitions for a figure whose life is today obscure.

The text written by de Brion is a description of various sites of interest in the Holy Land, with a more scholarly than devotional purpose. It is organized alphabetically and may have been used as a reference text in scriptural study. Each site is described according to more or less the same template: after the place is named, its geographical position is detailed in relation to other known locations; a significant biblical event that occurred in the place is mentioned; and, in many entries, greater detail of the event is provided, occasionally in original verses by de Brion, followed by a citation of the biblical book, chapter and verse in which it is described. Prefacing the text is a dedication to Henry that praises his wisdom and appreciation for 'cosmographie'. Martin de Brion's gift of this volume was astute, given Henry's enthusiasm for cartography later in his life; in the wake of the invasion crisis of 1538–40, Henry amplified public perception of his dominion through patronage of maps and geographical treatises (see cat. nos. 95, 96). Indeed, this volume itself may have been accompanied by a map originally (Backhouse 1997). Contemporary references to a map by de Brion 'with lively colours, & bewtified with Gold' are tantalizing, but no such object has come to light (Karrow 1993).

The illumination of Henry's manuscript is both characteristically French and remarkably similar to the volume presented to King Francis. In the preface to each, Martin de Brion's words to the relevant King are written within an elaborate border, in gold ink, and against a ground of saturated colour: blue for the French King and red for the King of England (pictured; fig. 1.18). Borders throughout the remainder of the manuscripts are less elaborate, comprising a gold-bar frame from the corners of which spring either a rose, for Henry, or a fleur-de-lis, for Francis.

Unlike Francis's volume, the Royal *Tresample description* retains its original binding – a rare survival from the hundreds of once lavishly bound books in the English royal collection. The 1547 inventory of Henry's possessions describes the book as 'covered with vellat enbrawdred' – a concise characterization for the precious binding of crimson velvet, gold thread and seed pearls that is still extant today. Although relatively little is known about the procedures for having books dressed for the Old Royal library, it is possible that the binding for this volume was added after it was presented to the King. A rare record of the payment for bindings appears in the Great Wardrobe accounts from Edward IV's reign (Harley 4780; fig. 2.17), which details payments to a London stationer for binding, dressing with velvet, and providing clasps and other fittings for eleven manuscripts in the King's library (see the essay 'A European Heritage'). Perhaps dressing with precious textiles a book that lacked an elaborate binding preceded its incorporation into the royal collection, a way of enhancing its opulence and value. Henry VIII owned many books with jewel-encrusted bindings of luxurious textiles as well as leather-bound volumes, although it is not known whether he preferred cloth to the tooled-leather bindings that had become popular France (see cat. no. 147). Nevertheless, this rare survival gives an idea of the importance of such bindings; when closed, the royal books offered a sumptuous display that was crucial to projecting the King's wealth, power and identity to rivals and allies. *S.D.*

PROVENANCE:
Henry VIII.

Above:
Lower cover

Opposite:
Dedication to Henry VIII by Martin de Brion, f. 2

Au treſilluſtre Prince
HENRY huyctieſme de ce
nom Roy d'Angleterre et de
France, ſeigneur d'Hyberme,
& defenſeur de la foy MARTIN
DE BRION Pariſien donne
ſalut immortel

LE DESIR que iay long temps
a, SIRE, de faire ains que
mourir, a ſi vertueux Roy quelque cho
ſe qui luy agree: m'a faict puiſnague=
res mectre la main a la pleume pour
deſcripre les villes Portz, Fleuues,
Torrentz, prouinces, & Regions, qui
ſont en la terre ſaincte. bien ſachant
qu'entre mille ſciences eſquelles
voſtre cueur noble ſe delecte, La

147 Isocrates, *Ad Nicoclem* and *Nicocles*

(French translation by Louis le Roy)

Paris, 1550
480 x 340 mm

BRITISH LIBRARY, ROYAL 16 E. xxxii

Arms of Edward VI facing Le Roy's dedication to Edward VI, ff. 1v–2

What constitutes an ideal ruler? How should he govern the state? These questions engaged the Athenian orator Isocrates (436–338 BC), who wrote several famous discourses, founded a school in Athens and lived until the venerable age of ninety-seven. Isocrates favoured early forms of Athenian democracy, but criticized politicians of his own day. Sympathetic to monarchy, he famously stated 'even the gods are ruled by Zeus as king'. One of his most widely read treatises, *Ad Nicoclem* (To Nicocles), a book on the duties of kingship, was addressed to the young ruler of that name who succeeded his father as King of Cyprus in 374 BC. In a second, related work, entitled *Nicocles*, Isocrates asked how the Cyprians should behave towards their king. It is thought that Nicocles may have been a pupil of Isocrates; certainly Nicocles welcomed his advice and rewarded him with gifts.

Made in Paris in 1550 for presentation to the young Edward VI, this manuscript, which opens with a frontispiece featuring the royal arms and a dedication to the King framed by an illuminated scatter border (pictured) and retains its original French binding of tooled leather, contains treatises by Isocrates as well as an extract from the *Cyropaedia*, a biography of Cyrus the Great by Xenophon (*c.* 430–354 BC), a historian and contemporary of Isocrates (see cat. no. 145). *Ad Nicoclem* and *Nicocles* are early examples of advice manuals for rulers or 'mirrors for princes'. Since they shed light on the roles and responsibilities of a king and his subjects, they were eminently suited to the young English monarch. The texts were translated from Greek into French by the humanist Louis le Roy (d. 1577), who spent most of his career travelling with the peripatetic French court. On a visit to England in October 1550, Le Roy gave the volume to the young King. In his preface he praised the recent peace forged between France and England, and Edward's love of learning and proficiency in French.

Few children can have been welcomed into the world more heartily than Prince Edward, the longed-for son and heir of Henry VIII, who was born to Jane Seymour, Henry's third wife, on 12 October 1537. No aspect of Edward's upbringing was left to chance, and his education included lessons in French, Latin and Greek. His chief preceptor, Sir John Cheke (b. 1514, d. 1557), served as Regius Professor of Greek at Cambridge, and

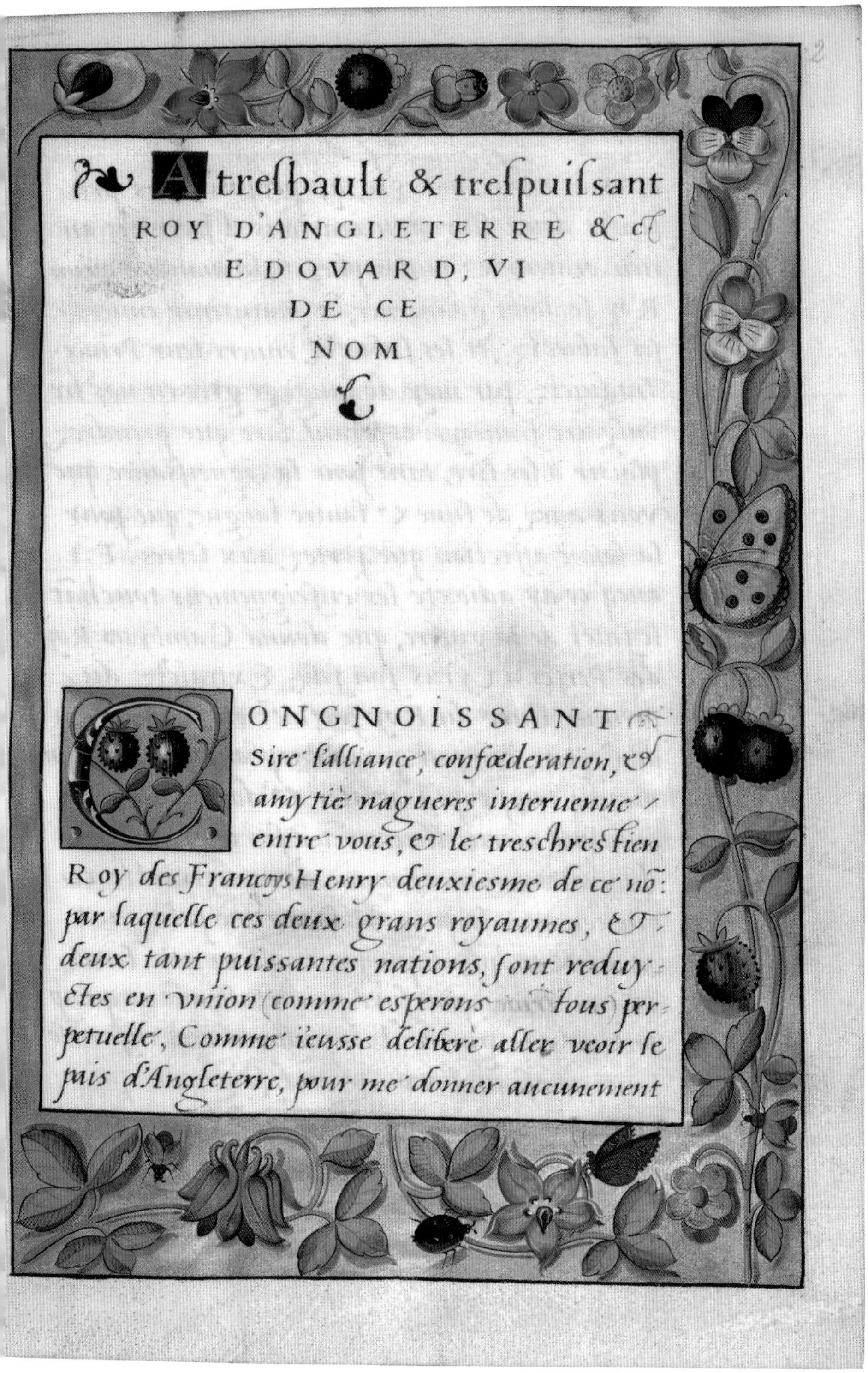
A treſhault & treſpuiſsant
ROY D'ANGLETERRE &c.
EDOVARD, VI
DE CE
NOM

CONGNOISSANT Sire l'alliance, confœderation, & amytie nagueres interuenue entre vous, & le treschres tien Roy des Francoys Henry deuxiesme de ce nō: par laquelle ces deux grans royaumes, & deux tant puissantes nations, sont reduyctes en vnion (comme esperons tous) perpetuelle, Comme ieusse delibere aller veoir le pais d'Angleterre, pour me donner aucunement

Roger Ascham (b. 1514/15, d. 1568), tutor of Edward's half-sister, Princess Elizabeth, is credited with introducing English readers to Isocrates (Whipple 1916). Edward excelled at his studies, and some of his notebooks, which have been preserved, reflect his seriousness (e.g. Additional 4724 and Arundel 510). Le Roy did not have Edward VI in mind, however, when he completed his translations of Isocrates. Instead, in 1547, he dedicated these to the French King, Henry II, to commemorate the latter's accession to the throne on the death of his father, Francis I. The manuscript presented to Henry II, containing Le Roy's translations, has survived in Paris (BnF, MS n.a.fr. 1843).

By dedicating works to members of the royal family and aristocracy, Le Roy hoped to win their favour and improve his financial situation. His efforts, however, were often overlooked. Happily, that was not the case in England. The only surviving letter in Le Roy's hand (Harley 6989, f. 148), addressed to Edward VI, who died before he reached his sixteenth birthday, records the French scholar's gratitude to the young King. He writes, 'You not only read and approved my little books when I was in England – a fact that is very honourable – but you also heaped a truly royal reward on the author, which I was not expecting' (Gundersheimer 1966).

Isocrates enjoyed a particular vogue with Renaissance humanists, who praised his works for their literary style. Sir Thomas Elyot (d. 1546), one of the foremost educational theorists of the time, argued that noblemen who studied great orators would more easily master the art of public speaking. Isocrates was one of Elyot's favourite authors, and as early as 1534 he published *The Doctrinal of Princes*, his English translation of *Ad Nicoclem*. According to Elyot, 'Isocrates, concerning the lesson of oratours, is every where wonderfull profitable, havynge almost as many wyse sentences as he hath wordes: and with that is so swete and delectable to rede, that, after him, almost all other seme unsavery and tedious' (Whipple 1916).

D.J.

PROVENANCE:

Edward VI.

148 The Psalter of the Earl of Arundel

London amd Paris (?), 1565
295 x 205 mm

BRITISH LIBRARY, ROYAL 2 B. ix

Arms of Henry Fitzalan, Earl of Arundel; Arundel as the penitent David, ff. 1v–2.

This elegant Psalter was made in London in 1565 by the Italian writer and calligrapher Petruccio Ubaldini (fl. 1545–99), who had first come to England in 1545 and settled there permanently in 1562. According to an inscription at the end of the volume, Ubaldini presented it to his then patron, Henry Fitzalan, 19th Earl of Arundel (b. 1512, d. 1580). Given the late date of the manuscript, which is written on paper, the text, complete with an index – an unusual feature for a Psalter manuscript – was probably copied from a printed edition of Jerome's Gallican Psalter.

The opening page of text showcases Ubaldini's beautiful cursive script, painterly skills and harmonious page layout. Decorative panels recall late antique wall-paintings, and the splendour of the page is enhanced by the large, gold initial '*B*'(eatus) and the alternating lines of gold and silver script of the first lines of Psalm 1. In the lower border are inscribed the opening words of the Book of Wisdom, 'Diligite Iustitiam, qui iudicatis terram' (Love justice, you that are the judges of the earth). This admonition would have served as an apt reminder to Arundel, a wealthy magnate who held key political appointments.

Although the Psalter was made in England, the two full-page miniatures at the beginning of the volume (pictured) were painted by an anonymous artist working in an ornate style favoured by the French court, and one that was equally attractive to English patrons eager to emulate French fashions. The first consists of Arundel's arms, motto and monogram, and the second, an image of King David beseeching an avenging angel to spare the city of Jerusalem (as recounted in 2 Kings 24:16). The artist responsible for these paintings has not been identified with certainty, but questions of attribution should not eclipse the most important point: few illustrated Psalters were produced in the sixteenth century and this one is a rarity (Orth 2004).

Is it a coincidence that King David bears a resemblance to Arundel, whose appearance is recorded in several extant portraits? David's prominent nose, long beard, high forehead, large ears and curly hair look very much like Arundel's as depicted, for example, in a portrait of 1550 by the Netherlandish artist Hans Eworth, which shows the Earl in another guise – that of the Emperor Marcus Aurelius (The Berger Collection at the Denver Art Museum, TL-17953). Devotional books commissioned or owned by both Francis I and Henry VIII include depictions of them in the guise of the biblical king (see Paris,

BnF, MS n.a.lat. 82, f. 152v and cat. no. 45), and it is possible that the Davidic image in the present manuscript is also a veiled portrait. The fact that the miniature faces Arundel's arms supports this interpretation. Unlike Francis and Henry, however, Arundel was not a king.

Success as Henry VIII's deputy of Calais, as well as his participation in campaigns against the French, led to Arundel's appointment as Lord Chamberlain, a post he also occupied under Edward VI. During the reigns of Mary and Elizabeth I he served as Lord Steward, but fostered greater ambitions because he saw himself as a suitable husband for Elizabeth. Not all of his contemporaries were convinced. The Austrian Baron Breuner, for example, scathingly remarked: 'He and he alone entertains this hope, for he is somewhat advanced in years and also rather silly and loutish, is not well-favoured, nor has a handsome figure' (von Klarwill 1928).

In 1564 Arundel, who had abandoned the idea of marrying the Queen, resigned his post as Lord Steward, invoking the displeasure of Elizabeth, who confined him to house arrest at his estate, Nonsuch, Surrey, the palace with Italianate gardens, sculptures and stuccoes begun by Henry VIII and completed by Arundel. Shortly afterwards, Ubaldini presented him with the Psalter. There is no record of Arundel's response to the gift, but we can be certain that the book, with its French miniatures and Italian script, was in keeping with his taste. Besides, Nonsuch Palace, one of the most exceptional witnesses to Arundel's interest in the culture of the Italian Renaissance, albeit filtered through a Netherlandish sensibility, is the Eworth portrait showing him as Marcus Aurelius and bearing the Latin inscription 'Invidia torquet autorem' (Let envy torment its author), an allusion to Arundel's political enemy, John Dudley, Earl of Warwick. The inclusion of this pointed inscription strongly suggests that Arundel dictated the terms of the painting and elected to be portrayed 'in full gilded Roman field armour', a unique occurrence in English painting of the sixteenth century (Boyle 2002). Arundel left his library to his son-in-law Lord Lumley, and his unusual Psalter is one of many manuscripts that passed from Lumley to Henry Frederick, Prince of Wales. *D.J.*

PROVENANCE:

Henry Fitzalan, 19th Earl of Arundel (b. 1512, d. 1580); John, 1st Baron Lumley (d. 1609); Henry Frederick, Prince of Wales (d. 1612).

149 Vasco da Lucena, *Les Fais d'Alexandre le grant*

(French translation of Quintus Curtius Rufus, *Historiae Alexandri magni*)

Amiens or Bruges, 1475–80
430 x 335 mm

BRITISH LIBRARY, ROYAL 15 D. iv

In the prologue to *Les Fais d'Alexandre le grant* the Burgundian courtier Vasco da Lucena sought to prepare his readers for a distinctive aspect of his account of Alexander. In contrast to the 'fables made up by men ignorant of the nature of things ... the present history is much more useful. For it tells us how in reality Alexander conquered the whole of the East and how in our day a ruler could really achieve such conquests.' A modern Alexander was to do so 'without flying in the air [and] without going under the sea'. By this means Vasco da Lucena clearly signalled how his account of the deeds of Alexander the Great would differ from the centuries-old tradition of the *Romance of Alexander* (cf. cat. nos. 75, 91, 143). Based principally on the authority of the classical author Quintus Curtius, his work was to adhere to truthful, not fantastic accounts of the past – to constitute *historia*, not *fabula*. Completed in 1468 and dedicated to Charles the Bold, Duke of Burgundy, Vasco's text forms a landmark in humanistic writing produced in northern Europe. His zealous pursuit of a rational approach to the story of Alexander opened up to the dynastic elite new perspectives not only on the great Macedonian leader, but also on models of secular greatness and magnificence. Vasco kept the north abreast of cultural developments in Italy too; there, Curtius's text had achieved a renewed success among rulers and their courtiers, and the *Romance* was received with devastating scorn within cultured circles.

Vasco's text proved notably popular. No fewer than thirty-four manuscripts of his translation of Curtius survive (McKendrick 1996). All were produced within the translator's lifetime by professional book producers in northern Europe, and all of their known early owners were members of the French-speaking nobility there. Most are large, luxury volumes; many are profusely illustrated. By far the largest proportion was made in the southern Netherlands, and no other Burgundian court text survives in similarly large numbers or was so frequently and extensively illustrated. Apparently no other such text was transmitted in such large numbers outside the Burgundian Netherlands.

The present manuscript is a typically lavish copy of Vasco's text. Dating from the second half of the 1470s, it includes an impressive campaign of seventeen large and thirty-two small illustrations. All these miniatures have been attributed securely to the Rambures Master, an illuminator principally active in Amiens but also known to have collaborated closely with Bruges illuminators (Kren and McKendrick 2003). Together they form one of the most extended and inventive campaigns of illustration of Vasco's text that was produced in the southern Netherlands. The text, written in a handsome script typical of south Netherlandish library books, is very closely related to that of another copy (Royal 17 F. i), which was transcribed at Lille by the copyist Jan Du Quesne (cf. cat. nos. 48, 76). Also the figures in the borders may have been executed by the miniaturist responsible for the illustrations of the volume copied by Du Quesne.

Thanks to Backhouse's careful re-examination of this manuscript (Backhouse 1994), we now know that its first identified owner was Guillaume de la Baume, *chevalier d'honneur* of Margaret of York. Very soon afterwards it passed from him to Sir John Donne, a close associate of Margaret's brother Edward IV, at which point both Margaret and Mary of Burgundy inscribed in the book friendly greetings to Donne. It is likely that this transfer of ownership took place during either Donne's embassy to the Low Countries in 1477 or Margaret's visit to England in 1480. In addition to a well-known triptych painted by Hans Memling and a fine Book of Hours illuminated by Simon Marmion, two other library books of Netherlandish origin are known to have belonged to Donne (Campbell 1998). Like at least one of these volumes (Royal 20 B. ii), the present manuscript passed into the Old Royal library during the reign of Henry VIII. At this point an English illuminator added to its opening illuminated border (f. 11, pictured) a crowned escutcheon bearing the royal arms and supported by a red dragon and white greyhound. He also concealed the arms of de la Baume with an elaborate decorative panel that includes both Tudor roses and the pomegranate emblem of Catherine of Aragon (f. 219). One of Donne's sons – both of them served Henry VIII – may have thought the present biography of Alexander an appropriate gift for the Tudor monarch. *S.McK.*

PROVENANCE:

Guillaume de la Baume, Lord of Irlain (d. before 1501); Sir John Donne (d. 1503); Henry VIII.

Opposite:
Charles the Bold receiving Vasco da Lucena's text, f. 11

Cy commence le volume intitule des faiz du grant alexandre qui contient
en soi ·ix· livres particuliers Et premiers commence le prologue du
translateur
Treshault tres
puissant et tres
excellent prince
et mon tres re
doubte seigneur
Charles par la
grace de dieu duc de bourgongne
de lotrich de brabant de lebourg
et de luxembourg conte de flan
dres dartois et de bourgongne
palatin de henault de hollande
de zellande et de namur vasq
de lucene portugalois humble

150 Charles Soillot, *Le Débat de félicité*

Bruges, between 1464 and 1467
350 x 260 mm

BRITISH LIBRARY, ARUNDEL 71

The *Débat de félicité* (Debate on Happiness) is typical of didactic texts written at the court of Philip the Good, Duke of Burgundy. Dedicated to Philip's son Charles the Bold before he succeeded his father as Duke, the *Débat* was completed between 1464 and 1467. Its verse and prose text was compiled by Charles Soillot (b. 1434, d. 1493), successively secretary to Philip, Charles and Charles's daughter Mary of Burgundy, as well as author of a translation of Xenophon's *Hiero* also dedicated to Charles. The subject of the text is a debate on true happiness that the author purported to have witnessed in an extended dream. In this debate, personifications of the Three Estates of medieval society, the Church, Nobility and Labour, each seek to persuade a court held by the Twelve Sciences that it holds the key to happiness. The final judgement of the presiding judge, Theology, is that happiness in this world is possible only through contemplation of God, the Virgin Mary and heaven.

To judge from surviving copies, Soillot's *Débat* had a very limited circulation. Besides the present volume, only one untraced and three extant manuscript copies are known. An edition printed at Antwerp in *c.*1489–92 survives in only one copy. Moreover, only the Arundel copy and one other manuscript that formed part of the library of Philip the Good (Brussels, KBR, MS 9054) preserve the original dedication to Charles as Count of Charolais and apparently date from before he became Duke. The other two manuscripts date from after the death of the Duke and each has a different dedication, one to Louis of Gruuthuse (d. 1492) and the other to Philip of Croÿ (d. 1483), Count of Chimay.

The present copy of the *Débat* deserves greater scholarly attention than it has received to date. Of the two earliest copies only this one is written on parchment. Of all the surviving copies only it illustrates Soillot's dream, the other two illustrated copies each containing solely a presentation miniature. Moreover, although the Brussels copy is a large, handsomely presented volume worthy of its incorporation in the Burgundian ducal library, it cannot be more than an initial offering by the author, given its execution on paper and lack of any illustration. In contrast the Arundel volume, with its three finely illuminated openings, has the appearance appropriate to a copy commissioned by its dedicatee. In addition to an opening large miniature in which Soillot is depicted presenting his book to Charles, two equally large miniatures illustrate the court proceedings at the beginning of the text's second and third books. Each illustration, which is accompanied by a finely illuminated four-sided border, is attributable to an anonymous illuminator named the Hiero Master after his contribution to two copies of Soillot's translation of Xenophon (Brussels, KBR, MSS 9567, 14642). Within this artist's attributed oeuvre his contribution to a collection of treatises on nobility (Brussels, KBR, MS 10977–9) is particularly close to that in the Arundel volume. According to contemporary records all three of these manuscripts were present in the Burgundian ducal library shortly after Philip the Good's death in 1467.

To date, the provenance of the Arundel *Débat* is imperfectly understood. Most previous scholarship on the present manuscript has identified its first known owner as Margaret of York, Duchess of Burgundy, based on its inclusion until 1947 of a Gradual leaf that incorporates in its illuminated border her heraldic arms (cat. no. 151). Yet the association of the manuscript volume and the now-detached leaf is unlikely to date from before the sixteenth century; the leaf's survival is certainly best explained as the result of English antiquarian interest. Previously unremarked is that the copy of the *Débat* recorded in the 1535 partial inventory of Richmond Palace's library (Carley 2000) must be the present volume. As noted earlier, Soillot's text had a very restricted circulation; the likelihood of two copies reaching England by such an early date is therefore very small. Given its documented association with volumes at Richmond that once formed part of the collections of Edward IV and Henry VII, the Arundel volume may be a further instance of a Burgundian court text that reached England relatively soon after its composition. Like the Royal copy of Du Quesne's *Commentaires* (cat. no. 76), it may have entered the royal library under Edward IV. Also like it, the Arundel *Débat* may have been first owned by Charles the Bold and later given to Edward by his sister Margaret after her husband's death. *S.McK.*

PROVENANCE:

Henry VIII; Henry Savile, of Banke (b. 1568, d. 1617); Thomas Howard, 2nd Earl of Arundel (b. 1586, d. 1646); Royal Society, London; purchased for the nation in 1831.

Opposite:
The Three Estates plead their cases before the Court of Sciences, f. 24

151 Leaf from a Gradual

Ghent, between 1480 and 1483
445 x 300 mm

BRITISH LIBRARY, ARUNDEL 71, f. 9

This single leaf is a remarkable survival. Bearing the arms of Margaret of York as formulated after her marriage in 1468 to Charles the Bold, Duke of Burgundy (see also cat. no. 35), it constitutes the only known remains of a book for public liturgy commissioned by a member of the house of York. It is also one of very few such books to survive from the late Middle Ages that have a direct connection with the English royal family. In addition, the precise religious context for which it was made may be known.

Of imposing dimensions well suited to its use by a choir in the sung liturgy, the leaf preserves the Introit for the first Sunday in Advent, 'To thee, O Lord, have I lifted up my soul' (Psalm 24). Undoubtedly it marked the opening of a fine Gradual. The Introit is the first text in the Gradual's opening section, the Proper of Time. At the centre of its upper border decoration the rubric foliation 'iii' confirms the leaf's original placement towards the front of its parent volume.

The recto of the present leaf was magnificently illuminated by south Netherlandish painters. Its border of gold acanthus and naturalistically depicted flowers casting shadows over a coloured ground is a fine example of a type developed by these artists in the late 1470s and early 1480s. Within a large initial 'A', David, the supposed author of the Psalms, has been represented with his hands lifted in prayer outside an imposing moated gateway and in front of a deeply receding river landscape. Echoing the words of the opening Psalm, David raises up his soul to God. Once considered the work of one of the greatest masters of Netherlandish illumination, the Master of Mary of Burgundy, this historiated initial is now attributed to a loose artistic grouping known as the Ghent Associates. As their name suggests, the works of these artists are associated with production in the town of Ghent. Although of uneven quality, the initial includes high-quality painting, particularly on the figure and harp of David, the finely detailed and naturalistic treatment of which echoes contemporary early Netherlandish painting. The striking imposition of a red cloak over David's cloth of gold gown is apparently based on an invention made within the circle of the Master of Mary of Burgundy.

On the verso several inscriptions added in the sixteenth and seventeenth centuries provide further information about the history of the volume of which the present leaf appears to be the sole remains. First, a scattering of pen trials, encompassing fragmentary text mainly in English, attests to the presence of the leaf in England by the sixteenth century. Combined with the marks of earlier folding still visible on the leaf, these inscriptions suggest that it was by then detached from the rest of the volume and being used as a wrapper for another book. Second, an addition by a seventeenth-century hand emulating Gothic letter forms is apparently that of an English antiquarian. According to it, 'Ther was a Booke called a graile given unto the graie observant friers of Greenwich by Margaret duchesse of Bourgoigne sister unto k[ing] Edward 4.' Implicit in this text is a connection of the present leaf, as part of what was then known in England as a Graile, with the first house established in England by the reformed Franciscans. Having secured papal approval early in 1481 for its foundation at Greenwich, Edward IV had assigned land for this establishment next to the royal palace at Greenwich. The following year he handed it over to the friars sent from the Continent to initiate the community. Until its suppression by Henry VIII the foundation was the focus of sustained royal patronage and its church the setting of many royal marriages and baptisms.

Margaret of York's commissioning of the Gradual would conform to such royal patronage and also to her documented association with the Observant Friars of Greenwich following her visit to England in 1480. The prominent purse that the artist of the initial included in his depiction of David, a significant divergence from contemporary iconography, may have been intended to allude to the generosity of another King, Margaret's brother, as the founder of the friary. The riverside setting of David's prayer (pictured) may also be a reference to the location of the Greenwich foundation. After the suppression of the Observants' house the Gradual may have been transferred to the nearby royal palace. Under Edward VI such a book would have fallen victim to the purge of liturgical books and been able to survive only through reuse as binding material. *S.McK.*

PROVENANCE:

Grey Friars, Greenwich (?); Henry VIII (?); Henry Savile, of Banke (b. 1568, d. 1617); Thomas Howard, 2nd Earl of Arundel (b. 1586, d. 1646); Royal Society, London; purchased for the nation in 1831.

Opposite:
Introit for the first Sunday in Advent, David at prayer, f. 9

152 *La Vie de notre seigneur Jésus Christ* and *La Vengeance de la mort de Jésus Christ*

Ghent, 1479
385 x 275 mm

BRITISH LIBRARY, ROYAL 16 G. iii

Transcribed at Ghent in 1479 by David Aubert (b. *c.* 1413, d. *c.* 1479), the former *escripvain* of Philip the Good, Duke of Burgundy (see cat. no. 51), the present manuscript contains two complementary texts relating the story of salvation, *La Vie de notre seigneur Jésus Christ* (The Life of Our Lord Jesus Christ), and *La Vengeance de la mort de Jésus Christ* (The Vengeance for the Death of Jesus Christ). These two works were both intended for use in personal devotions and composed in the orbit of the Burgundian court. *La Vie* is a French adaptation of the Latin treatise by the Augustinian monk Michele Benucci di Massa (d. 1377) (Straub 1998), which David Aubert attributed to his father, Jean Aubert, in an earlier copy of the *Vie* dedicated in 1461 to Philip the Good (Brussels, KBR, MS IV.106). Inspired by the *Golden Legend*, the anonymous *Vengeance* was adapted from another work dedicated to the Duke, Jean Mansel's *La Fleur des histoires* (The Flower of Stories) (see cat. no. 59).

The same two texts appear together in two other manuscripts commissioned by members of the Burgundian court: Guillaume de Ternay (fl. 1456–81), former governor of Baudouin and Jean, Bastards of Burgundy, and *prévôt* of Lille in the service of Charles the Bold and his daughter Mary (Cracow, Biblioteka Czartoryskich, MS 2919 V); and Louis of Gruuthuse (d. 1492), councillor to Philip the Good and Charles the Bold (Paris, BnF, MS fr. 181). The two books, produced respectively in 1478 and *c.* 1480, are closely related to the Royal manuscript not only in their textual contents, but also in the style and iconography of their illuminations. Although the three manuscripts differ in the number of miniatures, some illustrations – such as the quadripartite image that starts with the *Entry into Jerusalem* and that of the *Life of Judas* at the beginning of the *Vengeance* – clearly followed common visual models. Two partially preserved marginal notes in the Royal manuscript show that written instructions were also used to direct the illuminators.

The illustrations in the Royal and Cracow copies and some miniatures in the Parisian manuscript were attributed to the Master of the Flemish Boethius as the artist's early works (Kren and McKendrick 2003). Despite strong stylistic similarities (each manuscript includes, for example, slim human figures with oval heads and emotionless expressions), closer examination of the use of colour and creation of pictorial space in the Cracow miniatures casts doubt on the common authorship of the three cycles (Płonka-Bałus 2004). Regardless of whether they were illuminated by one workshop or a group of related associates, the three volumes share strikingly similar border decoration and script. This similarity suggests that although the manuscripts in Paris and Cracow are not David Aubert's autograph copies, they may have been written in his Ghent *officine*.

Virtually the same borders, decorated by slender branches of gold and blue acanthus and delicate flowers, are found in a group of manuscripts copied by David Aubert for Margaret of York, Duchess of Burgundy, between 1475 and 1476 (Brussels, KBR, MS 9106, Jena, Universitätsbibliothek, MS El. fol. 85; and Oxford, Bodleian Library, MS Douce 365). This remarkable resemblance to books in Margaret's own library, and the fact that the Royal *Vie de notre seigneur* was listed in the royal collection at Richmond in 1535, has caused some researchers to suggest that this manuscript was a gift from the Duchess to her brother Edward IV (Backhouse 1987, Straub 1998). Its production in 1479 would certainly have made it available for Margaret of York's visit to England in 1480 and also have coincided with the key period of Edward's acquisition of manuscripts from the Burgundian Netherlands. Although the book corresponds well to the King's new taste for the sumptuous courtly art of illumination, it differs from his own Bruges purchases in its artistic style and devotional contents. The choice of text would be more likely to reflect Margaret's interests than Edward's (see cat. no. 35). Also, unlike in a copy of *Les Fais d'Alexandre le grant* (cat. no. 149), which Margaret probably gave to the English aristocrat John Donne on her visit to England, no heraldic device or note of dedication confirms any involvement of the Duchess in the commission or presentation of the Royal manuscript. In addition, the miniature at the beginning of the text (f. 8, pictured) clearly identifies the recipient of the book as a young nobleman. Although it is likely that the *Vie de notre seigneur* was incorporated into the royal collection by Edward IV, it is uncertain how this manuscript came into the King's possession and who was its original addressee. *J.F.*

PROVENANCE:

Edward IV (?); Henry VIII.

Opposite:
The author in his study; presentation of the book, f. 8

Cy apres sensieult le pro
logue du liure Traittant
de la venue du benoit filz
de dieu A prendre char
humaine ou monde. De
sa vie et conuersation.
De ses oeuures et trauaulz
Et de sa passion et mort
Resurrection et apparitions
pour le sauuement du
monde. Prologue
a vie et conuer
sation de nostre
seigneur Jhesucrist filz
de dieu dieu et homme nez
de marie vierge Rachateur
et sauueur de lumain li
gnage au monde. Est fon
dement ferme droite Regle
Exemple cler esperance
vraye Et seure attendue
de sauuement pour tous
bien voeullans. Et ne est
point daultre Sicomme dit
pol en lepistre as corinthiens
dist ou tiers chapitre.
Fundamentum enim aliud
nemo potest ponere preter
MVSEVM
BRITAN
NICVM

153 Choirbook of Petrus Alamire

Southern Netherlands, *c.* 1513–25
370 x 260 mm

BRITISH LIBRARY, ROYAL 8 G. vii

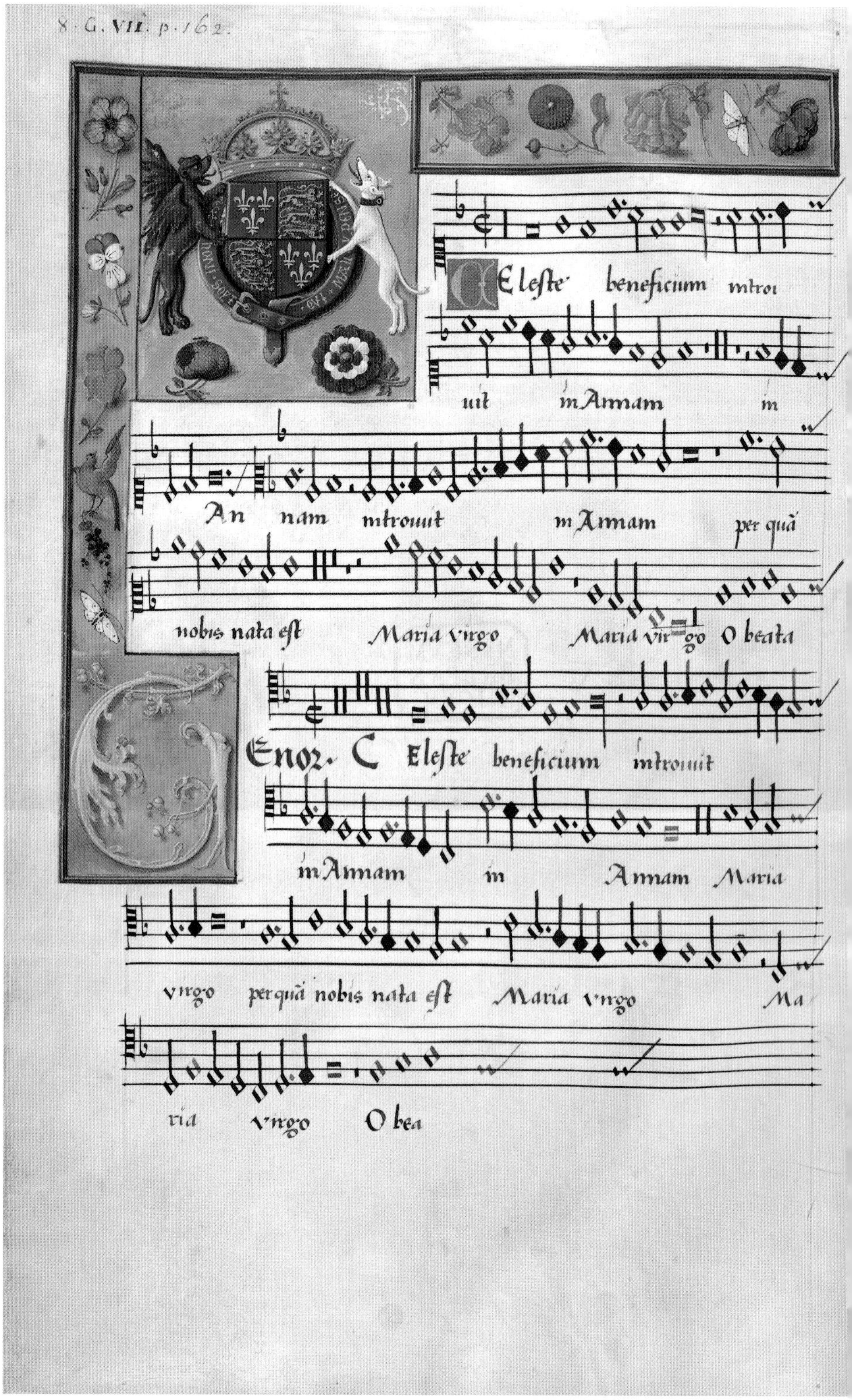

Motet 'Celeste beneficium' by Jean Mouton, ff. 2v–3

This magnificent choirbook was produced for Henry VIII and Catherine of Aragon in the workshop of Petrus Alamire, a famous music scribe who made several similar choirbooks for other European courts. Born into the Nuremberg merchant family of Imhof, Peter adopted the *nom de plume* 'Alamire' as a musical pun on the notes 'A la-mi-re'. He settled in the Low Countries in the 1490s and worked at the court of Margaret of Austria, Regent of the Netherlands. From 1509 Alamire was employed in the chapel of the Archduke Charles (later the Emperor Charles V) as 'scribe and keeper of the books', where he oversaw the production of numerous books of Franco-Flemish polyphony. His position put him in close contact with many important figures, and he also found employment as a diplomatic courier and merchant. Four autograph letters in Latin from Alamire to Henry VIII and Cardinal Wolsey, together with several letters from English ambassadors in the Low Countries, show that between 1515 and 1518 Alamire not only supplied musical manuscripts and instruments, but also acted as a spy, informing Henry of the movements of Richard de la Pole, exiled pretender to the English crown.

Henry VIII received a thorough musical education and spared no expense in bringing the finest musicians in Europe to play and sing in his court. His desire to model his court on the Burgundian and Habsburg courts was well known, and a grand collection of recently composed Continental music would have made a perfect gift for the King. The Royal manuscript contains twenty-eight motets by Josquin des Prez, Pierre de la Rue and other leading Continental composers of the day, together with an extraordinary series of five different settings of Dido's lament from Virgil's *Aeneid*, and another text from the *Aeneid*, 'Fama malum'. The inclusion of these classical texts in a collection of otherwise sacred pieces is unusual and has aroused much discussion; one recent study suggests that they may be intended as songs of mourning directed towards Catherine of Aragon, who was bereaved of her first husband, Henry's elder brother Arthur, as well as having suffered the deaths of several children in infancy or at birth (Thomas 2005).

The first piece in the book, the motet 'Celeste beneficium' by the French composer Jean Mouton, is a text more

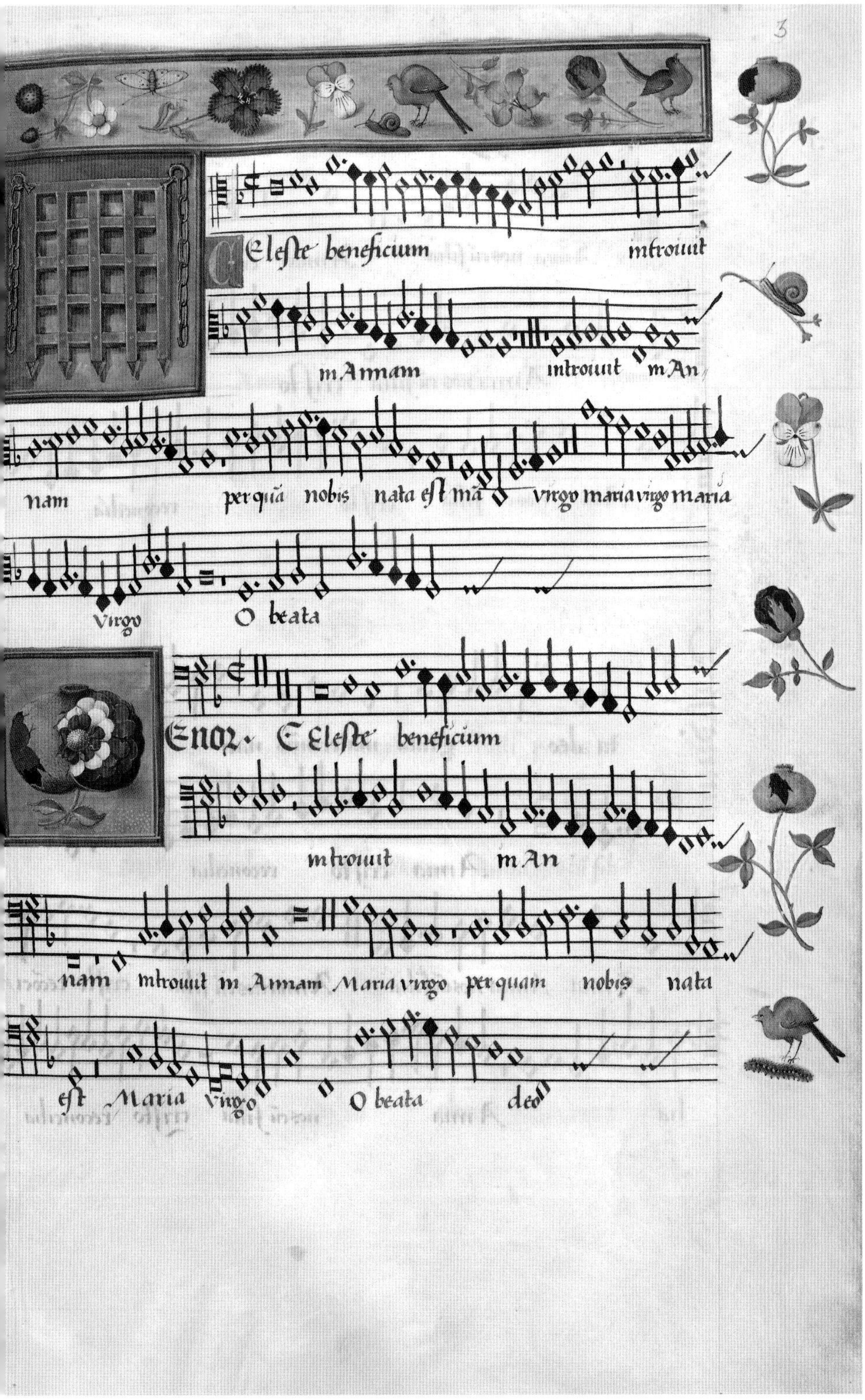

directly associated with the theme of childbirth. It was originally composed for Anne of Brittany and Louis XII of France, and calls upon St Anne, mother of the Virgin Mary, to help bring forth children. The following two motets continue this theme, and show that the choirbook was carefully planned to appeal to Henry VIII's need for Catherine to provide him with a male heir to ensure the continuation of the Tudor dynasty. Several later works are associated with Margaret of Austria and the Archduke Charles, and may have been intended as a way of establishing a connection between the book's donors and its recipient.

The opening pages of the choirbook are the most richly decorated (ff. 2v–3, pictured). Marginal flora and fauna common to the south Netherlandish style of illumination are combined with Tudor symbols such as the dragon, greyhound and portcullis. Catherine of Aragon's emblem of the pomegranate appears beneath the royal arms, but is also fused on the right-hand page with a red-and-white rose in a symbolic union, another probable reference to the desire for progeny. The royal arms show various anomalies: the crown has strawberry leaves in place of crosses and a single arch instead of double, while the lions on the shield are facing sinister (Tirro 1981). This error is a surprising flaw in an otherwise beautifully prepared book. The music is written in an astonishingly elegant hand, not by Alamire himself but by one of the scribes in his workshop, and the text hand is a *bastarde* script characteristic of choirbooks of this period. The remainder of the book has no painted initials, but each piece is introduced with elaborate strapwork initial letters (Kellman 1987; DIAMM).

Various hypotheses have been put forward for the date and occasion on which the choirbook may have been presented to Henry and Catherine. One proposal dates the book as early as 1513, but others have assumed that it was more likely to have been presented at one of the ceremonial meetings between the Archduke Charles or Margaret of Austria and Henry or Cardinal Wolsey, between 1516 and 1522 (Kellman 1999). Whatever the case, there can be little doubt that this book would have greatly appealed to the King. *N.B.*

PROVENANCE:

Henry VIII.

154 Motets for Henry VIII

Southern Netherlands (?Antwerp), 1516
490 x 355 mm

BRITISH LIBRARY, ROYAL 11 E. xi

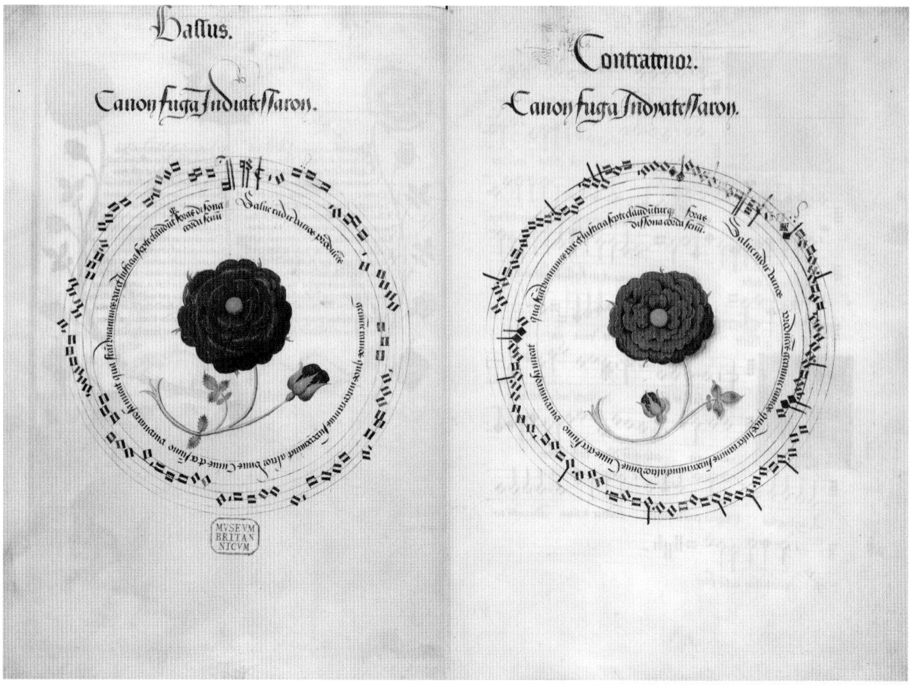

Above:
Salve Radix, the Rose Canon, ff. 2v–3

Opposite:
The Crowned Rose, f. 2.

This choirbook was produced for Henry VIII in 1516 by a Flemish merchant named Petrus de Opitiis. It is a slender volume of only seventeen leaves, but a manuscript of the grandest possible conception, containing two motets specially composed in honour of the King and a further four carefully designed to appeal to his concerns at the time. Its richly symbolic frontispiece (f. 2) provides a visual interpretation of the motet texts, making full use of the menagerie of heraldic emblems that had come to be associated with the Tudor dynasty during the reign of Henry VII.

Petrus de Opitiis, whose initials are found on the front flyleaf of the book, was a successful tradesman from Monferrato in northern Italy who had settled in Antwerp. One motet in the choirbook is ascribed to his son Benedictus, who became Henry's court organist at around the time the book was made. It is likely that another son, Johannes, wrote the lengthy poem inscribed between the stems of the rose-bush, a musical setting of which takes up most of the first half of the book. The poem extols the virtues of the red-and-white rose, representing Henry's position as the first monarch to have the hereditary right to combine the red rose of Lancaster with the white rose of York (Bell and Skinner 2009).

From the earliest years of his reign, Henry had shown a keener interest in the workings of the great European courts than in matters closer to home. The magnificent ceremonial of the court of the Holy Roman Emperor held a particular appeal to the young King, and it was well known that the Emperor Maximilian was something of a role model for Henry. The Opitiis family had compiled a similar presentation volume the previous year as a tribute to Maximilian, and there are several respects in which the present volume was clearly modelled on the volume presented to Maximilian – as well as one major difference: the book for Maximilian was printed, exploiting the Emperor's known predilection for woodcuts, while the later volume was an illuminated manuscript, better suiting the King's love of colour and pomp.

The frontispiece to Henry's choirbook (pictured opposite) presents an allegorical montage dominated by a rose with stems curved in the shape of a lyre (Backhouse 1993). At the centre, a single red-and-white rose stands higher than the others, surmounted by a jewelled crown of royal purple, with fleurs-de-lis on its inner petals symbolizing Henry's claim to the kingdom of France. Around the stems of the rose, a ribbon proclaims a second verse, 'Salve, radix', in praise of the root of the rose, which stands in the garden of England, 'where peace and justice stand enclosed and harmonious'. On the following pages this text is set to music in a double canon for four voices, the music written in a circle to surround and protect the royal rose.

To the side of the rose grows a pomegranate tree heavy with fruit. The pomegranate was the symbol of Catherine of Aragon, and this tree, along with a number of motets later in the volume reflecting on the theme of childbirth, may be seen as allusions to the urgent need for Catherine to produce a male heir to ensure the continuation of the Tudor line. Nearer the rose are a daisy (or *marguerite*) and a marigold, symbols of Henry's sisters Margaret (widow of James IV of Scotland) and Mary, whose husband Louis XII of France had died only two months after their marriage in 1514. In May 1516 the three surviving children of Henry VII were reunited for the first time in thirteen years, and a courtly entertainment the following Christmas included a pageant with very close parallels to the imagery of this frontispiece, presenting 'a Gardeyn artifical, called the Gardeyn of Esperance' (Dumitrescu 2007). The combination of poetic and visual artistry with the contrapuntal virtuosity of the 'rose canon' cannot have failed to impress the King.

N.B.

PROVENANCE:

Henry VIII

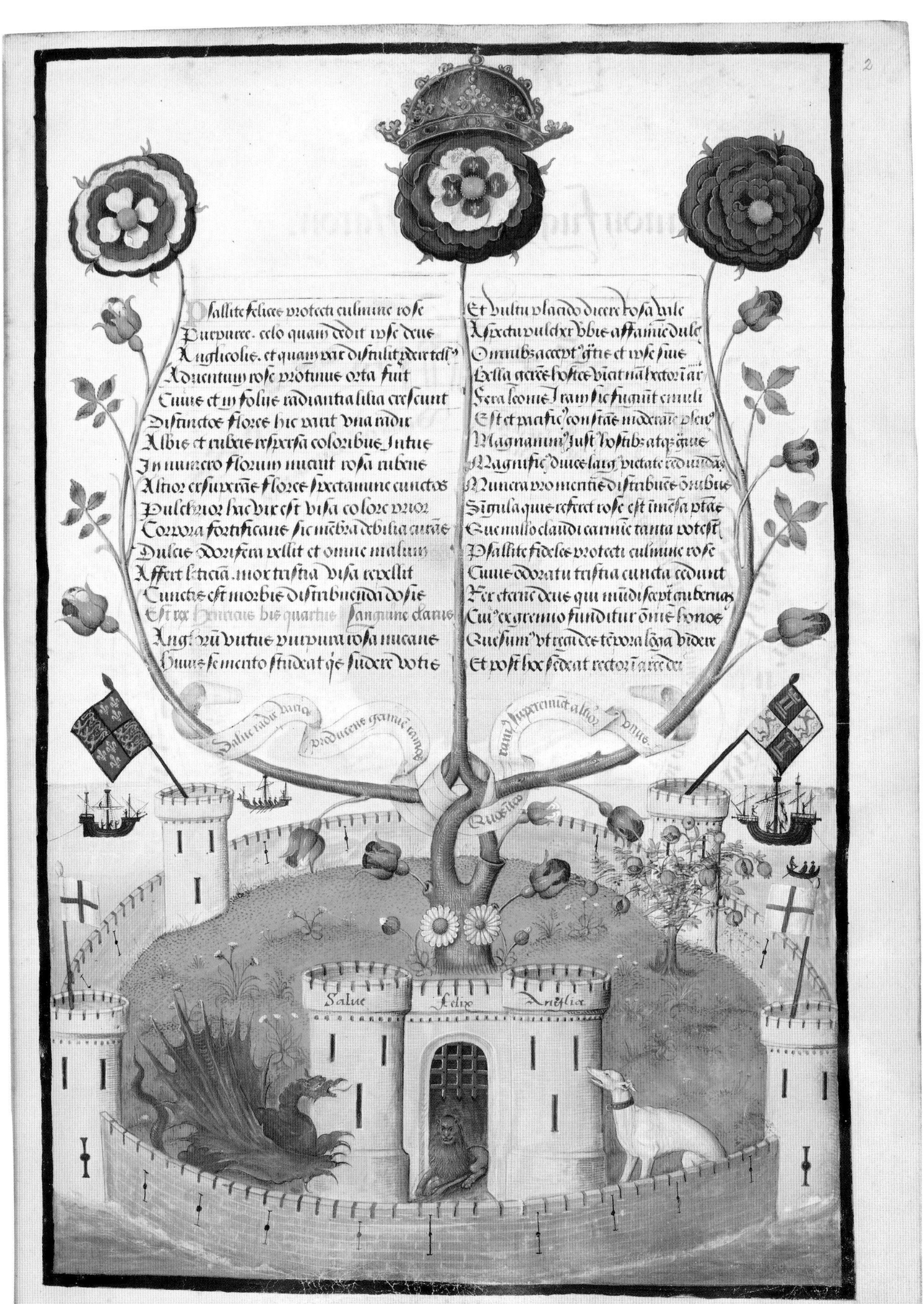
Salue Felix Anglia

Bibliographies to the Catalogue Entries

The following should be consulted for Royal manuscripts, but is not cited in individual entries:

George F. Warner and Julius P. Gilson, *Catalogue of Western Manuscripts in the Old Royal and King's Collections*, 4 vols (London: British Museum, 1921).

CAT. NO. 1
An Insular Gospel-Book
Royal 1 B. vii
Keynes, 'King Athelstan's Books' (1985); Gameson, 'Royal 1 B. vii Gospels' (1994); Brown, *Lindisfarne Gospels* (2003).

CAT. NO. 2
The Canterbury Royal Bible
Royal 1 E. vi
Alexander, *Insular Manuscripts* (1978), no. 32; Budny, '*Biblia Gregoriana*' (1999); Gameson, *Earliest Books* (2008), no. 1.

CAT. NO. 3
The Athelstan Psalter
Cotton Galba A. xviii
Keynes, 'King Athelstan's Books' (1985); Koehler and Mütherich, *Karolingischen Miniaturen*, VI (1994); Deshman, 'Galba Psalter' (1997).

CAT. NO. 4
The Athelstan or Coronation Gospels
Cotton Tiberius A. ii
Wormald, 'Coronation Oath-books' (1951); Wormald, *English Drawings* (1952), pp. 22–23; Schramm and Mütherich, *Denkmale* (1962), no. 64; Lapidge, 'Latin Poems' (1981), pp. 93–97; Keynes, 'King Athelstan's Books' (1985), pp. 147–53; Hoffmann, *Buchkunst* (1986), I, pp. 9–10; Brown, 'Sir Robert Cotton' (1998), pp. 285–90, 295; Puhle, *Otto der Grosse* (2001), II, pp. 121–23 (Katalog III. 13).

CAT. NO. 5
The New Minster Charter
Cotton Vespasian A. viii
Miller, *Charters of the New Minster* (2001); Rumble, *Property and Piety* (2002); Scragg, *Edgar* (2008).

CAT. NO. 6
Regula S. Benedicti, Regularis concordia and other Devotional, Practical and Educational Texts for Monastic Use
Cotton Tiberius A. iii
Ker, *Catalogue of Manuscripts* (1957), no. 186; Symons and others, *Regularis Concordia* (1984); Gneuss, 'Origin and Provenance' (1997); Liuzza, *Anglo-Saxon Prognostics* (2010).

CAT. NO. 7
The Cnut Gospels
Royal 1 D. ix
Brooks, *Early History* (1984); Heslop, '*De luxe* Manuscripts' (1990); Gerchow, 'King Cnut' (1992); Dumville, *Caroline Script* (1993), pp. 116–28; 139–40.

CAT. NO. 8
The New Minster *Liber Vitae*
Stowe 944
Gerchow, 'King Cnut (1992); Keynes, *Liber Vitae* (1996); Parker, 'Gift of the Cross' (2002); Karkov, *Ruler Portraits* (2004).

CAT. NO. 9
The Goda Gospels
Royal 1 D. iii
Thorpe, *Registrum Roffense* (1769); Glunz, *History of the Vulgate* (1933), no. 20; Richards, *Texts* (1988), pp. 45, 65; McGurk, 'Disposition' (1993), p. 255; Carley, *Libraries* (2000), H2. 643.

CAT. NO. 10
The Grimbald Gospels
Additional 34890
Keynes and Lapidge, *Alfred the Great* (1983); Barker, *York Gospels* (1986); Gameson, 'Colophon of the Eadwig Gospels' (2002); Keynes, 'Power of the Written Word' (2003).

CAT. NO. 11
The Shaftesbury Psalter
Lansdowne 383
Warner, *Illuminated Manuscripts* (1903), pl. 13; Kauffmann, *Romanesque Manuscripts* (1975), no. 48; Avril, Barral, and Gaborit-Chopin, *Le Monde Roman* (1983), pp. 213–14, pl. 179; Henderson and Heslop, 'Decoration and Illustration' (1992), pp. 28 n. 8, 30 n. 16, 31 n. 23; Kauffmann, 'British Library, Lansdowne Ms. 383' (2001), 256–58; Kauffmann, *Biblical Imagery* (2003), pp. 118–36, 156–57, 191, 228, figs 88, 91, 94, 96, 98–102, 123, 126, 128, 131, 134, 135, 137, 138, pl. VI.

CAT. NO. 12
The Westminster Psalter
Royal 2 A. xxii
Legg, 'Inventory' (1890), pp. 233–35; Millar, *English Illuminated Manuscripts* (1926), pp. 42–43, 60, 90–91, 100, pls 62–63, 90a, 90b; Oakeshott, *Winchester Bibles* (1981), p. 70; Morgan, *Early Gothic Manuscripts* (1982–88), I, no. 2; II, no. 95; *English Romanesque Art* (1984), no. 82; Binski and Panayotova, *Cambridge Illuminations* (2005), pp. 97, 183, 249; Pfaff, *Liturgy* (2009), pp. 229–33.

CAT. NO. 13
Psalter
Royal 2 B. ii
Vitzthum, *Die Pariser Miniaturmalerei* (1907), p. 101; Millar, *Souvenir de l'exposition* (1933), no. 22, pl. 22; Branner, 'Copenhagen Corpus' (1969), p. 116, fig. 25; Branner, *Manuscript Painting* (1977), pp. 116, 117, 235, fig. 342; Stratford, 'Royal Library' (1994), pp. 194–96.

CAT. NO. 14
Genesis and Exodus, with the *Glossa ordinaria*
Royal 3 E. i
Jayne and Johnson, *Lumley Library* (1956) p. 49; Ker, *Medieval Libraries* (1964) p. 124; De Hamel, *Illuminated Manuscripts* (1986) p. 134; Kauffmann, *Biblical Imagery* (2003), p. 148; Michael, 'Urban Production' (2008) p. 178 n. 63.

CAT. NO. 15
The Bible of William of Devon
Royal 1 D. i
Bennett, 'Additions' (1972), pp. 31–33, 37, figs 2, 3, 9, 12; Branner, 'Johannes Grusch Atelier' (1972), pp. 24, 26, fig. 2; Morgan, *Early Gothic Manuscripts* (1982–88), no. 159; Temple, 'Further Additions' (1984), pp. 344, 346, fig. 4; Carley, *Libraries* (2000), H2. 972.

CAT. NO. 16
Peter Comestor, *Historia scholastica*
Royal 3 D. vi
Verdier, Brieger and Montpetit, *Art and the Courts* (1972), no. 27; Sandler, *Gothic Manuscripts* (1986), no. 2; Lowden, *Making of the* Bibles moralisées (2000), I, p. 209; Carley, *Libraries* (2000), H2. 518; Sylwan, *Petri Comestoris* (2005), pp. xxxi–xxxii.

CAT. NO. 17
The Alphonso Psalter
Additional 24686
Bond, 'Description' (1863); Hutchinson, 'Attitudes toward Nature' (1974); Sandler, *Gothic Manuscripts* (1986), I, pp. 24, 27; II, no. 1; Alexander and Binski, *Age of Chivalry* (1987), no. 357; Goodall, 'Heraldry in Decoration' (1997); Parsons, *Eleanor of Castile* (1997).

CAT. NO. 18
Genesis to Ruth
Royal 1 E. iv
Warner and Gilson, *Western Manuscripts* (1921), I, p. 20; Pächt and Alexander, *Illuminated Manuscripts* (1966–73), III, no. 714, p. 64; Sotheby's, *Western Manuscripts* (1980), lots 3 and 4, p. 8; Sandler, *Gothic Manuscripts* (1986), no.100; Michael, 'Artists' (1987), I, p. 103; Dennison, 'Stylistic Sources' (1988), p. 70; Manion, Vines and de Hame., *Medieval and Renaissance* (1989), pp. 93–95; Rex, *John Fisher* (1991), p. 166; Carley, *Libraries* (2000), p. xxxi n. 33, H2. 1286; Doran, *Henry VIII* (2009), no. 109 (James P. Carley catalogue entry).

CAT. NO. 19
The Psalter of Philippa of Hainault
Harley 2899
Vale, *Edward III* (1982), pp. 42–56; Alexander, 'Painting and Manuscript Illumination' (1983), p. 143; Michael, 'Wedding Gift' (1985), pp. 589 n. 31, 590; Sandler, *Gothic Manuscripts* (1986), no. 110; Melis, 'Alexander Manuscript' (2002), p. 973 n. 50.

CAT. NO. 20
Bohun Psalter and Hours
Egerton 3277
Sandler, *Gothic Manuscripts* (1986), no. 135; Sandler, 'Political Imagery' (2002), pp. 117–18, 122–26, 135–45; Dennison, 'Egerton MS 3277' (2003); Sandler, 'Bared' (2006).

CAT. NO. 21
The Princess Joan Psalter
Royal 2 B. viii
Kuhn, 'Herman Scheerre' (1940), p. 154, figs 45, 46; Scott, *Later Gothic Manuscripts* (1996), no. 14; Mooney, *Kalendarium* (1998), pp. 18–19, 48, 50–51, 65–66; Rouse and Rouse, *Manuscripts* (2000), I, pp. 297–99; II, pp. 116, 124.

CAT. NO. 22
Bible historiale: Genesis to the Apocalypse
Royal 17 E. vii
Berger, *La Bible française* (1884), pp. 202, 212, 218, 286, 387–88; Stechow, 'Shooting' (1942); Gibson, *Bible in the Latin West* (1993), no. 21; Backhouse, *Illuminated Page* (1997), no. 105; Komada, 'Illustrations' (2000), III, no. 36; Annexe 6 (pp. 533–46); O'Meara, *Monarchy* (2001), pp. 265–71, 332 n. 7, figs 101, 102.

CAT. NO. 23
The 'Great Bible'
Royal 1 E. ix
Kuhn, 'Herman Scheerre' (1940), pp. 138–56; Wright, 'Big Bible' (1986); Stratford, 'Royal Library' (1994), pp. 187–97; Vertongen, 'Herman Scheerre' (1995), pp. 255–57; Scott, *Later Gothic Manuscripts* (1996), no. 26.

CAT. NO. 24
Bible historiale: Genesis to the Psalms
Royal 19 D. iii
Berger, *La Bible française* (1884), pp. 163, 179, 182–86, 206, 257, 392–93; Burgio, 'Ricerche' (1998), pp. 153, 157–60; Carley, *Libraries* (2000), H1. 24; Komada, 'Illustrations' (2000), III, no. 41, pp. 773–74; Annexe 6, pp. 533–46.

CAT. NO. 25
The Beaufort/Beauchamp Hours
Royal 2 A. xviii
Kuhn, 'Herman Scheerre' (1940), p. 151; Rickert, 'Beaufort Hours' (1962); Alexander, 'William Abell' (1972), p. 166; Rogers, 'Books of Hours' (1982), pp. 84–91; Smeyers and Vertongen, 'Meester van de Beaufortheiligen' (1992); Vertongen, 'Herman Scheerre' (1995); Scott, *Later Gothic Manuscripts* (1996), no. 37; Backhouse, 'Patronage and Commemoration' (2007).

CAT. NO. 26
Bedford Psalter and Hours
Additional 42131
Turner, 'Bedford Hours' (1962); Turner, 'Wyndham Payne Crucifixion' (1976), pp. 21–22; Stratford, 'Manuscripts' (1987), p. 342; Wright, 'Author Portraits' (1992); Scott, *Later Gothic Manuscripts* (1996), no. 54.

CAT. NO. 27
The Hours of Catherine of France
Additional 65100
Rogers, 'Trinity B.11.7' (1994), pp. 181–82; Scott, *Later Gothic Manuscripts* (1996), no. 72; Villela-Petit, 'Devises' (2001), pp. 80–92.

CAT. NO. 28
The Hours of Elizabeth the Queen
Additional 50001

Marks and Morgan, *Golden Age* (1981), p. 110, pl. 36; Orr, 'Hours of Elizabeth' (1989); Orr, 'Hours of Elizabeth: Evidence for Collaboration' (1995), pp. 619–33; Scott, *Later Gothic Manuscripts* (1996), no. 55.

CAT. NO. 29
Jean Galopes, *Le Livre doré des meditations*
Royal 20. B. iv
Meiss, Smith and Beatson, *French Painting* (1974), I, p. 391; Alexander, *Medieval Illuminators* (1992), pp. 66, 68–69, 186; Pearsall, 'Regement of Princes' (1994), pp. 386–410; Boulton, 'Jean Galopes' (2002/03).

CAT. NO. 30
John Lydgate, The Lives of Sts Edmund and Fremund
Harley 2278
Scott, 'Lydgate's "Lives"' (1982); Seymour, 'Some Lydgate Manuscripts' (1983–85); Scott, *Later Gothic Manuscripts* (1996), no. 78; Rogers, 'Bury Artists' (1998); Carley, *Libraries* (2000), p. xlviii, H2. 290; Edwards, *Life of Saint Edmund* (2004).

CAT. NO. 31
'Salve Regina' Prayer Roll for Margaret of Anjou
Oxford, Jesus College, MS 124
Rock, *Church* (1849), III, pt 1, pp. 312–14; Alexander, 'William Abell' (1972), pp. 166–68; Laynesmith, *Medieval Queens* (2004), p. 253, pl. 2; McGerr, 'Statute Book' (2006), p. 35.

CAT. NO. 32
Selection of Psalms, Litanies and Prayers for Humfrey of Gloucester
Royal 2 B. i
De la Mare and Hunt, *Duke Humfrey* (1970), no. 8A; Alexander, 'Painting and Manuscript Illumination' (1983), p. 150; Scott, *Later Gothic Manuscripts* (1996), no. 83; Stratford, 'Early Royal Collections' (1999), p. 266; Morgan, 'Devotional Images' (2002), p. 100, fig. 35; Petrina, *Cultural Politics* (2004), pp. 195–96

CAT. NO. 33
The St Omer Psalter
Yates Thompson 14
Saunders, *English Illumination* (1928), pp. 94, 100–02, 105–07, 111; pls. 113–14; Pächt, 'Giottesque Episode' (1943), pp. 52–53, 57, pl. 14d; Rickert, *Painting in Britain* (1965), pp. 130–32, 134, 181–83, pls. pp. 133, 182(a); Sandler, *Gothic Manuscripts* (1986), no. 104.

CAT. NO. 34
The Psalter of Isabel of York
Royal 2 B. xiv
Woodger, 'Henry Bourgchier' (1974); Scott, *Later Gothic Manuscripts* (1996), II, p. 190; Carley, *Libraries* (2000), p. xxxvi n. 48.

CAT. NO. 35
Nicolas Finet, *Dialogue de la duchesse de Bourgogne*
Additional 7970
Cochran, *Catalogue* (1829), no. 647; *Exposition de reliures* (1931), no. 112; Smith, 'Margaret of York' (1992), p. 50; Kren and McKendrick, *Illuminating the Renaissance* (2003), no. 51, pp. 215–16; Eichberger, *Women of Distinction* (2005), no. 83; Marti, Borchert and Keck, *Charles le Téméraire* (2008), no. 72.

CAT. NO. 36
Register of the Fraternity of the Holy Trinity, Luton
Luton Museum, 1984/127
Gough, *Register* (1906); Sotheby's, *Catalogue of Bute Collection* (1983), lot 19; Lunn, 'Luton Fraternity' (1984); Campbell, *Early Flemish Pictures* (1985), p. 45; Marks, 'Guild Registers' (1998); Alexander, 'Foreign Illuminators' (1999), p. 57; Scott, 'Illustration and Decoration' (2000); Marks and Williamson, *Gothic* (2003), no. 347.

CAT. NO. 37
Jean de Meun, *Sept articles de la foy*
Royal 19 A. xxii
Gallarati, 'Nota bibliografica' (1978); Hamel, 'Arthurian Romance' (1990), p. 356 n. 60; Backhouse, 'Illuminated Manuscripts (1995), p. 180, pl. 50; Scott, 'Manuscripts for Henry VII' (2007), p. 281.

CAT. NO. 38
Speculum humanae salvationis
Harley 2838
Lutz and Perdrizet, *Speculum Humanae Salvationis* (1907), no. 61; Breitenbach, *Speculum Humanæ Salvationis* (1930), p. 5 no. 61; Wright and Wright, *Diary* (1966), I: 1715–23, p. 8; Cardon, 'Het *Speculum Humanae Salvationis*' (1987), p. 463 n. 45; Backhouse, 'Illuminated Manuscripts' (1995), pp. 177–78; Scott, 'Fifteenth-Century English Manuscripts' (2002), p. 200; Broekhuijsen, *Masters* (2009), pp. 20–21, 222–27.

CAT. NO. 39
Ordinances of the Confraternity of the Immaculate Conception
Oxford, Christ Church, MS 179
Scott, 'Illustration and Decoration' (2000); Broekhuijsen, *Masters* (2009); Colson, 'Alien Communities' (2010), pp. 121–24, 136–41; Hanna, *Descriptive Catalogue* (<http://www.chch.ox.ac.uk/library/western-manuscripts>)

CAT. NO. 40
Proper of the Mass for the Immaculate Conception
Royal 2 A. xix
Henderson, 'Retrieving' (2002), p. 249; Scott, 'Manuscripts for Henry VII' (2007), p. 282; Colson, 'Alien Communities' (2010), pp. 136–41.

CAT. NO. 41
Quadripartite Indenture between Henry VII and John Islip
Harley 1498
Wright, *Fontes Harleiani* (1972), p. 191; Van Leeuwen, 'Bookbinding' (1989), pp. 293–94; Carley, *Libraries* (2000), p. 285; Condon, 'God Save the King' (2003), pp. 76–78.

CAT. NO. 42
Gospel Lectionary
Royal 2 B. xiii
Clode, *Merchant Taylors* (1888), II, pp. xv–xvi, 22–38; Broekhuijsen-Kruijer and Korteweg, 'Twee boekverluchters' (1989), pp. 49–76; Marks and Williamson, *Gothic* (2003), no. 143; Furdell, 'Jenyns' (2008); Broekhuijsen, *Masters* (2009), pp. 20–21, 228; Pfaff, *Liturgy* (2009), p. 494.

CAT. NO. 43
Bible
Royal 1 C. v
Gumbert, *Dutch and their books*(1990), p. 40 n. 52, pl. III; Obbema, 'Panel Painting' (1991), p. 387 n. 21; Carley, *Libraries* (2000), H2. 978; Carley, *King Henry VIII* (2004), p. 14, pl. 3.

CAT. NO. 44
Prayer-roll of Henry VIII
Additional 88929
Charlton, 'Roll of Prayers' (1858); Stork, 'Realienkundliches' (2004), p. 186; Skemer, *Binding Words* (2006), pp. 259–67; Starkey, *Virtuous Prince* (2008), pp. 199–205; Doran, *Henry VIII* (2009), no. 35 (David Starkey catalogue entry).

CAT. NO. 45
The Psalter of Henry VIII
Royal 2 A. xvi
Backhouse, 'Two Books of Hours' (1966–67), p. 93; Tudor-Craig, 'Henry VIII' (1989), pp. 194–205; Walker, *Pervasive Fictions*, (1996), pp. 80–89; Carley, *Prayer Book* (2009); Doran, *Henry VIII* (2009), no. 194 (James P. Carley catalogue entry); Sharpe, *Selling the Tudor Monarchy* (2009), p. 73.

CAT. NO. 46
The Cotton Genesis
Cotton Otho B vi
Tikkanen, 'Rappresentazioni della Genesi' (1888), pp. 212–23, 257–67, 348–63; Weitzmann and Kessler, *Cotton Genesis* (1986); Lowden, 'Concerning the Cotton Genesis' (1992); Carley and Tite, 'Wakefield' (2002), pp. 262–65; Kessler, 'Memory and Models (2009).

CAT. NO. 47
Jean de Wavrin, *Recueil des croniques d'Engleterre*, vol. 1
Royal 15 E. iv, vol. 1
Sutton and Visser-Fuchs, 'Richard III and the Knave of Cards' (1999), figs 1, 2, 7–9, 16, 17; Carley, *Libraries* (2000), H1. 12; Visser-Fuchs, 'Warwick and Wavrin' (2002); Kren and McKendrick, *Illuminating the Renaissance* (2003), pp. 276–80, no. 75; Hans-Collas and Schandel, *Manuscrits enluminés* (2009), pp. 157–58, 256–72.

CAT. NO. 48
Jean de Wavrin, *Recueil des croniques d'Engleterre*, vol. 3
Royal 14 E. iv
Carley, *Libraries* (2000), pp. xxv, 5–6, H1. 43; Visser-Fuchs, 'Warwick and Wavrin' (2002); Kren and McKendrick, *Illuminating the Renaissance* (2003), pp. 278–79, 289, 296 n. 6; Hans-Collas and Schandel, *Manuscrits enluminés* (2009), pp. 157–58, 256–72.

CAT. NO. 49
Jean Froissart, *Chroniques*, book 4
Royal 18 E. ii
Pächt, 'La Terre' (1978), p. 14; Le Guay, *Princes de Bourgogne* (1998), pp. 38–43, 169, 185–86; Kren and McKendrick, *Illuminating the Renaissance* (2003), pp. 282, 286, 288 n. 9; Wijsman, 'Two Petals' (2008), p. 68; Wijsman, *Luxury Bound* (2010), p. 582.

CAT. NO. 50
La Grande histoire César
Royal 17 F. ii
Flutre, *Manuscrits* (1932), pp. 42–44; Guenée, 'Culture historique' (1976); McKendrick, '*Grande histoire*' (1990); Brinkmann, *Flämische Buchmalerei* (1997), p. 295; Carley, Libraries (2000), H1. 30; Hughes, *Arthurian Myths* (2002), pp. 238–63.

CAT. NO. 51
Romuléon
Royal 19 E. v
Durrieu, *Miniature flamande* (1921), p. 61, pl. LXV; McKendrick, 'Romuléon' (1994); Carley, Libraries (2000), H1. 32; Wijsman, 'Lord Hastings' (2002); Kren and McKendrick, *Illuminating the Renaissance* (2003), p. 289; McKendrick, 'Charles the Bold' (forthcoming).

CAT. NO. 52
Antiquités judaïques et la guerre des Juifs, vol. 2
London, Sir John Soane's Museum, vol. 135
Millar, 'Les Manuscrits' (1925), pp. 9–14; Deutsch, *Iconographie* (1986); Martens, *Lodewijk van Gruuthuse* (1992), pp. 153–55, 186–89, no. 15; McKendrick, 'Lodewijk van Gruuthuse' (1992), pp. 153–55; Carley, *Libraries* (2000), H1. 5; Kren and McKendrick, *Illuminating the Renaissance* (2003), pp. 292–94, no. 81; Hans-Collas and Schandel, *Manuscrits enluminés* (2009), pp. 226–32.

CAT. NO. 53
Bible historiale : Tobit to Acts
Royal 15 D. i
Berger, *La Bible française* (1884), pp. 162, 177, 179, 203, 296, 389–90; Carley, *Libraries* (2000), H1. 31; Kren and McKendrick, *Illuminating the Renaissance* (2003), no. 82, pp. 224–25, 282, 295, 297–98, 299, 304.

CAT. NO. 54
Bible historiale: Genesis to Ruth
Royal 18 D. ix
Carley, *Libraries* (2000), H1. 45; Kren and McKendrick, *Illuminating the Renaissance* (2003), no. 83, pp. 224–45, 295, 297, 300–03, 304; McKendrick, *Flemish Illuminated Manuscripts* (2003), pl. 48; Hans-Collas and Schandel, *Manuscrits enluminés* (2009), pp. 175, 204, 208.

CAT. NO. 55
Histoire tripartite
Royal 18 E. v
Bayot, 'Première Partie' (1904); Foulet, 'Baldwin' (1946); Carley, *Libraries* (2000), H1. 1; Kren and McKendrick, *Illuminating the Renaissance* (2003), p. 292; McKendrick, *Flemish Illuminated Manuscript* (2003), pl. 28; Noirfalise, 'Family Feuds' (2009).

CAT. NO. 56
Trésor des histoires
Cotton Aug. A. v
Ross, 'Geographical' (1969); Pächt, 'La Terre' (1978); Carley, *Libraries* (2000), pp. xxv, 5–6, H1. 23; Kren and McKendrick, *Illuminating the Renaissance* (2003), pp. 283–84; Kren, 'Landscape' (2007), pp. 121–23; Noirfalise, 'Family Feuds' (2009).

CAT. NO. 57
Miroir historial, vol. 1
Royal 14 E. i
Chavannes-Mazel, 'Miroir historial' (1988), pp. 106–10; McKendrick, '*Romuléon*' (1994), pp. 161–65; Carley, *Libraries* (2000), H1. 26; Kren and McKendrick, *Illuminating the Renaissance* (2003), pp. 289, 296 n. 6; Brun and Cavagna, 'Pour une édition' (2006); Hans-Collas and Schandel, *Manuscrits enluminés* (2009), pp. 24–36.

CAT. NO. 58
St Augustine, *La Cité de Dieu*
Royal 17 F. iii, vol. 2
de Laborde, *Manuscrits à peintures* (1909), no. 52; Smith, 'Illustrations' (1974); Carley, *Libraries* (2000), H1. 34 or 64; Wijsman, 'Lord Hastings' (2002); Kren and McKendrick, *Illuminating the Renaissance* (2003), p. 289.

CAT. NO. 59
St Gregory the Great, *Homilies* and *Dialogues*
Royal 15 D. v
de Poerck, 'Introduction' (1935); Brinkmann, *Flämische Buchmalerei* (1997); Carley, *Libraries* (2000), H1. 51; Deam, 'Mapping the Past' (2001).

CAT. NO. 60
Simon de Hesdin and Nicolas de Gonesse,

Faits et dits mémorables des romains
Royal 18 E. iv
Schullian, 'Revised List' (1981), p. 709; Bloomer, *Valerius Maximus* (1992); McKendrick, 'Romuléon' (1994), pp. 161 n. 68, 162, ns 74, 75, 65, n. 101; Carley, *Libraries* (2000), H1. 29; Kren and McKendrick, *Illuminating the Renaissance* (2003), p. 290 no. 80; Walker, *Valerius Maximus* (2004); Scott, *Medieval Dress* (2007), p. 153.

CAT. NO. 61
Des Cas des nobles hommes et femmes
Royal 14 E. v
Durrieu, *Miniature flamande* (1921), pl. LXVI; Winkler, *Flämische Buchmalerei* (1925), pp. 137, 179; Bozzolo, *Manuscrits de Boccaccio* (1973); Reynolds, 'Boccaccio Manuscripts' (1988), pp. 153–59; McKendrick, 'Romuléon' (1994), p. 162 ns. 75, 76; Carley, *Libraries* (2000), H1. 33; Kren and McKendrick, *Illuminating the Renaissance* (2003), no. 78, pp. 224, 282, 284–86, 289, 304; Reynolds, '*Boccaccio visualizzato*: Edward IV of England's *Des cas*' (2005).

CAT. NO. 62
Jean de Courcy, *Le Chemin de vaillance*
Royal 14 E. ii
Kekewich, 'Edward IV' (1971), p. 484; Dubuc, 'Chemin de Vaillance' (1994); Sutton and Visser-Fuchs, *Richard III's Books* (1997), pp. 77–83; Kren and McKendrick, *Illuminating the Renaissance* (2003), p. 289.

CAT. NO. 63
Pseudo-Aristotle, *Secretum secretorum*
Additional 47680
James, *Milemete's Treatise* (1913), pp. xxxviii–lxiii, pls. 159–86; Sandler, *Gothic Manuscripts* (1986), no. 85; Michael, 'Iconography of Kingship' (1994); Escobedo, 'Audience and Patronage' (2006).

CAT. NOS. 64 AND 65
Thomas Hoccleve, *Regement of Princes*
Royal 17 D. vi and Arundel 38
Seymour, 'Hoccleve's Regiment of Princes' (1974), pp. 263–64 and 272–73; Seymour, 'Chaucer and Hocceleve' (1982), pp. 618, 622, pl. 45; Harris, 'Patron of British Library' (1984); Pearsall, 'Hoccleve's Regement of Princes' (1994), pp. 395–97, 402; Scott, *Later Gothic Manuscripts 1390–1490* (1996), no. 50; Perkins, *Hoccleve's Regiment* (2001).

CAT. NO. 66
Friar Laurent, *La Somme le roi*
Royal 19 C. ii
Stones, 'Stylistic Context' (1998), p. 545; Carley, *Libraries* (2000), H2. 1404; Rouse and Rouse, *Manuscripts and their Makers* (2000), esp. I, p. 170, II, App. 9A.; Brayer and Leuroquin-Labie, *La Somme le roi* (2007), p. 493.

CAT. NO. 67
Guillaume de Nangis, *Gesta S. Ludovici et Regis Philippi*
Royal 13 B. iii
Pannier, 'Les joyaux' (1874); Delisle, *Quelques manuscrits* (1878), pp. 36–38; Carley, *Libraries* (2000), H2. 1114; Villela-Petit, *Le Bréviaire* (2003); *Paris 1400* (2004), no. 68.

CAT. NO. 68
Miroir des dames
Royal 19 B. xvi
Delisle, 'Durand de Champagne' (1888); Henderson, 'Retrieving' (2002); Scott, 'Manuscripts for Henry VII' (2007), p. 280 n. 10; Siddons, *Heraldic Badges* (2009), I, pp. 148–50.

CAT. NO. 69
Hugues de Lannoy, *Enseignement de la vraie noblesse*
Royal 19 C. viii
Kipling, *Triumph of Honour* (1977), pp. 37, 43; Backhouse, 'Founders' (1987), pp. 32–33, 35; Carley, *Libraries* (2000), H1. 88; Kren and McKendrick, *Illuminating the Renaissance* (2003), no. 121; Sterchi, 'Hugues de Lannoy' (2004); Visser-Fuchs, '*Enseignement*' (2006), pp. 339–41, 344–53.

CAT. NO. 70
Des Cleres et nobles femmes
Royal 20. C v
Bozzolo, *Manuscrits de Boccaccio* (1973), pp. 23–25, 153–54; Meiss, Smith, and Beatson, *French Painting* (1974), I, p. 370; Reynolds, 'Illustrated Boccaccio Manuscripts' (1988), pp. 113–81 (pp. 171–80); Branca, *Boccaccio Visualizzato* (1999), I, pp. 109, 110, 136; III, pp. 12, 42–46, 53, 54, 267, 316; Carley, *Libraries* (2000), p. xxiv, H2. 301; Brown, *Boccaccio* (2001), p. 11.

CAT. NO. 71
Des Cleres et nobles femmes
Royal 16 G. v
Reynolds, 'Illustrated Boccaccio Manuscripts (1988), pp. 159–64; Avril and Reynaud, *Les Manuscrits* (1993), pp. 169–71; Branca, *Boccaccio Visualizzato* (1999), I, p. 136; III, pp. 46, 53–55, 105, 267, 316; Brown, *Boccaccio* (2001), p. 251; Dubois, 'De Rouen' (2009).

CAT. NO. 72
Des Cas des nobles hommes et femmes
Royal 18 D. vii
Gathercole, 'Frenchman's Praise' (1963); Longnon and Cazelles, *Les Très Riches Heures* (1969); Bozzolo, *Manuscrits de Boccaccio* (1973), pp. 137–38; Meiss, Smith and Beatson, *French Painting* (1974), I, p. 21; Reynolds, 'Illustrated Boccaccio Manuscripts (1988), pp. 164–66; Branca, *Boccaccio Visualizzato* (1999), I, p. 136; III, pp. 83–86, 96–98, 104–05; Carley, *Libraries* (2000), H1. 41; Hedeman, *Translating the Past* (2008), pp. 162–64.

CAT. NO. 73
John Lydgate, *Troy Book* and *Siege of Thebes*
Royal 18 D. ii
Lawton, 'Illustration' (1983), pp. 54–58, 60, 66, 68–69; Scott, *Later Gothic Manuscripts* (1996), no. 102; Kren and McKendrick, *Illuminating the Renaissance* (2003), no. 130; Naylor, 'Scribes and Secretaries' (2009), pp. 166–84

CAT. NO. 74
Bible historiale : Proverbs to the Apocalypse
Royal 19 D. iii, vol, 2
Berger, *La Bible française* (1884), pp. 163, 179, 182–86, 206, 257, 392–93; Burgio, 'Ricerche' (1998), pp. 153, 157–60; Carley, *Libraries* (2000), H1. 24; Komada, 'Illustrations' (2000), III, no. 41, pp. 773–74; Morgan, 'French Interpretations' (2000), p. 142.

CAT. NO. 75
Le livre et la vraye hystoire du bon roy Alixandre
Royal 20 B. xx
Meiss, Smith and Beatson, *French Painting* (1974), I, pp. 390–91; Ross, *Alexander historiatus* (1988), p. 55.; Reynolds, 'English Patrons' (1994), p. 304; Schmidt, *Legend* (1995), no. 46, pp. 185–86; McKendrick, *Alexander the Great* (1996); Carley, 'Marks in Books' (1997), Appendix I, pp. 603–05; Carley, *Libraries* (2000), p. 33, H2. 298; Ross and Stones, '*Roman d'Alexandre* (2002), p. 346; Pérez-Simon, 'Prose' (2005); Pérez-Simon, 'Savant philosophe' (2010).

CAT. NO. 76
Jan Du Quesne, *Les Commentaires de César*
Royal 16 G. viii
Bossuat, 'Commentaires' (1943); Schmidt-Chazan, 'Guerre des Gaules' (1980); Carley, *Libraries* (2000), H1. 66; Kren and McKendrick, *Illuminating the Renaissance* (2003), no. 74; Montigny, 'Traduire César' (2007); Wijsman, 'Pierre de Luxembourg' (2007), pp. 619–20.

CAT. NO. 77
Raoul Lefèvre, *Le Recueil des histoires de Troyes*
Royal 17 E. ii
Kekewich, 'Edward IV' (1971), p. 484; Backhouse, 'Founders' (1987), pp. 25, 27, 40, pl. 6; Aeschbach, *Recueils* (1987); Jung, *Légende de Troie* (1996); Brinkmann, *Flämische Buchmalerei* (1997), p. 115, fig. 35; Carley, *Libraries* (2002), H1. 44; Kren and McKendrick, *Illuminating the Renaissance* (2003), p. 289.

CAT. NO. 78
Legendary
Royal 20 D. vi
Meyer, 'Versions' (1906), pp. 279, 280, 286, 411, 414; Branner, *Manuscript Painting* (1977), pp. 58, 61, 63, 81, 123, 207, 209, 220, fig. 108, 115, 208; Carley, 'Marks in Books' (1997), pp. 583–606; Thompson, 'Recent Discovery' (1998); Thompson, 'Introduction' (1999), pp. 11–38.

CAT. NO. 79
La Légende dorée
Royal 19 B. xvii
Caxton, *de Voragine, Legenda aurea sanctorum* (1483); Delisle, *Recherches* (1907), p. 149, nos. 907–13; Meiss, *French Painting* (1967), I, p. 328; Painter, *William Caxton* (1976), pp. 143–45; Maddocks, 'Illumination' (1986); Hamer and Russell, 'Critical Edition' (1989); Maddocks, 'Pictures for Aristocrats' (1991); Hamer, 'Vignay's *Légende dorée*' (1993); Powell, 'Lady Margaret Beaufort' (1998), p. 233; Carley, *Libraries* (2000), H1. 99; Fisher, *Medieval Flower Book* (2007), p. 52.

CAT. NO. 80
Bestiary with Theological Texts
Royal 12 C. xix
Millar, *Thirteenth Century Bestiary* (1958), pp. 2, 11 n. 1, 13–15, 17–44, pls LXXXII–XCII; Morgan, *Early Gothic Manuscripts* (1982–88), no. 13; Muratova, 'Les Manuscrit-frères' (1986–90), pp. 72, n. 14, 81, 82; Faraci, *Il bestiario medio inglese* (1990), p. 258, pl. 13; Baxter, *Bestiaries* (1998), pp. 100, 110, 117–24, 147, 170; Clark, *Medieval Book* (2006) p. 120.

CAT. NO. 81
Bestiary and Lapidary ('The Rochester Bestiary')
Royal 12 F. xiii
McCulloch, *Medieval Latin* (1962), pp. 37, 74, n. 15, 188, 189; Morgan, *Early Gothic Manuscripts* (1982–88), no. 64; Baxter, *Bestiaries* (1998), pp. 147, 150, 152, 170, 174, 175–76, 192; Carley, *Libraries* (2000), pp. xl–xli, H2. 767; Clark, *Medieval Book* (2006), 26, 46, 61, 64, 73–75, 83, 107.

CAT. NO. 82
Psalter
Royal 2 B. iii
Haseloff, *Die Psalterillustration* (1938), p. 67; Carlvant, 'Some Modest Psalters' (1986), p. 90 n. 5; Carlvant, 'Brabantine Illuminator' (1987), pp. 262–63, fig. 14; Stones, 'Full-page Miniatures' (2004), pp. 300, 305, 307.

CAT. NO. 83
Psalter with Prefatory Miniatures
Royal 1 D. x
Rickert, *Painting in Britain* (1965), pp. 98–99, pl. 99B; Hoffmann, *Year 1200* (1970), no. 261; Morgan, *Early Gothic Manuscripts* (1982–88), no. 28; Kauffmann, *Biblical Imagery* (2003), p. 167.

CAT. NO. 84
The Psalter of John of Dalling
Royal 2 B. vi
Brieger, *English Art* (1957); Hunt, 'Library of the Abbey' (1978), p. 264; Morgan, *Early Gothic Manuscripts* (1982–88), no. 86; Lewis, *Art of Matthew Paris* (1987), pp. 25–26, 304, 425–26, 427, 436, 441, 442, 471, 476 ns 88, 101, fig. 5.

CAT. NO. 85
The Queen Mary Psalter
Royal 2 B. vii
Warner, *Queen Mary's Psalter* (1912); Roberts, 'Literary Source' (1973), pp. 361–65; Dennison, 'Illuminator' (1986), pp. 287–314; Sandler, *Gothic Manuscripts* (1986), no. 56; Smith, 'History' (1993), pp. 147–59; Stanton, 'Codicology' (1995), pp. 250–62; Stanton, *Queen Mary Psalter* (2001); Stanton, 'Queen Mary' (2009).

CAT. NO. 86
The Queen Mary Apocalypse
Royal 19 B. xv
Delisle and Meyer, *Apocalypse en français* (1901), no. 25; Warner, *Queen Mary's Psalter* (1912), p. 7; James, *Apocalypse* (1931); Laing, 'Queen Mary Apocalypse' (1971); Sandler, *Gothic Manuscripts* (1986), no. 61; Dennison, 'Apocalypse' (1994); Carley, *Libraries* (2000), H2. 22; Morgan, *Douce Apocalypse* (2006).).

CAT. NO. 87
The Welles Apocalypse
Royal 15 D. ii
Delisle and Meyer, *Apocalypse en français* (1901), no. 24; James, *Trinity Apocalypse* (1909), pp. 9, 26; Egbert, '*La lumiere*' (1936), pp. 446, passim; Egbert, *Tickhill Psalter* (1940), pp. 95–100, 182–88; Sandler, *Gothic Manuscripts* (1986), no. 34; Carley, *Libraries* (2000), H2. 291; Alexander, Marrow and Sandler, *Splendor* (2005), p. 207 n. 7.

CAT. NO. 88
Isidore of Seville, *Etymologiae*
Royal 6 C. i
James, *Ancient Libraries* (1903), p. 517; Carley, *Libraries* (2000), p. xxxvi, n. 48; Gneuss, *Handlist* (2001), no. 469; Barker-Benfield, *St Augustine's Abbey* (2008), BA I.427, p. cii.

CAT. NO. 89
Rabanus Maurus, *De rerum naturis*
Royal 12 G. xiv
Thomson, *Manuscripts* (1982), I, p. 48, no. 31; Schipper, 'Annotated Copies' (1997), pl. 6a; Carley, *Libraries* (2000), pp. xxxi–xxxii, n. 33, H2. 1099.

CAT. NO. 90
Gerald of Wales, *Topographica Hibernica*
Royal 13 B. viii
Morgan, *Early Gothic Manuscripts* (1982–88), no. 59(a); Carley, *Libraries* (2000), H2. 1116, H4. 33–34; Brown, 'Marvels of the West' (2002).

CAT. NO. 91
Roman d'Alexandre en prose and Other Texts
Royal 19 D. i
Ross, 'Book-Production' (1952), pp. 63–71; Ross, 'Nectanebus' (1952), pp. 68–72, fig. 16b; Ross, *Alexander Historiatus* (1963), pp. 13, 30, 41, 55, 88 n. 63, 90 n. 124, 97 n. 263, 98 ns.

276 and 279; Dutschke, 'Truth' (1998); Carley, *Libraries* (2000), H1. 91; Rouse and Rouse, *Manuscripts* (2000), I, pp. 212, 244–47, 250, 254, 380 n. 86, 390 n. 86, 391 n. 105; II, App. 9A; Melis, 'Alexander Manuscript' (2002), p. 972; Brun and Cavagna, 'Pour une édition' (2006); Pérez-Simon, *Mise en roman* (2011), pp. 438–40.

CAT. NO. 92
James le Palmer, *Omne bonum*
Royal 6 E. vi
Sandler, '*Omne bonum*' (1990), pp. 183–200; Sandler, *Omne Bonum: Encyclopedia* (1996); Carley, 'Marks in Books' (1997), pp. 597–98; Carley, *Libraries* (2000), H2.1326.

CAT. NO. 93
Livre des proprietez des choses
Royal 15 E. iii
Winkler, *Die Flämische Buchmalerei* (1925), pp. 137, 179; Meyer, 'Die illustrierten lateinischen Handschriften' (1996); Carley, *Libraries* (2000), H1.53; H1.61; Kren and McKendrick, *Illuminating the Renaissance* (2003), p. 311; Holbrook, 'Properties of Things' (2006); Hans-Collas and Schandel, *Manuscrits enluminés* (2009), p. 200.

CAT. NO. 94
Maps of an Itinerary from London to Apulia in Italy
Royal 14 C. vii
Vaughan, *Matthew Paris* (1958); Lewis, *Art of Matthew Paris* (1987); Carley, *Libraries* (2000), H2. 1041; H4.17; Connolly, *Maps of Matthew Paris* (2009).

CAT. NO. 95
Jean Rotz, *Boke of Idrography*
Royal 20 E. ix
Wallis, *Maps and Text* (1981); Wallis, 'Rotz Atlas' (1982); Carley, *Libraries* (2000), H2. 994; Toulouse, *Marine Cartography* (2007).

CAT. NO. 96
Jean Mallard, *Le Premier Livre de la cosmograpphie*
Royal 20 B. xii
Taylor, *Tudor Geography* (1930), pp. 71–72, pl. opp. p. 72; Cooper, 'Jean Mallard' (2003); Carley, *Prayer Book* (2009), pp. 44–59; Doran, *Henry VIII* (2009), no. 241 (James P. Carley catalogue entry).

CAT. NO. 97
Liber iudiciorum
Royal 12 C. v
Sandler, *Gothic Manuscripts* (1986), II, p. 175; Carey, *Courting Disaster* (1992), pp. 69, 183; Eberle, 'Richard II' (1999), p. 242 n. 31

CAT. NO. 98
William Parron, *Liber de optimo fato Henrici Eboraci ducis et optimorum ipsius parentum*
Royal 12 B. vi
Armstrong, 'Italian Astrologer' (1960); Avril and Stirnemann, *Manuscrits enluminés* (1987), p. 192; Carey, *Courting Disaster* (1992), p. 161; Scott, *Later Gothic Manuscripts* (1996), I, pp. 347, 365.

CAT. NO. 99
Collection of Astrological Treatises
Arundel 66
Talbot and Hammond, *Medical Practitioners* (1965), pp. 194–95; North, 'Alfonsine Tables' (1989); Scott, *Later Gothic Manuscripts* (1996), no. 140.

CAT. NO. 100
Aldobrandino of Siena, *Livre de physique*
Royal 19 A. v
Féry-Hue, 'Régime du corps' (1987); Nicoud, *Régimes de santé* (2007), II, p. 964; Scott, 'Manuscripts for Henry VII' (2007), pp. 280–81.

CAT. NO. 101
Smaragdus of St Mihiel, *Expositio in regulam S. Benedicti*
Royal 10 A. xiii
James, *Ancient Libraries* (1903), pp. 31, 507; Kauffmann, *Romanesque Manuscripts* (1975), no. 92; Zarnecki, *English Romanesque Art* (1984), no. 71; Ramsay and Sparks, *Image of Saint Dunstan* (1988); Budny and Graham, 'Dunstan' (1993), p. 88, fig. 7; Barker-Benfield, *St Augustine's Abbey* (2008), III, pp. 1723–24; Gameson, *Earliest Books* (2008).

CAT. NO. 102
The Rochester Bible
Royal 1 C. vii
Kauffmann, *Romanesque Manuscripts* (1975), no. 45; Richards, 'Decorated Vulgate' (1981); Cahn, *Romanesque Bible Illumination* (1982), no. 33, pp. 259–63; Zarnecki, *English Romanesque Art* (1984), no. 24; Kauffmann, *Biblical Imagery* (2003), pp. 87, 94, pl. 62, Appendix 2.

CAT. NO. 103
Peter Lombard, Gloss on the Pauline Epistles
Royal 4 E. viii
Casley, *Catalogue* (1734), p. 58; Ayres, 'Tanner Manuscript' (1969), p. 42, pl. 5c; De Hamel, *Glossed Books* (1984); Ker, 'Migration of Manuscripts'(1985), p. 467; Carley, *Libraries* (2000), pp. 171–72; Cahn, 'Romanesque Art' (2008).

CAT. NO. 104
Peter Lombard, Gloss on the Pauline Epistles
Royal 4 D. viii
Avril, 'A quand remontent' (1976), pp. 38–40; Rouse and Rouse, *Manuscripts and their Makers* (2000), I, pp. 31–32, 34–35, II, App. 1 D.

CAT. NO. 105
Peter Lombard, Gloss on the Pauline Epistles
Royal 4 E. ix
Avril, 'Un manuscrit' (1975), pp. 268–69 n. 10, fig. 31; Ayres, 'Parisian Bibles' (1982); De Hamel, *Glossed Books* (1984), p. 35; Brown, *Western Historical Scripts* (1990), pl. 32.

CAT. NO. 106
Gratian, *Decretum*; Bartholomew of Brescia, *Glossa ordinaria*
Royal 10 D. viii
Branner, *Manuscript Painting* (1977), pp. 102–07; Nordenfalk, 'Anthony Melnikas' (1980); Carley, *Libraries* (2000), H2. 984.

CAT. NO. 107
Gregory IX, *Decretals* ; Bernard of Parma, *Glossa ordinaria*
Royal 10 D. vii
Schadt, *Arbores* (1982), pp. 208, 238, 243, 251; *L'Art au temps des rois maudits* (1998), p. 265; Linehan, 'GAR' (1998); Carley, *Libraries* (2000), H2. 110..

CAT. NO. 108
The Smithfield Decretals
Royal 10 E. iv
Sandler, *Gothic Manuscripts* (1986), no. 101; Bovey, 'Didactic Distractions' (2000); Carley, *Libraries* (2000), H2. 1059; Bovey, 'Pictorial *Ex Libris*' (2002).

CAT. NO. 109
Athanasius, Theological Treatises
Royal 5 F. ii
Weiss, *Humanism in England during the Fifteenth Century* (1967), pp. 39–70; de la Mare and Hunt, *Duke Humfrey and English Humanism* (1970); Sammut, *Unfredo Duca di Gloucester* (1980), 74, 105, 137, 160–61; de la Mare and Gillam, *Duke Humfrey's Library* (1988), no. 32; Scott, *Dated and Datable* (2002), pp. 56–57, pls XVa, b.

CAT. NO. 110
Filippo Alberici, *Tabula cebetis, De mortis effectibus*
Arundel 317
Sider, 'Interwoven with Poems' (1990); Carlson, *English Humanist Books* (1993), pp. 20–37, 167–68, 171–74, 187 n. 1, figs 1–2, 6–11; Sider and Obrist, *Corpus Librorum Emblematum* (1997), p. 43, no. 147; Rundle, 'Filippo Alberici' (2005).

CAT. NO. 111
Filippo Alberici (?), *Hieroglyphica* and Emblematic Inscriptions
Royal 12 C. iii
Jayne and Johnson, *Lumley Library* (1956), p. 216; Sider and Obrist, *Corpus Librorum Emblematum* (1997), p. 77, no. 254.

CAT. NO. 112
Pauline and Catholic Epistles
Royal 1 E. v
Trapp, 'Notes on Manuscripts' (1975), no. 6; Gibaud, *Inédit d'Erasme* (1982); Brown, 'Latin Translation' (1984), pp. 351–54, 356–57, 360, 365–70, fig. 2; Trapp, *Erasmus* (1991); Kren and McKendrick, *Illuminating the Renaissance* (2003), p. 436; Trapp, 'Colet' (2004).

CAT. NO. 113
Pandolfo Collenuccio, *Apologues*; Lucian of Samosata, *Dialogues*
Royal 12 C. viii
Wolpe, 'Royal Manuscript' (1958); Kren, *Renaissance Painting* (1983), no. 17; Rummel, *Erasmus* (1985), p. 50; Starkey, *Henry VIII* (1991), no. II.15; Alexander, 'Foreign Illuminators' (1999), p. 55.

CAT. NO. 114
Matthew Paris, *Historia Anglorum*
Royal 14 C. vii
Vaughan, 'Handwriting of Matthew Paris' (1953); Vaughan, *Matthew Paris* (1958); Lewis, *Art of Matthew Paris* (1987); Carley, *Libraries* (2000), H2. 1041; H4.11.

CAT. NO. 115
Images of English Kings, from Edward the Confessor to Edward I
Cotton Vitellius A. xiii
Sandler, *Gothic Manuscripts* (1986), no. 9; Cavanaugh, 'Royal Books' (1988), p. 308; Michael, 'Iconography of Kingship' (1994), p. 44 n. 64; Dean and Boulton, *Anglo-Norman Literature* (1999), no. 31; Higgitt, *Murthly Hours* (2000), pp. 226–27.

CAT. NO. 116
Peter of Langtoft's *Chronicle, the Lament of Edward II*
Royal 20 A. ii
Wright, *Langtoft* (1866–68); Loomis and Loomis, *Arthurian Legends* (1938), fig. 385; Aspin, *Political Songs* (1953), pp. 93–104; Thiolier, *Le Règne* (1989), as 'C', and pl. at p. 332; Stones, 'Arthurian Art' (1991), pp. 21–78; Summerfield, *Kings' Lives* (1998), p. 217; Carley, *Libraries* (2000), H2. 1046; Stones, 'Egerton Brut' (2006), pp. 168, 172, 176; Delcourt, *La Légende* (2009), p. 21.

CAT. NOS. 117 AND 118
Genealogical Chronicles of the English Kings
Royal 14 B. v and Royal 14 B. vi
Carley, *Libraries* (2000), H1. 15; Tyson, 'Manuscript Tradition' (2001), p. 107; de Laborderie, 'Ligne de reis' (2002); de Laborderie, 'Normandes' (2003); Bovey, *Chaworth Roll* (2005); de Laborderie, 'New Pattern' (2008); Siddons, *Heraldic Badges* (2009), II, part 1: *Royal Badges*, pp. 211–12.

CAT. NO. 119
John Capgrave, *Liber de illustribus Henricis*
Cotton Tiberius A. viii
Hingeston, *Illustrious Henries* (1858); Hingeston, *Johannis Capgrave* (1858); de Meijer, 'John Capgrave' (1957); Lucas, *Author to Audience* (1997), esp. pp. 38–43; Carley, *Libraries* (2000), H1. 80; Winstead, *Capgrave's Fifteenth Century* (2007), pp. 157–61.

CAT. NO. 120
Jean Chartier, *Chronique de Charles VII*
Royal 20. E vi
Backhouse, 'Founders' (1987), pp. 34–35; Hedeman, *Royal Image* (1991), p. 181; Sutton and Visser-Fuchs, 'Choosing a Book' (1995); Scott, 'Manuscripts for Henry VII' (2007), pp. 279–86.

CAT. NO. 121
Documents on Royal Politics, Legislation and Ceremony
Cotton Nero D. vi
Scattergood, 'Literary Culture' (1983); Sandler, *Gothic Manuscripts* (1986), no. 151; Archer, 'Parliamentary Restoration' (1995); Eberle, 'Richard II' (1999), pp. 234–35, 238–39.

CAT. NO. 122
Liber regalis (Coronation order of English kings)
London, Westminster Abbey, MS 38
Rickert, *Carmelite Missal* (1952), pp. 77–79; Ullmann, *Liber Regie Capelle* (1961), pp. 22–23; Simpson, *Connections between English and Bohemian Painting* (1984); Sandler, *Gothic Manuscripts* (1986), no. 155; Binski, *Westminster Abbey* (1995), pp. 126–30; Binski, '*Liber regalis*' (1997).

CAT. NO. 123
Liber legum antiquorum regum
Cotton Claudius D. ii
Catto, 'Andrew Horn' (1981); Ker, 'Liber Custumarum' (1985); Sandler, *Gothic Manuscripts* (1986), no. 68; Dennison, 'Liber Horn' (1990).

CAT. NO. 124
Nova Statuta Angliae
Hargrave 274
McKenna, 'Piety and Propaganda' (1974); Scott, *Mirroure of the Worlde* (1980), pp. 66–67; Scott, *Later Gothic Manuscripts* (1996), no. 133; Skemer, 'Reading the Law' (1999).

CAT. NO. 125
Flavius Vegetius Renatus, *De re militari*
Cambridge, Fitzwilliam Museum, MS Marlay Add. 1
Thorpe, 'Mastre Richard' (1952); Morgan, *Early Gothic Manuscripts* (1982–88), no. 150; Reeve, 'Transmission' (2000), pp. 315–16; Allmand, '*De re militari*' (2004).

CAT. NO. 126
Jean de Meun, *Les establissemens de chevalerie*
Royal 20 B. xi
Löfstedt, *Vegesce Flave René* (1977); Avril, 'Gli autori classici' (1996), p. 91; Richardot, *Végèce* (1998); Carley, *Libraries* (2000), H2. 759; Allmand, '*De re militari*' (2004).

CAT. NO. 127
The Book of Vegecye of Dedes of Knyghthode
Royal 18 A. xii
Science, *Boethius* (1927), pp. xlv–l; Sutton and Visser-Fuchs, 'Richard III's Books' (1987); Sutton and Visser-Fuchs, *Richard III's Books: Ideals* (1997), pp. 17, 79, 89 n. 63, 282–83, fig. 35; Allmand, 'English Versions' (1998).

CAT. NO. 128
William Bruges's Garter Book
Stowe 594
Wagner, *Catalogue* (1950), pp. 83–86; Vale, *Edward III* (1982), pp. 76–91; Begent, 'Creation' (1995); Scott, *Later Gothic Manuscripts* (1996), no. 84; Selwyn, 'Heralds' Libraries' (2006).

CAT. NO. 129
Guillaume de Lorris and Jean de Meun, *Roman de la Rose*
Royal 19 B. xiii
Ward and Herbert, *Catalogue of Romances* (1883–1910), I, p. 874; Rickert, 'Richard II's Books' (1932–33); Green, 'Richard II's Books' (1976), pp. 235–39; Scattergood, 'Literary Culture' (1983), pp. 36, 41; Krochalis, 'Books and Readings' (1988), p. 51; Dahlberg, de Lorris and de Meun, *Romance of the Rose* (1995); Carley, *Libraries* (2000), H1. 81; Blamires and Holian, *Romance* (2002).

CAT. NO. 130
Guillaume de Lorris and Jean de Meun, *Roman de la Rose*; and *La Bataille d'Annezin*
Royal 20 A. xvii
Ward and Herbert, *Catalogue of Romances* (1883–1910), I, pp. 880–84; Langlois, *Roman de la Rose* (1910), pp. 142, 238; Chailley, 'Etudes musicales' (1948); Duncan, 'Review' (1988); Dahlberg, *de Lorris and de Meun, Romance of the Rose* (1995); Blamires and Holian, *Romance* (2002).

CAT. NO. 131
Lancelot du Lac
Royal 20 D. iv
Sandler, *Gothic Manuscripts* (1986), no. 136; Carley, *Libraries* (2000), H1. 89; Melis, 'Alexander Manuscript' (2002); Stones, 'A Note' (2002); Sandler, 'Lancastrian Heraldry' (2003).

CAT. NO. 132
Lancelot-Grail Cycle
Royal 14 E. iii
Stones, 'Another Short Note' (1987), pp. 187–88; Sutton and Visser-Fuchs, 'Most Benevolent Queen' (1995), pp. 228–30; Meuwese, 'Three Illustrated Prose Lancelots' (1999), pp. 98, 101 n. 6; Carley, *Libraries* (2000), H1. 93; Middleton, 'The Manuscripts' (2006), p. 85 n. 8.

CAT. NO. 133
Charles of Orleans, Poems
Royal 16 F. ii
Champion, *Charles d'Orléans* (1923–27), pp. x–xii; Sutton and Visser-Fuchs, 'Device' (1997); Backhouse, 'Charles of Orléans' (2000); Carley, *Libraries* (2000), H1. 77; Kren and McKendrick, *Illuminating the Renaissance* (2003), no. 119, pp. 394, 398–400, 403.

CAT. NO. 134
Carmina regia: Address of the City of Prato to Robert of Anjou
Royal 6 E. ix
Frugoni, 'Convenevole da Prato' (1969); *Regia carmina* (1982); Saenger, 'Robert von Anjou' (1988); Eichberg, 'Bedeutung' (1999).

CAT. NO. 135
Histoire ancienne jusqu'à César
Royal 20 D. i
Saxl, 'The Troy Romance (1957), I, pp. 135–36; Avril, 'Trois manuscrits napolitains' (1969), p. 295 n. 3, 300–07, 309, 311–14; Williams, 'A Case of Mistaken Identity'(1984), 60, 61, 62; Avril, 'Un atelier 'picard' à la cour Angevins de Naples', (1986), p. 76, fig. 2; Saggese, 'L'Enluminure à Naples' (2001), p. 127; *Paris 1400* (2004), nos. 118 and 164; Elliott and Warr, *Church of Santa Maria Donna Regina* (2004); Morrison and Hedeman, *Imagining the Past* (2010), no. 50; Saggese, 'Cristophoro Orimina' (2010), pp. 113–25.

CAT. NO. 136
Les Grandes chroniques de France
Royal 16 G. vi
Viard, *Les Grandes Chroniques* (1953); Lejeune and Stiennon, *La Légende* (1966); Hedeman, *Royal Image* (1991), pp. 51–73, 213–21; Carley, *Libraries* (2000), H1. 58; Rundle, 'Habits of Manuscript-collecting' (2004), pp. 110–11, 120–21 ns 21, 22.

CAT. NO. 137
Bible historiale: Genesis to the Apocalypse
Royal 19 D. ii
Fastes du Gothique (1981), no. 277; Carley, *Libraries* (2000), H1. 67; Komada, 'Illustrations' (2000), III, no. 40; Rouse and Rouse, *Manuscripts* (2000), 1, pp. 270–73; 2, pp. 51–52; O'Meara, *Monarchy and Consent* (2001), pp. 209, 215, 217, 228, 261, 332 n. 1, 336 n. 10, ills 60, 96.

CAT. NO. 138
Coronation Book of Charles V
Cotton Tiberius B. viii, ff. 35–80
Dewick, *Coronation Book* (1899); Sherman, 'Coronation Book' (1977); *Fastes du Gothique* (1981), no. 279; Jackson, *Vive le roi!* (1984), pp. 26–34; Jackson, *Ordines* (2001), II, pp. 454, 462, 466–69; O'Meara, *Monarchy* (2001).

CAT. NO. 139
Le Songe du Vergier
Royal 19 C. iv
Sherman, 'Representations' (1971), p. 91; Schnerb-Lièvre, 'Évrart de Trémaugon' (1980); *Fastes du Gothique* (1981), no. 282; Schnerb-Lièvre, *Le Songe* (1982); Carley, *Libraries* (2000), H2. 260; *Paris 1400* (2004), no. 11.

CAT. NO. 140
Philip de Mezieres, *Epistre au Roi Richart*
Royal 20 B. vi
Avril, 'Trois manuscrits' (1969), p. 307; Palmer, *England* (1972), pp. 180–210; Coopland, Philippe de Mézières,(1975); Camille, *Master of Death* (1996); Keen, 'Wilton Diptych' (1997), pp. 191–92, ills 112, 113; Carley, *Libraries* (2000), H1. 79.

CAT. NO. 141
The Psalter of Henry VI
Cotton Domitian A. xvii
Porcher, *Les Belles Heures de Jean de France* (1953), pp. 26–27, fig. 16; Meiss, 'French and Italian Variations on an Early Fifteenth-Century Theme' (1963), p. 149; Pächt, 'Zur Entstehung des "Hieronymus in Gehäus"' (1963), pp. 137–38; Spencer, 'Master of the Duke of Bedford: The Salisbury Breviary' (1966), p. 612; Turner, *Illuminated Manuscripts Exhibited in the Grenville Library* (1967), no. 54; Meiss, Smith and Beatson, *French Painting* (1974), I, pp. 375, 405; Reynolds, 'English Patrons' (1994), pl. 19; Clark, 'The Influence of the Limbourg Brothers' (2005), pp. 217–23, figs. 11, 12; Backhouse, 'Psalter of Henry VI' (2004), pp. 329–36; Reynolds, 'Très Riches Heures' (2005), p. 529 n. 22; Stirnemann and Rabel, 'Très Riches Heures and Two Artists' (2005), p. 538.

CAT. NO. 142
The Bedford Hours
Additional 18850
Gough, *An Account of a Richly Illuminated Missal* (1794); Spencer, 'The Master of the Duke of Bedford' (1965); Backhouse, *Bedford Hours* (1990); Reynolds, 'Très Riches Heures' (2005); Stirnemann and Rabel, 'Très Riches Heures and Two Artists' (2005); Reynolds, 'The Workshop of the Master of the Duke of Bedford' (2006); König, *Bedford Hours* (2007).

CAT. NO. 143
The Shrewsbury Book
Royal 15 E. vi
Reynolds, 'The Shrewsbury Book' (1993); Marks and Williamson, *Gothic* (2003), no. 42; Pérez-Simon, *Mise en roman* (forthcoming); Hedeman, 'Collecting Images', (2011); Taylor, A., 'The Time of an Anthology' (2011); Taylor, C., 'The Shrewsbury Book' (2011); Fresno, 'Christine de Pizan' (2011).

CAT. NO. 144
The Egerton Hours
Egerton 1070
Avril and Reynaud, *Les Manuscrits* (1993), no. 122; Backhouse, 'Illuminated Manuscripts' (1995), p. 182; Smeyers, *Flemish Miniatures* (1999), p. 265, pls 45, 46 on p. 264; *Paris 1400* (2004), no. 165; Campbell, *Henry VIII* (2007), p. 83; *Splendeur* (2009), pp. 196, 206–11.

CAT. NO. 145
Xenophon, *Anabasis*
Royal 19 C. vi
Scheller, 'Ensigns' (1983); Avril and Reynaud, *Les Manuscrits* (1993), p. 345; Backhouse, 'Illuminated Manuscripts' (1995), p. 179; Dionisotti, 'Claude de Seyssel' (1995), p. 90; Boone, 'Ancient Historians' (2000); Carley, *Libraries* (2000), p. xxvi n. 15; Hochner, *Louis XII* (2006); Boone, *War* (2007).

CAT. NO. 146
Martin de Brion, *Tresample description de toute la Terre Saincte*
Royal 20 A. iv
Davenport, 'Embroidered Bindings' (1904), pp. 268–69; Karrow, *Mapmakers* (1993), pp. 94–95; Backhouse, 'Robert Cotton's Record' (1997), p. 232; Carley, *Libraries* (2000), H5. 140; Coron and Lefèvre, *Livres en broderie* (1995), pp. 25–26.

CAT. NO. 147
Royal Isocrates, *Ad Nicoclem* and *Nicocles*
16 E. xxxii
Whipple, 'Isocrates' (1916), pp. 15–27; Gundersheimer, *Louis le Roy* (1966) pp. 12, 145; Dowling, *Humanism* (1986); Livingstone, 'Voice of Isocrates' (1998); Sciacca, *Umanesimo* (2007), pp. 21, 60, 113.

CAT. NO. 148
The Psalter of the Earl of Arundel
Royal 2 B. ix
von Klarwill, *Queen Elizabeth* (1928), p. 113; *Livres d'heures* (1993), no. 28; Boyle, 'Hans Eworth's Portrait' (2002); Clough, 'Ubaldini' (2004); Orth, 'Primacy' (2004); Kurtz, 'Classical Past' (2008).

CAT. NO. 149
Vasco da Lucena, *Les Fais d'Alexandre le grant*
Royal 15 D. iv
Backhouse, 'Sir John Donne' (1994), pp. 49–51; McKendrick, *Alexander the Great* (1996), pp. 20, 24, 50, 102; Campbell, *Fifteenth Century* (1998); Carley, *Libraries* (2000), p. lv, n. 117, H1. 38; Kren and McKendrick, *Illuminating the Renaissance* (2003), pp. 255–56; Carley, *King Henry VIII* (2004), p. 113, fig. 100; Blondeau, 'Imiter' (2005), pp. 188–89; *Women of Distinction* (2005), pp. 243–44 no. 81.

CAT. NO. 150
Charles Soillot, *Le Débat de félicité*
Arundel 71
Watson, *Henry Savile* (1969), p. 63 no. 240; *Charles le Téméraire* (1977), pp. 73–77; Morgan, 'Texts of Devotion' (1992), p. 72 n. 16; Carley, *Libraries* (2000), H1. 120; Bousmanne and others., *La Librairie* (2003), pp. 61–66; Hans-Collas and Schandel, *Manuscrits enluminés* (2009), pp. 72–73 no. 15.

CAT. NO. 151
Leaf from a Gradual
Arundel 71, f. 9
Page, *Victoria County History* (1926), pp. 194–98; Pächt, *Master* (1948), p. 69 no. 20; van Buren, 'Master' (1975), p. 307 no. 7; Morgan, 'Texts of Devotion' (1992), p. 63.

CAT. NO. 152
La Vie de notre seigneur Jésus Christ and *La Vengeance de la mort de Jésus Christ*
Royal 16 G. iii
Backhouse, 'Founders' (1987), pp. 26, 40, pl. 8; Straub, *La Tradition* (1998), pp. 50–57, pl. VI; Carley, *Libraries* (2000), H1. 63; Kren and McKendrick, *Illuminating the Renaissance* (2003), p. 309; Płonka-Bałus, *Vita Christi* (2004), pp. 11, 22, 23, 38, 164, 180.

CAT. NO. 153
Choirbook of Petrus Alamire
Royal 8 G. vii
Tirro, 'Strawberry Leaves' (1981); Kellman, *London, British Library* (1987); Kellman, *Treasury* (1999), pp. 110–11; Thomas, 'Patronage' (2005); DIAMM.

CAT. NO. 154
Motets for Henry VIII
Royal 11 E. xi
Backhouse, 'Salute' (1993); Dumitrescu, *Early Tudor Court* (2007), pp. 117–47; Bell and Skinner, *Music* (2009); DIAMM.

Bibliography

A select bibliography only is included for each catalogue entry, sometimes including further reading. A much fuller bibliography, description and further images for manuscripts in the Royal, Arundel, Egerton, Hargrave, Harley, Lansdowne, Stowe and Yates Thompson collections can be found at http://www.bl.uk/catalogues/illuminatedmanuscripts/welcome.htm

Notes
Entries are under author(s) or editor(s). Entries without such attribution are by title, their order disregarding the definite or indefinite article.

Acts of the Privy Council of England, 1542–1631, 45 vols (London: HMSO, 1890–1964).

Aeschbach, Marc, ed., Raoul Lefèvre, *Le Recueil des histories de Troyes* (Bern: Peter Lang, 1987).

Alexander, Jonathan J.G., 'A Lost Leaf from a Bodleian Book of Hours', *Bodleian Library Record,* 8 (1971), 248–51.

Alexander, Jonathan J.G., 'William Abell "lymnour" and Fifteenth Century English Illumination', in *Kunsthistorische Forschungen: Otto Pächt zu seinem 70 Geburtstag,* ed. by Artur Rosenauer and Gerold Weber (Salzburg: Residenz, 1972), pp. 166–72.

Alexander, Jonathan J.G., *Insular Manuscripts 6th to 9th Century,* A Survey of Manuscripts Illustrated in the British Isles, 1 (London: Harvey Miller, 1978).

Alexander, Jonathan J.G., 'Painting and Manuscript Illumination for Royal Patrons in the Later Middle Ages', in *English Court Culture in the Later Middle Ages,* ed. by V.J. Scattergood and J.W. Sherborne (London: Duckworth, 1983), pp. 141–62.

Alexander, Jonathan J.G., *Medieval Illuminators and their Methods of Work* (New Haven, CT: Yale University Press, 1992).

Alexander, Jonathan J.G., 'Foreign Illuminators and Illuminated Manuscripts', in *The Cambridge History of the Book in Britain* (Cambridge: Cambridge University Press, 1987), III: *1400–1557,* ed. by Lotte Hellinga and J.B. Trapp (1999), pp. 47–64.

Alexander, Jonathan J.G., and Paul Binski, eds, *The Age of Chivalry: Art in Plantagenet England 1200–1400* (London: Royal Academy of Arts, 1987).

Alexander, Jonathan J.G., James H. Marrow and Lucy Freeman Sandler, eds, *The Splendor of the Word: Medieval and Renaissance Illuminated Manuscripts at the New York Public Library* (London: Harvey Miller, 2005).

Allmand, Christopher, 'The Fifteenth-century English Versions of Vegetius' *De re militari*', in *Armies, Chivalry and Warfare in Medieval Britain and France: Proceedings of the 1995 Symposium,* ed. by Matthew Strickland, Harlaxton Medieval Studies, n.s. 7 (Stamford: Paul Watkins, 1998), pp. 30–45.

Allmand, Christopher 'The *De re militari* of Vegetius in the Middle Ages and the Renaissance', in *Writing War: Medieval Literary Responses to Warfare,* ed. by Corinne Saunders, Françoise Le Saux and Neil Thomas (Woodbridge: Boydell and Brewer, 2004), pp. 15–28.

Archer, Rowena, 'Parliamentary Restoration: John Mowbray and the Dukedom of Norfolk in 1425', in *Rulers and Ruled in Late Medieval England: Essays Presented to Gerald Harriss,* ed. by R.E. Archer and S. Walker (London: Continuum International, 1995), pp. 99–116.

Armstrong, C.A.J., 'An Italian Astrologer at the Court of Henry VII', in *Italian Renaissance Studies,* ed. by F.F. Jacob (London: Faber and Faber, 1960), pp. 433–54.

L'Art au temps des rois maudits Philippe le Bel et ses fils: 1285–1328, Paris, Galeries nationales du Grand Palais 17 mars–29 juin 1998 (Paris: Réunion des musées nationaux, 1998).

Aspin, Isabel S.T., *Anglo-Norman Political Songs* (Oxford: Basil Blackwell, 1953).

Avril, François, 'Trois manuscrits napolitains des collections de Charles V et de Jean de Berry', *Bibliothèque de l'École des Chartes,* 127 (1969), 291–328.

Avril, François, 'Un manuscrit d'auteurs classiques et ses illustrations', in *The Year 1200: A Symposium* (New York: Metropolitan Museum of Art, 1975), pp. 261–82.

Avril, François, 'A quand remontent les premiers ateliers d'enlumineurs laïcs à Paris?', *Les Dossiers d'archéologie,* 16 (1976), 36–44.

Avril, François, 'Un atelier "picard" à la cour Angevins de Naples', in *'Nobile claret opus': Festgabe für Frau Prof. Dr Ellen Judith Beer zum 60. Geburtstag,* Zeitschrift für schweizerische Archäologie und Kunstgeschichte, 43 (1986), 76–85.

Avril, François, 'Gli autori classici illustrati in Francia dal XIII al XV secolo', in *Vedere i classici: L'Illustrazione libraria dei testi antichi dall'età romana al tardo medioevo,* ed. by Marco Buonocore (Rome: Palombi and Rose, 1996), pp. 87–98.

[Avril, François, and Jean Lafaurie], *La Librairie de Charles V* (Paris: Bibliothèque nationale, 1968).

Avril, François, and Nicole Reynaud, *Les Manuscrits à peintures en France 1440–1520* (Paris: Flammarion, 1993).

Avril, François, and Patricia Danz Stirnemann, *Manuscrits enluminés d'origine insulaire, VIIe–XXe siècle* (Paris: Bibliothèque nationale, 1987).

Avril, François, Xavier Barral i Altet and Danielle Gaborit-Chopin, *Le Monde Roman 1060–1200,* 2 vols (Paris: Gallimard, 1983), II: *Les Royaumes d'Occident.*

Ayres, Larry M., 'A Tanner Manuscript in the Bodleian Library and some Notes on English Painting of the Late Twelfth Century', *Journal of the Warburg and Courtauld Institutes,* 32 (1969), 41–54.

Ayres, Larry M., 'Parisian Bibles in the Berlin Staatsbibliothek', *Pantheon,* 40 (1982), 5–13.

Backhouse, Janet, 'Two Books of Hours of Francis I', *British Museum Quarterly,* 31 (1966–67), 90–96.

Backhouse, Janet, 'Founders of the Royal Library: Edward IV and Henry VII as Collectors of Illuminated Manuscripts', in *England in the Fifteenth Century: Proceedings of the 1986 Harlaxton Symposium,* ed. by Daniel Williams (Woodbridge: Boydell, 1987), pp. 23–41.

Backhouse, Janet, *The Bedford Hours* (London: British Library, 1990).

Backhouse, Janet, 'Sir Robert Cotton's Record of a Royal Bookshelf', *British Library Journal,* 18 (1992), 44–51.

Backhouse, Janet , 'A Salute to the Tudor Rose', in *Miscellanea Martin Wittek: Album de codicologie et de paléographie offert à Martin Wittek,* ed. by Anny Raman and Eugène Manning (Leuven: Peeters, 1993), pp. 1–14.

Backhouse, Janet, 'Sir John Donne's Flemish Manuscripts', in *Medieval Codicology, Iconography, Literature, and Translation. Studies for Keith Val Sinclair,* ed. by Peter Rolfe Monks and D.D.R. Owen (Leiden: E.J.Brill, 1994), pp. 48–53.

Backhouse, Janet, 'Illuminated Manuscripts associated with Henry VII and Members of his Immediate Family', in *The Reign of Henry VII: Proceedings of the 1993 Harlaxton Symposium,* ed. by Benjamin Thompson (Stamford: Paul Watkins, 1995), pp. 175–87.

Backhouse, Janet, 'Sir Robert Cotton's Record of a Royal Bookshelf', in *Sir Robert Cotton as a Collector: Essays on an Early Stuart Courtier and his Legacy,* ed. by C.J. Wright (London: British Library, 1997), pp. 230–37.

Backhouse, Janet, *The Illuminated Page: Ten Centuries of Manuscript Painting in the British Library* (London: British Library, 1997).

Backhouse, Janet, 'The Royal Library from Edward IV to Henry VII', in *The Cambridge History of the Book in Britain* (Cambridge: Cambridge University Press, 1987-), III: *1400–1557,* ed. by Lotte Hellinga and J. B. Trapp (1999), pp. 267–73.

Backhouse, Janet, 'Charles of Orléans Illuminated', in *Charles of Orléans in England (1415–1440),* ed. by Mary-Jo Arn (Cambridge, MA: Brewer, 2000), pp. 157–63.

Backhouse, Janet, 'Memorials and Manuscripts of a Yorkist Elite', in *St George's Chapel, Windsor, in the Late Middle Ages,* ed. by Colin Richmond and Eileen Scharff, Historical Monographs relating to St George's Chapel, Windsor Castle, 17 (Windsor: Dean and Canons of Windsor, 2001), pp. 151–60.

Backhouse, Janet, 'The Psalter of Henry VI (London, BL, ms Cotton Dom. A. XVII)', in *The Illuminated Psalter. Studies in the Content, Purpose and Placement of its Images,* edited by Frank O. Büttner (Turnhout: Brepols, 2004), pp. 329–36.

Backhouse, Janet, 'Patronage and Commemoration in the Beaufort Hours', in *Tributes to Lucy Freeman Sandler: Studies in Illuminated Manuscripts,* ed. by Kathryn A. Smith and Carol H. Krinsky (London: Harvey Miller, 2007), pp. 331–44.

Barker, Nicolas, ed., *The York Gospels, a Facsimile* (London: Roxburghe Club, 1986).

Barker, Nicolas, *Treasures of the British Library* (London: British Library, 2005).

Barker-Benfield, B.C., ed., *St Augustine's Abbey, Canterbury,* Corpus of British Medieval Library Catalogues, 13, 3 vols (London: British Library, 2008).

Barnes, Timothy, *Constantine and Eusebius* (Cambridge, MA: Harvard University Press, 1981).

Barron, Caroline, 'Introduction: England and the Low Countries 1327–1477', in *England and the Low Countries in the Late Middle Ages,* ed. by Caroline Barron and Nigel Saul (Stroud: Alan Sutton, 1995), pp. 1–28.

Baxter, Ron, *Bestiaries and their Users in the Middle Ages* (Stroud: Sutton Publishing, 1998).

Bayot, Alphonse, 'La Première Partie de la *Chronique dite de Baudouin d'Avesnes*', *Revue des bibliothèques et archives de Belgique,* 2 (1904), 419–32.

Begent, Peter J., 'The Creation of the Office of Garter King of Arms', *Coat of Arms,* n.s. 11 (1995), 134–40.

Bell, Nicolas, and David Skinner, eds, *Music for King Henry: BL Royal MS 11 E XI: Facsimile, Commentary and Performing Edition,* 2 vols (London: Folio Society, 2009).

Bell, Susan Groag, 'Medieval Women Book Owners: Arbiters of Lay Piety and Ambassadors of Culture', in *Women and Power in the Middle Ages,* ed. by Mary Erler and Maryanne Kowaleski (Athens, GA: University of Georgia Press, 1988), pp. 149–87.

Bennett, Adelaide L., 'Additions to the William of Devon Group', *Art Bulletin,* 54 (1972), 31–40.

Bennett, Michael, 'Isabelle of France, Anglo-French Diplomacy and Cultural Exchange in the Late 1350s', in *The Age of Edward III,* ed. by J.S. Bothwell (York: York Medieval Press, 2001), pp. 215–25.

Berger, Samuel, *La Bible française au Moyen Âge: étude sur les plus anciennes versions de la Bible écrites en prose de langue d'oïl* (Paris: Imprimerie Nationale, 1884).

Biblia de San Luis, facsimile edition, 3 vols (Barcelona: Moleiro, 1999), commentary, ed. by Ramón Gonzálvez Ruiz, 2 vols (Barcelona: Moleiro, 2002–04).

Binski, Paul, *Westminster Abbey and the Plantagenets: Kingship and the Representation of Power 1200–1400* (New Haven, CT: Yale University Press, 1995).

Binski, Paul, 'The *Liber regalis:* Its Date and European Context', in *The Regal Image of Richard II and the Wilton Diptych,* ed. by Dillian Gordon, Lisa Monnas and Caroline Elam (London: Harvey Miller, 1997), pp. 233–43.

Binski, Paul, and Stella Panayotova, eds, *The Cambridge Illuminations: Ten Centuries of Book Production in the Medieval West* (London: Harvey Miller, 2005).

Birrell, T.A., *The Library of John Morris: The Reconstruction of a Seventeenth-century Collection* (London: British Museum, 1976).

Birrell, T.A., *English Monarchs and their Books:*

From Henry VII to Charles II, The Panizzi Lectures 1986 (London: British Library, 1987).

Blamires, Alcuin, and Gail C. Holian, *The Romance of the Rose Illuminated: Manuscripts at the National Library of Wales, Aberystwyth* (Tempe, AZ: Arizona Center for Medieval and Renaissance Studies, 2002).

Blondeau, Chrystèle, 'Imiter le prince?: La Diffusion des *Faits et gestes d'Alexandre* de Vasque de Lucène à la cour de Bourgogne', in *Hofkultur in Frankreich und Europa im Spätmittelalter: La Culture de cour en France et en Europe à la fin du Moyen-Âge*, ed. by Christian Freigang and Jean-Claude Schmitt (Berlin: Akademie, 2005), pp. 185–208.

Bloomer, Martin, W., *Valerius Maximus and the Rhetoric of the New Nobility* (Chapel Hill, NC: University of North Carolina, 1992).

Boase, T.S.R., *English Art 1100–1216*, Oxford History of English Art, 2 (Oxford: Clarendon Press, 1957).

Boeckler, Albert , ed., *Das goldene Evangelienbuch Heinrichs III* (Berlin: Deutscher Verein für Kunstwissenschaft, 1933).

Bond, E.A., 'Notices of the Last Days of Isabella, Queen of Edward II, Drawn from an Account of the Expenses of her Household', *Archaeologia*, 35 (1854), 453–69.

Bond, E.A., 'Description of an Illuminated Latin Psalter, formerly in the Library founded by Archbishop Tenison, in the Parish of St Martin in the Fields, London', *Fine Arts Quarterly Review*, 1 (1863), 77–96.

'Books and Manuscripts', The Royal Collection, <http://www.royalcollection.org.uk/default.asp?action=article&ID=21> [accessed 9 April 2011]

Boone, Rebecca, 'Claude de Seyssel's Translations of Ancient Historians', *Journal of the History of Ideas*, 61 (2000), 561–75.

Boone, Rebecca, *War, Domination, and the Monarchy of France: Claude de Seyssel and the Language of Politics in the Renaissance* (Leiden: Brill, 2007).

Booton, Diane E., *Manuscripts, Market and the Transition to Print in Late Medieval Brittany* (London: Ashgate, 2010)].

Boren, Elizabethanne, 'Young, Patrick (1584–1652),', in *Oxford Dictionary of National Biography* (Oxford: Oxford University Press, 2004), <http://www.oxforddnb.com/view/article/30276> [accessed 9 April 2011].

Bossuat, Robert, 'Traductions françaises des Commentaires de César à la fin du XVe siècle', in *Bibliothèque d'humanisme et renaissance*, 3 (1943), 253–411.

Boulton, Maureen, 'Jean Galopes, traducteur des *Meditationes Vitae Christi*', in *Traduction, dérimation, compilation: La Phraséologie.* Actes du Colloque international, Université McGill, Montréal 2000, ed. by Giuseppe Di Stefano and Rose M. Bidler, Le Moyen Français 51–53 (Montréal: CERES, 2002/03), pp. 91–102.

Bousmanne, Bernard and others, eds, *La Librairie des ducs de Bourgogne. Manuscrits conserves à la Bibliothèque royale de Belgique* (Turnhout: Brepols, 2000-), II: *Textes didactiques*, ed. by Bernard Bousmanne, Frédéric Johan and Céline Van Hoorebeeck (2003).

Bovey, Alixe, 'Didactic Distractions framing the Law: The Smithfield Decretals (London, BL Royal MS 10 E IV)' (unpublished doctoral thesis, Courtauld Institute of Art, London, 2000).

Bovey, Alixe, 'A Pictorial *Ex libris* in the Smithfield Decretals: John Batayle, Canon of St Bartholomew's, and his Illuminated Law Book', in *Decoration and Illustration in Medieval English Manuscripts*, ed. by A.S.G. Edwards, English Manuscript Studies 1100–1700, 10 (London: British Library, 2002), pp. 60–82.

Bovey, Alixe, *The Chaworth Roll: A Fourteenth-century Genealogy of the Kings of England* (London: Sam Fogg, 2005).

Boyle, Andrew, 'Hans Eworth's Portrait of the Earl of Arundel and the Politics of 1549–50', *English Historical Review*, 117 (2002), 25–47.

Bozzolo, Carla, *Manuscrits des traductions françaises d'oeuvres de Boccaccio, XVe siècle*, Medioevo e Umanesimo, 13 (Padua: Antenore, 1973).

Branca, Vittore, ed., *Boccaccio visualizzato: Narrare per parole e per immagini fra Medioevo e Rinascimento*, Biblioteca di Storia dell'arte, 30, 3 vols (Turin: Giulio Einaudi, 1999).

Branner, Robert, 'The Copenhagen *Corpus*', *Konsthistorisk Tidskrift*, 38 (1969), 97–119.

Branner, Robert, 'The Johannes Grusch Atelier and the Continental Origins of the William of Devon Painter', *Art Bulletin*, 54 (1972), 24–30.

Branner, Robert, *Manuscript Painting in Paris during the Reign of Saint Louis: A Study of Styles* (Berkeley, CA: University of California Press, 1977).

Brayer, Édith., and Anne-Françoise Leurquin-Labie, eds, *La Somme le roi par Frère Laurent* (Paris and Abbeville: Société des textes français modernes, F. Paillart, 2008).

Bremmer, Rolf H. jun., 'Morris, John (*d.* 1658)', in *Oxford Dictionary of National Biography* (Oxford University Press, 2004; online edn, Jan 2008) <http://www.oxforddnb.com/view/article/71214> [accessed 13 April 2011].

Brewer, J. S., R.H. Brodie and J. Gairdner, eds, *Letters and Papers, Foreign and Domestic, of the Reign of Henry VIII*, 23 vols (London: HMSO, 1862–1932).

Breitenbach, Edgar, *Speculum humanæ salvationis: Eine typengeschichtliche Untersuchung* (Strasbourg: Heitz, 1930).

Brieger, Peter, *English Art 1216–1307*, Oxford History of English Art, 4 (Oxford: Clarendon Press, 1957).

Brinkmann, Bodo, *Die flämische Buchmalerei am Ende des Burgunderreichs: Der Meister des Dresdener Gebetbuchs und die Miniaturisten seiner Zeit*, 2 vols (Turnhout: Brepols, 1997).

Broekhuijsen, Klara H., *The Masters of the Dark Eyes: Late Medieval Manuscript Painting in Holland* (Turnhout: Brepols, 2009).

Broekhuijsen-Kruijer, Klara H., and A.S. Korteweg, 'Twee boekverluchters uit de Noordelijke Nederlanden in Duitsland. Een Zwarte-ogen-meester, Johannes Ruysch en het Graduale van de abdij Gross St. Martin te Keulen uit het jaar 1500', in *Annus Quadriga Mundi. Opstellen over middeleeuwse kunst opgedragen aan Prof. dr. Anna C. Esmeijer*, ed. by J.B. Bedaux and A.M. Koldeweij (Zutphen: Walburg Pers, 1989), pp. 49–76.

Brooks, Nicholas, *The Early History of the Church of Canterbury: Christ Church from 597 to 1066* (Leicester: Leicester University Press, 1984).

Brown, Andrew J., 'The Date of Erasmus' Latin Translation of the New Testament', *Transactions of the Cambridge Bibliographical Society*, 8 (1984), 351–80.

Brown, Michelle P., *A Guide to Western Historical Scripts from Antiquity to 1600* (London: British Library, 1990).

Brown, Michelle P., 'Sir Robert Cotton, Collector and Connoisseur?', in *Illuminating the Book: Makers and Interpreters. Essays in Honour of Janet Backhouse*, ed. by Michelle P. Brown and Scot McKendrick (London: British Library, 1998), pp. 281–98.

Brown, Michelle P., 'Marvels of the West: Giraldus Cambrensis and the Role of the Author in the Development of Marginal Illustration', in *Decoration and Illustration in Medieval English Manuscripts*, ed. by A.S.G. Edwards, English Manuscript Studies 1100–1700, 10 (London: British Library, 2002), pp. 34–59.

Brown, Michelle P., *The Lindisfarne Gospels: Society, Spirituality and the Scribe* (London: British Library, 2003).

Brown, Michelle P., ed., *In the Beginning. Bibles before the Year 1000* (Washington, DC: Freer Gallery of Art, 2006).

[Brown, T.J., and Margaret Scheele], *The Old Royal Library* (London: British Museum, 1957).

Brown, Virginia, ed. and trans., Giovanni Boccaccio, *Famous Women*, I Tatti Renaissance Library, 1 (Cambridge, MA: Harvard University Press, 2001).

Brun, Laurent, and Mattia Cavagna, 'Pour une édition du *Miroir historial* de Jean de Vignay', *Romania*, 124 (2006), 378–428.

Budny, Mildred O., 'The *Biblia Gregoriana*', in *St Augustine and the Conversion of England*, ed. by R.G. Gameson (Stroud: Sutton, 1999), pp. 237–84.

Budny, Mildred O., and Timothy Graham, 'Dunstan as Hagiographical Subject or Osbern as Author? The Scribal Portrait in an Early Copy of Osbern's Vita Sancti Dunstani', *Gesta*, 32 (1993), 83–98.

Buettner, Brigitte, 'Past Presents: New Year's Gifts at the Valois Courts, ca. 1400', *Art Bulletin*, 83 (2001), 598–625.

Buettner, Brigitte, 'Women and the Circulation of Books', *Journal of the Early Book Society*, 4 (2001), 9–31.

Burgio, Eugenio, 'Ricerche sulla tradizione manoscritta delle vite antico-francesi di Giuda e di Pilato. III: Le Hystoires Apocrifes nella Bible Historiale', *Annali de ca' Foscari*, 37 (1998), 153–213.

Burns, Robert I., ed., *Emperor of Culture: Alfonso X the Learned of Castile and his Thirteenth-century Renaissance* (Philadelphia: University of Pennsylvania Press, 1990).

Büttner, F.O., *The Illuminated Psalter: Studies in the Content, Purpose and Placement of its Images* (Turnhout: Brepols, 2004).

Cahn, Walter, *Romanesque Bible Illumination* (Ithaca, New York: Cornell University Press, 1982).

Cahn, Walter, 'Romanesque Art, Then and Now: A Personal Reminiscence', in *Romanesque: Art and Thought in the Twelfth Century: Essays in Honor of Walter Cahn*, ed. by Colum Hourihane, Index of Christian Art Occasional Papers, 10 (Princeton, NJ: Index of Christian Art, 2008), pp. 31–39.

Camille, Michael, *Master of Death: The Lifeless Art of Pierre Remiet Illuminator* (New Haven, CT: Yale University Press 1996).

Campbell, Lorne, *The Early Flemish Pictures in the Collection of Her Majesty the Queen* (Cambridge: Cambridge: University Press, 1985).

Campbell, Lorne, *The Fifteenth Century Netherlandish Schools* (London: National Gallery, 1998), pp. 374–91.

Cardon, Bert, 'Het *Speculum humanae salvationis* manuscript Harley 2838 in de British Library te Londen, een handschrift omstreeks 1500 in Engeland verlucht door een miniaturist uit de Nederlanden?', in *Miscellanea Neerlandica: Opstellen voor Dr Jan Deschamps ter Gelegenheid van zijn Zeventigste Verjaardag*, ed. by Elly Cockx-Indestege and Frans Hendrickx, 3 vols (Leuven: Peeters, 1987), I, pp. 441–63.

Carey, Hilary M., *Courting Disaster: Astrology at the English Court and University in the Later Middle Ages* (New York: Macmillan, 1992).

Carley, James P., 'The Royal Library as a Source for Sir Robert Cotton's Collection: A Preliminary List of Acquisitions', *British Library Journal*, 18 (1992), 52–73.

Carley, James P., 'Marks in Books and the Libraries of Henry VIII', *Papers of the Bibliographical Society of America*, 91 (1997), 583–606.

Carley, James P., 'The Royal Library under Henry VIII', in *The Cambridge History of the Book in Britain* (Cambridge: Cambridge University Press, 1987-), III: *1400–1557*, ed. by Lotte Hellinga and J.B. Trapp (1999), pp. 274–81.

Carley, James P., ed., *The Libraries of King Henry VIII*, Corpus of British Medieval Library Catalogues, 7 (London: British Library, 2000).

Carley, James P., *The Books of King Henry VIII and his Wives* (London: British Library, 2004).

Carley, James P., *King Henry's Prayer Book: BL Royal MS 2A XVI*, commentary volume (London: Folio Society, 2009).

Carley, James P. and Caroline Brett, ed. and trans. John *Leland, De viris illustribus (On Famous Men)*, Studies and Texts, 172, British Writers of the Middle Ages and the Early Modern Period, 1 (Toronto: Pontifical Institute of Medieval Studies, 2010).

Carley, James and Colin C.G. Tite, 'Thomas Wakefield, Robert Wakefield and the Cotton Genesis', *Transactions of the Cambridge Bibliographical Society*, 12 (2002), 242–65.

Carlson, David R., *English Humanist Books: Writers and Patrons, Manuscript and Print, 1475–1525* (Toronto: University of Toronto Press, 1993).

Carlvant, Kerstin, 'Some Modest Psalters from Thirteenth Century Flanders', *Scriptorium: Revue internationale des études relatives aux manuscrits*, 40 (1986), 88–95.

Carlvant, Kerstin, 'A Brabantine Illuminator of the Mid-thirteenth Century', in *Miscelanea Neerlandica: Opstellen voor Dr Jan Deschamps ter Gelegenheid van zijn Zeventigste Verjaardag*, ed. by Elly Cockx-Indestege and Frank Hendrickx (Leuven: Peeters, 1987), pp. 355–80.

Casley, David, *A Catalogue of the Manuscripts of the King's Library: An Appendix to the Catalogue of the Cottonian Library* (London: [n. pub.], 1734).

Catalogi librorum manuscriptorum Angliae et Hiberniae (Oxford: Sheldonian, '1697', but 1698?).

Catto, Jeremy, 'Andrew Horn: Law and History in Fourteenth-century England', in *The Writing of History in the Middle Ages: Essays presented to Richard William Southern*, ed. by R.H.C. Davis and J.M. Wallace-Hadrill (Oxford: Clarendon Press, 1981), pp. 367–91.

Cavanaugh, Susan H., 'A Study of Books Privately Owned in England, 1300–1450', 2 vols (unpublished doctoral dissertation, University of Pennsylvania, 1980).

Cavanaugh, Susan H., 'Royal Books: King John to Richard II', *Library*, 6th s., 10 (1988), 304–16.

Caxton, William, trans., Jacobus de Voragine, *Legenda aurea sanctorum, sive Lombardica historia* (*The Golden Legend*) (London: William Caxton, 1483).

Chailley, Jacques, 'Études musicales sur la chanson de geste et ses origines', *Revue de musicologie*, 30 (1948), 1–27.

Champion, Pierre, ed., *Charles d'Orléans: Poésies* (Paris: Champion, 1923–27).

Charlton, Edward, 'Roll of Prayers formerly belonging to Henry VIII when Prince', *Archaeologia Aeliana*, n.s. 2 (1858), 41–45.

Chattaway, Carol M., *The Order of the Golden Tree: The Gift-giving Objectives of Duke Philip the Bold of Burgundy* (Turnhout: Brepols, 2006).

Chavannes-Mazel, Claudine A., 'The *Miroir historial* of Jean le Bon: The Leiden Manuscript and its Related Copies' (unpublished doctoral thesis, Leiden University, 1988).

Christianson, C. Paul, *A Directory of London Stationers and Book Artisans* (New York: Bibliographical Society of America, 1990).

Christie's sale catalogue (London: Christie's, 24 June 1987).

Clanchy, Michael, *From Memory to Written Record, England 1066–1307*, 2nd edn (Oxford: Blackwell, 1993).

Clark, Gregory T., 'The Influence of the Limbourg Brothers in France and the Southern Netherlands', in *The Limbourg Brothers: Nijmegen Brothers at the French Court 1400–1416*, ed. by Rob Dückers and Pieter Roelofs (Amsterdam: Ludion, 2005), pp. 209–35.

Clark, Willene B., *A Medieval Book of Beasts: The Second-family Bestiary* (Woodbridge: Boydell, 2006).

Clode, Charles M., *The Early History of the Guild of Merchant Taylors of the Fraternity of St John the Baptist, London, with notices of the lives of some of its eminent members*, 2 vols (London: Harrison, 1888).

Clough, Cecil H., 'Baldassare Castiglione's Presentation Manuscript to King Henry VII', in Cecil H. Clough, *The Duchy of Urbino,* Variorum Collected Studies Series, 129 (London: Variorum, 1981), pp. XV.1–5 (first publ. in *Liverpool Classical Monthly*, 3 (1978), 269–72).

Clough, Cecil H., 'Ubaldini, Petruccio (*fl.* 1545–1599)', in *Oxford Dictionary of National Biography* (Oxford: Oxford University Press, 2004), <http://www.oxforddnb.com/view/article/27970> [accessed 23 May 2011].

Cochran, John, *A Catalogue of Manuscripts in Different Languages* (London: John Cochran, 1829).

Cockshaw, Pierre, Claudine Lemaire and Anne Rouzet, eds, *Charles le Téméraire: exposition organisée à l'occasion du cinquième centenaire de sa mort*, (Brussels: Bibliothèque Royale Albert 1er, 1977).

Colson, Justin, 'Alien Communities and Alien Fraternities in Later Medieval London', *London Journal*, 35 (2010), 111–43.

Condon, Margaret, 'God Save the King! Piety, Propaganda, and the Perpetual Memorial', in *Westminster Abbey: The Lady Chapel of Henry VII*, ed. by Tim Tatton-Brown and Richard Mortimer (Woodbridge: Boydell, 2003), pp. 59–97

Conklin, George, 'Ingeborg of Denmark, Queen of France, 1193–1223', in *Queens and Queenship in Medieval Europe*, ed. by Anne Duggan (Woodbridge: Boydell, 1997), pp. 39–52.

Connolly, Daniel, *The Maps of Matthew Paris: Medieval Journeys through Space, Time and Liturgy* (Woodbridge: Boydell, 2009).

Coopland, G.W. trans., Philippe de Mézières, *Letter to King Richard II: A Plea made in 1395 for Peace between England and France* (Liverpool: Liverpool University Press, 1975).

Cooper, Richard, 'Jean Mallard, poète et peintre rouennais', in *Première poésie française de la Renaissance: Autour des Puys poétiques normands.* Actes du colloque international organisé par le CÉRÉDI (Université de Rouen) 30 septembre –2 octobre 1999, ed. by Jean-Claude Arnould and Thierry Mantovani (Paris: Champion, 2003), pp. 193–213.

Cornwallis, Sir Charles, *The Life and Death of our late most incomparable and Heroique Prince Henry, Prince of Wales* (London: John Benson, 1641), repr. in *A Collection of Scarce and Valuable Tracts*, The Somers Collection of Tracts, ed. by Walter Scott, 13 vols (London: T. Cadell and W. Davies, 1809–1815, repr. New York: AMS Press, 1965), II (1809), pp. 225–52; Early English Books Online, *The life and death of our late most incomparable and heroique prince, Henry Prince of Wales. A prince (for valour and vertue) fit to be imitated in succeeding times. Written by Sir Charles Cornwallis knight, treasurer of his Highnesse household*, p. 101 <http://quod.lib.umich.edu/cgi/t/text/text-idx?c=eebo;idno=A34595.0001.001;rgn=div1;view=text;cc=eebo;node=A34595.0001.001%3A4> [accessed 28 April 2011]

Coron, Sabine and Martine Lefèvre, eds, *Livres en broderie: reliures françaises du Moyen Âge à nos jours*, (Paris: Bibliothèque nationale de France, 1995).

Coulter, Cornelia C., 'The Library of the Angevin Kings at Naples', *Transactions and Proceedings of the American Philological Association*, 75 (1944), 141–55.

Cox, Montagu H. and Philip Norman, eds, *Whitehall Palace: Buildings*, The Survey of London, 13 (London: Joint Publishing Committee, 1930), British History Online, Survey of London, 13 – St Margaret, Westminster, part II: Whitehall I <http://www.british-history.ac.uk/report.aspx?compid=67776> [accessed 28 April 2011].

Dahlberg, Charles, trans., Guillaume de Lorris and Jean de Meun, *The Romance of the Rose*, 3rd edn (Princeton, NJ: Princeton University, 1995).

Daniell, F.H., *Calendar of State Papers Domestic: Charles II, September 1, 1680–December 31, 1681* (London: HMSO, 1921).

Davenport, Cyril, 'Embroidered Bindings of Bibles in the Possession of the British and Foreign Bible Society', *Burlington Magazine*, 4 (1904), 267–80.

Davies, C.S.L., 'Review-Article: Representation, Repute, Reality', *English Historical Review*, 124 (2009), 1432–47.

De Beer, E.S., ed., *The Diary of John Evelyn*, 6 vols (Oxford: Clarendon Press, 1951).

De Hamel, Christopher, *Glossed Books of the Bible and the Origins of the Paris Book Trade* (Woodbridge: Brewer, 1984).

De Hamel, Christopher, *A History of Illuminated Manuscripts* (Oxford: Phaidon, 1986).

[de la Mare, Tilly, and Stanley Gillam], *Duke Humfrey's Library and the Divinity School 1488–1988,* an exhibition at the Bodleian Library June–August 1988 (Oxford: Bodleian Library, 1988).

[de la Mare, Tilly, and Richard Hunt], *Duke Humfrey and English Humanism in the Fifteenth Century: Catalogue of an Exhibition held in the Bodleian Library, Oxford* (Oxford: Bodleian Library, 1970).

de Laborde, Alexandre, *Les Manuscrits à peintures de la* Cité de Dieu *de Saint Augustin* (Paris: Société des bibliophiles français, 1909).

de Laborde, Alexandre, *La Bible moralisée conservée à Oxford, Paris et Londres: Reproduction intégrale du manuscrit du XIIIe siècle*, 5 vols (Paris: Société française de reproductions de manuscrits à peintures, 1911–27).

de Laborderie, Olivier, "Ligne de reis': Culture historique, représentation du pouvoir royal et construction de la mémoire nationale en Angleterre à travers les généalogies royales en rouleau du milieu du XIIIe siècle au début du XVe siècle' (unpublished doctoral thesis, École des hautes études en sciences sociales, Paris, 2002).

de Laborderie, Olivier, 'La Mémoire des origines Normandes des rois d'Angleterre dans les généalogies en rouleau des XIIIe et XIVe siècles', in *La Normandie et l'Angleterre au Moyen Âge, Colloque de Crécy-la-Salle (4–7 octobre 2001)*, ed. by Pierre Bouzet and Véronique Gazeau (Caen: Publications du CRAHM, 2003), pp. 211–36.

de Laborderie, Olivier, 'A New Pattern for English History: The First Genealogical Rolls of the Kings of England', in *Broken Lines: Genealogical Literature in Britain and France,* ed. by Raluca L. Radulescu and Edward D. Kennedy, Medieval Texts and Cultures of Northern Europe, 16 (Turnhout: Brepols, 2008), pp. 45–61.

de Lettenhove, Baron Joseph Kervyn, *Oeuvres de Froissart*, 29 vols (Brussels: Devaux, 1867–77).

de Meijer, A. 'John Capgrave, O.E.S.A.', *Augustiniana*, 7 (1957), 118–48, 531–75.

de Poerck, Guy, 'Introduction à la Fleur des histoires de Jean Mansel (XVe siècle)', *Annales du Cercle archéologique de Mons*, 54 (1935), 6–101.

De Ricci, Seymour, *English Collectors of Books and Manuscripts (1530–1930) and their Marks of Ownership*, Sandars Lectures 1929–30 (Cambridge: Cambridge University Press, 1930).

de Winter, Patrick, *La Bibliothèque de Philippe le hardi, duc de Bourgogne (1364–1404): étude sur les manuscrits à peintures d'une collection princière à l'époque du 'style gothique international'* (Paris: CNRS, 1985).

Deam, Lisa, 'Mapping the Past: The 'Fleur des histoires' (Brussels, Bibliothèque royale, ms 9231–9232) in the Context of Fifteenth-century Burgundian Historiography' (unpublished doctoral thesis, University of Chicago, 2001).

Dean, Ruth J., and Maureen B.M. Boulton, *Anglo-Norman Literature: A Guide to Texts and Manuscripts*, Anglo-Norman Text Society, Occasional Publications Series, 3 (London, 1999).

Delcourt, Thierry, ed., *La Légende du Roi Arthur* (Paris: Bibliothèque nationale de France, 2009).

Delisle, Léopold, *Le Cabinet des manuscrits de la Bibliothèque impériale* [nationale]: *Étude sur la formation de ce dépôt, comprenant les éléments d'une histoire de la calligraphie, de la miniature, de la reliure, et du commerce des livres à Paris avant l'invention de l'imprimerie*, 3 vols (Paris: Imprimerie nationale, 1868–71).

Delisle, Léopold, 'Notes sur quelques manuscrits du Musée Britannique', *Mémoires de la Société de l'histoire de Paris et de l'Ile de France*, 4 (1878), 183–238.

Delisle, Léopold, 'Durand de Champagne, franciscain', in *Histoire littéraire de la France*, 30 (1888), 302–33.

Delisle, Léopold, 'Notice sur un psautier du XIIIe siècle appartenant au comte de Crawford', *Bibliothèque de l'École des Chartes*, 58 (1897), 381–93.

Delisle, Léopold, *Recherches sur la librairie de Charles V*, 2 vols (Paris: H. Champion, 1907).

Delisle, Léopold, and P. Meyer, *L'Apocalypse en français au XIIIe siècle (Bibl. Nat. Fr. 403)* (Paris: Firmin Didot, 1901).

Dennison, Lynda, 'An Illuminator of the Queen Mary Psalter Group: The Ancient 6 Master', *Antiquaries Journal*, 66 (1986), 287–314.

Dennison, Lynda, 'The Stylistic Sources, Dating and Development of the Bohun Workshop' (unpublished doctoral thesis, University of London, 1988).

Dennison, Lynda, '"Liber Horn", "Liber Custumarum" and Other Manuscripts of the Queen Mary Psalter Workshops', in *Medieval Art, Architecture and Archaeology in London,* ed. by Lindy Grant, British Archaeological Association Conference Transactions for the Year 1984 (Leeds, Manley and Son, 1990), pp. 118–32.

Dennison, Lynda, 'The Apocalypse, British Library, Royal Ms. 19 B XV: A Reassessment of its Artistic Context in Early Fourteenth-century English Manuscript Illumination', *British Library Journal*, 20 (1994), 35–54.

Dennison, Lynda, 'British Library, Egerton MS 3277: A Fourteenth-century Psalter-Hours and the Question of Bohun Family Ownership', in *Family and Dynasty in Late Medieval England*, ed. by Richard Eales and Shaun Tyas, Harlaxton Medieval Studies, n.s. 9 (Donington: Shaun Tyas/Paul Watkins Publishing,, 2003), pp. 122–55.

Deshman, R., 'The Galba Psalter: Pictures, Texts and Contexts in an Early Medieval Prayer-book', *Anglo-Saxon England*, 26 (1997), 109–38.

Deuchler, Florens, *Der Ingeborgpsalter* (Berlin: de Gruyter, 1967).

Deutsch, Guy N., *Iconographie de l'illustration de Flavius Josèphe au temps de Jean Fouquet*, Arbeiten zur Literatur und Geschichte des hellenistischen Judentums, 12 (Leiden: Brill, 1986).

Dewick, E.S., *The Coronation Book of Charles V of France (Cotton Ms. Tiberius B.VIII),* Henry Bradshaw Society, 16 (London: Harrison and Sons, 1899).

DIAMM, *The Digital Image Archive of Medieval Music*: images of the complete manuscripts Royal 8 G. vii and Royal 11 E. xi <www.diamm.ac.uk> [accessed 9 April 2011].

Diebold, William, 'The Ruler Portrait of Charles the Bald in the S. Paolo Bible', *Art Bulletin*, 76 (1994), 6–18.

Dillon, Viscount, and W.H. St John Hope, 'Inventory of the Goods and Chattels belonging to Thomas, Duke of Gloucester, and Seized in his Castle at Pleshy, co. Essex, 21 Rich. II (1397); with their Values, as shown in the Escheator's Accounts', *Archaeological Journal*, 54 (1897), 275–308.

Dionisotti, A.C., 'Claude de Seyssel', in *Ancient History and the Antiquarian: Essays in Memory of Arnaldo Momigliano*, ed. by M.H. Crawford and C.R. Ligota (London: Warburg Institute, 1995), pp. 73–103.

Dodwell, C.R., *The Pictorial Arts of the West 800–1200* (New Haven, CT: Yale University Press, 1993).

Doran, Susan, ed. *Henry VIII, Man and Monarch* (London: British Library, 2009).

Dowling, Maria, *Humanism in the Age of Henry VIII* (London: Croom Helm, 1986).

Dubuc, B. Doris, 'Le Chemin de vaillance: mise à point sur la date de composition et la vie de l'auteur', in *Medieval Codicology, Iconography, Literature, and Translation: Studies for Keith Val Sinclair,* ed. by R. Rolfe Monks and D.D.R. Owen (Leiden: Brill, 1994), pp. 276–83.

Dubois, Anne, 'De Rouen vers les Pays-Bas bourguignons: Le Manuscrit 9078 de la Bibliothèque royale de Belgique', *In Monte Artium: Journal of the Royal Library of Belgium*, 2 (2009), 87–104.

Dumitrescu, Theodor, *The Early Tudor Court and International Musical Relations* (Aldershot: Ashgate, 2007), pp. 117–47.

Dumville, D.N., *English Caroline Script and Monastic History: Studies in Benedictinism, A.D. 950–1030*, Studies in Anglo-Saxon History, 6 (Woodbridge: Boydell, 1993).

Duncan, Thomas G., 'Review of John Stevens, *Words and Music in the Middle Ages: Song, Narrative, Dance and Drama, 1050–1350* (Cambridge: Cambridge University Press, 1986)', *Review of English Studies*, n.s. 39, 156 (1988), 531–33.

Durrieu, Paul, *La Miniature flamande au temps de la cour de Bourgogne (1415–1530)* (Paris: G. van Oest, 1921).

Dutschke, Consuelo W., 'The Truth in the Book: The Marco Polo Texts in Royal 19.D.I and Bodley 264', *Scriptorium: Revue internationale des études relatives aux manuscrits*, 52 (1998), 278–99.

Eberle, Patricia J., 'Richard II and the Literary Arts', in *Richard II: The Art of Kingship*, ed. by Anthony Goodman and James Gillespie (Oxford: Clarendon Press, 1999), pp. 231–53.

Edwards, A.S.G., ed., *Life of Saint Edmund, King and Martyr: A Facsimile,* (London: Folio Society, 2004).

Egbert, Donald Drew, 'The so-called "Greenfield" *La Lumiere as lais* and *Apocalypse*', British Museum, Royal MS. 15 d II', *Speculum: A Journal of Medieval Studies*, 11 (1936), 446–52.

Egbert, Donald Drew, *The Tickhill Psalter and Related Manuscripts: A School of Manuscript*

Illumination in England during the Early Fourteenth Century (New York: New York Public Library, 1940).
Eichberg, Barbara Bruderer, 'Die theologisch-politische Bedeutung des Allerheiligenbildes im panegyrischen Lobgedicht an Robert von Neapel: Ein Beitrag zur spätmittelalterlichen Herrscherikonographie', *Concilium medii aevi*, 2 (1999), 29–57.
Eichberger, Dagmar, ed., *Women of Distinction: Margaret of York and Margaret of Austria* (Leuven: Davidsfonds, 2005).
Eisenberg, Peter, *Itinerarium Galliae et Angliae* (Leipzig: Grosse, 1614).
Elliott, Janis, and Cordelia Warr, eds, *The Church of Santa Maria Donna Regina: Art, Iconography and Patronage in Fourteenth-century Naples* (Aldershot: Ashgate, 2004).
[Ellis, Henry and Francis Douce], *A Catalogue of the Lansdowne Manuscripts in the British Museum* (London: British Museum, 1819).
Escobedo, Libby Karlinger, '"To the Illustrious Lord Edward:" A Re-evaluation of Audience and Patronage in the Milemete Treatise and the Companion *Secretum Secretorum*', *Manuscripta*, 50 (2006), 1–19.
Evans, Mark, ed., *The Lumley Inventory and Pedigree. Art Collecting in the Elizabethan Age* (London: The Roxburghe Club, 2010).
Exposition de reliures, 2 vols (Brussels: Bibliothèque Royale de Belgique, 1931), II: *Du XVII siècle à la fin du XIXe*.

Faraci, Dora, *Il bestiario medio inglese (Ms Arundel 292 della British Library)* (Rome: Japadre, 1990).
Farnham, Willard, 'England's Discovery of the Decameron', *Proceedings of the Medieval Language Association*, 39 (1924), 123–39.
Les Fastes du Gothique: Le Siècle de Charles V, Galeries nationales du Grand Palais, 9 octobre 1981–1er février 1982 (Paris: Réunion des musées nationaux, 1981).
Faucon, Maurice, *La Librairie des papes d'Avignon: sa formation, sa composition, ses catalogues (1316–1420) d'après les registres de comptes et d'inventaires des archives vaticanes*, 2 vols (Paris: E. Thorin, 1886–87).
Ferdinand, C.Y., 'Library Administration (*c.* 1475 to 1640)', in *The Cambridge History of Libraries in Britain and Ireland*, ed. by Elisabeth Leedham-Green and Teresa Webber, 3 vols (Cambridge: Cambridge University Press, 2006), I: *To 1640.*, pp. 565–91.
Féry-Hue, Françoise, 'Le Régime du corps d'Aldebrandin de Sienne: Tradition manuscrite et diffusion', in *Santé, médecine et assistance au Moyen Âge: Actes du 110e Congrès national des sociétés savantes, Montpellier, 1985,* Section d histoire médiévale et de philologie, 1 (Paris: Comité des travaux historique et scientifiques, 1987), pp. 113–34.
Field, Sean L., 'Marie of Saint-Pol and her Books', *English Historical Review*, 125 (2010), 255–78.
Fisher, Celia, *The Medieval Flower Book* (London: British Library, 2007).
Flutre, Louis-Fernand, *Les Manuscrits des 'Faits des Romains'* (Paris: Hachette, 1932).
Focillon, Henri, *Le Peintre des Miracles Notre-Dame* (Paris: Paul Hartmann, 1950).
Foot, Mirjam M., 'Mearne, Samuel (1624–1683)', in *Oxford Dictionary of National Biography* (Oxford: Oxford University Press, 2004, online edition, January 2008) <http://www.oxforddnb.com/view/article/52143> [accessed 13 April 2011]
Foulet, Alfred, 'The Chronicle of Baldwin of Avesnes', *Record of the Museum of Historic Art, Princeton University*, 5 (1946), 3–5.
Fresno, Karen, 'Christine de Pizan's *Livre des fais d'armes et de chivalerie* and the Coherence of Brit. Lib. MS Royal 15 E. vi', in *Collections in Context: The Organization of Knowledge and Community in Europe (14th–17th Centuries)*, ed. by Karen Fresno and Anne D. Hedeman (Columbus, OH: Ohio State University Press, 2011), pp. 225–66.
Frugoni, Arsenio, 'Studi su Convenevole da Prato, maestro di Petrarca', *Bullettino dell'Istituto storico italiano per il Medio Evo e archivio muratoriano*, 81 (1969), 1–32.
Furdell, Elizabeth Lane, 'Jenyns, Sir Stephen (*c.* 1450–1523)', in *Oxford Dictionary of National Biography* (Oxford: Oxford University Press, 2004; online edition, Jan 2008) <http://www.oxforddnb.com/view/article/14767>[accessed 9 April 2011].

Gallarati, Silvia Buzzetti, 'Nota bibliografica sulla tradizione manoscritta del *Testament* di Jean de Meun', *Revue romane*, 13 (1978), 2–35.
Gamble, Harry, *Books and Readers in the Early Church: A History of Early Christian Texts* (New Haven, CT: Yale University Press, 1995).
Gameson, Richard G., 'The Royal 1 B. vii Gospels and English Book Production in the Seventh and Eighth Centuries', *The Early Medieval Bible: Its Production, Decoration and Use*, ed. by R.G. Gameson (Cambridge: Cambridge University Press, 1994), pp. 24–52.
Gameson, Richard G., 'The Colophon of the Eadwig Gospels', *Anglo-Saxon England*, 31 (2002), 201–22.
Gameson, Richard G., *The Earliest Books of Canterbury Cathedral: Manuscripts and Fragments to* c. *1200* (London and Canterbury: Bibliographical Society, British Library, Canterbury Cathedral, 2008).
Gameson, Richard G., *Manuscript Treasures of Durham Cathedral* (London: Third Millennium, 2010).
Gatch, Milton McC., 'John Bagford, Bookseller and Antiquary', *British Library Journal*, 12 (1986), 150–71).
Gathercole, Patricia M., 'A Frenchman's Praise of Boccaccio', *Italica*, 40 (1963), 225–30.
Gautier, Marc-Edouard, ed., *Splendeur de l'enluminure: Le roi René et les livres* (Angers: Ville d'Angers, 2009).
Gerchow, J., 'Prayers for King Cnut: The Liturgical Commemoration of a Conqueror', in *England in the Eleventh Century*, ed. by C. Hicks, Harlaxton Medieval Studies, 2 (Stamford: Paul Watkins, 1992), pp. 219–38.
Gibaud, Henri, *Un inédit d'Erasme: La première version du Nouveau Testament copiée par Pierre Meghen, 1506–1509: Contribution à l'établissement d'une édition critique du Novum Testamentum* (Angers: Moreana, 1982).
Gibson, Margaret T., *The Bible in the Latin West*, The Medieval Book, 1 (Notre Dame: University Press, 1993).
Gilson, Julius P, 'Introduction', in George F. Warner and Julius P. Gilson, *Catalogue of Western Manuscripts in the Old Royal and King's Collections*, 4 vols (London: British Museum, 1921), I, pp. xi–xxxii.
Glunz, H.H., *History of the Vulgate in England from Alcuin to Roger Bacon* (Cambridge: Cambridge University Press, 1933).
Gneuss, Helmut, 'Origin and Provenance of Anglo-Saxon Manuscripts: The Case of Cotton Tiberius A. III', in *Of the Making of Books: Medieval Manuscripts, their Scribes and Readers. Essays Presented to M.B. Parkes*, ed. by P.R. Robinson and R. Zim (Aldershot: Ashgate, 1997), pp. 13–48.
Gneuss, Helmut, *Handlist of Anglo-Saxon Manuscripts: A List of Manuscripts and Manuscript Fragments Written or Owned in England up to 1100*, Medieval and Renaissance Texts and Studies, 241 (Tempe, AZ: Arizona Center for Medieval and Renaissance Studies, 2001).
Goldfinch, John, 'Appendix II: Some Contemporary Sources for the Early History of the British Museum's Printed Collections', in *Libraries within the Library: The Origins of the British Library's Printed Collections*, ed. by Giles Mandelbrote and Barry Taylor (London: British Library, 2009), 424–28.
Gooch, Leo, *A Complete Patter of Nobility: John Lord Lumley (c. 1534–1609)* (Rainton Bridge: University of Sunderland Press, 2009).
Goodall, John A., 'Heraldry in the Decoration of English Medieval Manuscripts', *Antiquaries Journal*, 77 (1997), 179–220.
Gough, Henry, ed., *The Register of the Fraternity or Guild of the Holy and Undivided Trinity and Blessed Virgin Mary in the Parish of Luton* (London: Chiswick Press, 1906).
Gough, Richard, *An Account of a Richly Illuminated Missal Executed for John Duke of Bedford, Regent of France under Henry VI, and afterwards in the Possession of the Late Duchess of Portland* (London, 1794).
Goyau, Georges. 'Jacques-Auguste de Thou', *The Catholic Encyclopedia.* 18 vols (New York: Robert Appleton Company, 1912), XIV (1907–22) <http://www.newadvent.org/cathen/14706d.htm> [accessed 11 April 2011].
Grafton, Anthony, and Joanna Weinberg, 'Isaac Casaubon's Library of Hebrew Books', in *Libraries within the Library: The Origins of the British Library's Printed Collections*, ed. by Giles Mandelbrote and Barry Taylor (London: British Library, 2009), pp. 24–42.
Grasser, Johann Jacob, *Newe und volkom[m]ne Frantzösische und Englische Schatzkammer* (Basel: Waldkirch, 1610).
Grassi, Cesare, trans., *Regia carmina: dedicati a Roberto d'Angiò, re di Sicilia e di Gerusalemme* (Prato: Gruppo Bibliofili Pratesa, 1982).
Green Mary Anne Everett, ed., *Calendar of State Papers, Domestic Series, 1606–1610* (London: HMSO, 1857).
Green Mary Anne Everett, ed., *Calendar of State Papers, Domestic Series, 1649–1660*, 13 vols (London: HMSO, 1875–1886).
Green, R.F., 'King Richard II's Books Revisited', *The Library*, 31 (1976), 235–39.
Guenée, Bernard, 'La Culture historique des nobles: Le succès des "Faits des Romains" (XIIIe–XVI siècles)', in *La Noblesse au Moyen Âge (XIe–XVe siècles): Essais à la mémoire de Robert Boutruche*, ed. by Philippe Contamine (Paris: Presses universitaires de France, 1976), pp. 261–88.
Guiffrey, Jules, *Inventaires de Jean duc de Berry (1401–1416)*, 2 vols (Paris: Leroux, 1894–96).
Gumbert, J.P. *The Dutch and their Books in the Manuscript Age*, The Panizzi Lectures, 1989 (London: British Library, 1990).
Gundersheimer, Werner L., *The Life and Works of Louis le Roy* (Geneva: Librairie Droz, 1966).
Gwynne, Paul, 'The Frontispiece to an Illuminated Panegyric on Henry VII: A Note on the Sources', *Journal of the Warburg and Courtauld Institutes*, 55 (1992), 266–70.

Hamel, Mary, 'Arthurian Romance in Fifteenth-century Lindsey: The Books of the Lords Welles', *Modern Language Quarterly*, 51 (1990), 341–61.
Hamer, Richard, 'From Vignay's *Légende dorée* to the Earliest Printed Editions', *Le Moyen Français*, 32 (1993), 71–81.
Hamer, Richard, and V. Russell, 'A Critical Edition of Four Chapters from the Légende dorée', *Mediaeval Studies*, 51 (1989), 130–204.
Hanna, Ralph, *A Descriptive Catalogue of the Medieval Manuscripts in Roman Scripts of Christ Church, Oxford* <http://www.chch.ox.ac.uk/library/western-manuscripts> [accessed 17 April 2011]
Hans-Collas, Ilona, and Pascal Schandel, *Manuscrits enluminés des anciens Pays-Bas méridionaux* (Paris: Bibliothèque nationale de France, 2009-), I: *Manuscrits de Louis de Bruges.*
Harris, Kate, 'The Patron of British Library MS Arundel 38', *Notes and Queries*, n.s. 31 (1984), 462–63.
Harris, Kate, 'Patrons, Buyers and Owners: The Evidence for Ownership and the Rôle of Book Owners in Book Production and the Book Trade', in *Book Production and Publishing in Britain, 1375–1475*, ed. by Jeremy Griffiths and Derek Pearsall (Cambridge: Cambridge University Press, 1989), pp. 163–99.
Harris, P.R., *A History of the British Museum Library 1753–1973* (London: British Library 1998).
Harris, P.R., 'The First Century of the British Museum Library', in *The Cambridge History of Libraries in Britain and Ireland*, ed. by Giles Mandelbrote and K.A. Manley, 3 vols (Cambridge: Cambridge University Press, 2006), II: *1640–1850*, pp. 405–21.
Harriss, G.L., 'Henry V's Books', in K.B. McFarlane, *Lancastrian Kings and Lollard Knights* (Oxford: Clarendon Press, 1972), pp. 233–38.
Haseloff, Günther, *Die Psalterillustration im 13. Jahrhundert: Studien zur Geschichte der Buchmalerei in England, Frankreich und den Niederlanden* ([n.p.]:[n. pub.], 1938).
Haussherr, Rainer, *Bible moralisée: Faksimile-Ausgabe im Originalformat des Codex Vindobonensis 2554 der Österreichischen Nationalbibliothek*, facsimile and commentary, 2 vols, Codices Selecti, 40–40* (Graz: Adeva, 1973).
Haussherr, Reiner, *Bible moralisée: Prachthandschriften des Hohen Mittelalters* (Petersberg: Michael Imhof, 2009).
Hedeman, Anne D., *The Royal Image: Illustrations of the Grandes Chroniques de France, 1274–1422* (Berkeley, CA: University of California Press, 1991).
Hedeman, Anne D., *Translating the Past: Laurent de Premierfait and Boccaccio's De casibus* (Los Angeles: J. Paul Getty Museum, 2008).
Hedeman, Anne D., 'Collecting Images: The Role of the Visual in the Shrewsbury Talbot Book (Royal 15 E. vi)', in *Collections in Context: The Organization of Knowledge and Community in Europe (14th–17th Centuries)*, ed. by Karen Fresno and Anne D. Hedeman (Columbus, OH: Ohio State University Press, 2011), pp. 139–67.
Hellinga, Lotte, *William Caxton and Early Printing in England* (London: British Library, 2010).
Henderson, George, and T.A. Heslop, 'Decoration and Illustration', in *The Eadwine Psalter: Text, Image, and Monastic Culture in Twelfth-century Canterbury*, ed. by Margaret Gibson, T.A. Heslop and Richard W. Pfaff, Modern Humanities Research Association, 14 (London: The Modern Humanities Research Association, 1992), pp. 25–61.
Henderson, Virginia K., 'Retrieving the "Crown in the Hawthorn Bush": The Origins of the Badges of Henry VII', in *Traditions and Transformations in Late Medieval England*, ed. by Douglas Biggs, Sharon D. Michalove and A. Compton Reeves (Leiden: Brill, 2002), pp. 237–59.
Heslop, T.A., 'The Production of *de luxe* Manuscripts and the Patronage of King Cnut and Queen Emma', *Anglo-Saxon England*, 19 (1990), 151–95.
Higgitt, John, *The Murthly Hours: Devotion, Literacy and Luxury in Paris, England and the Gaelic West* (London: British Library, 2000).
Hingeston, Francis Charles, ed., *Johannis Capgrave, Liber de Illustribus Henricis,* (Rolls Series, 7) (London: Longman, Brown, Green, Longmans and Roberts, 1858).
Hingeston, Francis Charles, trans., John

Capgrave *Book of the Illustrious Henries* (London: Longman, Brown, Green, Longmans and Roberts, 1858).
Histoire des bibliothèques françaises, 4 vols (Paris: Promodis-Éditions du Cercle de la librairie,1989–92), I : *Les Bibliothèques Médiévales du Vie siècle à 1530*, ed. by André Vernet.
Hochner, Nicole, *Louis XII : Les Dérèglements de l'image royale, 1498–1515* (Paris: Champ Vallon, 2006).
Hoffmann, Hartmut, *Buchkunst und Königtum im ottonischen und frühsalischen Reich*, 2 vols, Schriften der Monumenta Germaniae Historica, 30 (Stuttgart: Anton Hiersemann, 1986).
Hoffmann, Konrad, ed., *The Year 1200: A Centennial Exhibition at the Metropolitan Museum of Art*, 12 February to 10 May 1970 (New York: Metropolitan Museum of Art, 1970).
Hofmann, Mara, *Jean Poyer: Das Gesamtwerk* (Turnhout: Brepols, 2004).
Holbrook, Sue Ellen, 'The Properties of Things and Textual Power: Illustrating the French Translation of *De proprietatibus rerum* and a Latin Precursor', *Patrons, Authors and Workshops: Books and Book Production in Paris around 1400*, ed. by Godfried Croenen and Peter Ainsworth (Leuven: Peeters, 2006), pp. 367–403.
Holladay, Joan A., 'Fourteenth-century French Queens as Collectors and Readers of Books: Jeanne d'Evreux and her Contemporaries', *Journal of Medieval History*, 32 (2006), 69–100.
Hughes, Jonathan, *Arthurian Myths and Alchemy: The Kingship of Edward IV* (Stroud: Sutton Publishing, 2002).
Hunt, R.W., 'The Library of the Abbey of St Albans', in *Medieval Scribes, Manuscripts and Libraries: Essays presented to N.R. Ker*, ed. by M.B. Parkes and Andrew G. Watson (London: Scolar Press, 1978), pp. 251–78.
Hutchinson, G. Evelyn, 'Attitudes toward Nature in Medieval England: The Alphonso and Bird Psalters', *Isis*, 65 (1974), 5–37.
Hutton, Ronald, *Charles the Second: King of England, Scotland, and Ireland* (Oxford: Clarendon Press, 1989).

Jackson, Deirdre E., 'Saint and Simulacra: Images of the Virgin in the *Cantigas de Santa Maria* of Alfonso X of Castile (1252–1284)' (unpublished doctoral thesis, Courtauld Institute of Art, London, 2002).
Jackson, Richard A., 'The "Traité du Sacre" of Jean Golein', *Proceedings of the American Philosophical Society*, 113 (1969), 305–24.
Jackson, Richard A., *Vive le roi!: A History of the French Coronation from Charles V to Charles X* (Chapel Hill, NC: University of North Carolina Press, 1984).
Jackson, Richard A., *Ordines Coronationis Franciae: Texts and Ordines for the Coronation of Frankish and French Kings and Queens in the Middle Ages*, 2 vols (Philadelphia: University of Pennsylvania Press, 2001).
James, M.R., *The Ancient Libraries of Canterbury and Dover* (Cambridge: Cambridge University Press, 1903).
James, M.R., *The Trinity Apocalypse* (Oxford: Roxburghe Club, 1909).
James, M.R., *Walter of Milemete's Treatise De nobilitatibus sapientibus et prudenciis regum* (Oxford: Roxburghe Club, 1913).
James, M.R., *A Descriptive Catalogue of the Latin Manuscripts in the John Rylands Library at Manchester* (Manchester: Manchester University Press, 1921).
James, M.R., *The Apocalypse in Art* (London: British Academy, 1931).
James, M.R., *The Romance of Alexander. A Collotype Facsimile of MS Bodley 264* (Oxford: Clarendon Press, 1933).
Jayne, Sears, and Francis R. Johnson, eds, *The Lumley Library: The Catalogue of 1609* (London: British Museum, 1956).
Jemolo, Viviana and Mirella Morelli, eds, *La Bibbia di S. Paolo fuori le mura* (Rome: De Luca, 1981).
Jervis, Simon, 'The English Country House Library', in Nicolas Barker, *Treasures from the Libraries of National Trust Country Houses* (New York: Royal Oak Foundation, 1999), pp. 12–33.
Jones, Michael, 'Entre la France et l'Angleterre: Jeanne de Navarre, duchesse de Bretagne et reine d'Angleterre (1368–1437)', in *Autour de Marguerite d'Écosse: Reines, princesses et dames du XVe siècle. Actes du colloque de Thouars (23 et 24 mai 1997)*, ed. by Geneviève and Philippe Contamine (Paris: Honoré Champion, 1999), pp. 45–72.
Jones, Michael K., and Malcolm G. Underwood, *The King's Mother: Lady Margaret Beaufort, Countess of Richmond and Derby* (Cambridge: Cambridge University Press, 1992).
Jung, Marc-René, *La Légende de Troie en France au Moyen Âge: Analyse des versions françaises et bibliographie raisonnée des manuscrits*, Romanica Helvetica, 114 (Basel: Francke, 1996).

Karkov, C.E., *The Ruler Portraits of Anglo-Saxon England*, Anglo-Saxon Studies, 3 (Woodbridge: Boydell, 2004).
Karrow, Robert W., Jr, *Mapmakers of the Sixteenth Century and their Maps: Bio-bibliographies of the Cartographers of Abraham Ortelius, 1570* (Chicago: Speculum Orbis, 1993).
Kauffmann, Martin, 'The Image of St Louis', in *Kings and Kingship*, ed. by Anne Duggan (London: King's College, 1993), pp. 265–86.
Kauffmann, C.M., *Romanesque Manuscripts 1066–1190*, Survey of Manuscripts Illuminated in the British Isles, 3 (London: Harvey Miller, 1975).
Kauffmann, C.M., 'British Library, Lansdowne Ms. 383: The Shaftesbury Psalter?', in *New Offerings, Ancient Treasures: Studies in Medieval Art for George Henderson*, ed. by Paul Binski and William Noel (Stroud: Sutton, 2001), pp. 256–79.
Kauffmann, C.M., *Biblical Imagery in Medieval England 700–1500* (London: Harvey Miller, 2003).
Keane, Marguerite, 'Most Beautiful and Next Best: Value in the Collection of a Medieval Queen', *Journal of Medieval History*, 34 (2008), 360–73.
Keen, Maurice, 'The Wilton Diptych and the Case for a Crusading Context', in *The Regal Image of Richard II and the Wilton Diptych*, ed. by Dillian Gordon, Lisa Monnas and Caroline Elam (London: Harvey Miller, 1997), pp. 189–96.
Kekewich, Margaret, 'Edward IV, William Caxton, and Literary Patronage in Yorkist England', *Modern Language Review*, 66 (1971), 481–87.
Kellman, Herbert, ed., *London, British Library, Ms Royal 8 G.vii*, Renaissance Music in Facsimile, 9 (New York: Garland, 1987).
Kellman, Herbert, ed., *The Treasury of Petrus Alamire: Music and Art in Flemish Court Manuscripts, 1500–1535* (Ghent: Ludion, 1999)
Kelly, Samantha, *The New Solomon: Robert of Naples (1309–1343) and Fourteenth-century Kingship* (Leiden: Brill, 2003).
Ker, N.R., *Catalogue of Manuscripts containing Anglo-Saxon* (Oxford: Oxford University Press, 1957).
Ker, N.R., ed., *Medieval Libraries of Great Britain: A List of Surviving Books*, 2nd edn, Royal Historical Society Guides and Handbooks, 3 (London: Royal Historical Society, 1964).
Ker, N.R., 'The Migration of Manuscripts from the English Medieval Libraries', in N.R. Ker, *Books, Collectors, and Libraries: Studies in the Medieval Heritage*, ed. by Andrew G. Watson (London: Hambledon, 1985), pp. 459–69.
Ker, N.R., 'Liber custumarum, and other Manuscripts formerly at the Guildhall', in N.R. Ker, *Books, Collectors and Libraries: Studies in the Medieval Heritage*, ed. by Andrew G. Watson (London: Hambledon Press, 1985), pp. 135–42 (first pub. in *Guildhall Miscellany*, 1 (1952–59), 37–45).
Kessler, Herbert L., *The Illustrated Bibles from Tours*, Studies in Manuscript Illumination, 7 (Princeton, NJ: Princeton University Press, 1977).
Kessler, Herbert L., 'Memory and Models: The Interplay of Patterns and Practice in the Mosaics of San Marco in Venice', in *Medioevo: Immagine e Memoria, Atti del Convegno internazionale di studi, Parma, 23–28 settembre 2008*, ed. by A.C. Quintavalle (Milan: Electa, 2009), pp. 463–75.
Keynes, Simon D., 'King Athelstan's Books', in *Learning and Literature in Anglo-Saxon England: Studies presented to Peter Clemoes on the Occasion of his Sixty-fifth Birthday*, ed. by Michael Lapidge and Helmut Gneuss (Cambridge: Cambridge University Press, 1985), pp. 143–201.
Keynes, Simon D., ed., *The Liber Vitae of the New Minster and Hyde Abbey, Winchester*, Early English Manuscripts in Facsimile, 26 (Copenhagen: Rosenkilde and Bagger, 1996).
Keynes, Simon D., 'The Power of the Written Word: Alfredian England 871–899', in *Alfred the Great. Papers from the Eleventh-centenary Conference*, ed. by T. Reuter (Aldershot: Ashgate, 2003), pp. 175–97.
Keynes, S and M. Lapidge, trans., *Alfred the Great: Asser's Life and Other Contemporary Sources*, (Harmondsworth: Penguin, 1983).
Kipling, Gordon, *The Triumph of Honour: Burgundian Origins of the Elizabethan Renaissance* (The Hague: Leiden University Press, 1977).
Kipling, Gordon, ed., *The Receyt of the Ladie Kateryne*, Early English Text Society, 296 (Oxford: Oxford University Press, 1990).
Klingshirn, William E., and Linda Safran, *The Early Christian Book* (Washington, DC: Catholic University of America Press, 2007).
Koehler, Wilhelm, and Florentine Mütherich, *Die Karolingischen Miniaturen*, 6 vols (Berlin: Deutscher Verlag für Kunstwissenschaft, 1930–99), II: *Die Hofschule Karls des Grossen*, ed. by Wilhelm Koehler (1958); VI: *Die Schule von Reims. Von den Anfängen bis zur Mitte des 9. Jahrhunderts*, ed. by Wilhelm Koehler and Florentine Mütherich, 2 vols (1994–99).
Komada, Akiko, 'Les Illustrations de *la Bible historiale*: Les Manuscrits réalisés dans le Nord', 4 vols (unpublished doctoral dissertation, University of Paris IV, 2000).
König, Eberhard, *The Bedford Hours: The Making of a Medieval Masterpiece* (London: British Library, 2007).
Kren, Thomas, ed., *Renaissance Painting in Manuscripts: Treasures from the British Library* (New York: Hudson Hills Press, 1983).
Kren, Thomas, ed., *Margaret of York, Simon Marmion and the Visions of Tondal* (Malibu, CA: J. Paul Getty Museum, 1992).
Kren, Thomas, *French Illuminated Manuscripts in the J. Paul Getty Museum* (Los Angeles: J. Paul Getty Museum, 2007).
Kren, Thomas, 'Landscape in Flemish Illuminated Manuscripts before Patinir', in *Patinir: Essays and Critical Catalogue*, ed. by Alejandro Vergara (Madrid: Museo Nacional del Prado, 2007), pp. 117–33.
Kren, Thomas, and Scot McKendrick, *Illuminating the Renaissance: The Triumph of Flemish Manuscript Painting in Europe* (Los Angeles: J. Paul Getty Museum, 2003).
Krochalis, Jeanne E., 'The Books and Readings of Henry V and his Circle', *Chaucer Review*, 23 (1988), 50–77.
Kuhn, Charles L., 'Herman Scheerre and English Illumination of the Early Fifteenth Century', *Art Bulletin*, 22 (1940), 138–56
Kurtz, Donna, 'The Concept of the Classical Past in Tudor and Early Stuart England', *Journal of the History of Collections*, 20 (2008), 189–204.

Laing, Aileen Hyland, 'The Queen Mary Apocalypse, London, British Museum, Royal MS 19 B. XV' (unpublished doctoral dissertation, Johns Hopkins University, Baltimore, 1971).
Langlois, Ernest, *Les Manuscrits du Roman de la Rose: Description et classement*, Travaux et mémoires de l'Université de Lille, n.s. I, 7 (Lille: Tallandier, 1910).
Lapidge, Michael, 'Some Latin Poems as Evidence for the Reign of Athelstan', *Anglo-Saxon England*, 9 (1981), 61–98.
Lawton, Lesley, 'The Illustration of Late Medieval Secular Texts with Special Reference to Lydgate's "Troy Book"', in *Manuscripts and Readers in Fifteenth-century England: The Literary Implications of Manuscript Study: Essays from the 1981 Conference at the University of York*, ed. by Derek Pearsall (Cambridge: D.S. Brewer, 1983), pp. 41–69.
Laynesmith, J.L., *The Last Medieval Queens: English Queenship 1445–1503* (Oxford: Oxford University Press, 2004).
Le Goff, Jacques, *Saint Louis* (Paris: Gallimard, 1996).
Le Guay, Laetitia, *Les Princes de Bourgogne, lecteurs de Froissart: Les Rapports entre le texte et l'image dans les manuscrits enluminés du livre IV des Chroniques* (Turnhout: Brepols, 1998).
Le Loup, Willy, 'De Relatie tussen Gruuthuse en Mansion: een *Status Questionis*', in Maximilaan P.J. Martens, *Lodewijk van Gruuthuse: Mecenas en Europees Diplomaat, ca. 1427–1492* (Bruges: Stichting Kunstboek, 1992), pp. 149–52.
Legaré, Anne-Marie, 'La Librairye de Madame', in *Women of Distinction: Margaret of York, Margaret of Austria*, ed. by Dagmar Eichberger (Leuven: Davidsfonds, 2005), pp. 207–19.
Legaré, Anne-Marie, 'Les Deux épouses de René d'Anjou et leurs livres', in *Splendeur de l'Enluminure: Le Roi René et les livres*, ed. by Marc-Édouard Gautier (Angers: Actes Sud, 2009), pp. 59–71.
Legg, J. Wickham, 'On an Inventory of the Vestry in Westminster Abbey taken in 1388', *Archaeologia*, 52 (1890), 195–286.
Lejeune, Rita, and Jacques Stiennon, *La Légende de Roland dans l'art du Moyen-Âge* (Brussels: Editions de l'Arcade, 1966), pp. 281–87.
Leland, John, *The Laboryouse Journey & Searche of Johan Leylande for Englandes Antquitees* (London, [n. pub.],1549, repr. Amsterdam: Theatrum Orbis Terrarum, 1975).
Lemaire, Claudine, 'De bibliotheek van Lodewijk van Gruuthuse', in *Vlaamse Kunst op Perkament. Handschriften en miniaturen te Brugge van de 12de tot de 16de eeuw* (Bruges: Schoonbaert, 1981), pp. 207–29.
Leroquais, Victor, *Les Breviaires manuscrits des bibliothèques publiques de France*, 6 vols (Paris: Protat, 1934).
Lewis, Suzanne, *The Art of Matthew Paris in the 'Chronica majora'* (Aldershot: Scolar Press, 1987).
Lewis, Suzanne, 'The Apocalypse of Isabella of France: Paris, Bibl. Nat. MS fr. 13096', *Art Bulletin*, 72 (1990), 224–60.
Lindsay. W.M., ed., *Isidori Hispalensis Episcopi Etymologiarum sive originum libri XX* (Oxford: Clarendon Press, 1911).
Linehan, Peter, '"GAR": A Case of Mistaken Identity', *Revista Española de Derecho Canónico*, 55 (1998), 749–54.
Liuzza, R.M., ed. and trans., *Anglo-Saxon Prognostics. An Edition and Translation of Texts from London, British Library, MS*

Cotton Tiberius A.III, Anglo-Saxon Texts, 7 (Cambridge: D.S. Brewer, 2010).
Livingstone, Niall, 'The Voice of Isocrates and the Dissemination of Cultural Power', in *Pedagogy and Power: Rhetorics of Classical Learning*, ed. by Yun Lee Too and Niall Livingstone (Cambridge: Cambridge University Press, 1998), pp. 263–81.
***Livres d'heures royaux: La Peinture de manuscrits à la cour de France au temps de Henri II*, ed. by M. Dickmann Orth and T. Crépin-Leblond (Paris: Réunion des musées nationaux, 1993).**
Löfstedt, Leena, *Li Abregemenz noble honme Vegesce Flave René des establissemenz apartenanz a chevalerie : Traduction par Jean de Meun de Flavii Vegeti Renati viri illustris Epitoma Institutorum Rei Militaris*, Suomalainen Tiedeakatemian Toimituksia, ser. B, 200 (Helsinki: Suomalainen Tiedeakatemia, 1977).
Longnon, Jean, and Raymond Cazelles, *Les Très Riches Heures du Duc de Berry* (London: Thames and Hudson, 1969).
Loomis, Roger Sherman, and Laura Hibbard Loomis, *Arthurian Legends in Medieval* Art (New York: Modern Language Association of America, 1938).
Lowden, John, 'Concerning the Cotton Genesis and other Illustrated Manuscripts of Genesis', *Gesta*, 31 (1992), 40–53.
Lowden, John, 'The Image and Self-image of the Medieval Ruler', in *Kings and Kingship in Medieval Europe*, ed. by Anne Duggan (London: King's College London, Centre for Late Antique and Medieval Studies, 1993), pp. 213–40.
Lowden, John, 'The Beginnings of Biblical Illustration', in *Imaging the Early Medieval Bible*, ed. by John Williams (University Park, PA: Penn State University Press, 1999), pp. 9–59.
Lowden, John, *The Making of the Bibles moralisées*, 2 vols (University Park, PA: Pennsylvania State University Press, 2000).
Lowden, John, 'The Apocalypse in the Early-thirteenth-century *Bibles moralisées*: A Re-assessment', in *Prophecy, Apocalypse and the Day of Doom: Proceedings of the 2000 Harlaxton Symposium*, ed. by Nigel Morgan, Harlaxton Medieval Studies, 12 (Donington: Shaun Tyas, 2004), pp. 195–219.
Lowden, John, 'The *Bible moralisée* in the Fifteenth Century and the Challenge of the *Bible historiale*', *Journal of the Warburg and Courtauld Institutes*, 68 (2005), 73–136.
Lowden, John, 'The Word made Visible: The Exterior of the Early Christian Book as Visual Argument', in *The Early Christian Book* (Washington: Catholic University of America Press, 2007).
Lowry, Martin, 'Sister or Country Cousin? The Huntington *Recuyell* and the Getty *Tondal*', in *Margaret of York, Simon Marmion and the Visions of Tondal*, ed. by Thomas Kren (Malibu, CA: J. Paul Getty Museum, 1992), pp. 103–10.
Lucas, Peter J., *From Author to Audience: John Capgrave and Medieval Publication* (Dublin: University College Dublin Press, 1997).
Lunn, J., 'The Luton Fraternity Register', *Bedfordshire Magazine*, 19 (1984), 177–82.
Lutz, J., and P. Perdrizet, *Speculum humanae salvationis: Texte critique, traduction inédite de Jean Miélot (1448): Les Sources et l'influence iconographique* (Mulhouse: J. Lutz, 1907).
[Lyte, H.C. Maxwell, ed.], *Calendar of the Patent Rolls Preserved in the Public Record Office*, Henry VII, 2 vols (London: HMSO, 1914–1916).

Madan, Falconer and others, *A Summary Catalogue of Western Manuscripts in the Bodleian Library at Oxford*, 7 vols (Oxford: Clarendon Press, 1895–1953).
Maddocks, Hilary, 'Illumination in Jean de Vignay's Légende dorée', in *Legenda aurea, sept siècles de diffusion. Actes du colloque international sur la 'Legenda aurea', texte latin et branches vernaculaires, à l'Université du Québec à Montréal, 11–12 mai 1983*, ed. by Brenda Dunn-Lardeau, Cahiers d'études médiévales, Cahier special, 2 (Montreal: Bellarmin, 1986), pp. 155–69.
Maddocks, Hilary, 'Pictures for Aristocrats: The Manuscripts of the Légende dorée', in *Medieval Texts and Images: Studies of Manuscripts from the Middle Ages*, ed. by Margaret Manion and Bernard James Muir (Sydney: Craftsman: 1991), pp. 1–23.
Manion, Margaret M., Vera F. Vines and Christopher de Hamel, eds, *Medieval and Renaissance Manuscripts in New Zealand Collections* (Melbourne: Thames and Hudson, 1989).
Marks, Richard, 'Two Illuminated Guild Registers from Bedfordshire', in *Illuminating the Book: Makers and Interpreters. Essays in Honour of Janet Backhouse*, ed. by Michelle P. Brown and Scot McKendrick (London: British Library, 1998), pp. 120–41.
Marks, Richard, and Nigel Morgan, *The Golden Age of English Manuscript Painting 1200–1500* (London: Chatto and Windus, 1981).
Marks, Richard, and Paul Williamson, eds, *Gothic: Art for England 1400–1547* (London: V&A Publications, 2003).
Martens, Maximiliaan P.J., *Lodewijk van Gruuthuse, Mecenas en Europees Diplomaat ca. 1427–1492* (Bruges: Stichting Kunstboek, 1992).
Marti, Susan, Till-Holger Borchert and Gabriele Keck, eds, *Charles le Téméraire: Faste et déclin de la cour de Bourgogne* (Brussels: Fonds Mercator, 2008).
Martin, Henri, *Les Joyaux de l'Arsenal*, 3 vols (Paris: Berthaud, 1909–21), I: *Psautier de Saint Louis et de Blanche de Castile*.
Mayor, J.E.B., ed., *Nicholas Ferrar: Two Lives by his Brother John and by Dr Jebb* (Cambridge: Cambridge University Press, 1855).
Mayr-Harting, Henry, *Ottonian Book Illumination*, 2 vols (London: Harvey Miller, 1991).
McCulloch, Florence, *Medieval Latin and French Bestiaries*, University of North Carolina Studies in the Romance Languages and Literatures, 33 (Chapel Hill, NC: University of North Carolina Press, 1962).
McFarlane, K. B., *Lancastrian Kings and Lollard Knights* (Oxford: Clarendon Press, 1972).
McFarlane, K.B., *The Nobility of Later Medieval England* (Oxford: Clarendon Press, 1973).
McGerr, Rosemarie, 'A Statute Book and Lancastrian Mirror for Princes: The Yale Law School Manuscript of the 'Nova Statuta Angliae"', *Textual Cultures*, 1 (2006), 6–59.
McGurk, Patrick, 'The Disposition of Numbers in Latin Eusebian Canon Tables', in *Philologia Sacra: biblische und patristische Studien für Hermann J. Frede und Walter Thiele zu ihrem siebzigsten Geburtstag*, ed. by Roger Gryson (Friedburg: Herder, 1993), pp. 242–58.
McKendrick, Scot, 'Edward IV: An English Royal Collector of Netherlandish Tapestry', *Burlington Magazine*, 129 (1987), 521–24.
McKendrick, Scot, '*La Grande Histoire Cesar* and the Manuscripts of Edward IV', in *English Manuscript Studies 1100–1700*, 2, ed. by Peter Beal and Jeremy Griffiths, (Oxford, Basil Blackwell, 1990), pp. 109–38.
McKendrick, Scot, 'Lodewijk van Gruuthuse en de Librije van Edward IV', in *Lodewijk van Gruuthuse, Mecenas en Europees Diplomaat ca. 1427–1492*, ed. by Maximiliaan P. J. Martens (Bruges: Stichting Kunstboek, 1992), pp. 153–54.
McKendrick, Scot, 'The *Romuléon* and the Manuscripts of Edward IV', in *England in the Fifteenth Century: Proceedings of the 1992 Harlaxton Symposium*, ed. by Nicholas Rogers, Harlaxton Medieval Studies, 4 (Stamford: Paul Watkins, 1994), pp. 149–69.
McKendrick, Scot, 'Tapestries from the Low Countries in England during the Fifteenth Century', in *England and the Low Countries in the Late Middle Ages*, ed. by Caroline Barron and Nigel Saul (Stroud: Alan Sutton, 1995), pp. 43–60.
McKendrick, Scot, *The History of Alexander the Great: An Illuminated Manuscript of Vasco da Lucena's French Translation of the Ancient Text by Quintus Curtius Rufus* (Los Angeles: J. Paul Getty Museum, 1996).
McKendrick, Scot, *Flemish Illuminated Manuscripts, 1400–1550* (London: British Library, 2003).
McKendrick, Scot, 'The Codex Alexandrinus, or the Dangers of being a Named Manuscript', in *The Bible as Book: The Transmission of the Greek Text*, ed. by Scot McKendrick and Orlaith A. O'Sullivan (London: British Library, 2003).
McKendrick, Scot, 'Reviving the Past: Illustrated Manuscripts of Secular Vernacular Texts, 1467–1500', in Thomas Kren and Scot McKendrick, *Illuminating the Renaissance: The Triumph of Flemish Manuscript Painting in Europe* (Los Angeles: J. Paul Getty Museum, 2003), pp. 59–78.
McKendrick, Scot, 'Charles the Bold and the *Romuléon*: Reception, Loss and Influence', in *Kunst und Kulturtransfer zur Zeit Karls des Kühnen*, ed. by Norberto Gramaccini and Marc Schurr (Bern: Peter Lang, forthcoming).
McKenna, John W., 'Piety and Propaganda: The Cult of King Henry VI', in *Chaucer and Middle English Studies: In Honour of Rossell Hope Robbins*, ed. by Beryl Rowland (London: Allen and Unwin, 1974), pp. 72–88.
McKitterick, Rosamond, *The Carolingians and the Written Word* (Cambridge: Cambridge University Press, 1989.
Meale, Carol M., 'Patrons, Buyers and Owners: Book Production and Social Status', in *Book Production and Publishing in Britain, 1375–1475*, ed. by Jeremy Griffiths and Derek Pearsall (Cambridge: Cambridge University Press, 1989), pp. 201–38.
Meiss, Millard, 'French and Italian Variations on an Early Fifteenth-century Theme: St Jerome in his Study', *Gazette des Beaux-Arts*, s. 6, 62 (1963), 147–70.
Meiss, Millard, *French Painting in the Time of Jean de Berry: The Late XIV Century and the Patronage of the Duke*, 2 vols (London: Phaidon, 1967).
Meiss, Millard, *French Painting in the Time of Jean de Berry. The Boucicaut Master* (London: Phaidon, 1968).
Meiss, Millard, Sharon Off Dunlap Smith and Elizabeth Home Beatson, *French Painting in the Time of Jean de Berry: The Limbourgs and their Contemporaries*, 2 vols (London: Thames and Hudson, 1974).
Melis, Tine, 'An Alexander Manuscript for a Powerful Patron (Oxford, Bodleian Library, MS. Bodl. 264)?', in '*Als Ich Can': Liber Amicorum in Memory of Professor Dr Maurits Smeyers*, ed. by Bert Cardon and others, 2 vols (Paris: Peeters, 2002), II, pp. 961–81.
Meuwese, Martine, 'Three Illustrated Prose Lancelots from the same Atelier', in *Text and Image: Studies in the French Illustrated Book from the Middle Ages to the Present Day, Bulletin of the John Rylands University Library of Manchester*, 81 (1999), pp. 97–125.
Meyer, Heinz, 'Die illustrierten lateinischen Handschriften im Rahmen der Gesamtüberlieferung der Enzyklopädie des Bartholomäus Anglicus', *Frühmittelalterische Studien*, 30 (1996), 368–95.
Meyer, Paul, 'Versions en vers et en prose des vies des pères', *Histoire littéraire de la France*, 331 (1906), 254–458.
Michael, Michael A., 'A Manuscript Wedding Gift from Philippa of Hainault to Edward III', *Burlington Magazine*, 127 (1985), 582, 584–99.
Michael, Michael A., 'The Artists of the Walter of Milemete Treatise', 2 vols (unpublished doctoral thesis, University of London, 1987).
Michael, Michael A., 'The Iconography of Kingship in the Walter of Milemete Treatise', *Journal of the Warburg and Courtauld Institutes*, 57 (1994), 35–47.
Michael, Michael A., 'Urban Production of Manuscript Books and the Role of the University Towns', in *The Cambridge History of the Book in Britain* (Cambridge: Cambridge University Press, 1987-), II: *1100–1400*, ed. by Nigel Morgan and Rodney M. Thomson (2008), pp. 168–94.
Middleton, Roger, 'The Manuscripts', in *The Arthur of the French: The Arthurian Legend in Medieval French and Occitan Literature*, ed. by Glyn S. Burgess and Karen Pratt, Arthurian Literature in the Middle Ages, 4 (Cardiff: University of Wales Press, 2006), pp. 8–92.
Millar, Eric G., 'Les Manuscrits à peintures des bibliothèques de Londres', *Bulletin de la Société française de reproductions de manuscrits à peintures*, 4 (1925), 5–81.
Millar, Eric G., *English Illuminated Manuscripts from the Xth to the XIIIth Century* (Paris: Van Oest, 1926).
Millar, Eric G., *Souvenir de l'exposition de manuscrits français à peintures organisée à la Grenville Library, (British Museum) en janvier-mars, 1932: Étude concernant les 65 manuscrits exposés* (Paris: Société française de reproductions de manuscrits à peintures, 1933).
Millar, Eric G., *A Thirteenth Century Bestiary in the Library of Alnwick Castle* (Oxford: Roxburghe Club, 1958).
Miller, Edward, *That Noble Cabinet: A History of the British Museum* (London: André Deutsch, 1973).
Miller, John, *Charles II* (London: Weidenfeld and Nicolson, 1991).
Miller, Sean., ed., *Charters of the New Minster, Winchester*, Anglo-Saxon Charters, 9 (London: British Academy, 2001).
Montigny, Séverine, 'Traduire César entre Moyen Âge et Renaissance: étude de la 'translation' de la Guerre des Gaules par Jean du Quesne (1473–1474) à partir de l'exemple du livre III (édition et commentaire)', (Rapport d'étape de thèse diplôme de conservateur des bibliothèques, Villeurbanne: École nationale supérieure des sciences de l'information et des bibliothèques, 2007), <http://enssibal.enssib.fr/bibliotheque/documents/dcb/montigny-dcb15.pdf> [accessed 17 April 2011].
Mooney, Linne R., *The Kalendarium of John Somer* (Athens, GA: University of Georgia Press, 1998).
Morgan, Nigel, *Early Gothic Manuscripts 1190–1250*, 2 vols, A Survey of Manuscripts Illuminated in the British Isles, 4 (London: Harvey Miller, 1982–88).
Morgan, Nigel, 'Texts of Devotion and Religious Instruction Associated with Margaret of York', in *Margaret of York, Simon Marmion and the Visions of Tondal*, ed. by Thomas Kren (Malibu, CA: J. Paul Getty Museum, 1992), pp. 63–76.
Morgan, Nigel, 'French Interpretations of English Apocalypses', in *Proceedings of the 1996 Harlaxton Symposium*, ed. by John Mitchell and Matthew Moran, Harlaxton Medieval Studies, 8 (Stamford: Shaun Tyas, 2000), pp. 137–56.
Morgan, Nigel, 'Patrons and Devotional Images in English Art of the International Gothic *c.* 1350–1450', in *Reading Texts and Images: Essays on Medieval and Renaissance*

Art and Patronage in Honour of Margaret M. Manion, ed. by Bernard J. Muir (Exeter: University of Exeter Press, 2002), pp. 93–121.
Morgan, Nigel, *The Douce Apocalypse: Picturing the End of the World in the Middle Ages* (Oxford: Bodleian Library, 2006).
Morgan, Nigel, and Stella Panayotova, *A Catalogue of Western Book Illumination in the Fitzwilliam Museum and the Cambridge Colleges* (London: Harvey Miller, 2009-) I, in 2 vols, I, part 2: *The Meuse Region. Southern Netherlands.*
Morrison, Elizabeth and Anne D. Hedeman, eds, *Imagining the Past: History in Manuscript Painting* 1250–1500 (Los Angeles: J. Paul Getty Museum, 2010).
Munby, A.N.L., *The Formation of The Phillipps Library Up to the Year 1840*, Phillipps Studies, 3 (Cambridge: University Press, 1954).
Muratova, Xenia, 'Les Manuscrit-frères: un aspect particulier de la production de Bestiaires enluminés en Angleterre à la fin du XIIe siècle', in *Artistes, artisans et production artistique au Moyen Âge: Colloque international*, ed. by Xavier Barral i Altet, 3 vols (Paris: Picard, 1986–90), III: *Fabrication et consommation de l'oeuvre*, pp. 67–92.
Murdoch, W.G. Blaikie, 'Two Royal Bibliophiles', *The Book-Lover's Magazine*, 6 (1907), 56–60.
Myers, A.R., ed., *The Household of Edward IV: The Black Book and the Ordinance of 1478* (Manchester: Manchester University Press, 1959).

Naylor, Pat, 'Scribes and Secretaries of the Percy Earls of Northumberland, with Special Reference to William Peeris and Royal MS 18 D. II', in *Tudor Manuscripts 1485–1603*, ed. by A.S.G. Edwards, English Manuscript Studies 1100–1700, 15 (London: British Library, 2009), pp. 166–84.
Neumayr von Ramssla, *Des durchlauchtigen hochgebornen Fürsten und Herrn, Herrn Johann Ernsten des Jüngern Hertzogen zu Sachsen ... Reise in Franckreich, Engelland und Niederland* (Leipzig: Jansonius für Gross, 1620).
Nicolas, Nicholas Harris, *Privy Purse Expenses of Elizabeth of York: Wardrobe Accounts of Edward IV* (London: William Pickering, 1830).
Nicholls, Mark, 'Knyvett , Thomas, Baron Knyvett (1545/6–1622)', *Oxford Dictionary of National Biography* (Oxford University Press, 2004); online edn, Jan 2008 <http://www.oxforddnb.com/view/article/15800> [accessed 9 April 2011].
Nichols, John, *Literary Anecdotes of the Eighteenth Century*, 9 vols (London: Nichols, Son and Bentley, 1812–15).
Nicoud, Marilyn, *Les Régimes de santé au Moyen Âge: Naissance et diffusion d'une écriture médicale en Italie et en France (XIIIe–XVe siècle)*, 2 vols (Rome: École Française de Rome, 2007).
Nixon, Howard M., 'Early English Gold-Tooled Bookbindings', in *Studi di Bibliografia e di Storia in Onore di Tammaro De Marinis*, 4 vols (Verona: Biblioteca Apostolica Stamperia Valdonega, 1964), III, pp. 283–308.
Nixon, Howard M., *English Restoration Bookbindings: Samuel Mearne and his Contemporaries* (London: British Museum, 1974).
Noirfalise, Florent, 'Family Feuds and the (Re)writing of Universal History: The *Chronique dite de Baudouin d'Avesnes* (1278–84)' (unpublished doctoral thesis, University of Liverpool, 2009).
Nordenfalk, Carl, 'Review of Anthony Melnikas, *The Corpus of Miniatures in the Manuscripts of Decretum Gratiani* (Studia Gratiana 16–18, Rome: Studia Gratiana 1975)', *Zeitschrift für Kunstgeschichte*, 43 (1980), 318–37.
North, John David, 'The Alfonsine Tables in England', in *Stars, Minds and Fate: Essays in Ancient and Medieval Cosmology*, ed. by John David North (London: Hambledon Press, 1989), pp. 327–60.
Nuvoloni, Laura, 'Pier Antonio Sallando o "il più excellente scriptore credo habia il mondo"', in *Il Libro d'Ore Durazzo.* Commentary volume, ed. by Andrea De Marchi (Modena: Panini, 2008), pp. 145–88.

Oakeshott, Walter, *The Two Winchester Bibles* (Oxford: Clarendon Press, 1981).
Obbema, Pieter F.J., 'Panel Painting and Book Illumination in a Monastic Workshop ca. 1440–85', in *Masters and Miniatures: Proceedings of the Congress on Medieval Manuscript Illumination in the Northern Netherlands* (Utrecht, 10–13 December 1989), ed. by Koert van der Horst and Johann-Christian Klamt (Doornspijk: Davaco, 1991), pp. 381–88.
Ollard, Richard, *The Image of the King: Charles I and Charles II* (London: Pimlico, 1979).
O'Meara, Carra Ferguson, *Monarchy and Consent: The Coronation Book of Charles V of France: British Library MS Tiberius B VIII* (London: Harvey Miller, 2001).
O'Meara, J.J., trans., Gerald of Wales, *The History and Topography of Ireland* (Harmondsworth: Penguin Classics, 1982).
Omont, H., 'Les Manuscrits français des rois d'Angleterre au château de Richmond', in *Études romanes dédiés à Gaston Paris* (Paris: É. Bouillon, 1891), pp. 1–13.
Orr, Michael T., 'The "Hours of Elizabeth the Queen"' (British Library Additional Manuscript 50001): The Workshop of Johannes and English Fifteenth-century Illumination' (unpublished doctoral dissertation, Cornell University, 1989).
Orr, Michael T., 'The Hours of Elizabeth the Queen: Evidence for Collaboration between English Illuminators and an Artist from the Gold Scrolls Group', in *Flanders in a European Perspective: Manuscript Illumination around 1400 in Flanders and Abroad*, ed. by Maurits Smeyers and Bert Cardon (Leuven: Peeters, 1995), pp. 619–33.
Orth, Myra Dickman, 'The Primacy of the Word in French Renaissance Manuscripts', in *The Illuminated Psalter: Studies in the Content, Purpose and Placement of its Images*, ed. by Frank O. Büttner (Turnhout: Brepols, 2004), pp. 397–403.
Ouy, Gilbert, *La Librairie des frères captifs: Les Manuscrits de Charles d'Orléans et Jean d'Angoulême* (Turnhout: Brepols, 2007).
Ovenden, Richard, 'The Libraries of the Antiquaries (*c.* 1580–1640) and the Idea of a National Collection', in *The Cambridge History of Libraries in Britain and Ireland*, ed. by Elisabeth Leedham-Green and Teresa Webber, 3 vols (Cambridge: Cambridge University Press, 2006), I: *To 1640*, pp. 527–61.

Pächt, Otto, 'A Giottesque Episode in English Illumination', *Journal of the Warburg and Courtauld Institutes*, 6 (1943), 51–70.
Pächt, Otto, *The Master of Mary of Burgundy* (London: Faber and Faber, 1948).
Pächt, Otto, 'Zur Entstehung des "Hieronymus in Gehäus"', *Pantheon*, 21 (1963), 131–42.
Pächt, Otto, 'La Terre de Flandres', *Pantheon*, 36 (1978), 3–16.
Pächt, Otto, and J.J.G. Alexander, *Illuminated Manuscripts in the Bodleian Library, Oxford*, 3 vols (Oxford: Clarendon Press, 1966–73).
Page, William, ed., *The Victoria County History of Kent*, 3 vols (London: St Catherine Press, 1908–32).
Painter, George D., *William Caxton: A Quincentenary Biography of England's First Printer* (London: Chatto and Windus, 1976).
Palmer, John Joseph Norman, *England, France and Christendom, 1377–99* (Chapel Hill, NC: University of Carolina Press, 1972).
Palmer, Richard, and Michelle P. Brown, *Lambeth Palace Library. Treasures from the Collection of the Archbishops of Canterbury* (London: Scala, 2010).
Pannier, Léopold, 'Les Joyaux du duc de Guyenne: Recherches sur les goûts artistiques et la vie privée du Dauphin Louis, fils de Charles VI', *Bibliothèque de l'École des Chartes*, 35 (1874), 158–70, 209–25, 306–20.
Paris 1400: Les Arts sous Charles VI, Musée du Louvre, 22 mars–12 juillet 2004 (Paris: Réunion des musées nationaux, 2004).
Parker, D.C., *An Introduction to the New Testament Manuscripts and their Texts* (Cambridge: Cambridge University Press, 2009).
Parker, D.C., *Codex Sinaiticus: The Story of the World's Oldest Bible* (London: British Library, 2010).
Parker, E.C., 'The Gift of the Cross in the New Minster Liber Vitae', in *Reading Medieval Images: The Art Historian and the Object*, ed. by E. Sears and T.K. Thomas (Michigan: University of Michigan Press, 2002), pp. 176–86.
Parsons, John Carmi, *Eleanor of Castile: Queen and Society in Thirteenth-century England* (London: Macmillan, 1997).
Pearsall, Derek, 'Hoccleve's Regement of Princes: The Poetics of Royal Self-representation', *Speculum*, 69 (1994), 386–410.
Pérez-Simon, Maud, 'Prose et profondeur temporelle: du Merveilleux à l'Histoire dans le *Roman d'Alexandre en prose*', in *Dire et penser le temps au Moyen-Âge, Frontières de l'histoire et du roman*, ed. by E. Baumgartner and L. Harf-Lancner (Paris: Presses de la Sorbonne Nouvelle, 2005), pp. 171–91.
Pérez-Simon, Maud, 'Le Savant philosophe et le prince savant: Aristote et Alexandre le Grand', in *Savoirs et savants dans la littérature (Moyen Âge – XXe siècle)*, ed. by Pascale Alexandre-Bergues and Jeanyves Guérin (Paris: Classiques Garnier, 2010), pp. 17–33.
Pérez-Simon, Maud, *Mise en roman et mise en image: Les Manuscrits du Roman d'Alexandre en prose: Pour une stylistique de la traduction* (Paris: Champion, forthcoming).
Perkins, Nicholas, *Hoccleve's Regiment of Princes: Counsel and Constraint* (Woodbridge: D.S. Brewer, 2001).
Petrina, Alessandra, *Cultural Politics in Fifteenth-century England: The Case of Humphrey, Duke of Gloucester* (Leiden: Brill, 2004).
Pfaff, Richard W., *The Liturgy in Medieval England: A History* (Cambridge: Cambridge University Press, 2009).
Płonka-Bałus, Katarzyna, *Vita Christi [et] Vengance de Nostre Seigneur Jhesu Christ: Zagadnienia treści, stylu i funkcji miniatur rękopisu 2919 w Bibliotece Czartoryskich* (Cracow: Universitas, 2004).
Plummer, Charles, ed., Fortescue, Sir John, *The Governance of England*, (Oxford, Clarendon Press, 1885).
Poole, Reginald, 'Review', *English Historical Review*, 37 (1922), 450–58.
Porcher, Jean, *Les Belles Heures de Jean de France, duc de Berry* (Paris: Bibliothèque nationale, 1953).
Powell, Susan, 'Lady Margaret Beaufort and her Books', *The Library*, 20 (1998), 197–240.
Prud'Homme, Caroline, '*Donnez, vous recevrez*: Les Rapports entre écrivains et seigneurs à la fin du Moyen Âge à travers le don du livre et la dédicace', *COnTEXTES* [online], 5 (2009), <http://contextes.revues.org/index4259.html> [accessed 7 January 2011].
Public Reference Office, *Calendar of the Patent Rolls Preserved in the Public Record Office*, Edward VI, 6 vols (London: HMSO, 1924–1929).
Puhle, Matthias, ed., *Otto der Grosse: Magdeburg und Europa*, 2 vols (Mainz: Philipp von Zabern, 2001).

Ramsay, Nigel, 'Libraries for Antiquaries and Heralds', in *The Cambridge History of Libraries in Britain and Ireland*, ed. by Giles Mandelbrote and K. A. Manley, 3 vols (Cambridge: University Press, 2006), II: *1640–1850*, pp. 134–57.
Ramsay, Nigel, and Margaret Sparks, *The Image of St Dunstan* (Canterbury: The Dunstan Millennium Committee, 1988).
Redington, Joseph, ed., *Calendar of Treasury Papers*, 6 vols (London: HMSO, 1868–1889).
Reeve, Michael D., 'The Transmission of Vegetius's *Epitoma Rei Militaris*', *Aevum: Rassegna di scienze storiche, linguistiche e filologiche*, 64 (2000), 243–354.
Rex, Richard, *The Theology of John Fisher* (Cambridge: Cambridge University Press, 1991).
Reynolds, Catherine, 'The Salisbury Breviary, Paris, BN, MS lat. 17294, and some Related Manuscripts' (unpublished doctoral thesis, University of London, 1986).
Reynolds, Catherine, 'Illustrated Boccaccio Manuscripts in the British Library (London)', *Studi sul Boccaccio*, 17 (1988), 113–81.
Reynolds, Catherine 'The Shrewsbury Book, London, British Library, Royal MS 15 E VI', in *Medieval Art, Architecture and Archaeology at Rouen*, ed. by Jenny Stratford, British Archaeological Association Conference Transactions, 12 (Leeds: Manley, 1993), pp. 109–16.
Reynolds, Catherine, 'English Patrons and French Artists in Fifteenth-century Normandy', in *England and Normandy in the Middle Ages*, ed. by David Bates and Anne Curry (London: Hambledon Press, 1994), pp. 299–313.
Reynolds, Catherine, 'England and the Continent: Artistic Relations', in *Gothic: Art for England, 1400–1547* (London: V&A, 2003), pp. 76–85.
Reynolds, Catherine, '*Boccaccio visualizzato*: Edward IV of England's *Des cas des nobles hommes et femmes*' (unpublished paper given at the Conference in Memory of Vittore Branca, Warburg Institute, London, 21–22 October 2005).
Reynolds, Catherine, 'The "Très Riches Heures", the Bedford Workshop and Barthélemy d'Eyck', *Burlington Magazine*, 147 (2005), 526–33.
Reynolds, Catherine, 'The Workshop of the Master of the Duke of Bedford: Definitions and Identities', in *Books and Book Production in Paris c.1400*, ed. by Peter Ainsworth and Godfried Croenen (Leuven: Peeters, 2006), pp. 437–72.
Reynolds, Catherine, and Jenny Stratford, 'Le Manuscrit dit "Le Pontifical de Poitiers"', *Revue de l'Art*, 84 (1988), 61–80.
Ribémont, Bernard, intro. and notes, *Le Livre des propriétés des choses: Une encyclopédie au XIVe siècle* (Paris: Stock, 1999).
Richardot, Phillipe, *Végèce et la culture militaire au Moyen-Âge (Ve–XVe siècles)* (Paris: Economica, 1998).
Richards, Mary P., 'A Decorated Vulgate Set from 12th Century Rochester, England', *Journal of the Walters Art Gallery*, 39 (1981), 59–67.
Richards, Mary P., *Texts and their Traditions in the Medieval Library of Rochester Cathedral Priory*, Transactions of the American Philosophical Society, 78, part 3 (Philadelphia: American Philosophical Society, 1988).

Rickert, E., 'King Richard II's Books', *The Library*, 4th s., 13 (1932–33), 144–47.
Rickert, Margaret, *The Reconstructed Carmelite Missal: An English Manuscript of the Late XIV Century in the British Museum, Additional 29704–5, 44892* (London: Faber and Faber, 1952).
Rickert, Margaret, 'The so-called Beaufort Hours and York Psalter', *Burlington Magazine*, 104 (1962), 238–48.
Rickert, Margaret, *Painting in Britain: The Middle Ages*, 2nd edn (London: Penguin Books, 1965).
Roberts, Colin H., and T.C. Skeat, *The Birth of the Codex* (London: British Academy, 1983).
Roberts, Julian, 'Extending the Frontiers: Scholar Collectors', in *The Cambridge History of Libraries in Britain and Ireland*, ed. by Elisabeth Leedham-Green and Teresa Webber, 3 vols (Cambridge: Cambridge University Press, 2006), I: *To 1640*, pp. 292–321.
Roberts, Marion, 'Towards a Literary Source for the Scenes of the Passion in Queen Mary's Psalter', *Journal of the Warburg and Courtauld Institutes*, 36 (1973), 361–65.
Rock, Daniel, *The Church of our Fathers, as seen in St Osmund's Rite for the Cathedral of Salisbury, with dissertations on the belief and ritual in England before and after the coming of the Normans*, 4 vols (London: C. Dolman, 1849).
Rogers, Nicholas J., 'Books of Hours produced in the Low Countries for the English Market in the Fifteenth Century' (unpublished master's dissertation, University of Cambridge, 1982).
Rogers, Nicholas J., 'The Artist of Trinity B.11.7 and his Patrons', in *England in the Fifteenth Century: Proceedings of the 1992 Harlaxton Symposium*, ed. by Nicholas Rogers (Stamford: Paul Watkins, 1994), pp. 170–86.
Rogers, Nicholas J., 'The Bury Artists of Harley 2278 and the Origins of Topographical Awareness in English Art', in *Bury St Edmunds: Medieval Art, Architecture, Archaeology and Economy*, ed. by Antonia Gransden, British Archaeological Association Conference Transactions, 20 (Leeds: British Archaeological Association, 1998), pp. 219–27.
Roskell, J.S., 'Sir John Cheyne of Beckford, Knight of the Shire for Gloucestershire in 1390, 1393, 1394 and in 1399, when Elected Speaker', *Transactions of the Bristol and Gloucestershire Archaeological Society*, 75 (1956), pp. 43–72.
Ross, Charles, *Edward IV* (London: Methuen, 1974).
Ross, D.J.A., 'Methods of Book-Production in a XIVth Century French Miscellany (London, BL, MS Royal 19. D. I.)', *Scriptorium: Revue internationale des études relatives aux manuscrits*, 6 (1952), 63–75.
Ross, D.J.A., 'Nectanebus in his Palace: A Problem of Alexander Iconography', *Journal of the Warburg and Courtauld Institutes*, 15 (1952), 67–87.
Ross, D.J.A., 'Some Geographical and Topographical Miniatures in a Fragmentary *Trésor des Histoires*', *Scriptorium: Revue internationale des études relatives aux manuscrits*, 23 (1969), 177–86.
Ross, D.J.A., *Alexander historiatus: A Guide to Medieval Illustrated Alexander Literature* (London: Warburg Institute, 1963; repr. Frankfurt: Athenäum, 1988).
Ross, D.J.A., and M.A. Stones, 'The *Roman d'Alexandre* in French Prose: Another Illustrated Manuscript from Champagne or Flanders *c.* 1300', *Scriptorium: Revue internationale des études relatives aux manuscrits*, 56 (2002), 345–56.
Rostenberg, Leona, *Literary, Political, Scientific, Religious and Legal Publishing, Printing and Bookselling in England, 1551–1700: Twelve Studies*, 2 vols, Burt Franklin Bibliography and Reference Series, 56 (New York: Burt Franklin, 1965).
Rouse, Richard H., and Mary A. Rouse, *Manuscripts and their Makers: Commercial Book Producers in Medieval Paris 1200–1500*, 2 vols (Turnhout: Harvey Miller, 2000).
Rumble, A.R., *Property and Piety in Early Medieval Winchester: Documents relating to the Topography of the Anglo-Saxon and Norman City and its Minsters*, Winchester Studies, 4.3 (Oxford: Oxford University Press, 2002).
Rummel, Erika, *Erasmus as a Translator of the Classics* (Toronto: University of Toronto Press, 1985).
Rundle, David, 'Habits of Manuscript-collecting: The Dispersals of the Library of Humfrey, Duke of Gloucester', in *Lost Libraries: The Destruction of Great Book Collections since Antiquity*, ed. by James Raven (Basingstoke: Palgrave Macmillan, 2004), pp. 106–24.
Rundle, David, 'Filippo Alberici, Henry VII and Richard Fox: The English Fortunes of a Little-known Italian Humanist', *Journal of the Warburg and Courtauld Institutes*, 68 (2005), 137–55.
Rye, William Brenchley, *England as Seen by Foreigners in the Days of Elizabeth and James the First* (London: John Russell Smith, 1865).

Sacred: Books of the Three Faiths: Judaism, Christianity, Islam (London: British Library, 2007).
Saenger, Ernst, 'Das Lobgedicht auf König Robert von Anjou : Ein Beitrag zur Kunst- und Geistesgeschichte des Trecento', *Jahrbuch des kunsthistorischen Sammlungen in Wien*, 84 (1988), 7–91.
Saggese, Alessandra Perriccioli, 'L'Enluminure à Naples au temps des Anjou (1266–1350)', in *L'Europe des Anjou: Aventure des princes angevins du XIIIe au XVe siècle*, ed. by Francesco Aceto and others (Paris: Somogy, 2001), pp. 123–33.
Saggese, Alessandra Perriccioli, 'Cristophoro Orimina: An Illuminator at the Court of Naples', in *The Anjou Bible: A Royal Manuscript Revealed, Naples 1340*, ed. by Lieve Watteeuw and Jan Van der Stock (Paris: Peeters, 2010), pp. 113–25.
Samaran, Charles, *Pierre Bersuire, prieur de Saint-Eloi de Paris (?1290–1362)*, Histoire littéraire de la France, 39 (Paris: Imprimerie nationale, 1962), p. 153.
Samman, Neil, 'The Progresses of Henry VIII, 1509–1529', in *The Reign of Henry VIII*, ed. by Diarmaid MacCulloch (Basingstoke, 1995), pp. 59–74.
Sammut, Alfonso, *Unfredo Duca di Gloucester e Gli Umanisti Italiani* (Padua: Antenore, 1980).
Sandler, Lucy Freeman, *Gothic Manuscripts 1285–1385*, 2 vols, A Survey of Manuscripts Illuminated in the British Isles, 5 (London: Harvey Miller, 1986).
Sandler, Lucy Freeman, '*Omne bonum*: *Compilatio* and *Ordinatio* in an English Illustrated Encyclopedia of the Fourteenth Century', in *Medieval Book Production: Assessing the Evidence*, ed. by Linda L. Brownrigg, Proceedings of the Second Conference of the Seminar in the History of the Book to 1500, Oxford, July 1998 (Los Altos Hills, CA: Anderson-Lovelace, 1990), pp. 183–200.
Sandler, Lucy Freeman, *Omne bonum: A Fourteenth-century Encyclopedia of Universal Knowledge*, 2 vols (London: Harvey Miller, 1996).
Sandler, Lucy Freeman 'Political Imagery in the Bohun Manuscripts', in *Decoration and Illustration in Medieval English Manuscripts*, English Manuscript Studies 1100–1700, 10, ed. by A.S.G. Edwards (London: British Library, 2002), pp. 114–53.
Sandler, Lucy Freeman, 'Lancastrian Heraldry in the Bohun Manuscripts', in *The Lancastrian Court: Proceedings of the 2001 Harlaxton Symposium*, ed. by Jenny Stratford (Donington: Shaun Tyas, 2003), pp. 221–32.
Sandler, Lucy Freeman, 'Bared: The Writing Bear in the British Library Bohun Psalter', in *Tributes to Jonathan J.G. Alexander: The Making and Meaning of Illuminated Medieval and Renaissance Manuscripts, Art and Architecture*, ed. by Gerald B. Guest and Susan L'Engle (London: Harvey Miller, 2006), pp. 269–82.
Saunders, O.E., *English Illumination*, 2 vols (Florence: Pantheon, 1928).
Savile, George, Marquis of Halifax, *A Character of King Charles the Second: And Political, Moral and Miscellaneous Thoughts and Reflections* (Dublin: James Esdall, 1750).
Saxl, Fritz, 'The Troy Romance in French and Italian Art', in *Lectures*, 2 vols (London: Warburg Institute, 1957), I, pp. 125–38.
Scattergood, V.J., 'Literary Culture at the Court of Richard II', in *English Court Culture in the Later Middle Ages*, ed. by V.J. Scattergood and J.W. Sherborne (London: Duckworth, 1983), pp. 29–43.
Schadt, Hermann, *Die Darstellungen der Arbores Consanguinitatis und Arbores Affinitatis* (Tubingen: Ernst Vasmuth, 1982).
Schaff, Philip and Henry Wace, eds, *Nicene and post-Nicene Fathers: **a select library of the Christian Church,*** 2nd s., 14 vols (Edinburgh: T & T Clark, 1890–1900, repr. Grand Rapids, MI: Eerdmans, 1979–1986), I: ***Eusebius: Church history, Life of Constantine the Great, and Oration in praise of Constantine***, trans. by Arthur Cushman McGiffert and Ernest Cushing Richardson.
Scheller, Robert W., 'Ensigns of Authority: French Royal Symbolism in the Age of Louis XII', *Simiolus: Netherlands Quarterly for the History of Art*, 13 (1983), 75–141.
Schipper, William, 'Annotated Copies of Rabanus Maurus' *De rerum naturis*', in *English Manuscript Studies 1110–1700*, 6, ed. by Peter Beal and Jeremy Griffiths (London: British Library, 1997), pp. 1–23.
Schmidt, V.M., *A Legend and its Image: The Aerial Flight of Alexander the Great in Medieval Art* (Groningen: Egbert Forsten, 1995).
Schmidt-Chazan, Mireille, 'Les Traductions de la Guerre des Gaules et le sentiment national au Moyen Âge', *Annales de Bretagne et des pays de l'Ouest*, 87 (1980), 387–407.
Schnerb-Lièvre, M., 'Évrart de Trémaugon et le Songe du Vergier', *Romania*, 101 (1980), 527–30.
Schnerb-Lièvre, M., trans. and ed. *Le Songe du Vergier*, 2 vols (Paris: Editions du Centre national de la recherche scientifique, 1982).
Schramm Percy Ernst, and Florentine Mütherich, *Denkmale der deutschen Könige und Kaiser: Ein Beitrag zur Herrschergeschichte von Karl dem Großen bis Friedrich II, 768–1250* (Munich: Prestel, 1962).
Schullian, Dorothy May, 'A Revised List of the Manuscripts of Valerius Maximus', in *Miscellanea Augusto Campana*, Medioevo e Umanesimo, 45 (1981), 695–728.
Sciacca, Enzo, *Umanesimo e scienza politica nella Francia del XVI secolo, Loys le Roy* (Castello: Leo S. Olschki, 2007).
Science, Mark, ed., *Boethius, De Consolatione Philosophiae translated by John Walton Canon of Osney*, Early English Text Society, 170 (London: Oxford University Press, 1927).
Scofield, Cora L., *The Life and Reign of Edward IV, King of England and of France and Lord of Ireland*, 2 vols (London: Longmans, 1923).
Scott, Kathleen L., *The Mirroure of the Worlde: MS Bodley 283 (England* c. *1470–1480): The Physical Composition, Decoration and Illustration* (Oxford: Roxburghe Club, 1980).
Scott, Kathleen L., 'Lydgate's "Lives of Saints Edmund and Fremund": A newly Located Manuscript in Arundel Castle', *Viator*, 13 (1982), 335–66.
Scott, Kathleen L., *Later Gothic Manuscripts 1390–1490*, 2 vols, A Survey of Manuscripts Illuminated in the British Isles, 6 (London: Harvey Miller, 1996).
Scott, Kathleen L., 'The Illustration and Decoration of the Register of the Fraternity of the Holy Trinity at Luton Church, 1475–1546', in *The English Medieval Book: Studies in Memory of Jeremy Griffiths*, ed. by A.S.G. Edwards, Vincent Gillespie and Ralph Hanna (London: British Library, 2000), pp. 155–83.
Scott, Kathleen L., *Dated and Datable English Manuscript Borders c. 1395–1499* (London: Bibliographical Society, 2002).
Scott, Kathleen L., 'Four Early Fifteenth-century English Manuscripts of the *Speculum humanae salvationis* and a Fourteenth-century Exemplar', in *Decoration and Illustration in Medieval English Manuscripts*, ed. by A.S.G. Edwards, English Manuscript Studies 1100–1700, 10 (London: British Library, 2002), pp. 177–203.
Scott, Kathleen L., 'Manuscripts for Henry VII, his Household and Family', in *The Cambridge Illuminations: The Conference Papers*, ed. by Stella Panayotova (London: Harvey Miller, 2007), pp. 279–86.
Scott, Margaret, *Medieval Dress and Fashion* (London: British Library, 2007).
Scragg, D., ed., *Edgar, King of the English 959–975: New Interpretations*, Publications of the Manchester Centre for Anglo-Saxon Studies, 8 (Woodbridge: Boydell, 2008).
Sed-Rajna, Gabrielle, 'Images of the Tabernacle/Temple in Late Antique and Medieval Art: The State of Research', *Journal of Jewish Art* (1997–98), 42–53.
Selwyn, David G., *The Library of Thomas Cranmer* (Oxford: Bibliographic Society, 1996).
Selwyn, Pamela, 'Heralds' Libraries', in *The Cambridge History of Libraries in Britain and Ireland*, ed. by Elisabeth Leedham-Green and Teresa Webber, 3 vols (Cambridge: Cambridge University Press, 2006), I: *To 1640*, pp. 472–85.
Selwyn, Pamela, and David Selwyn, 'The Profession of a Gentleman: Books for the Gentry and the Nobility (*c.* 1560 to 1640)', in *The Cambridge History of Libraries in Britain and Ireland*, ed. by Elisabeth Leedham-Green and Teresa Webber, 3 vols (Cambridge: Cambridge University Press, 2006), I: *To 1640*, pp. 489–519.
Serrano, Matilde López, *El Códice Aureo: Los Cuatro Evangelios siglo XI*, 3rd edn (Madrid: Editorial patrimonio nacional, 1987).
Seymour, Michael C., 'The Manuscripts of Hoccleve's Regiment of Princes', ***Edinburgh Bibliographical Society Transactions***, 4 (1974), 255–97.
Seymour, Michael C., 'Manuscript Portraits of Chaucer and Hoccleve', ***Burlington Magazine***, 124 (1982), 618–23.
Seymour, Michael C., 'Some Lydgate Manuscripts: Lives of SS Edmund and Fremund and Danse Macabre', *Edinburgh Bibliographical Society Transactions*, 5 (1983–85), 10–21.
Sharpe, Kevin, *Selling the Tudor Monarchy: Authority and Image in Sixteenth-century England* (New Haven, CT: Yale University Press, 2009).
Shaw, William A., ed., *Calendar of Treasury Books*, 32 vols (1904–1962).
Sherman, Claire Richter, 'Representations of Charles V of France (1338–1380) as a Wise Ruler', *Medievalia et Humanistica: Studies in Medieval and Renaissance Culture*, n.s. 2 (1971), 83–96.

Sherman, Claire Richter, 'The Queen in Charles V's "Coronation Book": Jeanne de Bourbon and the "Ordo ad reginam benedicendam"', *Viator*, 8 (1977), 255–98.
Siddons, Michael Powell, ed., *Heraldic Badges in England and Wales*, 4 vols (Woodbridge: Boydell Press, 2009).
Sider, Sandra, '"Interwoven with Poems and Picture": A Protoemblematic Translation of the *Tabula cebetis*', in *The European Emblem: Selected Papers from the Glasgow Conference, 11–14 August 1987*, ed. by B.F. Scholz, M. Bath and D. Weston (Leiden: Brill, 1990), pp. 1–17.
Sider, Sandra, and Barbara Obrist, eds, *Corpus Librorum Emblematum: Bibliography of Emblematic Manuscripts* (Montreal: McGill, 1997).
Simmons, Eleanor, *Les Heures de Nuremberg. Reproduction intégrale du calendrier et des images du manuscrit Solger 4.4° de la Stadtbibliothek de Nuremberg* (Paris: Éditions du Cerf, 1994).
Simpson, Amanda, *The Connections between English and Bohemian Painting during the Second Half of the Fourteenth Century*, Outstanding theses from the Courtauld Institute of Art (New York: Garland, 1984).
Skemer, Don C., 'Reading the Law: Statute Books and the Private Transmission of Legal Knowledge in Late Medieval England', in *Learning the Law: Teaching and the Transmission of Law in England 1150–1900*, ed. by Jonathan A. Bush and Alain Wijffels (London: Hambledon Press, 1999), pp. 112–31.
Skemer, Don C., *Binding Words. Textual Amulets in the Middle Ages* (Pennsylvania: State University Press, 2006).
Smeyers, Katrien, and Susie Vertongen, 'De Meester van de Beaufortheiligen en de Brugse miniatuurkunst', in *Boeken in de late Middeleeuwen, Verslag van de Groningse Codicologendagen*, ed. by J.M.M. Hermans and K. van der Hoek (Groningen: Egbert Forsten, 1992), pp. 275–84.
Smeyers, Maurits, *Flemish Miniatures from the 8th to the mid-16th Century* (Leuven: Davidsfonds, 1999).
Smith, Jeffrey Chipps, 'Margaret of York and the Burgundian Portrait Tradition', in *Margaret of York, Simon Marmion, and the Vision of Tondal: Papers delivered at a Symposium Organized by the Department of Manuscripts of the J. Paul Getty Museum, in collaboration with the Huntington Library and Art Collections, June 21–24, 1990*, ed. by Thomas Kren (Malibu, CA: J. Paul Getty Museum, 1992), pp. 47–56.
Smith, Kathryn A., 'History, Typology and Homily: The Joseph Cycle in the Queen Mary Psalter', *Gesta*, 32 (1993), 147–59.
Smith, Sharon Off Dunlap, 'Illustrations of Raoul de Praelles' Translation of St Augustine's *City of God*' (unpublished doctoral dissertation, New York University, 1974).
Sotheby's, London, sale catalogue, *Western Manuscripts and Miniatures* (London: Sotheby's, 10 December 1980).
Sotheby's, London, sale catalogue, *The Bute Collection of Forty-two Illuminated Manuscripts and Miniatures* (London: Sotheby's, 13 June 1983).
Spencer, Eleanor P., 'The Master of the Duke of Bedford: The Bedford Hours', *Burlington Magazine*, 107 (1965), 495–502.
Spencer, Eleanor, 'The Master of the Duke of Bedford: The Salisbury Breviary', *Burlington Magazine*, 108 (1966), 607–12.
Stahl, Harvey, *Picturing Kingship: History and Painting in the Psalter of St Louis* (University Park, PA: Penn State Press, 2008).
Stanton, Anne Rudloff, 'Notes on the Codicology of the Queen Mary Psalter', *Scriptorium: Revue internationale des études relatives aux manuscrits*, 48 (1995), 250–62.
Stanton, Anne Rudloff, *The Queen Mary Psalter: A Study of Affect and Audience* (Philadelphia, PA: American Philosophical Society, 2001).
Stanton, Anne Rudloff, 'Isabelle of France and her Manuscripts, 1308–58', in *Capetian Women*, ed. by Kathleen Nolan (New York: Palgrave Macmillan, 2003), pp. 225–52.
Stanton, Anne Rudloff, 'Queen Mary and her Psalter: A Gothic Manuscript in Tudor England', in *Medieval Art and Architecture after the Middle Ages*, ed. by Janet T. Marquardt and Alyce A. Jordan (Newcastle upon Tyne: Cambridge Scholars Publishing, 2009), pp. 18–38.
Starkey, David, *Henry VIII: A European Court in England* (London: Collins & Brown, 1991).
Starkey, D.R., ed., *The Inventory of King Henry VIIII: Society of Antiquaries MS 129 and British Library MS Harley 1419: The Transcript*, transcribed by P. Ward (London: Harvey Miller, 1998).
Starkey, David, 'Preface', in James P. Carley, *The Books of Henry VIII and His Wives* (London: British Library, 2004), pp. 7–8.
Starkey, David, *Henry: Virtuous Prince* (London: Harper Press, 2008).
Stechow, Wolfgang, 'Shooting at Father's Corpse', *Art Bulletin*, 21 (1942), 213–25.
Sterchi, Bernhard, 'Hugues de Lannoy, auteur de l'*Enseignement de la vraie noblesse*, de l'*Instruction d'un jeune prince* et des *Enseignements paternels*', *Le Moyen Âge*, 110 (2004), 79–117.
Stirnemann, Patricia, 'Les Bibliothèques princières et privées aux XIIe et XIIIe siècles', in *Histoire des bibliothèques françaises*, 4 vols (Paris: Promodis-Éditions du Cercle de la Librairie 1988–92), I, *Les Bibliothèques Médiévales du VIe siècle à 1530*, ed. by André Vernet (1989), pp. 173–91.
Stirnemann, Patricia, and Claudia Rabel, 'The "Très Riches Heures" and Two Artists Associated with the Bedford Workshop', *Burlington Magazine*, 147 (2005), 534–38.
Stones, Alison, 'Another Short Note on Rylands French I', in *Romanesque and Gothic: Essays for George Zarnecki*, 2 vols (Woodbridge: Boydell, 1987), I, pp. 185–192.
Stones, Alison, 'Arthurian Art Since Loomis', in *Arturus Rex: Koning Artur en de Nederlanden*, 2 vols (Leuven: University Press, 1987–91), II: *Acta conventus Lovaniensis 1987*, ed. by Willy van Hoecke, Gilbert Tournoy and Werner Verbeke, Mediaevalia Lovaniensia, Series 1, Studia 17, pp. 21–78.
Stones, Alison, 'The Stylistic Context of the Roman de Fauvel, with a Note on *Fauvain*', in *Fauvel Studies: Allegory, Chronicle, Music, and Image in Paris, Bibliothèque nationale de France, MS français 146*, ed. by Margaret Bent and Andrew Wathey (Oxford: Clarendon Press, 1998), pp. 529–67.
Stones, Alison, 'A Note on the 'Maître au menton fuyant', in '*Als Ich Can': Liber Amicorum in Memory of Professor Dr Maurits Smeyers*, ed. by Bert Cardon and others, 2 vols (Paris: Peeters, 2002), II, pp. 1247–71.
Stones, Alison, 'The Full-page Miniatures of the Psalter-Hours New York, PML, ms. M. 729: Programme and Patron', in *The Illuminated Psalter: Studies in the Content, Purpose and Placement of its Images*, ed. by Frank O. Büttner (Turnhout: Brepols, 2004), pp. 281–307.
Stones, Alison, 'The Egerton Brut and its Illustrations', in *Maistre Wace: A Celebration: Proceedings of the International Colloquium held in Jersey 10–12 September 2004*, ed. by Glyn S. Burgess and Judith Weiss (St Helier, Jersey: Société Jersiaise, 2006), pp. 167–76.
Stork, H.-W., 'Realienkundliches auf den Tafelbildern des Conrad von Soest, oder: Was auf den Bildern zu lesen ist', in *Conrad von Soest: Neue Forschungen über den Maler und die Kulturgeschichte der Zeit um 1400*, ed. by B. Huberl (Bielefeld: Verlag für Regionalgeschichte, 2004), pp. 166–94.
Stratford, Jenny, 'The Manuscripts of John, Duke of Bedford: Library and Chapel', in *England in the Fifteenth Century: Proceedings of the 1986 Harlaxton Symposium*, ed. by Daniel Williams (Woodbridge: Boydell, 1987), pp. 329–50.
Stratford, Jenny, *The Bedford Inventories: The Worldly Goods of John, Duke of Bedford, Regent of France (1389–1435)* (London: Society of Antiquaries, 1993).
Stratford, Jenny, 'The Royal Library in England before the Reign of Edward IV', in *England in the Fifteenth Century: Proceedings of the 1992 Harlaxton Symposium*, ed. by Nicholas Rogers, Harlaxton Medieval Studies, 4 (Stamford: Paul Watkins, 1994), pp. 187–97.
Stratford, Jenny, 'The Early Royal Collections and the Royal Library to 1461', in *The Cambridge History of the Book in Britain* (Cambridge: Cambridge University Press, 1987-), III: *1400–1557*, ed. by Lotte Hellinga and J. B. Trapp (1999), pp. 255–66.
Stratford, Jenny, 'Gold and Diplomacy: England and France in the Reign of Richard II', in *England and the Continent in the Middle Ages: Studies in Memory of Andrew Martindale. Proceedings of the 1996 Harlaxton Symposium*, ed. by John Mitchell (Stamford: Shaun Tyas, 2000), pp. 218–37.
Stratford, Jenny, 'Royal Books', in *Gothic: Art for England, 1400–1547*, ed. Richard Marks and Paul Williamson (London: V&A, 2003), pp. 180–81.
Stratford, Jenny, and Catherine Reynolds, 'The Foyle Breviary and Hours of John, Duke of Bedford', in *Tributes to Lucy Freeman Sandler. Studies in Illuminated Manuscripts*, ed. by Kathryn A. Smith and Carol H. Krinsky (London: Harvey Miller, 2007), pp. 345–71.
Stratford, Jenny, and Teresa Webber, 'Bishops and Kings: Private Book Collections in Medieval England', in *The Cambridge History of Libraries in Britain and Ireland*, ed. by Elisabeth Leedham-Green and Teresa Webber, 3 vols (Cambridge: Cambridge University Press, 2006), I: *To 1640*, pp. 178–217.
Straub, Richard E., *La Tradition manuscrite de la* Vie de Jésus-Christ *en sept parties* (Montréal: CERES, 1998).
Strong, Patrick and Felicity Strong, 'The Last Will and Codicils of Henry V', *English Historical Review*, 96 (1981), 79–102.
Strong, Roy, *Henry, Prince of Wales and England's Lost Renaissance* (New York: Thames and Hudson, 1986).
Summerfield, Thea, *The Matter of the Kings' Lives: The Design of Past and Present in the Early Fourteenth-century Verse Chronicles by Pierre de Langtoft and Robert Mannyng* (Amsterdam: Rodopi, 1998).
Sutton, Anne F., and Livia Visser-Fuchs, 'Richard III's Books: IV. Vegetius' *De re militari*', *Ricardian: Journal of the Richard III Society*, 99 (1987), 541–52.
Sutton, Anne F. and Livia Visser-Fuchs, 'A "Most Benevolent Queen": Queen Elizabeth Woodville's Reputation, her Piety and her Books', *Ricardian. Journal of the Richard III Society*, 10 (1995), 214–45.
Sutton, Anne F., and Livia Visser-Fuchs, 'Choosing a Book in Late Fifteenth-century England and Burgundy', in *England and the Low Countries in the Late Middle Ages*, ed. by Caroline Barron and Nigel Saul (Stroud: Alan Sutton, 1995), pp. 61–98.
Sutton, Anne F., and Livia Visser-Fuchs, *Richard III's Books: Ideals and Reality in the Life and Library of a Medieval Prince* (Stroud: Sutton, 1997).
Sutton, Anne F., and Livia Visser-Fuchs, 'The Device of Queen Elizabeth Woodville: A Gillyflower or Pink', *Ricardian: Journal of the Richard III Society*, 11 (1997), pp. 17–24.
Sutton, Anne F., and Livia Visser-Fuchs, 'Richard III and the Knave of Cards: An Illuminator's Model in Manuscript and Print, 1440s to 1990s', *Antiquaries Journal*, 79 (1999), 257–99.
Sylwan, Agneta, *Petri Comestoris scolastica historia liber Genesis* (Turnhout: Brepols, 2005).
Symons, T., S. Spath, M. Wegener and K. Hallinger, eds, *Regularis concordia Anglicae nationis*, Corpus Consuetudinum Monasticarum, 7.3 (Siegburg: Franz Schmitt, 1984).

Talbot, Charles Hugh, and Eugene Ashby Hammond, *The Medical Practitioners in Medieval England: A Biographical Register*, Publications of the Wellcome Historical Medical Library, n.s. 8 (London: Wellcome Historical Medical Library, 1965).
Taylor, Andrew, 'The Time of an Anthology: British Library MS Royal 15 E. vi and the Commemoration of Chivalric Culture', in *Collections in Context: The Organization of Knowledge and Community in Europe (14th–17th Centuries)*, ed. by Karen Fresno and Anne D. Hedeman (Columbus, OH: Ohio State University Press, 2011), pp. 169–91.
Taylor, Craig, 'The Shrewsbury Book (BL MS Royal 15 E. vi) and Chivalric Writing in Late Medieval England', *Collections in Context: The Organization of Knowledge and Community in Europe (14th–17th Centuries)*, ed. by Karen Fresno and Anne D. Hedeman (Columbus, OH: Ohio State University Press, 2011), pp. 193–223.
Taylor, E.G.R., *Tudor Geography 1485–1583* (London: Methuen, 1930).
Temple, Elżbieta, 'Further Additions to the William of Devon Group', *Bodleian Library Record*, 2 (1984), 344–48.
Thiolier, Jean-Claude, ed., *Le Règne d'Edouard Ier: édition critique et commentée* (Créteil: CELIMA, Université de Paris XII, 1989).
Thomas, Jennifer, 'Patronage and Personal Narrative in a Music Manuscript: Marguerite of Austria, Katherine of Aragon, and London Royal 8 G.vii', in *Musical Voices of Early Modern Women: Many-headed Melodies*, ed. by Thomasin LaMay (Aldershot: Ashgate, 2005), pp. 337–64.
Thompson, Edward Maunde, *An Introduction to Greek and Latin Palaeography* (Oxford: Oxford University Press, 1912).
Thompson, John Jay, 'The Recent Discovery of a Collection in Early French Prose, Wauchier de Denain's *Li Seint Confessor*', *Romance Notes*, 38 (1998), 121–37.
Thompson, John Jay, 'Introduction', in Wauchier de Denain *La Vie mon signeur seint Nicholas le benoit confessor*, ed. by John Jay Thompson (Geneva: Droz, 1999), pp. 11–38.
Thompson, J.W., *The Medieval Library* (Chicago: University of Chicago Press, 1939).
Thomson, Rodney M., *Manuscripts from St Albans Abbey, 1066–1235*, 2 vols (Woodbridge: D. S. Brewer, 1982).
Thorpe, J., ed., *Registrum Roffense: or, a collection of antient records, charters, and instruments of divers kinds necessary for illustrating the ecclesiastical history and antiquities of the diocese and cathedral church of Rochester* (London: Longman, 1769).
Thorpe, Lewis, 'Mastre Richard, A Thirteenth-century Translator of the *De Re Militari* of Vegetius', *Scriptorium: Revue internationale des études relatives aux manuscrits*, 6 (1952), 39–50.
Thurley, Simon, 'The Domestic Building Works of Cardinal Wolsey', in *Cardinal Wolsey: Church, State and Art*, ed. by S.J. Gunn and P.G. Lindley (Cambridge, Cambridge University Press, 1991), pp. 76–102.
Thurley, Simon, *The Royal Palaces of Tudor*

England: A Social and Architectural History (New Haven, CT: Yale University Press, 1993).
Tikkanen, J.J., 'Le rappresentazioni della Genesi in S. Marco a Venezia e loro relazione con la Bibbia Cottoniana', *Archivio storico dell'arte*, 1 (1888), 212–23, 257–67, 348–63.
Tirro, Frank, 'Royal 8.G.vii: Strawberry Leaves, Single Arch, and Wrong-Way Lions', *Journal of the American Musicological Society*, 67 (1981), 1–28.
Toulouse, Sarah, 'Marine Cartography and Navigation in Renaissance France' in *The History of Cartography*, 6 vols (Chicago: University of Chicago Press, 1987-), III: *Cartography in the European Renaissance*, ed. by David Woodward (2007), pp. 1550–68.
Trapp, J.B., 'Notes on Manuscripts written by Pieter Meghen', *Book Collector*, 24 (1975), 80–96.
Trapp, J.B., *Erasmus, Colet, and More: The Early Tudor Humanists and their Books. Panizzi Lectures, 1990* (London: British Library, 1991).
Trapp, J. B., 'The Humanist Book', in *The Cambridge History of the Book in Britain* (Cambridge: Cambridge University Press, 1987-), III: *1400–1557*, ed. by Lotte Hellinga and J.B. Trapp (1999), pp. 293–96.
Trapp, J.B., 'Colet, John (1467–1519)', *Oxford Dictionary of National Biography* (Oxford: Oxford University Press, 2004; online edition, Jan 2008) <http://www.oxforddnb.com/view/article/5898> [accessed 13 May 2011].
Tudor-Craig, Pamela, 'Henry VIII and King David', in *Early Tudor England: Proceedings of the 1987 Harlaxton Symposium*, ed. by Daniel Williams (Woodbridge: Boydell Press, 1989), pp. 183–206.
Turner, D.H., 'Bedford Hours and Psalter', *Apollo*, 76 (1962), 265–70.
Turner, D.H., *Illuminated Manuscripts Exhibited in the Grenville Library* (London: British Museum, 1967).
Turner, D.H. 'The Wyndham Payne Crucifixion', *British Library Journal*, 2 (1976), 8–26.
Tyson, Diana B., 'The Manuscript Tradition of Old French Prose *Brut* Rolls', *Scriptorium: Revue internationale des études relatives aux manuscrits*, 55 (2001), 107–18.

Ullmann, Walter, *Liber Regie Capelle: A Manuscript in the Biblioteca Publica, Evora*, Henry Bradshaw Society, 92 (London: Henry Bradshaw Society, 1961).

Vale, Juliet, *Edward III and Chivalry: Chivalric Society and its Context, 1270–1350* (Woodbridge: Boydell, 1982).
van Buren, Anne, 'The Master of Mary of Burgundy and his Colleagues: The State of Research and Questions of Method', *Zeitschrift für Kunstgeschichte*, 38 (1975), 286–309.
Van Leeuwen, Jan Storm, 'The Well-shirted Bookbinding: On Chemise Bindings and Hülleneinbände,' in *Theatrum orbis librorum: Liber amicorum presented to Nico Israel on the Occasion of his Seventieth Birthday*, ed. by Ton Croiset van Uchelen and others (Utrecht: HES Publishers, 1989), pp. 277–305.
Vaughan, Richard, 'The Handwriting of Matthew Paris', *Transactions of the Cambridge Bibliographical Society*, 5 (1953), 376–94.
Vaughan, Richard, *Matthew Paris* (Cambridge: Cambridge University Press, 1958).
Verdier, Philippe, Peter Brieger, and Marie Farquhar Montpetit, eds, *Art and the Courts: France and England from 1259 to 1328* (Ottawa: National Gallery of Canada, 1972).
Vertongen, Susie, 'Herman Scheerre, the Beaufort Master and the Flemish Miniature Painting: A Reopened Dabate', in *Flanders in a European Perspective: Manuscript Illumination around 1400, Flanders and Abroad: Proceedings of the International Colloquium, Leuven, 7–10 September 1993*, ed. by Maurits Smeyers and Bert Cardon (Leuven: Peeters, 1995), pp. 251–65.
Vetusta monumenta quae ad Rerum Britannicarum memoriam conservandam Societas Antiquariorum, 7 vols (London: n. pub., 1747–1906).
Viard, J., ed., *Les Grandes Chroniques de France*, 10 vols (Paris: Société de l'histoire de France, 1920–53)
Vidas, Marina, *The Christina Psalter: A Study of the Images and Texts in a French Early Thirteenth-century Illuminated Manuscript* (Copenhagen: Museum Tusculanum Press, 2006).
Villela-Petit, Inès, 'Devises de Charles VI dans les Heures Mazarine: La Personnalisation d'un manuscrit', *Scriptorium: Revue internationale des études relatives aux manuscrits*, 55 (2001), 80–92.
Villela-Petit, Inès, *Le Bréviaire de Châteauroux* (Paris: Somogy, 2003).
Visser-Fuchs, Livia, 'Warwick and Wavrin: Two Case Studies on the Literary Background of Anglo–Burgundian Relations in the Yorkist Period' (unpublished doctoral thesis, University of London, 2002).
Visser-Fuchs, Livia, 'The Manuscript of the *Enseignement de vraie noblesse* made for Richard Neville, Earl of Warwick, in 1464', in *Medieval Manuscripts in Transition: Tradition and Creative Recycling*, ed. by Geert H.M. Claassens and Werner Verbeke, Mediaevalia Lovaniensia, ser. 1, Studia 36 (Leuven: Leuven University Press, 2006), pp. 337–62.
Vitzthum, Bertold Georg, *Die Pariser Miniaturmalerei von der Zeit des hl. Ludwig bis zu Philipp von Valois und ihr Verhältnis zur Malerei in Nordwesteuropa* (Leipzig: Quelle and Meyer, 1907).
Von Bülow, Gottfried, ed., 'Diary of the Journey of Philip Julius, Duke of Stettin-Pomerania, through England in the Year 1602', *Transactions of the Royal Historical Society*, n.s. 6 (1982), pp. 1–67.
von Klarwill, Victor, ed., *Queen Elizabeth and some Foreigners, being a Series of Hitherto Unpublished Letters from the Archives of the Hapsburg family*, trans. by T.H. Nash (London: John Lane, 1928).

Wagner, Anthony Richard, *A Catalogue of English Medieval Rolls of Arms* (Oxford: Oxford University Press, 1950).
Walker, Greg, *Pervasive Fictions: Fiction, Faith and Political Culture in the Reign of Henry VIII* (Aldershot: Scolar, 1996).
Walker, Henry John, trans., Valerius Maximus, *Memorable Deeds and Sayings* (Indianapolis: Hackett Publishing, 2004).
Wallis, Helen, ed., *The Maps and Text of the Boke of Idrography presented by Jean Rotz to Henry VIII: Now in the British Library* (Oxford: Roxburghe Club, 1981).
Wallis, Helen, 'The Rotz Atlas: A Royal Presentation', *Map Collector*, 20 (1982), 40–42.
Walpole, Horace, trans., *Paul Hentzner's Travels in England During the Reign of Queen Elizabeth* (London: Edward Jeffery, 1797), <http://elfinspell.com/HentznerOriginal.html> [accessed 12 April 2011].
Ward, H.L.D., and J.A. Herbert, *Catalogue of Romances in the Department of Manuscripts in the British Museum*, 3 vols (London: British Museum, 1883–1910).
Warner, George F., *Illuminated Manuscripts in the British Museum*, ser. 1–4 (London: British Museum, 1899–1903).
Warner, George F., *Queen Mary's Psalter: Miniatures and Drawings by an English Artist of the 14th Century Reproduced from Royal MS. 2 B. VII in the British Museum* (London: British Museum, 1912).
Warner, George F., and Julius P. Gilson, *Catalogue of Western Manuscripts in the Old Royal and King's Collections* in the British Museum, 4 vols (London: British Museum, 1921).
Warnicke, Retha M., 'Anne [Anne of Cleves] (1515–1557)', *Oxford Dictionary of National Biography* (Oxford: University Press, 2004), <http://www.oxforddnb.com/view/article/558> [accessed 13 April 2011].
Watson, Andrew G., *The Manuscripts of Henry Savile of Banke* (London: Bibliographical Society, 1969).
Watteeuw, Lieve and Jan Van der Stock, eds, *The Anjou Bible: A Royal Manuscript Revealed*, (Paris: Peeters, 2010).
Weiss, Roberto, *Humanism in England During the Fifteenth Century* (Oxford, Blackwell, 1967).
Weitzmann, Kurt, and Herbert L. Kessler, *The Cotton Genesis: British Library Codex Cotton Otho B. V*, (Princeton, NJ: Princeton University Press, 1986).
Wheatley, Henry B., ed., *Diary of John Evelyn*, 4 vols (London: Bickers and Son, 1906).
Whipple, T.K., 'Isocrates and Euphuism', *Modern Language Review*, 11 (1916), 15–27.
Whitaker, Lucy, and Martin Clayton, *The Art of Italy in the Royal Collection: Renaissance and Baroque* (London: Royal Collection Publications, 2007).
Whitelock, *Memorials of the English Affairs* (London: J. Tonson, 1732).
Wieck, Roger S., William M. Voelkle and K. Michelle Hearne, *The Hours of Henry VIII: A Renaissance Masterpiece by Jean Poyet* (New York: George Braziller, 2000), pp. 26–27.
Wijsman, Hanno, 'William Lord Hastings: *Les Faits de Jacques de Lalaing* et le 'Maître aux inscriptions blanches': À propos du manuscript français 16830 de la Bibliothèque nationale de France', in *'Als Ich Can': Liber Amicorum in Memory of Professor Dr Maurits Smeyers* (Paris: Peeters, 2002), pp. 1641–64.
Wijsman, Hanno, 'Het psalter van Lodewijk de Heilige. Functie, gebruik en overlevering van een middeleeuws prachthandschrift', in *Bronnen van Kennis. Wetenschap, kunst en cultuur in de collecties van de Leidse Universiteitsbibliotheek*, ed. by Paul Hoftijzer and others (Leiden: Primavera, 2006), pp. 32–42.
Wijsman, Hanno, 'Les Manuscrits de Pierre de Luxembourg (ca 1440–1482) et les bibliothèques nobiliaires dans les Pays-Bas bourguignons de la deuxième moitié du XVe siècle', *Le Moyen Âge*, 113 (2007), 615–37.
Wijsman, Hanno, 'Two Petals of a *Fleur*: the "Copenhagen *Fleur des Histoires*" and the Production of Illuminated Manuscripts in Bruges around 1480', *Fund og Forskning*, 47 (2008), 17–72.
Wijsman, Hanno, *Luxury Bound: Illustrated Manuscript Production and Noble and Princely Book Ownership in the Burgundian Netherlands (1400–1550)* (Turnhout: Brepols, 2010).
Wild, Benjamin Linley, 'Gift Inventory' (2010), pp. 529–69.
Wilks, Timothy, 'Art Collecting at the English Court from the Death of Henry, Prince of Wales to the Death of Anne of Denmark (November 1612–March 1619)', *Journal of the History of Collections*, 9 (1997), 31–48.
Williams, Clem C., 'A Case of Mistaken Identity: Still another Trojan Narrative in Old French Prose', *Medium Aevum*, 53 (1984), 59–72.
Winkler, Friedrich, *Die flämische Buchmalerei des XV. und XVI. Jahrhunderts: Künstler und Werke von den Brüdern van Eyck bis zu Simon Bening* (Leipzig: E.A. Seemann, 1925).
Winn, Mary Beth, *Anthoine Vérard, Parisian Publisher, 1485–1512: Prologues, Poems and Presentations* (Geneva: Droz, 1997).
Winn, Mary Beth, 'Paint, Pen, and Print: Royal Presentations in France, 1470–1515', *Manuscripta*, 50 (2006), 191–212.
Winstead, Karen A., *John Capgrave's Fifteenth Century* (Philadelphia: University of Pennsylvania Press, 2007).
Wolpe, Berthold, 'A Royal Manuscript by Arrighi Vicentino in the British Museum', *Book Collector*, 7 (1958), 78–79.
Woodger, L. S., 'Henry Bourgchier, Earl of Essex, and his Family (1408–83)' (unpublished doctoral dissertation, University of Oxford, 1974).
Wormald, Francis, 'Coronation Oath-books', in *Essays in Honor of Georg Swarzenski*, ed. by Oswald Goetz (Chicago: Henry Regnery, 1951), pp. 233–37.
Wormald, Francis, *English Drawings of the Tenth and Eleventh Centuries* (London: Faber and Faber, 1952).
Wright, Cyril Ernest, *Fontes Harleiani: A Study of the Sources of the Harleian Collection of Manuscripts Preserved in the Department of Manuscripts in the British Museum* (London: British Museum, 1972).
Wright, Cyril Ernest, and Ruth C. Wright, eds, *The Diary of Humfrey Wanley 1715–1726*, 2 vols (London: Bibliographical Society, 1966).
Wright, Sylvia, 'The Big Bible Royal 1 E IX in the British Library and Manuscript Illumination in London in the Early Fifteenth Century' (unpublished doctoral thesis, University of London, 1986).
Wright, Sylvia, 'The Author Portraits in the Bedford Psalter-Hours: Gower, Chaucer and Hoccleve', *British Library Journal*, 18 (1992), 190–202.
Wright, Thomas. ed., *The Chronicle of Pierre de Langtoft, in French Verse, from the Earliest Period to the Death of King Edward I*, 2 vols (London: Longmans, 1866–68).

Zarnecki, George, Janet Holt and Tristram Holland, eds, *English Romanesque Art 1066–1200*, Hayward Gallery, London, 5 April – 8 July 1984 (London: Weidenfeld and Nicolson, 1984).
Zinzerling, Justus, (pub. pseudonymously as Jodocus Sincerus), *Itinerarum Galliae*, 4th edn (Amsterdam: Jodocum Jansonium, 1649).

General Index

Page numbers in **bold** refer to main catalogue entry.

Page numbers in *italics* refer to pages with illustrations.

Index of Manuscripts

MSS shelfmarks in **bold** refer to MSS with main catalogue entry.

Page numbers in **bold** refer to main catalogue entry.

Page numbers in *italics* refer to pages with illustrations.